Business Economics

This textbook aims to analyse rigorously topics of immediate interest to business. It also introduces realism into the analysis, thus indicating the power and usefulness of economics in formulating and taking business decisions. Concerned specifically with the economics of business enterprises, the author attempts to show how economic methodology can assist our understanding of the way in which business firms operate.

By synthesising traditional and modern approaches to the firm, the author has achieved a coherent analytical framework directly relevant to everyday business problems. This is compounded by real-world examples and enriched with empirical evidence drawn from a variety of sources in the UK and other countries, from the small firm to the international corporation. A unique feature of this textbook is the inclusion of applications, thirteen in all, which follow each chapter. These short case studies and the numerous questions and problems are designed to illustrate economic thinking, to assist business problem solving and to stimulate seminar discussions.

Aimed at second and third year undergraduates in business economics, business studies, accounting and other applied economics courses, the book will also be of interest to MBA students.

Maria Moschandreas studied economics in Athens and at the LSE and spent four years in auditing and consultancy work before embarking upon an academic career. She is a Senior Lecturer in Economics at Middlesex University Business School and has taught business economics to a variety of undergraduate and postgraduate courses.

To the memory of my mother
Ιωαυυα Κουβαριτακι

Business Economics

Maria Moschandreas

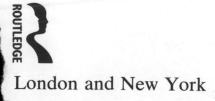

London and New York

First published 1994
by Routledge
11 New Fetter Lane, London EC4P 4EE

Simultaneously published in the USA and Canada
by Routledge
29 West 35th Street, New York, NY 10001

Typeset in Times by
J&L Composition Ltd, Filey, North Yorkshire
Printed and bound in Great Britain by
TJ Press (Padstow) Ltd, Padstow, Cornwall

British Library Cataloguing in Publication Data
A catalogue record for this book is available from the British
Library

Library of Congress Cataloging in Publication Data has been
applied for

Moschandreas, Maria, 1937–
    Business economics / Maria Mochandreas.
        p. cm.
    Includes bibliographical references and index.
    ISBN 0–415–10909–4. — ISBN 0–415–10910–8 (pbk.)
    1. Managerial economices.   I. Title.
HD30.22.M666 1994   93–38120
338.5'024658—dc20   CIP

Contents

Figures

Tables

Preface

Economic methodology as a means of formulating solutions to real-world problems is an indispensable tool of business education and as a result economics finds its way, under one guise or another, into virtually all business undergraduate programmes. Received economic theory, however, has serious limitations as a study of the business enterprises that populate modern society. Its assumptions of universal certainty and a world of costless information, where the firm is treated as a mathematical device converting inputs into outputs, contradict sharply common observation and experiences and makes it exceedingly difficult to generate and keep student interest in a subject which does not appear to be concerned with the complex business organisations of the real world. Students respond with claims that economics is too abstract and unrealistic a subject to be of any use to the real world of business. Student interest, is enhanced however, by exposure to the theoretical developments of the last two decades in the theory of the firm. By emphasising the lack of perfect knowledge, the existence of costs in the acquisition and communication of information, the bounds on individual rationality and the role of the entrepreneur, such developments greatly enhance our understanding of problems and forces operating in areas of particular interest to business. It becomes thus possible to enquire into the forces that contribute to the existence and diversity of firms, the influences bearing on internal organisational structures and their impact on behaviour, the formation of business strategy and the relationship of firms with their customers and suppliers. A synthesis of the diverse theoretical developments that make this possible and its introduction into textbooks, however, can be a rather slow process.

As a result there is a dearth of textbooks written for the business undergraduate which attempt to rigorously analyse topics of immediate interest to business and which aim to introduce realism into the analysis thus indicating the power and usefulness of economics in formulating and taking business decisions. This textbook aims to make a contribution towards filling this gap.

The book has grown out of a course in 'business economics' which I have given to business studies students at the Middlesex University Business

School over a number of years. While student response to the course has invariably been very encouraging, the growing student interest in the subject has always been accompanied by demands for assistance with the onerous task of amassing information from an unusually large variety of sources. It is hoped that this textbook will go some way in satisfying this demand.

The approach adopted comprises a synthesis of the traditional view with new theories of the firm and in particular the *transactions cost* approach and the *agency theory* of the firm. This approach emphasises that the forces which contribute to the emergence and growth of firms are not simply technological in nature. The firm is not a 'black box'; it is an institutional structure that comes into existence in order to economise on the costs of carrying out certain transactions. The way firms are organised and behave depends on human and environmental attributes. Human limitations and lack of information create costs which can be reduced by appropriate organisational structures and incentives. Organisational and behavioural issues are therefore as important as production efficiency.

The book is of an intermediate level aimed at second and final year undergraduates in business economics, business studies, accounting and other applied economics courses. Furthermore, the approach adopted, the use of short cases and real examples drawn from various companies, should make it suitable for MBA courses in its own right or as a supplement to a conventional (more narrowly focused) managerial economics text.

A limited prior knowledge of economics is assumed; an introductory microeconomics course should suffice. Although numeracy is a necessary skill for all business and economics students, the level of numeracy assumed is also very limited. Thus, the exposition adopted is, on the whole, verbal supported by a liberal use of diagrams and illustrated with many real world examples and empirical evidence. Only very simple numerical examples and a few algebraic manipulations are incorporated in the text. The more mathematically inclined reader is, however, occasionally offered further mathematical proofs, including simple differentiation, in notes and appendices. Guidance to references for a more advanced mathematical treatment of certain topics is given where appropriate.

DISTINCTIVE FEATURES OF THE BOOK

This book is concerned with the economics of business enterprises. It attempts to show how economic methodology can assist our understanding of the way in which business firms operate. As such it is quite different to textbooks in the area of business which are usually concerned with the description of business practices. It is also quite distinct to managerial economics textbooks which usually adopt a more technical and narrowly focused approach to business decision making. Further distinctive features of this book can be summarised as follows.

1 The analytical approach adopted is a synthesis of traditional and modern approaches to the firm. Traditional concepts and tools of analysis have been supplemented with new ones in an attempt to develop a coherent analytical framework capablc of dealing with questions of direct relevance to business problems and management practices.

   'Transaction cost economics' and, for some topics, the 'agency theory' provide the modern analytical concepts which are combined with traditional techniques to built the theoretical basis for the analysis of business behaviour and strategy.

2 The analysis has been illustrated throughout with real world examples and enriched with empirical evidence. Both examples and statistical evidence have been drawn from a variety of sources in the UK, Europe and other countries. They refer to small or large firms, national or international corporations and industries.

3 Each chapter is followed by an application which illustrates and, in some instances, expands the material introduced in the text. These applications, thirteen in all, are short case studies referring to investigations into real business problems, practices or other issues. They have been drawn from empirical investigations of firms and industries of various nationalities and published in academic journals or other relevant publications. Although space limitations have meant that some of the cases have been rather severely abbreviated, further references have been provided, whenever possible, for any reader who requires further information on a particular case or for the instructor who wishes to create a more extensive case according to the needs of a particular course.

4 The use of mathematics within the text has been restricted to a minimum; it consists of a few numerical examples and simple algebraic manipulations. It is hoped, however, that the clarity of the exposition has been safeguarded by the liberal used of diagrams and tables.

5 Each chapter concludes with a brief summary of the main issues raised in that chapter and gives, following the application, a guide to further reading.

6 Each chapter is accompanied by a number of questions and problems designed to fulfil a double aim. First, they are designed to illustrate how economic thinking can assist in business problem solving, thus enhancing a student's analytical abilities and problem-solving skills. Second, they are designed to stimulate seminar discussions or to be used as essay topics for individual or group assignments. Thus, while some end of chapter questions are intended to assist in the understanding of the tools of analysis and concepts introduced in the chapter, it is hoped that most provide clear illustrations of the usefulness of economic methodology for business decisions. There are ninety-eight questions and problems most of which have been tried, with encouraging results, on my students both in the classroom and as assesment material.

ACKNOWLEDGEMENTS

I would like to begin my acknowledgements by expressing my gratitude to my students who not only acted as my guinea pigs in testing new material and methods of presentation but also offered many useful comments on drafts of chapters they were given as lecture handouts. Of the many students from whose comments I have benefited I must single out Amrit Judge who read several chapters in addition to the lecture handouts and offered many comments and queries.

During the two years over which this book was written I also benefited from comments and encouragement offered liberally by many friends and colleagues. I am particularly indebted to Professor Michael Driscoll, Dean of the Middlesex University Business School, without whose encouragement and guidance this project would never have begun. My friend Professor Philip Arestis read several chapters and offered both encouragement and very perceptive comments and suggestions for which I am most grateful. I would also like to thank William Messom, a friend – and colleague till his recent retirement – who shared for a while the business economics course teaching with me and has contributed some of the end of chapter questions. My thanks and appreciation also go to the library staff of the Middlesex University Business School and in particular to Pauline Hollis, Michael Dunne and Maggie Jesson whose assistance in chasing sources of information often went beyond the call of duty. My husband has done a brilliant job in spotting inaccuracies in my 'art work' and has spent a great deal of time amending and re-drawing most of my diagrams. Furthermore, both he and our daughter have given me constant encouragement and support and have cheerfully endured my moods and impatience when progress of the project seemed to be desperately slow.

1 Introduction and book outline

INTRODUCTION

In Marshallian microeconomics the basic unit of analysis is the 'typical' firm whose behaviour, although sophisticated in some respects, is restricted, in the short run, to no more than selecting the output level at which the rising marginal cost is equal to the given market price. This is, probably, a close approximation to how contemporary firms operated in nineteenth-century Britain. The rise and growth of modern corporations has meant, however, that the 'typical' firm bears no resemblance to its real-world namesake and a theory based on this premise cannot address the diversity of enterprises that populate the modern business world. In neoclassical theory, the firm is defined in a way not intended to approximate the firm of the real world but as a theoretical institution in which production (for others) takes place. Such an abstraction from reality may be well justified when considering that the 'mission of neoclassical economics is to understand how the price system coordinates the use of resources, not to understand the inner workings of real firms' (Demsetz 1983, p. 377). Nevertheless, this renders microeconomic theory of little relevance to the analysis of business problems. In fact, as Demsetz's quote implies, neoclassical economic theory was not meant to be applied to problems of internal business organisation. Neither was it meant to be applied to an understanding of the complex relationships that develop between a firm and its suppliers or buyers. The theory did not lend itself to direct business applications.

The neoclassical view of the firm as a 'black box' which converts inputs into outputs, according to a specified rule and with no discretion over resource allocation questions, is made possible by the assumptions of perfect competition. Perfect and costless knowledge allows the innards of the firm to be ignored in order to facilitate the development of a theory of value in which issues of general resource allocation could be studied.

That general equilibrium theory was never intended to be a study of the inner workings of real business enterprises is not a controversial proposition. Machlup (1967), for example, comments that 'frankly, I cannot quite see what great difference organisational matters are supposed to make to the firm's price reacting to changes in conditions' (p. 13) and Ricketts (1987) observes that the theory of equilibrium price does not require a theory of the firm and that 'In a world of costless knowledge they [firms] have no rationale' (p. 18). Loasby suggests that in the conditions of perfect knowledge postulated by traditional economics the theory of the firm is very easy: there are no firms! It is indeed true that the traditional abstraction from time and uncertainty implies conditions of perfect, present and future, knowledge which leaves no scope for entrepreneurship, organisational features do not matter and there are no difficulties in devising and writing long-term contracts. There is simply no need for a theory of the firm.

The neoclassical view of the firm abstracts from present-day reality to an extent that has meant the neglect of the study of issues relevant to the working of business enterprises resulting in a very poor communication between economists and business practitioners. The vacuum created by this lack of communication has been filled, at least partly, by other disciplines. The study of enterprises since the 1950s has been divided among organisation theorists interested in the internal structure of firms, business historians studying the strategies of individual firms and biographers recording the entrepreneurial endeavours of individuals (Ricketts 1987). A notable exception has been the work of Michael Porter who has applied economics to the study of corporate strategy.

Meanwhile, discontent among economists with the black box view of the firm has been growing fast. Although the significance of the firm as an institution worth studying has been recognised since the 1930s – a decade during which Coase's seminal contribution to the theory of the firm and the work of Joan Robinson and Chamberlin on the economics of monopolistic competition were published – it was not till the 1950s and 1960s that dissenting voices began to have some impact. The new managerial theories were concerned with the impact of the divergence of interests between managers and owners while the behavioural theory viewed the firm as a coalition of individuals or groups of individuals with divergent and often contradictory objectives. Both offer serious challenges to the 'black box' view of the firm. The neoclassical theory of the firm has, however, on the whole withstood the assaults from the managerial theories and the behavioural theory of the firm. The more recent attacks from transaction costs and information economics have, however, made more headway.

Over the last fifteen years or so important developments have taken place on issues concerned with the internal functioning as well as the external relationships of the firm. In this respect Oliver Williamson's contribution via the development of the transaction costs approach to the theory of the firm is particularly significant. Williamson's writings postulate a world characterised by lack of knowledge and populated by self-interested humans who are less than perfectly rational as decision makers. On these premises he developed a body of literature that bears directly on the existence and functioning of business enterprises.

Lack of information or the existence of asymmetric knowledge among traders and its impact on the behaviour of individuals as agents or principals has been at the heart of the theories which view the firm as a 'nexus of contracts' or a 'nexus of treaties'; this view has gained prominence so that an important area of change and development in micro-economics relates to issues of the behaviour of individuals under conditions of asymmetric information. Divergences of interests coupled with lack of knowledge and asymmetric information imply contractual difficulties and agency costs which have a bearing on the internal organisation of firms, their sources of finance, growth prospects and other aspects of business behaviour.

The new developments in the theory of the firm cover an area which is diverse and very fertile. Despite this diversity and the absence of full integration of the new developments, two common themes are discernible: (a) a recognition of the need for a broader interpretation of the behaviour of individuals as decision makers, and (b) a concern for the nature and extent of our knowledge of the future. Although both these themes are likely to be developed and better integrated in the future (Wiseman 1991) they have already had an impact on business economics. The focus of transaction cost economics, for example, on the interplay between transaction characteristics with human attributes and environmental influences has made it possible to address questions which were never raised by or were alien to the neoclassical theory of the firm.

THE SCOPE OF BUSINESS ECONOMICS

The new institutional view of the firm is not necessarily a substitute for the neoclassical theory of the firm. On the contrary, the institutional view supplements the traditional approach by addressing questions the traditional approach did not purport to tackle. A synthesis, therefore, of neoclassical concepts and tools of analysis with the new concepts is not only possible but is also very fruitful since it expands the scope of the theory of the firm and the contribution that economics can make to a better understanding of the way in which business firms operate. To illustrate consider the decision to vertically integrate.

Traditional theory postulates that vertical integration depends on technological considerations which influence costs of production. In simple terms, vertical integration occurs in order to economise on production costs. Vertical integration may, for example, bring about substantial thermal energy savings in the production of steel. Similarly, the heterogeneity of bauxite coupled with a heavy weight which entails high transport costs implies that production efficiency will be served by locating an alumina refinery close to the bauxite mine. Locating succeeding stages of production next to each other is necessary, in both these examples, if substantial production cost savings are to be enjoyed. Locating in near proximity does not, however, necessitate common ownership. Transactional difficulties in exchanges between the two independently owned stages of production may, however, be sufficiently severe to induce common ownership. In the absence of integration substantial transaction costs may be incurred. These costs exist when the presence of specialised investments makes it difficult to contractually safeguard against the development of situations of moral hazard. Ignoring the fact that in addition to production costs integration may be induced by a desire to avoid the uncertainties and contractual difficulties which may surround market transacting is simply misguided. The decision of whether to make your own (integrate) rather than buy from other producers depends on contractual as well as on technological considerations. Technology alone cannot define the boundaries of the firm and explain its behaviour. It is a combination of transaction and production costs that determine the outcome of many important business decisions.

This book attempts to synthesise traditional and modern contributions to the theory of the firm in a way that is comprehensible to undergraduate students. The outcome of this synthesis is a part of economic knowledge which can address questions of immediate interest to business enterprises. Business economics can therefore be defined as that part of economic theory which focuses on business enterprises and inquires into the factors contributing to the diversity of organisational structures and to the relationships of firms with labour, capital and product markets. Business economics is, therefore, concerned with problems related with business organisation, management and strategy. Its enquiry includes issues such as the following: an exploration of the reasons why firms emerge; what contributes to their vertical, horizontal and spacial expansion; the role and function of entrepreneurship; the significance of organisational structure; the relationship of the firm with its employees, the providers of capital and its customers; and the interactions between firms and the industrial environment.

As already emphasised, while technology can have a bearing on these questions, the firm is not viewed as a technological 'black box'. It is recognised that technological relationships have a bearing on business affairs but they are not necessarily the decisive factor in many business decisions. Human behaviour in an environment characterised by uncertainty and informational asymmetries plays a crucial role. The nature of a firm's transactions, the extent to which they require specialised human and capital resources, the degree of frequency with which transactions occur and the uncertainty and complexity involved create contractual difficulties and costs which shape business behaviour. The theory of transaction costs and information economics is therefore at the heart of business economics.

Two assumptions of traditional microeconomic theory are challenged by the new approach to business behaviour: (a) the assumption that internal organisation is irrelevant for a firm's behaviour and its production decisions; and (b) the 'inhospitability' assumption (Williamson 1981), i.e. the belief that certain features of the corporation are necessarily the result of anti-competitive behaviour. A firm's features may be the result of either efficiency or the exercise of market dominance or a combination of the two.

The synthesis of neoclassical with modern theories of the firm incorporated in the approach to business economics adopted in this text implies that while the focus of business economics is on firms, the basic unit of analysis is the transaction. Informational asymmetries and other transactional characteristics coupled with human attributes create costs which play a central role in business decisions. Transaction costs influence both the internal structure of the firm and its external relationships.

Thus, the traditional view of the firm that hires labour in well-defined markets, at fixed or monopsonistically determined wages based on current production, has been replaced with the view of the firm as an employer managing a set of long-term employment relationships. Efficiency in personnel management requires contracts with incentives and rewards which do not necessarily reflect current productivity. Similarly, asymmetrically distributed information between the providers of capital and the managers who control its use create agency costs which have a bearing on the firm's cost of capital and the optimal capital structure.

The modern view of the firm has implications not only on questions of motivation and efficiency but on how the firm is likely to react to external environmental and policy changes. Business economics is therefore concerned with the relationship of the firm and its environment but, unlike the economics of industrial organisation which is 'concerned with the environmental setting within which enterprises operate and in how they behave in these settings as producers, sellers and buyers' (Bain 1959, p. vii), it is primarily concerned with business behaviour and the internal and external relationships of the enterprise.

THE PLAN OF THE BOOK

The book is organised as follows. Chapter 2 examines the industrial environment within which firms operate. Statistical information is used to illustrate the main market features and their evolution over time. It is emphasised that firms are dynamic institutions which while operating within the limits imposed by the industrial environment actively attempt to change that environment in ways that serve their purposes. The causal relationship postulated by the structure–conduct–performance paradigm is critically evaluated by focusing on the simultaneity of relationships between markets and firms thus setting the scene for the rest of the book.

The following three chapters (Chapters 3–5) introduce fundamental concepts while analysing the nature of entrepreneurship and the emergence and internal organisation of firms. The firm is defined as a nexus of contracts between buyers and sellers of inputs and outputs. The basic premise of this part of the book is that the interaction of human attributes with environment characteristics have efficiency implications which determine whether firms supersede the market as a resource allocation mechanism and what institutional arrangement (governance form) the firm will adopt. Chapters 6 and 7 revise and extend the theory of production and consumer choice respectively. The theory of costs has been extended to incorporate the costs of multi-product and multi-plant firms. Similarly, the theory of consumer choice has been extended to incorporate consumer behaviour under conditions of risk. Chapters 8–13 refer to business decisions in different market structures and include an analysis of principal–agent relationships. Agency theory is applied to the examination of the impact of divergencies of interests between shareholders and managers and between the firm and its employees, and the providers of capital. Government policies and in particular competition policies conclude the book (Chapter 14).

To be more specific, Chapter 3 lays the foundation for the transaction cost approach to the theory of the firm, thus introducing concepts utilised throughout the rest of the book. The analysis assumes that (a) decisions are taken by self-interest seeking individuals who, as decision makers, have limited capabilities, and (b) the environment is characterised by uncertainty and/or complexity, information is limited and often asymmetrically distributed, the number of traders can be small and transactions may require specialised investments. The exposition is illustrated with many examples including the input procurement policy of the US aerospace industry and the transportation of chemicals. Chapter 4 develops further the notion of transaction cost efficiency and employs it to explore the way in which firms are internally organised. The impact that a firm's internal organisational structure may have on business behaviour is also examined and illustrated with the early organisation of the railways. Chapter 5 supplements the examination of the forces contributing to the emergence and continued existence of firms by considering the role and function of entrepreneurship, both in the market and within firms. It is suggested that any individual, including managers, may act entrepreneurially but managers are not necessarily entrepreneurs. The nature and meaning of profit is explored and factors contributing to its size are examined. The end of chapter application illustrates the practical significance of entrepreneurship by examining managerial policies which have been identified as conducive to entrepreneurship and have operated successfully in practice.

Chapters 6 and 7 introduce some tools of analysis. The technology of the firm and its costs of production are examined in Chapter 6. The analysis has been extended to include the study of multi-product and multi-plant production costs which are usually omitted in intermediate microeconomics textbooks. Economies of scale and scope are analysed and their significance for business policy demonstrated with the example of the automobile industry. Chapter 7 is devoted to consumer behaviour. Traditional demand analysis is briefly reviewed. The elasticity concept is examined and illustrated with a large number of statistical estimates drawn from a variety of real-world markets. The analysis has been extended to situations involving risk. In particular, consumer behaviour under risk is examined and the concept of risk aversion and preference is introduced. Empirical work on the demand for health care in European Community (EC) countries has been used to illustrate how some of the concepts introduced in this chapter are applied.

Business behaviour in different market structures is the subject matter of Chapter 8. Given their predominance in industrial markets, oligopolies occupy a substantial part of this chapter. Cartels and price leadership models of behaviour are analysed and their significance illustrated with many examples. Their market impact is further explored in some of the end of chapter problems. Business strategic behaviour including limit pricing, strategic investment in advertising, excess capacity and other variables is also analysed in this chapter and the impact of potential entry on incumbent behaviour is explored. The application is drawn from recent evidence on the cartelization of the UK building industry.

While Chapter 8 explores inter-firm interactions Chapter 9 takes an intra-firm perspective. It explores the influence that professional managers may have on the behaviour of the firm. The focus is on principal–agent relationships and the agency costs which may arise in their presence. The function and impact of the market in corporate control are examined. It is suggested that external control mechanisms mitigate but do not necessarily eliminate the divergence of interests that may exist between managers and owners. Furthermore, varying attitudes to risk coupled with information asymmetry create the need for appropriate internal incentive and control mechanisms. Concepts related to effort incentives are introduced so that this chapter lays the foundation for Chapter 13. The existence of agency problems and their mitigation in oil and gas explorations provides the end of chapter case study.

Business decisions relating to vertical, horizontal and multinational expansion are examined in Chapter 10. The traditional approach to national and international expansion is supplemented by the transactions cost approach. The emphasis is on multinationals. The International Aluminium Industry provides the material for the end of chapter application. Business vertical, lateral and spacial expansion implies the creation of multi-product and multi-market firms which involve management in a variety of pricing and output decisions that do not arise within single-product enterprises. Such decisions are explored in Chapter 11. The pricing policies of multi-market firms including pricing of joint products, transfer pricing and pricing of heterogeneous but inter-related products within diversified firms are examined. The transfer pricing policies of two US companies provide the case study at the end of this chapter.

Chapters 12 and 13 explore the relationship of the firm with its owners and its employees in more detail. Ownership is defined in Chapter 12 as consisting of two rights: the right to control the firm and the right to receive its residual income. Any group of firm participants can become the owners of the firm and efficiency considerations imply that ownership is assigned to the group with the lowest transaction and monitoring costs. Ownership structure has an impact on the cost of capital and hence on its optimal capital structure. Asymmetric information between outside investors who provide the capital and the managers of the firm imply that both debt and equity finance is associated with agency and other transaction costs. The selection of financial structure is therefore important in determining the cost of capital and the value of the firm. The ownership structure and its relationship to the cost of debt finance in Japanese firms provides the case material of this chapter.

The firm as an employer who manages long-term employment contracts under conditions of asymmetric information is the focus of Chapter 13. To be efficient personnel management must adopt policies which discourage opportunistic behaviour and provide incentives. These include payment schemes that may deviate from current productivity such as deferred payments and hierarchical pay structures. The role and influence of trade unions is also analysed and found to have efficiency implications. The construction industry is used to illustrate several of the issues examined in this chapter.

Government policies, whether of an interventionist or 'a hands off' philosophy, can have a significant influence on the industrial environment within which firms operate. Government industrial and competition policy can create business opportunities or inhibit the efficient functioning of markets. The recent wave of privatisation and market liberalisation in the UK and elsewhere is a case at hand. It is therefore appropriate to conclude the book with an examination of competition policy and its impact on the industrial environment. Recent competition policy in the UK is examined and compared with competition policy in the EC and the USA. The privatisation and liberalisation of the UK industry which took place in the last decade is reviewed and evaluated. The electricity privatisation provides the end of chapter case that illustrates some of the issues examined.

A NOTE ON THE USE OF THE BOOK

As indicated in the preface the book has been based on a business economics course which I have taught over a number of years. For reasons of completeness and coherence the material has, however, been extended and it is hoped that the final product constitutes a coherent unit with a natural progression from concepts to more demanding models and applications. An effort, however, has been made to ensure that each chapter is, to a large extent, self-contained so that it is possible for an instructor to select material, depending on student background knowledge and interests, so as to build a coherent but shorter unit of study. Students on applied economics courses or those with a prior introduction to the traditional theory of the firm should be familiar with most of the material covered in Chapters 6 and 7 and the first section of Chapter 9. Similarly, students taking a module on industrial economics will be familiar with most of the material covered in Chapter 2. Since it is highly unlikely, however, that many students may be familiar with transactions cost economics it is essential that Chapters 3 and 4 are included even in a short course because transactions cost and efficiency concepts introduced in these chapters permeate throughout the rest of the book. Similarly, the second part of Chapter 9, on the agency theory of the firm, introduces fundamental concepts and is thus essential reading for subsequent chapters and especially for an understanding of the optimal capital structure of the firm examined in Chapter 12. These constraints notwithstanding, it is hoped that the book provides sufficient flexibility to meet the needs of a variety of course units.

2 Industrial and market structure

INTRODUCTION

Questions of how and why firms emerge, what factors contribute to the size and direction of their growth, what determines their output mix, what methods of production they utilise and how efficiently they organise their personnel and other affairs are at the heart of business economics. And, since the answers to these questions depend, at least partly, on the characteristics of the markets within which firms operate, this chapter examines briefly the main features of a firm's industrial environment and the controversies surrounding its impact on business behaviour.

The significance of market characteristics for the behaviour and efficiency of firms has occupied industrial organisation economists for half a century or more. The traditional view, clearly focused by the work of Bain (1956, 1959) and summarised by the structure–conduct–performance (SCP) paradigm, asserts that market structure (number and size of firms, barriers to entry, etc.) determines the conduct of firms (their policy regarding price, capacity, advertising, research and development (R&D) expenditure, etc.) which in turn determines the performance of the industry (its productive and allocative efficiency, for example). Although the proponents of this scheme would accept that causation may not be strictly one-way, they do emphasise the one-way link. This emphasis and the concomitant policy recommendations have been successfully challenged on both theoretical and empirical grounds in favour of the belief that there exists a simultaneity in relationships, of a nature indicated in Figure 2.1. Despite the doubts expressed, the SCP sequence can be a useful starting point when examining the environmental setting within which firms operate.

The structure of this chapter therefore, is, as follows. Markets and industries are defined first. This is followed by the definition of market structures and product differentiation. Concentration, one of the cornerstones of the SCP paradigm and an important influence on public policy, is analysed in the following section which also presents some evidence on UK, US and European Community (EC) concentration and its recent trends. Barriers to entry and an introduction to concepts derived from the

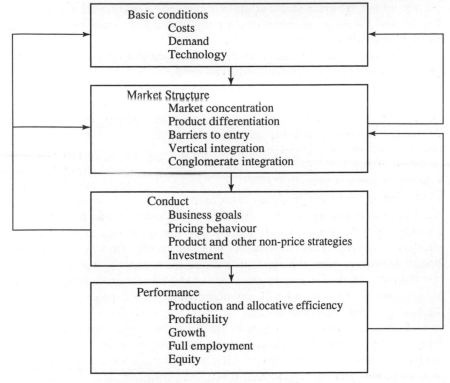

Figure 2.1 The simultaneity of relationships in the structure–conduct–performance paradigm
Source: Adapted from Scherer 1980, Figure 1.1, p. 4

controversial theory of market contestability are the subject matter of the next section. The penultimate section gives a critical appraisal of the SCP paradigm. The view that a reversal in causality can plausibly be argued is outlined but the main debate relates to the simultaneity of the relationships involved. The concluding section summarises the main points. The end of chapter application is a brief case study of the main features of the UK market for soluble (instant) coffee.

MARKETS AND INDUSTRIES

Definitions

A market can be defined as a group of buyers and sellers involved in exchanges. This definition, however, is rather vague since it fails to specify how the members of the group are to be identified. Intuition would suggest that all buyers and sellers of the 'same' product should be grouped together. But what is the same product? A variety of definitions each based

on any one of the many features that characterise a market transaction can
be devised. Some of these relate to the physical characteristics of the
product and others to buyer characteristics such as income, age or location,
or to producer characteristics such as the location of production, the
production process or the raw materials used.

Given the practical significance attached to the definition of the market,
the choice of a criterion must ultimately depend on the purpose for which
the definition is required. If the aim is to assist in the study of some aspect
of market behaviour then the market must be defined broadly enough to
embrace all the market participants likely to have an impact on the
problem at hand. Suppose, for example, that the purpose of defining the
UK car industry is to assist the suppliers of metal paints to estimate trends
in the demand for their products. If metal paints are suitable for any metals
used in vehicle production then the UK car industry should be defined to
include the UK producers of cars of any shape or size as well as the
producers of vans, trucks and buses. The same definition would be far too
broad, however, when the aim is to analyse the competitive process in the
car industry. In the latter case the price or the annual production of Rolls
Royce cars is unlikely to be of any significance to the producers of Mini
Metros or other small family cars.

Defining a market is no easy task, but once the market boundaries have
been drawn it becomes relatively easy to define an industry since an
industry consists of all the firms operating in a particular market. The terms
'industry' and 'market' are indeed often used interchangeably despite the
emphasis of the term 'industry' on sellers only.

The substitutability criterion

In analysing the behaviour of firms the need to group similar products
together arises because firms, as decision makers, select their decision
variables after considering the possible reactions of other competing firms.
But while all firms are likely to be affected to a certain extent by each
other's actions, it is infeasible or extremely costly for a decision maker to
consider the possible links and interactions of a large number of competitors.
Decision makers are more likely to confine their attention to those firms
whose behaviour they believe to have a significant influence on the result
of their own actions. It is reasonable therefore to assume that the extent
to which firms take each other's actions into consideration depends on the
extent to which products are considered as substitutes for each other by
their consumers or producers. A market should, therefore, be defined
broadly enough to embrace all those goods or services which are regarded
as substitutes by buyers or sellers.

If products are considered to be very similar by many buyers, product
substitutability will be strong and a firm's price setting ability will be
limited. A price increase in this case will induce customers to switch to

substitute products, thus curbing a firm's monopoly power. Similarly, a rival firm's price reduction may, unless matched, cause substantial sales reductions and losses. Clearly, strongly inter-related products should be part of the same market and the question of measuring the strength of product interactions arises. A specific measure used by economists to measure the extent to which the demand for one product responds to price changes of another product is the cross price elasticity of demand (e_c) This is defined as the ratio of the percentage change in the quantity demanded of one product x over the percentage change in the price of another product y assuming that other variables such as consumer incomes or preferences remain constant. That is,

$$e_c = \frac{dQ_x}{dP_y} \frac{P_y}{Q_x}$$

The cross-price elasticity is examined in more detail in Chapter 7 but it should be clear from its definition that the larger the absolute value of e_c the more closely inter-related the products are. Furthermore, e_c can be positive (denoting substitutability) or negative (denoting complementarity). High positive values of e_c indicate close substitutes and very high values indicate almost identical products since small price changes induce customers to switch between the two brands.

The value of the cross-price elasticity of demand is a useful guide in drawing market boundaries. There are, however, two caveats. First, its empirical estimation is fraught with difficulties. Second, even assuming that reasonable estimates of e_c for a group of products can be obtained the question remains as to where to draw the line between successive magnitudes of e_c in order to decide which products belong to the same market and which should be left outside. There is no theoretical guidance as to what value of e_c defines similar products.

Despite these difficulties, the substitutability criterion is often used to guide both public policy and business strategy. For example, the method of defining markets and measuring market shares incorporated in the US Justice Department Merger guidelines of 1982 (revised in 1984) is based on the substitutability criterion; the guidelines suggest that, in defining the market for product X, the possibility that consumers could switch to substitute products in response to a price increase in X should be taken into account. Furthermore, the guidelines require that producers of related products who could switch to the production of X should be given 'imputed' market shares based on the quantity of X they could produce in response to a given price increase. Producers of X located in different regions who could export to compete with X were also included in the definition. Thus, when DuPont was accused of operating a monopoly in the cellophane industry, in violation of US legislation, the company successfully argued in court that it did not have a monopoly because cellophane competed with a large number of other packaging materials such as wax paper, greaseproof paper, glassine, foil and saran. The court ruling conceded that 'every manufacturer is a sole producer of the particular commodity it makes, but its control . . . of the relevant market depends upon the availability of alternative commodities for buyers (i.e., whether there is a *cross-elasticity of demand* between cellophane and the other wrappings)' (Shughart 1990: 145). The market definition was broadened to include these substitutes thus reducing DuPont's share well below that associated with monopoly.

The court ruling, however, was different in the case of Alcoa which argued that it did not have an aluminium monopoly despite its 90 per cent share of the ingot market because of the existence of substitute metals. Judge Hand ruled that Alcoa's market consisted of all domestic aluminium ingot production plus ingot imports but it excluded other metals such as copper or steel despite the fact that the cross-price elasticity was calculated to be around 2.0.[1]

It should be clear that, in defining a market, substitutability both on the demand side and on the supply side of the market can play a role. Substitutability on the supply side can be measured by the cross-price elasticity of supply. The latter is defined as the percentage change in quantity supplied of one product in response to a given percentage change in the price of another product, *ceteris paribus*. A high cross-price supply elasticity shows that as the price of, say, product x increases the quantity supplied of product y decreases as producers switch resources from y to the production of the relatively highly priced product x. Thus, high inter-relationships on the supply side may denote a significant extent of potential competition in the market which may restrain monopolistic behaviour. A higher price–cost margin in women's shoes compared with men's shoes may not, for example, be sustainable since the producers of men's shoes use the same raw materials, techniques and expertise and are, presumably, able to switch their production in search of higher profits. A more illustrative example has been provided by the European Court of Justice in relation to the market of continental can. The court did not uphold the European Commission's ruling that the market for meat cans was separate from that for fish cans on the grounds that resources could easily be switched from the supply of one type of can to the supply of the other type (Vickers and Hay 1987). Each type of can provides a source of prompt potential competition.

The significance of substitutability on the supply side is perhaps indicated by the fact that national standard industrial classifications (SICs) assign firms into industries by grouping together establishments producing a product or products which are related by a technical process or raw materials. Table 2.1 indicates the structure of the UK SIC as revised in 1992. This is a hierarchical five-digit system based on the European Community Classification of Economic Activity (NACE) Rev 1 with the only difference being that a fifth digit has been added to form subclasses

Table 2.1 The UK standard industrial classification, 1992

The structure of the 1992 UK SIC (based on NACE)	
17 sections	A–Q
99 divisions	01–99
990 groups	01.1–99.0
9,900 subclasses	01.11–99.00

Example:			
Section A			Agriculture, hunting and forestry
01			Agriculture, hunting and related services activities
	01.1		Growing of crops; market gardening; horticulture
		01.11	Growing of serials and other crops not elsewhere classified
		01.12	Growing of vegetables, horticultural specialities and nursery products
		01.13	Growing of fruit, nuts beverage and spice crops
	01.2		Farming of animals
	01.21		Farming of cattle, dairy farming
	01.22		Farming of sheep, goats, horses, asses, mules and hinnies
02			Forestry, logging and related service activities
	02.0		Forestry and logging related service activities
		02.01	Forestry and logging
		02.02	Forestry and logging related service activities

Source: SIC, 1992, Central Statistical Office, London: HMSO

where necessary. The United Nations (UN) SIC and the US SIC are slightly different but are also based on supply side considerations. The SICs provide useful official classifications but they have shortcomings. They tend, for example, to assign each firm to one industry only, according to their main product line. But since many firms are multi-product enterprises, they operate in more than one industry at any point in time. Ignoring this fact produces groupings which are, occasionally, somewhat idiosyncratic and of limited use. For example, industry No. 4494 in the 1966 UK SIC groups together manufacturers of scarves, suspenders and artificial flowers (Needham 1978: 116).

MARKET STRUCTURE AND PRODUCT DIFFERENTIATION

Having determined the boundaries of a market we can begin to analyse its structure. A market structure can be defined as the set of those organisational features of the market which have a significant influence on the nature of competition (Bain 1959). Such features include (a) the extent of product differentiation, (b) the number of buyers and sellers operating in a market and their relative sizes (concentration), (c) the extent to which new competitors can enter the market or are impeded by barriers to entry, (d) whether production is subject to economies of scale and how important they are, and (e) the degree to which firms are vertically integrated and diversified.

We shall argue in subsequent chapters that entrepreneurship and dynamism, as well as human limitation in decision making, lack of information and informational asymmetries combined with the attributes of the transactions involved, have an important influence on behaviour and on market structure. In this chapter, however, we concentrate on some of the features traditionally considered as very significant, such as product differentiation, concentration and barriers to entry. Vertical integration and diversification are analysed in detail in Chapter 10.

Product differentiation refers to the extent to which products are perceived by buyers to be different. Whether they are different or not, in reality is immaterial. What is sufficient is that buyers believe them to be different. Furthermore, the more differentiated products are believed to be the more likely it is that consumer attachment to a particular product (brand loyalty) may exist, which has important implications for market behaviour and competition.

Two types of product differentiation – horizontal and vertical – can be distinguished (Shaked and Sutton 1987). *Horizontal differentiation* corresponds to the traditional view of differentiation. It exists when the mix of attributes of a particular product varies so as to satisfy the preferences of a particular group of customers. For example, variations in the news, pictures, advertisements or colour combinations of a newspaper or magazine constitute horizontal differentiation. The editor of each paper selects a different mix of, say, news and gossip columns in order to appeal to a particular readership. In other words, a firm may offer a different mix of product attributes in an attempt to create a brand that appeals to a particular group of customers (i.e. create a 'niche' in the market). *Vertical differentiation*, on the other hand, refers to quality differences which appeal to all consumers and are usually associated with differences in costs. A computer with a large memory is clearly different to one with a small memory. It is better and more expensive to produce.

Product differentiation plays an important role in business economics for several reasons.

1 It can assist in defining a market. The absence of strong product differentiation, indicated by high cross-price elasticities, identifies products which can be thought of as belonging to the same market. The higher the degree of differentiation the lower the e_c is and the more likely it is that products belong to different markets.

2 The extent of product differentiation has implications for the shape and position of a firm's demand curve. Clearly, given the total demand, the larger the number of consumers who prefer a particular brand the larger the market share of that brand will be. Furthermore, the stronger the consumer attachment to a brand is, the lower the price elasticity of the

demand for this brand is. Thus, the extent to which decision makers are likely to provoke reactions from 'near neighbours', the degree of interdependence and rivalry among products, depends on the distribution of consumer preferences among products and on the strength with which these preferences are held, i.e. on the extent of product differentiation.

Advertising is often used by firms in an attempt to affect this distribution and strength of consumer preferences. So far as it succeeds in concentrating preferences on existing products and in increasing a consumer's disutility to changes to other products, advertising enhances the phenomenon of 'brand loyalty', which reduces product substitutability and gives power to producers. Advertising can play such an important role as a business strategic variable and as a barrier to entry that some authors consider the advertising intensity of a market as a significant structural feature rather than as a surrogate for product differentiation.

3 Differentiation and brand loyalty can affect conditions of entry. The stronger the consumer preferences for existing products the more difficult it becomes for firms to enter, especially if there are economies of scale and firms must enter at a large scale in order to produce at minimum cost.

4 The extent of market concentration can be influenced by the nature of product differentiation. When, for example, the market demand expands and there are no barriers to entry, whether new entry may occur and to what extent depends on whether horizontal or vertical differentiation is possible. If horizontal differentiation is possible then new entry will occur. As Shaked and Sutton (1987) show, market expansion encourages the entry of firms offering new brands. Product proliferation increases giving consumers a wider choice of products that better satisfy their preferences. If, however, in the same circumstances only vertical differentiation is possible, since quality improvements require higher costs, a market expansion will be associated with increased costs. There may be no scope for new entry in which case concentration remains high.

INDUSTRIAL CONCENTRATION

Market concentration refers to the extent to which production in a particular market is controlled by a few firms. This is also known as seller concentration and is determined by the number and size distribution of sellers. Buyer concentration is similarly defined by the number and size distribution of buyers operating in a particular market.

Seller concentration has important implications for the behaviour of firms in both differentiated and homogeneous product markets; this is for several reasons.

The cost of search and acquisition of information by consumers may depend crucially on the number of firms operating in a market

When sellers are known to charge different prices for the same (or similar) product, consumers would benefit by the acquisition of relevant information which may be obtained by, for example, visiting or otherwise contacting firms prior to purchasing. Information can be acquired but at a cost. Clearly the more firms there are the more diffused and costly to gather the relevant information becomes. Consumers may find it impossible or very expensive to canvass all the firms before every purchase. The number of firms to be visited would depend on the relevant costs and benefits involved. A rational consumer would stop searching when the extra cost of a search is equal to the expected reduction in price associated with an extra unit of search. Assuming that marginal information costs increase while the expected marginal reduction in price quotes declines as search increases, the optimum number of firms to be visited will be less than the total number of firms. Informational costs imply that price differentials will persist. The prices of foodstuffs, for example, may vary among local supermarkets but owing to the costs involved, in terms of time and inconvenience in visiting all the local supermarkets, consumers are prevented from acquiring the full relevant information prior to purchasing.

While several factors may contribute to search costs the number of incumbent firms is very significant. The fewer the firms the easier it becomes for buyers to acquire price information from all sellers who, as a result, find it more difficult to maintain price differentials. Factors affecting the cost of time such as occupation, age and income level vary among individuals so that search costs may vary among markets with the same number of firms. Similarly, factors which facilitate the flow of information such as the localisation of markets (as, for example, in the wholesale fruit and vegetable markets) or improvements in information technology make consumer search easier which tends to reduce price differentials.

Seller concentration can influence oligopolistic interdependence and price–cost margins

When a few firms produce a homogeneous product which is sold at a uniform price, if one seller were to increase its output the market price and the revenues of all the other firms would fall, thus inducing them to consider an appropriate response. This effect on market price and competitors' revenues would, however, depend on the number of firms and on their relative sizes. Thus, a 20 per cent output expansion by a firm controlling, say, 10 per cent of the market, is unlikely to have a very significant impact on price and market shares while the same percentage expansion by a firm controlling, say, 50 per cent of the market, may have a sufficiently large impact to trigger fierce competitive reactions. In short, the extent of interdependence or 'the degree of oligopoly' depends on both the number and the relative market shares of the firms in a market.

A more rigorous explanation of the degree of oligopoly is given in Appendix 2.1 which shows that if each firm profit maximises so that each firm produces where marginal revenue equals marginal cost (MR = MC) and when deciding on its production level each firm expects its competitors to maintain their production at the current level (i.e. a Cournot model behaviour prevails), then the following relationship holds:

$$\frac{P - c_i}{P} = \frac{S_i}{e.}$$

That is, a firm's price–cost margin depends inversely on the price elasticity of demand and directly on its market share. Therefore, the larger a firm's market share the bigger its price–cost difference. When market shares are equal then, for a given market size, the fewer the firms the larger each share is and the wider the price–cost margin becomes.

For the industry as a whole, Appendix 2.1 shows that on average the MR and hence the average price–cost margin depends on the price elasticity of demand and on the extent of seller concentration:

$$\text{average MR} = P(1 + \frac{\Sigma s_i^2}{e})$$

where $i = 1, 2, \ldots, n$ is the number of firms in the market and $\Sigma s_i^2 = \text{HI}$ is the Herfindahl index of concentration. Since HI falls as n increases and tends to unity as n becomes very small, the more concentrated the industry the closer the price–cost mark-up approaches the monopoly mark-up.

This conclusion was derived on the assumption that each firm contemplating a production change expects its competitors to maintain their output levels constant. Other assumptions are possible, however. For example, when a firm changes its output it might expect its competitors to respond by a proportionate change a in their own output. Symbolically this means that

$$\frac{\mathrm{d}X_j}{X_j} = a \frac{\mathrm{d}X_i}{X_i}$$

for all j where $a \leqslant 1$. In fact it is claimed that the average industry mark-up IM depends on the strength of the competitive response a, the price elasticity of demand e and the market concentration. Davies (1988: 76) has shown that

$$\text{IM} = \frac{\text{HI} (1 - a)}{e} + \frac{a}{e}.$$

It should be noted that as the industry approaches a monopoly (HI → 1), IM approaches the monopoly mark which is inversely related to the price elasticity of demand; i.e. IM $\rightarrow$ $1/e$. In conclusion, concentration has an influence on profits but the extent of this influence depends on the way in which firms respond to each other's actions as well as on the strength of preference that consumers show for their product.

Concentration may considerably influence inter-firm knowledge

Information about rivals' behaviour regarding their pricing policies, advertising budgets, expenditure on R&D or productive investment decisions is usually not easily available. As a rule the cost of search and collection of information increases with the number of firms producing the same or a strongly similar product. This is particularly true when firms are of equal size, since when substantial differences in firm size exist it may be only necessary to consider the behaviour of the dominant firms.

As the number of firms declines a firm's own sales figures become a good source of information about rivals' behaviour. This is because given the general market conditions a loss in sale or market share might indicate successful changes in rivals' behaviour. Indeed the higher the concentration the smaller the probability of random sales fluctuations and the easier it becomes to detect secret price cutters. Thus, a high degree of concentration not only contributes to a strengthening of oligopolistic interdependence, it also facilitates co-operation by making easier (through its influence on information flows) the detection of chiselling.

Measures of concentration

Concentration is the single most frequently used feature of market structures, both by market analysts and by those implementing government monopoly and competition policy. To analyse its influence a measure of its size is required. Difficulties in constructing a unique measure have, however, led researchers to use a variety of indices some of which measure absolute inequalities in concentration while others measure relative inequalities in concentration. Some of the most popular ones are as follows.

The concentration ratio

The concentration ratio (CR_i) is simply the sum of the market shares of the i largest firms in a market, where i is a small number (usually 3–5). Thus, if $i = 5$ then $CR_5 = 0.90$ means that the five largest firms in the market control 90 per cent of the industry size. Industry size can be measured in terms of value or volume of sales, employment or capital employed. The five-firm concentration ratio, CR_5, is commonly used in the UK while CR_3 or CR_4 are more common in the USA and other countries.

Carbonated drinks	Market share (per cent)	Razors	Market share (per cent)
Coca Cola and Schweppes	43	Gillette	60
Britvic Soft Drinks	22	Wilkinson Sword	20
12 others, each with 1–2 per cent share	31	Biro Bic Ltd	15
Another 80 or so	4	Own Labels	3
		Supermac	1
		Schick	1
Total	100		100

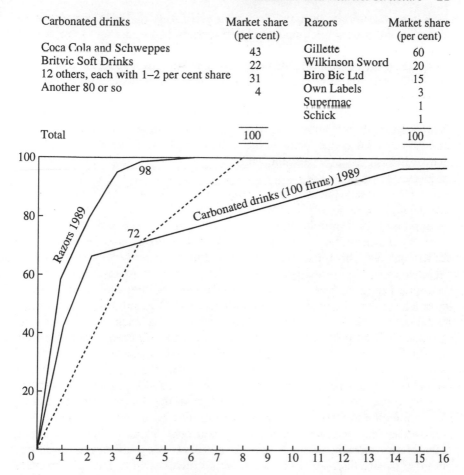

Figure 2.2 The UK razors and carbonated drinks concentration curves in 1989
Source: Monopolies and Mergers Commission reports (1991a, 1991c)

The CR is but one of a number of indices given by the concentration curve. The concentration curve is derived when we plot the cumulative sales (output or any other measure of market size) against the cumulative number of firms starting from the largest. Figure 2.2 gives the concentration curves for the UK carbonated drinks and razor industries in 1989 together with the data used to derive them. An examination of Figure 2.2 shows that the four-firm CR of the carbonated drinks industry is 98 per cent while the corresponding figure for the razors industry is 72 per cent. On the basis of the CR_4, the carbonated drinks industry is ~~more~~ less concentrated than the razors industry. In fact it is clear from Figure 2.2 that the same conclusion would be derived by calculating CR_5 or any other CR. Since the concentration curve of the carbonated drinks industry lies everywhere above the concentration curve of the razors industry we may conclude that the carbonated drinks industry was, in 1989, more concentrated than the razors industry, although both industries were highly concentrated.

A CR provides useful information regarding the extent of market or aggregate (national) concentration at a particular point in time as well as its trend over time. Compared with other indices, a CR has the advantage of simplicity in construction and interpretation. This simplicity, however, has been brought about at the expense of providing rather limited information since the focus of the CR is on a few firms rather than the whole industry. Care must therefore be taken in making inferences from a given CR or in making comparisons between industries when only one CR, rather than the entire concentration curve for each industry, is available.

Suppose, for example, that $CR_4 = 80$. This clearly indicates that the industry described is an oligopoly in which four firms control 80 per cent of the market. This is useful information, but can we infer from it the likely behaviour of this industry? The answer is most probably not, for two reasons. First, we have no information regarding the relative size of the four leading firms and it is known that relative size can have an important influence on the way in which firms respond to each other's actions. Competitive behaviour would be expected to be different when the four largest firms are of approximately equal size than when one firm controls, say, 40 per cent of the market with the other three accounting for the remaining 40 per cent. In the case of the UK razor industry for example, a CR_4 equal to 0.98 conceals the fact that the largest firm (Gillette) dominates the industry with a market share of 60 per cent. It also does not reveal the fact that the fourth largest firm controls an insignificant 3 per cent of the market. Second, the CR gives no information regarding the number or size distribution of the firms not included in it. It may, however, be of some significance to know whether a small or a large number of firms account for the market share not controlled by the x largest firms. Market behaviour could be very different when two rather than twenty firms account for the market share not included in the CR_4. Thus, it might be useful to know that the UK carbonated drinks industry includes approximately one hundred insignificantly small firms while it is dominated by two ($CR_2 = 0.65$). The CR_4 fails to reveal this information.

Another serious weakness of the CR relates to changes over time. A change in the relative shares of the leading firms or a takeover or merger among the smaller firms may not alter the size of the CR while it can have significant competitive implications. In the UK razors industry, for example, a merger between Gillette and Wilkinson Sword would produce a virtual monopoly (the largest market share following the merger would be 80 per cent and the second largest only 15 per cent). A merger between Wilkinson Sword and Biro Bic, on the other hand, would produce a duopoly (with the largest market shares at 60 and 35 per cent). In both instances the two-firm CR however, would be the same, $CR_2 = 0.95$, which fails to indicate the difference in market structure.

Care must be taken in comparing industries since the outcome of a comparison based on the CR may depend on how many firms are included in it. Thus, if the CR_4 is used to compare the carbonated drinks industry with the hypothetical industry X whose concentration curve is indicated by the broken line in Figure 2.2, the conclusion is that the two industries are equally concentrated. At CR_2, however, X is less concentrated than the carbonated drinks industry and at CR_6 X is more concentrated.

To sum up, the CRs place a heavy emphasis on the share of the few largest firms whilst ignoring the significance of relative shares and any influence that the smaller firms may have on industrial behaviour. Two summary indices, the Herfindahl and the Rosenbluth indices, are among several indices proposed to remedy the limitations of the discrete indices.

The Herfindahl index

The Herfindahl index ($HI = \Sigma s_i^2$ where $i = 1,2,3, \ldots, n$), also known as the Hirschman–Herfindahl index, is simply the sum of the squared market shares of all the firms comprising an industry. Thus, the Herfindahl index takes into account both the number and the size distribution of the firms in the industry. The squaring of the market shares implies, however, that the smaller a firm the smaller its contribution to the index. In other words, the weights attached to larger firms are higher implying that small firms do have an influence on market behaviour but their influence is not as significant as that of the larger firms.

The index varies between zero and one, i.e. $0 \leq HI \leq 1$. It is equal to $1/n$ when the firms have equal market shares and approaches one as the industry approaches a monopoly. The generalised form of this index is widely used in empirical research.

The Rosenbluth index

The Rosenbluth index is calculated using the following formula:

$$RI = \frac{1}{2\Sigma i s_i - 1}$$

where $i = 1,2,3, \ldots, n$ is the firm's rank when firms are ranked in descending order of size. Thus, the smaller a firm the larger its ranking which tends to increase its contribution to the index. The Rosenbluth index therefore attaches more significance to small firms than does the Herfindahl index. The Rosenbluth index, like the Herfindahl index, varies between zero and one and tends to $1/n$ as the firms become equally sized.

The comprehensive concentration index

The comprehensive concentration index, proposed by Professor J. Horvath in 1970,[2] is a mixture of a discrete and a summary index. It is calculated by adding to the market share of the largest firm a summary index covering the remaining firms in the industry. Thus,

$$CCI = si + \Sigma s_j^2 \, (2 - s_j)$$

where i denotes the largest firm and j the remaining firms. This index also varies between zero and one and approaches $1/n$ as the size distribution of firms approaches equality.

Relative measures of concentration

The indices described so far are all concerned with absolute inequality and the most fundamental difference among them refers to the weights they attach to the market shares of the firms. Other indices, however, have been devised emphasising relative inequality. Relative or inequality measures of concentration focus attention on the degree of size inequality that prevails rather than on the numbers of firms operating in a market. They are summary indices and their graphical representation is called the 'Lorenz curve'. A Lorenz curve relates the cumulative percentage of market output (or size) to the cumulative percentage of firms starting from the smallest.

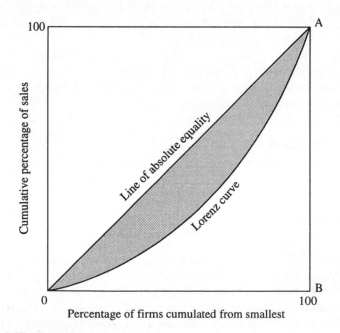

Figure 2.3 The Lorenz curve

In Figure 2.3 a hypothetical Lorenz curve is drawn. It lies below the diagonal line and is concave from below. Since equality exists when all the firms in a market have the same size, so that 10 per cent of the firms account for 10 per cent of the market size, 20 per cent of the firms control 20 per cent of the market and so on, the diagonal line represents absolute equality irrespective of the number of firms. It is thus known as the line of absolute equality. In a market of equally sized firms the Lorenz curve coincides with the diagonal line. Otherwise, it lies below it and the further away it is the higher the extent of inequality in the market it describes. Graphically, the larger the area between the two curves (the shaded area in Figure 2.3) the more significant the size inequality among the firms. The shaded area is called the area of inequality. An index of inequality commonly used is the Gini coefficient. This measures the area of inequality as a percentage of the total area below the diagonal (triangle 0AB):

$$\text{Gini coefficient} = \frac{\text{area of inequality}}{\text{area below the diagonal line}}$$

An obvious weakness of the Lorenz curve is that it ignores numbers altogether. An industry of four equally sized firms would have the same Lorenz curve as that consisting of forty equally sized firms. Thus, although extremely useful in studies involving large numbers such as studies of income or wealth distribution, it is more limited in the study of oligopolistic markets.

Evaluating concentration indices

Given the large variety of concentration indices the question arises as to which index should be used in each instance. There is no straightforward answer to this question since there is no ideal way of quantifying the extent of concentration that exists in a market. The appropriateness of an index must ultimately depend on one's belief as to which index is most likely to correspond to the system of relationships taken into account by business decision makers. The Rosenbluth index, for example, may be advocated by those who feel that small firms contribute significantly to the pattern of behaviour in a particular industry. Those who feel that the actions of small firms are unlikely to have a serious impact on market behaviour will advocate a Herfindhal index or a concentration ratio. Finally the comprehensive concentration index will be used when one believes that the largest firm exerts a dominant influence in the market.

There are advantages and disadvantages in the use of any index which cannot be resolved *a priori*. The choice depends on the problem under investigation. The best index would be the one which is most closely related to whatever aspect of behaviour is being investigated. This is an empirical question. Yet, an index must have some desirable properties. A set of such properties proposed by Hannah and Kay (1977) imply that a good index must fulfil the following criteria.

The concentration curve criterion

When the cumulative share of the x largest firms increases (where x can be any number of firms) a concentration index must show increased concentration. In other words, a shift of the entire concentration curve upwards must be indicated by an increase in the index since it reflects a real increase in market concentration.

The principle of sales transfer must hold

If the share of a firm increases at the expense of the market share of a smaller firm the concentration index must increase since the size distribution of firms has become more unequal.

The new entry criterion

Provided that the size distribution of existing firms remains unchanged, the entry of new relatively small firms must reduce the concentration index. However, as the size of a new entrant becomes smaller its influence on concentration should decline. The proviso that firms must be small should be intuitively obvious since the entry of a large firm may actually increase concentration.

Mergers should increase concentration

This criterion is actually implied by the first two criteria. Clearly if the merger is between a large and a small firm it is equivalent to a sales transfer or an upwards shift of the concentration curve and it should increase the concentration index. It is not, however, always true that a merger increases concentration since a merger between two or more small firms may improve the share distribution which is equivalent to a reduction in concentration.

The influence of random factors

If the growth of firms is influenced by random factors then concentration should increase, while random brand switching by customers reduces concentration.

Hannah and Kay have shown that a generalised Herfindahl index of the form $HK = (\Sigma s_i^2 a)^{1/(1-a)}$, where $a > 0$ and $a \neq 1$, satisfies all their criteria.

Concentration in the UK industry

Just as market concentration indices are used to measure the extent to which a market is dominated by a few sellers, aggregate concentration

Table 2.2 Comparisons of aggregate concentration levels in manufacturing, 100-firm concentration ratios

Year	USA	UK	EC
1947	23		
1949		22	
1953		27	
1954	30		
1958	30	32	
1963	33	37	
1967	33		
1968		41	
1970		41	
1972	33	41	
1975		42	34
1977	33	41	24
1980		41	25
1982		41	26

Source: Ferguson 1988, Table 3.2, reproduced by permission of Macmillan Press Ltd.

indices are used to measure the extent to which the whole economy or a large sector thereof is dominated by a few producers. Traditionally aggregate concentration refers to the share of total industrial output accounted for by the largest one hundred firms in the UK industry (largest 500 in the USA). Using this measure, aggregate concentration in the UK showed a steady increase from 16 per cent in 1909 to around 41 per cent in 1968 where it remained till the early 1980s (see Table 2.2). During the 1980s it stabilised around 40 per cent despite the existence of substantial variations among industries. In industries such as sugar, cigarettes, cement, cars, tractors, man-made fibres, etc. the leading five firms account for at least 90 per cent of the market (Table 2.3), while in non-electrical engineering, textiles and the brewing industry concentration is very small. Furthermore market concentration varies substantially among countries as Table 2.2 demonstrates.

Two important observations follow from Table 2.2. First, concentration in the UK shows a sharp increase in the period 1949–70 which is not paralleled in the US experience, and second, UK concentration levels have persistently been higher than those of the USA and the EC countries.

The stability of the concentration level during the 1970s is confirmed by a different sample of ninety-three three-digit industries which showed that the CR_5 increased by only 1 per cent between 1970 and 1979 (Davies 1988), while Table 2.4 shows a slight reduction in concentration during the 1970s and early 1980s.

Trends in aggregate concentration are of particular interest to (a) policy makers concerned with the political implications of the concentration of economic power in few hands and (b) to business economists since increased concentration implies increased firm size which raises questions

Table 2.3 Highly concentrated UK industries

Industry (four-digit)	Five-firm concentration ratio, 1975	Five-firm concentration ratio, 1983[a]
Tobacco	98.8	99
Cars	98.2	91
Man-made fibres	95.4	93
Cement	93	91
Cables for telecommunication	95.3	–
Telegraph and telephone installations	98.9	–
Tractors	95.7	–
Tyres and tubes	96.4	–
Breakfast cereal	91.4	–
Sugar	99.9	
Cigarettes	100.0 (7 firms)	

Source: Clarke, Roger 1985: Table 2.3; Ferguson, 1988; Table 3.5
Note: [a] The 1983 figures refer to three-digit industries so that they are not strictly comparable with the 1975 figures.

Table 2.4 Average five-firm concentration ratios for the UK adjusted for international trade

	1970	1973	1977	1979	1979[a]	1981	1983
CR$_5$	41.3	40.9	38.1	36.5	39.3	37.6	35.9

Source: Adapted from Ferguson 1988: Table 3.4
Note: [a] Data for 1970–9 based on SIC 1968; data for 1979–83 based on the (1980) revised SIC.

of business strategy in selecting the best method of growth, of internal organisation and of the allocation of resources by managers with possibly very little 'discipline' enforced by markets. Some evidence on highly concentrated UK industries is given in Table 2.3.

The increase in concentration during the 1950s and 1960s (indicated in Table 2.2) has been brought about by both internal and external expansion, the relative magnitude of which varies among industries. The data on Table 2.5, however, suggests that the increase in concentration between 1957 and 1969 was mainly due to mergers. Internal growth was in general relatively less important than expansion by merger and in eight out of the twelve industries indicated its effect was to reduce concentration.

The increase in firm size, implied by Table 2.5, has been brought about by an increase in the number of plants operated by each firm rather than by an increased plant size. This is true for both the UK and the USA since in both countries the concentration ratio of the largest hundred plants has remained constant at 9–10 per cent. This suggests that multi-plant operations are extensive. Indeed the largest 200 firms in the USA have an average of forty-five plants each and in the UK the number of plants

Table 2.5 Source of change in the CR_{10} in UK industry, 1957–69

SIC group	1957	Change due to merger	Change due to internal growth	1969
Food	62.1	+12.9	+5.5	80.7
Drink	40.8	+45.4	+1.0	87.2
Tobacco	100.0	–	–	100.0
Chemicals	80.6	+2.0	+3.8	86.4
Metal manufacturing	58.7	+16.7	−1.1	74.3
Non-electrical engineering	39.0	+6.0	−12.9	32.1
Electrical engineering	60.4	+22.0	−1.2	81.2
Shipbuilding	80.3	+10.5	+2.5	93.3
Vehicles and aircraft	67.2	+20.0	−1.4	85.8
Metal goods	67.2	+12.8	−2.9	77.1
Textiles	55.9	+23.4	−5.1	74.2
Building materials	71.2	+3.2	−9.4	65.0
Paper and publishing	63.6	+16.1	−1.6	78.1

Source: Adapted from Hay and Morris 1991: Table 15.1

operated by the largest one hundred firms has risen from an average of twenty-seven in 1958 to seventy-two in 1972 (Hay and Morris 1991: 556).

Determinants of concentration

The evidence on concentration raises many questions. Why is it that concentration varies among countries and among industrial sectors? Why is concentration in countries such as the USA, Germany or Canada lower than in the UK? A literature survey on the determinants of concentration reveals a number of disparate explanations with no attempt at integration, so that the theory of the determination of concentration has been likened to the Tower of Babel 'with different groups of contributors seemingly speaking in different and unconnected tongues' (Davies 1988: 91). Despite this state of affairs two broad strands of thought can be distinguished; the deterministic and the stochastic explanations of concentration. The deterministic approach embraces all those contributors who emphasise technological factors as having the predominant influence on concentration. In this school of thought we could include those who believe that past behaviour has played a role in shaping the existing number and size distribution of firms. The stochastic approach, on the other hand, is based on the notion that concentration reflects the net effect of a multitude of uncertain influences. Consider each in turn.

The deterministic approach

While technology and barriers to entry have been emphasised by the SCP paradigm as the main determinants of concentration, other economic influences, including government competition policy and merger activity, are also embraced by the deterministic approach to concentration. The focus, however, is on economic or 'natural' rather than chance factors, the main ones among these are as follows.

Technology (economies of scale)

Technology, through its influence on costs, is at the heart of the SCP paradigm. It is expected that efficiency seeking firms would select to operate at the minimum efficient scale of production (MES, see Figure 2.4(a)). If it is further assumed that all firms have access to the same technology so that their average cost curves are the same and U-shaped as indicated in Figure 2.4(a) and that the competitive price $p = c$ prevails, each firm produces q_c units of output. If the total market size is X, the number of firms will be exactly X/q_c. This is clearly determined by the size of MES in relation to the market.

This precise determinacy of the number of firms is undermined, however, if it is assumed that (a) the U-shaped cost curve describes the costs of a plant rather than the cost of a firm and that firms can expand by operating a number of plants, or (b) cost curves are L-shaped (Figure 2.4(b)). The number of single-plant firms in this case would be equal to X/MES only if all the firms were to operate at MES. But there is no efficiency reason why firms cannot produce more than MES. In fact they could produce efficiently anywhere along the horizontal part of the average cost curve. Thus, it is more realistic to assume that the number X/MES defines the upper limit rather than the exact number of firms in the industry. If costs increase steeply beyond output w (broken line) then cost minimisation is achieved up to this level of output and X/w determines the minimum number of cost minimising firms that this industry could sustain.

A serious criticism of the above analysis is that in the absence of a perfectly competitive market it is not necessarily true that firms will operate at MES. Profit maximising firms are more likely to restrict production to less than MES, and charge a price higher than c. Small firms may then be able to operate at suboptimal levels (such as q) especially if they can differentiate their product horizontally so as to service a particular 'niche' in the market.

It can therefore be argued that technology, although significant, cannot by itself determine concentration. This is particularly true when technology determines costs at the plant rather than the firm level since firms, as the evidence suggests, often operate more than one production plant. Thus, whatever the level of MES multi-plant operations can vary the extent of concentration.

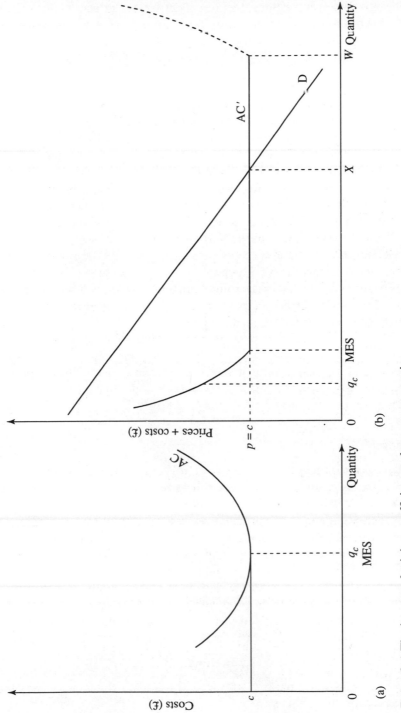

Figure 2.4 The impact of minimum efficient scale on concentration

Despite these reservations, technological factors or economies of scale have been shown by several empirical studies to have an important influence on the extent of concentration.

Entry barriers

Since entry barriers slow down or prevent new entry they may, *ceteris paribus*, contribute to a more concentrated market structure. When incumbent firms are protected from potential competition they are more likely to restrict production in order to charge a price higher than the competitive price ($p > c$). As a result the market size declines which tends to increase concentration. Furthermore, large incumbent firms may be able to expand output at a constant cost increasing their market share at the expense of smaller firms which enhances the existing size inequalities. The conclusion, however, that barriers to entry increase concentration can be erroneous since in the absence of pressures from potential entry a price higher than cost may make it possible for a suboptimal sector of smaller firms to survive, which increases numbers and may imply lower concentration. Thus, the influence of barriers on market concentration is not as straightforward as intuition might suggest.

Similarly the absence of barriers and the impact of new entry has an ambiguous effect on concentration. New entry increases the number of firms but at the same time it can increase size inequalities especially when the new entrant is an already established, financially strong firm diversifying into the new market at a large scale.[3]

Conduct

The traditional view that market structure determines conduct has been challenged by many industrial economists who argue that in many instances it is the conduct of firms that determines market structure rather than the other way round. In particular, it can be argued that the nature of competition that exists among incumbent firms can determine market shares and hence firm size inequalities and concentration. Clarke and Davies (1982), for example, have shown that if oligopolists select their production levels simultaneously and on the expectation that their competitors will maintain their production level (this is called a Cournot assumption), then for any given cost distribution and market demand curve the equilibrium number of firms will be inversely related to fixed costs. More importantly, concentration will be higher the more prone firms are to act in a 'co-operative way' (Davies 1988: 96). This is because (as Chapter 8 shows) collusive output restrictions tend to favour the larger firms which increases size inequalities.

Mergers

Merger activity can have a significant positive influence on concentration as Table 2.5 indicates. It is believed, for example, that the flurry of merger activity that followed the Second World War is one of the most important contributory factors to increased aggregate concentration in the UK.

The more permissive attitude towards mergers adopted by the UK government compared with that of the USA, especially during the 1960s, encouraged a wave of mergers that resulted in the higher concentration level of the UK economy compared with that of other European countries and the USA.

It cannot, however, be concluded from this general trend that the impact of merger activity at the industry level always increases concentration. For if a medium-sized firm merges with, or takes over, a small firm or if two or more small firms combine their operations the concomitant improvement in market share equality may over-compensate for the related reduction in numbers and reduce overall concentration.

Government policy

In addition to encouraging or inhibiting mergers, government policy can create barriers to entry and can influence directly or indirectly the extent of market concentration.

Technological change

Technological change has long been recognised as a major influence on market structure. Many economists, including well-known authorities such as Karl Marx, Arthur Burns and John Kenneth Galbraith, have argued that technological change tends to increase plant size and the level of industrial concentration. This is because the term 'technological change' usually refers to improvements in production processes which enhance economies of scale and increase the MES. Technological change can, however, manifest itself either as an improvement in production processes or in the introduction of new products. In the latter case the impact of new technology is not unequivocal. Major product innovations are almost by definition characterised by a uniqueness which gives monopolistic power to the producer. Not all new products, however, are major new innovations. Many are simply variants of existing products forming additions to an existing range of available brands. Their introduction increases competition and reduces concentration.

Research tends to confirm the hypothesis that major process innovations are scale expanding and tend to increase the MES and the degree of concentration while product innovations have an equivocal effect on concentration. Mansfield (1983) provides some evidence according to which

major process innovations in the UK chemical, petroleum and steel industries
has increased the MES and the four-firm concentration ratio. This is
because most of the innovations in these industries required large new
plants and heavy investment and the innovators were the inventors which
usually were the largest firms in the industry. Product innovations,
however, had a varied effect. In the petrol and steel industries they tended
to increase concentration while in the chemical industry they tended to
either have no impact or to reduce concentration. The explanation of why
the percentage of concentration-increasing innovation was very low in the
chemical industry was that in over half the cases the innovators were firms
established in other industries so that the new product represented new
entry into the market. Moreover when the innovator was in the same
industry, in one-sixth of the cases, it was not one of the four largest firms.

Vertical integration

Vertical integration can influence both the nature and the strength of
oligopolistic interdependence and the ease or difficulty with which new
firms can enter the market. Vertical integration can be a strong influence
on concentration through its impact on barriers to entry (see Chapter 10).

Market growth

Market size has always been recognised as a factor of concentration. As
indicated above market size in relation to MES can influence the number
of firms operating in a market. For a given MES the larger the market the
larger the number of firms can be. What is also important, however, is the
relative rate of growth or decline of industry size (Curry and George 1983).
The fact that the post-war growth of the UK market has been much slower
than that of the German or French markets is thought to have contributed
to the higher concentration of the UK economy partly by encouraging
merger activity and partly by reducing opportunities for new entry.

The stochastic approach

Stochastic explanations of concentration appeared during the 1950s but
have only recently gained attention from mainstream economists. In
contrast to the deterministic approach which attempts to explain the forces
that determine the equilibrium level of concentration, the stochastic
approach is concerned with actual concentration change. At the centre of
stochastic models is the notion that concentration change reflects the net
effect of a multitude of uncertain influences which affect the decisions and
growth rates of firms. Factors such as the effectiveness of advertising
campaigns, the successful launch of new products, the impact of mergers,
changes in competitive behaviour or labour relations, the number of strikes

in a particular year, the exchange rate or other government policies, changes in managerial or other personnel and a host of other factors influence a firm's growth pattern.

The multiplicity and uncertain nature of these influences makes it both futile and unnecessary to attempt to examine the impact of each separately. The combined effect of all these influences may, however, obey certain rules. Several stochastic models postulating different rules have indeed been constructed in an attempt to capture this chance process. Popular among such models is the *Gibrat process* or the *law of proportionate effect*. In its simplest form the Gibrat process postulates that the net effect of the multitude of economic and chance factors which influence business behaviour implies that the rate of growth of firms is an independent random variable ε_t normally distributed with mean m and variance s^2, i.e.

$$\varepsilon_t = \log S_{i,t+1} - \log S_{i,t}$$

where $S_{i,t}$ and $S_{i,t+1}$ denote the size of firm i at times t and $t+1$.

The normality of ε_t derives from the central limit theorem[4] which holds if it is assumed that the proportionate growth of each firm (expressed here in logarithmic form) is a random variable independent of the size of the firm. In other words, it is assumed that each firm faces a probability distribution of proportionate growth which does not depend on its size. Thus, the chance that a firm will grow by a given percentage in a given time period is the same whatever its size. Some of the most important implications of the law of proportionate effect are as follows.

1 The process focuses on size inequalities rather than on firm numbers and it predicts that size inequality and therefore concentration increases over time. That is, chance factors contribute to a persistently increasing concentration. Although the law is one of proportionate rather than absolute size change, the increase in concentration does not derive from the proportionality assumption. Concentration will increase over time provided that firms grow at different rates which do not depend on their size, so that a small firm has the same probability of growing as fast or as slow as a large- or a medium-sized firm. The actual growth rates vary, however, within any industry and some firms may be lucky enough to experience a series of positive growth rates and become much larger than the majority of firms in the industry.

2 The Gibrat process, similarly to other more sophisticated stochastic models, predicts that the frequency distribution of firm sizes will have a positive variance and skewness similar to that of the lognormal distribution shown in Figure 2.5. The industrial structure portrayed in Figure 2.5 consists of many small and medium-sized firms and only a few large ones. This pattern seems to reflect the pattern of concentration of many real-world industries.

3 The assumption that growth is independent of firm size contrasts sharply

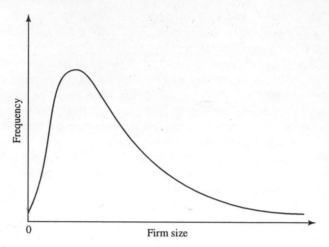

Figure 2.5 A lognormal distribution

with the determinist approach to concentration and in particular with the view that large firms are more likely to enjoy economies of large scale production. The law of proportionate effect predicts an increase in concentration even if all firms have the same unit costs. If economies of scale do exist that would be an additional reason for increased concentration.

4 There is some debate regarding the policy implication of this model with Davies (1988) claiming that the model 'has nothing of interest for the policy maker intent on controlling concentration' while for Roger Clarke (1985) 'the theory suggests that *laissez faire* policies may not be sufficient to protect the competitiveness of the economy'. The policy implication is that if the process of increased concentration is to be reversed the entry of new firms must be facilitated and existing small firms must be protected and encouraged to expand rapidly. In short, a commitment to maintaining a competitive economy may require a positive support for small business.

The working of the law of proportionate effect can be illustrated by the following fictitious example popularised by Prais (1976: ch. 2). An industry consists of 128 firms of equal size, each employing one hundred employees. Each firm faces the same probability distribution that its size may change in each time period, which is as follows: there is a 50 per cent chance that it may experience no change in its size so that the number of employees remains the same, a 25 per cent chance that its size will increase by eleven-tenths and a 25 per cent that it will decline by a factor of 10/11. Table 2.6 shows how the sizes of the 128 firms in the industry change over time under this stochastic process. To start with (at period 0) the Herfindahl index is very small: $100,000HI = 100,000(1/128) = 781$. By the fifth time period

Table 2.6 The Gibrat process

Year	42	46	51	56	62	68	75	83	91	100	110	121	133	146	161	177	195	214
										Number of employees								
0										128								
1									32	64	32							
2							8	32	48	32	8							
3							2	12	30	40	30	12	2					
4							5	13	28	35	28	13	5					
5						1	5	15	26	31	26	15	5	1				
6						2	6	15	25	29	25	15	6	2				
7					1	3	7	15	23	27	23	15	7	3	1			
8					1	4	8	15	22	25	22	15	8	4	1			
9					2	4	9	15	21	24	21	15	9	4	2			
10					2	5	9	15	20	22	20	15	9	5	2			
11				1	2	5	10	15	20	21	20	15	10	5	2	1		
12				1	3	6	10	15	19	20	19	15	10	6	3	1		
13			1	1	3	6	10	14	18	20	18	14	10	6	3	1	1	
14			1	2	3	6	10	14	17	18	17	14	10	6	3	2	1	
15			1	2	4	7	10	14	17	18	17	14	10	7	4	2	1	

this has increased to 796 which is still very small but the index keeps on rising with time. The increase in concentration is solely due to increased size inequalities since, by assumption, there is no entry. Allowing new entry or altering the relevant probabilities of growth would speed up the process of concentration.

The empirical evidence on concentration

The question remains as to whether concentration does indeed increase over time and if so whether the process of concentration is a chance one or whether it can be attributed to specific economic factors. The answer must be sought in empirical evidence. A survey of recent empirical work on concentration, undertaken by Davies (1988), reveals some interesting findings, of which the main ones are summarised here.

1 Many studies using cross-section data involve linear regression equations roughly of the form

$$C = a_0 + a_1 \left(\frac{MES}{X}\right)_j + \Sigma a_2 B_{ij} + \Sigma a_3 Z_{ij}$$

where MES is the minimum efficient scale, X is a measure of size, B represents barriers to entry and Z stands for a variety of other variables. Two important findings emerge from such studies: (a) MES/X is nearly always found to be a strongly significant determinant of concentration giving some credence to the deterministic approach. Because MES, however, is difficult to observe there are serious limitations in the data used which cast some doubt on the validity of the estimates. (b) There is widespread evidence that barriers to entry, mainly in the form of capital requirements and product differentiation, are inversely related to the rate of entry in a market and positively related to the degree of concentration.

2 Among the very few studies which attempt to test the validity of the stochastic approach is the one carried out by Weiss using US data for 1947–54. This study has found that the largest increases in concentration had occurred in the consumer durable and durable equipment industries. This is considered by the author to be consistent with the stochastic approach since 'it is precisely these types of industry in which one might expect substantial inter-firm variability in growth rates, and thus in size inequality' (Davies 1988: 107). This variability is in turn attributed to the frequency with which new product designs are introduced and to the large advertising campaigns which accompany the launch of new products.

3 Time series studies have mainly adopted the case study methodology. Evidence from the UK indicates that concentration in many instances tended to increase with economies of scale and market contraction, increased forward integration and permissive government attitude to merger activity. Factors leading to reductions in concentration included market growth, low entry barriers and high initial levels of concentration.

4 The impact of mergers on concentration has attracted a substantial amount of work often producing controversial results. A consensus, however, has been emerging according to which during the 1950s and 1960s mergers were one of the main factors that contributed to increased aggregate concentration in the UK.

BARRIERS TO ENTRY

The theory of entry barriers originates from the seminal work of Joe Bain which he developed in order to explain his empirical observations on pricing. His observation that firms tended to price their products at a level lower than the profit maximising level he attributed to the influence of potential entry. When entry into a market is possible, he suggested, firms may choose to charge a price lower than the full monopoly price in order to discourage or prevent entry so as to maximise their long-term profitability. His observation that potential competition did not force firms to charge the competitive price he attributed to the existence of entry barriers.

Bain (1956) defined barriers to entry in relation to the extent to which new entrants may be disadvantaged relative to established firms. More specifically, he defined barriers as 'the extent to which established sellers can persistently raise their prices above a competitive level without attracting new firms to enter the industry'(p.3). Barriers are therefore anything that allows a high price to persist in the long run. Indeed Bain defined the *height* of entry or the *condition of entry E*, as the percentage mark-up of the maximum entry forestalling price over the minimum attainable average cost of the established firms, i.e.

$$E = \frac{P_L - \min AC}{\min AC}.$$

Bain's definition, however, is somewhat problematic since it incorporates both market conduct and market structure. It presumes that firms will charge the maximum entry forestalling price. Firms may decide, however, for competitive or other strategic reasons to charge a lower price. They may decide, for example, to charge less than the highest possible price in order not to attract the attention of the regulatory authorities. Alternatively, barriers to entry may be so high that the profit maximising (monopoly) price, which firms may collusively adopt, is lower than the entry forestalling price. In this case entry is said to be 'blockaded' and there is no need for strategic pricing. On the other hand, when barriers are low or non-existent entry may be 'ineffectively impeded' or 'effectively impeded'. The first exists when firms select to charge a price higher than that impeding entry, thus taking higher profits at present whilst allowing entry to occur in the future. Only when firms decide to adopt the maximum entry forestalling price entry is described as 'effectively impeded'.

Despite this implied interdependence between conduct and structure, or perhaps because of it, Bain's definition enjoys widespread popularity. Yet, several other definitions of barriers to entry have been proposed which are independent of business conduct. Demsetz (1982), for example, has suggested that barriers to entry are always related to government-based restrictions. In the absence of such restrictions competition would prevail and monopoly rents would be eliminated in the long run. Thus, any restriction imposed by Government which increases costs of production constitutes an entry barrier. For example, the requirement in the USA to acquire a medallion in order to have the right to operate a taxi, constitutes a barrier, even if there are no restrictions on the number of medallions available. Similarly, according to this view, any safety regulations like the UK MOT tests on cars or regulations regarding safety at work constitute entry barriers. Most economists would agree, however, that this is too narrow a definition of barriers to entry.

Stigler (1968) defines an entry barrier as 'a cost of producing (at some or at every rate of output) which must be borne by a firm which seeks to enter an industry but is not borne by firms already in the industry' (p. 67). According to this definition when established firms and potential entrants face the same cost and demand conditions there are no barriers to entry. Thus, transport costs may be a barrier (for firms located at a distance) but taxi medallions aren't if all firms are required to obtain them. Similarly, an absolute cost advantage by incumbents is a barrier to entry but economies of scale are not. As Chapter 6 shows, however, economies of scale can under certain conditions constitute a barrier to entry. In brief, Stigler's definition can be too narrow.

More recently economists interested in the welfare implications of business behaviour and in questions of whether and under what conditions governments are justified in intervening to regulate the economy have defined barriers to entry in terms of their welfare implications. The laws on patents may be used to illustrate this. Patents are barriers to entry. They provide protection to innovators from imitation and competition by prohibiting entry over a certain time period. They therefore give monopoly power to patent holders. Such power, however, is justified in terms of its welfare enhancing potential. A system of patents and the assumed protection of monopoly profits it offers to innovators is expected to encourage R&D which leads to new inventions and innovations contributing to technical progress and economic growth. Thus, it can be argued that entry into a market can, in certain circumstances, be socially suboptimal because a particular activity is not sufficiently protected while in other circumstances a barrier to entry may be suboptimal because incumbent firms are overly protected.

The welfare implications of barriers to entry are explicitly introduced in the definition adopted by Weizsacker (1980) according to which barriers are 'socially undesirable limitations of entry, which are attributable to the protection of resource owners already in the industry' (p. 400). Clearly this definition extends the concept of barriers by considering explicitly their desirability. It is therefore more controversial than Bain's definition although the latter also incorporates some value judgements.

Bain's barriers refer to cost advantages over potential entrants or product differentiation which enhances consumer choice, thus implying that barriers do not necessarily have adverse welfare effects. It is for this reason that they are called 'innocent' or 'natural' barriers. Furthermore, in order to emphasise that they are created by technological factors they are alternatively called structural or exogenous barriers to entry. In contrast, barriers created by the behaviour of firms such as limit pricing are known as endogenous or behavioural or strategic barriers. Strategic barriers are discussed in Chapter 8 which examines business strategic behaviour. For present purposes we focus attention on the main structural barriers.

Product differentiation

As already indicated, product differentiation refers to the extent to which consumers perceive products to be different. Whether real or imagined, product differentiation can have a significant influence on consumer preferences which in turn influence the shape and position of each firm's demand curve and consequently the distribution of market shares and the degree of market concentration. To influence consumer preferences through product differentiation firms may need to incur higher costs since quality improvements may require additional resources and reputational effects may be sought through increased advertising or increased expenditure on R&D and other promotional activities. To the extent that firms succeed in concentrating preferences on their products, consumers become reluctant to switch to new products and the phenomenon of 'brand loyalty' arises. Brand loyalty reduces substitutability among products.

Strong product differentiation and brand loyalty affect the extent of barriers to entry for various reasons. First, to enter a heavily advertising industry potential entrants will need to raise sufficient capital to be able to match the advertising campaigns of the incumbent firms. Second, even assuming no advertising, differentiation can provide incumbents with the means of adopting a successful entry prevention strategy. This is true whether differentiation is vertical or horizontal.

Vertical differentiation (VD), it will be recalled, refers to product quality variations which are assumed to be known and equally valued by all customers. If it is further assumed that quality variations among existing products are known but there is some uncertainty regarding the quality of a new and untried brand, then VD can constitute a significant barrier to entry since it provides incumbent firms with a first mover advantage. Due to the uncertainty regarding the quality of the new product, the pioneer product enjoys a premium over and above that expected by the new entrant. Thus, by pricing at a little less than a potential entrant's average cost plus this premium, an incumbent firm can make new entry unattractive whilst maintaining price above minimum cost. A simple numerical example may help illustrate this point. Suppose that AC = £10 for both incumbent and new entrant. The maximum value consumers place on a unit of the incumbent's product is V_1 = £20 and that on a unit of a new product is V_2 = £14. The premium enjoyed by the incumbent is higher than that of the entrant's by $V_1 - V_2$ = £6. Now, assuming that buyers prefer to buy the product which gives them the greatest benefit, i.e. the greatest $V - P$ (known as the consumer's surplus), the incumbent can impede entry by pricing at just under $P = \text{AC} + (V_2 - V_1)$ = £10 + £6 = £16, i.e. by giving consumers a surplus of just over £4. This is because if the new product is to offer at least as much consumer surplus (£4) as the incumbent product, its selling price must be a little less than £10 (i.e. £4 below V_2 = £14) which is insufficient to cover the average cost of production. Schmalensee (1982) shows that the height of the barrier to entry in these circumstances increases with scale economies and with the infrequency of transactions.

A similar situation arises in horizontally differentiated markets in which consumer preferences are not equally distributed among products. Brand preferences and brand loyalty provide an obvious impediment to entry. In the case of two brands, a strong consumer preference for brand 1 implies that its demand is everywhere higher than the demand for brand 2, or that when $q_1 = q_2$ then $p_1 > p_2$. Clearly brand 1 enjoys an advantage in the form of a price premium. If brand 2 is the product of a potential entrant, the incumbent firm can, by adjusting this premium, select a price p_1 such that p_2 lies always below the entrant's cost curve, thus making entry unattractive.

An alternative method of impeding entry arises when a firm decides to produce a range of horizontally differentiated products rather than a single brand. The selection of a range of products known as 'product proliferation' can be used strategically especially when there are sunk costs in production.[5] To discourage entry incumbents may select their product range so as to fill the product space in a way that leaves gaps in the market which are too narrow to support a new brand but which are large enough to give a generous market to each of the incumbent's products. The US ready-to-eat breakfast cereal industry seems to follow a strategic use of product space. Data for 1972 show that the leading six firms control among themselves eighty brands and 95 per cent of the market (Lyons 1988).

Product differentiation is exceedingly difficult to quantify in practice so that empirical evidence regarding its impact as an entry barrier is rather limited and indirect. Anecdotal evidence supports the view that the stronger the consumer preference for existing products the more difficult new entry becomes, especially if there are economies of scale, and firms must enter at MES. Diversified entry can overcome such obstacles but it requires substantial financial strength.

Advertising expenditure which has often been used as a proxy for differentiation and brand loyalty has been found to impede new entry in several industries among which is the UK detergents industry.

Strong consumer preference, however, may exist even if advertising expenditure is relatively small. Strong preferences for Nescafe over other soluble coffee brands has been attributed by the MMC to its superior quality rather than to advertising. Strong brand preferences, attributed to various reasons, are usually associated with products such as cars, cigarettes, spirits, tractors, typewriters, etc. while moderately strong preferences are found in tyres, detergents, petroleum refinery, metal containers, etc.

Absolute cost advantage

Incumbent firms may be able to achieve lower per unit of production costs compared with potential entrants for various reasons which include the following.

1 They may have an exceptionally skilled management team or other scarce resources (e.g. the richest bauxite mine) which new entrants cannot reproduce. Unpatented expertise which newcomers could not imitate was shown to be a barrier to entry in the UK for sophisticated machinery, mass-produced components and bulk chemical processes (Lyons 1988).

2 They may possess superior techniques and know-how possibly protected by patents. Ownership of patented superior resources confers a double advantage to the firm: a cost differential and protection from imitation.

Patents are by their nature barriers to entry intended to provide innovators with protection from imitators for a certain period of time. As already noted above, despite their restrictive influence on competition, patents may actually improve consumer welfare since the prospect of protection of expected profits may encourage further expenditure on R&D which is necessary for continued innovation and economic progress. It is possible, however, that patents may be used strategically with adverse effects on competition and innovation. DuPont provides an example of patent manipulation intended to create monopolistic advantages. After their invention of nylon, DuPont followed a strategy of close investigation of any possible molecular variations which could have properties similar to nylon, 'blanketing their findings with hundreds of applications to prevent other firms from developing an effective substitute' (Scherer 1980: 451).

3 They may have control of the supply of raw materials. Monopolisation of an essential raw material may imply higher costs for competitors since they have to use either more expensive or inferior substitutes. Furthermore, if control of an essential raw material is combined with vertical integration then the producer of the resource can refuse to supply its competitors at the succeeding stage of production or can supply them under unfavourable terms. An explanation of how the adverse effect on competition can be magnified when control of resources is combined with vertical integration is provided in Chapter 10.

4 The cost of capital may be lower for existing firms. It is often the case that incumbent firms can build a good reputation which, especially when combined with financial strength, implies that incumbents are able to raise capital at a lower cost compared with new entrants. This kind of barrier to entry, however, is created by imperfections in the capital market rather than by the structure of the producer sector or the behaviour of producers.

5 The production costs of incumbent firms may be lower to the cost of potential entrants due to the beneficial effects of vertical integration. Bain found that in industries such as copper, cars and petroleum refinery backward integration by the entrant is necessary if serious cost disadvantages were to be avoided. But vertically integrated entry implies that entry at a large scale must be contemplated which creates the need for larger initial capital requirements which can impede entry altogether.

Initial capital requirements

The existence of imperfect capital markets implies that when firms need to raise substantial sums of capital in order to start production, entry into a market will be difficult. This is confirmed by empirical studies which show that initial capital requirements are an obstacle to entry in the case of the production of steel, automobiles, oil refining, tractors, cigarettes, etc. The significance of this barrier is confirmed not only by case studies but by cross-section evidence. Orr (1974), for example, who used cross-section data from seventy-one Canadian industries to examine barriers to entry, suggests that initial capital requirements, advertising and concentration are the most significant entry barriers.

Economies of scale

When economies of scale are important so that the volume of production at MES is large compared with the market size, the industry may be able to sustain only a small number of efficiently operating firms. Potential entrants may find it difficult to enter even if they can produce at the same cost as incumbents. This is particularly true since existing firms may be able to adopt a price which is both profitable and prevents new entry. The circumstances under which this is possible are analysed in the 'limit pricing' section of Chapter 8. For present purposes it is sufficient to note that when MES occurs at large volumes, new entry must be at a large scale if the potential entrant is to achieve the same per unit cost as an incumbent operating at or near MES. But, given the market size, this implies a substantial increase in output and a concomitant reduction in price. If price is expected to fall below the average cost of production the prospect of losses can discourage new entry. The extent of this barrier to entry depends both on the size of the MES in relation to the market and on the price elasticity of demand.

The significance of economies of scale as an entry barrier enjoyed widespread acceptance for over 25 years. During the 1980s, however, the theory of market contestability, developed by Baumol (1982) and some of his colleagues, has shed some doubt on the entry prevention power of economies of scale. As indicated in the next section, market contestability theorists claim that under certain circumstances the presence of economies of scale may not constitute a barrier to entry.

Despite this, economies of scale are still considered to be an important barrier to entry in many industries especially when they are produced by the existence of sunk costs and are combined with product differentiation. As already noted cross-section evidence supports the view that economies of scale are an important barrier to entry. Major studies of UK industries have suggested that MES in the production of electronics calculators, television sets, aircraft, diesel engines and machine tools is more than 100 per cent of the entire UK market (Hughs 1988). Similarly industries such as dyes, individual machine tools, turbo generators, electronic capital goods and single plastic products are believed to require output levels of more than 100 per cent of the size of the UK market in order to minimise average cost (Lyons 1988).

Vertical integration

Both the efficiency and the possible market power motives for integration as well as its impact on market structure are analysed in some detail in Chapter 10. It is therefore sufficient for present purposes to note that vertical integration can have an important influence on structure since it can create substantial barriers to entry, either strategic or structural. Vertical integration is used strategically when, for example, incumbents integrate backwards in order to acquire control of a resource and thus prevent potential competitors from entering the intermediate stage market. When integration is induced by efficiency considerations, potential entrants need to enter fully integrated in order to be competitive. Entry at more than one stage of production implies, as already noted above, a larger firm size and the need to raise sufficient initial capital which may impede entry.

BARRIERS TO ENTRY AND MARKET CONTESTABILITY

Although the existence of barriers to entry has been empirically verified for many industries, there is often no consensus of opinion regarding either the nature or the significance of barriers to entry. For reasons elaborated in Chapter 8, it is possible to argue that many entry barriers can be overcome by a diversifying entrant who is financially strong. It is only when barriers are so substantial that the cost of entry to the diversifying entrant becomes very high or when the incumbents can credibly threaten retaliatory entry into the potential diversifier's primary market that entry can be limited.

More importantly, under a certain set of circumstances barriers to entry may not exist even when production is subject to substantial economies of scale. This, according to Baumol (1982), occurs under the following conditions.

1 All producers and potential entrants have access to the same technology and the same average cost of production.
2 There are no sunk (non-recoverable) costs even though there may be economies of scale in production. Thus, the average cost may fall with the volume of output because of, for example, fixed recoverable costs, such as the rent on office space, but there should be no sunk costs (such as the cost of investment specific to the firm). Since sunk costs are non-recoverable their presence makes exiting the market expensive.
3 Existing suppliers can change their price but only with time lags, while consumers respond instantaneously to any price change. That is, consumers are assumed to have perfect knowledge and no attachment to existing products.

Under these conditions there are no barriers to entry and exit from the market is costless. The market is therefore perfectly contestable which means that in the long run incumbents cannot earn positive profits, for if $p >$ AC entry will occur and the price will decline till it is equal to average cost. This is because a new entrant, by undercutting the existing price slightly, can take all the customers away from the incumbent firm and will remain in the market earning positive profit until the incumbent has time to respond, at which point the newcomer leaves the market without incurring exit costs. In brief, positive profits cannot be sustained in perfectly contestable markets because of the threat of 'hit-and-run' competition. Provided that these three conditions prevail there are no barriers to entry and the threat of entry implies pricing at average cost in the long run.

It is the non-fulfilment of these conditions which implies the existence of barriers to entry and the non-contestability of markets. Accordingly, if barriers to entry exist they are to be found in cost advantages that existing firms may have over potential entrants (as Bain suggested long ago) or in the existence of sunk costs which makes exit expensive (thus inhibiting hit-and-run competition) or in the ability of incumbents to instantaneously adjust their prices in response to competition or to maintain consumer loyalty in the face of new entry.

Perfect contestability has thus shifted the emphasis from structure as the sole determinant of performance to focus on a combination of barriers to entry and behavioural features. The postulated absolutely free entry and costless exit are, however, unlikely to be descriptive of many real-world oligopolies. Baumol (1982) has indeed conceded that contestability is an ideal or benchmark of wider applicability than the perfectly competitive model rather than a description of real oligopoly. This wider applicability derives from the contention that potential competition can exert a significant influence on the behaviour even of the most concentrated markets. The policy implication of this contention is that government competition policy should focus on opening the markets by enhancing flexibility in the movement of firms and strengthening competitiveness between incumbents and potential entrants rather than by attempting to directly influence the extent of market concentration. The influence of contestability on public policy has been significant in many countries, an example being the recent UK privatisation programme (see Chapter 14).

THE STRUCTURE–CONDUCT–PERFORMANCE DEBATE

The most important contribution of contestability theory, especially for public policy, is its implication that industry structure is determined endogenously and simultaneously with the pricing, output, advertising expenditure and other decisions of the firms comprising an industry. This claim contrasts with older theories of industrial organisation such as the SCP paradigm which provided an analytical and empirical framework that dominated industrial economics for many years. According to this paradigm industry structure, which is exogenously given, determines the conduct of firms and the performance of the industry. This implies that the fewer the firms in a market the more likely it is that they will tend to collude. Prices will therefore tend to be above the competitive level and entry prevention and other anti-competitive strategies will be more prevalent the higher the degree of industrial concentration. Furthermore, lack of competitive pressures may contribute to managerial slack and inefficiency in production. Low concentration, on the other hand, implies competitive behaviour and pricing according to marginal cost, the absence of supernormal profits and control of managerial discretion leading to production efficiency. Market structure determines, therefore, the conduct of firms and the extent to which industrial performance leads to allocative efficiency and the maximisation of social welfare.[6]

A voluminous empirical work has attempted to test the prediction that structure determines performance. But since it is not possible to construct an index which encompasses all, or even the main, structural features of an industry many empirical studies attempt to infer the relationship between structure and performance by examining the impact of one feature, usually concentration, on some measure of performance, usually profitability. Research carried out over three decades or more by Bain, Stigler, Mann, Weiss and others has consistently indicated a positive although occasionally weak association between concentration and profits.

There are, however, dissenting voices. Several studies report an insignificant negative (Holtermann 1973; Clarke 1984) or positive (Khalilzadeh-Shirazi 1974) relationship between concentration and profits while others (Geroski 1981) have found that the relationship is non-linear. That is, the effect of concentration on profits alternates between positive and negative over several ranges of concentration. Furthermore other studies (Brozen 1971) dispute both the universal validity of the hypothesis that a positive association between concentration and profits exists and its stability over time. Brozen, on the basis of estimates which he derived (in 1970) using a sample of ninety-eight industries which included Bain's original sample of forty-two industries, claims that there is no association between concentration and profits. He also claims that the profitability of the industries studied was not stable over time. The industries examined, however, had become less concentrated over time which may simply indicate that new entry reduces profitability confirming the view that barriers to entry have a bearing on profits.

In addition to empirical evidence the theory of market contestability casts doubt on the causal links of the SCP paradigm. For, when markets are perfectly contestable, their performance, in the long run, is the same as the performance of perfectly competitive markets whatever the number of firms in the industry. Even monopolists cannot raise prices above marginal costs without attracting 'hit-and-run' competition.

Despite theoretical objections and the empirical problems of data collection and specification, the sheer volume of evidence showing an association between structure and performance points to the conclusion that such a relationship exists. The existence of an association between two variables is not, however, proof of causation. Either variable can cause the other to move or both may be influenced by a third variable. If concentration and profit move in the same direction it does not necessarily follow that concentration affects profits. Profits may cause an industry to become more concentrated. A reversal in causation can indeed be advocated.

Thus, Demsetz (1983) argues that a positive association between concentration and profits is no proof of profit enhancing collusive behaviour among firms. A firm's superior ability to lower costs or to improve product quality, whether due to sheer luck or to entrepreneurial or managerial ability, increases profits and growth. This can affect market structure since efficient firms may expand by drawing sales from less efficient firms whose market shares and profitability decline and some of which are taken over. Size inequalities are thus exasperated or numbers decline or both.

In brief, Demsetz's argument is that efficiency affects structure rather than the other way round. For, if concentration facilitates collusive price fixing which causes the increase in profitability then small as well as large firms would benefit from the higher prices. This would mean that small firms operating in highly concentrated industries should be more profitable than small firms operating in less concentrated industries. Since his empirical evidence shows that small firms in concentrated industries do not perform better than small firms in other industries, he concludes that his claim that performance affects structure is valid.

Scherer's work also emphasises the significance of behaviour for market structure, so much so that he described himself as a 'behaviouralist' while he considered Bain as a 'structuralist'. More recently, the group of economists associated with what is known as the 'new industrial organisation' theory treat conduct as an equilibrium concept exogenously determined. (The non-co-operative Nash equilibrium is commonly adopted.[7]) In their models conduct and the initial demand and supply conditions determine the performance of the market and the number of firms that will exist in the long run. Thus, conduct affects structure.

The transactions cost approach to business organisation has also shed doubts on the simple one-way causation implied by the SCP paradigm. Contractual and other transaction costs have an important bearing on industrial organisation. But, as the next two chapters will show, transaction costs are not exogenously determined. They are rather the result of the interplay of human attributes and environmental features. Limitations in human rationality, for example, coupled with complexity and uncertainty create transaction costs which may lead firms to expand by internalising transactions, thus affecting the number and size distribution of firms in the market. Thus, behaviour affects structure. But at the same time a more

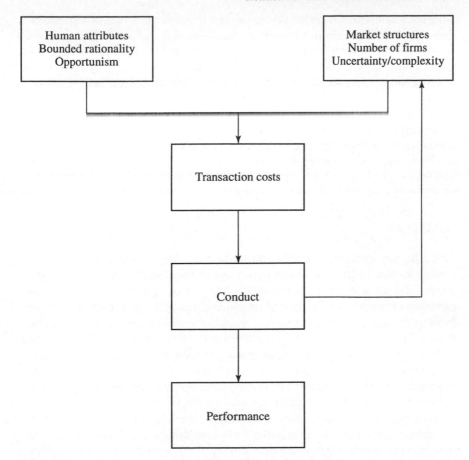

Figure 2.6 A transaction costs model of industrial organisation

concentrated structure implies the existence of small numbers of traders which coupled with information asymmetries can induce opportunistic behaviour and protracted bargaining situations which create substantial transaction costs. To avoid or reduce these costs firms may decide to supersede the market by producing their own requirements rather than buying them from third parties. In other words, structural features affect the size of transaction costs which in turn affects business behaviour and market structure. We have come full circle. There is simultaneity in the relationships of a nature indicated in Figure 2.6. Behaviour as an influence on structure is certainly important in industries populated by dynamic firms run by entrepreneurs or by entrepreneurial managers who may actively attempt to alter their industrial environment. Business decisions regarding mergers and vertical or horizontal expansion can have a direct impact on the number of firms or their size distribution. Advertising, product proliferation and R&D can create barriers to entry. Predatory pricing can eliminate competition. Price decisions can influence the size of the market thus altering the initial demand conditions. Intensified R&D and the concomitant innovation can influence cost conditions, product quality and variety and hence product differentiation. Transactions costs have a bearing on structure and structure affects transaction costs. In short, the linkages among the elements of SCP are more complex and the interdependencies more prevalent than Figure 2.1 may suggest. In the following chapters we shall explore some of these linkages. To be able to do so we must begin by examining the nature of transaction costs and the reasons why firms emerge (Chapter 3), how they are organised and whether organisation matters for business behaviour (Chapter 4).

SUMMARY

This chapter examines briefly the industrial environment within which firms operate. Markets and industries are defined and their main features analysed with particular emphasis on market concentration. Alternative methods of measuring the extent of seller concentration are discussed and evaluated and some evidence on concentration in the UK and other countries is presented before enquiring into the causes of concentration. Two schools of thought – the deterministic approach and the stochastic approach to concentration – are explored. Despite some supporting evidence, for each, reference to the facts has not yet provided a definitive answer to the question of what determines concentration.

Evidence from specific industries and aggregate concentration figures from several countries indicate a diversity of concentration rates. It appears though that, despite some slight reduction during the late 1970s and early 1980s, aggregate concentration in the UK and in particular in UK manufacturing has been consistently higher than that in the USA and the EC.

Technology and the size of MES have been shown to have a significant influence on concentration in particular industries while a consensus has been emerging according to which the merger flurry of the 1950s and 1960s was the main factor contributing to the high increase in UK concentration during that period.

The nature and influence of barriers to entry are also examined focusing on 'endogenous' or 'natural' barriers. Product differentiation, cost differentials, integration and patents are among the most commonly observed significant barriers to entry. The main impact of barriers is to restrict entry, thus rendering markets non-contestable and contributing to enhanced concentration.

The absence of barriers to entry and sunk costs would render the market vulnerable to 'hit-and-run' competition which would eliminate profits in the long run, according to market contestability theory. Although this assertion points to the significance of barriers to entry for profitability, perfect contestability casts serious doubts on the significance of structural features and in particular concentration as a determinant of market behaviour and efficiency since even monopolies can be perfectly contestable.

Further doubts on the validity of the SCP paradigm were expressed by Demsetz who argues that a reversal in the causation implied by the SCP paradigm is plausible. He contends that efficiency leads to concentration rather than the other way round. The section on the evaluation of the SCP paradigm concludes with the suggestion that transaction costs create simultaneity in the relationships among the various elements of the SCP. This will become clearer after the nature and significance of transaction costs has been explored in the following chapters.

APPLICATION: THE UK MARKET FOR SOLUBLE COFFEE

The high profitability of Nestlé and the slow adjustment of soluble coffee prices following reductions in the world price of green coffee beans, especially in the summer of 1989, prompted a Monopolies and Mergers Commission investigation aiming to establish whether the market for soluble (instant) coffee is a monopoly and if so to consider whether it operated against the public interest. The Commission's report of January 1991 has provided the information for this case study which illustrates several of the points raised in this chapter. Consider the following.

The definition of the market

The first task of the Monopolies and Mergers Commission was to define the market under investigation. Since the purpose of the study was to examine profitability and competition in the supply of soluble coffee, all UK manufacturers supplying soluble coffee to retailers in 1989 were included in the definition. This means manufacturers of branded coffee as well as coffee sold under distributors' own labels. The suppliers of soluble coffee suggested that other products such as roast and ground (R&G) coffee, tea, fizzy drinks and other drinks should be part of the market since they are close substitutes to coffee. Had this suggestion been adopted, soluble coffee would be only a small part of the market since, during 1975–89, it comprised just over 20 per cent of the drinks market. The Commission did not, however, accept this recommendation for several reasons. To begin with, the R&G coffee was excluded as an insignificant part of the market. R&G coffee provides the bulk of coffee consumption in other EC countries, but it comprises only about 10 per cent of the UK market. Other drinks were excluded because the cross-price elasticity between coffee and other drinks was thought to be very small. Soluble coffee, although slightly more expensive than tea, at 3p or 4p per cup (including sugar and milk), is significantly cheaper than other drinks such as Coca Cola for example. This led to the conclusion that it was highly unlikely that competition from such products would be effective in constraining the price or the profitability of soluble coffee. Indeed the industry indicated that adult coffee consumption has remained constant over time, at 8.3 cups of coffee per day on average. Thus, in defining the market the Commission defined 'the supply of soluble coffee for retail sale as supply by manufacturers located in the United Kingdom or by importers' (p. 8).

Market concentration

The suppliers identified according to the above definition, and their major brands, are summarised in Table 2.7. The market includes about twelve firms which offer a vast range of products. It is therefore

Table 2.7 Market shares by supplier and major brand in the UK soluble coffee market in 1989

	Sales (£m)	Average price (£/100 g)	Shares
Nestlé	**270.0**	**1.46**	**56.0**
Nescafe	196.2	1.41	40.8
Nescafe decaffeinated	14.0	1.52	2.9
Gold Blend	34.3	1.65	7.1
Gold Blend decaffeinated	11.7	1.72	2.4
Blend 37	6.4	1.66	1.3
Others	7.4	1.48	1.5
GFL UK	**119.0**	**1.22**	**24.7**
GFL branded sales, GB	93.8	1.34	19.5
Maxwell House	42.0	1.24	8.7
Maxwell House decaffeinated	2.5	1.40	0.5
Kenco regular	11.0	1.54	2.3
Kenco decaffeinated	5.4	1.69	1.1
Cafe Hag granules	16.5	1.44	3.4
Cafe Hag Freeze dried	3.0	1.71	0.6
Mellow birds	11.5	1.22	2.4
Other	2.0	1.17	0.4
For distributors' own label	22.0	0.93	4.5
Brooke Bond	**27.6**	**1.24**	**5.7**
Red Mountain	22.2	1.25	4.6
Red Mountain Decaffeinated	3.6	1.41	0.7
Lyons Tetley	**40.0**	**0.80**	**8.3**
Other suppliers	**24.8**	**0.72**	**5.2**
Total	482.1	1.24	100

Source: Monopolies and Mergers Commission 1991b

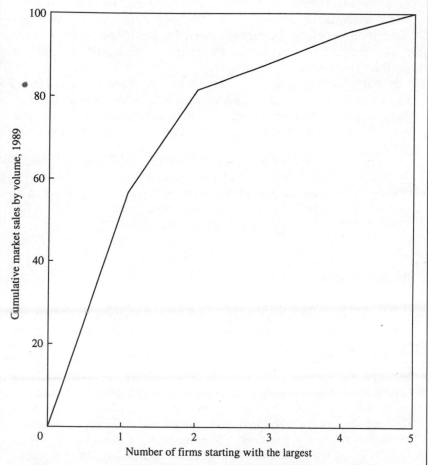

The UK supply of soluble coffee:

Company	Market share
Nestle	56.0
GFL (and associated companies)	24.7
Lyons Tetley	8.3
Brook Bond	5.7
Other suppliers	5.2
	100.0

Figure 2.7 The seller concentration curve in the UK market for soluble coffee in 1989

Source: Monopolies and Mergers Commission 1991b

a differentiated oligopoly but since the dominant firm, Nestlé, controls 56 per cent of the value of sales (and almost 50 per cent of the volume of sales), legally the market is considered to be a monopoly. In any case, market concentration is very high as indicated by the concentration curve, in Figure 2.7. CR_2 is 80.7.

Product differentiation is extensive and in some instances very strong

Although 32.2 per cent of the market is accounted for by Nescafe, the main brand of Nestlé, over 200 other products exist. The bulk of soluble coffee is sold through supermarkets which, typically, offer the consumer a choice of between thirty-three and thirty-eight types of coffee. This normally includes eight to nine brands from Nestlé and a similar number from GFL, approximately nine types of distributors' own brands, three to four Brook Bond types and between two and nine other types from smaller suppliers. Even excluding tea and other drinks the industry offers a vast range of products of different qualities and prices.

Product differentiation appears to be a competitive weapon. Launches of new products and withdrawals or re-launches by the main suppliers have been occurring in almost every year since the early 1970s. About a dozen new products have been introduced in the last two years.

Despite this variety of choice there is a strong consumer preference for Nescafe which is believed to be of a higher quality compared with other products. Indicative of this preference is the fact that when in May 1987 the price of coffee sold under distributors' own labels fell by 10 per cent more than the price of Nescafe, the sales of Nescafe were not affected at all.

Barriers to entry

Entry into the market is possible and has occurred recently not only via new products launched by existing firms but via new firm entry. A recent new entrant was Food Brands which obtained supplies from imports.

The cost of establishing a new plant, however, is rather high, at between £30 million and £60 million depending on the method of production. The minimum efficient size, according to Nestlé, is approximately 10 per cent of the market. In addition, launching a new product nationally would require an advertising campaign estimated at about £5 million. Large-scale entry does not appear to be very easy. Entry at a local or regional level, however, is possible without television advertising. In general entry is thought to be easier by importing soluble coffee from overseas although imported coffee may cost more than that produced in the UK. Distributors may also

Table 2.8 Profitability in the supply of soluble coffee to UK retailers

Company	As percentage on capital employed	Year	Comments
Nestle	114	1989	Nescafe accounted for 95% of total profit
GFL	29	1989	
Sol-Tenko	10	1990	
Brooke Bond	9	1988	
	3	1989	

Source: MMC 1991b

ask for higher profit margins as an incentive to stock new products. Entry seems to occur at small scale rather than in direct competition with Nestlé for a large market share. But the Commission concludes that 'there is no evidence that entry has been deterred by Nestlé's strong position in the market, or that Nestlé has taken action to prevent entry' (p. 101).

Market performance

The high degree of concentration indicated in Figure 2.5 coupled with strong product preferences would, according to the SCP paradigm, lead to the prediction that the dominant firm has market power which may be manifested in high price–cost margins. The existence of high profits, among the main suppliers, which has led to the Monopolies and Mergers Commission investigation is documented in Table 2.8. The profitability of Nestlé is far higher than that of its closest competitors and much higher than the average profitability of the food, drink and tobacco industry which was 17 per cent on capital employed in 1989.

Does structure affect performance?

The question of interest to the Monopolies and Mergers Commission inquiry was whether the high profitability of Nestlé was brought about by the exercise of dominance to the detriment of the consumer.

Profitability in the industry has been increasing over time, partly because of falling world prices of green coffee beans especially during 1989. The high profitability of Nestlé was derived from three main factors.

1 Nestlé had higher sales revenues per tonne of coffee compared with the other three main suppliers. This was attributed to product quality difference for which consumers were prepared to pay a higher price. The higher price of Nescafe was not considered to be exploitative

because consumers were offered a wide choice of products (even though of somewhat inferior quality) at a range of lower prices.

2 Nestlé's costs of production per tonne were lower than those of the two other main suppliers.

3 Nestlé had lower advertising costs than its competitors (except for Sol-Tenco which did not advertise).

In brief, a quality product was produced at lower costs and marketed very effectively resulting in enhanced overall efficiency.

There was no evidence of restrictive practices or unfair competition and the industry's claim to compete in terms of 'value for money' rather than simple price competition seemed justified. The MMC conclusion is that 'Nestlé's prices and profitability reflect its success in meeting consumer preferences in a market characterised by effective competition and a wide degree of consumer choice' (p. 1). Any intervention was therefore thought to be counterproductive. On the contrary, it was suggested that Nestle's profitability might actually provide an incentive for other firms to compete in this market.

In short, in this industry dominance seems to have been brought about by better quality and efficiency implying a reversal in the causation suggested by the SCP paradigm.

FURTHER READING

Clarke, Roger (1985) *Industrial Economics*, Oxford: Blackwell,
Hay, D.A. and Morris, D.J. (1991) *Industrial Economics and Organisation: Theory and Evidence*, Oxford: Oxford University Press. 2nd edn.
Scherer, F.M. (1980) *Industrial Market Structure and Economic Performance*, Skokie, IL: Rand McNally. 2nd edn.
Shughart, W.F.S. (1990) *The Organisation of Industry*, Homewood, IL: Richard D. Irwin.

QUESTIONS

1 Define 'concentration' and 'barriers to entry' and discuss the advantages and disadvantages of alternative methods used to measure each.

2 Suppose that an industry consists of three firms with the following output shares: the first firm has 50 per cent, the second firm has 30 per cent and the third firm has 20 per cent. Show that the value of each of the following concentration indices is correct and explain which, if any, is the most 'appropriate' one to use: HI = 0.38, RI = 0.4167, CCI = 0.695.

3 The three–firm sales CR in the UK canned potatoes industry is 45 per cent, almost identical to that of the packaged cakes industry which is 44 per cent. Does this imply that the two industries are equally competitive? If not why not?

4 Use the data in Table 2.6 to construct the concentration curves describing the industry in time periods 5 and 10 and interpret your findings.

5 Evaluate the importance of new technology as a determinant of seller concentration.

6 'Given that a multitude of uncertain factors may influence the size distribution of firms, seller concentration will tend to increase over time, even in the absence

of concentration increasing technological change. Thus, *laissez-faire* policies may not be sufficient to protect the competitiveness of industry.' Discuss.

7 It is often argued that 'industry structure influences market conduct and economic performance'. A reversal in the direction of causation can, however, be plausibly argued. Discuss.

8 'Since markets cannot be contestable in the presence of barriers to entry, potential competition can have no impact on the behaviour of existing firms when production is subject to economies of scale.' Critically evaluate this statement.

9 Suppose the market shares in an industry consisting of four firms are as follows: firm 1 has 0.40, firm 2 has 0.30, firm 3 has 0.15 and firm 4 has 0.15. The product is homogeneous and is sold at the uniform price of £10.00. It is known that the price elasticity of demand for this product is −1.5.

  Making any other necessary assumptions determine (a) the average cost and the profitability of each firm (hint: see Appendix 2.1) and (b) the average profitability of the industry.

10 Comment on the view that the nature and internal organisation of firms are important determinants of business behaviour.

APPENDIX 2.1: CONCENTRATION AND 'THE DEGREE OF OLIGOPOLY'

Suppose an industry consisting of N firms produces a homogeneous product. Each firm's production decisions are based on the expectation that competitors will maintain their existing production level (this is known as the Cournot model of behaviour). The market price is determined by the demand curve, i.e. $P = f(X)$ where $X = \Sigma X_i$, X_i is the output and X_i/X is the market share of the ith firm.

  The profit of each firm can be written as

$$\Pi_i = PX_i - c_iX_i - FC_i$$

where c_i is the average variable cost and FC_i denotes the total fixed cost for firm i. The first order condition for profit maximisation requires that

$$\frac{d\Pi_i}{dX_i} = \frac{dP}{dX}\frac{dX}{dX_i}X_i + P - c_i = 0$$

but $dX/dX_i = 1$ so

$$\frac{dP}{dX}X_i + P - c_i = 0$$

$$\frac{dP}{dX}X_i + P = c_i$$

where

$$\frac{dP}{dX}X_i + P = MR_i \tag{A2.1}$$

Equation (1) can be written as

$$MR_i = P\left(1 + \frac{dP}{dX}\frac{X_i}{P}\frac{X}{X}\right)$$

or

$$MR_i = P\left(1 + \frac{dP}{dX}\frac{X}{P}\frac{X_i}{X}\right)$$

where $(dP/dX)(X/P) = -(1/e)$ is the inverse of the price elasticity of demand and $X_i/X = S_i$ is the market share of the ith firm. Therefore, $MR_i = P(1 - S_i/e)$ and, since $MR_i = c_i$, $c_i = P(1 - S_i/e)$ which implies that

$$\frac{P-c}{P} = \frac{S_i}{e} \qquad\qquad (A2.2)$$

Equation (2.2) implies that a firm's price–cost margin depends on its own market share and the elasticity of the market demand.

When size inequalities exist we can calculate the average price–cost margin for the industry as a whole by averaging the profit–cost margin of the individual firms using their market shares as weights. Thus, multiplying equation (A2.1) by X_i/X and summing over i gives

$$\text{average MR} = \Sigma P \, \frac{X_i}{X} + \Sigma \, \frac{X_i^2}{X} \frac{dP}{dX}$$

noting that $\Sigma (X_i/X) = 1$ this can be written as

$$\text{average MR} = P \left(1 + \Sigma \, \frac{X_i^2}{X} \frac{X}{X} \frac{dP}{dX} \frac{1}{P} \right)$$

or

$$\text{average MR} = P \left(1 + \frac{H}{e} \right)$$

and

$$\frac{P-c}{P} = \frac{H}{e} \qquad\qquad (A2.3)$$

where H is the Herfindahl index of concentration. (Equation (2.3) can also be derived by averaging equation (2.2); see Davies 1988.)

NOTES

1 For evidence and further details see Shughart (1990: 66).
2 As quoted by Needham (1978: 125).
3 For a formal proof of this statement see Davies (1988: 93–4).
4 Broadly speaking the central limit theorem states that any variable which represents the sum total effect of many other independent variables will have a normal probability distribution.
5 For a concise review of recent contributions to the theory of product proliferation see Lyons (1988).
6 The simplest form of a social welfare function usually postulated is the sum of consumers' and producers' surpluses.
7 A market is said to be in Nash equilibrium when each firm's decision variable is optimised given the decision variables of its rivals.

3 The nature of the firm

INTRODUCTION

Neoclassical economic theory assumes that prices constitute the control mechanism through which market transacting directs the allocation of resources. In the world of certainty and costless information postulated, firms become simple production functions which, on the assumption of profit maximisation, convert inputs into outputs. At this level of analytical abstraction, structural features and internal organisational forms are of no relevance so that the firm is simply viewed as a useful 'black box' whose innards are of no interest. Clearly such an approach, although possibly quite constructive for some purposes such as problems of general equilibrium theory, is extremely limiting for the study of real-world business problems. Indeed it renders the theory of the firm of no value to the analysis of factors contributing to the emergence and evolution of firms, the diversity of firm size and governance structure,[1] the internal organisational features and other attributes of modern corporations which may significantly contribute to business success or failure. Such issues can and have been recently addressed by the new approaches to the theory of the firm which recognise the significance of informational imperfections and the limitations of human decision makers.

One such approach is what Williamson (1984a) called 'transaction cost economics'. Williamson's approach recognises that business is carried on in an environment characterised by uncertainty and complexity and that, because of the limitations of human nature, decision makers cannot be perfectly rational. The interaction of decisions, taken by non-perfectly rational human beings, with environmental attributes can generate substantial transaction costs. Attempts to economise on such costs figure prominently in explaining the variety of organisational forms we observe in modern business, the dilemma posed by the separation of ownership from control, the degree of business integration, the emergence of multinational enterprises and other major features of the business world (Williamson 1981).

This chapter introduces the basic concepts of transaction cost economics and examines the economic factors that contribute to the emergence of firms. As such, it is based on the work of the main contributors and proponents of this theory, such as Oliver Williamson (1975, 1981, 1984a), Neil Kay (1982, 1984) and others. Important insights are provided by the work of some of their predecessors, especially Ronald Coase who, as far back as 1937, laid the foundations of the modern transaction cost approach to the theory of the firm in his pioneering work on 'The Nature of the Firm'. Thus, after defining a firm this chapter gives a brief outline of Coase's seminal contribution to the nature of the firm and proceeds to outline, briefly, Alchian and Demsetz's 'team production'. Williamson's approach to the question of the emergence of firms is introduced in the following section which analyses the basic concepts and factors contributing to the existence of transaction costs. The next section examines the transactions cost approach to the emergence of internal organisations in general, while efficiency considerations for the emergence of simple hierarchies are examined in the penultimate section. The chapter concludes with a brief summary.

THE FIRM AND ITS EMERGENCE

The term 'firm' is commonly used to refer to such diverse organisations as IBM, British Telecom, Mr A. Jones' grocery shop, etc. If the small grocery shop and a large multinational enterprise are both 'firms', what do they have in common, one might ask. What is the economic as opposed to the legal definition of a firm?

Ronald Coase (1964) defined the firm as 'the system of relationships which comes into existence when the direction of resources is dependent on an entrepreneur' (p. 339). This system of relationships refers to the co-operation of several factors of production. Owners of resources, such as labour, capital, land, and raw materials, co-operate within the firm not through contracts signed among themselves but through bilateral contracts between each resource owner and a single contractual agent. Within the limits of their contractual obligations resource owners co-operate in the collection of information regarding all aspects of the business such as the tastes of consumers and their demands, the state of technology, the attributes of employees, the state of the economy, etc. This information is then transmitted to the decision makers who in turn choose and implement the business plan. Resources within the firm may move from one use to the other according to the dictates of the corporate plan. Thus, resource allocation takes place as a response to the conscious decisions of planners. This process contrasts sharply with the complete decentralisation of the market mechanism.

The fact that resource owners enter freely into contractual arrangements which can be voluntarily terminated has led some authors (Alchian and Demsetz 1972) to emphasise co-operation rather than the authoritative relationships that may exist within a firm. An element of authority exercised by some member(s) to the contract, however, is essential for the enforcement of contracts and possibly for settling disputes. This is indeed what distinguishes the set of contractual relationships which define the firm from the contractual arrangements of market exchanges. That is, the contractual arrangements which define the firm are non-specific[2] in nature and are enforced internally by the exercise of authority (Fitzroy and Mueller 1984). These two contractual features imply that the co-ordination and direction of resources within a firm is dependent on conscious planning. Conscious planning and resource direction and allocation which is dependent on the 'visible hand' of the manager or entrepreneur is the element that all firms, whatever their size or organisational structure, have in common.

While resource allocation within a firm is subject to planning, the market allocation of resources is decentralised and directed by the price mechanism. The way this operates is as follows. If the price of a factor of production, say X, becomes higher in the production of good A than in the production of good B then the owner of X in order to benefit from the price differential will seek to move X from B to A. The incentive to do so persists and more of X will be transferred until the price differential is eliminated. Resources are re-allocated and directed as though by 'an invisible hand' to their best use, instantaneously and costlessly. In reality, for factor X to move from one use to another its owner may need to terminate a contract (in the production of B) and seek to initiate a new contract (in the production of A). Thus, the movement of resources requires market exchanges based on contractual arrangements; they do not occur instantaneously and costlessly. Similarly, market transacting, with the relevant information being transmitted through price movements, takes place when semi-finished products move from one firm to another. Such market transacting is not, however, required when either inputs or semi-finished products move between departments or divisions of the same firm; movements are then co-ordinated by planning.

Firms as co-ordinators and planners perform a resource allocation function similar to that performed by markets through prices. The question then arises as to why two alternative methods of resource allocation exist. Since prices can perform this allocative function, why do firms emerge as an alternative to the price mechanism and what is the optimum mix of these two alternative methods of allocating resources? Coase (1964) suggested that 'the main reason why it is profitable to establish a firm would seem to be that there is a cost of using the price mechanism' (p. 336) and that by organising production under the direction of an entrepreneur these marketing costs can be reduced. Terminating a contract and initiating a new one is part of these costs, other costs include the following.

Costs related to discovering the relevant market prices

The owner of X, in the previous example, will need to acquire information regarding the change in the prices offered before he or she can consider moving X from B to A. When transactions are internalised, however, the firm supplies itself and the relevant information is more readily available. For example, information about the marginal cost of a resource or a semi-finished product which moves from one division to the other within the same firm should be easily available in the supplying division.

Costs of negotiating and concluding contracts for each market transaction

For the factor X to be re-allocated, its owner incurs costs in order to terminate its contract of employment in the production of B and initiate a new one in the production of A. Such costs need not occur when A and B are divisions of the same firm. More importantly perhaps, in market transacting, contracts may have to be negotiated and concluded among all the co-operating resource owners so that for one resource to move several contracts may need to be terminated and re-negotiated. Thus, in the previous example, if X was one of ten factors co-operating in a market contractual arrangement for the production of product B, then nine contracts may have to be terminated in the production of B and several new contracts may need to be initiated in the production of A before X can move from B to A. Contracts are not, however, required among resource owners co-operating within a firm. Workers do not contract with each other or with other input owners. Instead, there is a long-term contract between each factor owner and the firm which means that even when a resource moves between firms only one contract need be terminated and a single new one initiated.

Uncertainty and risk attitudes

Suppliers of goods or services may prefer a long-term contract to a series of short-term contracts in order to save on contractual costs and to reduce the risks associated with forecasting future events. This may not be possible, however, in circumstances in which buyers find it difficult to forecast in detail their future requirements. In such cases, a long-term contract may become feasible if the details of future requirements are not of particular significance (within limits) to the supplier so that the service to be provided is expressed in general terms with the details to be decided by the buyer later on. For example, a bricklayer may be prepared to sign a long-term contract with a construction firm specifying that, for a certain daily payment, he or she will be prepared to provide a certain amount of bricklaying services under the following conditions: (a) the work takes place at any location within the bounds of a specified city, (b) it is in co-operation with a team of unspecified membership (i.e. other brick-layers, plasterers, architects, electricians, plumbers, etc.) and (c) it is under supervision by a team member to be appointed in the future. This arrangement may reduce the risk of unemployment for the bricklayer and save on the costs of renewing a series of short-term contracts.

In brief, the firm has emerged as a means of economising on transaction costs. The emergence of firms does not, however, imply that all market transacting will be superseded. Firms and markets co-exist for two reasons.

1 Depending on the nature of business, replacing market transacting by internal transacting may involve no cost saving or the cost saving may not be of sufficient magnitude to compensate for internal organisational costs. In the absence of net cost benefits transactions will be carried on under the price mechanism (through market exchanges). Examples are provided by the existence of self-employment.
2 The existence of decreasing returns to the entrepreneurial function will imply that cost savings may decline as the firm expands. The firm will keep expanding up to the point where the marginal cost of an extra transaction carried on in the firm is equal to the marginal cost of the same transaction carried on in the market or by another firm. Increasing organisational costs limit the size of the firm so that several firms may co-exist and inter-firm trading (market transacting) takes place.

In brief, for Coase, transaction costs are responsible both for the emergence of firms and for the determination of the size distribution of the firm.

RECENT CONTRIBUTIONS TO THE EMERGENCE OF FIRMS

Coase's contention that efficiency is the motivating force behind the emergence of firms is widely accepted although there are differences of opinion regarding the nature of the efficiency gains. Alchian and Demsetz (1972), for example, claim that it is not so much transactions cost savings but the benefits derived from working together as a team that create firms Williamson (1975) on the other hand, while acknowledging the benefits of team production is more inclined to accept Coase's claim that the emer-gence of firms is due to transaction cost economising. His concept of transaction costs, however, is much broader than that of Coase's, as will be explained below.

Team production

Firms, for Alchian and Demsetz, emerge because technology is such that efficient production involves people working together as a team. Total production is the result of co-operative effort in which the contribution of each co-operating resource cannot be easily identified. More precisely, team production is said to exist when inputs belonging to several resource owners co-operate in production whose technology is such that total output is not the sum of the separate contributions[3] of the co-operating inputs. Consequently, the productivity of each factor of production cannot be easily observed and measured. The example given is that of two workmen shifting a heavy cargo. Since effort exerted is not easily observable payment according to marginal productivity may not be possible. Moreover, assuming that leisure enters an individual's utility function, resource owners have an incentive to shirk.[4] This is because output reduction brought about by shirking cannot be attributed to those guilty of shirking and it is shared by all the members of the team. Thus the opportunity cost of leisure time declines for the shirker who will therefore be inclined to take more leisure. To illustrate, suppose that ten inputs, owned by ten different individuals, co-operate in production. Productivity cannot be easily observed and total production is shared equally among the members of this team. Suppose that one team member reduces his or her work effort and as a result total production declines by 20 per cent per time period. Since output is equally shared every team member experiences a reduction in income equal to 2 per cent of total output. The person who shirked (by enjoying more leisure or putting time and energy in pursuit of other tasks) bears only a fraction of the true cost of his or her shirking. So, Alchian and Demsetz claim that all team members will have an incentive to shirk and as a result production declines substantially and all members suffer. The whole team would therefore benefit if shirking were eliminated.

Market competition cannot, however, be relied upon to resolve the shirking problem for two reasons: (a) potential competitors lack the relevant information to displace the shirker since neither effort nor productivity is easily observable, and (b) new team members will have a similar tendency to shirk. What is required is a monitor who will observe behaviour, meter productivity and apportion rewards. To perform his or her duties effectively the monitor should also have the power to discipline resource owners by terminating their contracts and hiring alternatives. To eliminate the monitor's incentive to shirk she or he must become the residual income earner.

This contractual arrangement which, in the presence of team production, resolves the shirking information problem better than the non-centralised contractual arrangement, is what Alchian and Demsetz called the classical capitalist firm. One of its most important features is the existence of a monitor who has the right to negotiate any input contracts independently of contracts with other input owners, who has the residual claim on income and who has the right to sell his or her central contractual status.

Alchian and Demsetz' contribution, like that of Coase's, implies that a firm with a hierarchical internal structure will evolve in response to market failures which occur in the presence of technological non-separability.

Technology, however, is only one specific instance of market failure rather than a generalised instance. Other human and environmental factors can contribute to failures that necessitate the emergence of firms or the decision to internalise transactions (to make rather than to buy). The most complete explanation of the reasons for the existence of firms and the forces contributing to the adoption of particular internal structures has been offered by Oliver Williamson (1975).

The transaction costs approach to the emergence of firms

Williamson builds upon and extends Coase's idea that firms emerge as an alternative organisational method to the price mechanism in response to transactional costs. He disagrees with Alchian and Demsetz when they claim that it is mainly the benefits of team production, i.e. the non-separability of marginal products that cause groupings of workers to exist. He maintains that it is the size of transaction costs rather than the nature of technology that determines the efficiency of exchange by one organisational method as compared with another. This does not mean that technology is unimportant. It does mean, however, that technological non-separabilities are rarely the decisive factor (1975: chs 4–5). What is distinctive about Williamson's approach (which he called the 'organisational failures framework') is that transaction costs (or market failures) have been attributed to the interplay of human with environmental factors. Human attributes and behaviour in decision-making situations coupled with certain environmental factors can create costs. ' . . .it is always the joining of human with environment factors, not either taken by itself that poses transactional problems' (1975: 20). If, for example, some individuals are inclined to behave in a rather deceitful way in relation to the quality or price of their product, this will not create problems in a trading situation involving large numbers of competitors. Competition will ensure that the deceit is soon discovered and the deceitful trader will not trade for long. However, if the opportunist is the single supplier or if there is widespread uncertainty about the quality or any other attribute of the transaction then the dishonesty will create problems. In such circumstances bilateral bargaining can be expensive and information regarding quality or other aspects of trade is costly. Therefore, the question as to whether to buy an input in the market or to make your own arises and the answer may be in favour of making your own. Thus, the proclivity of individuals to act opportunistically will create problems (transactional costs) in monopolistic rather than in competitive situations. Similarly, lack of ability on the part of decision makers will manifest itself and create problems only when decisions are complex or uncertainty is present.

When the interaction of human and environment factors create substantial costs in market exchanges 'internal organisations' (firms) will emerge as an alternative to markets in order to economise on transaction costs.

As Coase suggested long ago, the significance of transaction costs does not end with the decision to internalise. Transactions have a variety of different characteristics so that the extent of cost saving following inter-nalisation may well vary depending on the way in which transactions are organised. Thus, having taken a decision to internalise a transaction, the question of how to organise this internal transaction arises. The answer is that the organisation should be such as to minimise the costs associated with this transaction. To put it differently, of the variety of possible administrative structures the most efficient one should be chosen. This optimal structure is not, however, unique. It rather depends on the nature of the transactions and, since the attributes of transactions vary, an assessment of alternative organisational forms will indicate the most efficient one in each case.

For Williamson efficiency in the form of economising on transaction costs is both the reason why firms emerge and the main contributing factor to the evolution of different internal organisational structures. Further-more, economising on transaction costs can be an important influence on decisions such as vertical or horizontal business expansion, conglomerate mergers, multinational enterprises and business strategy and control.

To understand the nature and the significance of transaction costs it is essential to analyse, in some detail, the factors which contribute to their existence. The relevant concepts will then be utilised in the subsequent section of this chapter to indicate how efficiency considerations may lead to the emergence of internal organisations.

FACTORS CONTRIBUTING TO MARKET FAILURES

Human attributes

Of the extremely rich set of human attributes two are of particular significance for the transaction cost approach to the theory of the firm; lack of competence (bounded rationality) and trustworthiness (opportunism). When these attributes co-exist with certain environmental factors such as uncertainty, small-numbers exchange relationships (monopolistic situa-tions) or asset specificity, market exchange problems occur and efficiency considerations will favour alternative organisational forms. To be able to understand these issues we need to define, in more detail, the human and environment factors whose interplay causes market failures.

Bounded rationality is a term used to describe the behaviour of individuals who wish to act rationally but whose ability to be rational is limited. As decision makers, individuals may experience limitations in their ability to process information and to formulate and solve problems. This is due to cognitive and language limitations which restrict (a) the capacity of humans to receive, store, retrieve and process information without error (Simon 1957), and (b) their ability to articulate knowledge and feelings.

Bounded rationality creates problems (i.e. costs) only when the bounds are reached. When decisions have to be taken with incomplete knowledge or in the presence of uncertainty and complexity then bounded rationality will exist. The problem of complexity can be demonstrated by considering a game of chess. To construct a table containing all the possible opening moves and then for each opening move record all the possible responses allowed by the rules of the game and to each response record the possible counter moves and so on to the end of the game involves such a large number of moves that even the best chess player operates under bounded rationality; she or he has to make decisions in the absence of a complete list of future contingencies.

A Managing Director considering whether to recommend a takeover bid, a consumer deciding to buy a new product, a multinational enterprise deciding to invest in a new country, are examples of business decisions which may encounter problems of incomplete information and uncertainty which imply the existence of bounded rationality.

Opportunism is a motivational attribute. It refers to the behaviour of individuals who seek their self-interest in deceitful ways. As Williamson (1981) puts it, 'Opportunism effectively extends the assumption of self-interest seeking to make allowances to self-interest seeking with guile' (p. 1545). Opportunism exists when some individuals are not trustworthy so that they are likely to make a misrepresentation of intentions in the form of false or empty promises regarding future contact. Distorting information or disclosing selective pieces of information (being economical with the truth) is opportunistic behaviour. It should be noted that it is not assumed that all individuals are inclined to behave opportunistically. Indeed the problems are actually compounded if opportunistic behaviour varies among individuals since in this case it will be beneficial to expend resources in order to discriminate among types of individuals.

Characteristics of transactions

The efficiency of market transacting can be influenced significantly by the nature of the transactions carried out. Business transactions differ in their attributes and in particular in the following.

1 *Uncertainty and/or complexity* While some uncertainty and/or complexity may be common in most business transactions the extent to which these attributes exist varies substantially with significant consequences.
2 *Frequency* Some transactions are repetitive but others are not.
3 *Numbers of transactors* When the number of market participants is small bilateral monopoly situations may arise which create uncertainty and, given opportunistic behaviour, can result in substantial transaction costs.
4 *Asset specificity* When a transaction is supported by 'specific' investment

or contributes to the development of 'specific' know-how or on-the-job training, asset specificity is said to exist. 'Specific' investment refers to investment which has very little or no value in alternative uses. Similarly, know-how and on-the-job training is specific if it is not transferable to other uses or users.

There are in fact three types of asset specificity. Know-how and on-the-job training specific to a firm or to a particular transaction is known as *human asset specificity*. Equipment specifically designed to produce a product that can be bought by only one buyer is said to involve *physical asset specificity*. An example could be a car engine which can only be used by Rolls Royce cars. Finally, *site specificity* exists when technologically separable stages of production are located in close proximity in order to save on transportation and other costs.

Palay (1984) gives two interesting examples of physical asset specificity from the transportation of cars and chemicals. Motorcars moved by rail require special racks which have no other use than to carry cars. Once built their value in the next best use is roughly equal to their scrap value. Moreover, the railcars have to be fitted with decks and tie-downs which make it almost impossible to use them to transport different car makes or models. Tank cars, used to transport chemicals, are constructed to be substance specific. They are fitted with specialised equipment such as glass or rubber lining, special pressure valves and damage control equipment. Quality control and safety concerns prevent the use of the same tank cars for the transport of several chemicals or their use by other manufacturers.

A final point regarding asset specificity is that it should not be confused with fixed costs. Assets that give rise to fixed costs are not necessarily asset specific because they can usually be redeployed to alternative uses. Office space, for example, gives rise to fixed costs but is not characterised by asset specificity, since it can be re-deployed. On the other hand variable costs may contain a non-salvageable asset or firm specific part. Human knowledge of aspects of the firm or of the way a particular team functions could give rise to variable costs (by adjusting hours of work) but can be of a non-transferable nature.

Environmental characteristics

Atmosphere refers to the nature of the exchange process itself. It touches on peoples' perceptions of qualitative aspects of the environment within which transactions take place. The atmosphere can influence the way people interact, by influencing the attitudes and behaviour of individuals. If the atmosphere of a particular organisation is such that it induces respect for human dignity and a sense of belonging then the organisation may be more successful since individuals are likely to perform better in these conditions. Moreover, some people may be prepared to sacrifice monetary rewards for a work environment that is characterised by such an atmosphere. Thus, atmospheric differences may affect both production and transaction costs and should contribute to the choice of a particular mode of organising transactions.

Derivative conditions

Information impactedness is a derivative condition. It exists when decision makers are inclined to act opportunistically in the presence of uncertainty/ complexity and small-number exchange relationships. It arises when one participant to a transaction is better informed, in relation to this transaction, than another participant who cannot acquire the same information without substantial costs because the informed participant cannot be relied upon to fully and honestly disclose the relevant information. It should be noted that for information impactedness to exist two conditions must be fulfilled; information acquisition must be costly and opportunistic behaviour must be present (bounded rationality may also contribute). The following examples may clarify the concept.

The problem of adverse selection

This is a problem usually discussed in relation to insurance although it may occur in other markets. Consider insurance first. Potential buyers of insurance are likely to be better informed than sellers about their personal characteristics (such as health etc.). Unless this information can be acquired costlessly by the seller, information asymmetry implies uncertainty for the potential seller. If, moreover, buyers are likely to behave opportunistically so that poor risk individuals do not disclose their true characteristics, then the probability of the insured risk occurring increases. As a result premiums increase and potential buyers with good risk characteristics refuse to take up insurance. Adverse selection has occurred. Bad risk individuals drive out of the market good risk individuals and the volume of trade declines.

The same problem may arise in any market in which distinguishing between good and bad quality is difficult. The second-hand car market (Akerlof 1970) may suffer from adverse selection. Owners of second-hand cars are better informed about the quality of their cars than potential buyers. Given the average price of cars owners of bad cars (what the Americans call 'lemons') will be more inclined to sell than owners of good cars. Thus, the average quality of second-hand cars declines and the price declines and this will reduce the numbers of good car owners who wish to sell. Thus lemons have driven good cars out of the market. Trade will decline unless alternative institutional arrangements can ameliorate this problem by, for example, offering warranties of quality etc. to remedy this market problem.

Moral hazard

Like adverse selection,[5] the term moral hazard originated in the insurance literature. It refers to the behaviour of parties (such as insurance buyers) who exploit information differentials opportunistically. Assume, for example, that the occurrence of a loss insured depends to a certain extent on steps taken by the buyer to mitigate risks but that the relevant information is not available to the insurer except at high costs. This could be the case of a contract insuring house or office contents against theft or fire. Moral hazard will exist if the buyer acts carelessly or diverts any loss mitigating resources (such as the financing of alarm systems or employment of night porters) to other uses so that the probability of the insured losses occurring increases.

First mover advantages

Suppose that a project is to be contracted out by tender and that a perfectly competitive situation exists. As a result a large number of equally well-informed and competent participants respond to the tender invitation (an efficient allocation takes place). If, however, the project requires specialised investment or involves learning-by-doing or the development of know-how then the first winner of the contract acquires knowledge and other advantages which other parties will lack at the point of the renewal of the contract. Information asymmetry and a small-numbers (monopolistic) bargaining situation have evolved. There is information impactedness.

THE ADVANTAGES OF INTERNAL ORGANISATION

When information is imperfect or complex business decisions are involved individuals may lack the ability required for efficient decision making and some may be induced to act opportunistically. As a result substantial transaction costs occur and the market mechanism fails to be an efficient method of organising transactions. In these circumstances 'internal organisation', i.e. an organisational method involving planning and authority in the administration of transactions, may have advantages over market transacting. That is, internal organisation may be able to influence human behaviour favourably and as a result economise on transaction costs. When this reduction in transaction costs is sufficient to compensate for increased administrative expenses then internal structures emerge as alternatives to market transacting. In other words, transaction cost economics suggests that internal organisation of transactions will supersede market transacting for reasons of efficiency. Efficiency takes the form of economising (i.e. reducing rather than eliminating) on transaction costs.

In order to understand the emergence of internal structures we may begin by considering the circumstances which produce high transaction

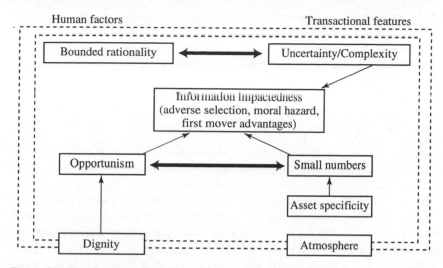

Figure 3.1 Factor interactions that may result in market failure

costs in market exchanges. We will then enquire as to whether and how internal structures may be able to alter these circumstances so as to reduce transaction costs sufficiently.

As already noted transaction costs arise by the interaction of human and environmental factors. Such interactions can be analysed by reference to Figure 3.1. The following examples may help to illustrate.

1 Consider how a business decision involving bounded rationality combined with uncertainty or complexity will create transaction costs. A firm requires the services of an architect (or an accountant or a solicitor) on a long-term basis. The details of the work are not known and cannot be precisely specified over the long run. Since the details of future requirements are not known with any degree of accuracy (a relevant decision tree cannot be constructed), long-term market contracting will not be feasible. A series of short-term market contracts on the other hand is expensive and can be hazardous because of the possibility of the development of first mover advantages. That is, the person awarded the first short-term contract may gain such knowledge of the intricacies of the firm that she or he may have a monopolistic advantage over other accountants at the contract renewal time. Internalisation of this transaction (an employment contract rather than market contracting) offers the possibility that a series of short-term contracts are replaced by a long-term contract expressed in general terms. That is, the solicitor or accountant will be expected to provide legal or accounting services the precise nature of which will be specified in the future as the firm's needs unfold over time. Thus, a long-term contract becomes feasible since the two parties need not form

detailed expectations about a distant future in order to negotiate its terms. In general, within an internal structure decisions are taken sequentially as time unfolds thus reducing bounded rationality.

Similarly, market transacting in conditions of uncertainty or complexity requires that all parties to a transaction form their own expectations about future events and act accordingly. This can, however, result in a set of mutually incompatible decisions. Agreement could eventually be reached but only after a series of costly adjustments and bargaining. Internalisation can reduce these costs by shortening the adjustment period. This can be achieved by assigning decision-making responsibility to one member of a team.

2 Consider opportunism combined with small-number exchange relations. The only control of opportunistic behaviour in market transacting is the threat of severing a contract at the contract renewal time. That is, deceitful traders may be controlled by the fear of losing their customers. However, in monopolistic situations (small-number exchange relations) a threat of withdrawal from the contract will not be credible. This can occur when asset specificity is present in which case there are either no alternative sources of supply or, if there are, the costs involved are much higher.[6] In these circumstances internalising the relevant transactions may attenuate opportunistic behaviour for several reasons. First, members to the exchange may have no direct claim to the outcome (profit) of their actions. This will be, for example, the case if both buyer and seller belong to the same organisation (two divisions of the same firm). Besides, internalisation may create a feeling of belonging which may induce more co-operative behaviour. Second, the existence of better auditing systems within firms will tend to discourage opportunism. Third, management can intervene to resolve prolonged disputes without the need to resort to the courts.

3 Information asymmetry does not create problems unless combined with opportunistic behaviour in which case information impactedness occurs. To the extent that internal organisation reduces opportunism it attenuates the information impactedness problem. Even if conditions of information impactedness remain they are unlikely to give rise to strategic behaviour.

To summarise, internalisation, a form of transacting which supplants the market, may emerge as a method of economising on transaction costs associated with uncertainty, bounded rationality, opportunism and strategic behaviour.

THE HIERARCHICAL STRUCTURE OF FIRMS

Internal structures supersede markets because they can deal better with problems arising from bounded rationality and opportunistic behaviour.

This does not, however, imply that such behaviour can be totally eliminated. The extent to which bounded rationality and opportunism are controlled within firms will vary with the particular features of the internal organisational structure adopted. Internal structures may in turn involve different degrees of complexity and may or may not be hierarchically organised.

As noted earlier both Coase (1964) and Alchian and Demsetz (1972) suggested that the internal structures which replace the market mechanism will be hierarchically organised. It is only recently, however, that the notion of efficiency in the form of economising on transaction costs has been utilised in order to (a) explain why a variety of structures (both simple non-hierarchical and hierarchical) may develop and (b) explore their implications for business behaviour.

A non-hierarchical structure, what Williamson called a 'peer group' of workers, may have advantages over market transacting in certain circumstances. However, as the complexities of business increase, peer groups may be replaced by simple hierarchies. Increased complexity and uncertainty may in turn imply the linking of simple hierarchies into more complex (multi-stage) hierarchical structures.

Peer groups are associations of individuals which act collectively and co-operatively so that they are characterised by the absence of subordination. Decision making is democratic. A peer group is a form of internal organisation and as such it must have advantages over market exchanges or it would not emerge as an alternative to the market. Peer groups may emerge for several reasons. Specialisation in production is a well-known advantage of working in groups but there are other incentives such as advantages due to indivisibilities, risk bearing or associational gains. Let us consider each briefly.

1 *Indivisibilities* When production involves the use of large indivisible assets (either physical assets or 'set-up' costs for collecting and handling information) full capacity utilisation which will bring about lower per unit costs may require that assets be used by more than one producer. For example, the minimum accommodation and other costs involved in setting up a legal practice in a big city could be sufficient for say three solicitors to work together. In principle full utilisation could be achieved if one individual (solicitor) acquired the asset and contracted its use to the rest of the group. Such market contracting, however, may be faced with problems. Bounded rationality will make long-term contracting (complex contingent type) infeasible and spot (short-term) contracting may be exploited opportunistically by the monopolist. Co-operation alleviates these problems.

2 *Risk reduction* The group may be able to better reduce risks compared with the individual, so that team members may earn more when working as a team than when working individually. If the group members are

involved, for example, in related or integrated tasks, they will have the knowledge to select group members. The problem of adverse selection will thus be mitigated. Moreover, despite errors, a deliberate attempt will be made to choose well-motivated productive co-workers. As a result the team will consist of a group of workers of more than average efficiency. Insurance costs, therefore, may be lower in group effort compared with individual effort.

3 *Associational gains* Associational gains refer to the atmosphere that prevails in such groups. Some individuals may value co-operative action and feel a sense of belonging and responsibility that results in higher productivity. Alternatively, members may dislike subordination and control (which exist in a hierarchical structure) and be prepared to sacrifice monetary rewards for the advantages of working collectively and co-operatively.

Such advantages imply that efficiency improves when 'peer group' organisational structures supersede market transacting. However, as the size and the complexity of business increase, peer groups may face substantial transactional costs which may be reduced by an organisation which involves some authoritative relationship. Consider how such costs may occur and why they can be reduced by a simple hierarchical structure.

The lack of subordination that characterises peer groups implies that all members participate in decision making. Universal participation is not only time consuming, it may create substantial costs related to the collection and dissemination of information among all members of the team. Effective participation in decision making requires that all team members should be well informed. A two-way communication system among all the members requires the establishment of an all channel network. As Figure 3.2(a) indicates, fifteen two-way flow connections are required when there are six team members. As the number N of membership increases the number of connections increases by $N(N-1)/2$. After a point the

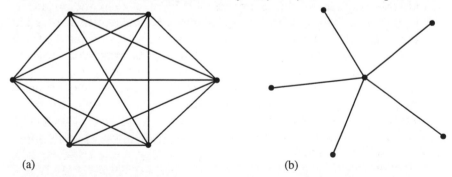

(a)   (b)

Figure 3.2 Alternative information communication systems: (a) all channel network; (b) wheel network

opportunity cost of wasted time in communicating everything to and from everyone, in order to reach collective decisions, becomes prohibitive.

To economise on communication costs (especially when membership is large) a wheel network may be adopted. Information is communicated to one individual (at the hub of the wheel) who takes all the decisions and communicates them back to the rest of the team. This reduces the number of communication channels to $N-1$ with substantial savings on related costs but at the same time it replaces collective by individual decision making. To avoid subordination so as to preserve the associational gains, members may take turns to act as the 'hub' of the wheel. Examples of this are provided by the administration of university departments where the headship rotates among the members of the department. Such an administrative scheme will be both feasible and efficient when all members are equally qualified as administrators and equally efficient as decision makers. That is, when bounded rationality differences do not exist. Otherwise efficiency will be sacrificed for democracy. If substantial differentials in bounded rationality exist so that one member (or a few members) is permanently assigned a decision-making role then a simple hierarchy emerges.

Similarly, when some members of the group cannot be trusted to perform their duties to the best of their ability, free rider problems exist and the need arises to control shirking. A monitor is needed to assess performance and adjust compensations over time. Unless all the members of a peer group are equally able to act as monitors and auditors, a central monitor will be required or there will be losses in production. Appointing a monitor compromises the democratic character of a group and implies the emergence of a hierarchy.

Thus, when peer group efficiency in making and implementing decisions improves, through comparative advantage gains, hierarchies emerge by establishing an elite.

This does not, however, imply that efficiency dictates that all firms should be hierarchically organised. It is possible that peer groups are more efficient than hierarchies in certain circumstances. This will happen when democratic decision making and the absence of auditing and subordination act as inducements which improve productivity.

It should also be noted that Williamson's notion of efficiency employed so far can be criticised as too narrow. When individuals are prepared to sacrifice monetary rewards for associational benefits, or when democracy is valued in itself as an organisational form, in certain instances the meaning of efficiency should be modified to incorporate this value. Such considerations will be emphasised in subsequent chapters especially when we examine monitoring and incentives mechanisms. Meanwhile we examine in the next chapter how efficiency in the form of transaction cost economising can have an important influence in determining the internal organisation and behaviour of a firm.

SUMMARY

The view that firms emerge as alternatives to markets for reasons of efficiency is examined in this chapter. Particular emphasis is placed on the concept of transaction costs, the way they arise and their significance for the choice of organisational form.

When the market gives rise to serious transaction costs the administration of transactions becomes internalised. The resultant internal structure may be non-hierarchical (peer group). Bounded rationality differentials and opportunism, however, may create problems especially as the size of a peer group expands. When the benefits derived from co-operation and the absence of subordination fail to compensate for increasing transaction costs, peer groups may also be supplanted by simple hierarchies. A 'simple hierarchy', defined as a group of individuals working under the supervision and assessment of one (or a few) monitor(s), is what Williamson called a firm.

The emergence of firms does not imply that all transactions are or should be internalised. Indeed the co-existence of market transacting with firms and peer groups enhances efficiency. This is because transactions differ in their attributes so that transaction cost economising requires a variety of organisational forms. The influence of the nature of transactions on organisational structure is further explored in the next chapter.

APPLICATION: ASSET SPECIFICITY IN THE US AEROSPACE INDUSTRY AND IN TRANSPORT

An important proposition, advanced in this chapter, is that the decision as to whether a transaction will be internalised depends on the characteristics of the transaction. The realism of this proposition can be illustrated with the following two cases.

1 The input procurement policy of the US aerospace industry was investigated by Masten (1984). Not surprisingly, he reported that asset specificity was found to be an important influence on the decision as to whether a producer would make their own inputs or buy them from another producer.

To be more specific, there are two stages in the input procurement policy in the US aerospace industry. First, the government selects a prime contractor to be responsible for a particular programme and, second, the prime contractor manages the whole system including the administration of subcontracts. Masten investigated the procurement policy of both the federal government and the prime contractors and found that the method of procurement depended on the nature of inputs. The system he analysed consisted of 1,887 components for each of which a decision as to whether to make or buy had to be taken by a group of company representatives. It was found that the general reluctance on the part of administrators to internalise transactions was overcome by exposure to the hazards of market exchange when components were specialised and complex. More precisely, the probability that a particular item would be sourced-in-house rather than bought varied substantially with the characteristics of the item. The more complex or site specific the item was the higher the probability that it would be produced internally. In particular, Masten calculated that 'The lack of alternative uses for a component increases the probability that it will be procured internally from less than 1 per cent to 31 per cent for relatively uncomplex items and from 2 per cent to 92 per cent for more complex components' (p. 411). He concluded that 'Overall the data on the aerospace system supports the contention that design specificity and complexity are necessary, if not sufficient, conditions for the breakdown of cooperation in market-mediated exchanges and the subsequent integration of production within the firm' (p. 417).

2 Asset specificity was also found to be present in the transportation of chemicals (Palay 1984). But in this industry problems of asset specificity were dealt with partly by internalisation and partly by the development of mutual trust and a desire to maintain a good business reputation and good relations. Thus, partial internalisation was observed in the movement of chemicals while the enforcement of other aspects of agreements relating to requirements for specialised handling and co-ordination in the transport of chemicals relied mainly on the mutuality of interest and trust relations that had developed. Trust relations were also observed in the transport of motorcars, where verbal promises and legally non-enforceable commitments involving substantial sums of money were regularly honoured in the interest of good business relations.

Awareness of the detrimental effects of opportunistic behaviour led those involved in the transport of both cars and chemicals to behave honestly. 'In order to maintain reputations shippers and carriers simply did not take advantage of the ex-post small-numbers bargaining conditions. Instead trust relations developed' (Palay 1984: 276).

FURTHER READING

Alchian, A.A. and Demsetz, R. (1972) 'Production, Information Costs and Economic Organisation', *American Economic Review*, LXII (5): 777–95.
Coase, R.H. (1964) 'The Nature of the Firm', *Economica*, New Series, IV: 386–405; reprinted in *Readings in Price Theory, The American Economic Association*, London: Allen and Unwin, 1964. This is essential reading since it lays the foundations on which transaction costs economics is built.
Ricketts, M. (1987) *The Economics of Business Enterprise*, Brighton: Wheatsheaf, ch. 2.

Williamson, O.E. (1975) *Markets and Hierarchies: Analysis and Antitrust Implications*, New York: Free Press. This gives a detailed although more advanced treatment of the issues covered in this chapter.

QUESTIONS

1 Compare and contrast (briefly) Coase's and Alchian and Demsetz's explanations of the emergence of business firms.
2 Transactions cost economics suggests that when markets fail to organise transactions efficiently firms supersede market transacting.
   Take some relevant factors (such as asset specificity) and explain how they may contribute to a market failure and hence to the emergence of firms.
3 Use examples to illustrate the problem of 'moral hazard' and 'adverse selection'.
   Do you agree with the view that racial or sexual discrimination in employment may be an entrepreneurial response to the 'adverse selection' problem? Explain.
4 Explain and critically evaluate the role of 'opportunism' in transaction cost economics.
5 'Neither the emergence of business firms nor the way in which they organise themselves can be attributed solely to the benefits of team production.' Comment.
6 Comment on the view that the forces contributing to the emergence and growth of firms are not simply technological in nature.

NOTES

1 'The term governance is a shorthand expression for the institutional framework in which contracts are initiated, negotiated, adapted, enforced, and terminated' (Palay 1984).
2 The necessity for non-specific contracts will become clearer once the nature of transaction costs is explained. Fitzroy's and Mueller's (1984) definition of a firm is 'a cooperative productive agreement in which . . . formal contracts specifying the actions of all individuals are inefficient, and implicit contracts, enforced by members of the cooperative itself, are only used to coordinate and monitor the activities of its members'.
3 A production function $Q=f(L,K)$ is said to be non-separable when $\partial Q/\partial L\partial K \neq 0$; i.e. when the marginal product of a factor of production depends on the marginal product of another factor. An example of a non-separable production function often used by economists is the Cobb–Douglas function

$Q = AL^a K^{1-a}$.

The function is non-separable since

$$\frac{\partial Q}{\partial L} = aAL^{a-1}K^{1-a}$$

$$\frac{\partial Q}{\partial K} = (1-a)AK^{-a}L^a$$

and

$$\frac{\partial Q}{\partial L\partial K} \neq 0$$

An example of a separable function is

$Q = aL^2 + bK^2$

which is separable since it can be written as $Q = Q_1 + Q_2$ where

$$Q_1 = aL^2$$
$$Q_2 = bK^2$$

and the marginal product of L is $\partial Q/\partial L = 2aL$ independent of K
and that of K is $\partial Q/\partial K = 2bK$ independent of L.

4 The incentive to shirk is derived from the assumption that leisure enters an individual's utility function. The more leisure one enjoys the higher his or her utility is. But leisure like any other commodity has a price. When shirking cannot be detected easily so that its full cost is not borne by the person responsible for shirking, the realised cost of leisure is less than its true cost. Consequently individuals will tend to acquire more leisure. Since the cost of shirking to the person who shirks is lower the more numerous the team is, it follows that the incentive to shirk will increase with the size of a team.

5 Moral hazard in its broader sense includes adverse selection.

6 It should be noted that human dignity, a desire to act fairly and the benefits of establishing a good reputation may overcome opportunistic tendencies and the need for internalisation. Palay (1984) found some evidence which supports this claim. He reports (1984: Section 8) that considerations of goodwill and respect for personal (managerial) and corporate reputations have managed to overcome asset specificity problems in the cases he examined.

4 The internal organisation of firms

INTRODUCTION

It was suggested, in the previous chapter, that when transaction costs render market transacting expensive and hazardous, alternative methods of organising transactions evolve. The organisations which supersede the market may adopt a non-hierarchical internal structure (peer groups), but as the size of peer groups increases the benefits of working in a co-operative and non-authoritarian environment may fail to compensate for transaction costs associated with increases in bounded rationality differentials and opportunism. When this occurs efficiency may indicate that peer groups should be supplanted by hierarchies. The mere adoption of a hierarchical structure does not, however, ensure that the organisation of transactions will be efficient. Hierarchical structures vary in the way they administer transactions and in their internal procedures and control systems. Moreover, as we have already seen, transaction costs vary with the nature of business. That is, costs depend on the frequency of trade, the extent of uncertainty and complexity involved and the requirements for specific investment. Efficiency requires that internal administrative structures should match the characteristics of the transactions they govern so as to minimise costs. An optimum structure is the one that minimises bounded rationality while safeguarding against opportunistic behaviour (Williamson 1983b). The optimum administrative structure is not unique and universally applicable. Rather the opposite is true. Administrative structures will vary with the particular characteristics of the firm so that different structures may co-exist.

Moreover, an optimum internal structure does not remain optimal indefinitely. As the size of the firm increases, synergies develop and more complex tasks are tackled, the control of transaction (and production) costs requires adaptations of the administrative structure. Thus, more layers may be added to the administrative pyramid, simple hierarchies may join up and more sophisticated control and monitoring systems develop. The modern corporation is the result of this evolutionary process.

At any point in time, however, firms of different sizes and complexity exist which implies that a variety of structures should co-exist. Many of the internal structures encountered in business today, however, fall into two broad groups; the unitary (U-form) and the multidivisional (M-form) structures although combinations of the two are not uncommon. U- and M-form firms are examined in the following two sections. The significance of structure for business objectives and behaviour is then analysed and some empirical evidence on the impact of organisational structure on business performance is presented. A brief summary follows and the chapter concludes with an application: the organisation of railroads.

THE UNITARY FORM FIRM

Although a hierarchy, almost by definition, involves some authority and conscious planning, Williamson claims that the hierarchical relation which defines a firm is not rigidly authoritarian. He therefore disagrees with Coase (1964) who likened the relationship between the monitor and other members of the team to the relationship between a master and his servant. At the same time he does not accept the opposite view expressed by Alchian and Demsetz (1972), i.e. that the relation between employer and employees involves no authority but is a series of short-term implicit contracts which are renewed every time an employee accepts to perform a certain task.

Neither the view of a master–servant relationship nor that of a series of implicit contracts serve a useful analytical purpose. Whether a member of a team is seen as accepting instructions or as renegotiating an implicit contract, in practice contracts are periodically renegotiated explicitly. Negotiations may involve bargaining and substantial transaction costs. This will be particularly true when employees do not trust employers or when workers acquire specialised knowledge and expertise over time. When employment involves on-the-job training, employers may find themselves bargaining, at contract renewal time, in a situation of asymmetric information with employees having first mover advantages. Thus, the productivity advantages of a well-trained and experienced workforce may put an employer in a weak bargaining position. It should be clear from Chapter 3 that employers cannot resolve this problem by drawing up a contract with a complete list of tasks to be performed by employees. This is because information is revealed over time and is asymmetrically distributed. Internal structures, however, will mitigate these informational problems if they create an environment which gives incentives to both employees and employers to act co-operatively rather than opportunistically. Employers cannot operate simply as givers of instructions; they rather need to provide an environment within which opportunistic behaviour is discouraged. In other words, employers in addition to their role as monitors must act as providers of incentives. The 'employment relation' (i.e. the set of contractual relationships which characterises a firm) incorporates such a system of incentives and control mechanisms which labour economists call an 'internal labour market'.

The main features of an internal labour market which contribute to a suppression of conflict and the attenuation of opportunistic behaviour include the following.

1 *Collective bargaining*   Individual contracts are replaced by collective contracts. Employers do not bargain with individuals. Employees are, on appointment, offered a grade in the hierarchy and are expected to accept the conditions of service and the collectively agreed upon remuneration attached to that particular grade. The lack of individual bargaining reduces employees' incentives to act opportunistically by misrepresenting their knowledge or by threatening to resign when they have firm-specific advantages over potential replacements. Employees cannot capitalise on knowledge or other advantages they have over equally qualified outsiders who lack the on-the-job experience. At the same time collective agreements include grievance procedures and dispute settling mechanisms which tend to reduce bounded rationality.

2 *Promotion ladders and ports of entry*   Collective bargaining implies that individuals lose their job-specific rights. Moreover, auditing and monitoring may offend some individuals and inhibit the development of a sense of belonging and trust. Trust is particularly significant when substantial on-the-job training is involved and the firm is paying less during the training period with the promise to pay more later on. To ensure a better atmosphere, the development of trust and a sense of belonging, part of the incentives system is that higher level positions are usually filled by internal promotions. New appointments are normally restricted to lower level posts. This restriction of 'ports of entry' to lower levels has the additional advantage that the firm can avoid or reduce risks since decisions on internal promotions are based on better information provided by a firm's monitoring and experience rating system. This means that individual abilities and other personal attributes can be assessed more effectively. Thus, appointment errors will be restricted to lower level posts while the problem of adverse selection in internal promotions will be attenuated.

When such an 'employment relation' exists across all stages in a hierarchy the resulting internal structure is known as a 'unitary form' or 'U-form' enterprise. This structure in its simplest form is illustrated in Figure 4.1. At the top of the hierarchy is the chief executive officer (CEO) who acts as a central monitor. The next layer, immediately below, consists of the several functional areas of the firm such as production, marketing, personnel and finance.

The CEO is responsible for both long-term (strategic) decisions and the day-to-day running of the functions. Each function has a general manager who reports to the CEO. The functional manager collects and passes

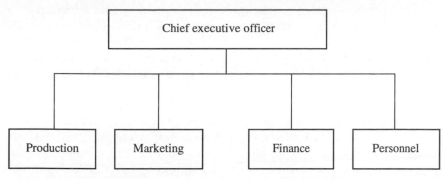

Figure 4.1 A U-form firm

information to the CEO and receives instructions. The links among the functions, if existent, are rather weak.

Although references to occasional examples of enterprises (in England and Japan) with complex hierarchical structures go as far back as the early eighteenth century,[1] economic historians consider that the first enterprise to be organised along functional lines was the US railroad in 1840 (see the application at the end of this chapter).

The U-form structure confers advantages of (a) specialisation, both managers and staff specialise in the work of a functional area, and (b) communication, which is established along functional lines. A production manager, for example, communicates primarily with production workers and does not require detailed information about finance. A functional manager reports to the CEO and may participate in the work of the CEO. Since each manager is allowed to concentrate on specific links related to a particular area of the work of the firm the problem of bounded rationality is mitigated so that the U-form structure remains effective, within limits, as business enterprises grow in size.

Technological innovations, however, have facilitated growth by diversification. Diversification increases complexity because (a) the personnel of each functional area are involved with a variety of products and (b) the need arises for closer co-ordination between functional divisions. Within a U-form firm this implies that more of the top management's time is required for functional co-ordination and less is devoted to strategic planning. However, so long as the degree of diversification is not very extensive the U-form structure remains efficient. Thus, the U-form was the typical organisational structure adopted during the second half of the nineteenth century and the first half of the twentieth century both in the USA and in the UK. By 1932 most USA large corporations were organised as U-form enterprises (Williamson 1981). Even today the U-form organisation is quite widespread in Western countries, especially among small and medium-size enterprises.

As firms continue to grow by diversification they may reach a size such that information-related problems, complexity and heavier administrative loads imply that senior executives become unable to handle their responsibilities effectively. As Chandler (1962) puts it, 'problems of co-ordination, appraisal, and policy formulation too intricate for a small number of top officers to handle both long-run entrepreneurial, and short-run operational administration activities' (p. 383) may present themselves. Moreover, problems due to complexity and bounded rationality are not confined to the senior executives. They permeate throughout the hierarchy. Suppose, for example, that a firm producing and marketing cosmetics diversifies into drugs usually dispensed by doctor prescription. The marketing skills involved in selling cosmetics are quite different to those of selling drugs. Communicating information to customers in the case of cosmetics would probably be most effective through the mass media while the dissemination of information relating to drugs may require personal visits to physicians. With increasing size the marketing personnel may find it productive to specialise within their functional area, so that two areas emerge – marketing of cosmetics and marketing of drugs. Since effective marketing to physicians may require a good knowledge of the product those involved with the marketing of drugs may find themselves communicating more with the production department than with the cosmetics marketing staff. Thus, links between functional areas may begin to become much stronger. As diversification increases so does the requirement for a diverse range of marketing skills. Bounded rationality will eventually limit the ability of the functional (marketing) manager to effectively co-ordinate and control a diverse set of activities. Similar problems are faced by the managers of all the other functional departments as they attempt to cope with a variety of distinct businesses. At the same time the CEO experiences increased difficulties in the co-ordination of individual businesses across departments.

One solution to the informational and control problems that arise is to add more levels to the hierarchy. But adding levels means that information will need to go through more steps both before reaching the top decision makers and as decisions are communicated back for execution. This may encourage opportunistic behaviour. Information may be delayed or distorted in pursuit of personal goals. In Williamson's terminology, bounded rationality gives rise to finite span of control. There is control loss which may lead to subgoals and alter the character of strategic decision making. Since the profitability of functional divisions is neither directly observable nor measurable, functional managers may pursue expansion of their divisions beyond the level consistent with corporate profitability. Permissive attitudes towards slack may develop leading to a resource allocation which is suboptimal.

In short, problems of bounded rationality and information impactedness will arise as firms expand and the acquisition of job specific skills and knowledge (job idiosyncrasy) may accentuate opportunistic behaviour. Increases in transaction costs render the U-form structure suboptimal.

THE MULTIDIVISIONAL STURCTURE (M-FORM)

When the inherent weaknesses of the U-form structure became critical the DuPont company, under Pierre S. DuPont, and General Motors, under Alfred P. Sloan, Jr., developed in the 1920s what is known as an M-form or multidivisional organisational structure. More recent examples include Johnson and Johnson and Microsoft. Siemens has re-organised into sixteen mini-corporations and IBM have currently embarked on a process of reorganisation along multidivisional lines.

A multidivisional structure is based on the principle of decomposition. In its simplest form it consists of a general office (see Figure 4.2) and a number of operating divisions. The general office is assigned responsibilities of strategic decision making and control of the operating divisions. It consists of the main directors and a small number of specialists ('elite' staff). It has superseded the board of directors as the main co-ordinating body. The operating part of the firm is decomposed into a number of semi-autonomous divisions each responsible for operating decisions.[2] Each division controls strongly interacting activities such as activities relating to one product or one geographical area. Divisions are self-contained and organised along functional lines. They are run by a head who is responsible for the divisional performance. The essence of this structure is a separation of long-term (strategic) decisions from the day-to-day operating decisions which are left to the divisional managers. Two important advantages derive from this separation.

1 *Economising on bounded rationality of top officers*   Freed from the burden of their involvement in the everyday running of the firm, the general office staff can concentrate on strategic planning and implementation.

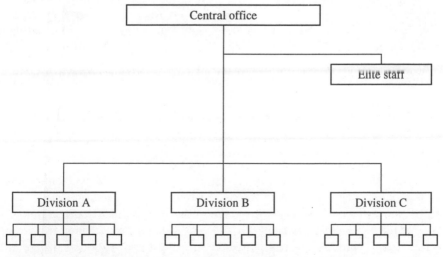

Figure 4.2 A multidivisional organisational structure (M-form firm)

2 *Economising on informational costs*　　Divisional managers are in closer contact and, therefore, have better information about developments taking place in their external competitive environment. They are able to act quickly within the limits of their brief. Many decisions and their execution can be speeded up since neither information nor instructions need be transmitted through all the levels of the hierarchy to the top officers and back.

In addition, the independence of each division contributes to an improved allocation of resources. The profitability of each division becomes observable in this structure, so that direct comparisons between product or geographical divisions are both possible and significant. Resource allocation can improve by investing in profitable areas and by encouraging less efficient divisions to improve their performance or by moving resources from less efficient to more profitable areas.

Since the M-form structure reduces the workload of top officers, growth is facilitated. Top officers only concerned with strategic decisions have more time to consider growth. Additionally, growth by diversification becomes easier since new products can be introduced by forming new divisions. Expansion along existing product lines, however, can increase the size of each division to such an extent as to create all the problems of the large U-form firm. Further decomposition may have to be introduced into the divisions to alleviate these problems.

Decomposition is a necessary feature of the M-form firm. However, when inter-relationships, what Kay (1982) called *synergies*, exist between operating divisions decomposition cannot be established without costs. Some of these costs may be reduced by the adoption of appropriate interdivisional rules regarding, for example, pricing and other decisions. Rules however, may be difficult to devise and implement when the synergies which exist between divisions are strong creating the need for extensive interactions. In the presence of strong interactions the information exchange requirements of the M-form structure may be different to those of the U-form firm but not necessarily less significant than those arising within U-form firms. The associated control loss potential need not be better and could be easily worse (Williamson 1971).

In such cases costs may be reduced by the adoption of a hybrid U-form and M-form structure. The circumstances favouring a hybrid form can be indicated by a fictional example (constructed by Kay 1982). Firm X produces and sells lemonade (A), potato crisps (B) and chocolate (C) to children. The market is the same for the three products but the technology is assumed to be completely different. An optimal organisational structure for X, indicated on Figure 4.3, groups together the 'natural decision units'. Strong marketing synergies suggest the establishment of a selling function while the technological independence of the three products suggests decomposition along the three product divisions.

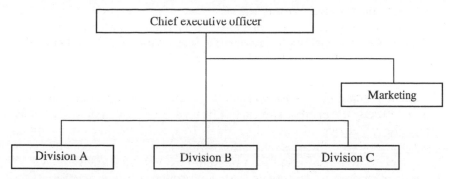

Figure 4.3 A hybrid U/M-form organisational structure

Although decomposition is a necessary feature of the M-form firm the main advantages of this organisational structure do not derive from decomposition alone. As will be explained in the next section, the efficiency of divisionalisation depends crucially on the adoption of internal mechanisms which ensure (a) the separation of strategic from operational decision making, (b) the introduction of an internal control system to assess divisional performance and (c) the adoption of an efficient resource allocation system. Therefore, the attributes of the M-form structure are quite different to those of its predecessors. Pure M-form structures are very sophisticated organisation systems which may explain why its diffusion was rather slow.

Thus, although the M-form was invented in the 1920s it was not very widely adopted until about 1945. The period of 1945–60 witnessed the adoption of the M-form structure by most large corporations in the USA. By 1970 the vast majority (85 per cent) of the US *Fortune 500* firms were organised along divisional lines (Hill 1984). The diffusion of the M-form in Europe was much slower than in America. Between 1950 and 1970, however, the percentage of the one hundred UK manufacturing firms organised along divisional lines increased from 59 per cent to 72 per cent, while in a sample of 144 firms drawn from the top 500 public-quoted companies in 1982, Hill (1984) found that 82.6 per cent operated along divisional lines and only 1.6 per cent had a traditional U-form structure (the rest were holding companies).

ORGANISATIONAL STRUCTURE AND BUSINESS BEHAVIOUR

While the multidivisional structure is now prevalent among large diversified firms many small and medium-sized firms are functionally organised. This may be quite consistent with efficiency (in the form of economising on transaction costs) but since the control mechanisms and the incentive systems differ between these two organisational structures, the question arises as to whether structural differences have an impact on business behaviour and resource allocation.

To answer this question we must examine how the main features of each structure may influence its behaviour. To begin with consider functionally organised firms. Their main features are as follows

1 One of the most important characteristics of unitary organised firms is that the profitability of each separate product or geographical division is not directly observable and cannot be measured. This implies not only that the efficiency of each functional area must be judged on other criteria but that the relevant information available to top officers is incomplete and insufficient for optimum resource allocation.

2 Another important feature is that departmental heads participate in the making of strategic decisions. Consequently, resource allocation depends on a process of bargaining among departmental heads, so that power relations and empire building may influence the relevant decisions.

3 Perhaps more importantly, as many economists[3] have suggested, managers may pursue objectives consistent with their own self-interest rather than profit maximisation, i.e. managerial moral hazard may be present. If departmental heads derive status, prestige and power as well as monetary rewards from the size of their departments, they will have a strong incentive to expand beyond the size indicated by overall corporate profitability. To achieve their aims functional managers create slack and in order to justify excess staff they create discretionary investment. Thus, managerial objectives influence the overall objective of the firm. Firms do not profit maximise. They aspire to grow even if this reduces overall profitability. This, naturally, influences the character of decision making and the behaviour of the firm. A more extensive analysis of the impact of managerial objectives on business behaviour is undertaken in Chapter 9. For present purposes it is sufficient to note that the existence of managerial discretion is possible because of transaction costs which prevent the product and the capital markets from adequately disciplining non-profit maximising firms.

4 Although managerially run U-form firms may place more emphasis on growth, the U-form structure itself tends to inhibit growth. This is because as the firm expands, top officers (managers) tend to spend a disproportionate amount of their time on operating decisions (which need immediate attention) and on co-ordinating the progressively more complicated interactions among divisions. As a result long-term decisions receive less attention.

In brief, informational and bounded rationality problems inherent in U-form firms may inhibit profit maximisation. Much more significantly, managerial motivation is such that U-form firms are unlikely to seek profit maximisation. Managerial discretion in setting and pursuing business objectives is possible because of transaction costs which prevent the product and capital markets from adequately disciplining non-profit maximising firms.

The reasons why managerial control mechanisms may be ineffective are explored in some detail in Chapter 9. It should, however, be noted here that the capital market is a rather inefficient control mechanism because an information impactedness condition exists. Business enterprises are complex organisations and their performance depends on external economic conditions and rival behaviour as well as on managerial objectives and competence. It is therefore difficult to detect managerial discretionary behaviour by simply observing performance. Moreover, the control mechanisms available, i.e. a proxy battle to replace the incumbent management and a takeover bid, are both costly and subject to opportunism. Shareholders lack the necessary information and the time or inclination to collect and interpret the relevant facts. Their decisions are therefore dependent on an interpretation of the facts as presented to them by the incumbent management or by a bidder in the case of a hostile takeover bid. In either case they cannot easily distinguish between accurate and opportunistic interpretations. Even in the absence of opportunistic behaviour, capital markets have informational disadvantages since share-holders' power to conduct audits of a firm's affairs is limited and they have restricted access to the firm's incentive and resource allocation systems.

Since many of the shortcomings of the U-form structures do not exist in the M-form structure, the supersession of unitary-organised firms by multidivisional firms has important implications for business behaviour through its influence on strategic decision making. It is actually claimed that the improved features of the M-form organisational structure imply that the behaviour of multidivisional firms is similar to that of the neoclassical profit maximising firm so that resource allocation within M-form firms is optimal. As Williamson (1975) put it,

> The organisation and operation of the large enterprise along the lines of the M-form favors goal pursuit and least cost behavior more nearly associated with the neoclassical profit maximising hypothesis than does the U-form organisational alternative.

> (p. 150)

This claim is known as the M-form hypothesis. It is a strong claim. It suggests that managerial discretion can only exist among functionally organised firms and that the incidence of M-form firms implies cost efficiency and a change in business behaviour. Firms are no longer profit satisfying. They are, like the traditional theory postulates, attempting to maximise their profits. This improves resource allocation. Significant policy implications follow from these claims. Government policy relating to mergers and takeovers, for example, should be more permissive since these amalgamations facilitate the creation of multidivisional firms with the associated improvements in resource allocation.

In order to evaluate the M-form hypothesis we must examine those features of the M-form structure which lead to the implications of the M-form hypothesis. The relevant empirical evidence is also reviewed in the next section.

Perhaps the most important claim in favour of the M-form firm is that it operates an internal capital market which is more efficient than the external capital market. Central office has informational advantages over external markets since it employs specialists (elite staff) and has auditing powers over divisions. In particular, the advantages of the M-form firm are attributed to three strategic controls (Williamson 1975).

1 *An internal incentives and control system* which can be used to encourage behaviour consistent with the overall objective of the firm. Both pecuniary and non-pecuniary rewards and penalties may be included in this system. Salaries and bonuses may be adjusted, whenever possible, to reflect differences in operating performance. An example of a deliberate manipulation of the incentives system given by Williamson (1975) is the replacement of a division manager who 'may be managerially competent but unco-operative (given, for example, to aggressive subgoal pursuits in ways that impair overall performance)' (p. 145). Replacements of this nature or for managerial incompetence would not occur often and although the central office should not be directly involved it can have a great indirect influence. In short, the CEO can discipline quickly and effectively non-profit maximising divisions and enforce profit maximising objectives better than the external capital market which is limited by significant displacement costs.

2 *An internal monitoring system* which includes internal auditing. Internal auditing is more extensive and efficient compared with external auditing for two reasons: first, division managers are subordinates and all their accounting records and files are available for scrutiny. Shareholders on the other hand have no direct access to this information. Their demand for access to even non-classified information may be resisted by management. Second, central office can expect more co-operation from its employees than would external auditors. Thus, while the disclosure of sensitive information to internal auditors will be regarded as necessary for the efficiency of the firm and will be encouraged, its disclosure to external auditors may be viewed as a hostile act against the firm and will be strongly resisted.

3 *A resource allocation system* based on profitability. This requires that resources are allocated by central office to the divisions on the basis of an objective analysis of actual and potential performance. Investment proposals from the divisions are evaluated on the basis of objective investment criteria such as the internal rate of return on investment. These proposals together with those initiated in central office relating to diversification or divestment constitute the range of activities over

which cash flows are allocated. This range will be narrower compared with the range available to shareholders outside the firm, even in the case of a firm actively diversifying into new product lines and divesting from old ones. The central office, however, will be better informed about the productive potential of the relevant proposals and can allocate funds accordingly. The fact that investment finance comes, at least partly, from retained profits should not be allowed to interfere with the allocation process. Efficiency, therefore, requires that profits be remitted from the divisions back to central office for re-investment according to current as well as potential profitability.

In brief, the allocational advantages claimed by the M-form hypothesis will exist when departmental heads remit profits to the central office, top officers are completely removed from operating decisions which are decentralised to the divisions and the reallocation of funds among the competing claims of the divisions is based on objective and impersonal profit criteria.

A further claim in favour of the M-form (elaborated on in Chapter 9) is that it enhances the effectiveness of takeovers as a mechanism controlling managerial discretion. This is because divisionalisation facilitates the expansion which follows an acquisition. An acquired firm can easily be incorporated, as a new division, within an existing M-form structure.

There are, however, serious doubts as to whether multidivisional firms operate under the strict decentralisation system described. Some of the reasons why the main benefits of the M-form, efficient resources allocation, profit orientation, effective planning and achievement of growth, may be compromised in practice are as follows.

1 Top officers may get involved in the operating affairs of divisions in which case personal loyalties may develop. Favouritism towards a particular division plays havoc with the idea of a resource allocation strictly dependent on objective investment criteria. The arms-length assessment and control of divisions will be violated and subgoals may be pursued.

2 Similarly, subgoals may intrude when the semi-autonomous divisions which are organised along functional lines grow very large in size. In this case all the problems of the functionally organised firm will reappear at the divisional level unless further divisionalisation and decentralisation, along the lines of the M-form hypothesis, takes place.

3 Much more importantly, top officers may not have the profit orientation that the M-form hypothesis assumes. There is no obvious reason why top officers should identify closely with shareholders and pursue profit maximisation. Top officers may well favour corporate goals associated with a satisfactory level of profits and the attainment of other objectives such as faster growth or larger market share or an increased size of the enterprise. In this case they may deliberately decide to cross-subsidize[4]

between divisions in pursuit of market power or in order to eliminate competitors in certain areas in order to enhance the growth potential of their enterprise. Other forms of anti-competitive behaviour within the divisions may be tolerated, if not encouraged, in pursuit of market power. Such behaviour will result in a less than optimal allocation of resources.

4 Firms may operate what Hill (1984) termed 'latent economic systems'. These are said to exist when there is no general reallocation of resources by the central office. There are two reasons why profits may not be remitted to the centre for general reallocation. Either top officers fail to see its advantages and the system is not introduced or they may fail to convince powerful divisional heads of the advantages of the system. In the latter case divisional heads of profitable divisions may claim priority on the allocations of profits they generate.

EMPIRICAL EVIDENCE

Are the above criticisms a fair description of reality, or do divisionalised firms operate as the M-form hypothesis suggests? Several empirical studies have emerged over the last two decades or so attempting to investigate the impact of organisational structure on performance in general and the predictions of the M-form hypothesis in particular. If M-form firms pursue profit maximisation more vigorously than U-form firms, then statistically M-form firms should outperform firms of other organisational structures. It should perhaps be reiterated that this will be the case when divisionalisation is accompanied by decentralisation and an appropriate internal control and monitoring system, but not otherwise. In reality divisionalisation is not always accompanied by the adoption of the necessary control mechanisms so that many so called multidivisional firms may lack the necessary characteristics associated with the 'M-form hypothesis'. It is therefore not very surprising that several studies fail to confirm that M-form firms in general outperform other firms. Armour and Teece (1978), for example, studied a sample of twenty-nine USA petroleum firms and found that during the period 1955–73 (i.e. in the period of diffusion of the M-form) there was a positive relationship between profitability and M-form structure and that pure M-form structures, i.e. those embracing most of the features associated with the M-form hypothesis, showed significantly increased profitability. When their study concentrated, however, on the period 1969–73 they found that the M-form firms performed no better than other firms. Amour and Teece concluded that during this period there was no differential performance because all the firms in their sample were 'appropriately organised'.[5] This can be interpreted to mean that each firm had adopted the organisational structure appropriate for its size and complexity.

Another study by Channon (1978) on a sample consisting of unitary,

holding company and multidivisional UK firms, found that unitary organised firms had the best profitability while the multidivisional firms performed better in terms of growth of sales, assets and dividends. Channon's
is an interesting study since it followed the same investigation as Rumelt
(1974), who studied the financial performance of approximately 40 per cent
of the US *Fortune 500* firms, but concluded with totally different results.
Rumelt's study indicated that multidivisional firms outperformed the
others on all conventional measures of profitability and growth.

Two further studies from the UK failed to show that divisionalised firms
perform generally better than other firms. Grinyer *et al*. (1980) found that
growth in net profits and in the rate of return on investment was negatively
related to divisionalisation. Hill (1984) suggests that an earlier study of his
of a sample of 144 UK firms found no association between organisational
form and growth and that holding companies performed best and divisionalised firms worst in terms of profitability.

The above evidence clearly cannot confirm the M-form hypothesis but
neither can it reject it. The reason is that many of the sample firms had
not adopted the organisational features postulated by the M-form hypothesis. They were 'corrupt M-form' structures. As noted earlier, the M-
form hypothesis only applies to those multidivisional structures which have
also adopted strict decentralisation and proper internal monitoring and
control systems. It is these 'pure' M-form structures that are expected to
outperform the unitary and other organisational form firms.

Empirical studies specifically designed to test for the M-form hypothesis,
rather than divisionalisation in general, tend to confirm its predictions. For
example, Hill (1984) found that when adjustments were made so that pure
M-form firms in his sample were compared with other firms they tended
to outperform the non M-form firms in both the profit margin and the rate
of return on capital employed. Similarly, Steer and Cable (1978), who
investigated eighty-two UK firms between 1967 and 1971, have reported
that optimally organised M-form firms could expect to substantially
outperform non-optimally organised firms. They could expect their rate of
return on investment to be 6–7 per cent higher than average (their sample
mean was 16.9 per cent) and their rate of profit to be 2–3 per cent higher
than average (which was 6 per cent in the sample studied).

More recently a study by Dunsire *et al*. (1991) has found some evidence
that a structural change from a functional towards a 'profit-centre' (multidivisional) structure was associated with improvements in performance in
five UK enterprises: HMSO, ROF, Post Office and Telecommunications,
London Transport and British Aerospace.

It would appear from this evidence that pure M-form firms may indeed
outperform otherwise organised firms. What empirical evidence has yet to
establish is how widespread the pure M-form actually is. Such evidence
would be significant given the policy implications derived from the M-form
hypothesis.

SUMMARY

The transaction cost approach was utilised to analyse the internal organisation of firms. An 'employment relation' across all the stages of a hierarchy was seen to define a U-form firm. It was argued that unitary-form structures are optimal when specialisation advantages exist and information flows need to be established within functional areas. Diversification, increased size and complexity can render the U-form firm inefficient. When this happens transaction cost economising may be enhanced by adopting a multidivisional structure. M-form firms are characterised by decomposition but their full benefits are only achieved when further internal monitoring and allocation mechanisms are adopted. Divisions, which consist of strongly interacting activities, must be autonomous profit centres and there must exist a separation between strategic and operating decision making. When divisional profits are remitted to the central office for reallocation on the basis of objective investment criteria the M-form firms operate an internal capital market. Because the internal capital market has informational and other advantages over external capital markets, it can be claimed that the diffusion of M-form firms can substantially improve resource allocation.

The internal organisation of firms was found to have important implications for business objectives and behaviour. Organisational improvements can potentially bring about improvements in resource allocation. However, Williamson's claim that M-form firms are profit maximisers and their behaviour is similar to the neoclassical firm cannot be accepted unequivocally. This claim, known as the M-form hypothesis, is only valid under a set of organisational features that may not be present in all divisionalised enterprises. Both empirical evidence and *a priori* reasoning shed doubt on the universality of the validity of the M-form hypothesis. An important determinant of this doubt relates to the motivation and entrepreneurship of top management. Indeed both the organisation and the conduct of firms and markets depend on the entrepreneurship of their participants. Consequently the next chapter attempts to define entrepreneurship and examine its role in order to lay the foundations for the analysis of business behaviour.

APPLICATION: THE RAILROADS

Railroads were among the first enterprises both in the USA and in Britain and Western Europe to hire large numbers of managers and to adopt a complex internal organisational structure. As such they provide a good example illustrating some of the ideas developed in this chapter.

According to Chandler (1977) the first 'natural' railroad units which appeared in the USA in the early 1840s were lines of about 50 miles long. They employed, on average, fifty workers each and were 'administered by a superintendent who had under him a manager responsible for each of the road's major activities: transportation and traffic, maintenance of way, and maintenance of locomotives and rolling stock' (p. 96).

Long hauls required the joining up of these lines which in principle could be achieved contractually. In practice, however, '[T]he resulting contracts would be tightly bilateral . . . since investment in site specific assets by each party were considerable' (Williamson 1981: 1552). To economise on transaction costs, long hauls were created by joining up end-to-end lines under common ownership. The complexity of the operations was, however, such that long haul companies had to overcome tremendous organisational problems. Take as an example the early operation of the Western and Albany road which was over 150 miles long and built in three sections, each operated as a distinct division with its own managers. Trains were running on a single track and on mountainous roads. Without the benefit of the telegraphic signal, scheduling was so hazardous that it resulted in several accidents. A head-on collision on 5 October 1841, acted as a springboard for substantial organisational innovations intended to improve safety. It was thus recognised that the safe movement of goods and passengers by rail required the creation of a large administrative organisation to co-ordinate several functionally distinct activities such as maintaining the lines, scheduling the passenger trains, arranging the carriage of freight, buying fuels and other

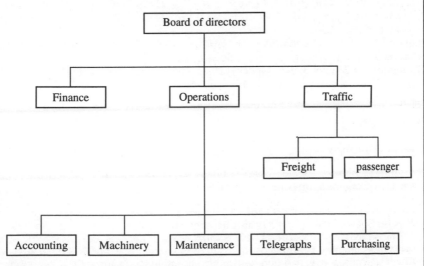

Figure 4.4 A simplified illustration of the functional organisation of a railroad
Source: Adapted from Fig 2, Chandler, 1977

raw materials, selling tickets and so on. A hierarchical structure was introduced with a comparable set of functional managers on each of the three geographical areas and the creation of a headquarters to monitor and co-ordinate the activities of the managers. This is a typical U-form structure.

As the intensity of traffic and the volume of freight increased, organisational innovations, intended to reduce costs and improve safety, were introduced in a piecemeal fashion. By the 1870s 'the decentralised line-and-staff divisional form of organisation' was widely used. This was a relatively complex structure but a simplified version is given in Figure 4.4. This shows three departments (operations, finance, traffic) as well as the functional areas in each. Lines of responsibility are not shown but the characteristic of the line-and-staff concept is that managers on the line of authority are responsible for monitoring employees involved with the basic functions of the enterprise while functional managers are responsible for setting standards. For example, the division superintendent is on the direct line of authority from the president through the general superintendent.

FURTHER READING

Chandler, A.D. (1977) *The Visible Hand: The Managerial Revolution in American Business*, Cambridge, MA: Belknap Press. This is a classical book on the organisation of firms. Chapter 3 is particularly relevant to the material of this chapter.
Hill, C.W.L. (1984) 'Organisational Structure, the Development of the Firm and Business Behaviour', in J.F. Pickering and T.A.J. Cockerill (eds) *The Economic Management of the Firm*, Oxford: Philip Allan. This adopts a similar perspective to that of this chapter.
Ricketts, M. (1987) *The Economics of Business Enterprise; New Approaches to the Firm*, Brighton: Wheatsheaf, esp. Section 7.2.
Williamson, O.E. (1981) 'The Modern Corporation: Origins, Evolution, Attributes', *Journal of Economic Literature* 19: 1537–68.

QUESTIONS

1 Empirical evidence suggests that while a high proportion of large enterprises have adopted an M-form administrative structure many firms still operate with a unitary, or some other, organisational structure. Can the existence of this variety of organisational form be attributed to economic efficiency? Explain.
2 IBI, the manufacturer of product X, have just decided to expand vertically by taking over all the distributors of X. This is a substantial expansion since product X is one of the main products produced by IBI.

The Managing Director of IBI is currently considering the possibility of a substantial internal reorganisation of the post-merger firm and has been advised that 'the internal organisation has important implications not only for corporate strategy but also for profitability and competitive behaviour and that in order to enhance the efficiency of the company a multidivisional structure should be adopted'.

Critically evaluate the advice given to the Managing Director, noting in particular the structural attributes consistent with the M-form hypothesis.
3 It has been suggested that once firms exceed a certain size their profitability tapers off. A proposed response to this problem is an organisational structure based on the principle of decomposition into a number of divisions, each acting as an independent profit centre, and a chief executive consisting of a small number of elite staff.

(a) Can you offer an economic explanation for the suggested change in organisational structure?

(b) Explain in what circumstances, if any, the proposed divisional structure may not lead to the adoption of a global profit maximisation objective.

4 Prior to its nationalisation in 1971, Rolls Royce had an organisational structure described as 'effectively multidivisional' with a number of profit centres and a chief executive board which being 'heavily overweight with engineers . . . did not receive the information that . . . Aero-Engines was running the whole company into dire trouble; and what it did receive it discounted' (Dunsire *et al.* 1991). After years of bad performance the company adopted a mixed structure with the main production and design activities functionally organised and with three more autonomous divisions, Aero Engine, Small Engines and Industrial and Marine Engines, responsible for developing new products.

Explain why the pre-1971 Rolls Royce structure was described as 'effectively multidivisional' rather than simply multidivisional and comment on the possible merits of the mixed structure it subsequently adopted.
5 'The recently (late 1980s) increased rate of merger activity, both nationally and internationally, suggests that many business enterprises will adopt a multi-divisional internal structure. The implication of this divisionalisation must be that modern business firms are more likely to adopt goal pursuits and least cost behaviour associated with the neoclassical profit maximisation hypothesis.' Critically evaluate this statement.

NOTES

1 Two examples quoted by Williamson (1981: 1538) are (a) a reference to the 'Genesis of Divisional Management and Accounting Systems in the House of Mitsui, 1710–1730', attributed to an unpublished manuscript by Sadao Takatera and Nobaru Nishikawa, and (b) the description of the 'East India Company as a Multidivisional Enterprise' at the beginning of the eighteenth century, attributed to G. Anderson, R. E. MacCormick and R. D. Tollison.
2 'Strategic' decisions refer to decisions which affect the overall strategy of the firm and the concomitant allocation of resources. Strategic decisions affect the long-term prospects of the firm. 'Operating' decisions on the other hand are decisions related to the use of resources already allocated to a department or other area.
3 See Baumol (1959), Marris (1964), Williamson (1964) and Cyert and March (1963)
4 Williamson (1975) does not accept this criticism on the grounds that 'the M-form structure is seriously compromised if predatory cross-subsidization is attempted' (p. 165).
5 This conclusion is consistent with the view that the M-form innovation is not more efficient under all circumstances (Rickett 1987) and that a variety of efficient organisational structures may co-exist.

5 Entrepreneurship and profit

INTRODUCTION

The entrepreneur is nothing if not an opportunist.

Reekie

Chapters 3 and 4 examined the reasons why firms exist, how they emerge and what organisational adaptations successful firms have to undertake as their environment and their size change. This chapter takes a closer look at the individuals who initiate all these changes. Of the many individuals who co-operate in the functioning of firms only a few may have the foresight, ability or inclination to pursue beneficial changes. Adaptation of organisational structure in response to uncertainty, complexity and other transaction costs presupposes action by individuals who are alert to opportunities for beneficial change and who are motivated enough to initiate the required changes. They are the entrepreneurs. But what motivates individuals to become entrepreneurs and what is the nature of entrepreneurship? Do entrepreneurs also operate in the market or is the 'invisible hand' devoid of entrepreneurship? Such questions will be addressed in this chapter with a view to facilitating a better understanding of the function of entrepreneurship and the nature of profits.

THE ENTREPRENEUR

The term *entrepreneur* was coined by the French economist J.B. Say almost 200 years ago. Say defined the function of the entrepreneur as being that of reallocating resources so as to improve productivity and yield. An element of newness and change is essential in resource reallocation. Entrepreneurship, the function of the entrepreneur, is therefore something more than venturing. It requires doing something differently rather than imitating existing tasks or behaviour. Entrepreneurial ventures are new and remote from existing or past ventures which means that entrepreneurship is by its very nature unpredictable. This novel and unpredictable nature of entrepreneurship makes it impossible to give a precise and universally acceptable characterisation of its activities and of the persons who practice it. As a result there exist a substantial diversity of opinion regarding the definition of the entrepreneur.

Schumpeter (1943), for example, considers the entrepreneur as a very exceptional person, a revolutionary innovator who overturns known ways of production and brings about disequilibrium in the economy. The rare psychological force that motivates such behaviour is threefold: a desire to build private kingdoms; a desire to conquer; and the sheer joy of creating or simply excercising one's energy and ingenuity.[1] Boldness, confidence, personal leadership and force characterise this innovator of new products and new processes which are often introduced in the face of substantial animosity and opposition. Similar traits characterise Williamson's (1983a) innovator of new organisational methods.

An inclination to foresee uncertain events in pursuit of profit rather than the implementation of change is the main attribute of an entrepreneur for Knight (1921). The entrepreneur is, therefore, a bearer of uncertainty. But since uncertainty characterises the world we live in, it can be argued that the actions of all market participants, if not all human actions, carry some risk. Politicians or military commanders are involved in risk taking but are not necessarily entrepreneurs. Uncertainty for Knight is not, however, the same as risk. Uncertainty involves total ignorance. It relates to decisions which involve new and unique events for which probabilities, calculated as relative frequencies, do not apply. It exists in situations when probabilities cannot be assigned to expectations so that future events cannot be insured. It is this uncertainty, or uninsurable risk, which entrepreneurs are willing to bear for a reward. They make judgements about an uncertain future. If they are right they are rewarded by profit, if not, they bear a loss.

Judgemental decisions in the presence of uncertainty is also an essential element in Mises (1966) writings on entrepreneurship. For Mises '[t]he term entrepreneur . . . means: acting man exclusively seen from the aspect of the uncertainty inherent in every action'. Kirzner (1979), who belongs to the group of economists known as Austrians and whose writings are inspired by Mises, places less importance on uncertainty and more on alertness as the motivating force for entrepreneurship. An entrepreneur is alert to opportunities for profit. If a product is trading at two different prices, an alert individual will spot the opportunity for profit by buying at the lower price and selling at the higher price. Alertness, however, does not only refer to the identification of opportunities overlooked until now because of error. It extends to opportunities involving the future and therefore uncertainty. In this context entrepreneurial alertness is 'the endeavor to secure greater correspondence between the individual's future as he envisages it and his future as it will in fact unfold' (Kirzner 1982).

While for Kirzner the entrepreneur is especially alert, for Shackle he or she has a particularly creative imagination. Human decisions involve choice among actions the consequence of which are not known with certainty; they are only expected or imagined. We choose on the basis of the imagined consequences of our actions. Opportunities, therefore, are not so much perceived as anticipated or imagined. The planning of action is the work of imagination which for Shackle (1984) is subject to only one constraint: 'that what it [the imagination] creates in thought must be deemed possible by the planner' (p. 71). The novelty and uniqueness of entrepreneurial actions implies that probabilities (in the sense of frequency distributions) are not applicable. A particular course of action whose outcome is deemed desirable will be taken provided that its outcome is believed to be possible. Possible does not mean probable. Possible means that the decision maker does not see any fatal obstacles to the occurrence of a desirable outcome. Thus the traditional concept of probabilities is rejected by Shackle who suggests that the entrepreneur selects from a '*stein of imagined sequels deemed possible*' (p. 76), a notion that corresponds to the business practice of considering a few possible scenarios in deciding how to use the company's resources rather than any kind of averaging of probabilistic events.[2]

The most important elements of the theories on entrepreneurship just mentioned have been brought together by Casson (1982). He synthesises those elements which are particularly relevant in examining the role of the entrepreneur within the firm and the nature of the entrepreneurial reward. Casson's positive theory of entrepreneurship begins by defining the entrepreneur as '*someone who specialises in taking judgemental decisions about the coordination of scarce resources*' (p. 23, italics in original). Judgemental decisions imply, strictly speaking, that two individuals who have the same objectives and share the same information would arrive at different decisions. This is due to different perceptions (or imagination) of the situations which arise because of different interpretations of the same information. More generally, though, information asymmetry and uncertainty are incorporated in the concept of 'judgemental decision'. When opinions differ about the most appropriate course of action, uncertainty exists whether the action relates to a unique or to a repetitive event. Additionally, since co-ordination means reallocation of resources which is a dynamic concept as opposed to the static concept of allocation, Casson's entrepreneur, like Say's, is an agent of change.[3]

Since the entrepreneur is an agent of change and the quest of newness an essential part of entrepreneurship, it is unlikely that, in a world of uncertainty and information asymmetry, individuals totally averse to risk taking could function as entrepreneurs. However, apart from this ability to undertake risk, individuals of differing traits have been observed to perform well as entrepreneurs in different situations.[4] The high incidence of entrepreneurial talent among immigrant and other disadvantaged groups have led some writers to conclude that environmental conditions may induce entrepreneurship. As Ronen (1989) put it, 'entrepreneurial traits are sparked off (brought to light for all to see) by certain forces of the environment, such as the set opportunities and knowledge thereof, the stage of the individual's life and career, and the number of constraints, legal or otherwise'.

Whether entrepreneurial traits are innate or can be enhanced or acquired by education and training, most writers agree that they are scarce. It is the possession of scarce traits that gives an advantage to some individuals in becoming an entrepreneur. For a person specialising in judgemental decision making these scarce traits include imagination, foresight, delegation skills and organisational skills. Of these the first two, imagination and foresight (or alertness to opportunities according to Kirzner), are very difficult to screen for and to enhance by training.

THE ROLE AND FUNCTION OF THE ENTREPRENEUR

Whatever their traits, the presence of entrepreneurs is manifested through their actions. It is therefore essential to examine how entrepreneurs function and what the consequences of their actions are. In other words, what is the entrepreneurial role or the function of entrepreneurship?

Entrepreneurship is an elusive concept to define, despite the fact that its presence is always noticed. This is because entrepreneurs act for personal gain and their actions are novel and varied. Rather than try to define the way in which entrepreneurs behave it may be more appropriate to define entrepreneurship in terms of the outcome or the effect of the entrepreneurial presence. Entrepreneurship can therefore be defined as the co-ordination of economic activity (Casson 1982). Such co-ordination takes place both through market transacting and within firms.

Entrepreneurship in the market

In a world of perfect knowledge with no transaction costs, arbitrage among well-informed producers and consumers will lead to an optimum allocation of resources. That is, production will be maximised and its distribution will be the best possible in the sense that no re-distribution can be devised which could make some individual better off without making somebody else worse off. To put it differently, the best methods of production will be known to, and adopted by, all producers so that the economy will be on the production possibility frontier, PP on Figure 5.1.[5] Moreover, costless transactions among producers and costless exchanges among consumers will lead to the most preferred configuration, a point such as A on curve PP (known as Pareto optimum). Given perfect knowledge and the absence of transaction costs, Pareto optimality will be achieved without the assistance of entrepreneurs. This is a well-known result of neoclassical economics and the reason why neoclassical economics is not concerned with the study of entrepreneurship. However, when knowledge is not perfect so that the best technology is not instantaneously utilised by all producers and transaction costs prevent beneficial exchanges, production

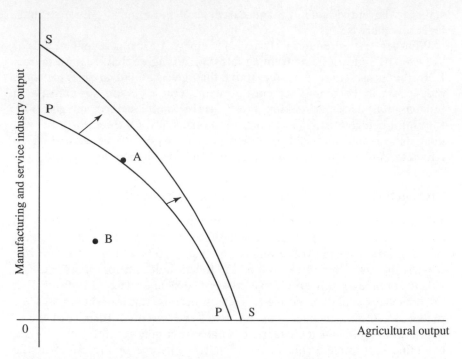

Figure 5.1 Entrepreneurship and the production possibility curve

may be less than the maximum possible. In terms of Figure 5.1, the economy may be within the frontier, at a point such as B. Resources may be unemployed, best methods of production may not be universally adopted or resources may not be efficiently utilised within firms. There are errors and disequilibrium prevails. It is in these circumstances that entrepreneurship plays an instrumental role in assisting to improve resource allocation. Entrepreneurs, i.e. alert individuals motivated by personal gain, will spot the available opportunities for profit. As producers they will seize the opportunity of increasing production by using different techniques or better organisational methods and as middlemen they will initiate beneficial trade. As a result more will be produced from the given limited resources and output distribution will improve. In other words, entrepreneurship moves the economy from point B inside the frontier towards a point on the frontier PP. If the output thus produced is not distributed in accordance with individual tastes and preferences, entrepreneurship will initiate beneficial exchanges among consumers. Lack of information and other transaction costs may inhibit such trade but the activities of entrepreneurs will tend to economise on transaction costs and hence to facilitate beneficial trade.

The role of the entrepreneur is not, however, limited to initiating changes that move the economy towards equilibrium. Entrepreneurship is a double-sided function. One side is stabilising and the other destabilising. As innovators, entrepreneurs adopt new ideas, discover new resources, produce new products, recognise new needs and create new markets. In the process they create turbulence where calm and equilibrium may have previously existed. Thus, even if the economy had reached a state of equilibrium (a point on PP), entrepreneurship is likely to move the frontier itself outwards creating disequilibrium and further opportunities for entrepreneurship and economic growth.

Entrepreneurs as middlemen

The stabilising or equilibrating nature of entrepreneurship can be indicated by examining the role of the entrepreneur as a middleman. That entre- preneurs can initiate beneficial trade when a given output is not optimally distributed, i.e. when the distribution is not in accordance with individual tastes and preferences, can be illustrated by a simple example. Suppose that two products, apples and oranges, are distributed between two individuals, Peter (P) and Jane (J). The preferences of P and J are different and such that the valuation that each places on extra units of oranges in terms of apples is as shown in Figure 5.2(a). Each point on the valuation curve shows the maximum apple value of oranges for each individual concerned. P's marginal valuation curve indicates that he values oranges more than J does and that he would be prepared to exchange apples for oranges, at the indicated rates. Since J's marginal valuations are much lower, she would be willing to accept apples, in smaller quantities than P could offer, in exchange for oranges. There is scope for beneficial trade with P a demander and J a supplier of oranges in exchange for apples. In fact the quantities demanded and supplied at the corresponding rates can be deduced from the marginal valuation curves. These are shown in Figure 5.2(b). Thus, provided that P and J knew each other and that they could communicate freely and costlessly they might start swapping apples for oranges, not unlike the way children swap car cards for marbles in the school playground. These exchanges will naturally depend not only on individual tastes but also on the initial individual endowments. To clarify, consider Figure 5.2 in more detail. Suppose that the initial endowments are indicated by points P_1 and J_1 on Figure 5.2(a). That is, P is endowed with 10 kg of oranges and 25 kg of apples while J has 10 kg of oranges and 5 kg of apples. The apple value of an extra kilogram of oranges is 21.25 for P but only 3.75 for J. It is clear that P would be prepared to give up to 21.25 kg of apples for one extra kilogram of oranges while J would be glad to give up a kilogram of oranges in exchange for anything in excess of 6.25 kg of apples. The potential for trade, beneficial to both P and J, exists. Once initiated, trade will be carried up to the point where the marginal valuations of the two individuals are equal. In our example this happens when both P's and J's marginal valuation of oranges is 10 kg of

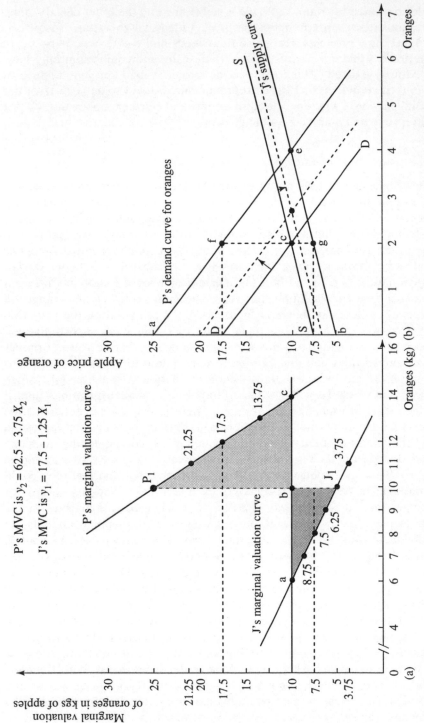

Figure 5.2 The role of the entrepreneur as middleman: (a) marginal valuation curves; (b) individual demand and supply curves

apples. Assuming that a uniform exchange rate prevails, it will be 10 kg of apples per kilogram of oranges. At this rate P will be prepared to buy exactly the same amount of oranges as Jane is prepared to sell (see figure 5.2(b)); 4 kg of oranges will be traded and both traders will benefit. Peter will have acquired oranges which he values at 62.50 kg of apples (21.25 + 17.5 + 13.75 + 10) by sacrificing only 40 kg apples. Similarly Jane will have exchanged oranges which she valued at 32.5 kg of apples (6.25 + 7.5 + 8.75 + 10) for 40 kg of apples. In Figure 5.2(a) P's benefit is indicated by the area bP_1c and J's by the area abJ_1. As expected free trade has benefited both traders although not equally.

If, however, P and J are not alert enough to see the opportunity 'that stares them in the face' the benefit from trade will not materialise. Moreover, in reality they may not know of each other's existence and differences in tastes and endowments. They may need to advertise and to incur other expenses such as those related to negotiating, initiating and implementing of relevant contracts. The presence of transaction costs will restrict, if not totally discourage trading. Suppose for example that Peter incurs transaction costs equivalent to 7.5 kg of apples per kilogram of oranges exchanged and Jane's cost of trading is 2.5 kg of apples per kilogram of oranges. If the price were to remain at 10 kg of apples, the effective cost of oranges would be 17.5 kg of apples for P while J would receive a net price of 7.5 kg of apples per kilogram of oranges. As Figure 5.2(a) indicates only 2 kg of oranges will change hands at such prices. An alternative derivation of the same result is illustrated in Figure 5.2(b). Since transaction costs increase the buying price and reduce the selling price at any volume of trade, the demand curve moves inwards (to DD) and the supply curve moves upwards (to SS). DD is the net demand curve and SS the net supply curve. Their intersection indicates that the quantity to be exchanged is 2 kg of oranges. Trade and its concomitant benefits have been restricted. The total net benefit is equal to the area of triangle DcS (reduced from area aeb). Transaction costs are shown by the area of the rectangle DfgS (which is equal to 20 kg of apples).

When ignorance or transaction costs prevent or restrict trade an entrepreneur, i.e. an individual who thinks that he or she can economise on transaction costs, may intervene. In our example, Eddy (E) may approach J and offer to buy oranges at a price slightly more than 7.5 kg of apples per kilogram of oranges. She sells just over 2 kg. E then approaches P and offers to sell oranges at slightly less than 17.5 kg of apples per kilogram of oranges. P and J would benefit from this intervention and E will have a surplus of somewhat less than 20 kg of apples. Provided that E's perception was correct so that the relevant transaction costs were indeed reduced to less than 20 kg of apples, trade volume increases to the benefit of both traders and middleman. The extent of the increase depends on the extent of cost saving. So long as there are transaction costs, however, trade will be restricted compared with its volume in the absence of transaction costs.

The reduction in transaction costs brought about by E's intervention is indicated in Figure 5.2(b) by a shift of the net demand and the net supply curve to the right to positions indicated by the dotted lines. The extent of the shift depends on the extent of cost savings.

A perceptive reader may enquire at this point as to how did E acquire the first apples he offered to J at the beginning of the trade? Does this mean that the entrepreneur must have a stock of resources and if so does this not make E a capitalist and the surplus obtained by trading a return on capital invested? The brief answer to this question is that although capital may be a requirement of entrepreneurship the entrepreneur is not necessarily a capitalist. In our example E may be penniless but successful in persuading J to supply the oranges in advance of the date delivery to P must take place. In this case J has effectively become a creditor and she may require some compensation before accepting such an agreement. This compensation is interest on the capital lent and it may also include some premium to cover risks. Thus, an entrepreneur may indeed be faced with problems of raising finance and interest may have to be paid on funds raised. When E provides the capital himself, his surplus includes interest. But interest is not part of the entrepreneurial reward. (For an expansion on this theme and the determination of the cost of capital see Chapter 12.)

Whether the initiator of trade happens to provide the required capital or not is immaterial. The function of the entrepreneur is quite distinct to that of the capitalist. Entrepreneurship exits when an individual perceives a possibility for personal gain and acts upon it. It involves risks, since the perception may prove to be wrong. In our example trader E perceived an opportunity for gain. However, neither the marginal valuation curves nor the endowments were known to him with certainty. Additionally, time may have elapsed between the two exchanges during which preferences may well have changed. When E negotiated the purchase of oranges from J he acted on the *ex ante* belief that P's preferences would be such at the time of bargaining (next time period) that he could be persuaded to buy oranges at a high enough apple price. So, E acted in the hope of gain, in conditions that Mises called 'heterogeneous ignorance', and in so doing he induced beneficial changes.

It should be emphasised that the entrepreneurial function could have been performed by either one of the three individuals involved. It is also possible that all three could have acted entrepreneurially and reaped entrepreneurial rewards. In an exchange situation no one needs to be totally passive. But it is possible, as in our example, that only one person (E) plays the entrepreneurial role and reaps the entrepreneurial reward. E is the entrepreneur. The fact that both P and J benefited from the trade does not make them entrepreneurs. Their benefit is simply a windfall gain. Our example also illustrates the significance of information and the fact that E must have the foresight to keep the two traders in the dark. The services of the entrepreneur were needed because P and J did not know of each other's existence and differences in preferences and endowments. If at the time of bargaining they were made aware of the price differentials offered by E they might approach each other to trade directly to the exclusion of E. Barring communication between P and J (i.e. keeping information secret) as well as the possession of negotiating skills are crucial determinants of the size of the entrepreneurial reward.

Entrepreneurs as innovators

The role of the entrepreneur as a trader or middleman described above was restricted to perceiving past errors and facilitating exchanges. In this process technology, know-how, preferences and marginal valuations formed the background to the entrepreneurial act. As a result entrepreneurship tended to move the economy from disequilibrium (point B) to a position of equilibrium (point A on the PP curve). However, Schumpeter's view of the entrepreneur is much more revolutionary and destabilising than this. For Schumpeter (1943) entrepreneurs are the individuals who adopt inventions. They introduce new products or processes and new or improved management techniques; they open up new markets and new sources of supply. Whether innovations are at a grand scale such as the introduction of railroads, or at a small scale such as the use of known materials (synthetic fibres) to produce new products (a tooth brush), entrepreneurship is creative but disruptive. The introduction of a new product may displace an old one; new technology may improve the use of resources but it disrupts the old methods of production. Innovative entrepreneurship upsets any equilibrium. In terms of Figure 5.1 the impact of innovative entrepreneurship is to change both the shape and the position of the production possibility curve. PP shifts outwards to curve SS and any point on PP represents now a point of disequilibrium.

Similarly to the middleman, the entrepreneur who innovates makes decisions in ignorance of basic data. Consumer tastes and responses to the introduction of new products, for example, are unknown and cannot be estimated by market research. Market research is not possible for something genuinely new and when carried out is likely to be grossly inaccurate. For example, a scientific research carried out by the American company Unica in 1950 concluded that about 1,000 computers will be sold by the year 2000. By 1984 actual sales were about 1 million (Drucker 1985).

Innovative behaviour is fraught with uncertainty. However, despite the difficulty of estimation, or possibly because of it, the entrepreneur forms his or her own perception of the likely outcome of an innovation and acts upon this conviction. When their convictions are correct entrepreneurs gain and the whole economy benefits. There is evidence to suggest that the greatest part of economic growth in the USA between 1874 and 1953 was due to improved know-how and innovations shifting the production possibility curve outwards (Reekie 1984).

In brief then, our discussion so far has indicated that the function of entrepreneurship is to perceive a possibility for change and to act upon it in the hope of capturing (an uncertain) gain. In terms of its impact, entrepreneurship means the co-ordination of economic activity. The exercise of entrepreneurship may require capital but entrepreneurship is quite distinct to capital ownership. Capital owners may or may not be entrepreneurs. Neither is the commonly assumed identification of owner– managers with entrepreneurs always correct. Professional managers may act entrepreneurialy while owner–mangers may not, as the next section attempts to show.

Entrepreneurship in the firm

The entrepreneurial function is not restricted to market transacting. Entrepreneurs both act within firms and are responsible for the birth of firms. The person who believes that a group of people would produce more working together as a team rather than in isolation, who forms the team by contracting with each of its members, who monitors behaviour and assesses individual performance and who receives the increase in output brought about as a result, is an entrepreneur.

Firms are brought to life by entrepreneurs who spot the opportunity for personal gain by internalising market transactions. In team production the instigator of the firm is also the monitor who is entitled to any residual income. As a monitor, the entrepreneur enters into mutually beneficial contracts which move the firm towards its objectives. The function of entrepreneurship within the firm is in this respect similar to that of the middleman or market transactions facilitator who moves the market towards equilibrium. But it is more than that. Firms, rather than isolated market transactors, innovate, introduce new products, adopt new technologies and new organisational methods, thus contributing to the obsolescence of existing products and methods of production. Entrepreneurship contributes to the success of the firm and the demise of the non-entrepreneurial firm. Schumpeter's process of 'creative destruction' is firmly rooted in the firm.

The fact that entrepreneurs create firms has led to the commonly held but erroneous belief that anyone who starts his or her own small business is an entrepreneur. Entrepreneurship is not, however, synonymous with venturing. Entrepreneurship involves novelty and imagination which business venturing may lack. Venturing into existing product or business practices characterises enterprisers not entrepreneurs. Starting a new Chinese take-away restaurant in a London suburb may involve risks but is not entrepreneurial since all it involves is imitating something that has already been done many times over. Enterprisers are the same as Schumpeter's imitators as opposed to his innovators who are entrepreneurs. To be entrepreneurial a new venture must involve new ideas, producing new products, satisfying needs in novel ways or creating new markets and involving risks. The person who conceived of and initiated the McDonalds chain was an entrepreneur. Entrepreneurship is neither exclusive to small firms nor restricted to manufacturing or retailing. It may well be practised within old large firms like General Electric or Marks and Spencer as well as within educational institutions, hospitals and the government sector.

When the creation of a firm is entrepreneurial and any innovative aspects of entrepreneurship within the firm are carried out by its founder then the firm's founder is the entrepreneur. However, successful firms usually outlive their founders, and their heirs, either because they lack entrepreneurial talents or for other reasons, quite often sell their contractual rights. Entrepreneurial elements, however, may survive within the firm. Successful firms continue to adapt to changing circumstances and to induce innovative change. Their size increases, their organisational structures change. The history of General Electric, one of the world's largest companies established over a hundred years ago, and that of the Ford Motor Company provide two examples of a series of such entrepreneurial innovative actions. So the question arises as to who are the individuals who bring about these changes? Are the buyers of firms entrepreneurs? Who is the monitor and the initiator of mutually beneficial gain in the modern corporation which is managed by directors with a small and a progressively diminishing shareholding in the firm they run. Who if anybody is the entrepreneur in modern business firms?

Are managers entrepreneurs?

Entrepreneurship may exist throughout the organisation. Any member of the team (firm) may be alert to opportunities for personal gain when contracting his or her membership of the team. Contracts will differ to reflect differences in talents, risk attitudes, wealth, alertness and other personal traits. Some members of the team (employees) will agree to perform tasks under close direction and supervision by other members of the team (employers or employees) for a fixed reward. Their contractual agreements may leave little scope for entrepreneurship. Even managerial posts may leave no scope for entrepreneurship. However, not all managerial posts fit this description. Indeed many managers (middle or junior) and other employees will be able to exercise 'alertness' in pursuit of personal gain within any organisational structure. This is true even when the structure is hierarchical with decision making centralised at the top as for example in the U-form firm. In this case (as explained in Chapter 4) decision making depends on information which is not readily available at the top but emanates from sources closer to individuals at lower levels of the hierarchy. Information must flow from the bottom of the hierarchical ladder to the top where decisions are taken. Similarly, instructions issued at the top pass through several layers of the hierarchy in the opposite direction. Individuals in key positions, therefore, may influence these flows of information and policy instructions, in pursuit of personal gain. Information may be delayed, distorted or selectively withdrawn. The personal gain derived from such acts may take the form of promotion or shirking (increased leisure), enhancement in status and prestige, etc.

More significantly perhaps, individual entrepreneurial action may be positively encouraged as for example within the M-form organised firms. As firm size and complexity increase the founder of the firm will need such a diversity of information and expertise that bounds on rationality and increasing transaction costs will necessitate decentralisation and delegation of authority. Delegation can take two forms: (a) delegates may be given detailed instructions as to exactly what information they need and how to process it, in this case delegates exercise no discretion at all, and (b) delegates may be given discretion with regard to information collection and processing. This will happen either because it is practically impossible to supervise them or because the entrepreneur who delegates (the principal) may not have the know-how to lay down precise procedures to be followed. Additionally, principals may expect changes but cannot anticipate where the relevant information can be found or by which delegate. In this case delegates are expected to use their judgement as to what piece of information may be relevant to their principal and to act upon such information. Henry Ford, for example, the founder of the Ford Motor Company, probably realising his lack of expertise in areas of the firm other than engineering and manufacturing appointed James Couzens who as a manager introduced many innovative policies (often attributed to H. Ford), such as the $5–a-day wage in 1913 and the pioneering distribution and service policies (Drucker 1985).

Since, however, entrepreneurs act for personal gain the question arises as to why they should act in the interest of their employer rather than pursue their own personal interest either within firms or as self-employed. One possibility is that individual delegates may not be able to exploit their full potential in external markets because of barriers to entrepreneurship and difficulties in obtaining finance. Such delegates are Casson's 'unqualified entrepreneurs' who work as managers. They exercise discretion and they need to be motivated if they are to act in the interests of their principals. They must be rewarded by at least as much as they could expect to earn in external markets or other managerial posts. Decentralisation must be accompanied by managerial compensation packages which include performance-related rewards intended to encourage entrepreneurial behaviour.

The Austrian claim that anyone can be 'alert' and act entrepreneurially is as valid within firms as it is in the marketplace. James Couzens, although an employee, was undoubtedly an entrepreneur. His continuous search for change and innovation is believed to have led to his dismissal in 1917. His dismissal was in turn followed by a continuous decline in the fortunes of the Ford Motor Company which lasted for nearly thirty years. It cannot be claimed, however, that all managers are necessarily entrepreneurs. Delegates who are allowed no discretion or managers whose job it is to allocate scarce resources to known ends are administrators rather than entrepreneurs. Their job is that of the managerial economist, i.e. the comparison of marginal costs to known (even if only probabilistically) marginal benefits. This is not an entrepreneurial task. Reekie (1989) put it rather vividly. 'Compared to the entrepreneur the managerial economist is no more than a pompous inventory clark' (p. 157).

In brief, non-owner managers, as well as other employees, may act entrepreneurially but all managers are not necessarily entrepreneurs.

Are firm owners entrepreneurs?

The German word for the entrepreneur – Unternehmer – means the person who both owns and runs the firm. This means an owner–manager. Indeed writers associated with the Austrian school of thought identify the entrepreneur as the owner or the shareholder as the following passage from Reekie (1989) testifies.

> In the final analysis, Mises argues, the entrepreneur is the owner. He alone determines the grand strategy of the business. He may call on managerial advice but the decisions are his. Decisions as to 'what lines of business to employ capital [in] and how much capital to employ . . . [decisions as to] expansion and contraction of the size of the total business, and its main sections . . . [decisions as to its] financial structure' fall upon the entrepreneur alone.
>
> (p. 189)

To claim that ownership coincides with entrepreneurship seems to contradict the Austrian contention that any individual may act entrepreneurially. On the other hand if the owner is not the entrepreneur then who is the entrepreneur? This question acquires particular significance in the modern joint stock company whose directors have little if any shareholding interest.

The divorce of ownership from control does not seem to matter to those identifying ownership with entrepreneurship since dispersed shareholdings are seen as the optimal consequence of the need of modern corporations to raise large sums of capital.[6] According to this view, dispersed shareownership implies that individual shareholders find it too expensive to perform their monitoring and control duties by participating personally in the running of the firm. They therefore delegate part of their duties to senior managers and directors while retaining sufficient control over the activities of top management via two control mechanisms: the managerial labour market and the market in corporate control. The details of the way in which these and other control mechanisms operate and the extent of their effectiveness are examined in some detail in Chapter 9. For present purposes it is sufficient to give a very brief outline of the Austrian claim of the insignificance of the divorce of ownership from control.

Within a firm building a good reputation is essential for (a) promotion to higher posts including the Board of Directors, and (b) sending the right signals to the managerial labour market. Competition within the firm, therefore, encourages managers to fulfil their contractual obligations, i.e. to act in accordance with shareholder interests. Additionally, entrepreneurship is induced by compensation packages which include performance-related rewards intended to minimise any diversion of interests (see Chapter 13 for details). Across firms, the market in corporate control also disciplines managers. If managers do not pursue wealth maximising policies, the stock value of the firm will decline. Sooner or later other entrepreneurial firms will spot the opportunity for profit by taking over the undervalued firm which they believe they can manage better than the incumbent management. A successful takeover bid may be launched and managers may lose their jobs. Alternatively, shareholders may congeal power at the Annual General Meeting to replace managers who do not pursue wealth maximising policies. This twin threat to job security is supposed to eliminate managerial discretion.

Austrians do not, therefore, attribute much significance to the divorce of ownership from control which they consider more apparent than real. They see the modern corporation as a 'marriage of productive convenience between internal labour markets and entrepreneurship' (Reekie 1989: p. 188). They assert that any member of the team can act entrepreneurially but shareholder control and award incentives ensure that managers' entrepreneurial activities are reconciled with shareholder interests. Moreover, managers act on delegated authority and are not answerable for losses incurred; they cannot, therefore, be the entrepreneur.

To claim that the owners are the entrepreneur while at the same time proclaiming that any member of a firm – workers, junior and senior managers and shareholders – may act entrepreneurially and that personal gains accrue to any alert individual exploiting opportunities either as an employer or as an employee, is paradoxical if not outright contradictory. But according to Reekie the paradox is resolved by noting that 'anticipated gain is not synonymous with anticipated corporate profits. The latter is only a subset of the former' (p. 190). In his view corporate profit seems to define entrepreneurship. He claims that shareholders are the entrepreneur even if the market in corporate control cannot eliminate managerial discretion. They are the entrepreneur since in their judgement it is still more profitable to employ managers rather than run the firm themselves or incur the additional costs required to eliminate managerial discretion.

The view that ownership coincides with entrepreneurship is not, however, universally accepted, as the following quote indicates.

Clearly the single owner of the classical capitalist firm who supplies the capital and performs routine managerial tasks *may* also exercise entrepreneurial skills. But the owner is not necessarily the entrepreneur. . . . Especially in large firms entrepreneurship, alertness to new opportunities, may exist throughout the organisation.

(Ricketts 1987: 73)

Continuous change in the business environment requires continuous adaptation by the firm. Firms cannot survive without some entrepreneurial talent in making judgemental decisions. The makers of judgemental decisions may own the resources they direct in which case owner–managers are entrepreneurs. That the Rothschilds, who financed with their own money the railways they built, were entrepreneurs is in no doubt. But the first bankers such as the brothers Pereire who founded in 1857 the Credit Mobilier in France or Gearg Siemens the founder of Deutsche Bank were not interested in ownership. They acquired money from other people and allocated it in areas of higher yield.

Ownership is not a necessary condition for entrepreneurship. Non owner–managers may exercise discretion so that they, to a large extent, are responsible for decisions relating to the expansion or contraction of the business, its financial structure and administrative adaptations. They specialise in judgemental decision making relating to innovation which is one of the main instruments of entrepreneurship. They gain personally when their decisions are correct and they suffer personal loss when they are wrong. They are entrepreneurs.

THE MARKET FOR ENTREPRENEURSHIP AND THE MEANING OF PROFIT

Entrepreneurs, whether owners or managers, are motivated by personal gain so that the factors which determine the size of the entrepreneurial reward are significant in encouraging entrepreneurial activity. Expected rewards are likely to depend on the characteristics of the economy as well as on the number and behaviour of active entrepreneurs. To analyse the entrepreneurial market Casson's diagrammatic analysis is utilised in Figure 5.3. It should be emphasised that the analysis refers to total market rather than individual behaviour which, by the very nature of entrepreneurship, cannot be predicted. Thus, although it cannot reasonably be assumed that a particular person will enter the entrepreneurial market when the prospect of entrepreneurial gains improves, it is reasonable to assume that higher expected gains will induce some individuals to enter entrepreneurship and increase the number of active entrepreneurs.

Curve DD in Figure 5.3 indicates the relationship between the size of the expected entrepreneurial reward and the number of active entrepreneurs. It assumes that (a) the economy is dynamic and evolving but

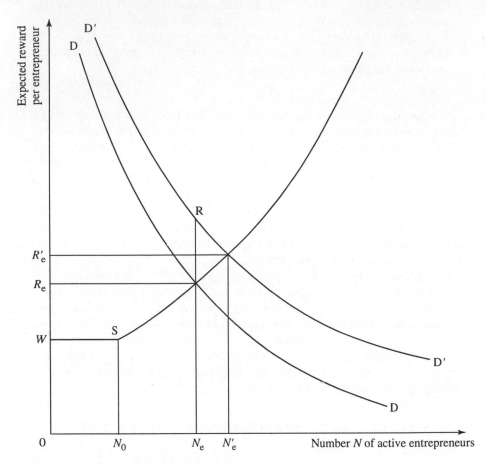

Figure 5.3 The market for entrepreneurs

there is a *given pace* of change, and (b) each entrepreneur can spot only a fraction of the available opportunities. It follows that as the number of active entrepreneurs increases a higher proportion of the opportunities available at each point in time is exploited and the longer it will take for each entrepreneur to spot another opportunity. Therefore, the larger the number of active entrepreneurs the lower the expected entrepreneurial reward will be. This is shown by the negative slope of the DD curve. When the existing opportunities are few so that a given increase in the number of active entrepreneurs brings about a large reduction in expected gains, DD is steep. On the other hand when opportunities are plentiful, any reduction in expected gains due to increased numbers of entrepreneurs will be small and the DD curve will be relatively flat. The position of the DD curve depends on the pace of change in the economy. The faster the pace of change the further away from the origin DD will be.

Curve SS on Figure 5.3 is the supply curve of 'active entrepreneurs'. For each level of expected reward it shows the number of individuals with the necessary personal traits who decide to acquire command of the required resources (either as owners or through borrowing or employment in large corporations) and to act as entrepreneurs. SS is flat at the prevailing wage rate because it is assumed that no individual would decide to act as an entrepreneur when the entrepreneurial reward is expected to be less than the current national wage rate. A number of individuals (no more than N_0) would enter the market when the expected reward is equal to the wage rate. The positive section of SS indicates that as the expected reward (R_e) becomes higher so more individuals with the necessary traits will leave paid employment or leisure activities to act as entrepreneurs (N_e). The rate of increase of N_e as R_e increases (that is the slope of SS) will depend on social and institutional factors which may affect the willingness of individuals to become entrepreneurs and the extent of barriers to entry into entre- preneurship. The position of SS depends on (a) the number of individuals who possess the necessary traits to become entrepreneurs and (b) the proportion of the potential entrepreneurs who can acquire control of the necessary resources to qualify as entrepreneurs. Capital may be either owned or borrowed. Borrowing may be acquired through social contacts with wealthy people or from financial institutions which screen for entre- preneurial traits. Finally command over resources may be possible through the acquisition of a senior position in a large corporation. Any social or institutional changes that have an impact on these sources of finance will affect the position of SS. Thus, the supply of entrepreneurs will be influenced by changes in wealth distribution, social mobility and educa- tional opportunities since educational qualifications are used as screening devices by large corporations and financial institutions.

The number of active entrepreneurs and the size of the entrepreneurial reward will be determined by the intersection of DD and SS. This long- run equilibrium is achieved at R_e and N_e in Figure 5.3. A change in either DD or SS will disturb this position and will tend to produce a new equilibrium. For example, if DD shifts to the right to D'D' the level of expected rewards corresponding to N_e increases (to R) which induces more entrepreneurs to become active. As N increases R falls and a new equilibrium is established at R_e' and N_e'[7] involving more entrepreneurs and higher expected rewards.

Profit as an entrepreneurial reward

Entrepreneurial activity includes both the identification and the imple- mentation of judgemental decisions, i.e. decisions about which there is diversity of opinion. Entrepreneurial decisions, therefore, can be thought of as bets. When the entrepreneurial judgement is correct others have to pay up. This payment, which is a reward to superior entrepreneurial judgement, is profit. To protect this reward it is essential for the entrepreneur to keep secret the different pieces of information and the way they were synthesised and utilised in forming the superior judgement. Secrecy is important to avoid competition from imitators especially when the exploitation of an opportunity is an on-going process. However, the very act of exploiting commercial information alerts other people to the existence of a profitable opportunity. Imitators move in and bid away the activity from the entrepreneur. Thus, when information about the existence of profitable opportunities cannot be kept secret and the exploitation is a continuous process, competition will bid the profit away unless there are barriers to entry. Barriers to entry can take the conventional form (see Chapter 2). That is, the entrepreneur can (a) apply for a statutory monopoly such as a patent, (b) acquire control of a scarce resource which is necessary in the activity involved, (c) decide to exploit the activity at such a large scale that entry would imply overexpansion and the expectation of losses for potential entrants (see Chapter 8 for other forms of strategic behaviour) or (d) utilise initial profits to create a good reputation. The erection of barriers to entry is important in protecting the entrepreneur's lead over competitors. The size of the entrepreneurial profit depends crucially on the monopoly power the entrepreneur has acquired over both the information and the situation to which it applies.

In the long run, however, high rewards will attract more entrepreneurs into the market. The greater the number of entrepreneurs the higher the probability that two or more of them may identify the same opportunity for profit simultaneously. If two entrepreneurs attempt to exploit the same opportunity independently, they compete against each other and thus reduce the level of their reward. A collusive agreement may be entered into to reduce the effects of competition. But collusion presupposes that each entrepreneur knows that the other has the same information and judgemental ability. This may not be possible since each entrepreneur may believe his or her judgement to be superior. Besides, when more entrepreneurs compete collusive agreements become difficult to implement and sustain in practice (see Chapter 8).

In the long run expected rewards decline because (a) the proportion of opportunities identified by each entrepreneur decreases as the number of active entrepreneurs increases and (b) competition among entrepreneurs increases. Provided that a long-run equilibrium is established the expected level of reward is no more than a reward for time and effort spent in identifying and implementing judgemental decision making.

In brief, entrepreneurship is a factor of production which relates to the co-ordination of resources through judgemental decision making. The expected long-run entrepreneurial reward is a reward to that factor of production. Social and institutional changes that enhance the pace of change in the economy affect the number of entrepreneurs and the level of their reward. Pure profit, in excess of the entrepreneurial reward, may however exist in the short run. Such profit is a reward for superior (monopoly) knowledge. Its size depends on barriers to entrepreneurship.

Profit as a reward to entrepreneurship is clearly a residual reward. This view of profit incorporates influences from antecedent theories on entrepreneurship and its rewards and especially those developed by Knight, Schumpeter and the Austrians. The following three views on the nature and meaning of profit have been influential in shaping Casson's theory.

1 *The monopoly theory*   According to this view profit is the result of market frictions and imperfections. Barriers to entry, lack of information, business strategic behaviour and the resultant high market concentration cause imperfect competition. Markets are prevented from approaching equilibrium and profit is the result of monopoly pricing.

2 *The view that profit is a reward for uncertainty*   Since time is involved in entrepreneurial activity, entrepreneurs or firms co-ordinate production at one point in time to satisfy future needs, so that they undertake risks. Profit is the reward for such risk taking. Uncertainty is not, however, simply involved in production for the market. Significant risk taking may, for example, be involved in personnel recruitment and delegation. Directors who recruit and supervise managers undertake the risk of employing the wrong person and are faced with moral hazard problems when they delegate the managerial function. Their compensations are profit related and thus they effectively bear the consequences of their actions. They are recipients of pure profit.

   In this view, profit is an inducement to function. Since on the whole risk taking is a socially desirable activity, profit is viewed as a just reward.

3 *Profit as a reward for innovation*   Innovation includes products, processes or 'all things' that make it possible to produce more out of existing resources. All factors involved in the process of innovation are paid their opportunity cost and the excess is the reward of the entrepreneur innovator. This Schumpeterian profit is of course competed away by the process of 'creative destruction'. As innovations become known, in the absence of barriers, imitators appear who increase the production of the innovative products or processes reducing their prices and eliminating the residual income.

Since Casson's model of entrepreneurship discussed above incorporates innovation, risk taking and structural features of the market such as barriers to entrepreneurship, it can justifiably be argued that the concept of profit he developed represents a synthesis and generalisation which corresponds nearer to the reality of profit. This view is consistent with behaviour in the presence of informational asymmetries and 'transaction costs' which characterise the modern business enterprises.

SUMMARY

The entrepreneur is someone who specialises in judgemental decision making about the co-ordination of resources. He or she perceives opportunities for change and acts upon them in the hope of personal gain. As market facilitators entrepreneurs assist the market to correct errors and move the economy towards equilibrium. But as innovators they move the economy away from equilibrium.

Entrepreneurs operate both in the marketplace and within firms. Any member of a firm may act entrepreneurialy. Entrepreneurship can be delegated. When delegates are given discretion in the collection and interpretation of information and in decision making they can act entrepreneurialy. Delegate managers may be entrepreneurs but all managers are not entrepreneurs. Similarly, owners may be entrepreneurs but all firm owners are not necessarily entrepreneurs.

Although entrepreneurship requires finance, the entrepreneurial function is quite distinct from the function of capital and the entrepreneurial reward is distinct from interest on capital used. The analysis of the market for entrepreneurs has indicated that in the long run the entrepreneurial reward is a reward for time and effort spend in judgemental decision making. In the short run pure profit may exist. This is a reward to superior (monopoly) judgement whose size depends on the existence of barriers to entrepreneurship.

APPLICATION: ENTREPRENEURIAL MANAGEMENT

Contrary to popular belief large- and medium-sized firms can be, and often are, entrepreneurial. To foster entrepreneurship, however, a firm must both reward its entrepreneurs and adopt managerial policies and administrative structures which facilitate innovative actions. The following management policies have been identified as conducive to entrepreneurship and have been observed by Drucker (1985) to operate successfully in practice. They include both management practices and appropriate administrative structures.

1 Policies conducive to entrepreneurship include practices which do the following.

(a) *Focus attention on opportunities*   While the management of almost any firm devotes time and effort to analysing failures to meet targets the same cannot be said about unexpected successes. Analysis of unexpected success, however, is equally if not more important. An example of a company focusing on opportunities as they present themselves is that of company X.[8] X is a medium-sized company supplying health-care products to physicians. Its top management holds monthly meetings to discuss areas where the company is doing better than expected. The CEO has been quoted as saying that the opportunities spotted at these meetings are not nearly as important as 'the entrepreneurial attitude which the habit of looking into opportunities creates throughout the management team'. It should be noted that this company is so successful that it has grown tenfold in twenty years.

(b) *Generate an entrepreneurial spirit throughout the firm*   Company X holds, twice yearly, a two-day conference for all executives in charge of divisions, markets, major products, etc. The aim is to receive reports from the most successful executives and to analyse the reasons for their success. Additionally ideas for change and ways leading to success are discussed. The gain from these meetings is also perceived to be a positive impact on attitudes and values.

(c) *Facilitate the flow of information*   Direct communication between top management and junior employees from all the functional areas of the firm is such a practice. Its purpose is to listen to new ideas, aspirations, views on the existence of new opportunities, ideas about the developing of new products, new designs, processes, etc. An equally important aim is to directly inform juniors of top level policies, position in the marketplace, technologies used, etc. Once more the gain from these meetings is not the direct generation of entrepreneurial ideas as much as the fostering and encouragement of an entrepreneurial spirit.

2 Administrative structures which separate new projects from existing ones are necessary not only to overcome problems of bounded rationality but in order to enable the assessment of the new venture and to design appropriate rewards. Typically, successful initiatives bring yields only after a period of very low or negative returns. To reward entrepreneurial effort according to current rates of return, as usually suggested, would be inappropriate since it would mean financial penalties for a number of years for those responsible for the new venture. This would stifle entrepreneurship. A method successfully utilised by 3M and Johnson and Johnson is to promise to the employees who successfully develop new products, markets or services that they will become the head of the business based on their new venture. This means general manager, vice president or division president, with the compensation, bonuses and stock options appropriate to that level of responsibility. This can be a very substantial reward and it does not commit the company to anything if the new business is a failure.

FURTHER READING

Casson, M. (1982) *The Entrepreneur: An Economic Theory*, Oxford: Martin Robertson.

Drucker, P.F. (1985) *Innovation and Entrepreneurship: Practice and Principles*, London: Heinemann.
Ricketts, M. (1987) *The Economics of Business Enterprise: New approches to the Firm*, Brighton: Wheatsheaf.
Ronen, J. (ed.) (1983) *Entrepreneurship*, Price Institute for Entrepreneurial Studies, Lexington, MA: Lexington Books.

QUESTIONS

1 Compare and contrast the role of the entrepreneur in the market with his or her role in the firm.
2 Use examples to distinguish between an enterpriser and an entrepreneur (Drucker (1985) may be a good source of material).
3 Use Casson's model of the entrepreneurial market to analyse the impact on the number of entrepreneurs and on the expected reward per entrepreneur of (a) social and institutional advancements which enhance the pace of change in the economy and (b) an increase in the level of real wages in the economy.
4 Define profit and comment on factors that may influence its size.

NOTES

1 For an expansion on this point see Casson (1982).
2 Shackle (1984) suggests the Shell's decision-making policy which consists of considering a very small number (2–3) of possible scenarios is very close to his notion of entrepreneurial decision making. It is evidence that refutes traditional ideas about decisions made on the basis of probabilistically calculated expected returns.
3 This view is supported by the responses that Ronen (1983) culled from interviews contacted with chief executive officers of large- and medium-sized companies. The following response of an anonymous interviewee is typical: 'I think the primary objective of the entrepreneur is to create, to develop something new, to push back the frontiers and to see that creation resolved in some commercial . . . application' (p. 171).
4 Drucker (1985) gives many practical illustrations of this point. Drucker views entrepreneurship as a practice and his book is concerned with entrepreneurial management and strategy. Based on experience and the author's long contact with many US companies (including two large hospitals, IBM, General Electric, etc.) as well as American and European Banks and Japanese multinationals the book provides large number of mini cases and numerous examples of entrepreneurial management.
5 The production possibility curve, PP, shows all the combinations of different commodities that can be produced assuming that all the available resources are fully and efficiently utilised.
6 In a highly geared firm lenders would bear unacceptably high risks so that lending at current rates of interest would not be forthcoming. High risk premiums would have to be charged making this method of finance unattractive.
7 It should be pointed out that further assumptions are necessary to ensure that a new equilibrium will be achieved after a disturbance. As Ricketts (1987) has pointed out it is possible to show that this model can produce cyclical patterns with bouts of entrepreneurial activity followed by recessions. Other patterns of market functioning similar to those postulated by the cobweb theorem of traditional economics are possible.
8 The name has been withheld for reasons of corporate confidentiality.

6 Production and costs

INTRODUCTION

Up to this point we have adopted the 'transaction' as the basic unit of analysis and have postulated that transactions cost economising is a force which motivates entrepreneurship. Transacting must not, however, be narrowly defined to mean only exchanges; it should rather be broadly interpreted to incorporate production. Economic activity encompasses both exchange and production and it can be argued that entrepreneurs create firms to use them as their production instruments (Reekie 1989: 191).

Production, if broadly defined to include any transformation of resources into products and services, can indeed be seen as the essence of any business enterprise. The force that motivates production is the residual income received after all resources, including any entrepreneurial labour time and capital invested, have been paid as much as they would have received in their best alternative use. This chapter examines the nature of such payments or costs and the way they vary with the volume of output and/or its composition.

The chapter begins with the traditional theory of production and costs. This focuses on the co-ordination of known scarce means aiming for known ends so that the question pursued is how best to organise resources of a given quality to produce a certain volume of a product. In organising production it is further assumed that the state of technological knowledge or 'the state of the arts' is known so that entrepreneurship is subsumed to the role of discovering, over time, either new methods of organising production which enhance output or new products.

This approach to production and costs although relevant to certain decisions and useful in providing conceptual tools of analysis is often unnecessarily restricted to the study of the costs of a single-plant single-product firm. Given that in reality firms commonly operate a number of plants producing a variety of products, we extend the analysis to cover multi-plant and multi-product operations. We begin by considering the technological relationships between inputs and outputs in the short and the long run. These form the basis for the derivation of a firm's cost curves.

PRODUCTION TECHNOLOGY

Production can be defined as the act of transforming inputs (goods and services of one kind) into outputs (goods and services of another kind). The set of all possible ways of carrying out this transformation, known as technology or 'the state of the arts' can be viewed as the technological constraint under which firms operate. Each member of this set is a different method of transforming inputs into outputs, called a production process or a production method. A production process specifies the quantities of various inputs required to produce a certain output and since several processes may be available at any point in time the problem of selecting one arises. It is assumed that in selecting a production process (method) from among all the feasible ones the firm aims to be technically efficient.

Isoquants and technical efficiency

To define the concept of technical efficiency, consider a firm whose technology is such that two inputs can be used in different proportions to produce a given output X. The inputs are machine hours K and labour hours L and the output is measured in tons of product X. There are five production processes available, P_0, P_1, P_2, P_3, P_4, the input requirements of which are specified in Table 6.1. Process P_1, for example, requires twenty machine hours and ten labour hours to produce 10 tons of X.

If it is further assumed that (a) the available inputs and outputs are divisible so that each production process can be operated at any output level and (b) a given percentage increase in all inputs increases output by the same percentage so that a doubling, say, of all inputs doubles output, then the technology described in Table 6.1 can be represented as in Figure 6.1 where each ray through the origin describes one production process. Ray P_1, for example, is the process which requires 20 units of K and 10 units of L to produce 10 tons of X, as shown by point a. Doubling all inputs ($K = 40$, $L = 20$) doubles output ($X = 20$) as shown by point b, whereas trebling all inputs trebles output (point c).

Since capital is measured on the y axis, the steeper the ray the more capital intensive the production method it represents is while the flatter a ray the more labour intensive the production method is. In other words,

Table 6.1 Example of input requirements of five production processes with P_4 being inefficient

	K	L	X	K/L
P_0	30	5	10	30/5 = 6
P_1	20	10	10	20/10 = 2
P_2	10	20	10	10/20 = 0.5
P_3	5	30	10	5/30 = 1/6
P_4	20	20	10	20/20 = 1

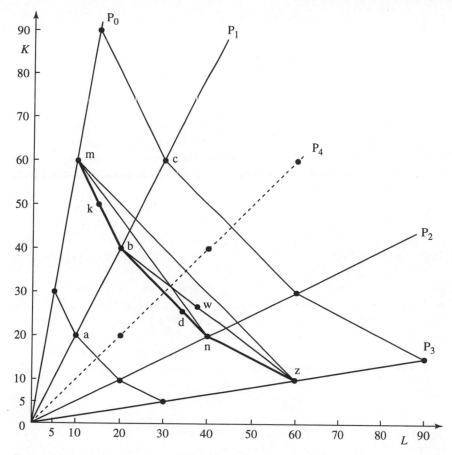

Figure 6.1 A five-production process technology (P$_4$ is inefficiency)

the capital intensity of each process is indicated by the slope of each ray which shows the capital to labour (K/L) ratio that this production method requires. Thus, if process 2 (P$_2$) were to be used in the production of X the K/L ratio would be 1/2 while if process 3 (P$_3$) were used it would be 1/6 (see Table 6.1). If it is possible, however, to combine production processes so as to produce part of the output by one process and part by another, a firm may be able to achieve a K/L ratio different to any of those depicted in Table 6.1. Thus, if it is possible to produce, say, 10 tons of X by P$_1$ and another 10 tons by P$_0$, 20 tons of X will be produced using 50 units of K and 15 units of L. The K/L ratio has thus become 50/15 = 3.33, as indicated by the coordinates of point k, which is different to the input requirements of either of the two processes used. In fact if it is possible to produce say one-third of total output by P$_0$ and two-thirds by P$_1$ or to alter the proportions in which P$_0$ and P$_1$ are combined, the K/L ratio would vary accordingly. All the possible input combinations that can be achieved by the linear combinations of P_0 and P_1 are indicated by the coordinates of the line segment mb. Similarly, the input combinations that can be achieved by combining P_0 and P_3 are indicated by the coordinates of the line segment mz and so on.

When production processes can be combined in the way suggested above, all the technically feasible input combinations that could be used to produce a given output level are indicated by the coordinates of points on the line segment which joins any two processes such as bz, mn, bn, etc. All feasible input combinations are not, however, technically efficient. In fact not all production processes need be efficient.

A method of production is technically inefficient if when compared with another method it requires more of at least one factor of production and not less of any other to produce the same output. In Table 6.1, for example, process P_4 is inefficient since compared with process P_1 it uses more labour and the same capital to produce any given level of output. Using more of one input and no less of any other is clearly wasteful and therefore process 4 must not be included in the set of technically efficient methods of production. In fact any process combination that involves a technically inefficient process is also inefficient and therefore inadmissible in the efficient set. It is for this reason that in considering combinations of processes in Figure 6.1, we ignored P_4 (the broken line) and combinations involving P_4. But perhaps more significant and less obvious is the fact that combinations of technically efficient processes may be technically inefficient and should not be included in the efficient production set.

A combination of processes is technically inefficient if, when compared with a production process or with another combination of processes, it uses more of at least one input and not less of any other to produce the same output. In Figure 6.1, any combination of P_1 and P_3 (points on the line bz) is inefficient. Compare, for example, point w with point d. Clearly w is inefficient since it requires more of both resources to produce the same output. The same is true for points on the line mn or mz etc. In fact all the technically efficient methods of producing 20 tons of X are indicated by the thick kinked line mbnz. This line traces the locus of points indicating the minimum input requirements of the given output level. All the line segments above this line represent inefficient methods of production while points below the line indicate infeasible input combinations.

The technically efficient methods of producing each of three different levels of output are indicated in Figure 6.1. Each curve consists of the linear combinations of the four technically efficient processes and is called an *isoquant*. By its construction, an isoquant denotes all the technically efficient input combinations which could be utilised to produce a given level of output. Since technically inefficient methods of production are not used an isoquant has a *negative slope* which means that as less of one input is used more of the other must be employed if output is to remain the same.

Inspection of Figure 6.1 indicates that isoquants are made up of a series of straight line segments. The larger the number of efficient methods of production available, the larger is the number of straight line segments contained in each isoquant and the shorter each one becomes so that in the limit the isoquant approaches a smooth curve. Indeed, isoquants are commonly drawn as continuous curves convex to the origin which makes the mathematical treatment of production and cost theory simpler.

Convexity is an important property of isoquants. It indicates the extent to which inputs can be substituted for each other on the assumption that only technically efficient methods of production are used. The rate at which L can be substituted for K as we move along an isoquant is equal to the slope of the isoquant at each point. In Figure 6.1 it changes at the kinks.

Since a firm can operate at any point along an isoquant it can produce a given product by a capital intensive method, say P_0, or if capital is expensive or insufficient it can move to a less capital intensive method. Moving from point m to point b the firm is producing the same output by substituting labour for capital. The rate of substitution is defined as $-\Delta K/\Delta L$ and is constant along a straight line segment. Thus along segment mb it is equal to $-20/10 = -2$ while along segment bn it becomes $-20/20 = -1$.

When isoquants are continuous curves the rate of substitution is different at each point along the isoquant. In considering very small input substitution we refer to substitution at the margin and the ratio that measures it is known as the marginal rate of technical substitution (MRTS). In other words, in the limit substitutability is quantified by 'the marginal rate of technical substitution' of capital for labour which is equal to the slope of the isoquant at a point.

In Figure 6.1 as capital per man hour (K/L) increases and we move up the isoquant its slope $(\Delta K/\Delta L)$ increases (ignoring the minus sign). That is, as the substitution of capital for labour continues larger and larger increments of capital are needed per unit reduction in labour in order to maintain constant output. This is known as the diminishing marginal rate of technical substitution of capital for labour or the diminishing marginal productivity of capital. Alternatively, as we move along an isoquant from left to right, the ratio K/L falls and the absolute value of the MRTS of labour for capital diminishes. In other words, the phenomenon of diminishing marginal productivity applies to any factor of production of which more is used in conjunction with a constant or a diminishing quantity of another input. Diminishing productivity has efficiency implications which must be further examined, but to analyse this phenomenon in more detail we need to examine the fundamental features of technology, i.e. the relationship between inputs and output when the quantities of all inputs can vary.

Returns to scale

The time period required for a firm to adjust all its inputs is referred to as the 'long run'. The actual calendar time involved depends on the most inflexible inputs, such as plant or machinery. In the meantime output can be increased by increasing some inputs while keeping others constant. It may be possible, for example, to produce more with a given plant by using an extra labour shift. The time period involved in increasing output by utilising more of only one input is determined by the most flexible input and is called the 'short-run'.

Returns to scale is the term used to describe the effect on output of an equiproportional increase in all inputs. In constructing the isoquants of Figure 6.1 it was assumed that production processes can be operated in such a way that a given proportionate increase of all inputs increases output in the same proportion. When this is the case the production technology is said to exhibit 'constant returns to scale' (CRS). Returns to scale are not, however, always constant. It is possible that output may expand faster or slower than an equiproportionate increase of all inputs in which case returns to scale are said to be increasing or decreasing, respectively.

Decreasing returns to scale are usually attributed to managerial bounded rationality. As the scale of operations increases inefficiencies may arise from delayed or distorted information flows and the intrusion of managerial subgoals. Problems of control loss were discussed in relation to the expansion of the U-form firm in Chapter 4, where it was suggested that they can be mitigated by an appropriate re-organisation of the internal structure of the firm. Mitigation does not, however, mean elimination. Thus, whatever the internal structure managerial bounded rationality problems may appear beyond a certain level of expansion, causing decreasing returns to scale.

On the other hand there are several reasons why increasing returns to scale (IRS) may occur. As the scale of operation expands it may be possible to divide up tasks into more specialised activities thereby enhancing labour productivity. Moreover a larger size may enable a firm to acquire more sophisticated (and hence more productive) equipment. Combine harvesters, for example, can be used on large farms to reduce costs but not on small farms. Technological indivisibilities may also appear as IRS. In addition a simple technical–geometric relationship between particular equipment and the inputs required to produce and install it can create IRS. Such relationships are common in the 'process industries' such as the petroleum industry, gas transmission, chemical industries, etc., in relation to the construction of storage tanks, reaction chambers, transmission pipes, etc. The labour and materials required increase in the same proportion as the size of the area that such plants occupy while the volume of these plants (which determines their output) increases by more than the increase in the area.

The law of diminishing marginal productivity

In the short run a firm may be able to increase output by using more of the variable factor(s) in conjunction with the given quantity of the fixed factor(s). The term 'returns to a variable input' is then used to describe the effect that increased utilisation of an input in conjunction with some fixed input has on output. To illustrate consider Figure 6.2 which shows that X is produced using two inputs L and K by a constant returns to scale technology so that points b, c, etc. indicate equiproportionate increases in inputs and output. Suppose that production is at point a and that K is an inflexible input, the amount of which currently available is equal to $0K$, and the firm wishes to increase X in the short run (a period of time long enough to increase L but too short to increase K). The only way to increase X, in this case, is to use a more labour intensive method of production as indicated by point b′ (point b is not feasible). Any further increases in X can be achieved by moving along the horizontal line KK, i.e. by increasing L and reducing the K/L ratio. Inspection of Figure 6.2 indicates that equal additions to output with K constant (moving along the KK line) require progressively larger increments of the labour input. Thus, to increase output by X units (from X to $2X$) requires that L increases to $2.8L$. That is, to double output the labour input more than doubles. A further increase of output by X units (to $3X$) requires L to increase by $3L$ (see point c′).

Looked at from a slightly different perspective, equal increments of the variable input yield decreasing increments of output. As already noted this phenomenon is known as decreasing marginal productivity or decreasing returns to a variable input.

In Figure 6.2 decreasing returns to the variable factor were derived on the assumption that the technology exhibited CRS. It can be shown that had it exhibited decreasing returns to scale then the decreasing returns to the variable factor would have been accentuated. It should also be intuitively clear that it is possible for increasing returns to scale to offset the decreasing returns to the variable factor so that a given increase in the variable factor increases output proportionately. It should be noted, however, that unless increasing returns to scale increase at the same rate at which returns to the variable input decrease, which is rather improbable, then even in the presence of increasing returns to scale, the returns to the variable input will at some output level decline. It is for this reason that although returns to scale may increase, decrease or be constant, the returns to a variable factor are *eventually* diminishing, a phenomenon also known as the 'law of variable proportions'.

Economically efficient methods of production

A technically inefficient method of production, i.e. a method which is wasteful in resources, is economically inefficient whatever the input prices. Such a process should not be adopted if the aim of the firm is to produce a given output at minimum possible cost. In selecting the input combination to be adopted the firm must therefore consider only the technically efficient methods of production.

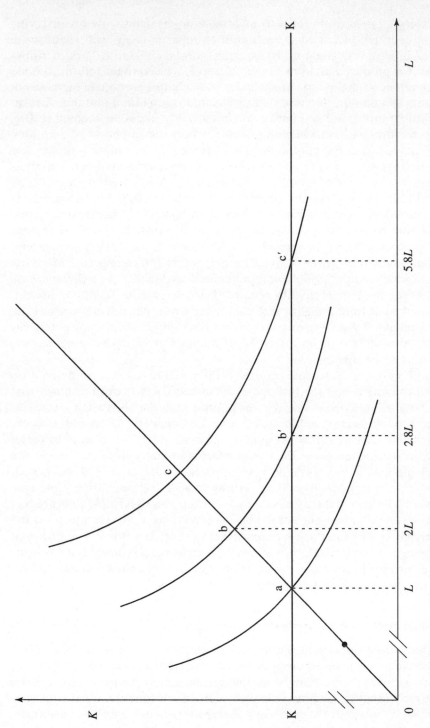

Figure 6.2 The law of diminishing marginal productivity

Since each technically efficient method of production involves a different combination of input quantities, given the input prices the cost of production will vary depending on which production method is used. Economic efficiency requires that from all the technically efficient input combinations the one which minimises the cost of producing a given output is selected. This combination, known as the 'optimum' input combination, clearly depends on input prices as well as on input quantities. Information on the cost of input requirements is summarised in the budget line.

A firm's budget or isocost line

Suppose that input prices are constant and independent of the input quantities used and that they are denoted by w and r where w is the hire price of labour services per period (hour or day) and r is the hire price of capital services per period (hour or day). Thus, r is not the price of a machine (just as w is not the price of a person) but rather the rental charge the firm has to pay out per period of time were it to hire the machine, or if the firm owns the machine the rental charge it forgoes by using it instead of hiring it out. Then the cost of any given level of output which is produced by using L hours of labour time and K machine hours per time period is given by

$$C = wL + rK \tag{6.1}$$

Since the quantities of L and K can vary at will, equation (6.1) describes the cost of any given specific combination of L and K. Viewed from a somewhat different perspective, equation (6.1) is the firm's budget line since for a given outlay C and input prices (w and r) it indicates all the maximum combinations of L and K that the firm can acquire.

Equation (6.1) can be re-arranged to give

$$K = \frac{C}{r} - \frac{w}{r} L \tag{6.2}$$

which is a straight line (under the given assumptions) with slope $(-w/r)$ equal to the inverse of the input price ratio. In Figure 6.3(a) it is shown as line (C/r) C/w. Since every point on a budget line indicates the same total outlay (C), the budget line is also known as an *isocost line*. Clearly the higher C the larger the attainable set of inputs and the further away from the origin the budget line will lie. Moreover, since the slope of the isocost line is equal to the negative of the price ratio, any change in relative prices will change the slope of the line. A lower w, for example, with the same r swings the line to the right and an increase in w swings it to the left, changing the set of attainable input combinations. If, for example, w doubles the budget line (C/r) C/w pivots around point C/r and becomes line (C/r) $C/2w$.

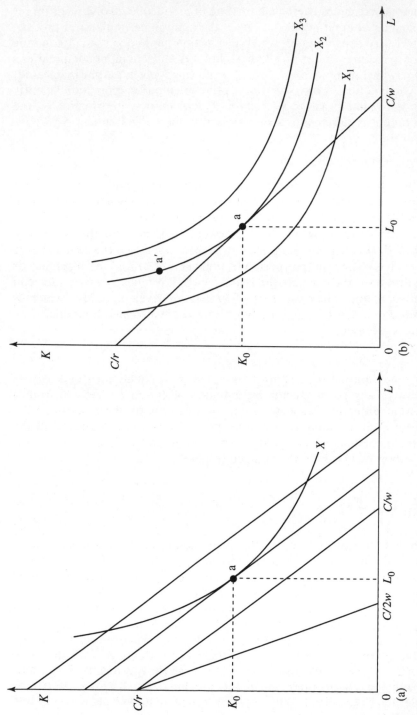

Figure 6.3 Economically efficient production: (a) input combination $K_0 L_0$ maximises output given the outlay C; (b) input combination $K_0 L_0$ minimises the production cost of output X

Economic efficiency

A firm's production function (described by a set of isoquants) indicates the relationship between the technically efficient input combinations (K and L, say) and the volume of output (X). Symbolically $X = f(K,L)$. Given the production function and the input prices the question of selecting the most economic method of production arises. Economic efficiency, in relation to production, can be approached in two different ways.

1 *Minimise the cost of a given X^1*   minimise the cost of a given X. For a certain output level, economic efficiency requires that the given output is produced at minimum cost. That is, from all the technically efficient input combinations on the isoquant representing the given output the one with the lowest cost must be selected. Now, since budget lines nearer the origin indicate lower total costs, the least expensive input combination is the one located on the lowest budget (isocost) line. In Figure 6.3(b) output $2X$ is produced at minimum cost if K_0 units of K and L_0 units of L are used since any other point on the isoquant lies on a higher budget line. As indicated, the optimum input combination is determined by the tangency of the given isoquant with the lowest budget line.
2 *Maximise output given the total outlay C^2*   Given a cost outlay C and input prices, production takes place under a given budget constraint. Economic efficiency in these circumstances is achieved if output is the highest possible. Since isoquants further away from the origin indicate higher levels of output that input combination must be selected, from among the available ones, which lies on the highest isoquant. This is achieved when the given budget line reaches the highest isoquant possible. This is once more determined by the point of tangency between the given budget line and an isoquant as indicated by point a in Figure 6.3(b).

Either way economic efficiency occurs at a point of tangency between an isoquant and an isocost line which implies that at this point the slope of the two curves must be equal. Now, since the slope of the budget line is the same as the negative of the input price ratio and the slope of the isoquant is $dK/dL = MP_L/MP_K$, where MP_L and MP_K are the marginal products of L and K respectively, the condition for economic efficiency is that

$$\frac{MP_L}{MP_K} = \frac{w}{r} \text{ or } \frac{MP_L}{w} = \frac{MP_K}{r} \tag{6.3}$$

Condition (6.3) means that input proportions must be such that the ratio of the marginal products of the two inputs is equal to the ratio of their prices or that the output gained from the last unit of money spent on labour

(MP_L/w) must be equal to the output gained from the last unit of money spent on capital (MP_K/r). If the slope of the isoquant for any given output is less than the slope of the isocost line, as for example at point a' (Figure 6.3(b)), then the input combination required, though technically efficient, is economically inefficient since it requires a higher cost compared with point a which, given the isocost line, is infeasible anyway.

Clearly a change in either the isoquant (brought about by new technologies, say) or in the budget line will result in a change in the economically efficient method of production. Let us consider a change in the budget line on the assumption of given isoquants. Suppose, for example, that the available outlay is increased by 50 per cent to $1.5C$ (see Figure 6.4(a)). This will cause a parallel rightward shift in the budget line enabling the firm to reach a higher isoquant. Given a CRS technology, the new economically efficient input combination at point b will lie on a straight line through point a and the origin. Further increases in outlay will result in the selection of input combinations on higher indifference curves but on the same straight line through the origin (denoted as OEP). Ray OEP is called the *optimum expansion path* of the firm since its slope shows the economically efficient input combination to be adopted as output expands.

The slope of the optimum expansion path will change in response to a change in relative prices. An increase in the price of labour with the price of K and total outlay C remaining the same is illustrated in Figure 6.4(b). The budget line pivots inwards towards the origin and the initial equilibrium at point a will shift to point c, resulting in a reduction of output and a switch to a more capital intensive production process. Subsequent increases in outlay will shift the new budget line outwards and will cause an efficient firm to follow the new expansion path OEP_{21}, i.e. to use a more capital intensive method of production.

THE COSTS OF PRODUCTION

The optimum expansion path incorporates sufficient information to derive a firm's optimum input mix and, given input prices, the cost of production as output expands. Since, however, the relationship between cost and output, known as the *cost curve*, is an important element in business decision making we must examine it in more detail. The cost–output relationship, similarly to the input–output relationship, will depend on whether a short- or long-term adjustment to inputs is considered. Additionally the behaviour of costs in relation to output depends on whether the firm is a single- or multi-plant enterprise and on whether more than one product is produced by the same inputs. To begin with we follow the traditional approach to costs which assumes single-plant and single-product operations but subsequently we examine multi-plant and multi-product firm cost curves.

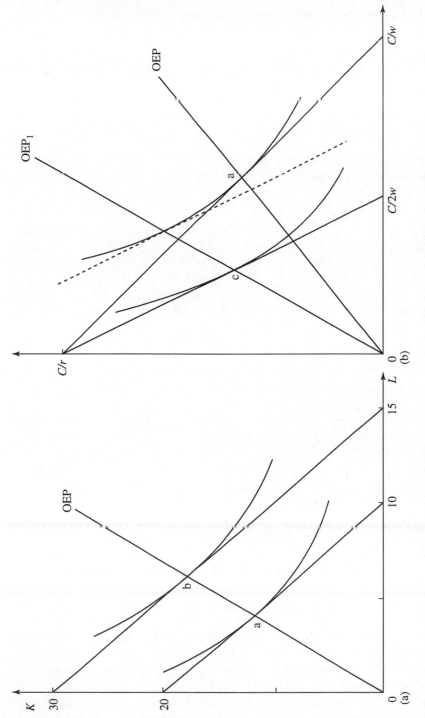

Figure 6.4 (a) An optimum expansion path, OEP; (b) the impact of an increase in w on the firm's optimum expansion path

The cost curves of a single-plant single-product firm

When examining a firm's cost curves the following definitions are commonly used. Total cost refers to the sum of all costs involved in the production of a given output Q. The total cost (TC) curve specifies the relationship between total cost and total output: $TC = f(Q)$. The average cost (AC), or total average cost, is the cost per unit of production, $AC = TC/Q$. The marginal cost (MC) is the rate of change of total cost. Thus $MC = dTC/dQ$ or for small changes $df(Q)/dQ$. Often we think of dQ as a unit change in output so that marginal cost shows the change in total cost when output changes by one unit.

If there are costs which do not vary with output (mortgage payments on the plant for example), then the sum of all such costs is called the total fixed cost TFC to distinguish it from the cost that varies with output (cost of raw materials or some kind of labour cost, for example) known as the total variable cost TVC. It follows that $TC = TFC + TVC$. To every total cost there corresponds an average cost so that we define the per unit of production fixed cost as $AFC = FC/Q$ and the per unit variable cost as average variable cost $AVC = AC/Q$. Since marginal cost refers to the rate of change of total cost it is not related to fixed costs. It is derived from the variable cost of production.

The long-run cost curves

Costs depend both on the quantities of the various inputs used and on their prices. But when input prices are constant the behaviour of costs is solely determined by the quantities of inputs used to produce any given output level. As indicated above the way in which input requirements vary as output expands in the long run will depend on the returns to scale. Thus, if we assume that input prices remain unchanged as the firm adjusts its scale of operations, then the behaviour of the long-run total production cost (LRTC) will also depend on the returns to scale. If output, for example, is doubled and returns to scale are constant then input requirements will double and, given unchanged prices, the total cost of production will double leaving the average cost the same. If there are *increasing returns to scale* then doubling output requires a less than doubling of inputs and therefore the LRTC less than doubles implying a falling average cost. With *decreasing returns to scale* input requirements increase faster than output so that doubling of output more than doubles the LRTC bringing about an increase in the per unit cost of production. In brief, the average cost of production will be constant, increasing or decreasing depending on whether the technology exhibits constant, decreasing or increasing returns to scale, respectively.

To illustrate, consider the following fictitious example. A firm's price of capital is $r = £100$ a unit per time period and price of labour is $w = £50$

Table 6.2 The impact of returns to scale on costs

	Q = 10	Q = 20	Q = 30
Constant returns to scale			
Labour (L)	10	20	30
Capital (K)	5	10	15
LRTC	1,000	2,000	3,000
LRAC = TC/Q	100	100	100
LRMC	–	100	100
Decreasing returns to scale			
Labour (L)	10	22	36
Capital (K)	5	11	18
LRTC	1,000	2,200	3,600
LRAC	100	110	120
LRMC		120	140
Increasing returns to scale			
Labour (L)	10	18	24
Capital (K)	5	9	12
LRTC	1,000	1,800	2,400
LRAC	100	90	80
LRMC		80	60

a unit per time period. The efficient input requirements for 10 units of output are 10 units of labour and 5 units of capital. Thus, the total cost of producing 10 units of the product (Q = 10) is TC = 50(10) + 100(5) = £1,000 and AC = TC/Q = 1,000/10 = £100. Suppose now that the firm wishes to increase output and is considering two alternatives, namely 20 or 30 units of output Q. Table 6.2 gives the input requirements of each level of output and the corresponding production costs on the assumption that returns to scale are constant (CRS), decreasing (DRS) or increasing (IRS).

The data in Table 6.2 has been used to draw the total cost curve under constant, increasing and decreasing returns to scale shown in Figure 6.5(a). The corresponding average and marginal costs are given in Figure 6.5(b). Clearly total cost increases with output but its rate of increase varies according to whether returns to scale are constant or not. When CRS are present total cost increases at the same rate as output so that the average cost of production is constant and equal to the marginal cost. With increasing returns to scale total cost increases but at a slower rate than that at which output expands so that the average cost declines. Finally, when returns to scale are decreasing the total cost rises faster than output so that both the average and the marginal costs are rising.

In the above illustrations it was assumed that returns to scale of the same kind prevailed as output changed from 10 units to 20 units to 30 units. It cannot, however, be inferred from this that returns to scale must be of the same kind over the whole range of production. On the contrary, it is quite

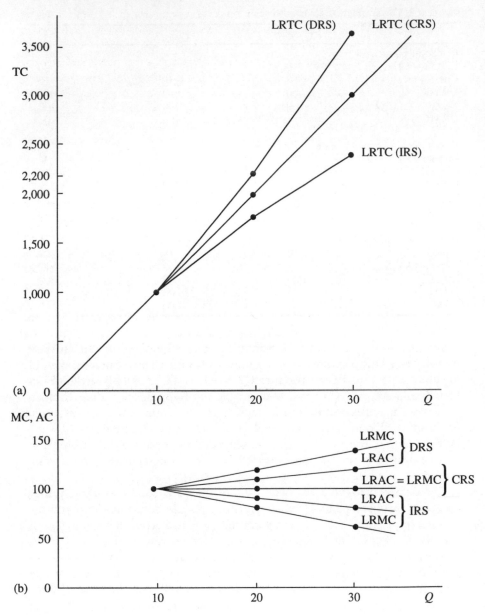

Figure 6.5 A firm's cost curves in the long run
Source: Table 6.2

possible that the nature of the input–output relationship is different at different levels of output. Indeed, traditional economic theory assumes that returns to scale are increasing at small scales of operation (as the size of a small plant increases) but decreasing at relatively large scales of operation (as the scale of large plants becomes even larger). This is sometimes thought to occur because at small plant size technical economies due mainly to indivisibilities may predominate whereas at large scale managerial diseconomies due to the proliferation of hierarchical levels, information distortions and control loss would outweigh any technical economies. According to this view, assuming unchanged input prices and production technology, the long-run total cost curve will increase initially at a diminishing rate and eventually at an increasing rate. This is shown in Figure 6.6(a) while the corresponding average and marginal cost curves are given in Figure 6.6(b).

At production levels smaller than Q_1 equiproportional increases in all inputs (including plant size) yield increasing returns to scale, so that as Q increases total cost increases at a diminishing rate which means that the marginal cost decreases and so does the average cost. Beyond output Q_1, however, increasing returns to scale become progressively insignificant so that the marginal additions to total cost start to increase. Marginal cost is therefore rising but since it is still lower than the average cost the latter continues to fall up to output level Q_2. At Q_2 decreasing returns to scale set in and both marginal and average costs start to rise.

Inspection of the figures shows that when production is subject to economies of scale (output up to Q_2) the marginal cost is lower than the average cost and the opposite is true when there are diseconomies of scale. In fact, the relationship between average and marginal cost indicates whether economies or diseconomies of scale prevail. In particular, the firm experiences economies of scale, constant costs or diseconomies of scale as the ratio S of the average to marginal cost is[3] more than, equal to, or less than one

$$S = \frac{AC}{MC} \gtreqless 1.$$

The assumption that $S > 1$ at small levels of output falls to unity as output expands and becomes less than unity at higher volumes of output is the kind of analysis that has produced the well-known hypothesis of traditional economic theory, namely that the long run average cost curve is U-shaped.

The short-run cost curves

If the firm desires to change output in the short run, say in response to a temporary change in demand or as an interim response to a permanent change, then because at least one input will be unadjustable the firm will be unable to move along its optimal expansion path. The way that costs behave in this case depends on (a) the relationship between output and the variable input, (b) the price of the variable input and (c) the cost of the fixed input.

According to the law of diminishing marginal productivity discussed above, beyond a certain level of output additions to a variable input will

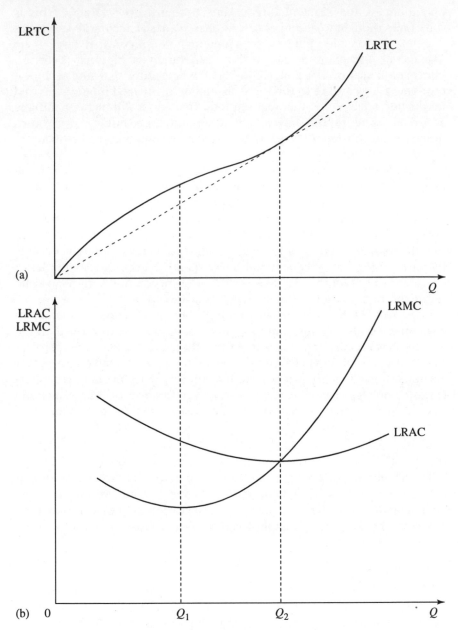

Figure 6.6 Traditional long-run cost curves

increase output by a smaller proportion. This means that there will be diminishing returns to the variable factor. It is possible, however, that returns to a variable input can be increasing. Consider for example the relationship between labour (L) and output (Q) assuming that the plant

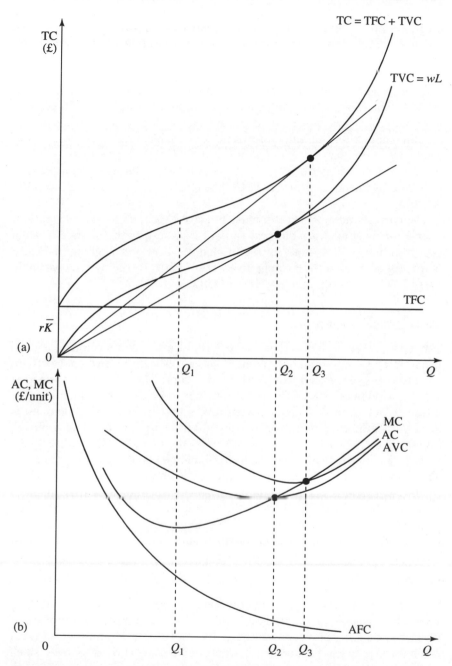

Figure 6.7 Short-run average and marginal cost curves of a single-product single-plant firm

size K (capital) is fixed. If the quantity L used is small compared with the plant size, the plant is underutilised so that an expansion in L by, say, 20 per cent may increase output by more than 20 per cent. Thus, at small levels of production the relationship between output and the variable factor L will be characterised by increasing returns to the variable input but beyond a certain level of output, diminishing returns set in.

If it is assumed that there is only one variable factor (L) and that its price w is given and does not vary with the quantity L then the total variable cost (TVC = wL) will vary with output as indicated in Figure 6.7. It initially increases slower than output due to increasing returns to the variable input but eventually returns to the variable input decrease, so that doubling L less than doubles output and TVC rises faster than Q. Since the fixed factor does not vary with output its cost rK is constant and is indicated by the horizontal line TFC. The total short-run cost is TC = TVC + TFC.

The corresponding short-run marginal cost (MC), defined as the rate of change of the total variable cost (= $\triangle$TVC/$\triangle Q$) or the change in total cost resulting from a small short-run change in output, is given in Figure 6.7(b) together with the average fixed cost (TFC/Q), the average variable cost (TVC/Q) and the average cost (TC/Q).

Costs of multi-plant firms

The cost curves derived above were based on the assumption that each firm operates one production plant. It was also shown that whenever there are resources specialised to a plant the AC curve of that plant is U-shaped and the optimum size of the plant and hence of the single-plant firm is uniquely determined. This analysis implies that if the market demand is large it is technically necessary for several firms to operate. The premise, however, that each firm can operate only one plant is wildly unrealistic, since large firms typically operate more than one plant at any point in time. Thus, in 1972 the one hundred largest UK firms operated on average seventy-two plants each. Similarly, US evidence indicates that in more than half the US industry sectors the average leading firm has more than four plants (Hay and Morris 1991: 38). Once we allow for the existence of multi-plant firms we can no longer assume that a firm's average cost curve is U-shaped. Thus, a firm can expand its size by operating several plants efficiently which means that there are no natural impediments to monopoly.

There are several reasons why firms select to operate a number of plants. Geographically dispersed markets combined with significant transportation costs may be a significant contributing factor. In general, multi-plant firms often evolve when production is more efficiently carried out in small specialised units of production and common ownership of a number of small production units economises on organisational and other transaction costs.

To simplify the analysis of the cost curves of the multi-plant firm we shall maintain the assumption that input prices are given and independent of the quantities of inputs that the firm may demand.

In the short run, the existence of specialised resources implies that each plant operates with some fixed cost which the multi-plant firm bears whether a particular plant is utilised or not. Not surprisingly, therefore, fixed costs have no bearing on the decision as to whether all or only some of the plants should be operated in the short run. That is, for a given level of total output, it would be efficient for the firm to produce no output in one of its plants, even in the short run, provided that increased production in the remaining plants brings about sufficient cost savings. The implication is that at any point in time the firm must decide not only on the total level of output that it wishes to produce but on how much to produce in each plant and whether production in some plants must cease.

To consider these decisions it would be helpful to begin by examining how any level of output can be optimally allocated among a number of plants. If the given number of plants happens to be the same as the number of plants in existence then this allocation will also determine the firm's short-run marginal cost curve. The assumption that all existing plants are operated can be justified either on the grounds that demand is sufficiently large to make this efficient or because of technical reasons which may impede temporary closures. If, for example, the demand for coal is temporarily low closing down a pit and re-allocating its output to other pits may be inefficient since for technological reasons closed pits cannot be re-opened in the future when demand expands.

The marginal cost of a multi-plant firm

Figure 6.8 shows a firm with two plants both of which must be operated. If the firm wishes to produce 35 units of output in the cheapest possible way the question then arises as to how much it should produce in each plant.[4] Recalling that the marginal cost indicates the increase in total cost brought about by a unit increase in output, it should be intuitively obvious that the allocation of output should be such that the marginal cost of producing output in plant 1 is equal to the marginal cost of producing output in plant 2. In other words the allocation must be such as to ensure that $MC_1 = MC_2$. To prove that this rule (known as the equimarginal rule) must hold for an optimum allocation of output between the two plants, suppose that it does not hold so that $MC_1 > MC_2$. This means that the addition to total cost brought about by the last unit of Q produced in plant 1 was larger than the addition brought about by the last unit produced in plant 2. Thus, by producing 1 unit less in plant 1 and 1 unit more in plant 2 the firm can reduce its total cost while maintaining output at the same level. Clearly, an output reallocation from the high marginal cost plant to the low marginal cost plant will be beneficial and should continue till the marginal cost equality between the two plants is restored.

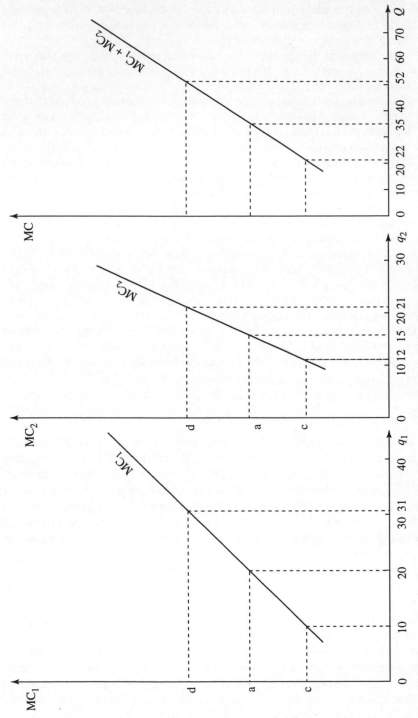

Figure 6.8 The marginal cost of a two-plant firm, assuming that both plants must be operated

In terms of Figure 6.8 this means that to produce a total of 35 tons plant 1 should produce 20 tons and plant 2 should produce 15 tons, in which case the marginal cost is the same in each plant and equal to a. Alternatively, at a marginal cost of £c the firm can produce 22 units of output when the allocation among plants is optimal (plant 1 produces 10 units and plant 2 produces 12 units). At marginal cost d, a total output of 52 units can be produced optimally and so on. Clearly to derive a multi-plant firm's marginal cost curve assuming that all plants must be operated and that the allocation of production among plants is such as to minimise the cost of production, we simply add up horizontally all the marginal cost curves. Optimality does not, however, require that all the existing plants must be operated. The opposite may in fact be true, even in the short run.

The average cost of a multi-plant firm

In addition to deciding on their desired level of overall output, multi-plant firms have to decide how many plants to operate and how to allocate a given volume of production among the plants which will be operated in each time period. Although the maximum number that can be operated is fixed in the short run, firms usually have the option of selecting how many of the existing plants they wish to operate. And, since by definition fixed costs cannot be avoided whether a plant operates or not, fixed costs have no bearing on either the decision of how many plants the firm will optimally operate or on the allocation of output among plants. Such decisions depend entirely on variable costs. To illustrate this and to indicate how a multi-plant firm's short-run cost curves can be derived a fictitious example will be used.

Assume that a firm has three identical plants the cost curves of which vary with output as indicated in Table 6.3. The firm can operate one, two or all three plants and it is assumed that it would select the number that minimises the cost of production. To derive the average cost curve we must, therefore, find out what allocation among plants minimises the total cost of each level of output. If at small output levels there are increasing returns to scale so that costs fall as output expands then clearly production in one or a small number of plants will minimise costs.

Suppose, for example, that the firm of Table 6.3 wishes to produce 3 units of output per time period. By operating only one plant the average variable cost is £52.8 while if one unit were to be produced in each plant the average variable cost would be £57.2. In either case the fixed cost would be £300 so that total cost is minimised if only one plant operates. In fact, inspection of Table 6.3 shows that for output of up to 10 units the total cost is minimised by operating only one plant. The cost of producing 10 units remains the same at £80 whether production is concentrated in one plant or is shared equally between two plants (the average variable cost of producing 5 units in each plant is £50 and the average fixed cost is

Table 6.3 The cost curves of a three-plant firm (for each plant TC = $100 + 60Q - 3Q^2 + 0.2Q^3$)

Output Q	One plant operating				Two plants operating			Three plants operating			Minimum	Minimum	MC
	AFC	TVC	AVC	AC_1	TVC	AVC	AC_2	TVC	AVC	AC_3	AC	TC	MC
1	2	3	4	5	6	7	8	9	10	11	12	13	14
0													
1	300.00	57.20	57.20	357.20	58.55	58.55	358.55	59.02	59.02	359.02	357.20	357.20	
2	150.00	109.60	54.80	204.80	114.40	57.20	207.20	116.18	58.09	208.09	204.80	409.60	52.40
3	100.00	158.40	52.80	152.80	167.85	55.95	155.95	171.60	57.20	157.20	152.80	458.40	48.80
4	75.00	204.80	51.20	126.20	219.20	54.80	129.80	225.42	56.36	131.36	126.20	504.80	46.40
5	60.00	250.00	50.00	110.00	268.75	53.75	113.75	277.78	55.56	115.56	110.00	550.00	45.20
6	50.00	295.20	49.20	99.20	316.80	52.80	102.80	328.80	54.80	104.80	99.20	595.20	45.20
7	42.86	341.60	48.80	91.66	363.65	51.95	94.81	378.62	54.09	96.95	91.66	641.60	46.40
8	37.50	390.40	48.80	86.30	409.60	51.20	88.70	427.38	53.42	90.92	86.30	690.40	48.80
9	33.33	442.80	49.20	82.53	454.95	50.55	83.88	475.20	52.80	86.13	82.53	742.80	52.40
10	30.00	500.00	50.00	80.00	500.00	50.00	80.00	522.22	52.22	82.22	80.00	800.00	57.20
11	27.27	563.20	51.20	78.47	545.05	49.55	76.82	568.58	51.69	78.96	76.82	845.05	45.05
12	25.00	633.60	52.80	77.80	590.40	49.20	74.20	614.40	51.20	76.20	74.20	890.40	45.35
13	23.08	712.40	54.80	77.88	636.35	48.95	72.03	659.82	50.76	73.83	72.03	936.35	45.95
14	21.43	800.80	57.20	78.63	683.20	48.80	70.23	704.98	50.36	71.78	70.23	983.20	46.85
15	20.00	900.00	60.00	80.00	731.25	48.75	68.75	750.00	50.00	70.00	68.75	1,031.25	48.05
16	18.75	1,011.20	63.20	81.95	780.80	48.80	67.55	795.02	49.69	68.44	67.55	1,080.80	49.55
17	17.65	1,135.60	66.80	84.45	832.15	48.95	66.60	840.18	49.42	67.07	66.60	1,132.15	51.35
18	16.67	1,274.40	70.80	87.47	885.60	49.20	65.87	885.60	49.20	65.87	65.87	1,185.60	53.45

19	15.79	1,428.80	75.20	90.99	941.45	49.55	65.34	931.42	49.02	64.81	64.81	1,231.42	45.82	19
20	15.00	1,600.00	80.00	95.00	1,000.00	50.00	65.00	977.78	48.89	63.89	63.89	1,277.78	46.36	20
21	14.29	1,789.20	85.20	99.49	1,061.55	50.55	64.84	1,024.80	48.80	63.09	63.09	1,324.80	47.02	21
22	13.64	1,997.60	90.80	104.44	1,126.40	51.20	64.84	1,072.62	48.76	62.39	62.39	1,372.62	47.82	22
23	13.04	2,226.40	96.80	109.84	1,194.85	51.95	64.99	1,121.38	48.76	61.80	61.80	1,421.38	48.76	23
24	12.50	2,476.80	103.20	115.70	1,267.20	52.80	65.30	1,171.20	48.80	61.30	61.30	1,471.20	49.82	24
25	12.00	2,750.00	110.00	122.00	1,343.75	53.75	65.75	1,222.22	48.89	60.89	60.89	1,522.22	51.02	25
26	11.54	3,047.20	117.20	128.74	1,424.80	54.80	66.34	1,274.58	49.02	60.56	60.56	1,574.58	52.36	26
27	11.11	3,369.60	124.80	135.91	1,510.65	55.95	67.06	1,328.40	49.20	60.31	60.31	1,528.40	53.82	27
28	10.71	3,718.40	132.80	143.51	1,601.60	57.20	67.91	1,383.82	49.42	60.14	60.14	1,583.82	55.42	28
29	10.34	4,094.80	141.20	151.54	1,697.95	58.55	68.89	1,440.98	49.69	60.03	60.03	1,740.98	57.16	29
30	10.00	4,500.00	150.00	160.00	1,800.00	60.00	70.00	1,500.00	50.00	60.00	60.00	1,300.00	59.02	30
31	9.68	4,935.20	159.20	168.88	1,908.05	61.55	71.23	1,561.02	50.36	60.03	60.03	1,361.02	61.02	31
32	9.38	5,401.60	168.80	178.18	2,022.40	63.20	72.58	1,624.18	50.76	60.13	60.13	1,324.18	63.16	32
33	9.09	5,900.40	178.80	187.89	2,143.35	64.95	74.04	1,689.60	51.20	60.29	60.29	1,389.60	65.42	33
34	8.82	6,432.80	189.20	198.02	2,271.20	66.80	75.62	1,757.42	51.69	60.51	60.51	2,357.42	67.82	34
35	8.57	7,000.00	200.00	208.57	2,406.25	68.75	77.32	1,827.78	52.22	60.79	60.79	2,127.78	70.36	35
36	8.33	7,603.20	211.20	219.53	2,548.80	70.80	79.13	1,900.80	52.80	61.13	61.13	2,200.80	73.02	36
37	8.11	8,243.60	222.80	230.91	2,699.15	72.95	81.06	1,976.62	53.42	61.53	61.53	2,276.62	75.82	37
38	7.89	8,922.40	234.80	242.69	2,857.60	75.20	83.09	2,055.38	54.09	61.98	61.98	2,355.38	78.76	38
39	7.69	9,640.80	247.20	254.89	3,024.45	77.55	85.24	2,137.20	54.80	62.49	62.49	2,437.20	81.82	39
40	7.50	10,400.00	260.00	267.50	3,200.00	80.00	87.50	2,222.22	55.56	63.06	63.06	2,522.22	85.02	40

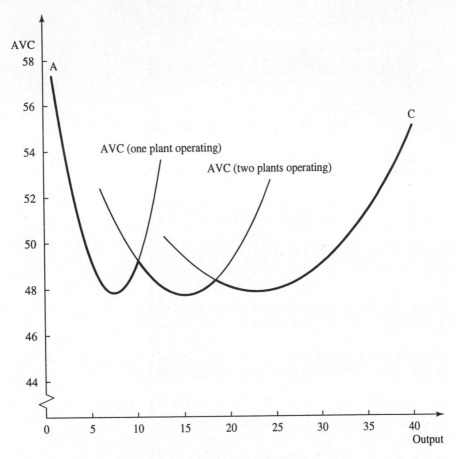

Figure 6.9 The average variable cost of a three-plant firm

£30). For outputs between 10 and 18 units cost is minimised if production is shared equally between any two of the three plants as a comparison of columns 5 (which gives the average cost when all production is in one plant) and 8 (indicating the average cost when output is shared equally between two plants) confirms. For output larger than 18 units optimality requires that all (three) plants operate, each producing one-third of the total output (see column 11). The optimum plant size (or MES) is 10 units of Q so that if the firm wished to produce 30 units the total cost would be minimised if each plant produced 10 units.

The relationship between output and the corresponding minimum average variable cost (which can be achieved when production is optimally allocated among plants) is indicated in Figure 6.9 by curve AC (the thick outline of the lower part of the graph which is reproduced, together with

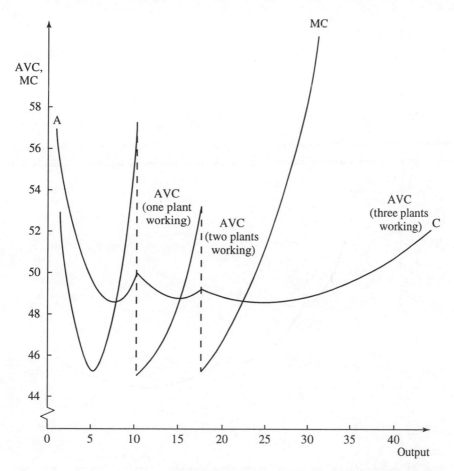

Figure 6.10 The average variable cost and the marginal cost of a three-plant firm

its marginal cost, in Figure 6.10). Now, by adding to the minimum average variable cost the average fixed cost of each output level the minimum average total cost has been derived. This is shown in column 12 of Table 6.3 and has been drawn in Figure 6.11. Clearly the average variable cost curve of a multi-plant firm is not U-shaped. On the traditional assumptions of initially increasing and eventually decreasing returns to scale in each plant the firm's average variable cost curve will be shaped as indicated by curve AC which is reproduced in Figure 6.10. Inspection of this figure shows that the average variable cost curve will be approaching a straight line as the number of identical (equally efficient) plants a firm owns becomes very large.

The marginal cost corresponding to curve AC is the discontinuous line indicated. Each section of the marginal cost curve can be derived on the

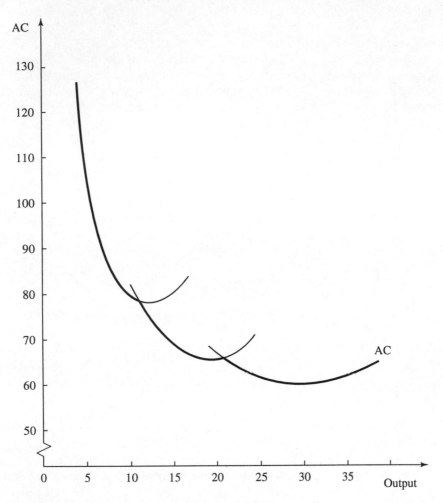

Figure 6.11 Short-run cost curve of a three-plant firm

assumption that one, two or three plants are used in production. The relevant cost figures are given in column 14 of Table 6.3. It should be noted that the shape of the total average cost curve approximates that of a U-shaped curve because of the influence of the fixed cost.

The long-run cost curves of a multi-plant firm

The cost of production of the three–plant firm of our example is minimised when production is 30 units so that all three plants are operated at the minimum efficient scale of operation (MES). At output levels lower than 30 units the per unit costs increase because the average fixed costs increase as output falls. But if a lower production is expected to be maintained in the long run then it may be possible to economise on costs by closing down one or more plants. If long-term production is, say, 20 units then one plant can be closed down with a saving of £100 on fixed cost and if output were to be reduced permanently to around 10 units then two plants should be closed down saving £200 on fixed cost. The opposite is also true. When a firm's size (sales volume) is large compared with the MES, production at minimum long-run average cost can be maintained constant (£80 in our example) by operating an appropriately larger number of plants.

An implicit assumption in the derivation of the long-run average cost of a multi-plant firm is that the costs of each plant do not vary as the firm adjusts the number of plants it operates. In particular, it is assumed that common ownership of a number of plants is associated neither with transaction costs savings nor with increased managerial bounded rationality or moral hazard. The existence of transaction cost savings can be thought of as an economy of scale external to the plant, although internal to the firm. Thus, if bringing several plants under common ownership brings in an economy of scale the long-run average cost of the three-plant firm will be lower than that of the two-plant firm and so on. The opposite is true if increasing the number of plants is associated with diseconomies internal to the firm but external to the plant. The minimum per unit of production cost of a four–plant firm would in this case be higher than that of a three–plant firm and so on.

ECONOMIES OF SCALE AND SCOPE IN MULTI-PRODUCT FIRMS

The analysis so far has focused on single-product firms which limits its scope since modern enterprises typically produce a range of related or unrelated products. The reasons for the emergence of multi-product firms vary but, as Chapter 10 shows, they can be attributed to the pursuit of efficiency or market power or both. Whatever its rationale multi-product production has an impact on production efficiency. It is therefore important that in analysing a firm's costs reference must be made to the multi-product nature of firms and the influence that the heterogeneity of output may have on costs. In other words, it is important to examine whether total costs are sensitive not just to the scale of production but to the composition of output as well. Cost changes brought about by alterations in the composition of output while the size (scale) of the firm is constant are described by the 'returns of scope'. Similarly to the returns to scale, returns of scope can be positive or negative.

While economies of scale or scope may co-exist it is important to distinguish cost changes associated with the output mix from cost changes associated with the size of the firm. It would be of some significance, for example, for management to know that total cost may be reduced by altering the output mix (economies of scope) rather than by expanding all production lines proportionately (economies of scale).

Economies of scale in multi-product firms

Some of the cost definitions introduced at the beginning of this chapter are inappropriate or meaningless in the context of a multi-product firm while others can be easily extended to cover multi-product operations. There is, for example, no meaningful definition of a multi-product firm's average cost curve because there is no uniquely correct way of aggregating the output of a number of diverse products. For how can we aggregate the output of a firm producing, say, ladies shoes, handbags and belts and tights? The marginal cost of each product, on the other hand, is both meaningful and useful. As in the case of a single-product firm, the marginal cost of a multi-product firm is defined as the rate of change of the total cost when the output of one product changes while the output of all other products remains constant. Thus, for a two-product firm if the total cost of producing products X and Y is denoted by $C(X,Y)$, the marginal cost of product X shows the additions to $C(X,Y)$ as X changes by a small amount while Y is kept constant. Formally,

$$MC_x = \frac{dC(X,Y)}{dX} .$$

Economies of scale is another cost concept that can be extended to the case of multi-product firms. To do so, however, we need to specify how scale (size) changes occur since a multi-plant firm can expand its size by an equiproportional increase in all outputs, in which case the output composition is maintained constant, or by adopting different growth rates for different products thus changing the composition of its output. By observing the behaviour of costs in each case we can define two different concepts of multi-product economies of scale; ray economies of scale or product specific economies of scale.

When the size of the firm increases but the output mix remains the same, the impact on the firm's total output of an equiproportional change in the quantity of all inputs is described by the term *ray returns to scale*. Ray returns to scale can be constant, increasing or decreasing. The existence of increasing ray returns to scale implies a less than proportionate increase in costs as output expands so that there exist *ray economies of scale*.

When changes in the size of the firm involve changes in the output mix then the behaviour of costs depends on product specific requirements and changes. Thus, economies brought about by an expansion in the output of one product while the output of all other products is constant are described by the term *product specific economies*.

This section examines both ray and product specific economies assuming for simplicity a two-product firm, although the analysis can be extended to

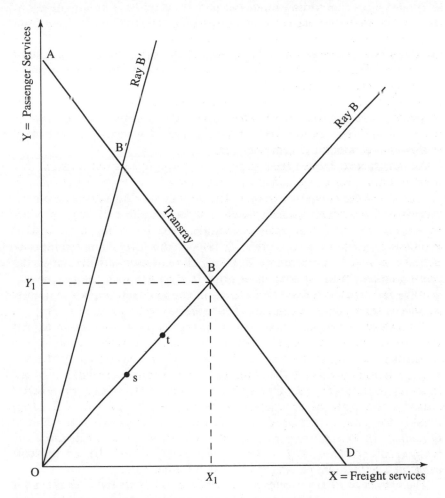

Figure 6.12 The output composition of a two-product firm

firms producing any number of products. Following Bailey and Friedlaender (1982) we can use the example of a railway firm which is providing passenger and freight transport services on an uncongested rail track.

Ray economies of scale

Ray scale economies or diseconomies indicate how total cost behaves as the scale of the firm expands but the output composition remains constant. In Figure 6.12 a proportional increase in the output of both X and Y is shown by a movement along the ray OB. Since OB is a straight line through the origin it indicates that the output composition remains constant as the scale of operation expands. We can then think of the firm as producing a composite output the unit of which is a bundle of goods (two in our example) produced in a given proportion. Thus, moving from point s to point t on ray OB indicates that the bundle of goods has increased but its composition has remained the same. In the example of the railway firm suppose that the number of railcars used for passenger services is twice the number used for freight. A composite unit can then be thought of as consisting of two passenger cars and one freight car. Assuming that the track is in place before any transport service can be provided, multiples of this unit can be thought of as referring to changes in the scale at which the firm operates.

As already noted when the composition of output remains constant, ray scale returns refer to the effect on total cost of a change in the scale of production of the composite output. The definition of ray scale economies, therefore, is a straightforward extension of the definition of single-product economies of scale. Ray scale economies exist when the total cost of production increases at a decreasing rate as the level of the composite output expands. If, for example, doubling all outputs less than doubles the firm's total cost then ray economies exist. In the railways example, the fact that the rail track is a fixed factor even in the long run implies that costs decline as traffic density expands. There are ray economies of scale.

The extent of ray economies can be quantified in a way similar to that used to measure the single-product economies of scale. That is, ray economies can be measured by the ratio of an appropriately defined average and marginal cost. The average cost of a composite unit is referred to as *ray average cost* (RAC) and is defined as $RAC = C(tQ)/t$, where t indicates the scale of production of the composite unit Q and $C(tQ)$ denotes the total cost of producing tQ. In our railways example a unit of Q consists of two passenger cars and one freight car and t denotes any multiple of Q. Thus, if $t = 1,000$ then $C(tQ)$ would denote the cost associated with 2,000 passenger and 1,000 freight cars.

The existence of ray economies to scale means that RAC declines for movements along a ray and that the corresponding marginal cost is lower than the RAC of output. In the railways example, provided that uncongested trackage exists, doubling the number of passenger and freight cars less than doubles total cost bringing about a reduction in RAC. This implies that, just as single-product economies of scale can be measured by the ratio of the average to the marginal cost of production, so the degree of ray economies of scale can be defined as the ratio of RAC to an appropriate marginal cost.

Since the marginal cost of each product can be determined, the marginal cost of the combined output can be defined as the weighted average of the marginal costs of the individual products with the weights being equal to the output of each product. Thus ray returns to scale are defined as

$$S = \frac{RAC}{\Sigma Q_i MC_i}$$

which in the two product case can be written as

$$S = \frac{RAC}{MC_X X + MC_Y Y.}$$

Thus, the degree of ray economies or diseconomies is the ratio of RAC to the weighted marginal cost of all the products produced using as weights the quantity of each product. In other words, the degree of overall scale economies is equal to the ratio of total cost to the revenue that would be generated by pricing each product at its marginal cost. Clearly ray returns to scale may be increasing, constant or decreasing as indicated by S. An $S > 1$ denotes economies of scale, if $S = 1$ there are constant returns to scale while an $S < 1$ indicates diseconomies of scale.

To illustrate, Table 6.4 gives the values of S, i.e. the ray returns to scale, which Drake (1992) has estimated for the UK building societies. Societies are classified by asset size. The value of S is around 1 implying neither increasing nor decreasing returns. Thus, on the whole there are no economies of multi-product expansion. Only building societies with assets in the range of £120–£500 million have experienced some very mild extent of economies of multi-product expansion.

Table 6.4 Economies of scale and scope in UK building societies, 1988

Societies (by asset range)	Estimated S value (ray returns to scale)	Economies of scope (Sc)
£5 billion and above	1.0114	−0.0689
£500 million to £5 billion	0.9873	−0.0920
£120 million to £500 million	1.0420[a]	0.0761
£50 million to £120 million	1.0370	−0.0787
Less than £50 million	1.0424	−0.1034

Source: Drake 1992: Tables 1, 4 and 5
Note: [a] Statistically significant at the 0.05 level.

Product specific economies

Ray returns to scale indicate how costs behave as output expands or contracts while its composition remains the same. When firms change their scale of operation, however, they often do so by altering the composition of output. The production of some products may increase while that of others may be restricted and new products may be added to the existing range. In other words an expansion (or contraction in size) is often accompanied by a change in output mix. Since each ray corresponds to a unique output mix, when expansion involves a change in output mix the firm moves from one ray to another. Thus, in Figure 6.12, the ray describing an output mix consisting of two products produced in the ratio of two to one (ray B) is different to that corresponding to an output of two to three (ray B'), and so on.

Mix changes, such as an expansion involving an increase in the output of one product while all other outputs are constant, relate to a *transray* movement. In terms of Figure 6.12 the effect on total cost of an output expansion along the line Y_1B or X_1B (which implies transray movements) is described by the *product specific returns of scale*. When a given percentage increase in the output of one product increases total cost by a smaller proportion 'product specific economies of scale' are said to exist. To measure the extent of product specific economies we need to identify the average cost of each product. Since, as already indicated, this cannot be uniquely defined in a multi-product context where typically joint costs[5] exist a new cost concept has been utilised: the *average incremental cost* (AIC).

The average incremental cost of a product X is defined as the addition to total cost associated with producing a certain output level of X compared with the size of the total cost when the output of X is zero, divided by X. That is, for a firm producing products X and Y the average incremental cost of X is given by

$$AIC_X = \frac{C(X,Y) - C(0,Y)}{X}.$$

A numerical example may help illustrate this concept. Suppose that a firm produces 10 units of product X and 20 units of product Y, at a total cost of £1,000. Suppose that it is known that if the division producing X were closed down so that the firm ceased to produce product X, the cost of producing the 20 units of Y becomes £800. The average incremental cost of X is then $AIC_X = (1,000 - 800)/10 = £20$.

Having defined the average incremental cost the product specific returns to scale, for any particular product, are given by the ratio S of the average incremental cost and the marginal cost (Panzar and Willig 1977). Thus, for product X,

$$S_X = \frac{AIC_X}{MC_X}.$$

Where S_X will be greater than, equal to or less than unity as there are increasing, constant or decreasing returns to product X.

Drake (1992), who investigated the cost structure of the UK building societies, has estimated that the S_Xs related to mortgage lending and 'other commercial assets' are equal to 0.9906 and 1.2257. But since both were statistically not significantly different than unity he concluded that building society lending and 'other commercial assets' are characterised by constant returns to scale. Their holding of liquid assets, however, was subject to economies of scale ($S_x = 1.8564$) which implied that efficiency would improve by expanding their holdings of liquid assets compared with other assets.

Economies of scope

Since in reality expanding firms often change the scale and the composition of output simultaneously, the full impact of economies of scale in a multi-product setting may incorporate changes in both the scale and the composition of output. Changes in composition may be brought about by the introduction of new products or by changing the output proportions of an existing range of products. In either case to assess the likely effect of changes in the composition of output on costs, the scale of operation must be kept constant. That is, to assess whether diversification reduces costs we must compare the total cost of a diversified firm with the sum of the cost of single-product firms producing the same output level. When the total cost of producing two products under common ownership is lower than the sum of the cost of producing each product separately production is said to exhibit *economies of scope*. Thus, economies of scope for a firm producing two products, X and Y, are defined as

$$C(X,Y) < C(0,Y) + C(X,O).$$

That is, economies of scope imply that joint production is cost efficient. The proportion S_c of total cost saved by producing jointly the two products can be used as a measure of the extent of economies of scope:

$$S_c = \frac{C(0,Y) + C(Y,0) - C(X,Y)}{C(X,Y)}.$$

Thus, $S_c > 0$ denotes the existence of economies of scope and the larger its value the more significant is the extent of economies of scope. A negative Sc quantifies the degree of diseconomies of scope and $S_c = 0$ signifies the absence of economies or diseconomies of scope.

The presence of economies of scope indicates that diversification is efficient since the total cost of the diversified firm is low compared with a group of single-product firms producing the same output. Economies of scope are created by the existence of semi-public resources or other spare resources such as information or know-how which cannot be traded through market transacting. In the railways example providing passenger and freight on the same track is cheaper than providing each on a separate track. Since jointness in production reduces costs, when contractual difficulties make it difficult (expensive) for one firm to own the rail track and to rent out the spare capacity to another firm, the firm owning the track should provide both products.

Unlike the railways, there seems to be no jointness in the production of services provided by the UK building societies, according to the evidence reported in Table 6.4 (all the coefficients indicating economies of scope are not significantly different than zero). On the basis of this evidence it would appear that the diversification strategies which building societies adopted following the 1986 Building Society Act do not seem to be justified in terms of cost efficiency.

To recapitulate, two sources of cost economising resulting from a change in the composition of output have been identified in multi-plant firms: product-specific economies of scale and economies of scope. When both exist a multi-product firm's expansion will be associated with substantial cost economies. In fact it can be shown that, in the two-product firm, the overall degree of scale economies is equal to a weighted average of the degrees of product-specific scale economies pertinent to each product magnified by economies of scope by the factor $1/(1 - S_c)$. Thus, economies of scope and decreasing average incremental cost to each product can account for the existence of economies of scale in a multi-product firm. More interesting perhaps is the observation that strong economies of scope can compensate for constant or decreasing returns to scale to individual products conferring scale economies on the composite output. Thus, expansion by diversification may appear to confer economies of scale when in fact the cost reduction is solely due to the impact of diversification rather than to the size of the firm. The opposite may also be true. Diseconomies of scope can counterbalance any constant or increasing returns to scale conferring scale diseconomies overall.

We must conclude by re-emphasising that the cost curves of the multi-product firm can be sensitive both to the composition and to the scale of output. Economies of scale and scope may co-exist at some scale of output but it is also possible that economies may be the result of strong economies of scope combined with product-specific diseconomies of scale. A full understanding of costs requires, therefore, an explicit treatment of the multi-product nature of the firm.

It is thus not surprising that the multi-product analysis of the cost curves of building societies indicates only mild economies of scale for medium-sized societies while earlier single-product analysis had suggested significant economies of scale for societies with assets over £280 million. Similarly, as indicated in the application at the end of this chapter, Ford's cost disadvantage compared with other major automobile manufacturers, in 1979, was due to the composition of its output rather than to the scale of its operation. Had Ford adopted an output mix similar to that of General Motors it would have enjoyed enhanced efficiency (Friedlaender *et al.* 1982)

A NOTE ON THE EVIDENCE ON COSTS

Much empirical work has attempted to verify the traditional cost hypothesis, namely that a firm's long-run and short-run average cost curves are U-shaped. The majority of studies, however, fail to unequivocally confirm this hypothesis.

Many studies show that, at low output levels, the long-run average cost falls as output expands and reaches a minimum level at which it stabilises. In other words, the long-run average cost curve is L-shaped.

With the exception of a minority of studies which suggest eventually rising costs (at very high levels of output) the evidence is that costs decline as output expands but only at small output levels. The implication is that either economies of scale are exhausted at rather low levels of output beyond which there are constant returns to scale, or that beyond the minimum efficient scale of operation any diseconomies of scale are offset by economies of scale keeping the average cost constant.

Despite the voluminous evidence in its support, the L-shaped cost curve has not been accepted as sufficiently strong evidence to reject the traditional view on the shape of the cost curves. This is because empirical research is fraught with difficulties not least of which is the lack of appropriate data. Researchers in their attempt to overcome these difficulties adopt a variety of statistical methods and techniques of analysis. The resulting studies are therefore exposed both to methodological and to statistical criticisms. For example, studies utilising time series data (attempting to observe how the long-run average cost behaves as the firm expands over time) are often criticised on the grounds that they fail to account properly for the impact of the introduction of new technology or changing prices. Since production methods are likely to improve over time it is suggested that the introduction of more productive techniques may conceal the effect on costs of diseconomies of scale. Inappropriately accounted for price changes may also distort the estimates.[6]

To overcome these problems several studies take a cross-section of firms with different plant sizes at a single point in time and observe how costs change with size. A common criticism of this approach is that it assumes that all firms use the same (up-to-date) technology. In reality this may not be correct since larger firms are more likely to utilize more up-to-date technology. Moreover, it has been suggested that the lack of a rising cost may be attributed to the fact that fears of sharply rising costs may prevent firms from operating beyond optimal capacity. The implication is that diseconomies of scale though present will not be observed, while economies of scale if present will be observed since many firms begin production at a rather small scale and expand over time.

The evidence on short-run cost curves indicates that the average variable cost is constant over the relevant range of production. This is thought to be intentional and is considered as a rational response to the uncertainties surrounding a business. Since the firm is unlikely to know its demand with any degree of certainty, it is suggested that it makes sense for firms to organise production in a way that ensures flexibility. Therefore, firms may adopt flexible techniques capable of producing a range of output at constant variable cost.[7]

A most important criticism of both short-run and long-run studies is that the multi-product nature of firms is not properly accounted for. Although the empirical work on multi-product cost curves is limited, it strongly suggests that seriously biased estimates of costs (with significant implication for policy) result when the multi-product nature of the firm is ignored. In the trucking industry for example the evidence (quoted by Bailey and Friedlaender 1982) shows that treating the firm as a single-product producer is very misleading. When physical output such as ton–miles is used in cost estimation and the heterogeneity of the various ton–miles is ignored, large firms appear to be more efficient compared with small firms. But larger firms in this industry tend to offer output with different characteristics to that of smaller firms. They tend, for example, to utilise longer hauls and larger shipment sizes. Thus, when a multi-product approach to cost estimation is adopted so that output with different characteristics, such as shipment size, average load, average haul, traffic, etc., is treated as a different product the lower cost of the larger firms is found to be due to the different nature of the products they offer rather than to their size. Similarly the evidence from the UK building societies quoted above and from the US automobile industry discussed in the application to this chapter indicate that the multi-product approach not only provides more robust empirical results but also provides better insights into the industry.

SUMMARY

Production technology and costs are examined in this chapter. A firm's production technology is described by a set of isoquants (an isoquant map) each indicating all the technologically efficient methods of producing a given output. On the assumption that only technologically efficient methods of production will be adopted by the firm, it is shown that the nature of technology can be such that when all inputs change by a given proportion output may change by the same, a larger or a smaller proportion. That is, 'returns to scale' may be constant, increasing or decreasing.

In the short run output changes can be brought about by using more of one input while keeping other inputs constant. It is shown that as input utilisation increases output may expand faster than the variable input but eventually diminishing returns to a variable factor of production set in.

After considering technology the chapter proceeds to examine economic efficiency and costs. Given the set of technologically efficient methods of production (either in the short run or in the long run) economic efficiency requires that production should be organised in a way that it utilises inputs in such a combination as to ensure that $MP_X/MP_Y = P_X/P_Y$. The input combination that satisfies this condition is then called 'optimal'.

When firms operate efficiently, for any given level of output, the minimum cost of production is indicated by the total cost curve. In the long run the average cost curve is U-shaped because it is assumed that returns to scale are increasing at small levels of output but decreasing at relatively large scales of production. In the short run cost curves are U-shaped because returns to a variable factor of production are eventually diminishing.

The cost curves of multi-plant and multi-product firms are the main focus of this chapter. To begin with the marginal cost of a firm producing a single product in a number of plants is examined and found to be equal to the horizontal summation of the marginal cost curve of all the plants operated. The production decision of a multi-plant firms involves, however, the selection of both the volume of total output to be produced per time period and the number of plants to be operated. Multi-plant analysis indicates that the average variable cost can no longer be assumed to be U-shaped.

In the short run both the marginal cost and the average variable cost of a multi-plant firm are discontinuous lines, the exact shape of each depending, among other things, on the number of plants a firm can operate efficiently. This depends, in turn, on a firm's size in comparison with MES. As the number of plants increases, the average variable cost tends to become constant at the level corresponding to the minimum efficient scale of production. The existence of fixed costs, however, would imply a falling average cost as output expands even in the short run. It is only when output expands so much that plants are operated at outputs beyond MES that short-run costs rise with output.

Since firms produce a variety of products the behaviour of costs in the long run can be influenced by both the size of the firm and its output mix. Economies of scale in the multi-plant context are of two kinds: ray economies (or diseconomies) and product specific economies (or diseconomies).

Ray economies exist when a proportionate increase in all outputs is associated with a less than proportionate increase in total costs. Product specific economies exist when an increase in the scale of production of one product, keeping all other outputs constant, is associated with a less than proportionate increase in total cost.

Economies of scope exist when the total cost of producing two or more products in the same firm is less than the sum of the cost of producing each product by a separate firm. Economies or diseconomies of scope relate, therefore, to changes in the composition of output (i.e. on a firm's diversification strategy). Cost changes resulting from output changes while the scale of operation is constant are described by the combined effect of economies of scope and product specific economies of scale.

Economies of scale and scope may co-exist but it is also possible that economies of scale may cancel out diseconomies of scope or vice versa. The policy implications of distinguishing between the various causes of cost changes are very significant as the application to this chapter indicates.

APPLICATION: ECONOMIES OF SCALE AND SCOPE IN THE AUTOMOBILE INDUSTRY

The organisation of production in the US automobile industry incorporates the co-existence of two concepts: one developed by

General Motors emphasises the production of a variety of cars to satisfy all types of consumers; and the other developed by Ford focuses on economies related to large-scale production of a standard line of car. This means that both economies of scale and scope may influence the cost structure and the competitiveness of the industry as a whole.

A major study of the cost structure of the three largest US car producers, General Motors, Ford and Chrysler, was undertaken by Friedlaender and two of her colleagues at the Massachusetts Institute of Technology in 1982. The aim of the research was to discover whether the unprecedented difficulties facing the industry at that time (large import penetration mainly from Japan and heavy losses, with Chrysler close to bankruptcy) were due to a competitive disadvantage. The analysis of the structure of costs and technology of the three major producers shows costs to be sensitive to both the scale and the composition of output.

Contrary to tradition, the study uses the firm rather than the plant as the unit of analysis which permits the incorporation of any organisation economies as well as any pure technological economies to be related to the scale of operation of a particular plant. The period covered is 1955–79 and long-run cost curves are estimated. Due to data limitations and estimation problems the final estimates relate to three generalised product lines: full size and luxury cars, compact and subcompact cars, and trucks.

Several interesting results have emerged. The marginal cost associated with production at the sample mean level of output was estimated to be $2,262, $4,282 and $5,499 for small cars, large cars and trucks respectively.

The technology is such that there is complementarity between labour and capital and between labour and materials. There is some degree of substitutability, however, between capital and materials. The strength of the relationship between factors of production as measured by the elasticity of substitution E was found to be as follows:

$$E_{LK} = 2.19$$
$$E_{LM} = 0.71$$
$$E_{KM} = -0.54.$$

Furthermore the demand for labour and capital is quite responsive to price changes (elasticities are −1.49 and −9.04 respectively) but not the demand for materials ($e = -0.80$). Productivity estimates show that Ford and to some extent General Motors have enjoyed productivity growth throughout the decade studied while Chrysler has suffered from poor productivity and increasing costs for most of the decade.

Production is subject to economies of scale. Table 6.5 shows that General Motors and to a much larger extent Chrysler enjoy economies

Table 6.5 Economies of scale in the US automobile industry

	General Motors	Ford	Chrysler
At 1979 output	1.10	0.79	7.44
At sample mean	1.23	0.88	1.16

Source: Friedlaender *et al.* 1982: Table 5a

or scale, but this is not true for Ford whose production both at the sample mean level and at its 1979 level exhibits decreasing returns to scale.

The evidence in Table 6.5 suggests that if General Motors and Chrysler were to expand the output of all their products by the same proportion so that they maintained the same output mix, they would find that their total cost would increase less than proportionately bringing a reduction in unit costs. This is not the case for Ford, however, whose costs would rise more than proportionately if it increased output in the same way.

The above evidence on economies of scale appears counter-intuitive since it indicates that the smallest firm (Chrysler) and the largest firm (General Motors), but not the medium-sized one (Ford), are subject to economies of large-scale production. This result would indeed be paradoxical if the output of the three firms had the same composition. Ford's output mix, however, was quite different to that adopted by General Motors which can have significant cost implications in an industry subject to economies of scope. There is indeed evidence of economies of scope in this industry. There are economies of scope from combining the production of large cars with 'small cars and trucks' and diseconomies of scope from combining the production of trucks with the production of 'small and large cars'. This is true for all firms at the sample mean data. It appears, however, that at the 1979 output level, Chrysler has achieved economies of scope throughout its product line but Ford has not (Table 6.6).

Since the industry is subject to economies of scope, what appears as diseconomies of scale is simply indicative of Ford's production policy failure to exploit the existence of economies of scope. To prove this point the researchers calculated the multi-product economies of scale for Ford and Chrysler on the assumption that they would adopt General Motors' output mix. The coefficients of multi-product economies were 1.76 and 4.40 for Ford and Chrysler respectively. What this means is that had Ford adopted, in 1979, the same output mix as General Motors they would have enjoyed substantial efficiency gains without any change to the size of the firm. Similarly, Chrysler would have benefited both by an expansion in output and by a change in the output mix along the lines indicated by General Motors' output composition.

Table 6.6 Economies of scope in the US car industry in 1979 at the 10 per cent and 1 per cent output level

	(Small cars) + (large cars + trucks)		(Large cars) + (small cars + trucks)		(Truck) + (small car and large car)	
	10%	1%	10%	1%	10%	1%
General Motors	−0.10	−0.15	0.53	0.68	−0.31	−0.42
Ford	−0.41	−0.50	0.52	0.77	−0.64	−0.66
Chrysler	0.82	0.82	1.01	1.06	0.79	0.78

Source: Adapted from Friedlaender *et al.* 1982: Table 6a

FURTHER READING

The traditional single-plant single-product firm cost curves are well covered in any intermediate level good microeconomics text. See, for example, Koutsoyiannis (1979) or Varian (1990). A good summary and interpretation of the new theoretical concepts and tools of analysing costs and efficiency in the multi-product enterprise is given by Bailey and Friedlaender ('Market Structure and Multiproduct Industries', *Journal of Economic Literature* XX (1982): 1024–48). The authors also show the significance of the new concepts for the analysis of market structures.

QUESTIONS

1 A new and more capital intensive method of producing cogs has been developed which means that there are now four ways of making cogs that differ only in terms of their input requirements of machine and man hours.
   The exact input requirements per cog of each method are as follows:

Process	Man hours	Machine hours
1	13.5	3.0
2	9.0	4.5
3	6.0	7.5
4	4.5	10.5

   (a) Define an isoquant and construct one for the cog making industry on the assumption that returns to scale are constant.
   (b) Define an isocost line and construct one on the assumption that both machine and man hours cost £7 each. Indicate which production process will be used and how much it will cost to produce 150 cogs.
   (c) Which is the newly developed process and by how much must the price of labour change before it will be used?

2 Cranks plc is typical of firms in the jig-making industry in the sense that it has three different ways of making jigs which differ only in terms of their input requirements of machine and man hours.
   Crank's input requirements per jig are as follows:

   Process A   2 man hours, 8 machine hours,
   Process B   6 man hours, 4 machine hours,
   Process C   12 man hours, 2 machine hours.

(a) Construct an isoquant for Cranks plc specifying the assumptions that you are making.
(b) Construct an isocost line and determine the least cost process for the current rates of £5 per man hour and £10 per machine hour.
(c) As a consequence of the recent steep increase in interest rates Cranks plc expect the machine hour rate to increase to £16. Calculate the effect of such an increase on the firm's costs and input requirements and say what effect you expect this change to have on the jig-making industry and the level of unemployment.

3 Suppose that a firm's costs vary with output in the following way: $TC = Q^2 + 1$. Derive and plot on a diagram the average variable cost, average cost and the marginal cost of this firm.

4 Electra is a small recycling company engaged in the extraction of precious metals (gold, silver, etc.) from electronic scrap which comprises disused or faulty printed circuits, microchips, etc. The firm's weekly output (Q), measured in kilograms, varies directly with labour input (L), measured in hours per week, in the following way:

Q	1	2	3	4	5	6	7	8	9	10
L	110	190	240	320	460	640	880	1,190	1,580	2,060

The production costs comprise the hourly wage of £1, weekly interest charges of £50, weekly land rent of £35 and weekly rates of £15.
  Assuming that there are no other production costs, estimate the following

(a) the level of labour input at which diminishing returns to labour commence;
(b) the amount of labour that the firm would employ in both the short run and the long run if the price obtainable for output (Q) were:
  (i) £180 per kilogram
  (ii) £80 per kilogram.

Finally, explain how diminishing returns to labour and diminishing returns to scale affect a firm's cost curves.
5 Define economies of scope and economies of scale of a multi-product firm and comment on their significance.
6 Suppose that a composite unit of production of a firm producing X and Y consists of twice as many units of Y as X and the total cost of production is given by $TC = 1000 + 20X^2 + X^3 + 10Y$.
  Calculate the following:

(a) the ray average cost (RAC) of production when $t = 1, 10, 20, 30, 40$;
(b) the marginal cost of each product;
(c) S when $t = 10$ and explain whether production is subject to RAC economies or diseconomies of scale;
(d) the product specific economies of scale.

Comment on the significance of your findings for the production policy of this firm.

NOTES

1 Mathematically the problem is to determine L and K so as to minimise $C = Lw + Kr$ subject to $X = f(K,L)$, where X is given. Using the Lagrange method, this is equivalent to minimising the expression $Z = Lw + Kr + \mu[X - F(L,K)]$. Assuming the second-order conditions for a minimum are satisfied the necessary conditions are as follows:

$$\frac{\partial Z}{\partial L} = w - \frac{\partial f}{\partial L} \quad = 0 \quad (1)$$

$$\frac{\partial Z}{\partial K} = r - \frac{\partial f}{\partial K} \quad = 0 \quad (2)$$

$$\frac{\partial Z}{\partial \mu} = X -. F(L,K) = 0 \quad (3)$$

where $\partial Z/\partial L$ and $\partial Z/\partial K$ denote the marginal product of labour (MP_L) and capital (MP_K) respectively. Dividing (1) by (2) gives

$$\frac{w}{r} = \frac{MP_L}{MP_K}.$$
                                                                QED

2 Mathematically the solution is found by max $X = f(L,K)$ subject to the budget constraint $C = Lw + Kr$. To solve, form the Lagrange expression and determine the values of L, K and μ that maximise $Z = f(K,L) + \mu(C - Lw - Kr)$. Assuming the second-order conditions for a maximum are satisfied then set the first-order conditions as

$$\frac{\partial Z}{\partial L} = \frac{\partial f}{\partial L} \quad - \mu w = 0 \qquad (1)$$

$$\frac{\partial Z}{\partial K} = \frac{\partial f}{\partial K} \quad - \mu r = 0 \qquad (2)$$

$$\frac{\partial Z}{\partial \mu} = C - Lw - Kr = 0. \qquad (3)$$

Dividing equation (1) by equation (2) gives

$$\frac{w}{r} = \frac{MP_L}{MP_K}.$$
                                                                QED

3 Formally, total cost is defined as $C = C(Y)$ where Y is aggregate output and other influences on costs are ignored. Average cost is $AC = C(Y)/Y$ and $MC = dC/dY$. Economies or diseconomies are then simply measured as $S = AC/MC = [C(Y)/Y]dC/dY$. S is therefore the reciprocal of the elasticity of cost with respect to output (elasticity is defined in Chapter 7).

4 Mathematically the problem is to minimise
    $TC(Q_1) + TC(Q_2)$ subject to $Q_1 + Q_2 = Q$.

5 As Chapter 11 shows an optimum allocation of joint costs depends on the market demand of each product as well as on business objectives.

6 Recall that the traditional long-run curve assumes both unchanged technology and constant factor prices. New techniques or lower factor prices shift the cost surves downwards.

7 This is so reasonable an assumption that it is suggested that the new theory on costs postulates a saucer shaped average variable cost, with a range of outputs characterised by constant average variable cost corresponding to the desired reserve capacity. See Koutsoyiannis (1979) for an expansion on this point.

7 Consumer behaviour and the market demand

INTRODUCTION

Resource allocation within markets or firms takes place by the interaction of individuals who in pursuit of personal objectives act as entrepreneurs, producers, consumers or providers of labour, capital and other resources. Self-interest motivates all market participants but their behaviour will vary among markets according to the extent of complexity, uncertainty, opportunism and information asymmetries which characterise each market.

Individuals acting as buyers for large corporations may specialise, for example, in purchasing and contracting and may therefore have acquired a deep knowledge of the technical characteristics and contractual features of the products and services in which they are dealing. Such specialisation mitigates against informational asymmetries and tends to improve transacting conditions. On the other hand, since these buyers act on behalf of their firms they may behave in ways intended to serve their own interests to the detriment of the interests of their firms. Intermediate product markets may as a result suffer from the existence of what are known as 'agency costs'. Agency costs are unlikely to exist in final product markets in which individual consumers buy commodities mainly for themselves or their families. Lack of buyer specialisation and technical knowledge, however, can make the cost of information very high in these markets.

In analysing markets, therefore, it is important to distinguish between intermediate markets in which transactions take place between firms and buyers who are likely to be less numerous and better informed and final product markets in which transacting takes place between firms and individual buyers who are likely to be numerous, less well informed and more reliant on market signals (Williamson 1985).

In this chapter we examine the behaviour of final product consumers who come to the market with some preconceived ideas regarding their material needs and the commodities they would like to acquire in order to satisfy them. What needs they may be able to satisfy, however, and to what extent will depend not only on the resources they command and on their preferences but on the availability of commodities as well, which is reflected on prices. The set of commodities demanded by consumers is therefore determined by consumer preferences as constrained by prices and incomes.

The chapter begins with an examination of consumer behaviour under conditions of certainty. The indifference curve approach is utilized in the first section to analyse consumer behaviour. Budgetary constraints are examined in the second section and the concept of consumer equilibrium is introduced in the third section. A consumer's response to price and income changes is subsequently analysed before proceeding to the derivation of a consumer's and the market demand curve. The following section examines some problems that arise in aggregating consumer demands in order to derive the market demand for a product. The concepts of elasticity and cross-price elasticity are introduced next and their applications indicated. Since risk is commonly present in business transacting and risk concepts are utilised in subsequent chapters of this book, consumer behaviour under conditions of risk is analysed in the penultimate section. The final section gives a brief summary of the main points. The end of chapter application has been drawn from the demand for health care in the European Community.

THE INDIFFERENCE CURVE APPROACH TO CONSUMER CHOICE IN THE CASE OF CERTAINTY

Consumer preferences under certainty

The traditional (neoclassical) concept of consumer rationality is based on the assumption of consistency or transitivity of choice. More accurately, a rational consumer is said to be an individual whose preferences satisfy the following set of assumptions.

(i) The axiom of choice

This states that an individual must be able to make choices. More precisely, it is assumed that for every pair of alternatives A and B which could be offered, a consumer is able to say that either A is preferred to B or B is preferred to A or that the two are equally valued so that one can be selected at random. The latter indicates indifference between the two commodities. Using R to denote preference and I to denote indifference this assumption can be stated thus: for any two alternatives A and B, either ARB or BRA or AIB.

(ii) The axiom of greed

This states that a consumer's wellbeing improves as the quantity of goods acquired increases. In other words, the consumer is not fully satiated.

Moreover commodities such as noise, pollution, risk and others which may affect wellbeing adversely are not considered. Furthermore, any benevolent feelings which might induce an individual to demand less so that others might be able to consume more, are ignored.

(iii) The axiom of transitivity or consistency of choice

Consumer choices are said to be consistent or transitive when, for any three alternatives A,B,C, if A is preferred to B and B is preferred to C then A must be preferred to C. Similarly, AIB and BIC implies AIC. If, for example, a consumer states that going to the theatre is preferred to going to the cinema and that going to the cinema is preferred to visiting a bingo hall then his or her choices are consistent if when offered the choice between going to the theatre or visiting the bingo hall the first is chosen in preference to the second.

(iv) Diminishing marginal rate of substitution

The marginal rate at which a consumer is prepared to substitute one commodity for another is diminishing. This is based on the assumption that the willingness of consumers to exchange commodities depends on the quantities already acquired. In particular it is assumed that the more of a commodity A and the less of commodity B a consumer has acquired, the more willing he or she will be to exchange A for B, but this willingness declines as more of A is given up and more of B is acquired. This decline in willingness to substitute A for B implies that larger compensations are required for substitution to proceed. More precisely, the number of units of B that must be acquired to compensate for an extra unit reduction in A increases as more B is substituted for A. That is, the rate of substitution of B for A falls as the quantity of A falls and that of B increases. In Figure 7.1(a), a move from point R to point S on curve II means that the consumer is prepared to give up RT units of A for 1 unit of B while the smaller quantity SW is given up for an extra unit of B (move from S to Z). For a move from R to S the rate of substitution is RT/ST. In the limit this rate, called the marginal rate of substitution of B for A (MRS_{AB}), is measured by the slope of the indifference curve at a given point. The convexity of the indifference curve means that the absolute value of the MRS declines for movements along an indifference curve from left to right.

Definition and shape of indifference curves

When assumptions (i)–(iv) are satisfied consumer preferences can be described by an order preserving function U, called utility. U is an ordinal ranking such that $U(A) > U(B)$ if and only if A is preferred to B. The utility

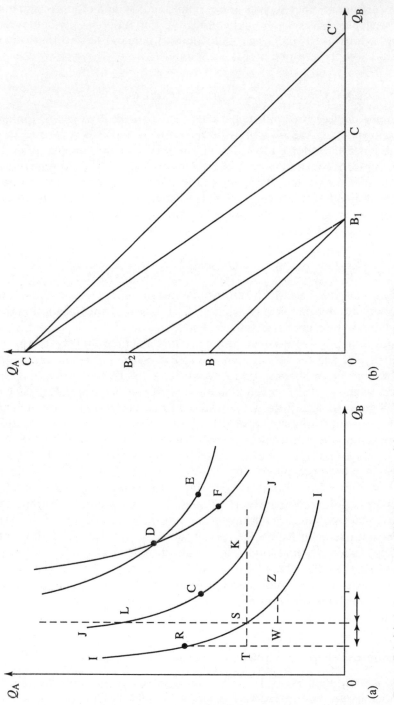

Figure 7.1 (a) A consumer indifference map; (b) a set of consumer budget lines

numbers attached to different commodity bundles indicate the order of preference but not the strength of preference. If, for example, the utility number attached to A is 2 and that attached to B is 1, we can infer that A is preferred to B but we cannot say that the preference for A (or the satisfaction derived from it) is twice as strong as that for B.

Since higher utility numbers indicate more preferred positions, consumer *rationality* (or self-interest seeking or utility maximisation) is nothing more than the assumption that consumers act in such a way as to achieve their most preferred product combination. Consequently, to analyse consumer behaviour we need to examine how this most preferred position is selected given the budgetary constraints which consumers typically face. For simplicity it is assumed that individual choices are restricted to two commodities, A and B. The analysis can be extended to cover a large number of products but the use of calculus is then required. (The mathematical analysis is given in Appendix 7.1).

If preferences obey assumptions (i)–(iv) they can be represented by a set of indifference curves each corresponding to a different level of preference (or satisfaction). *An indifference curve is defined as the locus of points indicating all the combinations of commodities among which a consumer is indifferent.* Thus, in Figure 7.1(a) the consumer is indifferent among the commodity combinations A and B indicated by the coordinates of points R, S and Z or between the commodity bundles indicated by points C and K. Consider, however, points R and C which lie on different curves so that they are not indifferent to each other. At point R the consumer has more of A and less of B compared with point C. Which is preferred? To answer this question we must examine the properties of indifference curves in more detail. The following four properties are characteristic.

Indifference curves have a negative slope

This follows from the assumption (i) that both commodities are desirable. This means that as more of either commodity is acquired without a compensating reduction in the other the consumer becomes better off. Thus any commodity bundle which, compared with R in figure 7.1(a), contains more of A with the same B or more B and no less A or more of both is preferred to R and should lie on an indifference curve other than II. Thus, any point on the broken lines SK or SL or on the LK plane corresponds to a commodity bundle which the consumer prefers to that corresponding to S. In particular, any point to the right of S must be preferred to S unless it is a point like Z which lies below the SK line and contains sufficiently less of A to be indifferent to S.

In brief, for indifference to prevail, more of one good must be combined with less of another which implies that indifference curves must have a negative slope.

Indifference curves are convex to the origin

This means that the absolute value of the slope of an indifference curve diminishes for movements from left to right along the curve. That is, the curve is flatter at point Z than at point S. Convexity follows from the assumption of a diminishing marginal rate of substitution (assumption (iv) above). If the rate at which consumers would be prepared to exchange one good for another were constant, indifference curves would be straight lines with a slope indicating the constant MRS.

Indifference curves do not meet or intersect

This means that only one curve passes from each point on the *xy* plane. This follows from the assumption of transitivity of choice. To see why assume that two curves do intersect at point D in Figure 7.1(a) and compare D with points E and F. Since D and E are on the same indifference curve E is indifferent to D (EID). But D and F must also be indifferent to each other (DIF) since they lie on the same indifference curve. But if EID and DIF then transitivity implies that the condition EIF must also hold. Point E, however, contains more of both commodities compared with point F and should, by the axiom of greed, be preferred to F. But since F cannot be both indifferent and preferred to E a contradiction arises indicating that the transitivity assumption has been violated.

Indifference curves further away from the origin indicate preferred combinations of goods (higher utility)

This follows from the assumption of non-satiety (axiom (ii) above). The reason becomes apparent by considering points R on indifference curve II and L on curve JJ. Since L lies above and to the right of R it contains more of both A and B and must be preferred to R. But any point on the indifference curve JJ is indifferent to L and must, by the transitivity assumption, be preferred to R and to any other point on curve II. Therefore, curve JJ indicates more preferred positions compared with curve II.

Since indifference curves further away from the origin indicate preferred combinations of goods, the assumption of rationality (or maximisation of utility) simply means that consumers acting according to their preferences will attempt to reach a position on the highest indifference curve possible. Two questions, however, remain: (a) which is the highest indifference curve possible and (b) given the highest indifference curve how is a point on it selected? The answer to both these questions is determined simultaneously by the budgetary constraint.

Consumer budget lines

A preference map cannot by itself determine consumer behaviour because it does not contain information about prices and income. The map is a simple ranking of preferences. It may, for example, indicate a preference for fast cars compared with less powerful ones but whether the consumer will select to buy a more or less powerful model will depend not only on the indicated preference for fast cars but on the price of each and the available income. In other words, consumer demand patterns depend on constrained preferences, the constraint been determined by relative prices and income. The constraint under which consumers operate is known as a budget or price line.

A budget line indicates all the combinations of maximum quantities of two or more different commodities which a consumer can buy for a given income and product prices. It follows that, for n products and income M, the budget line is $M = \Sigma P_i Q_i$ where $i = 1, 2, \ldots, n$, P_i represents the price of the ith commodity and Qi the corresponding quantity.

Assuming two commodities, A and B, the consumer budget or price line is

$$M = P_A Q_A + P_B Q_B$$

where M, P_A and P_B are assumed to be known parameters independent of quantities demanded.

By rearranging terms this becomes

$$Q_A = \frac{M}{P_A} - \frac{P_B}{P_A} Q_B.$$

Since prices are constant this is a straight line with slope $- P_B/P_A$ and constant term M/P_A, shown on Figure 7.1(b) as line BB_1. Point B indicates the maximum quantity M/P_A of A and point B_1 the maximum quantity (M/P_B) of B that could be bought if all the income were spent on A or B respectively. The straight line which passes through points B and B_1 gives all the combinations of maximum quantities of A and B which the consumer can buy with the given income and prices.

Clearly changes in relative prices alter the slope of the budget line while changes in money income, with constant prices, shift the line parallel to itself. In particular, higher incomes cause a rightward parallel shift from BB_1 to CC, for example, (Figure 7.1(b)) while lower incomes shift the budget line inwards towards the origin. A change in relative prices make the line steeper or flatter. A reduction in the price of B, for example, with the price of A and income being the same, swings the line outwards from CC to position CC′, while a reduction in the price of A *ceteris paribus* pivots the budget line B_1B to position B_1B_2.

Consumer equilibrium

The position of the budget line determines the set of choices available to a consumer. The complete range of attainable combinations of Q_A and Q_B is enclosed by (and includes) the budget line and the axes. In Figure 7.2(a) this is area OBB. Points such as k, lying to the right of the budget line, indicate commodity combinations which are unattainable. The selection of a point among those available will depend on consumer preferences. Thus, an individual whose indifference curves are illustrated in Figure 7.2(a) wishing to make the most of the available money income will select that combination of commodities which is on the highest indifference curve. This is indicated by point e on indifference curve JJ with corresponding quantities demanded, X_1 and Y_1. The convexity of the indifference curves implies that any other points, such as a or b, indicate a commodity combination which lies on a lower indifference curve and is therefore less preferred than that at e (the consumer is less well off at a or b compared with e). When the purchasing plan is as indicated by point e, the consumer is said to be in equilibrium since the quantities demanded are the best (most preferred) under the given budget constraint so that the consumer is not motivated to revise the purchasing pattern adopted. As indicated in Figure 7.2, equilibrium is achieved when the budget line is tangent to an indifference curve. Thus, at the equilibrium point the slope of the budget line is equal to the slope of the indifference curve. But as already shown the slope of the budget line is the same as the negative of the price ratio $(-P_X/P_X)$ and the slope of the indifference curve represents the MRS of Y for X. Therefore, equilibrium is achieved when the quantities of the two commodities demanded are such as to ensure that the ratio of their prices is equal to the rate at which the consumer is prepared to substitute one commodity for the other. That is, in equilibrium the quantities demanded are such that

$$-\frac{P_X}{P_X} = \text{MRS}_{XX}. \tag{E}$$

It follows that a change in relative prices, if not accompanied by a change in consumer preferences, will render the current purchasing plans suboptimal since the above equilibrium condition will no longer be satisfied. The consumer will then have an incentive to respond to the price change by changing the quantities demanded till equilibrium is restored.

Similarly changes in consumer preferences alter the MRS and violate condition (E) inducing consumers to adapt their optimal demand plans till condition (E) is once more satisfied. Therefore, to predict how the quantities demanded will change in response to changes in prices and/or income we must examine how the equilibrium condition (E) is affected in each case.

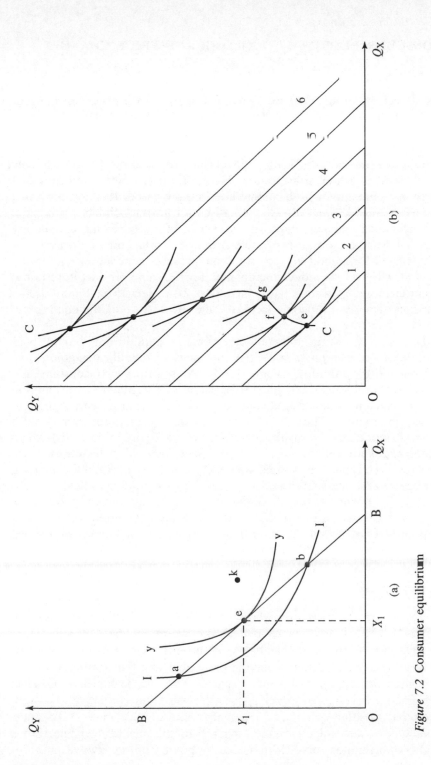

Figure 7.2 Consumer equilibrium

CONSUMER RESPONSE TO INCOME AND PRICE CHANGES

Income changes

As already noted an increase in money income, with prices unchanged, moves the budget line outwards expanding the consumer choice set. Real income thus increases since the consumer can move to a higher indifference curve by revising the purchasing plan adopted. Starting at point e, an increase in income shifts the budget line to position (2) and a new equilibrium is achieved at point f (Figure 7.2(b)). Point f indicates that consumer demand for both commodities has increased. It is not, however, necessary that demand always increases with income. Indeed, it is quite possible that as income increases the demand for a particular commodity may fall. Furthermore, it is possible that an individual may increase his or her demand for a good in response to an increase in income when income is at a low level, but reduce the demand for the same product in response to an increase in income when income is at a high level. Figure 7.2(b) illustrates a series of income increases and the corresponding equilibrium points.

The line CC, which joins all the points of equilibrium, is known as the *income–consumption line*. It is the locus of equilibrium points corresponding to different income levels when prices are constant and consumer preferences are given. The slope of the income–consumption line indicates how the desired consumer purchases change with changes in consumer income. Thus, a positively sloping CC denotes commodities whose demand increases with income (see curve Cg in Figure 7.2(b)). Such commodities are called 'normal' goods. Beef and veal or health care are, according to Table 7.1, normal goods. A negatively inclined CC line, on the other hand, indicates 'inferior' goods, i.e. commodities whose demand declines as income increases. Bread was, in 1987, an inferior good in the UK. As indicated in Figure 7.2(b), it is possible for a good to be normal at some level of income and inferior at another level of income. Moreover, the same good may be normal for some individuals and inferior for others.

Price changes

In Figure 7.3 the consumer whose preference map includes indifference curves I and II and whose budget constraint is line BB will be in equilibrium at point e demanding a_1 of product A and b_1 of product B. Now if the price of B falls while the price of A and the consumer income remain unaltered, the budget line becomes BB' and the consumer is better off. Point e becomes suboptimal since the consumer can move to a more preferred position (climb onto a higher indifference curve). The new equilibrium, determined by the tangency of the new budget line with a higher indifference curve, is indicated by point z and it involves more of

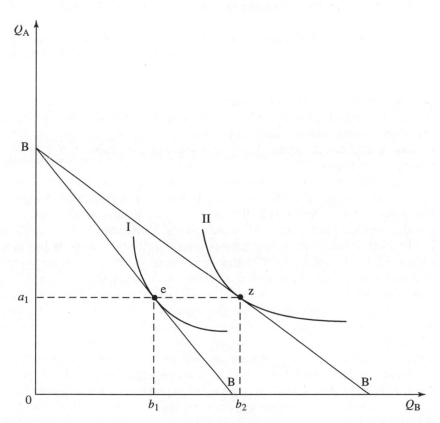

Figure 7.3 A consumer's response to a price reduction

commodity B and the same of A. This is consistent with the common view
that a lower price induces an increase in the quantity demanded. The
question, however, arises as to whether this outcome is always true. Does
a consumer always demand more of the relatively cheaper good and
does the quantity demanded of A (or any other goods) remain the same?
The answer to both questions depends on the shape of the indifference
curves which reflects the preferences of the individual concerned. Inspection of Figure 7.3 indicates that, depending on the curvature of II,
equilibrium could be to the right or to the left of point z, implying that the
quantity of A can either increase or decline. It would, however, be rather
difficult though not inconceivable for the quantity demanded of B to fall
as its price falls. To explain why this is so we must investigate in more
detail the reasons why the quantity of a commodity changes as its price
changes.

The income and substitution effect of a price change

Price changes alter the optimum purchasing pattern for two reasons. First, in the absence of compensating money income changes, a price change causes real income to change. Price reductions enhance real income since more of the cheaper and/or other commodities can be bought with the existing money income while price increases reduce the purchasing power of a consumer. There is thus a real 'income effect' associated with a price change. Second, relative price changes alter the choice set available to a consumer enhancing the scope for substituting the relatively cheaper good for other goods. This is the 'substitution effect' of a price change. The overall 'price effect' is the combined income and substitution effect, illustrated in Figure 7.4.

A reduction in P_B reduces the slope of the budget line in Figure 7.4(a) which swings to position BC. The new budget line is tangent to a higher indifference curve. As a result the consumer equilibrium moves from e to z which implies that the quantity demanded of X increases by $b_2 - b_1$. That is, the overall price effect induces this consumer to buy more of B when its price falls. But how much of this increase is due to the income effect and how much to the substitution effect of the price change?

To be able to answer this question we must separate, even if only conceptually, the two effects. To do so, assume that as price changes money income changes in the opposite direction and by an amount sufficiently large to keep real income constant. Keeping real income constant implies that any change in the optimum purchasing pattern observed must be attributed to the substitution effect of the relative price change. Having thus determined the substitution effect, the income effect can be derived as the difference between the total price effect and the substitution effect.

To proceed, however, we must identify what is the 'appropriate' amount by which money income must change in order to keep real income constant. One possibility is to alter income by an amount sufficient to ensure that the consumer remains on the same level of satisfaction, i.e. on the same indifference curve he or she was prior to the price change. For a price reduction this means that income must be reduced to an extent indicated in Figure 7.4(a) by an inward shift of budget line BC until it is tangent to curve I_1 (to position WW). The income reduction involved is BW and is known as Hicks' compensating variation (HCV) in income.[1]

In reality, since indifference curves are not known, compensation is such as to ensure that consumers can continue to buy the bundle of commodities they bought prior to the price change. In either case the question arises as to whether consumer equilibrium will change following a compensated price change.

Suppose, for example, that the cost of 'home heating' goes up and the government, fearing that old age pensioners may be unable to keep their

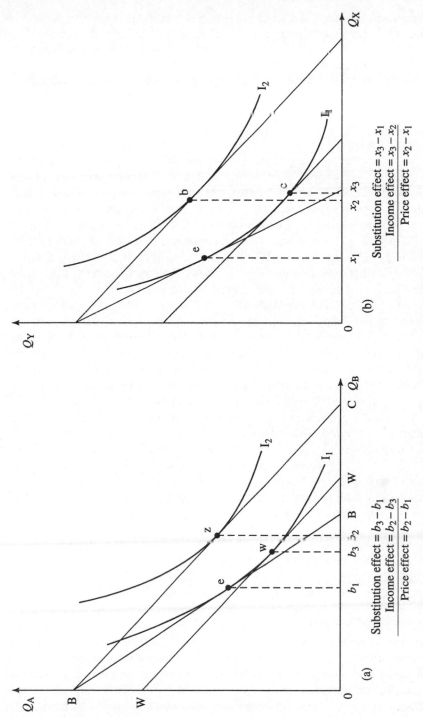

Figure 7.4 The income and substitution effect of a price change: (a) normal good; (b) inferior good

homes warm in winter, decides to increase pensioner income by a sufficient amount to compensate them for the increase in the cost of heating. The question then arises as to whether old age pensioners would continue to buy the same quantity of 'heating' or whether they would respond by buying less 'heating' despite the fact that they have been compensated for the price increase so that their real income has not changed. Similarly, suppose that the average price of textbooks falls and this is followed by an 'appropriate' reduction in student grants (!). Would the demand for textbooks change?

The answer to these questions is most probably yes. People are likely to change their consumption following an HCV in income because of the substitution effect of a price change. To see why consider Figure 7.4(a) again and suppose that the x axis refers to books and the y axis refers to all other commodities (or photocopied materials). Suppose that consumer equilibrium is at point e and that the average price of textbooks falls so that the price line swings to BC. The new equilibrium is at point z which indicates an increased demand for textbooks. That is, the effect of the price reduction is to increase the quantity of books demanded by $b_2 - b_1$. To find out what part of this overall price effect is due to the substitution effect we must consider how the consumer would respond in a situation in which real income had remained constant despite the price reduction. To this end suppose that the price reduction is accompanied by a sufficient reduction in money income so that the consumer is neither better off nor worse off following the price reduction (i.e. real income remains the same). Put differently, following a price reduction student grants are reduced sufficiently for a student's real income to remain the same, i.e. for equilibrium to remain on the indifference curve it was on prior to the price change. This is illustrated using Figure 7.4(a), by shifting the budget line parallel to itself inwards until it is tangent to curve I_1.[2] In other words, money income is reduced until the new budget line is WW and the new equilibrium is at point w indicating an increase in the quantity demanded of books equal to $b_3 - b_1$. This increase brought about by a move from point e to point w (along the same indifference curve) indicates the substitution effect of the price change.

Now imagine that the income withheld from student grants is given back (or that the price compensating income reduction never really occurred) so that the final consumer equilibrium is at point z. The increase in quantity b_3 to b_2 is due to the increase in real income since the price ratio is the same at points z and w.

In this example both the income and the substitution effect have induced the consumer to buy more of the commodity whose price has fallen. This is because the income effect is positive (more is demanded as income increases), re-enforcing the negative substitution effect and giving an overall negative price effect (quantity demanded increases as price falls and vice versa). Can we infer from this example that the price effect is always negative or that consumers will always demand more of a good when its price falls?

To answer this question let us examine each effect more closely beginning with the substitution effect. Provided that prices do not vary with the quantity demanded so that the budget line is a straight line negatively inclined, a relative reduction in the price of A will be represented by a new budget line flatter than the initial one (WW is flatter than DD). And, since indifference curves become flatter as we move from points on the top left of the curve towards points to the right (i.e. the MRS diminishes), it follows that the tangency between the same indifference curve and a flatter budget line must be to the right of the initial point of tangency. Thus, the substitution effect, when present, induces consumers to buy more of the relatively cheaper good.[3]

The same is not, however, true of the income effect. As already indicated an increase in income may induce a consumer to buy more of a normal good but less of an inferior good. It follows that for normal goods the price effect is negative, i.e. quantity demanded varies inversely with the price because the substitution effect of the price change is re-enforced by the income effect. In case of an inferior good, however, although the substitution effect is still negative, inducing the consumer to buy more of a good as its price falls, the income effect works in the opposite direction inducing a reduction in demand as income rises (see Figure 7.4(b)). For the overall price effect to be negative (i.e. for demand to increase as price falls) the income effect must not be as strong as the substitution effect of the price change. That is, the quantity demanded of an inferior good will increase as its price falls only if the substitution effect is stronger than the income effect but not otherwise.

We may conclude that, for normal goods, we can expect the quantity demanded to increase as its price falls, other things being equal. For inferior goods, however, the income and the substitution effect work in opposite directions so that it is theoretically possible that the income effect may be larger than the substitution effect resulting in a reduction in quantity demanded when the price falls (positive price effect). In this case the inferior product is termed a 'Giffen good'. It is difficult, however, to find many examples of Giffen goods in reality.

A CONSUMER'S DEMAND CURVE

Although focused on one product our analysis of price and income effects clearly implies (see Figures (7.2)–(7.4)) that a change in the price of one good may affect the quantity demanded of another and that income changes can affect both commodities. By extending the analysis to incorporate a number of products we can show that the overall demand for any product depends not only on its own price and the level of the consumer income but on the prices of all other goods and on any variables (such as advertising) which may affect consumer preferences.

To emphasise the fact that many variables affect consumer or market demand we refer to the demand function which is denoted symbolically as

$$Q^d_x = f(P_x, P_1, P_2, \ldots, M, T)$$

where Q^d_x refers to the quantity demanded of product X, P_x denotes the price of X, P_1, P_2, etc. are the prices of other goods, M is the consumer income and T denotes individual preferences.

The relationship between a product's own-price and the quantity demanded is of particular significance both for producers of the commodity and for consumers since price may have a strong influence on consumption patterns. The curve that illustrates how the quantity demanded of a good varies as its price varies when all other influences on demand are assumed to be constant is known as the *demand curve*.

A consumer demand curve can be derived from a consumer's preference map by tracing out the optimum purchasing patterns corresponding to different product prices. Thus, in Figure 7.5 when the prices of the two goods are P_B and P_A the budget line is mm$_1$ and equilibrium is at point a. This means that a consumer with the preference map and the budgetary constraint illustrated will be demanding a quantity of B equal to B_1 when the price of B is P_B. Quantity B_1 and price P_B correspond to a point on the consumer demand curve (since the demand curve shows the quantity demanded at each price given incomes and prices of other goods) shown in Figure 7.5(b) as p. When the price of B falls to P_B' while the price of A remains the same, the budget line becomes mm$_2$, consumer equilibrium is at point b and the quantity demanded of B increases to B_2. This corresponds to point q on the consumer demand curve. More points on the demand curve can be derived by altering the price of B. The line which connects all points such as p, q and r, is the consumer demand curve for product B.

The analysis so far has been restricted to two commodities in order to be able to use diagrammatic explanations. In the general case of n commodities, preferences can be described mathematically by an ordinal index (utility function) $U = f(Q_i)$ and the budget constraint becomes $M = \Sigma P_i Q_i$ where $i = 1, 2, 3, \ldots, n$. The problem is then to find the set of Q which is associated with the highest index (see Appendix 7.1).

We expect a consumer demand to be negatively sloped whether the product is normal or inferior since the income effect of a price change, for most commodities, is small so that even if negative it cannot swamp the substitution effect and give rise to a Giffen good.

Problems may, however, arise when a consumer's income is not fixed in terms of money but derives from the sale of a product part of which is kept for consumption purposes. In this case the individual comes to the market as both a buyer and a seller of a particular commodity. Suppose, for example, that an individual has a fixed stock of a commodity X (such as labour or an agricultural product) some of which is retained for individual

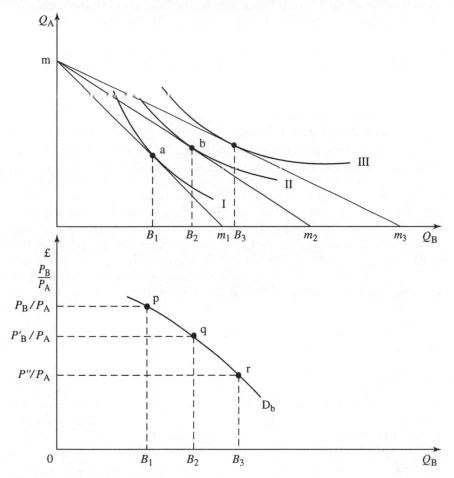

Figure 7.5 Derivation of consumer demand curve

consumption (in the form of leisure, say) and some is sold for income. A price change, say a price reduction, will in this case be associated with a substitution effect, which as always is non-positive (inducing the buyer to buy more), and two income effects. The first is the income effect of the price change which benefits the individual as a consumer of part of the product stock and the second is a reduction in money income which the individual, as a seller of the rest of the stock, suffers. Thus, assuming that X is a normal good, both the income and the substitution effect of the price change will induce the individual to buy more of X as its price falls but the adverse effect on money income which results from the sale of X will induce the individual to buy less of X since X is not an inferior good. In brief, the two income effects work in opposite directions unless the good is inferior in which case they work in the same direction. Additionally, there is no presumption that the change in nominal income (resulting from the sale of X) is likely to be smaller than the income effect of the price change. On the contrary the opposite should normally be true. It is therefore likely that as the price falls the combined impact of the substitution and the two income effects will result in a reduction in the demand for X.

To illustrate consider Figure 7.6 which derives an individual's supply of labour (or demand for leisure). Leisure is a normal good. Its price can be thought of as the income foregone in order to acquire leisure time. As leisure hours per day increase work hours decline and vice versa (see the direction of the arrows). At point B work hours are zero and the individual earns no labour income. As hours worked per day increase income increases and given the wage rate w_1 the maximum daily income is OB_1. When the wage rate increases to w_2 the maximum income becomes OB_2 and so on. Thus, the slope of the budget line is determined by the wage rate. Higher wages cause the budget line to swing from BB_1 to BB_2 to BB_3 to BB_4. The consumer equilibrium moves accordingly from point e to point f to g to h indicating that labour supply increases initially but, for this individual at least, it eventually declines as the wage rate increases.

MARKET DEMAND AND A FIRM'S DEMAND IN DIFFERENT MARKET STRUCTURES

The market demand

At any given price the market demand is simply the sum of the quantities demanded by all the consumers in a market. It is therefore tempting to suggest that it can be derived as the simple horizontal summation of the individual demand curves, its size depending on the number of customers operating in the market and its shape determined by the characteristics of the individual demand curves. Thus, if individual demands fall as price rises, the market demand should have a negative slope. Even if there were some pathological cases of positively sloping individual demand curves it can be expected that the shape of the market demand will resemble that of the majority of the buyers' demand curves. This would indeed be the case if individual preferences obeyed the assumptions described above and consumers acted according to the inherent qualities of the goods rather than being influenced by the behaviour of other individuals. Demand motivated exclusively by the inherent qualities of the good was called *functional* by Leibenstein (1950). Difficulties in deriving at the total market demand by a simple addition, however, may arise when the individual consumer demand is not wholly functional but is influenced by the purchasing behaviour of others. When consumers select products not entirely on the basis of their attributes but rather because of what other consumers do, consumer demand curves are inter-related and an additivity

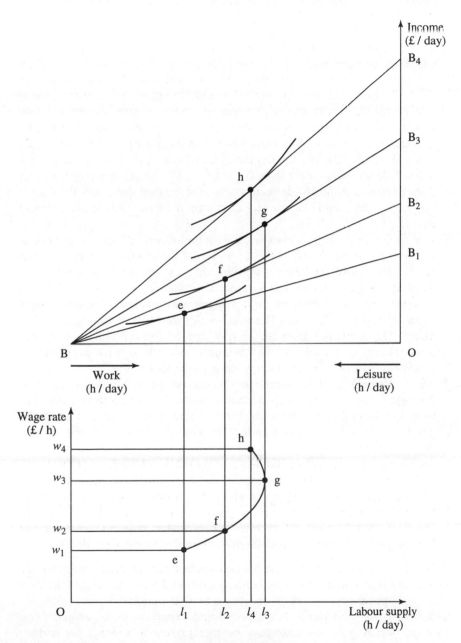

Figure 7.6 A backwards bending labour supply curve

problem exists. Several reasons may induce such consumer behaviour. Significant among these are the following.

1 *The bandwagon effect*   Individuals may buy more of a good when they observe others buying it. This is because they may wish to conform or be fashionable or friendly or simply follow the lead of others. Whatever the reason, their purchasing plans are influenced by what others do which means that they buy more of a good as its market demand expands. Thus, in Figure 7.7(a) suppose that market demand is D^a when consumers believe correctly that total demand is a. As price falls from P_1 to P_2, however, and quantity demanded expands to q, some individuals who wish to conform join the market and some of the existing buyers may buy more. The bandwagon effect causes D^a to shift to D^b. The quantity demanded increases to b. Similarly a price reduction to P_3 shifts D^b to D^a. The market demand incorporating the bandwagon effect is line DD which is flatter than D^a or D^b or D^c. Since each point on DD derives from a different demand curve, the market demand DD cannot be derived by simple horizontal summation of the individual demand curves.

2 *The snob effect*   This is associated with an individual's desire to appear to be different so that it is the opposite of the bandwagon effect. The snobs' pursuit of exclusivity implies that as the total demand for a product increases some snobs leave the market. In Figure 7.7(b) as quantity demanded expands, following a price decline, demand moves from D^a to D^b to D^c, etc. The market demand incorporating the snob effect, D_s, is steeper than the simple sum of the individual consumer demand curves. That is, market demand responds to price changes to a lesser extent when buyers behave in a snobbish fashion.[4]

3 *The Veblen effect*   This effect exists when consumers buy something just because it is expensive. This is another term for conspicuous consumption. Purchasing plans are related to a desire to show off so that as the price increases more is demanded. In Figure 7.7(c) D_3 is the market demand when price is P_3. As price increases (to P_2) it shifts upwards as indicated. The market demand including the Veblen effect is D_v.

Since it is reasonable to expect that for some products the market may include individuals belonging to all three groups, it is conceivable that the market demand can have a positive slope. For this to happen, however, the Veblen effect must be stronger than the sum of the bandwagon and snob effects which is unlikely for most products.

In addition to the above interdependencies our analysis excludes the possibility that individuals may behave irrationally in the sense that they buy on impulse or as a result of whims or that demand is speculative in which case demand depends on individual expectations regarding price movements. A price increase may be interpreted as a signal for further price increases in which case speculative demand would increase.

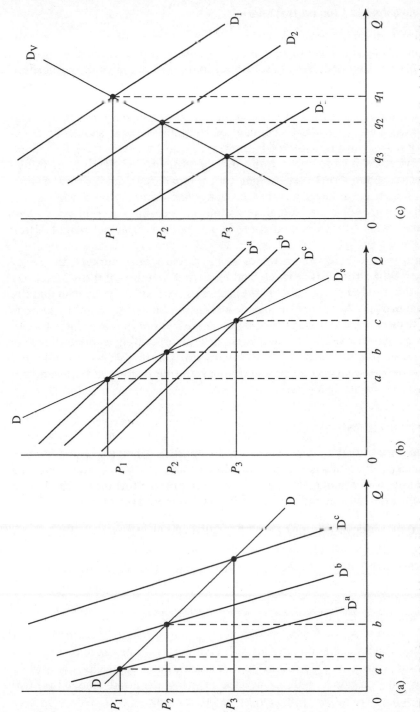

Figure 7.7 Consumer demand interdependences and the market demand: (a) the bandwagon effect; (b) the snob effect; (c) the Veblen effect

A firm's demand (or market share)

A firm's demand or market share, although part of the total market demand, may have characteristics which differ from the characteristics of the market demand. For a given total market demand both the position and the shape of a firm's market share may differ from market to market according to the structural features of each market. In a monopoly market, for example, the firm's demand coincides with the market demand and assuming away speculative demand or Veblen effects it should be negatively related to price. Suppose, however, that the same market demand is serviced by a large number of firms operating in a perfectly competitive industry. Each firm is so insignificantly small that any output change undertaken by a single firm has no appreciable impact on market price. Each firm in effect can sell all its output at the going market price. This means that a firm's demand curve is a straight line at the height of the market price.

In between these two extremes lie most real-world markets, the oligopolies. When the market is serviced by a small number of firms there may be a difference between the market share as perceived by the firm and the actual market share (see the discussion on the kinked demand hypothesis in Chapter 8). Additionally the market shares within the same industry can vary among firms. The demand curve of firms operating as price followers will be similar to that of a perfect competitor (perfectly elastic) while that of the leader will depend on the number and behaviour of followers and may not be a straight line.

ELASTICITIES

Having identified that a firm's, or the market, demand depends on a number of variables the next most obvious piece of information required for business decision making is an indication of the effect that each of these variables has on demand. Thus, business firms would be interested to know not only that quantity demanded may fall when price increases but how large this reduction is likely to be since this will determine whether the value of $P_X Q_X$ which represents the gross revenue of a firm (or total expenditure from the point of view of consumers) will be affected.

An obvious way to measure this responsiveness is to compare the change in quantity demanded brought about by a given change in price, i.e. we can use the ratio $\Delta Q / \Delta P$. The difficulty with $\Delta Q / \Delta P$, however, is that it deals with absolute changes which makes it difficult to compare this responsiveness across commodities. It is rather meaningless to compare an increase of, say, 3,000 pints of beer consumption a day following a £0.30 reduction in its price with an increase in the sales of lady shoes by 1,000 pairs a day when their price fell by £5.00 per pair.

Besides, by looking at absolute changes it is difficult to say whether the demand is responsive to a price change or not. In the beer example an increase of 3,000 pints may represent a substantial expansion, if total consumption prior to the price change were say 6,000 pints, or a minor one, if initial consumption were say 100,000 pints per day. Similarly, a £0.30 price reduction may represent a minor or a significant price change.

Such considerations have led to the conclusion that an appropriate measure of the responsiveness of one variable to a change in another must employ percentages rather than absolute changes. The measure that compares percentage changes in two variables has been termed *elasticity*.

Own-price elasticity of demand (E_p).

Own-price elasticity of demand (E_p) measures the responsiveness of quantity demanded to price changes assuming that other variables which might affect demand are constant. Thus, elasticity can be defined as

$$E_p = \frac{\text{Percentage change in quantity demanded}}{\text{Percentage change in price}}$$

$$= \frac{100\Delta Q/Q}{100\Delta P/P} = \frac{\Delta Q/Q}{\Delta P/P}$$

$$= \frac{\Delta Q}{\Delta P} \frac{P}{Q} . \tag{7.1}$$

Since price and quantity are inversely related E_p is a negative number. The larger the absolute value of this number the more responsive demand is to price changes. Thus, an $E_p = -5$ indicates a very responsive demand since a 10 per cent reduction in price will induce a 50 per cent increase in quantity demanded. An $E_p = -0.2$, on the other hand, means that the response is much weaker since a 10 per cent price reduction will, in this case, increase demand by only 2 per cent. An elasticity of -1 indicates that the proportionate change in demand is equal to the proportionate change in price. It is thus the size of the absolute value of the price elasticity that is significant in indicating how strongly demand responds to price changes. It is for this reason that some authors put a minus sign at the beginning of equation (7.1) so as to make elasticity a positive number, i.e. they select to use the absolute value of the elasticity. Since this can create confusion we have not followed this convention here so that the price elasticity is given with its appropriate (usually negative) sign. When we refer to a higher price elasticity, however, we shall mean a higher absolute value ignoring the negative sign. For example an elasticity of -5 is referred to as higher than an elasticity of -2.

To indicate the application of equation (7.1) consider the demand curve

$Q = a - bP.$

For any given price P_1 we can calculate the corresponding quantity Q_1 and apply formula (7.1) to find the elasticity. Thus, since $\Delta Q/\Delta P = -b$,

$$E_\text{p} = -b\frac{P_1}{Q_1}$$

which implies that the price elasticity of this demand curve[5] is different at each price. To illustrate how the elasticity varies and what impact it has on total revenue, the above demand curve has been drawn, in Figure 7.8(a), with price on the vertical axis and quantity on the horizontal axis. The gradient of the demand curve, $-1/b$, is the same at any point along the line but since P/Q is different at each point elasticity varies along the line as indicated. Figure 7.8(b) indicates the corresponding changes in total revenue. It should be clear that total revenue is maximised when price elasticity is equal to 1 and that price increases reduce total revenue when demand is elastic ($E_\text{p} > 1$) and increase revenue when demand is inelastic ($E_\text{p} < 1$). The opposite is valid for price reductions.

It is worth noting the following.

1 If the demand curve should shift to the right due, say, to an increase in income, the price elasticity of demand on the new curve will be less than that on the original demand curve whereas the opposite is true when the demand curve shifts to the left.
2 Demand curves need not be straight lines. Elasticity may vary along a non-linear demand curve but if the demand is a hyperbola then elasticity is the same at any price level.
3 In calculating an elasticity when only a pair of prices and quantities are known (rather than the whole demand curve) the initial pair of values of Q and P is conventionally used as the base to derive the percentage changes. But this creates the problem that the elasticity will be different for a price reduction (from a to b in Figure 7.8, when P_1 and Q_1 are used) than for a price increase (from b to a, since then P_3 and Q_3 are used in the formula). This inconsistency occurs because in calculating the elasticity for a price change from a to b we are in effect calculating an average elasticity for all the points in the arc ab. A better approximation is therefore achieved by using the average of the initial and terminal price–quantity pairs, i.e. $(P_1 + P_2)/2$ and $(Q_1 + Q_2)/2$ in the elasticity formula. Thus, price elasticity becomes

$$E_\text{p} = \frac{\Delta Q}{\Delta P}\frac{P_1 + P_2}{Q_1 + Q_2}$$

and is called *arc-price elasticity* to distinguish it from

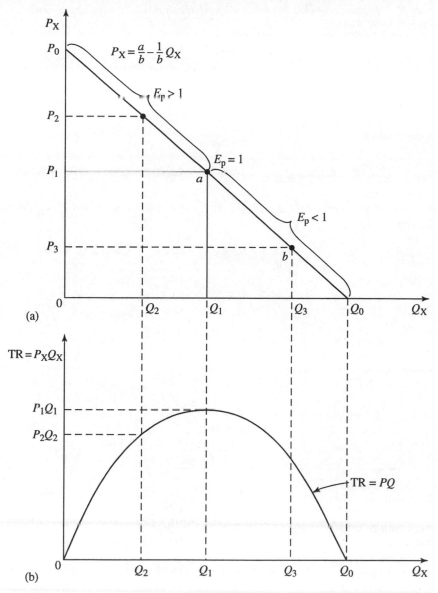

Figure 7.8 The relationship between price elasticity of demand and total revenue

$$E_p = -b\frac{P}{Q}$$

which is known as point price elasticity.

4 Empirical estimation of price elasticities indicates that they vary widely

Table 7.1 Estimated price and income elasticities of demand (selected form international markets)

Commodity demanded	Elasticity value	Country	Year	Reference
Price elasticities				
Beef and veal	−1.24	UK	1982–7	Harrison 1989
Bread	−0.25	UK	1982–7	Harrison 1989
Greek tourism demanded by West Germans	−0.63	West Germany	1985	Bakkal 1991
Italian tourism demanded by West Germans	−0.35	West Germany	1985	Bakkal 1991
Residential electricity	−1.19	USA	1987	Chang and Hsing 1991
Telephone usage				
day	−0.56			
evening	−0.46	USA	1985	Chen and Walters 1992
night	−0.45			
Entertainment	−1.4		1975	Jones 1989
RSC performances	−0.66	UK	1965–80	Jones 1989
Gasoline SR	−0.10	USA	1985	Jones 1989
Gasoline (demand over 10 years)	−0.82	USA	1985	Jones 1989
Income elasticities				
Beef and veal	0.82	UK	1987	Harrison 1989
Bread	−0.18	UK	1987	Harrison 1989
Tourism in Greece	1.53	West Germany	1985	Bakkal 1991
Margarine	−0.22	UK	1987	Harrison 1989
Health care in EC	0.77	EC	1963–81	Karatzas 1992
Cross-price elasticities				
Beef and veal with respect to pork	0.10	UK	1987	Harrison 1989
Pork with respect to beef and veal	0.25	UK	1987	Harrison 1989
Electricity with respect to gas	0.30	USA	1985	Chang and Hsing 1991
Greek tourism with respect to Italian tourism	−1.25[a]	West Germany	1966–85	Bakkal 1991
Day electricity with respect to evening prices	0.35	USA	1985	Chen and Walters 1992

Note: [a] Note that this is a surprising result since it indicates complementarity.

among products. Table 7.1 documents this variety to which several factors may contribute.

(a) The number of substitute products influences the size of the elasticity. The more substitutes there are for a product the larger the quantity adjustment in response to a price change is likely to be (the higher the elasticity). Thus the more narrowly defined a product is the higher its own price elasticity will be.

(b) The price elasticity is larger the larger the proportion of consumer income that is spent on a particular commodity. Thus, the reason why the price elasticity of the demand for bread is low (−0.25) may be that bread takes a small part of a customer's income (at least in the UK). In addition to being an affordable good, bread does not have very many substitutes.

(c) The number of uses to which a commodity may be put also has an influence on the size of the elasticity. The larger the number of uses the more elastic the demand is thought to be (wool).

(d) Time is a further influence. The immediate consumer response to a price change is likely to be smaller than the longer term response. This is because it takes time for price changes to become known and for individuals, once informed, to adjust their consumption patterns. This is particularly true when a commodity is consumed in conjunction with durables such as different kinds of fuel used in conjunction with different heating systems at home. Not surprisingly therefore, the price elasticity of the demand for residential electricity has been found to decline significantly over time, from −2.13 in 1950 to −1.19 in 1987 (Chang and Yu Hsing 1991).

Income elasticity of demand (E_I)

As the income–consumption curve of Figure 7.2(b) indicates, the relationship between quantity demanded and income, *ceteris paribus*, can be expressed as $Q = f(I)$.

The effect of a change in income on quantity demanded can then be expressed in terms of the income elasticity of demand which is defined as

$$E_I = \frac{\Delta Q}{Q} : \frac{\Delta I}{I} = \frac{\Delta Q}{\Delta I} \frac{I}{Q}$$

or, for small changes,

$$E_I = \frac{dQ}{dI} \frac{I}{Q}$$

The income elasticity of demand can be a positive number indicating a normal good (a positively sloped income-consumption curve) or a negative number indicating an inferior good (a negatively inclined income–consumption curve). For example, the demand for Greek tourism by West Germans is a normal good since Table 7.1 shows that the income (expenditure) elasticity of the West German demand for Greek tourism was 1.53 in 1985. This means that a 10.0 per cent increase (reduction) in German national income would increase (reduce) the demand for Greek holidays by 15.3 per cent. Similarly, beef and veal in the UK in 1987 was a normal good since its income elasticity of demand was 0.26 while margarine, fresh potatoes and bread were considered by customers as inferior goods since their income elasticities were −0.22, −0.43 and −0.18 respectively.

Cross-price elasticity of demand (E_c)

When two commodities are inter-related so that the price of one depends on the quantity of the other a cross-demand relationship exists such that $Q_x = f(P_y)$. The quantity demanded of fountain pens, for example, may depend on the price of, say, ball point pens. A measure of the strength of this relationship is given by $E_c = (\Delta Q_x/\Delta P_y) \, P_y/Q_x$. This is known as the cross-price elasticity of demand and may be a positive number indicating that as the price of one good falls the quantity demanded of the other also falls. The two commodities are then called substitutes since the reduction in the price of the first has presumably increased its consumption to the detriment of the consumption of the other. Electricity and gas, for example, are substitutes in domestic use. The cross-price elasticity of the demand for residential electricity with respect to the price of natural gas has been estimated to be approximately 0.30 in the long run (see Table 7.2 in Question 4). This means that a 10 per cent increase in the price of natural gas will bring about, in time, a 3 per cent increase in the demand for residential electricity. Thus although the two products are substitutes the extent of their relationship is not very strong.

A negative cross-price elasticity indicates that the goods are complementary since changes in their consumption move in the same direction. Thus, an increase in the price of cars may lead to a reduction both in the demand for cars and in the demand for petrol by motorists.

Two further observations should be noted before concluding this section: (a) Elasticity, as a measure of responsiveness, can be used to measure the impact which any one variable is likely to have upon another variable. The responsiveness of imports to a change in national income can thus be measured by the income elasticity of imports. Similarly, the responsiveness of investment to changes in the interest rate can be quantified by the interest elasticity of investment. The interest elasticity of the demand for money or the risk elasticity of the demand for assets such as bonds or shares can be defined analogously. (b) Elasticities are very significant in business decision making but their impact must be carefully assessed especially in situations in which a given price change is accompanied by income or other price changes. The demand for telephone usage varies, for example, according to the time of the day, with day, evening and night demand being substitutable to a certain extent. Thus, the price elasticity of the day demand was estimated to be -0.56 (for Bell Telephone company customers in the USA) which implies that a price increase of 10 per cent would decrease telephone usage by 5.6 per cent. This is valid, however, only if the price increase applied to the day time demand while the evening and night rates remained constant. A 10 per cent increase across the board would lead, according to Chen and Watters (1992), to only a 4.4 per cent decrease in day usage since fewer customers would have an incentive to switch to the relatively cheaper evening and night/weekend periods.

CONSUMER BEHAVIOUR UNDER CONDITIONS OF RISK

Up to this point we have assumed that consumers have full knowledge of the price, quality, sources of supply and all other attributes of the goods they may be interested to buy. In fact, it has been assumed that a particular consumer action (choice) leads to a particular outcome known in advance. Commonly, however, choices have to be made among alternatives whose outcomes are dependent on the occurrence of some event which is not known in advance. The existence of such alternatives, or 'contingent' events, means that consumer choices are made in the absence of perfect knowledge. Lack of perfect knowledge may, but does not necessarily, imply total ignorance. The state of 'unknowledge' within which entrepreneurs thrive was discussed in Chapter 5. Here we examine consumer behaviour in situations in which lack of perfect knowledge does not necessarily imply total ignorance. That is, individuals are assumed to be able to form a view as to the likelihood with which each potential outcome may occur.

If probabilities can be attached to the outcomes of a contingent plan the relevant choices are said to be made under conditions of risk. That is, when consumers have no perfect knowledge regarding product quality or other aspects of trade but have formed a view as to how likely it is that a particular product may be of the specified characteristics, they are making choices under conditions of risk. An example can be drawn from the car market. The lack of information about quality is widely acknowledged when considering the market for second-hand cars. Risks, however, are involved even when purchasing a new car since all cars of a particular model produced within the same plant do not necessarily have the same performance characteristics. Due to production process mistakes which occur randomly and which may not be detected at the quality control stage, a small number of new cars may have sub-standard performance. The identity of these cars is not known to a potential buyer who, if aware of this risk, is facing the problem of whether to buy a new car and undertake the risk of acquiring a sub-standard car or not to buy at all. Three possibilities therefore exist: the first (A) is to buy a new car which happens to be of standard performance, the second (B) is not to buy a car and use other means of transport instead and the third (C) is to buy a car which may be of sub-standard performance.

In other words, the consumer has a choice between a certain event (B) which is not to buy a car and an uncertain event which is to buy a new car and undertake the risk that the car may (A) or may not (C) be of the specified performance.

Buying insurance against house fire involves a similar choice but the risky event in this case is not to buy insurance since there is then a chance of a loss should the fire occur. Suppose that the probability that a house may be destroyed by fire is 0.01. A consumer with a house worth £100,000 and other wealth worth £10,000 can insure against the house fire risk by paying a premium of £1,000. The choice involved in this simple example is thus twofold: (a) to buy insurance which means that the consumer wealth becomes £109,000 (£100,000 + 10,000 − 1,000) whether the fire occurs or not, and (b) not to buy insurance in which case there is a small risk that the house will be destroyed by fire. The choice not to insure is a risky event with two outcomes. The first (A) involves a small probability (1 per cent) of a substantial loss, i.e. the loss of the house, and the second (B) involves a high probability (99 per cent) that the fire will not occur and the consumer's wealth will be £110,000.

Risky events of the kind described can be thought of as lotteries and can be represented by the triplet (P, A, B) which denotes a lottery offering outcome A with probability P (where $0<P<1$) and outcome B with probability $1-P$. Thus, in the fire risk insurance example the choice not to insure can be represented by L (0.01, £10,000, £110,000).

In both these examples the choice was between a certain and a risky event. Consumer choices may also involve only risky alternatives. Investing in bonds or company shares relates to such risky alternatives. The study of consumer behaviour under risk must, therefore, be general enough to embrace choices between risky alternatives.

UTILITY FUNCTIONS AND BUDGET LINES ASSOCIATED WITH RISKY EVENTS

Whether the house fire insurance in the above example is bought or not will depend partly on budgetary constraints, i.e. on existing income and the size of the insurance premiums required, and partly on consumer attitudes towards risk and the chances that the insured risk may occur. Let us consider each of these influences in turn.

A budget line in case of risky alternatives

The example of the purchasing of house insurance is used in Figure 7.9 to describe a budget line between two risky events which may occur if insurance is not bought. The endowment refers to the person's wealth (or consumption) in each of the two possible states that may occur if insurance is not acquired. One is the bad state (C_b) in which the risk occurs, that is, the house is destroyed by fire and the consumer's wealth falls to £10,000. The other is a good state (C_g) in which the risk does not occur and the consumer's wealth is £110,000.

Now, if it is assumed that any amount of wealth can be insured and that the premium is v per cent for the purchase of £K worth of insurance, the consumer has to decide whether to insure and if so how much insurance to buy. The choice set facing the consumer includes all the points along the line C_bC_g. A higher K indicates that a higher part of the value of the house (or of general wealth) is insured. The premium paid (vK) increases with K which reduces wealth if the risk does not occur but increases wealth when the risk does materialise. The premium v can therefore be thought of as the price of acquiring more wealth in the bad state while the price of acquiring more wealth in the good state is $1 - v$. The slope of the budget line, $dC_g/dC_b = -v/(1 - v)$, indicates the rate at which wealth in one state can be exchanged for wealth in the other state.

At point c, the individual's wealth is the same in the two states, £110,000

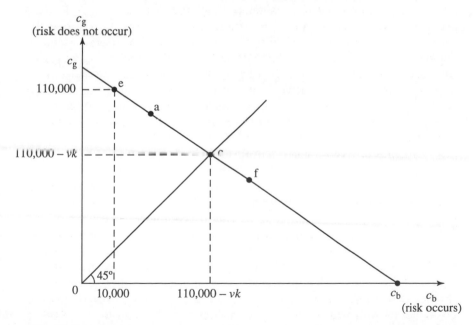

Figure 7.9 A budget line indicating insurance at premium v per cent of insured value k

$- vK$, whether the fire occurs or not. Thus c lies on the 45° line through the origin and indicates a choice involving no risk (the level of wealth is certain). The individual who selects point c is fully insured. Point a indicates partial insurance. That is, individual wealth is higher when the insured event does not occur than when it does occur. Point f indicates over-insurance, in the sense that wealth is higher when the risk does occur. The question then arises as to how much insurance individuals faced with the budget line C_gC_b will buy.

The answer depends on how individuals feel about undertaking risks and what preferences they have regarding the outcomes of the risky events. Consumer preferences in situations involving risk can, under certain conditions, be described by a utility function and indifference curves can be drawn which turn out to have similar properties as the indifference curves which describe consumer preferences over non-risky alternatives. Given a consumer's preference map the most preferred point on the budget line will be the one which lies on the highest indifference curve.

Consumer preferences in conditions of risk

In constructing an individual's preference map it is assumed that the ranking of risky alternatives will be influenced by individual preferences over the riskless outcomes involved in each case. This means that for any two risky alternatives, if the outcome associated with the risky alternative A is preferred to the outcome associated with the risky alternative B, then provided that the risks involved are the same A will be preferred to B. If, for example, an individual prefers tea to coffee then if offered a choice between two lotteries one of which offers tea and the other coffee as prizes with equal chances of success then he or she should select the first lottery in preference to the second. With regard to money wealth this assumption implies that more wealth is preferred to less since it represents a larger bundle of goods (recall the axiom of greed). Thus, in the case of the house insurance example £110,000 will be preferred to £10,000. Since, however, the outcomes are no longer certain it is reasonable to assume that preferences will be influenced by the extent to which the individual is confident that each outcome will occur. In other words whether you insure your house or not may depend on how likely you think it is that the house may be destroyed by fire. Finally, the psychological make up of an individual may have an important impact on this decision. Persons who dislike risky situations may choose to buy a lot of insurance while others may be more inclined to gamble and avoid buying insurance altogether.

In sum, we have identified three factors which influence consumer choices under risk: (a) preferences over the outcomes involved, (b) the probabilities with which outcomes may occur and (c) consumer attitudes with regard to risk.

Professors von Neumann and Morgenstern have shown that these factors can, under certain conditions, be combined to construct a cardinal utility index which ranks risky alternatives according to consumer preferences. To explain, the following notation will be used. A risky event or a gamble I, whose outcomes c_1, c_2, c_3 will occur with probabilities p_1, p_2, p_3 respectively, is denoted as $I = (p_1, p_2, c_1, c_2, c_3)$.

Two important conditions must be satisfied before a utility index, known as a von Neumann–Morgenstern utility index, can be constructed.

First, consumer preferences over riskless alternatives must be ranked by a utility index. That is, for any risky event $I = (p, c_1, c_2)$ we must identify (by, for example, interviewing the consumer) whether c_1 is preferred to c_2 or not so that we can assign a utility index to each riskless outcome, denoted by $U(c_1)$, $U(c_2)$.

Second, for any risky event which involves more than two possible outcomes, the choice between any two outcomes must be independent from a third available choice.

The house insurance example, which involves three outcomes, can be used to illustrate. Wealth is c_1 or c_2 depending on whether the fire does or does not occur in the absence of insurance and the third possibility is that wealth will be c_0 for certain if insurance is bought. Symbolically the event is $I=(p_1,p_2,c_0,c_1,c_2)$. The decision as to how much insurance to buy (what value to insure) implies a decision as to how much current consumption should be sacrificed in order to buy more consumption in case the house does burn down. This is a trade off between c_0 and c_1. The assumption made is that a consumer's choice between c_0 and c_1 (buying more insurance or not) is independent of c_2, i.e. of what value the wealth would be if the fire did not occur. If this assumption is valid, i.e. if the trade-off between any two alternatives, such as c_0 and c_1, does not depend on a third alternative c_2, then consumer preferences are said to be described by the *independence assumption*. This is a strong assumption to make since it may not hold true always.

If, however, consumer preferences satisfy the independence assumption then the utility function is 'additive' across the different contingent outcomes. That is, if c_1,c_2 and c_3 represent consumption at different 'states of nature' each of which may occur with probability p_1, p_2 and p_3 respectively, then the utility of the risky event takes the form

$$U(p_1,p_2,c_1,c_2,c_3) = p_1U(c_1) + p_2U(c_2) + p_3U(c_3).$$

This additive utility function is called *expected utility* and is the sum of the utility index of the outcomes each multiplied by its probability of occurrence. Similarly, for an event $L = (p, A, B)$ the expected utility is $EU(L) = pU(A) + (1-p)U(B)$.

In brief, the expected utility of a risky event is the actuarial value of the expected utilities of its outcomes.

To illustrate, consider the calculation of the utility index $EU(I)$ of the insurance option $I = (0.01, £10,000, £110,000)$ for an individual whose utility index over the riskless outcomes has been found to include the following:

U (£10,000) = 100 utils
U(£110,000) = 250 utils
U(£109,000) = 249 utils.

Then, since $p_1 = 0.01$, $p_2 = 1 - p_1 = 0.99$,

EU(I) = $0.01U$(£10,000) + $0.99U$(£110,000)
EU(I) = $0.01(100) + 0.99(250) = 248.5$.

This should be contrasted with the utility of the actuarial value of the outcomes which in this example is

$U(0.01 \times 10,000 + 0.99 \times 110,000) = U(100 + 108,900) = U(109,000) =$ 249 utils.

The calculation of expected utilities makes it possible to deal with consumer behaviour under conditions of risk for as von Neumann and Morgenstern have shown a utility function[6] can be constructed such that for any two alternatives L_1 and L_2

EU(L_1)>EU(L_2) if and only if L_1 is preferred to L_2.

It should be clear from the definition of expected utility that preferences over the riskless outcomes and the probabilities with which they occur are important determinants of consumer choices under conditions of risk. In general, expected utility increases with wealth and a desire for a high probability of success is assumed. The precise shape of the utility of wealth function, however, will vary among individuals so as to reflect their attitudes to risk. Thus, as utility increases with wealth, its rate of growth may be diminishing, increasing or constant reflecting risk aversion, risk preference or risk neutrality. Individuals are accordingly characterised as *risk averse*, *risk loving* or *risk neutral* individuals.

Risk aversion

A person who prefers a certain outcome to an uncertain one with the same expected value is called a *risk averter*. This implies that when risk is involved the risk averse person prefers the actuarial value of the risky event (also known as the *expected money value*) rather than the gamble. Risk aversion therefore exists when

$U[pA+(1-p)B] > pU(A)+(1-p)U(B)$

where U is the utility index indicating preference and p is the probability with which A occurs.

The person of the insurance example is a risk averter since for this individual the EU(I) = 248.5 utils while the utility of its actuarial value $U(p_1c_1 + p_2c_2)$ = 249 utils. That is, this person prefers to have £109,000 with certainty rather than undertake a gamble (by not insuring) which involves a high chance (99 per cent) of maintaining wealth at a high level (£110,000) coupled with a small chance (1 per cent) that wealth might be substantially reduced (£10,000).

A risk averter's utility of wealth function is illustrated in Figure 7.10(a). The graph shows that the expected utility of a lottery which offers a fifty–fifty chance of winning either £50 or £200 is 130 utils while the utility of its expected money value, UE[0.5(50) + 0.5(250)] = UE(125), also known as the *certainty equivalent*, is 110 utils. This means that a risk averter who maximises expected utility would prefer £125 with certainty to the lottery described.

It should be obvious that the expected money value of a gamble, or its certainty equivalent, changes with the probabilities with which the outcomes occur. In Figure 7.10(a) the certainty equivalents for different probabilities are indicated by the broken line which lies everywhere below the utility function, indicating that this individual is risk averse at any level of wealth. In other words this individual prefers the expected value of the gamble rather than the gamble itself whatever the relevant probabilities.

Risk aversion is indicated by the shape of the utility of wealth function which is concave from below. The more concave the utility function is the stronger the individual preference for the certainty equivalent or the more risk averse the person is. The utility function of Figure 7.10(b) refers to a risk-loving individual. This is a person who prefers a gamble to its certainty equivalent. Thus, a gamble which gives a fifty–fifty chance of winning either £100 or £250 has a higher utility (120 utils) to its expected money value. The expected value is £175 and its utility is 90 utils. This is because the shape of the utility function is convex from below. Again the curvature of this function indicates the strength of preference for risk of this individual.

It is possible, however, that an individual may be neither risk averse nor risk loving. A person may be indifferent between a gamble and its certainty equivalent in which case the utility of the expected money value will be the same as the expected utility of the gamble (EU(I) = UE(I)). The utility of wealth is then a straight line. Moreover, an individual may be risk averse at low levels of income and risk loving at high levels of income.

Indifference curves in the case of risky alternatives

By definition indifference curves represent sets of alternatives among which a consumer is indifferent, their shape reflecting variations in preferences. Thus, the rate at which one risky alternative may be substituted for another will vary among individuals and along a given indifference curve. It varies among individuals to reflect differences in risk attitudes and along an indifference curve to indicate how utility varies with the level of wealth of the individual concerned. Moreover, it is reasonable to assume

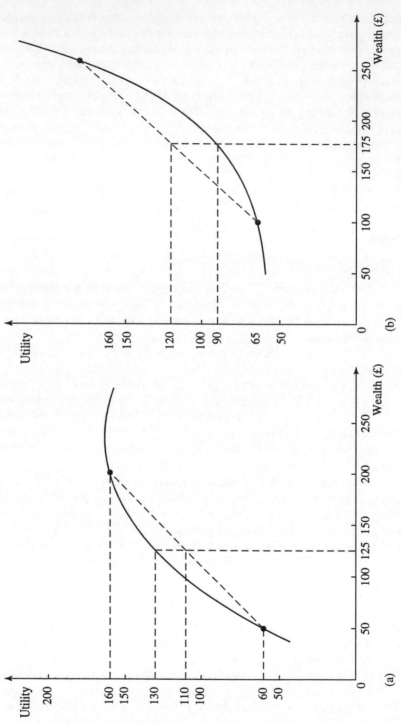

Figure 7.10 (a) Risk aversion: $U(125) = 130$ units, $EU(0.5, 50, 200) = 110$ units; (b) risk loving: $U(175) = 90$ units, $EU(0.5, 100, 250) = 120$ units

that the rate of substitution between risky alternatives may depend on the expected risks. The rate at which you may be prepared to substitute ice-cream if the weather is hot for ice-cream when the weather is cold may depend on how likely you think it is that the weather may turn out to be hot or cold.

In brief, the size of the MRS is dependent on risk attitudes, on individual preferences over the riskless alternatives involved and on the relative probabilities with which the risks may occur.

In the presence of risk the shape of indifference curves reflects a person's risk attitudes. The indifference curves of a risk neutral person, for example, would be straight lines with a slope equal to the ratio $-p/(1-p)$ to reflect the fact that the utility of wealth of a risk neutral person increases with wealth at a constant rate. In other words, the risk neutral individual is prepared to substitute money wealth available with a given probability for money wealth available with another probability at a rate indicated by the ratio of the relevant probabilities. Put differently, a risk neutral person is an expected money value maximiser. That is, for any $I=(p,A,B)$ this person attempts to maximise $E(I) = p(A) + (1 - p)(B)$. Therefore, along an indifference curve the rate of substitution between A and B is constant at $-p/(1 - p)$.

The indifference curves of a risk averse person, on the other hand, are convex to the origin and their convexity depends on the extent of risk aversion.

Figure 7.11 shows an indifference map for a risk averter. The slope of an indifference curve, as always, indicates the rate at which the individual is prepared to substitute one commodity for another. In this case the commodities are consumption (or wealth) in two different 'states of the world'. The utility index of the individual in Figure 7.11 can be written as

$$U(L) = p_A U(A) + p_B U(B) + p_C U(C)$$

where $L=(p_A,p_B,p_C,A,B,C)$ and A,B,C denote income or consumption levels available under different risk conditions. If the independence assumption is valid, the slope of the indifference curve is described by the MRS_{BA} which can be written as

$$\text{MRS}_{BA} = \frac{dU(L)/dA}{dU(B)/dB} \tag{7.2}$$

or

$$\text{MRS}_{BA} = \frac{p_A dU(A)/dA}{p_B dU(B/dB.} \tag{7.3}$$

But since on points such as b, or c, the MRS is -1, condition (7.3) becomes at these points

$$\frac{p_A dU(A)/dA}{p_B dU(B)/dB} = -1$$

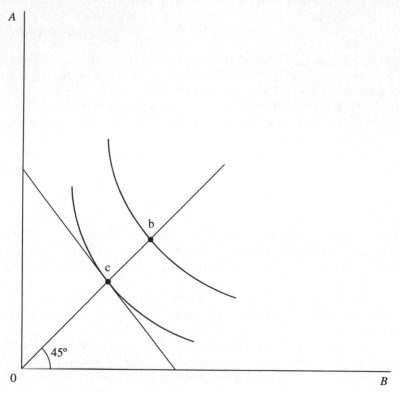

Figure 7.11 Equilibrium of a risk averse consumer

which in the case of two alternatives can be written as

$$\frac{p\,\mathrm{d}U(A)/\mathrm{d}A}{(1-p)\,\mathrm{d}U(B)/\mathrm{d}B} = -1.$$

Thus, the indifference curve slope varies according to an individual's preferences, over A and B, and the risks involved which are incorporated in p_A and p_B.

One property of these indifference curves worth emphasising is that at any point like c where the 45° line intersects the indifference curve, i.e. when income is the same whatever the risk (A and B are equal), the slope of the indifference curve is -1. This is because, given the independence assumption, utility depends only on the amount of income available in each state. Therefore, when income is the same the marginal utility is the same in each state which implies that the marginal rate at which the individual is prepared to substitute income in one state (A) for income in the other state (B) must be equal to one implying that the slope of the indifference curve (or the MRS_{BA}) at point c is equal to -1.

Consumer equilibrium

As in the case of certainty, consumer optimality is indicated by the tangency between an indifference curve and the budget line. That is, in equilibrium, the consumer will demand such quantities of the risky alternatives A and B as to ensure that their price ratio (i.e. the slope of the budget line) is equal to the marginal rate of substitution.

In the case of the insurance example of Figure 7.9 the price ratio is $-v/(1-v)$ where v is the insurance premium paid per $£K$ of insurance bought. Therefore, the optimum amount of insurance to be bought is determined by the condition that MRS $= -v/(1-v)$ or

$$\frac{P}{1-P} \frac{\mathrm{d}U(A)}{\mathrm{d}A} \frac{\mathrm{d}U(B)}{\mathrm{d}B} = \frac{-v}{1-v}$$

Clearly, if the price ratio is equal to the probability with which the risk may occur, i.e. if $v/(1-v) = p/(1-p)$, then the ratio of the marginal utilities of A and B is equal to -1 which implies that equilibrium is at a point on the 45° line. This means that $\mathrm{d}U(A)/\mathrm{d}A = -\mathrm{d}U(B)/\mathrm{d}B$ or that the marginal utility of an extra pound of income if the risk occurs is the same as the marginal utility of income when the risk does not occur. But since the utility of money is assumed to depend only on the level of income in each state, this implies that the individual will select to have the same income whether the risk occurs or not. He or she will be fully insured.

When insurance premiums are equal to the probability with which the risk occurs, the insurance is said to be fair. In general a *fair game* is defined to be a game in which the entry price (premium) is equal to the expected money value of the game. For example, if the price of a lottery ticket offering a fifty–fifty chance of winning £10 or £100 is £55 (which is the same as the expected money value of the game) the lottery is fair.

Since risk averse individuals prefer the certainty equivalent of fair games, they will be fully insured provided that insurance is available at a 'fair' rate but will not participate in a fair gamble. The opposite can be said of risk loving individuals.

Preferences in situations involving risk and the related risk attitudes have an important bearing on business behaviour as will become clear in subsequent chapters. Chapter 9, for example, utilises some of the concepts developed here to show that to be feasible and successful work incentive schemes must vary according to circumstances and to individual (employer and employee) preferences and risk attitudes.

SUMMARY

Consumer demand and the market demand for a product are derived and analysed in this chapter on the assumption that consumer preferences can be represented by an order preserving function known as utility. Consumer rationality is defined as a behaviour consistent with consumer preferences. To make the best of the available income a consumer demands such quantities of any two commodities as to ensure that the MRS of the two goods is equal to the negative of their price ratio. When this is achieved the consumer is said to be in equilibrium because there is no other consumption pattern that could bring him or her to a more preferred position.

An equilibrium position, however, will be disturbed by price or income changes. Consumers will, therefore, respond to price or income changes by appropriate adjustments to the quantities demanded.

A consumer's response to income changes is either positive (for a normal good) or negative (for an inferior good). A consumer's demand for a particular good is derived by observing how a consumer responds to a price change on the assumption that income and all other prices remained constant. It is shown that a consumer's demand curve for normal goods is negatively sloped since both the income and the substitution effect of the price change induce the consumer to buy more of a good when its price falls. For inferior goods, however, it is theoretically possible that the negative income effect may swap the substitution effect and induce a consumer to buy less of a good whose price has fallen. It is very difficult, however, to find examples of commodities for which this may be true in reality.

At each price the market demand shows the sum of the quantities demanded by all the individual consumers of a product. To arrive at this sum, any interactions between individual demand curves must be taken into account. The total market demand is shared by the firms operating in the same market in a way depending on market structure. A firm's demand curve, therefore, may differ, in shape and position, to the market demand.

A measure used to quantify the extent to which demand varies with price is known as the price elasticity of demand. It is defined as the percentage change in demand corresponding to a given change in price. Several other elasticities including the income elasticity of demand and the cross-price elasticity are defined and illustrated with real-world examples.

From consumer behaviour in conditions of certainty the chapter moves to choices involving risk. Three factors are shown to influence choices under risk: (a) individual preferences over the outcomes involved, (b) the probabilities with which outcomes may occur, and (c) consumer attitudes with regard to risk. These factors can be combined to construct a von Neumann–Morgestern utility function provided that preferences over the riskless outcomes are known and that such preferences fulfil the independence assumption.

The shape of the utility function varies with risk attitudes. Thus, for a risk averse person utility increases with wealth at an increasing rate while for risk lovers it increases at a decreasing rate and for risk neutral individuals it increases at a constant rate. It follows that the indifference curves of a risk neutral person are straight lines with a slope equal to the negative of the ratio of the probabilities associated with the risky alternatives. A risk averter's indifference curves are convex to the origin with a slope equal to −1 at points lying on the certainty line. Such individuals will be fully insured when insurance is available at a 'fair' rate but they will not participate in a fair game.

APPLICATION: THE DEMAND FOR HEALTH CARE IN THE EUROPEAN COMMUNITY

Consumer preferences, risk attitudes, income and relative commodity prices have a role to play in determining consumer demand. The demand for health care is no exception to this rule. It comes as no surprise that a number of factors have recently emerged as significant influences on the demand for health care in Europe. A review of recent studies carried out by Milne and Molana (1991) has identified five main influences on the demand for health care.

1 It has been suggested that the demand for health care may be supply induced. In European Community (EC) regions with more per capita physicians the demand for health care is *ceteris paribus* higher. This is not just because patients have easier access to their doctors. The market for health is fraught with informational asymmetries which apparently have induced physicians as agents to attempt to raise the level of demand for health care.

2 The demand for health care has an element of overall demand for health status. In this respect variables such as the level of education can have an influence on demand and for a more efficient use of health care.

3 In all of the EC countries at least part of the care is provided by third parties, either publicly financed or privately financed through insurance so that price at the point of access is lower than the true cost of the provision of health care. As the analysis in this chapter indicated, consumers respond to price at the point of access which implies a higher demand.

4 Income (as measured by gross domestic product (GDP)) is unanimously accepted to be an important influence although (as explained below) the income elasticity of demand is vivaciously debated.

5 Finally and not surprisingly, demography and in particular the age and sex distribution of the population are important determinants of the demand for health care. Indicative of the significance of age is the NHS expenditure per capita during 1982–3 which was in England as follows (Milne and Molana 1991: Table 1).

Age (years):   Births 0–4 5–15 16–64 65–74 75 and over all ages

Expenditure (£) 1,070 215 125   140   415   965   235

Since knowledge of factors influencing demand and their trends, are particularly useful in the formulation of EC policy a number of researchers have attempted to quantify their effects. Particular attention has been paid to the influence of income but the extent of this influence is still uncertain mainly because the multiplicity of factors affecting demand, data limitations and econometric problems have led to wide divergencies in numerical estimates.

Several studies have suggested that the income elasticity of demand for health care is higher than one implying that increases in income are accompanied by more than proportionate increases in demand. This view of health care as a 'luxury' good has been disputed on the grounds that the relevant empirical studies have not always accounted properly for relative price changes and have thus over-estimated the income effect. Milne and Molana, for example, argue that 'the demand for health care is homogenous of degree one in income and the relative price of health care'. This means that a given percentage increase in income and price will be associated with the same proportionate increase in the demand for health care. They therefore argue that health care is not a luxury. Others (like Parkin *et al.* 1987 or Karatzas 1992) argue that health care is a necessity. Using data from eight EC countries Karatzas, for example, has estimated the following relationship for health expenditure:

$$\ln(HE_t) = 8.846 + 0.771\ \ln(GDP_t) + 1.283\ \ln(DOC_t) + 4.890\ PUO_t$$
$$(2.330) \qquad\qquad (3.132) \qquad\qquad (1.508)$$

which has a good explanatory power ($R^2 = 0.954$). In this equation HE denotes expenditure in health care, GDP is the gross domestic product and PUO is a ratio of the population under 5 and over 65 years of age to the total population. Since the natural logarithmic form is used, the coefficients of the equation coincide with the elasticities of the corresponding variables. Thus, the income elasticity is equal to 0.771 which means that health care is a necessity. Four other equations were estimated in three of which the coefficient of $\ln(GDP)$ is around 0.9, suggesting that the income elasticity is not very different than 1. Since the policy implications for the provision and organisation of health care in the Community are significant and controversial, more research in this area is required.

FURTHER READING

Henderson, J.M and Quant, R.E. (1980) *Microeconomic Theory; a Mathematical Approach*, 3rd edn, New York: McGraw Hill. This gives a concise mathematical treatment of consumer theory.

Milne, and Molana ('On the Effect of Income and Relative Price on the Demand for Health Care: EC Evidence', *Applied Economics*, 23(1991): 1221–6) and Karatzas ('"On the Effect of Income and Relative Price on the Demand for

Health Care: EC Evidence." A comment', *Applied Economics*, 24(1992): 1251–3) are among the original sources of the case study on the EC Health care and as such give a more thorough account and further references to this topic.

Varian, Hal R., (1990) *Intermediate Microeconomics: A Modern Approach*, 2nd edn, London: Norton. This gives a thorough and more extended coverage of the traditional theory of consumer choice and demand theory. Chapter 12 on uncertainty is particularly good further reading.

QUESTIONS

1 In the example of Appendix 7.1 derive the demand for X_1.

2 Suppose that a consumer has £490.00 per month to spend on electricity and 'all other goods'. The price of electricity is 14 pence per unit and there are no standing charges. The price of a composite unit of 'all other goods' is 20 pence per unit.

   (a) On graph paper draw the budget line facing this consumer and assuming that the consumer preference function for electricity is known draw an indifference curve to indicate the quantity of electricity which this consumer will consume per month.

   (b) Suppose that because of recent events in the Gulf the government has instructed the electricity industry to reduce the total electricity production in order to save on fuels. To achieve this, while avoiding unnecessary hardship to small consumers, the following pricing scheme has just been introduced. The price of the first 1,000 units of domestic consumption per quarter of a year remains constant at 14 pence per unit while the price of any extra electricity consumed becomes 35 pence per unit. Draw the new budget line for the above consumer and explain whether your analysis indicates that the new pricing scheme will achieve its objective. (If you prefer assume that consumer preferences are given by $U = X_e X_o$ where X_e denotes a unit of electricity and X_o a unit of all other goods to work the above problem numerically.)

3 'Recent interest rate increases may fail to reduce the demand for housing since personal disposable income is still rising and housing is a normal good.' Explain what is meant by a 'normal good' and using mortgage repayments as the price of housing explain how a consumer's budget line will be affected by an increase in interest rates combined with an increase in personal disposable income. Determine the consumer optimum demand to evaluate the above statement.

Table 7.2 Long-run electricity elasticities, 1950–87, USA

Year	Long-run, own-price elasticity	Long-run income elasticity	Long-run, cross-price elasticity, with respect to the price of gas
1950	−2.13	1.29	0.40
1955	−1.83	1.17	0.37
1960	−1.64	1.10	0.34
1965	−1.47	1.06	0.32
1970	−1.26	1.00	0.28
1975	−1.24	0.98	0.27
1980	−1.20	0.96	0.29
1985	−1.22	0.97	0.30
1987	−1.19	0.97	0.29
Mean	−1.39	1.02	0.30

Source: Chang and Hsing 1991: Table 2

4 Table 7.2 gives information on the long-run own-price, income and cross-price elasticity of demand for residential electricity in the USA for the period 1950–87.

   (a) Explain how a 10 per cent increase in the price of electricity during 1987 may have affected the demand for residential electricity and the gross revenue of the electricity and the gas suppliers during 1987.
   (b) Examine the effect of rising real income on the demand for residential electricity.
   (c) Explain whether the information provided in the table may be useful to decision makers in determining the effectiveness of conservation programmes.

5 Oceanlink, a European car ferry consortium, operates two services between Dover and Ostend. The first, operated by conventional car ferry, costs the passenger £10 for a single journey and takes 3.5 hours. The second, operated by jet-foil, costs the passenger £16 for a single journey but takes only 1.5 hours. In 1992 the passenger traffic on the route was 500,000 by ferry and 120,000 by jet-foil.
   Oceanlink were disappointed with the 1992 jet-foil loadings and even though they do not anticipate any overall growth in demand next year have decided to reduce the jet-foil fare to £14 whilst holding the ferry fare at £10. They estimate the price elasticity of demand for the jet-foil service to be −2.5 and the cross-price elasticity of demand between the ferry and the jet-foil service to be 0.7.

   (a) Assuming no change in other possible influencing factors, what will be the change in revenue income from passenger carrying as a result of the change in the jet-foil fare? Illustrate your answer with diagrams.
   (b) Give details of the 'other possible influencing factors' mentioned in part (a) and indicate how they might affect your results.

6 Your friend whom you know to be a risk averter is offered the choice between a gamble that pays £2,000 with a 0.25 chance or £60 with a 0.75 chance and a cash payment of £545. Which do you think he will choose?

7 Construct the utility of wealth function of an individual who is a wealth averter at low levels of income but a risk lover at high levels of income.

8 The demand for the existing range of tours of a package tour operator has been declining for a number of years and the firm is faced with the choice of whether to continue with its present focus or to enter the market for remote island holidays.
   The firm's finance director and owner has produced the profit estimates given in Table 7.3 for the two strategies covering the next three years.

Table 7.3 Profit estimates

	Demand		
	High	*Moderate*	*Poor*
Existing strategy			
Anticipated profit (£000)	80	70	−10
Probability	0.5	0.3	0.2
New strategy			
Anticipated profit (£000)	110	80	30
Probability	0.1	0.4	0.5

Suppose that the managing director, who studied economics as an undergraduate, has assigned company utility value of 100 to profit of £110,000 and −10 to a loss of £10,000. In addition, she estimated that the owner would be indifferent between the certain outcomes and the corresponding chance prospects given in Table 7.4.

Table 7.4 Certain outcomes and chance prospects

Certain outcome	Chance prospect
£80,000 for certain	65% chance of £110,000 profit
	35% chance of £10,000 loss
£70,000 for certain	50% chance of £110,000 profit
	50% chance of £10,000 loss
£30,000 for certain	30% chance of £110,000 profit
	70% chance of £10,000 loss

(a) Using the expected monetary value approach which of the two options would you recommend the company to adopt?
(b) Would your advice differ if you had used the expected utility value decision rule?
(c) On the basis of the information given above, would you classify the owners as risk averters or risk takers? Explain why, illustrating your answer with a diagram.

9 Suppose that $U(A) = 50$ utils, $U(C) = 0$ utils and you observe the following for an individual X known to behave as a von Neumann–Morgenstern utility maximiser:

$L_1 = (A, C; 1/5, 4/5)\ I\ £180$
$L_2 = (A, £180; 3/5, 2/5)\ I\ £600$
$L_3 = (£600, £180; 1/2, 1/2)\ I\ L_4$
$L_4 = (A, N; 1/5, 4/5)$

where N denotes an evening out at the theatre, L is a lottery ticket and I denotes indifference.

Estimate the utility value of £180, £600 and for an evening out at the theatre.

10 Research has confirmed that in the country of Assumptia motorists behaviour can be described by the von Neumann–Morgenstern utility function and that motorists are risk averse individuals.

In response to the existence of widespread unauthorised street parking which causes serious traffic problems, the Transport Department has suggested that the Government should adopt one of two measures: one measure involves increasing on-the-spot parking fines by 20 per cent; the other would increase the probability of being caught, when illegally parked, by 20 per cent.

The minister responsible cannot see any difference between the two measures since the expected loss to motorists who park illegally is the same either way. Do you agree?

APPENDIX 7.1: THE ELEMENTARY MATHEMATICS OF DEMAND ANALYSIS

Most of traditional demand analysis is based on the consumer utility function

$$U = f(Q_1, Q_2, \ldots, Q_n) \tag{A7.1}$$

and the budget constraint

$$M = P_1Q_1 + P_2Q_2 + \ldots + P_nQ_n \tag{A7.2}$$

where Q_i denotes the quantity of good i demanded at price P_i and M is the consumer's money income. Consumers have perfect knowledge and act rationally. That is, they attempt to acquire those Qs that maximise their utility function. In other words, equation (A7.1) must be maximised subject to constraint (A7.2). Using the Lagrange method of optimisation this is equivalent to maximising the following Lagrange expression

$$\max L = f(Q_1, Q_2, \ldots, Q_n) + \lambda(P_1Q_1 + P_2Q_2 + \ldots + P_nQ_n - M) \qquad (A7.3)$$

Assuming that the second-order conditions for the maximisation are satisfied, the first-order condition is to set its partial derivatives equal to zero. Thus,

$$\partial L/\partial Q_1 = \partial f/\partial Q_1 + \lambda P_1 = 0$$
$$\partial L/\partial Q_2 = \partial f/\partial Q_2 + \lambda P_2 = 0$$
$$\vdots$$
$$\partial L_l/\partial Q_n = \partial f/\partial Q_n + \lambda P_n = 0$$
$$\partial L_l/\partial \lambda = P_1Q_1 + P_2Q_2 + \cdots + P_nQ_n - M = 0. \qquad (A7.4)$$

If any of the first $n-1$ equations in set (A7.4) is divided by its successor, if, for example, the first one is divided by the second, we get

$$\frac{\partial f/\partial Q_1}{\partial f/\partial Q_2} = \frac{P_1}{P_2}. \qquad (A7.5)$$

Since the left-hand side of this equation is the marginal rate of substitution, the equilibrium condition is that $\text{MRS}_{ji} = P_i/P_j$ which was derived less formally in the chapter.

Example Suppose that a consumer has £100.00 to spend on two commodities X_1 and X_2 whose prices are $P_1 = £5$ and $P_2 = £2$. Determine the quantities that this consumer would demand of each good if consumer preferences can be described by $U = X_1X_2$.

Answer Assuming that the consumer will act rationally, he or she will select such quantities of the two commodities as to maximise

$$U = X_1X_2$$

subject to the budget constraint

$$100 = 5X_1 + 2X_2.$$

To solve this problem numerically, we can form the Lagrange expression L and maximize it with respect to X_1, X_2 and λ; i.e.

$$\max L = X_1X_2 + \lambda(5X_1 + 2X_2 - 100)$$

The necessary condition for a maximum is

$$\frac{\partial L}{\partial X_1} = X_2 + 5 = 0 \qquad (A7.6)$$

$$\frac{\partial L}{\partial X_2} = X_1 + 2 = 0 \qquad (A7.7)$$

$$\frac{\partial L}{\partial \lambda} = 5X_1 + 2X_2 - 100 = 0 \qquad (A7.8)$$

Rearrange and divide equation (A7.6) by equation (A7.7) to derive $X_1/X_2 = 2\lambda/5\lambda$ or $X_1 = (2/5)X_2$. Substitute this in equation (A7.8) to derive

$$5\left(\frac{2}{5}\right)X_2 + 2X_2 - 100 = 0 \qquad (A7.9)$$

which gives $X_2 = 25$. Substitute into equation (A7.8) to derive $X_1 = 10$. Note that the general form of equation (A7.9) is

$$P_1(P_2/P_1)X_2 + P_2X_2 = M$$

which gives $X_2 = M/2P_2$. This is the demand for the second product.

NOTES

1 An alternative measure is the change in income which would have been necessary to take the consumer to the same level of satisfaction (in the absence of a price change) as did the price change. In terms of Figure 7.4(a) this is indicated by a shift of the line BB until it is tangent on indifference curve I_2. This money income change is known as Hicks' equivalent variation in income.

2 In reality indifference curves are not known and in practical applications the reduction in money income would be such as to let the consumer have sufficient money to acquire the same quantities he or she was buying at point e. That is, line BB' moves backwards till it passes through point e rather than become tangent to I.

3 Strictly speaking the substitution effect is non-positive.

4 A positive slope is inconsistent with the existence of a snob effect, since it would imply that a price reduction would reduce total demand in which case some snobs would demand more of the product reversing the reduction. (It is an expansion in demand that drives snobs away from the market.)

5 Generally, given Q = f (P) the price elasticity of demand E_p is defined as

$$E_p = \frac{dQ}{dP} \cdot \frac{P}{Q}$$

6 For a formal derivation of the expected utility function see Baumol (1972).

8 Business strategy in different market structures

INTRODUCTION

The view that market structure influences business contact and market performance has enjoyed widespread support over a number of years. Modern entrepreneurial firms may also, as we have argued in Chapter 5, consciously attempt to seize beneficial opportunities to modify the industrial environment so as to better achieve their objectives. But since beneficial opportunities vary with the characteristics of the industrial environment, there is a two-way causation between market structure and business conduct which makes it instructive to analyse business practices and policies under different market structures.

Since oligopolies dominate the industrial landscape of many countries today, the emphasis of this chapter is on oligopolies. Given, however, the normative significance of the perfectly competitive paradigm over much of economic theory and policy, the first section of this chapter begins with an examination of the perfectly competitive firm and market before proceeding to the analysis of monopolies. Both single-plant and multi-plant monopolies are analysed. The concept of monopoly power is defined and price discriminatory practices are examined in some detail. The second section is devoted to oligopolies. The interdependence which characterises oligopolies is examined and the significance of conjectures in business decision making is illustrated with the theory of the kinked demand curve. The uncertainty and risks which conjectural rivalry implies are often thought to contribute to collusion in oligopolies. The third section examines some commonly observed collusive agreements such as cartels and price leadership. It begins with some evidence on the existence and extent of collusive agreements and examines conditions which facilitate or hinder such arrangements. The following section focuses on strategic behaviour under oligopolistic interdependence. The traditional entry prevention pricing strategy is critically reviewed. This is followed by an introduction to a game strategic approach to entry deterrence. In this context strategic investment in productive capacity, reputation building and advertising are examined. Finally the theory of the perfectly contestable markets is introduced before the concluding section. The end of chapter application examines the cartelisation of the UK building industry.

PRODUCTION AND PRICING IN DIFFERENT MARKET STRUCTURES

A firm operating under conditions of perfect competition is extremely passive. In fact its only function is to take inputs of a homogeneous quality at the given market price and convert them into homogeneous outputs of a known market price. It is for this reason that a perfectly competitive firm has been likened to a 'black box' whose only purpose is to convert inputs into outputs and which makes the theory of the firm of no use to business practitioners. Given, however, the influence of the perfectly competitive model on public policy and its use as a yardstick for efficiency measurement, it is instructive to begin by briefly examining this 'ideal' and its efficiency qualities.

Perfect competition

When a large number of buyers and sellers are trading a homogeneous product under conditions of perfect knowledge and freedom of exit from and entry into the market, *perfect competition* exists. In perfectly competitive conditions no single firm has a perceptible influence on the market price. Firms are price takers with no market power. Given perfect knowledge there is no need to advertise or product differentiate and no agency problems arise. A firm's only decision variable is its output level and, in the long run, the choice of an appropriate plant size.

In the short run, given U-shaped cost curves, output Q is chosen so as to profit maximise. That is, output is at that level at which marginal revenue (or price) is equal to marginal cost. The mathematical proof of this marginalistic rule is simple. By definition total revenue $\text{TR} = PQ$ and total cost $\text{TC} = f(Q)$. Total profit Π is given by

$$\Pi = \text{TR} - \text{TC}.$$

To maximise

$$\Pi = PQ - f(Q)$$

where P is given (market determined) and $f'(Q) > 0$, the marginal cost of production, is eventually rising as output expands (see Chapter 6), the following condition must be fulfilled.

$$\frac{d\Pi}{dQ} = P - f'(Q) = 0$$

or

$$P = f'(Q).$$

Therefore, to maximise profits the firm produces that output at which price is equal to marginal cost. In Figure 8.1(a) this is shown by point a. Given the market price P the firm produces q_1 and enjoys a residual income known in traditional theory as super-normal profit. This is the excess of price over average cost (AC), when average cost has been calculated to include the opportunity costs of all the factors of production, including capital. At P_0 production is q_0 and at P_e it is q_e. In general, provided that the market price is higher than the average variable cost of production, the firm's output is indicated by its marginal cost (MC) curve. Thus, the marginal cost curve, above a certain point, coincides with the firm's short-run supply curve. The industry supply is the horizontal sum of the supply curves of all the firms in the industry. Its shape and position depends, therefore, on the shape of the cost curves of the individual firms and on the number of firms operating in the industry.

In Figure 8.1 if the market demand (labelled D) and the market supply (labelled S) are as shown so that the market clearing price is P each firm enjoys super-normal profits, the size of which is indicated by the shaded area. This is, however, a short-run equilibrium which cannot be sustained in the long run. If capital can earn a higher rate of return in this industry than in its best available alternative use and there are no obstacles to entry, new firms will enter this industry and existing ones may expand their operations. Total production and supply will therefore increase. In Figure 8.1(b) new entry means that the supply curve S moves to the right and, given D, the price starts to fall. The expansion will continue for as long as $P > AC$. When S has expanded to S', price has fallen sufficiently to equal the minimum average cost of production. At point P_e, output is q_e, normal profit is earned and there is no new entry into or exit from this industry. Provided that AC is the long-run average cost curve, firms have no reason to adjust the size of their plant, so that P_e and Q_e represent the long-run equilibrium market price and output. If AC refers to the short run and it can be reduced by altering the size of the firm then, given time, the firm will adjust its plant size so as to reduce costs and increase profits or eliminate any losses. In the long run the number of identical firms operating in this market is Q_e/q_e and the market price equals the minimum cost of production. Symbolically,

$$P_e = \text{SRMC} = \text{LRMC} = \text{SRATC} = \text{LRAC}_{min}.$$

It should be noted that industry-wide changes may affect the costs of each firm and have an impact on the market price. As the industry size expands some factor prices may increase while others may decline. Input requirements may also change. For example, congestion may occur thus increasing transportation time, or pollution and depletion of natural resources may increase the costs of production. On the other hand if expansion is backed by government provision of extra facilities or improved worker training, costs may fall so that expansion may bring about a reduction in the unit cost of production.

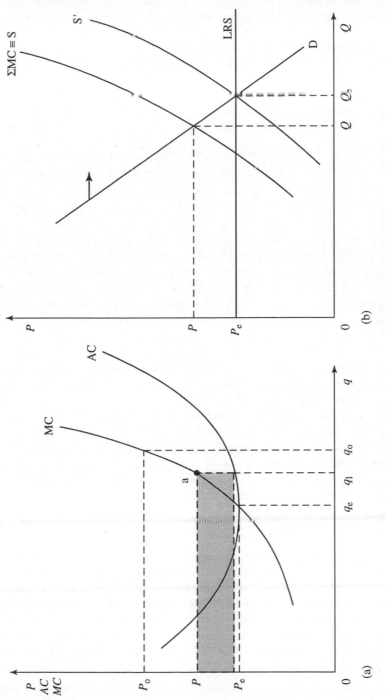

Figure 8.1 The short-run and the long-run supply curve of a constant cost competitive industry: (a) perfectly competitive firm; (b) perfectly competitive market

If industrial expansion has no effect on costs or its beneficial effects cancel out any detrimental effects, the industry size has no impact on a firm's cost curves. In this case the industry is known as a constant cost industry since extra output can be provided at the same price. To illustrate, suppose that demand increases so that, in Figure 8.1(b), D shifts to the right (direction of the arrow). The price and the firm's profitability increase. New firms enter, in the long run, and supply expands. S shifts to the right and price begins to fall until it becomes P_e again. In brief, an expansion in D causes S to expand, in due time, restoring the price level. The long-run supply curve is a horizontal line at P_e. Thus in the short run price changes in response to a change in demand but in the long run it tends to return to the same level provided the cost of production remains constant.

It is possible, however, that industrial expansion may alter the cost of production of each firm in the industry. When costs increase as the size of the industry expands, the market is said to be subject to external diseconomies of production. In this case, a demand expansion and the concomitant increase in price and profits attract new firms in the industry which may create resource shortages or other production difficulties which increase production costs. Thus, while the increase in supply halts or reverses the initial increase in price the increase in costs prevents it from reverting to its initial equilibrium level (if it did firms would incur losses and exit the industry forcing the price up). Equilibrium is established when the price becomes equal to the new minimum average cost of production. But since the new minimum average cost has increased, the new equilibrium price is at a higher level. More is supplied but at a higher price. The long-run supply curve is upwards sloping.

When industrial expansion is associated with decreases in the firm's cost of production the industry is subject to external economies of scale. In this case as new firms enter the industry increased supply tends to reduce the price and at the same time costs of production fall inducing a further reduction in price. More is supplied at a lower price. This implies a negatively inclined long-run supply curve.

The efficiency of competitive markets

The abstraction of the perfectly competitive theory from organisational issues, its failure to recognise the influence that human attributes may have on the affairs of the firm and its assumption of perfect knowledge restrict its interest to business practitioners. However, the efficiency characteristics of competitive prices are widely admired 'by customers, for they connote the absence of monopoly power; by lawyers, since the anti-trust laws are designed to achieve competition; and by economists' (Stigler 1966: 178) for two reasons.

1 Competitive prices lead to an optimal distribution of output among firms. Each firm's output is at the same marginal cost. Therefore, it is

impossible to reduce the cost of total production by reshuffling output among the existing firms. For a given cost structure, total production is at minimum cost.

2 Resource allocation is optimal (output is 'correct'). That resource allocation is the best possible follows from the presumption that firms operate where $P = MC$. That is, at the margin, price is equal to marginal cost. Now assuming that price is an indicator of the importance (or value) that consumers attach to marginal units of output and that marginal cost indicates the value (or opportunity cost) of the resources required to produce a marginal unit, $P = MC$ implies that output is optimal. At smaller volumes of output $P > MC$, which means that consumers value an extra unit of output by more than they value the resources required for its production. Thus, expansion in output would be beneficial. As output increases the gap between price and marginal cost diminishes. However, so long as $P > MC$ there are unexploited benefits which are eliminated only when production is such that $P = MC$. Similarly, if output were such that $P > MC$, the marginal unit of output is valued less than the resources required for its production. A reduction in output would therefore be beneficial.

The optimality properties of perfect competition should, however, be qualified on several counts.

1 As indicated in Chapter 7 consumer demand depends partly on preferences and partly on consumer incomes. What prices prevail, at any point in time, is determined by the existing income distribution. Indeed the optimality of competitive markets is derived on the assumption of a given income distribution. Thus, competitive prices are good indicators of society's desires for different commodities if the underlying income distribution is correct, but are not otherwise.

2 Marginal cost is a good indicator of the value of resources that must be used to produce a marginal unit of output only if properly calculated to include all the opportunity costs of production. In particular, any social costs of production, i.e. any costs which the firm does not bear itself but which it imposes on others without compensation, must be taken into account when calculating marginal costs. Pollution, noise, diminution of natural resources or the destruction of the environment provide examples of costs which producers may impose on others rather than bear themselves. In such cases the private costs deviate from the true social costs of production. When decisions are based on private rather than on social costs, production is likely to be too large.

3 The optimal properties of perfectly competitive industries do not hold true when industries are subject to external economies of production (i.e. when the industry supply curve is negatively sloping). In this case the total production is too small. The condition $P = MC$ fails to indicate that extra output would bring about a reduction in costs and prices.

Monopoly

A monopoly exists when there is a single firm in an industry. Monopolies are, almost by definition, large firms operating in markets protected by high barriers to entry and producing commodities for which there are few substitutes. In reality single firm control of an entire industry, although rare, occurs more frequently than perfect competition. Moreover, highly concentrated industries, which may behave monopolistically, are commonly observed.

Two types of monopolies can be distinguished: 'natural' and 'pure'. A *natural monopoly* exists when the minimum efficient scale (MES) of operation is so large compared with the market that only one firm can serve the market efficiently. In other words, if more than one firm existed each would operate at a suboptimal scale of production. In the case of single-product firms, natural monopolies emerge when economies of scale are significant; i.e. when the total cost $C(Q)$ of producing any output Q is less than the sum of the cost of two or more firms each producing part of this output, i.e.

$$C(Q) < C(Y) + C(Q - Y)$$

where $0 < Y < Q$. This condition must hold for all Y and for all $Q < Q^*$ where Q^* is the socially desirable output.

In the context of multi-product firms a natural monopoly exists when economies of scope are combined with decreasing average incremental costs of each product (see Chapter 6). As in the single-product case, production by a single firm is more efficient than production by two or more firms.

Examples of natural monopolies are provided by many public utilities such as transport, telecommunications, sewage, natural gas, electricity, etc.

Pure monopolies are all other monopolies. They owe their existence to barriers to entry and may be single- or multi-plant operations.

Monopolies are often dynamic firms whose behaviour may vary with their objectives, organisation and ownership structure. Since behaviour under alternative business objectives is examined in the next chapter, we assume here profit maximisation. Profit, in an accounting sense, is the difference between total revenue (PQ) and total cost (TC). That is, $\Pi = PQ - \text{TC}$, where the maximum price P corresponding to any output Q is determined by the demand function $P = g(Q)$, and costs vary according to output, i.e. $\text{TC} = f(Q)$. It follows that the firm aims to maximise $\Pi = g(Q)Q - f(Q)$ which implies that price will be set at such a level as to sell that output at which marginal revenue is equal to marginal cost. The derivation of this marginalistic rule is as follows. If we assume 'well-behaved' demand and cost functions, profit is maximised when the derivative of

$$\Pi = g(Q)Q - f(Q)$$

with respect to Q is set equal to zero. That is,

$$\frac{d\Pi}{dQ} = g'(Q)\,Q + g(Q) - f'(Q) = 0$$

or

$$g'(Q)Q + g(Q) = f'(Q)$$

where $g'(Q)Q + g(Q)$ is the marginal revenue and $f'(Q)$ is the marginal cost of production.

Single- and multi-plant monopolies

The equilibrium of a single-plant profit maximising monopolist, illustrated in Figure 8.2, is at output Q and price P. The profit maximising output Q is determined by the intersection of MR and MC and the corresponding

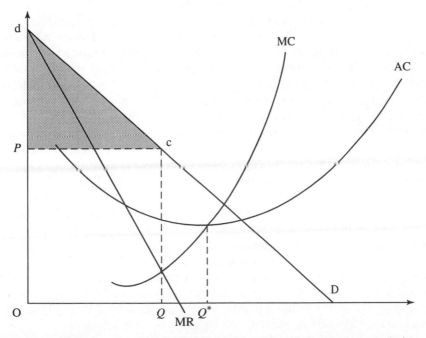

Figure 8.2 A single-plant monopolist (area *Pdc* indicates consumers' surplus)

price P is determined by the demand curve. That output Q is the profit maximising output becomes apparent by examining the profitability of alternative outputs. Consider, for example, the production of an extra unit of Q. Since its marginal cost is greater than its marginal revenue, it adds more to costs than to revenues, thus reducing total profit. Alternatively, producing one unit less than Q reduces revenues by more than it saves on costs, reducing total profitability.

Now if the cost curve, AC, indicates the lowest cost that can be achieved for any volume of output given the 'state of the arts', the plant size is optimal. That is, the cost of Q cannot be reduced by adjustments to the plant size. The firm produces Q for as long as demand and cost conditions remain the same. Price, in the example illustrated, is higher than marginal cost which implies allocative inefficiencies[1] and plant under-utilisation. Moreover, there is no reason for price and production to change either in the short run or in the long run. Excess capacity, however, is not a necessary feature of monopolies. Depending on the size of the market in relation to costs, monopolists could over- or under-utilise their facilities. Producing the cost minimising output, Q^*, could occur but only accidentally. That is, although a monopolist would if necessary adjust the size of its plant in order to lower the unit cost of a given production level, there is no market mechanism that ensures the efficient plant utilisation of a single-plant monopolist.

Production efficiency, however, improves in multi-plant operations. Indeed, monopolists often operate more than one plant of production for reasons of efficiency. This occurs when common ownership economises on transaction costs and small production units save on production costs. As Buckley (1989: 6) put it, 'multi-plant operation is often a rational response to problems of manufacturing highly specialised products with volatile demand or other features requiring close managerial supervision of technologies well suited to low volume production'. Moreover, the pursuit of profit induces multi-plant monopolists to adjust the number and size of their plants so as to produce an overall optimal output. Let us consider why. For simplicity assume a U-form organisational structure with centralised decision making producing a homogeneous product and wishing to profit maximise. The managerial problem of deciding the level of total production and its allocation among plants is illustrated in Figure 8.3. A two-plant firm is shown but the analysis applies to any number of plants. The market demand and marginal revenue are labelled D and MR respectively. At any level of output, plant 1 has a lower unit cost than plant 2. The curve ΣMC is the horizontal sum of MC_1 and MC_2. It is the overall marginal cost of the firm and, as explained in Chapter 6, it shows the maximum output that can be produced at each marginal cost when output is optimally allocated among plants. For example, at MC = £3.00 the firm can produce 28 units in plant 1 and 10 units in plant 2.

Consider now the determination of total production. To profit maximise

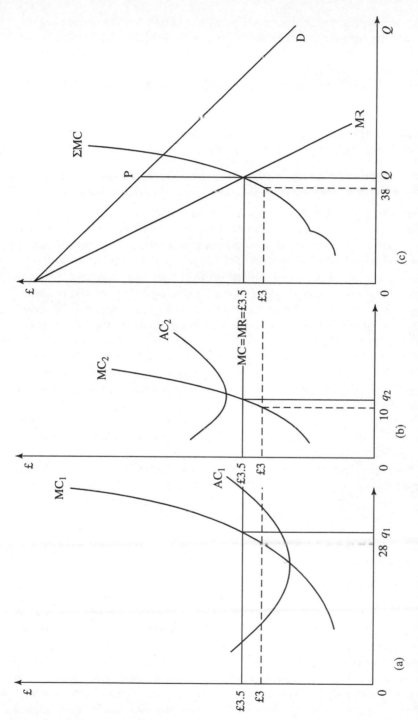

Figure 8.3 Short-run equilibrium of a monopolist operating two plants: (a) plant 1; (b) plant 2; (c) plant 1 + plant 2
Note: The horizontal scale in (c) is smaller than that shown in (a) and (b)

the firm must produce that level of output at which the marginal revenue is equal to its combined marginal cost, i.e. where $MR = \Sigma MC$. The profit maximising price is the maximum price that can be charged for this output, given the market demand.

Having decided to produce Q, management must ensure that the proportion of Q produced in each plant is such that total cost is minimised (which for a given revenue maximises profit). This is achieved when quotas are such that the marginal cost at each plant is the same and equal to the common marginal revenue. In other words, the following condition must hold:

$$MC_1 = MC_2 = MR.$$

It is not difficult to rationalise this condition. First, suppose that the equal marginal cost rule does not hold so that $MC_1 > MC_2$. Then a simple reallocation of production resulting in a lower output in plant 1 and a correspondingly higher output in plant 2 will reduce the total cost of a given level of output, Q, increasing its profits by an equal amount. Second, it should be obvious that as in the case of a single-plant firm, the common marginal cost must be equal to the firm's marginal revenue or production will not be profit maximising. (For a mathematical derivation of these results see Appendix 8.1.)

Inspection of Figure 8.3 clearly shows that in the short run each plant may be under- or over-utilised. In the long run, however, profits can increase by replacing high-cost plants by low-cost plants. In the limit the optimal plant size would be adopted for all plants, costs of production will tend to become identical and production levels equal across plants. The number of plants will also tend to be adjusted so as to produce at minimum average cost.

In brief, production efficiency improves in multi-plant, compared with single-plant, monopoly but the allocative inefficiency ($P > MC$) remains. The question then arises as to whether multi-plant monopoly production is less efficient than the perfectly competitive production.

Comparing perfect competition with monopoly

In comparing perfect competition with monopoly a multi-plant monopoly must be assumed even if small volume production is inefficient. Assume, for example, that a competitive industry consisting of n identical firms is taken over by a monopoly and that cost and demand curves remain the same after the take over.

Figure 8.4(a) shows one of the n firms and Figure 8.4(b) shows the industry. Prior to the takeover total production was Q_c, price was P_c and each firm produced q_c. Post-takeover, output declines to Q_m (where $MR = S$) and price rises to P_m. The reduction of output is distributed among the existing plants proportionately so as to maintain the equal marginal

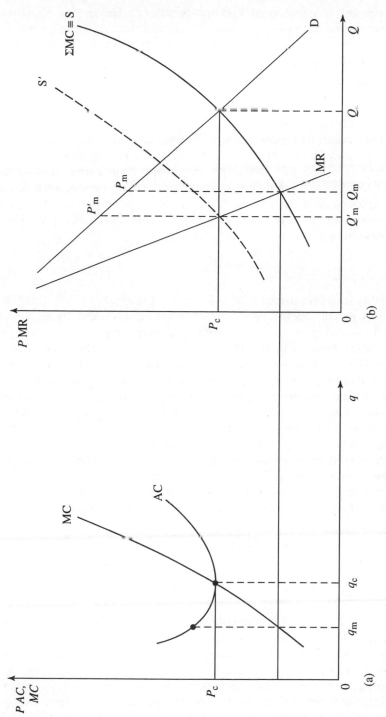

Figure 8.4 Monopolisation of a perfectly competitive industry

cost rule. As a result each firm produces q_m. This is the short-term response. In the long run some plants will be closed down to ensure that each of the remaining plants produces at minimum cost. This shifts the S curve to the left bringing a further reduction in total output to Q'_m. Price is P'_m.

A restriction in output and an increase in price is a well-known prediction of the monopolisation of a perfectly competitive industry. It should be noted, however, that this result may be mitigated by cost reductions associated with monopolisation. If cost reductions are substantial it is conceivable that output may remain constant or even increase. In either case, however, price remains higher than marginal cost. The allocative inefficiencies of monopoly remain so that any production efficiency improvements must be sufficiently high for the monopolisation of an industry to have an overall beneficial effect. (This is particularly significant for competition policy.)

Monopoly power

The ability of a firm to maintain price above marginal cost is indicative of *monopoly power*. Such power depends on the price elasticity of demand (which in turn depends on the availability of substitutes) and any competitive pressures under which a firm operates. The lower the price elasticity and the less competitive a market is, the higher the ability of a firm to charge prices in excess of costs. Since both price elasticity and competitive pressures from existing or potential competitors are difficult to quantify, it is difficult to measure a firm's monopoly power. The difficulties are compounded when firms decide not to exercise their full monopoly power in order, for example, to discourage potential competition or for fear of government intervention or a desire to built a good public image. It is, therefore, difficult to quantify the extent of the potential monopoly power of an industry. All that can be measured in practice is the power actually exercised. This can be quantified by the well-known Lerner index defined as

$$\text{monopoly power} = \frac{P - \text{MC}}{P}$$

where $0 \leqslant (P - \text{MC})/P \leqslant 1$. In perfect competition, since $P = \text{MC}$, the index is zero indicating the lack of monopoly power. As the deviation of price from marginal cost increases the index approaches unity indicating higher degrees of monopoly power. This performance orientation of the Lerner index constitutes both a weakness and a strength. It is a weakness since it shows the monopoly power a firm chooses to exercise rather than the monopoly power it could potentially exercise. It is a strength since 'it directly reflects the allocatively inefficient departure of price from marginal cost associated with monopoly' (Scherer 1980: 56).

Price discrimination

Firms often adopt a variety of monopoly power enhancing practices. Price discrimination is one such practice. It exists when the same product is sold at different prices, to different consumers, for reasons not associated with differences in costs. The non-discriminating firm of Figure 8.2 maximises profit at price P and output Q. Profits would, however, increase by an amount equal to area Pdc, if each unit of output, from O to Q, were sold at the highest price it could fetch. Total revenue would then be $OdcQ$ which is higher than revenue at the uniform price. The difference, $OdcQ - PQ$ (shaded triangle below the demand curve), indicates by how much the total value consumers place on Q units of production is higher than the total outlay they have to incur to acquire the Q units at the uniform price P. This is a benefit to consumers known as *consumers' surplus*. It arises because a condition of information impactedness exists. Consumers may know their true valuation of a product but are unlikely to voluntarily pass this information to producers. The cost involved in overcoming this lack of information, by for example organising an auction, is, for most products, higher than the expected increase in revenues. Thus, selling each unit at a different price, a practice known as 'first degree price discrimination', is impractical.

To appropriate part of the consumers' surplus while maintaining a uniform price, firms often charge an 'entrance fee' or a standing charge which is independent of consumption levels. The difficulty with this practice is that since the size of consumers' surplus varies among individual customers, a uniform fee drives out of the market those customers whose surplus is lower than the entrance fee. Setting a low entrance fee to mitigate against this risk implies that only a small part of consumers' surplus is transferred to suppliers. As a result suppliers often seek other discriminatory practices, such as charging different prices to the same customer for different quantities demanded (block tariffs) or different prices to different groups of customers (third degree price discrimination).

Block tariffs or second degree price discrimination

Block tariffs or second degree price discrimination exists when customers are charged a uniform price for the first x units consumed and a lower price for the next block of y units etc. The effects of this pricing scheme can be analysed with the help of Figure 8.5(a). A uniform price P_3 implies an outlay of P_3Q_3 and consumers' surplus of P_3Dc. Charging three different prices increases the total outlay (revenue to the supplier) by the shaded area and reduces the consumers' surplus by the same amount. This reduction in consumers' surplus does not affect all consumers equally unless they have identical demand curves. As Oni (1971) has shown, if all consumers had the same demand curve, say dd' in Figure 8.5(b), then the

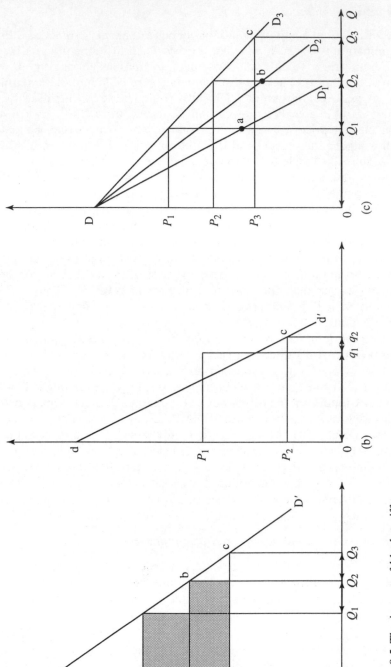

Figure 8.5 The impact of block tariffs

price for the first block of units, q_1, could be set at P_1 and that of the second block at P_2. The total demand would then be q_2 units provided that the total expenditure $P_1q_1 + P_2q_2$ were no higher than expenditure P_2q_2 plus the consumers' surplus indicated by area P_2dc. All consumers would then be affected equally.

In reality consumers have different incomes and different demand curves so that the impact of block tariffs and the way consumers respond to their imposition vary accordingly. Figure 8.5(c) indicates the demand curve of each of three consumers with different incomes. The poorest customer's demand is labelled D_1. The maximum outlay this consumer would be prepared to make, i.e. this consumer's reservation outlay, for Q_1 units is indicated by area $0DaQ_1$. Provided that the price charged for the first block of units, P_1, is such that the required expenditure P_1Q_1 is equal to the reservation outlay, the consumer buys Q_1 units and has no surplus; otherwise she or he demands less than Q_1. Similarly the second consumer will buy Q_2 units provided that his or her reservation outlay (area $0DbQ_2$) is no higher than the required expenditure $P_1Q_1 + P_2Q_2$. The richest consumer whose demand is D_3 will buy Q_3 units and will enjoy some surplus since the total outlay is less than area $0DcQ_3$.

Several implications of block tariff pricing have been noted by Hay and Morris (1991) and others. First, setting blocks in a way that maximises revenues is difficult in practice since information on market and consumer demand is limited. Second, block tariffs can extract all or most of consumers' surplus from the poorest consumers while leaving large proportions of their surplus to the richer ones. Moreover, customers in their attempt to maximise the difference between reservation outlays and required outlays are self-selecting. The firm does not need to distinguish between them.

The welfare implications of block tariffs can be serious especially when they apply to public utilities. Despite their potential adverse welfare implications and the difficulties encountered in their implementation, block tariffs are commonly adopted in the pricing of gas, electricity, telephone and other services. Table 8.1 gives, as examples, the pricing scheme of British Gas (North Thames region) valid on 1 April 1991 and British Telecom's charges introduced in September 1991.

Third degree price discrimination

This exists when different market segments are charged different prices for reasons not associated with differences in costs. This kind of discrimination is feasible only if markets can be effectively segregated so that resale from the lower to the higher priced market is not possible. Discrimination is profitable when the separated market segments have different demand elasticities. For example, electricity tariffs for business customers who are presumably less sensitive to price changes are often higher than tariffs charged to domestic customers, as Table 8.2 shows.

Table 8.1 Block tariff pricing

British Gas	
Consumption (therms)	Price per therm[a]
1–5,000	45.9p
Next 5,000	43.9p
Next 5,000	42.9p
Next 10,000	41.9p
British Telecom	
Units per quarter	Price per unit excluding VAT[b]
0–2,381	4.20p
2,382–6,140	3.99p
Each unit over 6,140	3.86p

Notes: [a] A standing charge of £9.40 per quarter was charged to each domestic customer.
[b] A standing charge, cheaper off-peak rates (which may or may not be discriminatory) and differential treatment of local and long distance calls were also applicable.

Table 8.2 Eastern Electricity tariffs for 1991–2 excluding VAT

Domestic	Business
D1 Domestic General Tariff Unit price 7.17p	*BE1 Business and Enterprise Tariff* Up to 1,001 units, unit price 9.61p Follow on, unit price 7.17p
D2 Economy 7 Tariff Day unit price 7.17p Night unit price 2.65p	*BE4 Business Day and Night Tariff* First 1,001 day units price 10.38p Over 1,001, follow on unit price 8.07p Night unit price (12 h) 3.92p Night unit price (10 h) 3.83p

The impact of third degree price discrimination can be analysed graphically. In Figure 8.6 the market is divided into two segments supplied by a single-plant monopolist. The demand and marginal revenue curves of each segment are D_1, MR_1 and D_2, MR_2 respectively, while the common marginal cost is MC. To determine the profit maximising output, the marginal revenues must be added horizontally (ΣMR) and compared with the marginal cost. The intersection of ΣMR and MC defines the optimal level of total production, Q. The distribution of this output among the two markets (q_1 and q_2) must be such as to ensure that the marginal revenue of each market is equal to the common marginal cost. That is, the rule $MR_1 = MR_2 = MC$ must hold. Graphically q_1 and q_2 are located at the points where a line parallel to the x axis drawn at the height of the intersection of MC and ΣMR meets MR_1 and MR_2 respectively.

The corresponding prices P_1 and P_2 are not equal. Price discrimination prevails. The mathematical derivation of the equal marginal revenue rule is given in Appendix 8.2. Intuitively, however, it should be clear that if sales distribution was such that marginal revenues were not equal a redistribution of total sales away from the low and towards the high

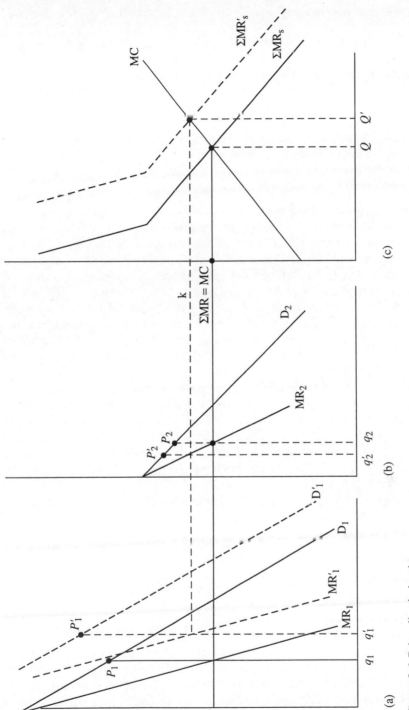

Figure 8.6 Price discrimination

marginal revenue market would increase the firm's total revenue and profits.

It should be noted that, unless marginal cost is constant, the two markets are inter-related in the sense that any change in demand conditions in one market has repercussions in the other. The broken lines in Figure 8.6 trace out the effects of an increase in demand in market 1. Since MR_1 increases, ΣMR increases and, given the same cost conditions, equilibrium occurs at the higher output Q'. More is sold in market 1 at a higher price. This expansion, however, is associated with higher per unit costs, which implies a higher price and lower sales in market 2.

In reality a variety of practices are adopted in order to facilitate price discrimination.

1 Product differentiation may be undertaken in an attempt to segment the market. Less price sensitive market segments can then be charged prices significantly higher than the cost of product differentiation. Since customers have different incomes, tastes, information, etc., changes in products may be introduced in order to appeal to different groups of customers. This kind of discrimination exists, for example, in the pricing of motorcars when the same basic car fitted with different features or extras (different engine sizes or luxury items such as carpets, radios, automatic switches, etc.) is sold at prices which reflect the income of different groups of customers rather than the difference in the cost of the extra features.
2 Charging a uniform price in different parts of the country, as some chain stores do, may imply price discrimination if transport costs differ.
3 Differentiation over time. Pricing according to the life cycle of a product may also constitute price discrimination. In pricing new products some firms adopt a skimming pricing policy and others a penetration pricing policy (Dean 1969). Skimming pricing is a policy of high prices when the product first appears and lower prices later on. The idea is to appeal to the highest income groups first and also attempt to discover the relevant elasticity of demand.

Oligopoly

The term oligopoly derives from the Greek word for 'a few' (oligos) and the Greek verb 'to sell' (polo), so it literary means a market with a few sellers. In economics 'a few' does not, however, refer to a particular number; it rather means a number small enough for there to be inter-dependence. Thus, an oligopoly is more accurately described as an industry in which each firm knows that its own actions may trigger competitive reactions which in turn influence the effectiveness of the initial action and must therefore be anticipated. Decision making is thus dependent on conjectures about rival behaviour. In other words, an oligopoly can be defined as a market consisting of a number of interdependent firms. The extent of this interdependence varies from market to market and may depend on the extent of product differentiation, the height of barriers to entry and exit, the extent of concentration and other market characteristics such as human attributes and informational channels. What is significant is that firms are aware that the outcome of any decision depends on the initial action and on the consequent competitive reactions. When selecting an advertising budget, for example, a firm considers the possibility that its own successful advertising campaign may impinge on competitors' market shares who are thus likely to respond by increasing their own advertising budgets which in turn may mitigate the initial success. Similarly, a price or output change may induce rival reactions which can mitigate the impact of the initial change.

It follows that, to be effective, decision makers must take into account competitive reactions despite the fact that such reactions are not generally known and can take a variety of forms. For example, the effectiveness of a price reduction by one firm will depend on whether competing firms react by (a) maintaining their prices unchanged, in which case an increase in sales and in the firm's market share may occur, (b) matching the price reduction, in which case market shares may be retained even though total sales may increase somewhat, or (c) reducing their prices to a greater extent in which case a price war may ensue.

In brief, oligopolistic market conduct depends on the particular form of business interactions that prevails at any point in time and since the set of likely reaction patterns can be very large it is not possible to construct a general theory of oligopoly. The significance of the conjectural interdependence of firms can be made clear by considering the classic Cournot and Edgeworth models of oligopoly.

The Cournot model assumes that each firm selects its output level on the expectation that its competitors will maintain theirs unchanged. On this assumption, after a series of actions and reactions the industry reaches a state of equilibrium known as 'Cournot equilibrium'. A Cournot equilibrium is said to exist when the output rates chosen by firms are such that, given the output rates of rivals, no firm can improve its profits by altering its production level. This is a stable equilibrium at a price lower than the monopoly price but higher than the competitive price. The exact price level depends on the number of firms.

An unstable equilibrium at a different price level, however, is achieved in the Edgeworth model which is the same as the Cournot model except that it assumes that each firm adjusts its price (rather than output) on the belief that its competitors will attempt to maintain their prices constant. The concept of equilibrium can be extended to embrace any variables, in which case we refer to a Nash equilibrium. For any decision variable a 'Nash equilibrium' is said to exist if any firm in the industry has no incentive to alter the size of its decision variable given the strategy of its rivals (Davies *et al.* 1988).

Rather than delve into the details of the more abstract oligopoly models we can illustrate the significance of conjectural interdependence by examining the theory of the kinked demand curve. This was developed by Paul Sweezy (1939) in order to explain why oligopolistic prices tend to be more stable than prices in other market structures. Price stability, however, was based on the assumption of a particular form of interdependence and is eliminated when this is relaxed.

Suppose that the products of an oligopolistic industry are very similar and that competitors' conjectures take the following form. Each firm expects that its price reductions would be exactly matched by its competitors so that any increase in sales would be small (total sales may expand somewhat but market shares will be maintained). A firm's perceived demand curve would, therefore, be rather inelastic. It could be curve DD' in Figure 8.7. When considering a price increase, however, the firm expects that its competitors will not have an incentive to match the price increase. This is because they would benefit by gaining new customers at the existing prices. Price increases, therefore, are expected to be associated with a substantial loss of customers to competitors. In other words, the demand curve for price increases is perceived to be rather elastic. This is indicated by curve dd' in Figure 8.7. The existing price is P, and the overall demand, as perceived by the firm, is dPD', with a kink at the prevailing price. The corresponding marginal revenue (MR) curve has a discontinuity (a vertical segment) at the existing production level. If marginal cost is MC, output Q maximises profits and the firm will be reluctant to change its price even if there were changes in costs. Thus, if costs change so that the marginal cost curve shifts up to MC' or falls to MC" the profit maximising output remains unchanged at Q. (At lower outputs MR > MC and at higher outputs MC > MR.) Price remains the same. It is also possible (although not certain) that demand conditions may change with no change in the price level.

A firm's expectations about competitor reactions, however, may be influenced by the state of the economy or the conditions of the industry. In inflationary periods, for example, or during periods of substantial expansions in product demand, a firm may expect that price increases will be followed by its competitors but not price reductions. In such circumstances there is a reversal in the kink. The demand, as perceived by the firm, is now DPd'. Prices are no longer stable. Firms tend to follow each other's price increases claiming to be passing on the real or imagined increases in factor prices.

The assumptions of the kinked demand curve, although restrictive and pessimistic (the firm expects the worst possible competitor reactions), may be realistic in certain industries and at certain points in time. They may be appropriate when inter-firm knowledge is very poor, which can occur when an industry is at its early stages of development or when a new and unknown rival enters the market. These circumstances are unlikely to

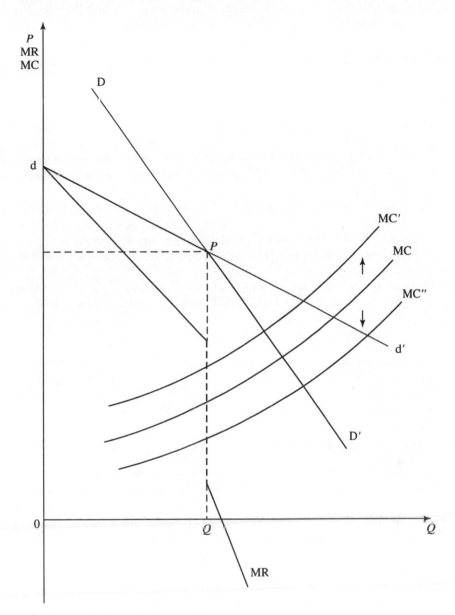

Figure 8.7 The kinked demand curve

persist in the long run, so that the kinked demand is at best a short-run phenomenon. There is some empirical evidence in support of this view. Stigler (1947), for example, analysed the price behaviour of several US oligopolies (such as cars, cigarettes, coal, steel, dynamite and gasoline) over a number of years and concluded that his evidence indicated instances where the assumptions of the kinked demand were verified but did not lend support to the general validity of the kinked demand curve.

Not only is there no evidence of the general validity of the kinked demand curve, the existence of price stability in the face of changing demand or cost conditions does not necessarily imply the existence of a kinked demand curve. Price stability may exist in oligopolistic markets even in the absence of a kinked demand curve for several reasons.

1 Price changes are expensive. Price labels need to be altered, catalogues reprinted, staff must become familiar with new prices and customers must be informed. Depending on circumstances it may be cost effective to maintain the same price in the face of small cost increases or other market changes.
2 Price instability adds to uncertainty. Oligopolistic firms may prefer non-price competition such as advertising, research and development (R&D) expenditure and other promotional activities which if successful may enhance product differentiation and a firm's image and goodwill thus reducing firm interdependence and uncertainty.
3 Price stability may also be the result of co-operative or price fixing agreements. Once an agreement has been arrived at, it will tend to persist despite changes in costs or demand conditions because of the expense and the risks involved in renegotiations.

In brief, oligopolistic market conduct is significantly dependent on conjectures regarding rival reactions, which may occasionally result in price stability or price wars and which implies that a general theory of oligopoly cannot be constructed easily.

COLLUSIVE AGREEMENTS

Oligopolistic interdependence creates uncertainty and rivalry which may result in price wars. To avoid such risks and to increase their market power, firms often enter into formal or informal collusive agreements. The nature of such agreements varies with the product, the characteristics of the market, the entrepreneurship of the market participants and any legal restriction that may exist. Collusive agreements can be explicit and formal (cartels) or tacit (price leaderships).

Cartels

Formal collusive agreements aimed at securing monopolistic prices have a history stretching back to Babylon, Ancient Greece and Rome (Utton 1970). During the 1930s in Germany nearly all raw materials and semi-finished products and almost a quarter of final products were covered by formal restrictive agreements. In Switzerland, in 1953, a government commission found 136 formal horizontal price fixing cartels. By 1967, several hundreds of price fixing agreements were registered in the European Economic Community (EEC) to avoid anti-trust prosecution by Article 85 of the EEC treaty. Following the 1956 Restrictive Practices Act many cases[2] heard by the UK Restrictive Practices Court involved highly developed, 'complete collusive' agreements (Utton 1970). The formal agreement of the thirteen oil producing and exporting countries (OPEC) and that of the international air transport association (IATA) are among the better known international cartels.

What is perhaps less well known is the impressively large number of illegal price fixing agreements operating currently in the UK and other countries. The following is part of a list of UK cartels recently revealed by the BBC (1992).

1983	Milk	Four major dairies secretly agreed not to compete.
1984	Ferries	Townsend Thorensen and Sealink fix prices on the Scotland–Northern Ireland route.
1986	Betting shops	Four major chains secretly agree to keep the same opening hours and not to compete with each other.
1987	Black top	157 price fixing agreements operated among companies making asphalt and macadam.
1988	Glass	Over forty companies admit to carving up the market and fixing the price at the customer's expense.
1991	Sugar	Two big companies, Tate and Lyle and British Sugar, admit to price rigging for over two years.
1991	Fuel oil	Seventeen companies in the north-east of England are involved in a price fixing agreement.
1991	Concrete	Companies all over the country admit to over sixty-five price fixing and market rigging arrangements.

The full list includes, among others, ICI's collusive agreements which span the history of the company since its creation. ICI, Britain's largest manufacturing company, is 'steeped in the cartel culture' (BBC 1992). In the last decade alone it has been caught in four major cartels, one of which has been going on for, literally, a hundred years. Since Victorian times ICI, in collusion with the Belgian company SOLVE, secretly fixed the price of soda ash, one of the raw materials used in the production of glass. They were discovered in 1990. Between 1970 and 1983 ICI was the prime mover in the European Polypropylene cartel. Between 1980 and 1987 ICI and Shell, the oil company, were fixing the price of PVC and between 1976 and 1987 they were fixing the price of plastic film. (ICI was fined a total of £22 million for its participation in these illegal practices.)

Perfect cartels

The term cartel is commonly used to describe a variety of collaborative agreements ranging from a weak link to a tightly neat formal collaboration pertaining to all aspects of production and trading. In fact, any formal agreement pertaining to price, output or other feature of a transaction is called a *cartel*. In its extreme form a cartel may attempt to operate as a monopoly. In this case, the aim of collusion is to maximise the joint profits of the group of firms participating in the agreement and the cartel is called a 'perfect' or a 'joint profit maximising' cartel. To achieve this aim the agreement attempts to establish a common price at the monopoly level, which implies that the cartel must operate as a multi-plant monopolist. To illustrate consider Figure 8.8 which assumes an industry made up of three firms producing a similar product under different cost conditions. The market demand is labelled D.

The operations of the cartel are usually co-ordinated by a central management or a cartel syndicate to which information regarding cost and demand conditions is communicated. To maximise the industry profit, the syndicate must charge the monopoly price and ensure that the correspond-ing output is produced at minimum cost. The profit maximising total output Q is determined by the intersection of MR and ΣMC (the horizontal sum of the three marginal cost curves). The corresponding price P_m is the monopoly price. To minimise the total cost of production, the allocation of Q among the three firms must be such that the marginal equivalence holds (see the discussion on multi-plant monopolies earlier). This requires production quotas q_1, q_2 and q_3, which imply that profits vary greatly and firm 3 incurs losses. To ensure the co-operation of the loss making firm the other two may need to subsidise it.

A profit sharing agreement is indeed often necessary if high-cost firms with small quotas and insufficient profits are to be persuaded to join the cartel and to resist the inherent incentive to cheat. An incentive to 'free ride' is always present in price fixing agreements since each member to the agreement can benefit by undercutting the common price, provided that all other members do not act similarly. Careful monitoring and policing of quotas and prices is thus necessary.

Free riding incentives and the costs and difficulties of policing agree-ments often lead to the view that perfect cartel agreements are, in reality, infeasible or can only be achieved with substantial compromises which prevent a cartel from arriving at the monopoly price. It is also argued that 'free riding' creates instability and a tendency for cartel agreements to break down. The reasons for such claims are as follows.

Difficulties of arriving at an agreement

Problems hindering cartel agreements are associated with large numbers of firms and significant differences in their cost structures.

The more firms there are in an oligopoly the more difficult it becomes to arrive at an agreement, since increased numbers increase the diversity of opinion as to what is fair and proper. Negotiations become lengthier

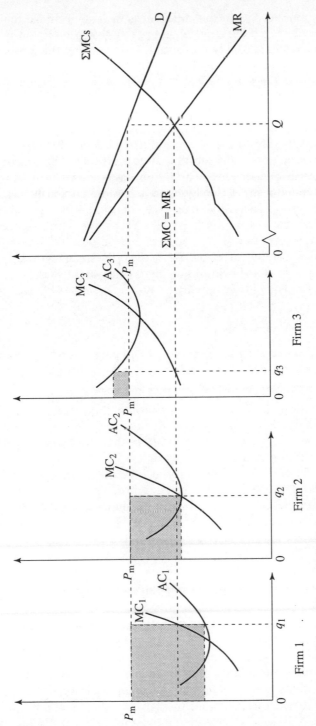

Figure 8.8 A joint profit maximisation cartel

and more expensive. Significant differences in costs increase the chances that some firms may be offered unacceptably low production quotas. A profit sharing agreement may not be able to overcome this problem. It is unlikely, for example, that a high-cost firm may accept, voluntarily, to exit the market so that the remaining firms may increase their profits. Yet there are instances when this happens. ICI, for example, under a pre-Second World War agreement, had promised to pay its potential competitors in the Soviet Union annual compensation payments in return for the Russian's agreeing not to export certain listed chemicals (BBC 1992).

Finally large numbers and substantial cost diversity may make a cartel agreement infeasible because of the high costs associated with effective policing and monitoring of the agreement in these circumstances.

It is thus often suggested that complete collusion is only practical where the number of firms is relatively small. Yet, there are instances where price agreements are successfully maintained despite large numbers. For example, price agreements existed in the UK manufacturing industry with carpet production having as many as fifty-eight members and the production of nuts and bolts having forty-four members (Utton 1970).

Factors hindering monopoly pricing

Several factors, including large numbers and cost diversity, opportunistic behaviour and the need for concessions, may contribute to a cartel's inability to charge the full monopoly price.

1 Since a firm's quota (and possibly its profitability) is larger the lower its costs, firms will have an incentive to under-report their true costs. In terms of Figure 8.8 this means a shift in the ΣMC curve to the right. Production increases and price falls below P_m.
2 The price elasticity of demand may also be over-estimated leading to a lower price. This may occur since each firm's perceived demand curve was, prior to the agreement, more elastic due to the existence of rivalry which will not exist after the agreement. Such mistakes and biases in demand estimation increase with the number of participating firms.
3 A profit sharing agreement may be difficult to implement in which case high-cost firms cannot be asked to produce a very small output or no output at all. In other words, production quotas may need to be realistic. Saudi Arabia, for example, one of the leading OPEC members, is often reported to produce less than its allotted petrol quota in order to compensate for over-production by other OPEC countries.
4 The fear of government intervention, the possibility of new entry or a desire to maintain a good public image may lead a cartel (like a monopoly) to avoid charging the full monopoly price.
5 Assuming that a cartel is able to arrive at the monopoly price, it is unlikely that it will be able to adjust this price, as frequently as a

monopolist would, in response to changing market conditions. Agreements often require expensive and protracted negotiations, and re-negotiations run the added risk that the initial agreement may break down. Cartel agreements, therefore, are normally reviewed at set intervals with the price remaining constant for the duration of the interval. This relative stability of cartel prices implies that they become obsolete and different to the monopoly price when demand and cost conditions change frequently.

The inherent instability of cartel agreements

Cartel agreements are periodically re-negotiated in order to respond to changing market conditions. Re-negotiations, however, carry the risk that differing views as to what the terms of the agreement should be can lead to an irreconcilable divergence of opinions which might threaten the very existence of a cartel. In 1988, for example, it was reported that for two years, during OPEC production re-negotiations, Iraq refused to accept an OPEC production quota unless it matched that given to Iran. She also defied the 1988 OPEC production limits in order to recoup production lost in the recent war with Iran and to help finance the post-war reconstruction programme (*Guardian* 27 September 1988).

Perhaps more seriously, the stability of the agreement is threatened by the 'free rider' problem hinted at earlier on. Since the cartel price is kept high (at P_m) by restricting production quotas, each firm is faced with a fixed price which is higher than its marginal cost. Each firm, therefore, can increase its profit by increasing production, provided that all other cartel members maintain their agreed quotas. This incentive to free ride on other firms may be particularly strong for small (high-cost) firms. But since extra sales may only be possible at a lower price firms may be induced to undercut the agreed price as indicated in Figure 8.9.

The collusive price is P_m and the firm's quota of production is q_1. Since $P_m > MC_1$ extra sales (up to q_3) would increase the firm's profits. To sell more, however, the prevailing price must be reduced to an extent dependent on the price elasticity of demand. In Figure 8.9(a), each unit of output after q_1 can be sold at the price indicated by the broken line cc'. Expanding production from q_1 to q_2 increases profits by an amount indicated by the shaded area. Since this analysis applies to all firms, they all have an incentive to expand by undercutting each other causing the agreed price to collapse. The stability of cartels, however, can be ensured by appropriate monitoring and policing. When, for example, the OPEC cartel failed, for a number of years, to stop the slide in the price of crude oil because several of its members over-produced, the ministerial conference of the thirteen countries involved agreed, in December 1984, a system whereby oil production quotas were monitored by independent auditors. In the Oxfordshire concrete cartel (discussed in the application

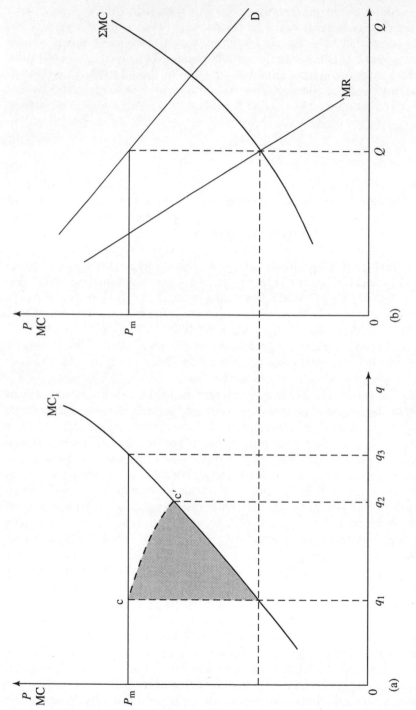

Figure 8.9 The incentive to undercut a collusively set price

section), on the other hand, monitoring of work across the area was based on recordings via an allocations book.

New entry can also have a destabilising effect on a cartelised market since new entrants have an incentive to undercut the existing cartel price in order to gain a market share. Retaliation by cartel members drives the price further down and may initiate a price war. To avoid warfare a new entrant may be asked to join the cartel. Such accommodating behaviour, however, may be an inappropriate strategy for incumbents to follow because it encourages further entry. Empirical evidence tends to confirm that free riding and new entry can lead to serious problems in practice. For example, it is often reported that chiselling and bickering among existing firms and new entrants are the main causes of the breaking up of numerous price fixing agreements.

Market sharing cartels

When the close co-ordination of activity required by perfect cartels is not feasible, looser forms of collusion, such as market sharing cartels, may occur. They can take different forms.

Regional sharing cartels

Regional sharing cartels are agreements intended to eliminate business rivalry by sharing the market regionally among the participating firms. Firms, however, retain the right to set their own price and select their product style, marketing activities and so on. Such a cartel operated, in pre-war years, whereby ICI in co-operation with the German company I.G. Farben and with DuPont shared the world market among themselves. ICI took the old British Empire, I.G. Farben operated in Europe and DuPont in the USA. Furthermore, regional sharing can also be part of a stronger collusive agreement. The Federation of the UK Cement Manufacturers, for example, which controlled cement prices very tightly for over fifty years, operated an agreement whereby each member sold within a particular region.

Non-price competition cartels

Non-price competition cartels are price fixing agreements in which firms remain free to select their own production levels, to pursue product differentiation and to adjust their selling and other promotional activities. That is, firms may compete in any other aspect of business except the price. Such agreements are less stable than perfect cartels since the fixed price can only be sustained by controlling the sales level. Without agreed quotas this will only be possible if all firms have identical cost curves in which case the monopoly price will emerge. When cost differences exist, however, low-cost firms favour a lower price than high-cost firms which causes price instability. Additionally, each firm would benefit if it were the only one to break the agreement by offering discounts. Free riding may lead to instability.

Quota cartels

Quota cartels are agreements pertaining to production levels. Firms agree on output quotas but retain control of their own prices. Any rule may be adopted in the determination of relative output quotas which are unlikely to be equal unless all firms are equally sized and have identical cost curves in which case the monopoly price may emerge. When costs are different, however, quotas and market shares have to be negotiated and may depend on bargaining skills and power. The level of past sales or existing production capacity and quotas can have an influence on the outcome of bargaining.

To sum up, cartel agreements are widespread and varied. They involve different degrees of collusion and stability. Despite their inherent instability many cartel agreements tend to survive for long periods of time so that we cannot conclude that formal collusion is necessarily impractical or unsuccessful. 'Notwithstanding predictions by economists that divisive forces and a 90 percent divergence between price and marginal cost would cause its early demise, the OPEC provides a spectacular counterexample' (Scherer 1980: 173).

Price leadership

Given that formal restrictive agreements are illegal in many countries, business activity is often co-ordinated by informal collusion. Informal collusion can take the form of price leadership, whereby one firm, the leader, announces the price or price change and the other firms in the industry follow the leader's initiative. Wide variations are possible regarding the stability of the leader's position, the reasons for its acceptance as a leader, the influence it has over other firms and its ability to maximise group profit. Three types of price leadership are commonly distinguished.

Barometric price leadership

Barometric price leadership exists when the price leader does no more than act as the industry's barometer. The leader is either one of the firms in the industry or it may belong to another industry. Its acceptance as a leader is due to its ability to reflect, in its pricing strategy, the changing market conditions promptly and effectively. When market conditions are depressed so that the number and amount of price concessions increase and it becomes difficult to maintain list prices, the leader revises list prices downwards and other firms follow. Similarly, in inflationary times, the leader responds to the economic pressures from industry costs by announcing price rises which are followed by the other firms. A classic example of a barometric price leader was the Standard Oil company in Ohio, USA, in the 1950s (Scherer 1980: 183). Its barometric role was particularly evident in periods of recession when it undertook to formalise, through list price announcements, changes that had already taken place in the form of concessions and informal price reductions across the industry.

Price leadership by a low-cost firm

A recognised low-cost firm is often in a position to discipline the industry through the credible threat of a price war. The higher cost firms may therefore have no option but to match the price announcements of the low-cost firm. The leader is effectively forcing the followers off their profit maximising position. In this case the industry price is kept lower than it would be in the absence of price leadership. General Motors' leadership of the American car industry since the Second World War has been described by Scherer as a low cost price leadership (p. 181).

Dominant firm price leadership

Dominant firm price leadership occurs when an industry consists of one large firm surrounded by a number of firms each of which is too small to view itself as having a perceptible influence on the market price. The dominant firm need not be a low-cost firm. It leads by virtue of its size and strength. Dunlop, for example, was found by a Monopolies Commission report, in 1956, to be a price leader in the rubber footwear industry by virtue of its size and financial strength rather than its cost efficiency.

The small firms known as the 'competitive fringe' respond to the price set by the leader in the same way as perfectly competitive firms respond to the market price. That is, they take the price as given and select their output so as to profit maximise. The dominant firm sets a price that best serves its objectives taking into account the possible supply of the 'competitive fringe'.

Figure 8.10 illustrates how a dominant firm price leadership operates. The leader's estimate of the possible supply of the fringe is indicated by curve S_f. Since each small firm produces that output at which $P = MC$, the marginal cost indicates each firm's supply curve and S_f is the horizontal sum of the marginal cost curves of the competitive fringe. The market demand is D. Curve dd in Figure 8.10(b) is a residual demand curve QRD. It indicates the difference between the quantity demanded at each price and

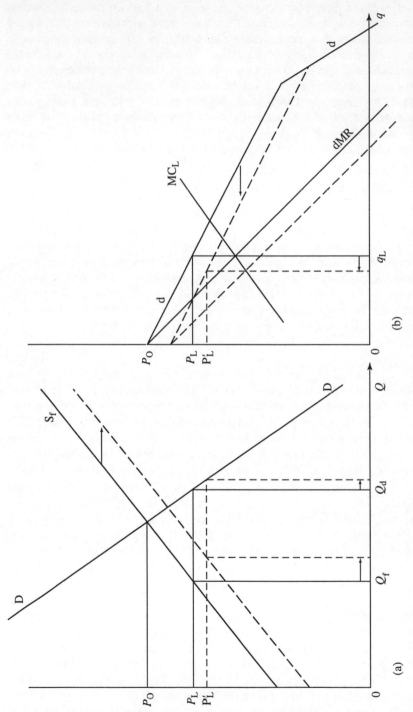

Figure 8.10 Dominant firm price leadership: DD, market demand; S_f, supply of the competitive fringe; MC_L, leader's marginal cost; dd = DD − S_f, residual demand; $Q_d = q_L + Q_f$

the estimated supply of the fringe. That is, each point on curve dd indicates the distance between D and S_f. If, for example, at P the market demand is 100 units and the supply of the fringe is 40 units the residual demand is 60 units. In general, $Q_{RD} = Q_D - Q_f$. Thus, at price P_0 since $Q_D = Q_f$ the residual demand is zero. At prices higher than P_0, the supply of the fringe is greater than the market demand so that there is excess supply whatever the output of the leader. At prices lower than P_0, if the leader were to produce a quantity indicated by curve dd and set the corresponding price, the fringe would produce the quantity indicated by S_f, so that total supply would equal total demand and the market would be in equilibrium. To profit maximise the leader would operate at a point on curve dd corresponding to the production level q_L *at which the leader's marginal cost equals the marginal revenue curve dMR. The market price would be* P_L.

It should be noted that short-run profit maximisation may be a short-sighted policy for the leader to follow since in the absence of barriers to entry a high P_L may attract new entrants into the industry and, even if entry is impeded, high profits might induce the competitive fringe to expand. In either case the fringe supplies more and the share of the leader declines (S_f shifts to the right and dd to the left as indicated by the broken lines). The fringe will continue to expand for as long as excess profits persist, putting pressure on the market price and on the leader's market share.

An illustration of such pressures has been provided by the international oil market. When OPEC, the world's price leader for oil, quadrupled the price of crude oil in the early 1970s, oil production became so profitable that the non-OPEC oil producing countries such as Britain, Mexico, etc. started pumping up oil at an accelerated rate. New, previously unprofitable, oil rigs came into production. As a result the OPEC oil production fell from an estimated 25,487,000 barrels per day (bpd) in 1972 to 16,972,000 bpd in 1984, while the total production of the non-Communist world increased from 15,302,000 to 22,148,000 bpd (Rosemary Clarke 1985). The increase in non-OPEC supply combined with a reduction in oil demand, due to a world economic recession and the world-wide search for alternative sources of energy, brought about a sustained decline in oil prices and a significant reduction in the OPEC's world market share.

STRATEGIC BEHAVIOUR BY FIRMS

In the absence of collusive agreements oligopolistic behaviour can best be described by what Schelling (1980) called a 'game of strategy' which he defined as 'a behavior situation in which each player's best choice of action depends on the action he expects the other to take, which he knows depends, in turn, on the other's expectations of his own' (p. 86). In other words, in a game of strategy the best course of action of each player depends on the expected actions of the other players. Players, therefore, may attempt to induce their opponents to act in a way that is beneficial to themselves. The moves employed to this end are called strategic moves. More precisely, a move taken by player A is a *strategic move* if it influences the choice of player B's actions in a way favourable to A, by affecting the expectations of B on how A will behave (Schelling 1980: 160).

Since an oligopoly is a market structure in which firms are interdependent and the outcome of their actions depends on competitors' reactions, an oligopoly involves a game of strategy in which each player can act strategically. A firm faced with potential competition, for example, may attempt to deter entry by influencing adversely the expectations of potential entrants regarding the post-entry profitability of the market. The action it adopts to achieve this aim (e.g. a threat of a price war) is a strategic move.

Entry deterrence provides good examples of business strategic decisions which can be analysed by game theory. Although the analysis of strategic decision making requires rather complex theoretical tools, useful insights into strategic business behaviour can be gained by analysing some simplified situations. Thus, after reviewing limit pricing behaviour as presented in the industrial economics literature, the entry deterrence decision is analysed from an introductory game theoretic perspective which forms the basis for the subsequent analysis of a firm's strategic investment decisions.

Limit pricing as a strategic response to potential competition

The study of potential competition as an influence on the behaviour of oligopolistic markets originates from the work of Joe Bain (1956), who suggested that firms may choose to charge a price lower than the full monopoly price in order to discourage new entry and protect their long-term profitability. Bain's work shows that the interdependence which characterises oligopolistic industries is not restricted to the incumbent firms; it rather extends to incorporate potential entrants. Whether firms contemplating entry will actually enter depends not on the existing price and profitability of a market but on conditions expected to prevail after entry. Expected losses deter entry. Similarly, the behaviour of incumbent firms may be influenced by the perceived impact of current decisions on potential entry. If, for example, high current prices are expected to entice new entry, incumbent firms may select a policy of lower prices in order to discourage entry.

Bain's ideas were formulated by Sylos-Labini into a model which was subsequently refined and generalised by Modigliani. The Bain–Sylos–Labini–Modigliani (B–S–M) model forms the basis of the traditional analysis of entry prevention strategy.[3]

The fundamental claim of limit pricing is that, in the absence of cost advantages or other barriers to entry, price can be used by incumbent firms as a strategic instrument to discourage potential new entry. The effectiveness of this instrument will depend, however, on how existing firms expect potential entrants to respond to their actions and on what expectations potential entrants have about the incumbent's behaviour post entry. Several reaction patterns are possible. Potential entrants may expect incumbent firms to (a) respond by reducing output somewhat but not sufficiently to prevent a post-entry price fall or (b) maintain price by reducing output as required thus accommodating new entry or (c) maintain output at its pre-entry level. Whether a limit price can successfully be adopted will depend on which one of these behavioural patterns prevails.

The assumptions made by the B–S–M model regarding the interaction between incumbent firms and a potential entrant is known as 'the Sylos postulate' and has two parts.

1 Existing firms expect that potential entrants will not enter with a plant size smaller than the minimum efficient scale of operation (MES). This is because entry at less than MES means that new firms will have higher per unit costs and will therefore be uncompetitive. Additionally, incumbent firms believe that potential entrants will not enter if they expect the post-entry price to be below average cost resulting in losses.
2 Potential entrants expect that post-entry established firms will maintain their output constant at the pre-entry level so that their entry will depress the market price.

In addition to the Sylos postulate the B–S–M model assumes the following: (a) technology and input prices are such that the long-run average cost curve is L-shaped and that it is the same for incumbent and potential new entrants, the assumption that existing firms have no cost advantage over potential entrants is made in order to isolate any premiums which incumbent firms may be able to extract because of the existence of an absolute cost advantage barrier to entry; (b) demand is constant; and (c) if there is more than one incumbent firm, the price is set by the largest one or by collusive agreement.

Given these assumptions existing firms can select their price in a way that prevents new entry while earning a premium. The level of the entry-preventing price (or limit price) and the size of the premium depend on demand and cost conditions. In Figure 8.11 the limit price is illustrated on the simplifying assumption that potential entrants will only contemplate entry at MES.

Figure 8.11(b) describes the prevailing cost conditions (assumed to be the same for incumbents and potential entrants). Line D is the market demand curve. The limit price P_L has been chosen so that the sales volume X_L is such that if a new firm entered at MES the post entry price would fall to just under the competitive price P_c. That is, the incumbent firm(s) aims to produce and sell an output X_L such that $X_L + \bar{x} \leq X_c$, where X_c is the output that could be sold at the competitive price (recall that $P_c = $ LRAC). Entry at MES implies an output higher than X_c and the

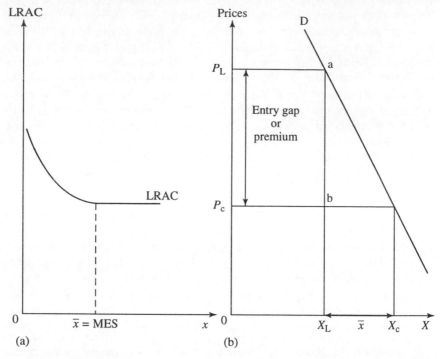

Figure 8.11 The B–S–M model of limit pricing: (a) firm, (b) $P_L = P_c (1 + \bar{x}/X_c^e)$; industry

expectation of zero profit or a loss means no entry. The entry gap or total premium that existing firms can enjoy without inducing entry, E, is equal to the rectangle $P_L ab P_c$. The determinants of the limit price and the entry gap can be seen from the diagram. They are as follows.

1 *The size of the market at the competitive price*   The larger the market the easier the entry of a firm with a given MES will be. This is because the impact of a given volume of additional production on price will be smaller the larger the market size prior to entry is.

2 *The price elasticity of the market demand*   The more inelastic the demand the more difficult new entry will be. That is, existing firms can charge high prices without inducing entry. This is because a relatively small additional output will be expected to reduce price substantially and make entry unprofitable.

3 *The minimum efficient scale of production*   The higher the MES the more difficult new entry will be. This is because, given the market demand, the larger the volume that must be sold by the new entrant the more the price will fall post-entry, increasing the likelihood of losses.

4 *Prices of factors of production and technology*   These determine the

position and the shape of the LAC curve and hence the MES and P_C and consequently the limit price and the entry gap. Mathematically,

$$P_L = f(X_c, e, \bar{x}, P_c)$$

where X_c is the competitive output, e is the price elasticity of demand, x denotes the MES, P_c is the competitive price and

$$\frac{\partial P_L}{\partial X_c} < 0$$

$$\frac{\partial P_L}{\partial e} < 0$$

$$\frac{\partial P_L}{\partial x} < 0$$

$$\frac{\partial P_L}{\partial P_c} < 0$$

The determinants of P_L can be combined into one relationship:[4]

$$※ \quad P_L = P_c\left(1 + \frac{\bar{x}}{X_c e}\right).$$

It can be seen that $\bar{x}/X_c e$ is equal to $(P_L - P_c)/P_c$. This is what Bain called the 'condition of entry' or the 'entry gap'. It indicates the premium over the competitive price which firms can extract without inducing entry.

Clearly if entry at less than MES were possible, the entry gap would be smaller than that indicated above to an extent dependent on how fast average cost increases as output declines below MES. For further elaboration on this point see Lyons (1988: 39).

Objections regarding the realism of the behavioural and other assumptions of the B–S–M model have led to claims that the limit price postulated is an over-estimate. Some of the most important criticisms are the following.

Conjectural interdependence

The proponents of the Sylos Postulate maintain that it is a realistic set of assumptions to make since they constitute a defensive strategy. There is nothing, however, in the pre-entry output that points to the necessity for its continuation post entry. On the contrary, provided that incumbent production is at constant average cost output it can be reduced after entry without a cost disadvantage. Besides, maintaining output at the pre-entry level implies that the incumbent firms are prepared to abandon their price strategy and let the new entrant's production determine the market price. It can be argued that a preferable strategy for the existing firm(s) is to retain some control over price and to adopt other actions such as a retaliation policy. Whether a price war will be initiated by incumbent firms will depend, of course, on how long price is expected to stay low, on the size of possible losses and on the abundance or scarcity of their financial reserves. Thus, an aggressive price cutting strategy cannot always be ruled out especially since it may have the additional advantage of discouraging further entry. Alternatively, a 'mixed strategy' may be adopted. That is, incumbent firms may partly reduce production and partly allow the price to fall. This strategy may allow for some excess profits (although less than those prior to entry) which can be utilised to mount a non-price competition to eliminate the new entrant.

Cross-entry has been ignored

The B–S–M model implies that the threat of entry comes mainly from the emergence of new (relatively small) firms and ignores the possibility that large firms already established in other markets may contemplate diversifying into other existing markets. The widespread phenomenon of diversification and multi-product production renders this assumption unrealistic. Cross-entry implies that the potential entrant may be a financially strong firm which may decide to enter at a suboptimal scale (i.e. output less than that corresponding to MES of operation) and be prepared to withstand short-term losses. Initial losses can indeed be considered as a necessary cost, or investment, which assists the entrant to establish a foothold in the new market. The prospect of an initial loss may not, therefore, deter cross-entry.

A classic example of diversified entry has been provided by the UK potato crisp market which in the 1950s was dominated by Smiths. Several local producers offered no challenge to the leadership of Smiths. In 1960 a large conglomerate, Imperial Tobacco, diversified into the market with Golden Wonder crisps, a better quality product with a longer shelf life. They advertised heavily pushing the average level of the industry's advertising from 0.11 per cent to 2.18 per cent. Within six years their market share increased to 45 per cent while that of Smiths fell from 65 to 34 per cent. The financial strength of the entrant has undoubtedly contributed to their success.

Lack of financial strength may imply that new specialist entry may fail even if supported by enormous entrepreneurial talent. Examples of such failures are the Rolls Razors and the Laker Airlines (Lyons 1988).

Number of firms

Neither the number of firms nor their relative market shares are among the determinants of limit price in the B–S–M model. In fact the number of existing firms is not even defined. It is simply assumed that the price is set collusively. However, in reality the accurate determination of a collusively set price may well depend on the number of firms and their relative strengths.

Consumer behaviour post-entry

The B S M model implies that as price falls post-entry market demand increases and new customers absorb the output of the new entrant. The possibility that the price reduction might cause existing customers to transfer their custom to the entrant (in chagrin) has not been considered.

Static nature of the model

Despite some dynamic considerations (discussed by Modigliani) the model is essentially static. It ignores the possibility of market expansion which would weaken the effectiveness of limit pricing.

The above criticisms imply that a firm's ability to prevent entry may be more limited than the model suggests. Consequently, some modifications and extensions have been incorporated into the basic model.

I   Bhagwati (1970), for example, has argued that P_L is an over-estimate for a variety of reasons which relate to what he called 'the attractiveness-of-entry factor'. He argues that 'the mere enjoyment of lucrative premiums by existing firms (no matter how amply justified in terms of difficulty of entry as defined previously) will attract firms into the market who may want to undergo initial losses with the view to driving some existent firms out, in the hope of surviving to earn the lucrative premiums that are being made in the industry'. In the case of cross-entry it is highly likely that the entrant may achieve such an objective for the following reasons.

1 When entry occurs, every firm makes losses. Which firm goes out of business is partly a matter of luck.
2 If a B–S–M strategy is pursued, it is actually likely that the entrant's losses will be less than those of incumbent firms. This will be the case if, prior to entry, the incumbent operates at the flat segment of the L-shaped cost curve (produces more than the MES output) while the entrant comes in at MES. As the price falls, the entrant suffers a relatively smaller loss.[5]
3 Since entrants are likely to be multi-product firms, they may be better able to survive these initial losses which are likely to be considered as a necessary entry investment.
4 Finally, multi-product firms enjoy a tax advantage compared with specialised firms since losses from one product are deducted from profits from other products before any tax liabilities are calculated. That is, part of the loss is borne by the Inland Revenue.

II   The model presumes that as prices fall post-entry the customers of existing firms do not change their allegiances and continue to buy from the same firms. If this is true then the new entrant's share of the market will be a share in the marginal increment of aggregate demand. However, Bhagwati and others argue that as price falls buyers may transfer their custom, being dissatisfied (in chagrin) because they were exploited prior to entry. Additionally, some of the new customers will buy from the incumbent firms. We can, therefore, assume that the increase in demand, due to a price reduction post entry, will be shared equally among existing firms and new entrants. Assuming N incumbents and denoting the chagrin effect by c, where c is the degree of reduction in the quantity sold by established firms as price falls, then it can be shown[6] that

$$ P_L = P_c \left[1 + \frac{\bar{x}}{X_c \left(\dfrac{e}{N+1} + c \right)} \right] $$

Thus, P_L can be seen to depend on the number of firms N and the chagrin effect c as well as the MES, the competitive price P_C and the price elasticity of demand. The limit price and the premiums vary directly with N and indirectly with the extent to which buyers may switch to new entrants as the price falls after new entry.

III   Finally the model can be extended to accommodate changes in demand. Suppose that market demand expands by w per cent per time period. If new entrants can take k per cent of this expansion, then the impact of new entry on price will depend on how many units of output kw is and how this compares with MES. If MES is $\bar{x}$ units, to find the limit price the expression $\bar{x} - kw$ must be substituted for $\bar{x}$ in the P_L formula. The implication is not simply that both P_L will be lower and entry will be easier the higher kw is, but more seriously than that, that if $kw > \bar{x}$ entry cannot be prevented by limit pricing since P_L would have to be lower than the competitive price. In this case the only entry preventing strategy will be for incumbent firms to ensure that the expansion of demand is appropriated by themselves rather than by potential entrants. The firm has in this case to look for non-price factors which determine the share of existing firms in the growing market and the way in which these are within the range of influence of the incumbent firms.

Despite these extensions and improvements there are still weaknesses in the traditional theory of limit pricing which fail to explain why firms can and do use other than price strategies to prevent entry, such as excess capacity, control of inputs, product differentiation, vertical integration and so on.

Strategic investment decisions

A serious weakness of the B–S–M model of limit pricing stems from its assumption that a potential entrant's expectations about incumbent actions are exogenously determined. In particular, a prospective entrant ('entrant' henceforth) is assumed to believe that the incumbent will, post entry, maintain output at its pre-entry level. But as already indicated this may not necessarily be correct. Post entry the best strategy of the incumbent may be either to co-operate with the entrant and reduce output or to fight by expanding output and initiating a price war. The Sylos postulate excludes co-operation and implies that any threats of a price war are either not made or, if made, are not believed. Threats of predatory behaviour, however, may occur and whether they are believed or not may depend on an incumbent's previous behaviour and in particular on commitments undertaken which render threats credible. In fact entry prevention involves firms in a game the outcome of which is determined by the series of moves and countermoves the players decide to adopt.

The essence of such behaviour is akin to that of a *game of strategy* which can be defined as a game in which each player's choice of action depends on the expected actions of the other players, so that there is scope for strategic moves. A move taken by player A is defined as a strategic move if it intends to influence the choice of player B's actions in a way favourable to A, by affecting the expectations of B on how A will behave (Schelling 1980: 160). Thus, a threat of a post-entry price war, if believed by a potential entrant, would be a strategic move. When, however, after entry the incumbent's optimal move is likely to be other than aggression, the threat of a mutually destructive war is unlikely to be believed. It is an empty threat. Empty threats, however, can be changed to credible threats by appropriate commitments. A firm, for example, may commit itself by devoting resources to excess productive capacity, in the form of sunk costs or asset specific investments, so that in the event of entry, production can be easily and costlessly expanded to sustain a price war.

For commitments to be effective they must be irreversible and known to all concerned. To illustrate consider the following bargain. A buyer negotiates the price of good X. The seller demands £20 for X but would consider a lower price, the lowest acceptable price being £15. The buyer offers £16 and declares that he or she cannot transact at a higher price. If it is known that the buyer's maximum available resources are £20 the threat of no completion of the transaction is an empty threat. To influence the outcome of bargaining to his or her favour the buyer strikes an agreement with a third party according to which, if the agreed price for X is more than £16, the buyer pays to the third party £5. This commitment, if legally enforceable, known to the seller and irreversible, has turned an empty threat into a credible threat. It has become impossible for the buyer to pay more and the seller knows it. The only choice is to transact at £16 or not at all.

A game can be represented diagrammatically by a decision tree. Figure 8.12 describes the decision tree of an entry deterrence game. On the assumption that a single firm is threatened with large-scale entry by an equally efficient entrant the tree indicates all the possible moves and the concomitant pay-offs. The relevant pay-offs, at the end of each sequence, are assumed to be known to both players. The first move is taken by the incumbent who has the choice either to attempt to deter entry or to remain passive and let the entrant make the first move. The sequence of moves following either choice is described by each of the two main branches of the tree. Let us begin by considering the left-hand side branch. The incumbent makes no strategic decision to influence entry and remains passive. The next move comes from the entrant who may decide to either enter or stay out. If the decision is to stay out, the incumbent earns R_m and the entrant earns nothing. If entry does take place the outcome of the game is determined by the incumbent's response to entry. This response may be accommodating (some form of co-operation or market sharing may take place) in which case each firm earns a positive return R_d. Alternatively, the incumbent may decide to fight the entrant by initiating a price war in which case both firms incur losses of R_w. It is assumed that $R_m > R_d > 0 > R_w$.

Before examining the other branch of the tree let us consider what sequence of moves will prevail. That is, let us consider whether entry will occur in a market in which the incumbent is passive to the prospect of entry and in which profits under duopoly are positive but lower than

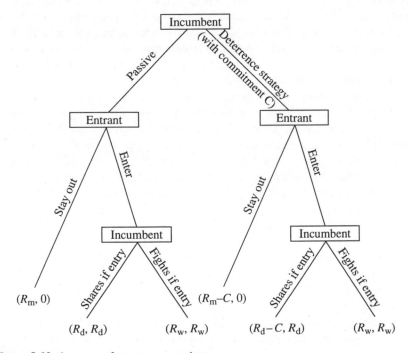

Figure 8.12 A game of entry prevention

monopoly profits. The behavioural assumption made throughout is that 'strict rationality' prevails. That is, it is assumed that at each point in the game 'each firm will act on the assumption that its rival will behave rationally from that point on' (Lyons 1987).

On the assumption of strict rationality, if the incumbent is passive entry will occur and the market will be shared in some fashion between the two firms. This is because given the postulated pay-offs, the pair of strategies 'enter' for the entrant and 'share if entry' for the incumbent is a pair of 'perfect' or 'sequential' equilibrium strategies. They satisfy the assumption of strict rationality. The alternative pair of strategies 'fight if entry' and 'stay out' for the entrant do not correspond to a perfect equilibrium since the entrant knows that it is to the incumbent's best interest to adopt an accommodating behaviour once faced with *de facto* entry. Even if the incumbent firm were threatening to initiate a price war, its threat would be an empty one which would not be taken seriously. To prevent entry the incumbent cannot rely on empty threats.

To consider the overall solution to the entry deterrence question the second branch of the decision tree must also be analysed. This traces out the consequences of the incumbent's decision to commit resources, worth say £C, in an attempt to prevent entry. Such resources may be invested in productive capacity, for example, to indicate readiness to initiate a price war. Again, the entrant has the choice to enter or to stay out. If entry does not occur the incumbent's pay-off will be $R_m - C$. That is, the commitment is costly since it lowers the monopoly profit. Resources have been expended on capacity which has little or no value in its best alternative use and which remains idle. If entry occurs the incumbent may fight or share the market. Sharing implies a pay-off $R_d - C$, for the incumbent and R_d for the entrant. A price war is associated with a pay-off of R_w for each (C does not lower the incumbent's pay-off if war occurs). An incumbent thus committed will find it optimal to fight in the event of entry only if $R_w > R_d - C$. That is, a price war will occur when the commitment makes sharing less profitable than war. Since the pay-offs are known, the entrant recognises that the incumbent's optimal strategy is to fight so entry will not occur and the incumbent will earn $R_m - C$. Clearly the incumbent, knowing the entrant's optimum strategy, will decide to commit resources only if $R_m - C$ is more than the pay-off R_d of a passive strategy.

In brief, entry would be deterred if the resource requirements of credible commitments do not lower monopoly profits by more than new entry would. Given the cost of potential commitments the higher the monopoly profit compared with the duopoly profit the more likely it is that firms will engage in strategic behaviour in order to deter entry. Clearly the feasibility of credible commitments will vary with the circumstances of production, the institutional arrangements and the nature of the product(s) produced. Sunk costs or asset specific investments, expenditures on advertising and R&D are examples of commitments which firms can adopt as part of their strategic attempts to prevent new entry into their markets.

Strategic investment in productive capacity

In the B–S–M model of limit pricing firms behave strategically by producing more than the monopoly output in order to induce a potential entrant to expect losses and thus decide to stay out of the market. Notwithstanding the criticisms regarding its effectiveness, this is an unnecessarily expensive strategy since (a) resources must be committed to install the extra productive capacity and (b) profits are further reduced because the pre-entry price is lower than the monopoly price. In a seminal article in 1977, Spence showed that a firm, like the one illustrated in Figure 8.11, can prevent entry by committing resources to excess productive capacity while pricing at the monopoly level. Excess capacity signals a commitment to increase production in the event of entry so that the threat of a price war becomes credible and the expected post-entry profitability zero or negative. Entry can, therefore, be forestalled while maintaining a monopoly price. That is, strategic entry deterrence behaviour by firms will result in excess capacity but not necessarily in lower pre-entry prices.

Excess capacity is an advance commitment intended to make the threat of extra production in the event of entry a credible threat. But, as Schelling (1980: ch.2) has shown, to achieve this aim the commitment must be such as to make the fulfilment of the threat optimal if not necessary. This means that (a) the excess capacity must be irreversible, i.e. once installed it cannot be used to produce other products and its scrap value is very small or zero, in other words, the excess capacity must be in asset-specific investments, and (b) the use of the excess capacity post entry must be optimal. That is, accommodating a new entrant must be a less profitable strategy for the incumbent firm than a price war. In terms of Figure 8.12, the condition $R_w > R_d - C$ must hold.

In brief, investment in excess capacity can under certain circumstances deter entry. It is, however, erroneous to suggest that the existence of excess capacity is sufficient for potential entrants to believe the threat of retaliatory post-entry policies and to be deterred from entering. Such a suggestion would imply that the Sylos postulate (i.e. the belief that the incumbent's output would be equal to Q_L post entry) has been maintained. But as the analysis of the game tree indicated this is not necessarily a correct assumption since it may contain an empty threat. For excess capacity to constitute a credible threat the condition $R_w > R_d - C$ must also hold. That is, the use of the excess capacity must be optimal.

Notwithstanding this comment, excess capacity can often play a strategic role in entry deterrence because it gives an initial leadership advantage to the incumbent firm. As Dixit (1979) put it, 'the role of an irrevocable commitment of investment in entry-deterrence is to alter the initial conditions of the post entry game to the advantage of the established firm, for any fixed rule under which the game is to be played'. Of particular significance is the commitment of resources to investment projects which reduce the marginal cost of production. A lower marginal cost gives an initial advantage to the incumbent firm because (a) a sufficient cost advantage may deter entry, (b) if entry does occur the incumbent can quickly and inexpensively increase output should post-entry aggression be an optimal response or (c) if co-operation is the post-entry optimal strategy, the incumbent is in a beneficial position since in most collusive models a low cost is an advantage which results in a larger market share and higher profits (see 'Cartels', pages 235–7).

An example of investment behaviour altering the initial conditions in favour of the incumbent (if not reducing marginal cost) is the behaviour of the Aluminium Company of America (ALCOA) for which Judge Learned Hand said 'we can think of no more effective exclusion than progressively to embrace each new opportunity as it opened, and to face every newcomer with new capacity already geared into a great organisation, having the advantage of experience, trade connections and the elite personnel' (as quoted in Shughart 1990: 30).

Strategic investment in reputation

The analysis of entry deterrence becomes much more complicated once the assumptions of a single period, no discounting, perfect knowledge and a single potential entrant are relaxed. A potential entrant, for example, may be unable to distinguish between a totally empty and a credible threat of a price war. The decision to enter or not will in this case depend on the entrant's belief as to how likely it is that the threat will be carried out. If the entrant believes that there is a certain probability (equal to p) that the incumbent will start a price war post entry then his or her expected return to entry is

$$pR_w + (1-p) R_d.$$

This is negative (entry unprofitable) as long as $p > R_d/(R_d - R_w)$.

Thus, if a price war is expected to be very likely (i.e. p is large) and expensive (R_w losses are large) entry will not occur. Now p is likely to be larger the more potential entrants there are. If, for example, it is recognised that there is a sequence of potential entrants, the pay-off of a price war against the first potential entrant may be much higher than that indicated in Figure 8.12. That is, short-run losses can be compensated by increased monopoly profits in the long run. Aggressive behaviour and initial losses may be viewed as a commitment which makes the threat of war a credible threat to other potential entrants.

Similarly, even a small probability that an incumbent is committed to a price war (smaller than $R_d/(R_d - R_w)$) may be sufficient to deter entry when the incumbent is threatened in more than one market at the same time and so wishes to build a reputation for aggressive behaviour (Lyons 1988).

The practical significance of predatory pricing in order to build a reputation, according to Schelling, has been demonstrated by the existence of anti-trust laws intended to curb it. This does not mean that such behaviour is not observed in practice. For example, the Monopolies and Restrictive Practices Commission (1956) found that BOC had used such practices extensively up to that year.

Strategic investment in advertising and research and development

The potential of advertising or R&D expenditure as a strategic decision variable acquires particular significance in the presence of an entry threat. The level of advertising may then be used rather than price or quantity as a weapon to deter entry. To indicate the strategic role of advertising, Funderberg and Tirole (1984) consider a market with an incumbent firm and a given number of potential customers. It is assumed that a customer can buy from a firm only if informed about its existence and that such information is passed on by advertising. The incumbent firm advertises therefore and reaches a certain number of potential customers. A proportion of the customers buying the product will not be interested to read further advertisements from potential entrants. They are happy with the incumbent's product or they have invested in its consumption and will remain attached even if a new entrant appeared. Such customers constitute an incumbent's 'captive' market. Advertising, by creating this captive market, has two important implications. First, the higher its captive market the less inclined the incumbent firm becomes to fight a price war post entry. Thus, large investments in advertising may serve as a signal that the incumbent has no incentive to fight. Funderberg and Tirole suggest that the incumbent's behaviour is akin to that of a 'fat cat' who is lazy and co-operative. Potential entrants expect a co-operative behaviour. The direct effect of advertising, therefore, is to encourage entry. There is, however, an 'indirect effect' of advertising which discourages entry. Increased advertising expenditure increases the incumbent's captive market and reduces the number of potential customers (market share) an entrant may expect to serve. The smaller the potential market the less attractive entry becomes.

Depending on circumstances and the significance of its direct and indirect effects over- or under-investment in advertising may be the strategic response to potential entry. Suppose, for example, that the incumbent is a multinational enterprise operating in a third world country and another larger and financially stronger multinational enterprise contemplates entry. The financial strength of the entrant renders the threat of a price war empty and entry becomes inevitable. The incumbent's strategic response may well be to increase advertising in order to increase its captive market. Post entry the incumbent firm will be passive rather than match the entrant's price and start a price war. The non-aggressive behaviour will benefit both firms.

When entry is not inevitable, however, two possibilities arise: either (a) the level of advertising may be reduced, so that the incumbent's signal to the potential entrant is that of 'a lean and hungry look' ready to fight, in other words under-investment in advertising is the strategic response to entry, or (b) if the indirect effect of advertising is strong, advertising may be increased in an attempt to reduce sufficiently the non-captive part of the market so as to discourage entry. In this case, over-investment in advertising becomes the appropriate strategy.

In reality the effects of advertising are more complicated than this simple model suggests and consequently advertising can be used in a variety of ways as a strategic variable. Lyons (1988), for example, suggests that if the production technology is such that the average cost is constant incumbents may be able to devise a large fixed cost by advertising, thus creating an economy of scale barrier. This, however, requires that the entrant believes that incumbents will not cut back on advertising post entry. Similarly, R&D expenditure may be directed towards the development of new large-scale technologies. In addition to its effects on entry, advertising may be an instrument of enhancing goodwill and product differentiation which can be used in a predatory way to enhance reputations. Empirical evidence suggests that increased advertising can create barriers to entry. The detergents industry in the UK seems to suffer from high barriers to entry initiated by extensive advertising.

THE CONTESTABILITY OF OLIGOPOLY MARKETS

The variety of strategic behaviour described above is aimed at influencing the conjectural interdependence that exists between incumbents and potential entrants in an attempt to deter entry and maintain profitability. Oligopolistic attempts to maintain price above cost depend, however, on whether new entry is possible or whether barriers to entry exist.

In the absence of barriers to entry the influence of potential competition can make it impossible for oligopolists to maintain prices above costs in the long run. In fact, strategic entry deterrence becomes impossible when an oligopoly market is perfectly contestable, i.e. when entry into the market is absolutely free and exit is absolutely costless (Baumol 1982). This absolute freedom of entry and exit exists when the following conditions are fulfilled (see Chapter 2).

1 All incumbent firms and potential entrants have access to the same technology, so that there are no cost (quality or other) disadvantages to entry.
2 Economies of scale may exist but there must be no sunk costs. The rent on office accommodation is a fixed cost which can cause unit costs to fall as output expands, but provided that it can be cancelled at short notice it is not a sunk and irrecoverable cost.

3 Incumbent firms can only change their prices with a time lag while consumers respond to price changes instantaneously.

When conditions (1)–(3) are fulfilled incumbents are open to 'hit-and-run' competition from potential entrants and there is no possibility of retaliation or other interactions. If incumbents fail to minimise the cost of their production, or attempt to cross-subsidise (so that price is less than marginal cost for a product) or set price above average cost, a potential entrant can undercut slightly the existing price, serve the whole market and exit quickly and costlessly when incumbents start to retaliate.

The possibility of hit-and-run competition frees oligopolistic structures and behaviour from their dependence on conjectural interdependence. Incumbents under the pressure of potential competition have no choice but to price according to marginal cost and earn only normal profits. Behaviour is therefore uniquely determined under perfect contestability and optimality depends neither on the number nor on the size distribution of firms operating in the industry. Two incumbent firms are enough to guarantee optimality. Even monopolies can, in certain circumstances, be induced to operate efficiently under the threat of potential entry.

Perfect contestability, however, has been proposed as a generalisation and simplification of the concept of the perfectly competitive market and not as a description of reality. As Baumol (1982) put it, 'real world markets are rarely, if ever, perfectly contestable. Contestability is merely a broader ideal, a benchmark of wider applicability than perfect competition.' Thus, although a number of industries, such as the passenger air traffic market between two towns, may approximate the theoretical structure in most real-world markets, production requires some sunk costs, i.e. specialised investments which can only be liquidated gradually, if at all, and at some cost. Moreover, consumers assimilate and respond to price changes with some delay and firms need time to calculate and implement price changes.

Perfect contestability, however, has important normative implications. As a benchmark for public policy it serves to focus regulatory policy towards the removal of artificial barriers to contestability and improvements to contestability when the industry is not conducive to it. As Chapter 14 shows, such ideas have had a pronounced impact on recent competition policy in the UK and elsewhere.

SUMMARY

Business behaviour under different market structures is analysed in this chapter beginning with the two extremes of perfect competition and monopoly. Firms in perfectly competitive markets are price takers operating where $MC = P$ and, in the long run, enjoy no super-normal profits. In general, competitive market prices reflect the costs of production and provided that these costs include both social and private costs the allocation of resources is the best possible for the existing income distribution. Monopolies, on the other hand, are price makers. To profit maximise they set prices higher than marginal costs, by a margin dependent on the price elasticity of demand. Monopoly prices imply an allocative inefficiency even though multi-plant monopolists may attempt to minimise production costs. Monopolists often charge different prices to different customers, or to the same customer for different volumes of purchases, for reasons not associated with differences in the costs of production. Some common discriminatory practices are examined.

Oligopolies, possibly the most common market structures, are characterised by the existence of recognised interdependence among firms. Each firm is aware that its actions are likely to trigger rival reactions which must therefore be anticipated in decision making. Since conjectures enter into decision making there is uncertainty and a risk of price warfare. To reduce such risks and to ensure that market prices are elevated above costs oligopolists often collude overtly or tacitly. Some commonly observed forms of cartels and price leaderships are analysed. Although the aim of such agreements is to reduce competition and, in many instances, to charge the monopoly price, monopoly pricing is difficult to implement in practice especially when the number of firms is large and their cost structures differ. Additionally, opportunistic behaviour and 'free rider' problems make restrictive agreements inherently unstable unless accompanied by effective control and monitoring systems and supplemented by profit sharing agreements. The formation and effective implementation of restrictive agreements are fraught with difficulties in practice and yet they can and do survive over long periods of time.

Oligopolistic markets, like monopolies, can be perfectly contestable. In the absence of sunk costs and other barriers to entry the possibility of 'hit-and-run' competition can force prices to equal the average cost.

When markets fail to be perfectly contestable and collusive agreements are infeasible or illegal, oligopolistic rivalry arises. In response to rivalry from existing or potential competition firms often behave strategically. That is, firms take actions intended to influence rivals' reactions in a way beneficial to themselves. Limit pricing, a form of strategic behaviour, is examined in some detail. In introducing other forms of strategic behaviour it is shown that threats are not sufficient to deter entry. Firms may need to commit resources by investing in excess capacity in order to signal that they are both willing and ready to act aggressively post entry. Advertising expenditure, R&D and reputational effects can play a significant role in business strategic behaviour.

APPLICATION: CARTELS IN THE UK BUILDING INDUSTRY

Building materials are fairly standardized, usually heavy, with high transportation costs which prevent imports and localise trade. They therefore provide fertile ground for the cultivation of cartel agreements.

Although cartels are, and have been for some time, illegal in the UK, the BBC (1992) has recently revealed evidence that cartels are extremely widespread. Even companies which were discovered in the past operating cartels and promised never to collude again have recently re-offended. Some of the worst offenders are to be found in the production of concrete. By the end of the 1970s many of the concrete cartels were discovered and companies promised not to collude again. But promises were not always kept. For example, in the Oxfordshire area during the 1980s four companies operated a neat cartel arrangement. They met monthly to fix the price and they shared the market among themselves as follows:

Smiths	43 per cent
Pioneer	21 per cent
RMC	21 per cent
Hartican	15 per cent

The strict allocation of work across the area was recorded and monitored via an allocations book. All large contracts were given to a member, according to the book. If a particular contract should, according to the cartel agreement, go to, say, Smiths and the buyer asked for tenders from the other members of the cartel, the other members would quote a price higher than the agreed cartel price so as to ensure that Smiths would win the contract. Thus, they adhered to the cartel agreement while pretending to compete. Three of the participating companies admitted the existence of the cartel when the Office of Fair Trading (OFT) investigated the industry after a tip off.

The Oxfordshire concrete cartel, however, is the tip of the iceberg. In 1991 British concrete companies owned up to fifty-two other price fixing agreements all over the country. RMC, the world's biggest supplier group of ready-made concrete, admitted the existence of nine restrictive agreements of its British subsidiaries. The Director General of the OFT called these and other cartels 'a matter of shame' (*Guardian*, 11 April, 1991) and was considering prosecuting RMC for breaking court orders made in 1978 banning the company from making such arrangements. The eight manufacturers of steel bars used in thousands of buildings admitted to running a cartel for six years during the 1980s. In 1990, the eighteen distributors in the £350 million thermal insulation business admitted they operated a four-year price fixing rig. In 1987 the OFT completed legal action against 200 companies supplying road-making materials like asphalt and macadam, whose price fixing agreements were deemed to be against the public interest. In the production of steel purlins three companies, Ayrshire, Wards and Metsec, ran a cartel for seven years (1983–90). They shared the market among themselves by operating a system of 'protected customers' whereby each customer was allocated to a particular company and the other members of the cartel did not effectively compete. If a customer was allocated to, say, Ayrshire 'the two other members of the cartel would actually quote a higher price than Ayrshire would do, therefore nine out of ten times, keeping the business within Ayrshire as it was one of their protected customers'. The cartel agreement extended to include an agreed behaviour *vis-à-vis* the small companies that operated outside the cartel. If any of these attempted to win a large contract any cartel member discovering this would bid below the agreed price in order to ensure that the small firms were unsuccessful. In case the price had to be below cost the losses were shared among the cartel members.

Perhaps one of the oldest cartels in this industry was that of the cement manufacturers established in 1934 and dissolved in 1987. When the agreement was examined by the Restrictive Practices Court, in 1961, the nine members of the Cement Federation produced virtually all of the UK's cement. The largest firm, Blue Circle, had a market share of 65 per cent and the CR_4 was 85 per cent. The Federation had divided the country into eleven regions within each of which delivered prices were agreed upon. According to Utton (1970) the price agreement was supplemented by schemes for determining margins for merchants and aggregated rebates to be allowed to different kinds of customers. Any members wishing a price adjustment had to seek the approval of the Federation. Until the early 1980s there was no evidence of any significant sales made on terms other than those laid down in the cartel agreement.

Firms cushioned from competition for so long tend to become complacent and inefficient and their management unwilling to carry out rationalisation and innovation. Besides, very high domestic prices can make imports profitable despite high transport costs and any duties. The breaking up of the cement cartel can be attributed to both of these causes. During the 1980s cement sales were declining for two reasons. First, substitute products, such as pulverised fuel ash and blast furnace slag used in the manufacture of concrete, appeared on the markets. Pulverised fuel ash produced by power stations improves the quality of concrete and also reduces the quantity of cement required. Taylor (1987) estimated that cement sales declined by 600,000 tonnes a year because of the use of pulverised fuel ash. Second, cheap imports from Poland, East Germany and Greece caused a further threat to domestic producers. Under these pressures firms started to behave opportunistically, including secret price concessions to customers and non-adherence to agreed quotas. The market share of Blue Circle started to decline and it became the driving force behind the decision to end the fifty-two year-old cartel.

FURTHER READING

Koutsoyiannis, A. (1979) *Modern Microeconomics*, 2nd edn, London: Macmillan. Unlike other traditional economics textbooks this book provides an extensive coverage of oligopoly markets.

Lyons, B. (1987) 'Strategic Behaviour by Firms', in R. Clarke and T. McGuinness (eds) *The Economics of the Firm*, London: Blackwell. This provides a concise but clear introduction to strategic business behaviour.

Scherer, F.M. (1980) *Industrial Market Structure and Economic Performance*, 2nd edn, Chicago, IL: Rand McNally.

QUESTIONS

1 A cost reducing new technology has been adopted by virtually all the firms of a perfectly competitive industry. Analyse the long-run effects of this improvement on market price, output and number of firms, stating clearly your assumptions regarding the impact of any industrial expansion on the cost curves of the individual firms. (Hint: is it a constant, increasing or decreasing cost industry?)

2 Product X is produced in three different plants in the UK. Plant A is located in Coventry, Plant B in Newcastle and Plant C in Glasgow. The Government have decided to impose a per unit of production tax but only on output of X produced by Plant A. The aim of this tax is to divert production from Coventry to the Newcastle and/or the Glasgow plants.

Explain whether the government objective will be achieved and what effect, if any, this tax would have on the price of X, in each of the following cases:

(a) All plants belong to a profit maximising monopolist.
(b) Each plant belongs to a different firm but the three firms operate as a perfect cartel.
(c) The three plants sell their output in a perfectly competitive international market.

3 'In the 1950s and 1960s, the (British) economy was run on a 'stop–go' pattern. . . . When the government wished to restrict domestic demand, a frequently used instrument was that of credit restrictions, either by requiring large deposits or by raising the interests rates for hire-purchase. . . . Whenever such restrictions were introduced, the motor industry was one of the first to suffer as demand for its products fell away. The government, however, was unsympathetic to the industry's protests and argued that producers could recoup any losses from falling home sales by increasing exports' (Rosemary Clarke 1985). Was the Government's claim correct?

To answer Clarke's question note that she and others have shown that the MES in this industry is large for the size of the market and that costs of production fall throughout the relevant area of production. It is also known that price discrimination takes place in the motor industry with domestic prices being higher than prices abroad.

4 Goulds is a small company in Kowloon which sells Fuji camcorders under licence in the local market at £1,144 each. Their unit costs (inclusive of licence fee) are constant at £1,140. The demand for these camcorders in Kowloon is given by

$$P_1 = £1{,}200 - 0.04Q_1.$$

The Fuji corporation produce their patented camcorders in Taiwan at a total cost C given by

$C = £6,400,000 + 10Q + 0.05Q^2$.

The demand for Fuji camcorders in Taiwan is given by

$P_2 = £1,500 - 0.025Q_2$.

Fuji are dissatisfied with Gould's sales performance and have notified Goulds of their decision to expand sales in Kowloon by supplying direct from Taiwan. Goulds have responded by accusing Fuji's of pursuing a 'dumping' policy and since the Chinese Government prohibits the import of 'dumped' products they (Fuji Corporation) will face bankruptcy if they implement their decision.

Evaluate Fuji's decision and Goulds response. (Hint: dumping takes place when the product price is below the marginal cost of production.)

5 The Maxton company produces its patented product in the UK with total cost C, inclusive of selling and distribution costs, given by

$C = 900,000 + 80Q + 0.05Q^2$

where Q denotes units of output. The company sells its product in continental Europe and in the UK. Its main sale effort, however, is concentrated in the UK where there are fewer substitutes. The demand curves for the product are

$P_1 = 2,000 - 0.2Q_1$
$P_2 = 500 - 0.02Q_2$

where Q_1 and Q_2 are the quantities supplied per month to their respective markets.

1 State which demand curve applies to the home market giving your reasons.
2 What is the maximum profit that the company can make?
3 Do you think that the company can be accused of dumping?
4 Would the activities of the company be affected by a legal instruction from the European Commission to sell it's output at a single price? If so specify the effects. If not explain why not.

6 Software plc have decided to produce computer diskettes and the Managing Director (MD) is considering the company's pricing and output strategy. He knows the costs of production are given by

$AC = 3.5 + Q/60$

and

$MC = 3.5 + Q/30$

where Q is the number of units of output, each unit consisting of a packet containing six diskettes.

Having attempted to estimate the demand curve for software diskettes, the MD believes that for prices higher than £6.00 the demand curve would be given by

$Q = 210 - 30P$

while for prices lower than £6.00 it would be

$Q = 90 - 10P$.

(a) On graph paper draw the demand curve facing Software plc together with the marginal and the average cost of production.
(b) Explain what kind of competitive reaction is anticipated by the MD of Software plc.
(c) Determine the profit maximising level of diskette output, the price that the MD has decided to charge in order to profit maximise and the total amount of profit.

7 Define a 'perfect cartel' and explain how the price of a product would be determined when an oligopoly industry is organised as a perfect cartel. Discuss the significance of a quota agreement and explain why cartel members have an incentive to over-produce.

8 In December 1984 the conference of ministers of the thirteen Oil Producing and Exporting Countries (OPEC) decided to appoint independent auditors in order to monitor that members to the oil cartel agreement would not exceed their agreed oil production quotas.

Use your answer to the previous question to evaluate the view that 'the decision to appoint independent auditors amply demonstrates the inherent instability of cartel agreements'.

9 Two firms producing the same product and controlling 100 per cent of industrial output form a perfect cartel. Their cost functions are given by

$$TC_1 = 40q_1 + 5q_1^2$$
$$TC_2 = 80q_2 + 2.5q_2^2.$$

The total demand for the product is

$$P = 200 - 5Q$$

where $Q = q_1 + q_2$.

(a) Determine
   (i) the total output of the cartel
   (ii) the market price of this product
   (iii) the output of each firm
   (iv) the total profit of the industry
(b) How would you expect your answer to be affected when
   (i) there is an increased demand for the product
   (ii) the costs of one of the firms increase.

10 Comment on the view that an industry with a three–firm concentration ratio of 100 per cent, in which the market share of the most efficient firm is more than 50 percent of total output, will most probably develop a price leadership model of behaviour.

Assuming that the largest firm (firm 1) does act as the leader calculate the price of this industry's product and the market share of each firm, given that the total market demand is

$$Q_d = 240 - 10P$$

where Q_d denotes total quantity demanded and P is the corresponding price. The marginal cost functions are:

Firm 1	$MC_1 . = Q_1/25$
Firm 2	$MC_2 = Q_2/6$
Firm 3	$MC_3 = Q_3/4$

11 Suppose that company A is the sole producer of commodity X and that the long-run average cost curve of X is L-shaped. The current production level of X is well above the MES and the price charged exceeds the average cost by a significant margin. In fact profits are maximised. However, the patent which secured the monopolisation of X is approaching its expiring date at which point the production technology of X will become easily available to potential competitors. As a result, new entrants into the market will have no cost disadvantage. Additionally, the Managing Director (MD) of company A has been informed that company B, a large diversified firm, is considering entry into the market for X. The MD is considering, therefore, whether to reduce the price of X in order to discourage company B and any other potential competitors from entering the market.

(a) Explain why a limit price calculated on the assumption of the Sylos postulate is likely to be rather ineffective in these circumstances.

(b) Making any other necessary assumptions construct a decision tree to indicate the firm's best strategy.

12 According to evidence, General Motors was until 1979 or 1980 the recognised dominant firm in the US automobile industry. It 'set a price that it thought would protect its market share and the other producers followed accordingly' (Friedlaender *et al.* 1982). During the early 1980s, however, this pattern of industrial behaviour was broken down as imports, mainly from Japan, rose dramatically.

Assuming a profit maximising objective use diagrammatic analysis to explain how General Motors may have determined the market price for a car of given specifications and indicate the pressures caused by higher imports that may have led to the disruption of the price leadership pattern of industrial behaviour.

13 Explain why strategic entry deterrence may result in excess capacity but not necessarily in lower prices.

14 Explain how firms may use advertising expenditure as a strategic weapon and use a decision tree to illustrate your answer.

APPENDIX 8.1: THE EQUILIBRIUM OF A TWO PLANT MONOPOLIST

Given the market demand $P = f(Q)$ and the cost of plant 1

$$TC_1 = g(q_1)$$

and plant 2

$$TC_2 = h(q_2)$$

where $q_1 + q_2 = Q$, the profit maximising firm is said to be in equilibrium when production and its allocation among the two plants is such that total profit is maximised. That is, q_1 and q_2 must be such as to maximise

$$\Pi = f(Q)Q - g(q_1) - h(q_2)$$

or

$$\Pi = f(q_1 + q_2)(q_1 + q_2) - g(q_1) - h(q_2).$$

Assuming well behaving functions so that the second-order conditions for a maximum are satisfied, the first-order conditions give

$$\frac{\partial \Pi}{\partial q_1} = f'(Q)Q + f(Q)\frac{\partial Q}{\partial q_1} - g'(q_1) = 0 \tag{A8.1}$$

$$\frac{\partial \Pi}{\partial q_2} = f'(Q)Q + f(Q)\frac{\partial Q}{\partial q_2} - h'(q_2) = 0 \tag{A8.2}$$

where $\partial Q/\partial q_1 = \partial Q/\partial q_2 = 1$ so that from (A8.1) and (A8.2) we get

$$f'(Q)Q + f(Q)\frac{\partial Q}{\partial q_1} = g'(q_1) \text{ or } MR = MC_1$$

$$f'(Q)Q + f(Q)\frac{\partial Q}{\partial q_2} = h'(q_2) \text{ or } MR = MC_2.$$

Solving these two equations simultaneously gives the profit maximising output of each plant. Substituting the sum of these into the common market demand we derive the monopoly price.

APPENDIX 8.2: DERIVATION OF THE EQUAL MARGINAL REVENUE RULE OF PRICE DISCRIMINATION.

Assume two markets or market segments have demand curves $P_a = f(Q_a)$ and $P_b = h(Q_b)$. Production takes place in a single plant with TC = $F(Q)$ where $Q = Q_a + Q_b$. It follows that $\Pi = f(Q_a)Q_a + h(Q_b)Q_b - F(Q)$
and to maximise profits the following two conditions must be fulfilled.

$$\frac{\partial \Pi}{\partial Q_a} = f'(Q_a)Q_a + f(Q_a) - F'(Q) \quad \frac{\partial Q}{\partial Q_a} = 0$$

$$\frac{\partial \Pi}{\partial Q_b} = h'(Q_b)Q_b + h(Q_b) - F'(Q) \quad \frac{\partial Q}{\partial Q_b} = 0$$

where $\partial Q/\partial Q_a = \partial Q/\partial Q_b = 1$. The first two terms of each equation denote the marginal revenue of each market. That is, Q_a and Q_b must be such that $MR_a = MC$ in the first equation and $MR_b = MC$ in the second equation. Therefore, for profit maximisation $MR_a = MR_b$.

NOTES

1 For negatively sloping demand curves the profit maximising price is always higher then marginal cost. To prove this recall that

   1 for profit maximisation MR = MC
   2 price elasticity is $e = (dQ/dP) P/Q$
   3 $MR = \dfrac{dTR}{dQ} = \dfrac{dP}{dQ} Q + P$

   or $MR = \dfrac{dP}{dQ} Q \dfrac{P}{P} + P = P(\dfrac{dP}{dQ} \dfrac{Q}{P} + 1)$.

   So $MR = P(1 + 1/e)$ but e is negative implying that $P > MR$, therefore, given i, $P > MC$.
2 The number of cases heard by 1983 was 4,958.
3 For references to this earlier literature and further details on the traditional limit pricing theory, see Scherer (1980: Chapter 8).
4 To derive the formula for the limit price, note that $e = (\triangle Q/\triangle P) P/Q$ but $\triangle Q = \bar{x}$ and $\triangle P = P_L - P_C$ while $Q = X_C$. Therefore, $e = [\bar{x}/(P_L - P_C)] P_C/X_C$ which gives, by re-arranging terms, $P_L = P_C (1 + \bar{x}/eX_C)$.
5 It is the same per unit loss but the volume of production is smaller for the entrant than the existing firm(s).
6 If the change $\triangle X$ in output is divided equally among $N + 1$ firms, i.e. $\triangle X/(N + 1) = x$ or $\triangle X = \bar{x}(N + 1)$ then the price elasticity of demand will be approximately equal to

   $$\frac{\triangle X}{X} : \frac{\triangle P}{P} = e + c(N + 1)$$

   therefore,

   $$\frac{\bar{x}(N + 1)}{X_C} : \frac{P_L - P_C}{P_C} = e + c(N + 1)$$

   and by arithmetic manipulation this gives

   $$P_L = P_c \left[1 + \frac{\bar{x}}{X_c \left(\frac{e}{N+1} + c \right)} \right]$$

9 The separation of ownership from control

Shareholders do not control the firm, and managers do not necessarily act in their interests

J.E. Stiglitz

SHARE-OWNERSHIP DISPERSION AND THE SEPARATION OF OWNERSHIP AND CONTROL

A large proportion of business enterprises are run by professional managers who have no, or a very small, share interest in their corporations. The possibility that they may not always act in the best interest of their shareholders was raised as far back as 1776 by Adam Smith who wrote

> The directors of such companies . . . being the managers rather of other peoples money than of their own, it cannot well be expected, that they should watch over it with the same vigilance with which the partners in a private copartnery frequently watch over their own. Like the stewards of a rich man, they are apt to consider attention to small matters as not of their master's honour, and very easily give themselves a dispensation from having it. Negligence and profusion, therefore, must always prevail, more or less, in the management of the affairs of such a company.[1]

Berle and Means (1932) also suggested that the separation of ownership from control produces a situation where the interests of owners may diverge from the interests of the managers in charge of modern corporations. This diversion is the result of (a) the existence of wide share dispersion with no individual or small group of shareholders owning a substantial percentage of total shares and (b) managers owning an insignificant proportion of total shares.

The Berle and Means propositions were derived from an investigation of the 200 largest US corporations (excluding banks) which showed that no shareholder had as much as 1 per cent of total shares and that the twenty largest shareholders had no more than 5.1 per cent of total shares. Despite their extensive empirical foundation the Berle and Means propositions, although well received, did not have a great influence on economists at the time of their publication. Until the late 1950s economists continued to analyse business behaviour on the assumption of profit maximisation, ignoring the possibility that the diversion between managerial and shareholder interests may influence business behaviour. Meanwhile ownership dispersion continued its upward trend both in the USA and in the UK. Thus, while in 1929 58 per cent of the 200 largest US non-financial corporations were 'corporations with no single important stock interest', this proportion had risen to 85 per cent by 1963.[2] By the middle of the twentieth century the dispersed joint stock corporation was prevalent in most industrial and commercial sectors. In 1951, for example, only 7 per cent of all UK companies with a share capital of over £3 million had a single majority shareholding. In only 5.5 per cent of the remaining companies did the largest twenty shareholders together have a majority position. For smaller companies (with a share capital between £0.2 million and £3 million) the corresponding figures were under 1 per cent and approximately 10 per cent respectively.[3] In 1981, a sample of fifty-four giant UK and US corporations were investigated by Cosh and Hughes (1987) who found that the median largest shareholding was 3.7 per cent for the UK sample and 5.1 per cent for the US sample. Such findings confirm that the process of increasingly dispersed share ownership continues. This implies boards of directors with an insignificant share ownership as indicated by Tables 9.1 and 9.2.

Table 9.1 shows that, based on a sample of fifty firms, the percentage shareholding of directors and managers in the USA in 1975 was on average 17.5 per cent. This percentage is much smaller (under 14 per cent) when firms too small to be included in the *Fortune 500* were excluded from the sample. The insignificance of shareholdings of directors and managers has been confirmed by Cosh and Hughes' (1987) sample of fifty-four giant UK and US corporations.

Table 9.2 shows that no board member, in the UK sample, controlled more than 5 per cent of shares and only in two instances did board members control approximately 1.4 per cent of the total shares of their

Table 9.1 Share ownership in the USA

Manufacturing firms on 1975 Fortune 500	*Percentage of shares held by directors and managers (unweighted average 1973–82)*
Ten largest	2.1
Middle ten	19.3
Last ten	20.4
Firms too small from 1975 *Fortune 500* (random sample)	32.5
Ten public utilities (randomly selected)	13.5
Average of all fifty	17.5

Source: Demsetz 1983: Table 1, p. 388

Table 9.2 Major shareholdings in fifty-four UK and US corporations

	UK sample		US sample	
	Number of holdings	*Sample median percentage of shares held by these holdings*	*Number of holdings*	*Sample median percentage of shares held by these holdings*
Holdings >5%				
Board	0	–	6	23.4
Internal funds[a]	1	17.7	2	18.5
Financial institutions	4	6.4	6	6.3
Other	4	31.1	2	5.3
Total	9	16.7	16	9.0
Holdings ⩾1%				
Board	2	1.4	12	7.4
Internal funds[a]	1	17.7	12	2.8
Financial institutions	201	10.9	224	14.8
Other	28	1.5	10	2.5
Total	232	16.8	258	24.5

Note: [a] Internally managed funds such as pension funds etc.
Source: Cosh and Hughes 1987: Table 12, p. 301

company. The corresponding US figures are somewhat higher. Further analysis (not included in Table 9.2) shows that the total percentage of shares controlled by the board, including the shares of internally managed funds, had a median value of 0.06 per cent and a mean of 0.85 per cent in the UK, and a median of 0.75 per cent and a mean of 8.1 per cent in the USA.

The dominance of the dispersed joint stock company is no longer disputed although its significance for business behaviour is vigorously debated. It can be argued, for example, that since share ownership is so widely dispersed, a small shareholding can give sufficient voting power and dominance over the affairs of a company. However, this small percentage may be in the hands of managers who can thus acquire more independence from shareholders to pursue their own rather than shareholder objectives.

Table 9.2 indicates that financial institutions (banks, pension funds, etc.), although infrequent holders of over 5 per cent of equity, are emerging as relatively significant shareholders. Four institutions in the UK and six in the USA control over 6 per cent of total shares and the vast majority (201 out of 232) of shareholders possessing more than 1 per cent of shares are financial institutions. Moreover, it can be argued that the power of financial institutions is actually more significant than Table 9.2 implies because of the existence of numerous inter-connections among financial institutions and corporate shareholders (such as shared director-ships). Thus, a small number of financial institutions was found by Cosh and Hughes to recur as significant owners and controllers of stock in the UK with the power to play a significant role in the determination of corporate behaviour. This potential power was rarely exercised, however, because very few institutions were prepared to undertake what they considered as 'the time-consuming and not always effective action of co-ordinated intervention' (p. 300). This contrasts sharply with the behaviour of financial institutions in Japan which take a very active role in the affairs of the companies they finance (see the Application section of Chapter 12 for more details).

Provided that financial institutions or other shareholders have neither the time nor the inclination to monitor managerial behaviour effectively, the assumption of profit maximisation cannot be relied upon to explain business behaviour. Alternative hypotheses, therefore, have been suggested by the behaviouralists and the managerialists. More recently transactions cost economics has shown that organisational features may influence the process of goal formation and business performance (see Chapter 4) and agency theory has shed serious doubts on the assumption of profit maximisation.

This chapter begins with a brief outline of alternative business objectives and proceeds to examine the business behaviour of managerially run firms. Three managerial theories, sales revenue maximisation, managerial utility maximisation and growth, form the basis for this analysis. The following section introduces the basic concepts of agency theory and examines business behaviour from the perspective of agency relationships. Various mechanisms controlling managerial discretion and their effectiveness are subsequently discussed. The final section gives a summary of the main points. The application illustrates the existence of agency conflict and its possible mitigation in oil and gas exploration partnerships.

THE IMPACT OF THE SEPARATION OF OWNERSHIP FROM CONTROL ON BUSINESS OBJECTIVES

The neoclassical theory of the firm is based on the assumption of profit maximisation which implies that the firm is a single unit with a sole aim. It assumes costless information and perfectly rational decision makers so that organisational features have no influence on behaviour. Furthermore, power relations are unimportant, empire building is insignificant and in general conflict among individual participants in a firm is either non-existent or inconsequential. This perfectly rational and anthropomorphic view of the firm has been rejected by many economists as bearing no resemblance to its real-world namesake.

Behaviouralists, such as Cyert and March (1963), view the firm as a coalition of individuals or groups of individuals with different and often contradictory objectives. The members of this coalition, which includes managers, workers, shareholders, customers, suppliers, lenders, tax-collectors and any others with an interest in the firm, make demands in the form of financial rewards or 'side payments', i.e. policy commitments. Such demands must be met if the coalition is to survive. The formation and continued existence of the coalition is the result of a process of bargaining and compromise by which the demands of each member, or subgroup, are defined. Since, however, information is costly and all individuals are boundedly rational, their demands take the form of 'aspirational levels'. Given that the aspirations of the coalition members vary, there is a multiplicity of objectives which take the form of aspiring to achieve satisfactory levels of performance in various aspects of the firm's work. The firm does not, therefore, aim to maximise anything. It simply operates under a number of constraints which it attempts to satisfy. The list of such constraints includes production, sales, market share, inventory level, profits, etc. Since these objectives can be contradictory, conflict in decision making may arise. The resolution of such conflict requires the existence of 'organisational slack'.

Organisational slack is the difference between the resources available and the resources which are necessary in order to meet the minimum payments required to ensure the continued existence of the coalition. In other words, slack takes the form of payments in excess of opportunity costs. If the aspirational level of any goal is not achieved, so that its performance is unsatisfactory, then the existing slack can be utilised to improve this performance without adversely affecting other goals. An example has been provided by the Ford Motor Company which, when faced with losses of $50 million for the first three-quarters of 1946, announced that they had found ways of reducing costs by about $20 million a year without reducing production.[4] Given that slack plays an important role in improving performance, its absence can affect adversely the very existence of a firm. It has, for example, been suggested that many UK firms are currently (early 1990s) facing liquidation being unable to reduce losses, apparently because of the absence of any slack. As John-Harvey Jones (a well-known and influential British business director) has observed,[5] these are efficient firms which three years ago modernised their plants and rationalised in preparation for the European integration in 1992.

While the behaviouralists maintain that firms do not maximise anything and slack can accrue to any member of the team, managerialists believe that any slack within the firm will be directed, as far as possible, towards the maximisation of the utility of management. The firm is viewed as a hierarchical structure in which top management sets the objectives and monitors lower level managers and other personnel. Managers are self-interest seeking individuals who attempt to maximise their own utility rather than profits, unless they happen to be the owners of the firm.

Managerialists suggest that managers are motivated by salaries, perquisites and other financial rewards as well as by a desire to enhance their status, prestige and power. Their policies, therefore, are influenced by these motives. They will be prepared to accept lower overall profits in pursuit of policies which enhance their own motives. In other words, managers may sacrifice profits in pursuit of policies which maximise their own utility. This does not, however, imply that the firm's profitability will be totally neglected. On the contrary, in order to secure their jobs, managers will wish to have a certain amount of net profits to distribute as dividends in order to keep their shareholders satisfied with the firm's performance. This is of paramount importance since dissatisfied shareholders may either replace the incumbent management or attempt to sell their shares causing a share devaluation and encouraging a hostile takeover bid. In either case managers risk losing their jobs. In brief, profitability is not ignored but profit has become a constraint rather than the sole objective of the firm.

All managerialists agree that subject to a satisfactory level of profits, managers will pursue policies consistent with their own motives. There is no consensus, however, regarding the way in which managerial motives manifest themselves in business decision making. Baumol (1961), for example, believes that managers aim to maximise sales revenue while Marris (1964) suggests growth maximisation. Williamson's earlier writings (1964) suggest that managers (especially of unitary organised firms) create discretionary funds for investment and spend excessively on emoluments and staff expenditure.

Agency theory views managers as the agents of shareholders and suggests that, whether ownership is dispersed or not, the separation of ownership from control means that they may try to pursue their own interests at the expense of the interests of their principals, the shareholders. This is consistent with self-interest seeking motivation and the existence of information asymmetry which hinders monitoring. As a result business objectives and decisions may not reflect shareholder interests. Therefore, an 'agency problem' exists whose solution depends on devising a system of incentives and control mechanisms capable of eliminating, or at least restricting, managerial discretion.

MANAGERIAL THEORIES OF THE FIRM

The diversity of views that managerialists hold regarding the way in which similarly motivated managers will behave has meant that a variety of managerial theories of the firm exist. The most influential ones will be briefly examined in this section.

Sales revenue maximisation

Baumol advanced the idea that managers would wish to maximise sales revenue subject to a profit constraint. That is, provided that profit does not fall below a certain level, management will devote all their energies to the expansion of sales. This is partly because increased sales increase the size of the firm which may improve its competitive position but mainly because managerial salaries, prestige and status are likely to be enhanced with increased size. At the same time a certain level of profit must be earned. This minimum profit is necessary to ensure job security for managers. Its size depends on Stock Market conditions and the level of dividends other firms are distributing to shareholders.

If the management of at least some firms pursue a sales maximising objective, the question then arises as to whether this will influence business decisions and policies. Do sales maximising firms pursue different policies and do they respond differently to environmental changes compared with profit maximising firms? To answer these questions we will examine the production, pricing and advertising policies of a sales maximising firm. We will also analyse possible responses to environmental changes and make some comparisons between sales and profit maximising firms.

Figure 9.1 illustrates a sales revenue maximising firm operating in monopolistic conditions. The total revenue (TR) curve has been drawn on the assumption that the firm's demand curve is negatively sloped. The shape of the total cost (TC) curve reflects the usual assumptions of a U-shaped average cost curve. Since profit Π is the difference between TR and TC, each point on curve Π corresponds to the distance between TR and TC. The larger this distance the higher the profit earned. The distance is the largest where the slope of a tangent on TR is the same as the slope of a tangent on TC (i.e. where MR = MC). This occurs at output Q_p. Profit, therefore, is maximised at this output level. (The broken lines should be ignored for the time being.)

Total revenue (TR = PQ), on the other hand, reaches its highest level at output Q_s, i.e. at that output level at which the price elasticity of demand is unity. But where elasticity is equal to 1 marginal revenue (MR) is 0. Indeed the sales maximising rule is that production should be carried to that output level at which MR = 0.[6] However, this will only be possible if the profit earned, as this output is sold, is sufficient to satisfy the minimum profit constraint. Otherwise, production will be reduced and price raised in order to raise profitability to its minimum acceptable level.

If stock market conditions are such that to keep shareholders satisfied with managerial performance a minimum amount of profit of £F is required, then the profit F_2 which is earned from the sales maximising output Q_s will not be sufficient. Management concerned about the shareholder response to a small dividend will not choose to produce Q_s. In an attempt to raise the price and improve profitability, production will be cut back to Q_s'. This is the production level that brings in the highest sales revenue while satisfying the profit constraint.

The profit maximising output is Q_p. This is the output that the firm would choose if the aim was to profit maximise. It is clear from Figure 9.1 that the firm would produce and sell more if the objective was to sales

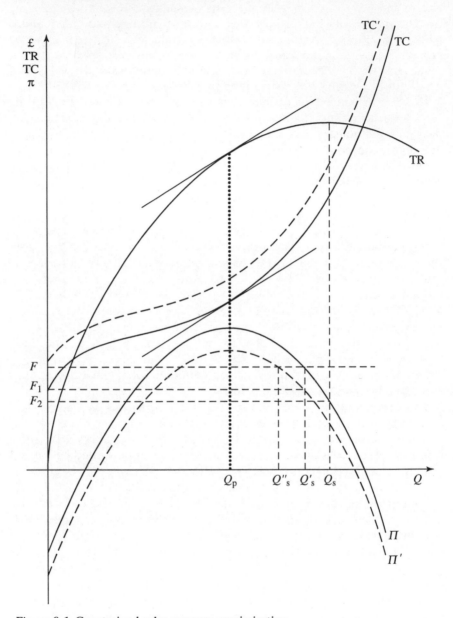

Figure 9.1 Constrained sales revenue maximisation

maximise rather than to profit maximise. Given a negatively sloping demand curve, this means that a sales maximising firm will charge a lower price for their product. The only case in which the production and pricing policy would be the same under profit and sales maximisation would be if the minimum profit constraint were equal to the maximum possible profit. This is highly unlikely since it is only feasible when the capital market is very well informed and operates perfectly efficiently or when other mechanisms exist which eliminate managerial discretion. We may conclude that in general the following holds.

Prediction 1 Sales maximisers produce more compared with profit maximisers and charge a lower price for their product.

Advertising and other sales promotional activities also depend on business objectives. Advertising campaigns are usually designed to stimulate demand and if successful the demand curve shifts to the right. This means that the firm can either sell the same output at a higher price or, as Baumol assumes, it can produce and sell more output at the same price. Thus, the higher the advertising budget the more output will be sold at a given price, but there may be diminishing returns so that total revenue increases but at a diminishing rate as advertising expenditure expands. This is shown in Figure 9.2 by the curve labelled TR. The TC curve includes production and advertising costs. Its shape assumes a U-shaped average production cost curve. The difference between TR and TC is the total profit Π.

Since increased advertising increases revenue, the TR curve on Figure 9.2 has no peak point (no maximum). This does not mean that the size of the advertising budget is unlimited or indeterminate. Sales maximisers cannot spend an unlimited amount of money on advertising since this will eventually add more to costs than to revenues and profit will start to fall. On the other hand it is assumed that any profit in excess of the minimum required will be used to improve demand conditions through advertising and other promotional activities. In Figure 9.2, profits reach a maximum at the advertising budget A_p and decline thereafter. To achieve the highest possible level of sales revenue while meeting the minimum profit constraint the advertising expenditure will be A_s. This is clearly smaller than the profit maximising advertising level A_p. In general the following holds.

Prediction 2 Sales revenue maximisers will tend to spend more than profit maximisers on advertising and other sales promotional activities.

The behaviour of sales maximisers differs to that of profit maximisers in many other respects. Consider, for example, the imposition of a lump sum tax (such as a licensing fee payable per year) or an increase in fixed costs. Since neither the fee nor fixed costs vary with output, marginal cost will not be affected by their changes and a profit maximiser will not respond to an increase in either. Price and output remain the same while net profits decline. Profit maximisers cannot pass on to consumers an increase in lump sum taxes or fixed costs. Students, sometimes, find this prediction difficult to accept since their intuition or personal experiences may contradict it. They tend to argue that in reality firms would respond to an increase in

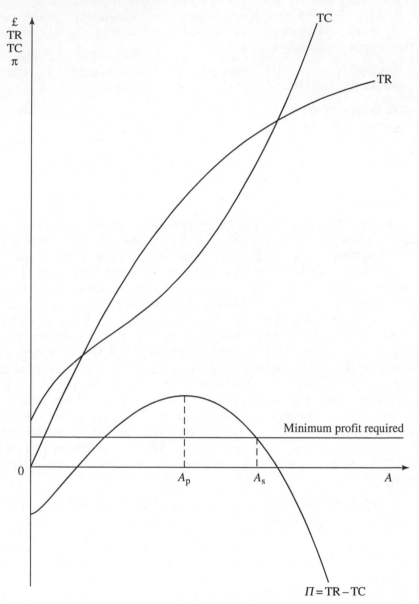

Figure 9.2 Advertising under sales revenue maximisation

fixed costs by increasing their prices. This is indeed what sales maximisers would be expected to do. Figure 9.1 may help explain why.

Suppose that the firm operates at point Q'_s meeting the profit constraint. An increase in fixed costs (or a lump sum tax) is shown by an upward shift

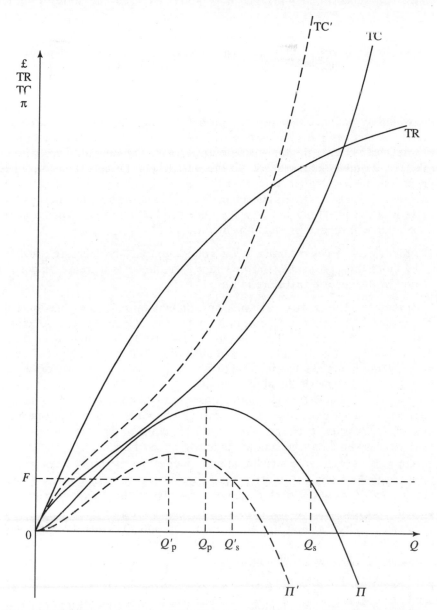

Figure 9.3 The impact of a per unit of production tax or an increase in variable costs, under sales revenue maximisation

in the total cost curve and a corresponding reduction in net profits. The new curves (broken lines) are denoted by TC′ and Π′ respectively. If price and output remain the same the minimum profit constraint will no longer be met since at Q_s profit is negative. To avoid this happening the firm will charge a higher price and aim to produce and sell the lower output Q_s''.

Prediction 3 Sales revenue maximisers will increase price and reduce production in response to increases in fixed costs or lump sum taxes.

When a per unit of production tax is imposed or when variable costs change the firm will respond by altering price and production. It is interesting, however, to note that the extent of this response will depend on whether management aims to profit or sales maximise. Figure 9.3 illustrates this case. An increase in variable costs means that the addition to total cost is larger the higher the output level. The new total cost curve (TC') shifts upwards and pivots to the left. If TR remains the same, the profit reduction is higher the higher the level of output; consequently the maximum level of profit is now achieved at a lower output. The new profit curve is Π'. A profit maximiser will reduce production to Q_p' while a sales maximiser will reduce production, by more, to Q_s'.

Prediction 4 Sales maximisers will reduce output and increase price by more than profit maximisers when variable costs increase or per unit of production taxes are imposed.

It can also be shown that (a) unlike profit maximisers, sales maximisers will respond to a change in corporation tax by altering their production and price level, and (b) the qualitative response to a change in market demand is the same but there is a quantitative difference. Appendix 9.1 gives the mathematical formulation of this model and a numerical example that illustrates some of the above points.

This static, single-period model has been extended by Baumol to incorporate a long-term sales maximising objective and a multi-period analysis.[7] However, the predictions of the dynamic model are very similar to those derived from the simple model discussed here.

A weakness of the sales maximisation model is that the profit constraint is rather vaguely defined. A more precise specification may therefore alter its predictions. Yarrow (1976), for example, has argued that the constraint will take the form of a deviation between the maximum possible stock market valuation of the firm and the actual valuation and that this deviation will depend on the size distribution of share ownership and the costs involved in replacing the incumbent management.[8] Yarrow's sales maximisers would behave somewhat differently to Baumol's. Similarly, business behaviour will be different if managerial objectives are other than sales maximisation. Williamson, for example, utilises the same constraint as Baumol but arrives at different conclusions since he assumes different managerial objectives.

Williamson's model of 'managerial discretion'

The existence of managerial discretion is prevalent in unitary organised firms, according to Williamson. As explained in Chapter 4, he distinguishes between the 'peak co-ordinator' and the 'process of co-ordination', which is a function. It is the function which is powerful and influential in goal formation. Although the peak co-ordinator participates in the function he or she does not dominate it, mainly because of bounded rationality. Thus, the preferences of the peak co-ordinator may be compromised. This is particularly true as the U-form firm expands. The need then arises for departmental heads to participate in the co-ordinating function which may change the top-level perspective from an enterprise one to a collection of partisan and possibly conflicting views. There is less check on empire building and related pursuits and as a result subgoals dominate the objectives of the peak co-ordinator. Since the aim of the peak co-ordinator is assumed to be profit maximisation, it is not so much the separation of ownership from control[9] that results in non-profit maximising objectives, it is rather the internal organisational features of the firm that may allow managers to sacrifice profits in pursuit of their own utility maximisation.

In common with other managerialists, Williamson assumes the managerial motives to be financial rewards, status, prestige, power and security. These motives are manifested in three policy variables which enter the managerial utility function:

1 salaries and other monetary rewards and the number and quality of staff reporting to a manager, a proxy variable for these is the expenditure on staff S;
2 discretionary investment funds I which are created in order to justify staff expansion and growth beyond the level required for profit maximisation;
3 expenditure on perquisites such as company cars, lavish offices and other emoluments M which enhance managerial status and prestige.

Managerial attempts to maximise utility by pursuing policies which increase expenditure on S, M and I will be constrained by considerations of job security. To secure their jobs managers try to achieve a level of profitability which will enable them to pay a sufficient level of dividends. But, unlike Baumol's sales maximisers, 'utility maximisers' will normally report profits higher than the minimum required level and the excess (after payment of relevant taxes) will be used as discretionary investment.

Managerial behaviour can be summarised as follows:

maximise $U = f(S, M, I)$
subject to $\Pi_r \geqslant \Pi_m + T$

Where U denotes utility, Π_r are the reported profits, Π_m is the minimum required level of profit and T denotes corporation tax. If Π_x is the maximum possible level of profit and Π_a the actual profit then, by definition,

$S = \Pi_x - \Pi_a$
$M = \Pi_a - \Pi_r$
$I = \Pi_r - \Pi_m - T.$

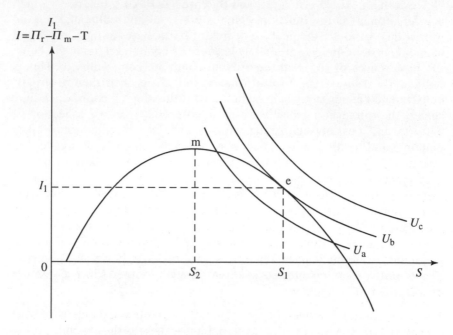

Figure 9.4 Managerial utility maximisation

The solution to the above maximisation problem requires some competence in mathematics and is, therefore, delegated to Appendix 9.2. Its main implications are summarised in Table 9.3. The behaviour of a utility maximising firm, however, can be appreciated by examining a simplified version of the full model. The simplification is achieved by assuming that emoluments are non-existent (see Figure 9.4).

Managerial utility is assumed to increase as S and I increase although the rate of this increase diminishes. So, the larger the expenditure on S and I the higher the managerial utility is. However, for any given level of profit, the amount devoted to S and I is fixed so that spending more on S implies less spending on I and vice versa. A choice has to be made. This choice will depend on the relative significance that management places on S and I or, to put it differently, on the extent to which managerial utility changes with marginal changes in S and I. Since both S and I are desirable, indifference curves with the conventional convex to the origin shape can be drawn to illustrate managerial preferences over S and I. Figure 9.4 shows a hypothetical set of indifference curves labelled U_a, U_b and U_c.

Profitability varies with the level of output X and expenditure on staff S. Production costs increase with output in the usual way. Expenditure on staff is assumed to have a small positive effect on demand so that as S increases a higher price can be charged for the same output.[10] Therefore, as X and S increase total profits increase up to a point. Beyond a certain level, however, increasing costs of production and the necessity to charge lower prices in order to sell higher volumes of output will bring about reductions in profits. Figure 9.4 shows the relationship between S and I. Recall that I (measured on the vertical axis) is equal to reported profits minus the minimum required profit and any tax on it. Therefore, point m indicates the maximum profit that can be reported after an amount equal to the minimum profit constraint plus taxation on it has been deducted.

Since the aim of management is to maximise utility they will choose to operate at point e which is on the highest possible indifference curve. Staff expenditure will be S_1 and discretionary investment will be I_1. Reported profits are maximised at point m. At e staff expenditure is higher than at m but reported profits are lower. In other words, managers will trade some profits (which would have provided funds for extra discretionary investment) for staff expenditure. Thus, S is higher than that required for profit maximisation and reported profit (i.e. $I = \Pi_{min} + T$) is less than the maximum possible.

In short, actual profit will be less than maximum possible profit because expenditure on staff (and also emoluments) is higher than necessary. Furthermore, part of the reported profit will be absorbed as discretionary investment. However, since reported profit is higher than the minimum required, actual profitability is higher, *ceteris paribus*, than in Baumol's model.

The response of the firm to changes in demand, taxes and fixed costs (derived from the full mathematical model) is summarised in Table 9.3. The corresponding response of the profit maximiser is also included for comparison. Some interesting inferences can be drawn from Table 9.3.

Table 9.3 Comparison of predictions of the utility and the profit maximisation models of firm behaviour

Variable affected	Increase in demand		Increase in profit tax		Increase in lump sum tax (or fixed cost)	
	Williamson	Profit	Williamson	Profit	Williamson	Profit
Output	+	+	+	0	−	0
Staff expenditure	+	+	+	0	−	0
Ratio Π_r/Π_a	−	0	−	0	+	0

1 Both utility and profit maximisers will respond to an increase in demand by producing more and spending more on staff. However, utility maximisers will reduce the ratio of reported to actual profits. In other words, a higher proportion of their profits will be absorbed as slack and discretionary investment. Profit maximisers do not change this ratio which is always equal to one. (They have no slack since their reported profit is always the same as actual profit.)

2 Profit maximisers do not respond to a change in corporation tax. However, since an increase in corporation tax penalises reported profits, utility maximisers will be induced to report less profits and to absorb more as staff expenditure, which increases output.

3 Profit maximisers do not respond to changes in lump sum taxes or fixed costs. However, since an increase in lump sum taxes (or any fixed costs) would violate the minimum profit constraint, utility maximisers would respond by reducing production, charging a higher price and increasing the ratio of reported to actual profits.

Williamson provides some empirical evidence in support of this model. Indeed several aspects of the postulated behaviour sound very realistic. However, the extent of the expected response is sometimes very small and it is difficult to collect information on a firm's 'discretionary' investment or 'slack' in order to estimate their size and significance. Some predictions, e.g. the suggestion that discretionary investment moves in opposite directions to output in response to a changed tax rate, seem to be rather unrealistic (Hay and Morris 1991). Williamson himself considers this model relevant only to U-form firms. He believes that the organisational attributes of M-form structures are sufficient to control managerial discretion. Organisational features may well influence behaviour and in particular they may mitigate against subgoal intrusion into top managerial perspective. The question, however, remains of why top managers should identify with shareholders. If they do not then their behaviour may deviate from that of an owner manager.

The growth of firms

To understand the process of growth we have to focus attention on the behaviour of 'active' firms which undertake research and development of their products, diversify, advertise, retain profits and acquire equity and debt finance. While active firms will seek growth whatever their overall objectives, a divergence of interests between management and shareholders will manifest itself in the rate at which a firm will attempt to grow. That is, growth policies need not resemble profit policies despite the existence of strong links between profitability and growth. To expand its productive capacity a firm needs to raise finance and this depends on profitability. On the other hand, to expand the market for its current range of products and to introduce new ones, the firm needs to increase promotional and other expenditures and to reduce its prices, thus reducing profit margins. This dual role of profitability, which implies a possible conflict between profitability and growth, was recognised by Downie (1958) and others and is at the heart of Marris's (1963) theory of the growth maximising enterprise. Marris contends that managerial motives of status, prestige and power will induce managers to attempt to maximise growth, but managerial growth policies will be constrained by bounded rationality and considerations of job security.

Growth involves an expansion of both the productive capacity and the demand for the products of a firm. To avoid over-capacity, existing resources must be brought in line with the demand placed upon them. Moreover, the rate at which both the productive capacity and the market demand grow must be equal, otherwise an ever growing over-capacity or excess demand may be created. Managers are assumed, therefore, to attempt to maximise a *balanced* growth rate. To facilitate the analysis, a *steady state growth* is assumed. That is, all the characteristics of the firm are assumed to grow at a constant exponential rate over time. Consequently, the ratio of any two characteristics such as the profit rate, the output to capital ratio, etc. become constant over time and are called 'state' variables. In reality state variables are not constant but any deviations may be thought of as changes in the firm's policies, in order to justify this simplifying assumption.

The rate at which a firm can grow will depend on how quickly and efficiently any obstacles to growth can be overcome. The main obstacles to growth will be analysed under three headings.

The managerial constraint

Growth implies increases in size and diversity which may result in complexity and bounded rationality especially in U-form firms. Increases in workloads and in the complexity of tasks to be carried out limit the rate of expansion which the existing managerial team can undertake. Expansion beyond this limit entails recruitment at all levels including the managerial team itself. But there are limitations to the rate at which the managerial team can expand. Such limitations are known as the 'Penrose effect'. Penrose (1959) believed that firms wishing to grow can always raise the necessary finance and increase their markets but they may face difficulties in expanding the size or the efficiency of the managerial team. For Penrose managerial limitations are the only constraint to growth. This view is not universally accepted since most business observers believe that both demand and financial difficulties may, at times, impede business expansion. However, the managerial constraint is quite often a serious impediment to growth.

Firms can grow, at a certain rate x, even with a constant managerial team for two reasons: first, managerial specialisation and experience mean that some managerial resources are released over time which can be devoted to expansion; second, as each new project becomes established its running becomes routine and less demanding on managerial time. Higher than x rates of growth are not, however, possible without an expansion of the managerial team.

The relationship between the expansion of management and growth can be analysed with the help of Figure 9.5. The *x* axis measures the growth rate and the *y* axis the growth of the managerial team. Point *x* is the rate corresponding to a constant managerial team. Curve A indicates that as the managerial team (*M*) expands growth increases but at a diminishing rate. There are two reasons for this.

The faster the growth rate the more managerial services are required to achieve a certain increase in absolute size

This is based on the assumption that the easiest to incorporate within the firm projects and the most productive ones will be undertaken first. As the rate of growth increases more difficult business opportunities will have to be explored which make excessive demands on managerial services.

The addition to managerial services provided by each new recruit decreases as the rate of recruitment increases

This is because the services which each new member can provide will increase the faster the training received and the quicker his or her overall integration within the managerial team is. The speed of integration of new managers will, therefore, depend on the time that existing managers can devote to the training and assimilation of new recruits. But this declines the faster the existing team attempts to grow.

There is also a negative relationship between the rate of expansion of management and the rate of growth, indicated by curve B. This is because increased demands on managerial time for training and integration of new members mean that less time will be devoted to other managerial duties such as the expansion of the firm. Given that a minimum amount of time has to be devoted to the absorption of each new manager, the faster the growth of management (*M*) the less time will be available for growth (*g*).

The overall effect on growth of an increase in *M* is the sum of two opposite effects. This is indicated in Figure 9.5 by curve C which is the horizontal sum of curves A and B. Curve C shows that a firm's growth rate can increase from *x* to *g** as the rate of managerial recruitment increases to *M**. Any faster expansion of the managerial team will have an overall negative impact on the growth of the firm. Thus, the maximum possible growth rate *g** is uniquely determined by the ease or difficulty with which management can expand itself.

Although the conclusion that growth is uniquely determined by the managerial constraint is debatable, managerial limitations can significantly impede a firm's expansion. When demand can expand by diversification and a reasonably well functioning capital market exists business growth can be slowed down by management limitations. In the 1960s, for example, when market conditions were buoyant in the UK and credit not very

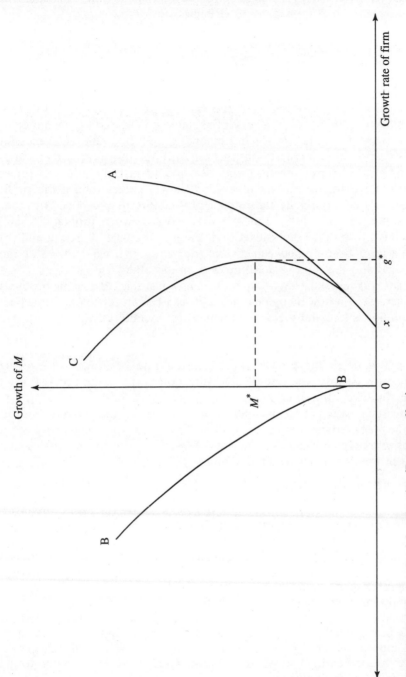

Growth of M

Growth rate of firm

C

A

B

M^*

B

0

x

g^*

Figure 9.5 The managerial constraint (Penrose effect)

difficult to obtain, many businessmen reported that 'suitable' management was the main check on expansion (Richardson 1964).

The demand constraint

Sustained growth requires a sustained expansion in the firm's markets. But competitive reactions and demand saturation may imply that this is not possible without an extension of the existing product range. Growth by diversification, therefore, is an essential element in Marris's growth model. To increase the rate at which demand grows the rate of successful diversification must increase. But this requires not only increased expenditure on product development, promotion and advertising but lower prices as well. Both increased expenditure and lower prices reduce the profit margin so that eventually the rate of profitability may decline. In other words, the reason why a trade-off may exist between profitability and growth is twofold: (a) diversification is the main vehicle of growth and (b) there is a relationship between current price and other expenditure on the one hand and the future rate of growth on the other.

In general demand growth depends on how fast sales of existing products can increase, on how many new products can be introduced per unit time and on how successful the new launches are. Symbolically,

$$g = x + kd \tag{9.1}$$

where g denotes the growth rate, x is the rate of growth of existing products, d denotes the rate of diversification and k is the proportion of successful diversification.

How successful a firm's diversification policy is depends on how innovative the management team is and on how fast it attempts to diversify, what prices it charges for each product and how successful its advertising and other promotional activities are. That is,

$$k = f(P, A, \text{R\&D}, W, d) \tag{9.2}$$

Now the relationship between k and d is a negative one, since the faster the firm attempts to diversify (the higher the d) the more likely it is that problems of bounded rationality will arise implying that products may not be researched very thoroughly so that the proportion of failures increases (k declines as d increases). In addition, equation (9.2) implies that a relationship exists between k and the profit margin m. On a *ceteris paribus* assumption, the proportion of successful diversification should increase as the product price P falls, advertising A and expenditure in R&D increase or the intrinsic value of new products (W) improves. But both a reduction in P and an increase in A, R&D or W imply a lower profit margin m. Therefore, the ratio of successful diversification is inversely related to the profit margin. Symbolically

$$k = f(m, d) \tag{9.3}$$

where $\partial k/\partial m < 0$ and $\partial k/\partial d < 0$. It follows from equations (9.1) and (9.3) that there is an inverse relationship between the growth of demand g and the profit margin m. This is because a higher profit margin reduces the chances of diversification success which in turn slows down the rate at which demand can expand. This trade-off between profitability and growth is indicated in Figure 9.6(a) by curve g_d, where

$$g_d = f_1(d, m).$$

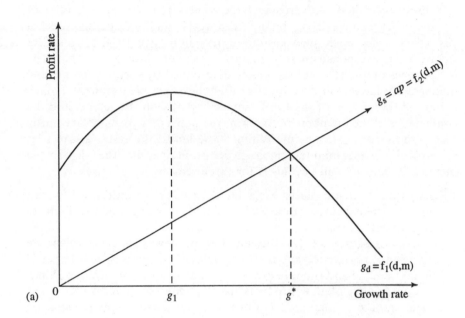

(a)

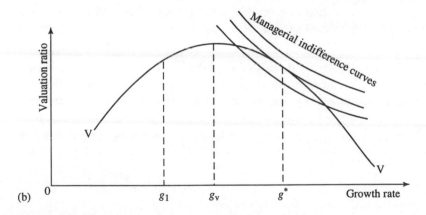

(b)

Figure 9.6 Marris's growth model: (a) the demand and finance constraints; (b) growth maximisation subject to a valuation constraint

The growth of demand (g_d) shows initially a positive relationship between profitability and growth. That is at low growth rates there may be (a) unused resources within the firm and (b) unexplored profitable market opportunities which means that a higher growth rate can increase profits. Beyond a certain point (g_1), however, growth requires intensified diversification which may only be possible at a declining rate of profit.

As already noted increased diversification increases the proportion of failures among new products unless they are well researched and effectively promoted. Advertising effectiveness refers to the number of customers each advertising budget can reach and on the number of customers which each new customer may introduce to the firm. But since customer responsiveness to advertising and emulation of the purchasing patterns of others is at least partly determined by socio-economic and demographic factors, or what Marris called the 'super environment' (which is beyond the control of the firm), and only partly on the talents and the competence of the members of the firm, the limits on expansion are partly due to the super environment. Within these limits, the faster a firm tries to diversify, while maintaining a given profit margin, the slower the increase in demand will be, this is for three reasons.

1 Faster diversification places excessive demands both on the R&D staff and on top management. Bounded rationality increases and the 'Penrose effect' manifests itself.
2 As a consequence of (1) the number of new products which are insufficiently researched and poorly promoted increases. The number of failures increase and the rate of successful diversification declines. Since the introduction of new products usually requires at least some new capital resources, increased failures imply increased unused capacity. The capital to output ratio increases and profitability declines.
3 In oligopolistic markets, the faster a firm diversifies the more likely it is to generate competitive reactions. To overcome these difficulties so as to increase the rate of growth of demand the firm will have to adopt a lower profit margin and eventually a lower rate of return on capital.

In brief, the position and the shape of the curve $g_d = f_1(d, m)$ depends on (a) the rate of diversification undertaken, (b) the Penrose effect, (c) the super environment, i.e. customer attachment to products resistance to advertising and informational circumstances, (d) barriers to diversification which can both afford protection to a firm's markets and make entry into new markets more difficult and (e) the extent of oligopolistic interdependence a firm faces.

The supply constraint

While increased growth of demand implies eventually lower profitability, the expansion of capacity (physical assets, financial assets, goodwill, know-how, etc.) requires increased profitability. The relationship between profitability and the growth of productive capacity is referred to as the growth of supply, or the 'financial security constraint'. This is denoted as g_s, in Figure 9.6(a), and is a straight line positively sloped reflecting the fact that higher profitability makes it possible to adopt a higher rate of capacity expansion. Thus, $g_s = ap$ where p is the rate of return on capital.

The slope of g_s (denoted as a) determines the maximum rate of growth that management could undertake at a given rate of profitability. A higher a indicates that more finance is raised and higher growth becomes possible. The curve $g_s = ap$ becomes flatter. The size of a is determined by managers and depends on three financial ratios:

$$\text{retention ratio} = \frac{\text{retained profits}}{\text{total profit}} < 1$$

$$\text{debt ratio} = \frac{\text{value of debt}}{\text{total assets}}$$

$$\text{liquidity ratio} = \frac{\text{liquid assets}}{\text{total assets.}}$$

Given the rate of profitability, to finance extra growth management can increase retentions and debt or reduce liquidity. There is, however, an upper limit to the total amount of finance that can be raised. A retention ratio approaching unity implies a very small or no dividend distribution. Shareholders may object to such a policy and may attempt to replace the incumbent management or, more likely, they may transfer their capital to other firms. The concomitant share sales will reduce the value of the shares and may encourage a hostile takeover bid which threatens managerial jobs. Similarly a high debt ratio or a low liquidity increase the possibility of bankruptcy and threaten job security. In brief, given the rate of profitability, the financial market (or considerations of job security) restricts managerial ability to raise finance.

The growth of supply is directly related to the rate of profit $p = \Pi/K$ where Π denotes total profit and K is the capital stock of the firm. We can, therefore, write $(\Pi/K)\ Q/Q = (\Pi/Q)x\ Q/K$. That is, p depends on Π/Q (the profit margin) and on Q/K (the inverse of the capital to output ratio v). Therefore, $p = m(1/v)$ where $v = Q/K$.

The capital to output ratio depends, in turn, on the rate of diversification, d. A small d may improve v but increased failures, associated with increasing d, imply that the growth of supply will eventually be negatively related to v. The growth of supply can therefore be written as

$$g_s = f_2(d, m).$$

The optimal growth rate, i.e. the maximum possible under the postulated constraints, is determined by the intersection of g_d and g_s. This is denoted as g^* on Figure 9.6(a). Note that a lower growth rate g_1 maximises profitability and potentially current dividends. However, we cannot presume that g_1 will be the rate preferred by shareholders who are more likely to opt for the growth rate that maximises their wealth.

Marris' 'balanced growth rate' can be summarized as follows:

1 $g_d = f_1(d, m)$ g_d increases as d increases but at a diminishing rate. g_d, beyond a certain point, is inversely related to m.

2 $g_s = f_2(d, m)$ g_s increases as profitability increases but, after a point, it declines as the rate of diversification expands.

The optimum growth rate (g^*) is determined by

3 $g_d = g_s$.

Growth maximisation subject to a valuation constraint

The growth rate, preferred by shareholders, depends on their objective which in a growth context is assumed to be the maximisation of their wealth. Shareholders' wealth depends not only on current dividends but on capital appreciation as well. The latter is the difference between the current value of the shares of a firm and their value at the time of sale. But since the price of a share at the time of sale depends on expected future returns, wealth maximisation means maximisation of the net present value of a stream of expected profits which accrue to shareholders as dividends. Ignoring tax complications and problems of defining an appropriate discounting rate, we can show (see Appendix 9.3) that the net present value V of a stream of dividends D which grows at the constant rate g is given by

$$V = \frac{D}{e - g}$$

where e is the discounting rate. A related ratio often used is the valuation ratio. This is defined as the value V of the firm divided by the book value of the firm's assets. The relationship between V (or the valuation ratio) and the growth of the firm known as the valuation curve is depicted in Figure 9.6(b). It shows that V is maximised when growth is g_v.

It is clear from the above formula that V increases as either D or g or both increase. However, D and g are inter-related. A low growth rate may be the result of under-utilisation of capacity and human talents so that as growth increases profitability may also increase, in which case the valuation ratio also increases. This occurs up to point g_1 in Figure 9.6(b). Beyond this point, however, higher growth is achieved at the cost of profitability. There is both a positive influence on the valuation ratio and a negative one. Which one will predominate? When the profit rate deviates only slightly from its maximum point it is reasonable to suppose that dividends may be maintained or that any necessary reduction will be small enough to be compensated for by the improved growth prospects, so that valuation may continue to increase. However, as the firm seeks to adopt ever higher growth rates at the cost of profitability, sooner or later its market valuation will start to fall. This is because declining profitability will necessitate higher retentions (and other forms of finance) and dividends may be reduced to an extent that cannot be compensated for by the prospect of higher growth. Dissatisfied shareholders may sell their shares bringing about a reduction in share prices. The valuation ratio declines (see Appendix 9.3). Shareholders wishing to maximise their wealth would wish the firm to grow at g_v per cent per time period while growth maximising managers will adopt the higher rate g^*.

It should be clear that the restrictions imposed on managers by the capital market can be expressed in two alternative but equivalent ways; either as a maximum amount of finance available (g_s on Figure 9.6(a)) or as a valuation constraint (valuation ratio, Figure 9.6(b)). When the emphasis is on the valuation ratio, the trade-off between growth and valuation which management have to face as they decide on their growth policies can be illustrated by a set of indifference curves. The optimum growth rate is then determined by the tangency of the valuation curve to the highest indifference curve. The optimum growth rate thus determined, g^*, is clearly the same as that determined by the intersection of the growth of demand and the growth of supply curves on Figure 9.6(a). In fact Figures 9.6(a) and 9.6(b) illustrate two alternative methods of determining g^*.

The shape of the indifference curves indicates the extent to which managers will be prepared to trade off increased growth for job security. That is, it reflects the risk taking attitudes of management. But the risks that management is actually undertaking by deviating from the growth rate that maximises the value of the firm depend on the efficiency of the capital market. The extent to which lack of information or the existence of informational and other enforcement costs impede the efficiency of the capital market is indicated by the shape of curve V. The more prepared management is to undertake risks and the less efficient the capital market control of management, the bigger the distance $g^* - g_1$ on Figure 9.6(b) will be and the more significant the extent of managerial discretion.

Evaluation and empirical evidence

Marris's growth model makes an important contribution to our understanding of business growth policies. The firm in his growth model is no longer assumed to passively respond to its environment. It is rather perceived as a dynamic unit which actively attempts to manipulate the environment in pursuit of its own objectives. The demand–growth relationship is also derived from a dynamic analysis of consumer behaviour. Moreover, the success of diversification and future growth are seen to depend on current marketing and other promotional expenditures which should therefore be treated as investment. Decision variables neglected or ignored by traditional theory are explicitly considered. Thus, profit as well as diversification and growth rates are decisions taken by the management. Problems of bounded rationality and financial considerations are introduced. Above all the emphasis is on the firm rather than on the industry.

There are, however, some weaknesses. The steady state growth assumption is effectively a *ceteris paribus* assumption. It means that particular values of decision variables today (such as R&D, advertising, profit margins, etc.) will be associated with a particular average growth rate in the future. That is, the possibility that external disturbances may mean that a given decision taken at one time period may bring about different growth rates in the future has been ignored. This weakness derives from the assumption that a part of the external environment is constant. The external environment consists of an 'immediate' environment and a 'super' environment. The immediate environment includes cost and demand curves, the extent of competition, barriers to entry, etc. The super environment consists of consumer attachment to a particular product, consumer resistance to advertising, the lack of information, human fallibility and institutional arrangements. While the firm tries to actively manipulate its immediate environment, the super environment is assumed constant.

Although it is reasonable to assume that the super environment cannot change by the actions of one firm it is not necessarily true that it will not be affected by the concerted efforts of a number of firms. Suppose, for example, that a given level of advertising undertaken by a firm leads to a given level of growth. If many firms decided to adopt this level of advertising the resulting increase in aggregate advertising may induce consumers to become either more susceptible to advertising or more resistant to advertising. Consequently, a given level of current advertising results in a different level of future growth. That is, the super environment has changed. Similarly, collective actions of firms can result in depletion of natural resources or destruction of the physical environment with consequent increases in costs and productivity. The super environment has once more been altered.

The absence of an analysis of collective actions has meant that the treatment of oligopolistic interactions between firms has been neglected. Competitive reactions to a firm's actions may influence profit margins and shift the growth of demand curve.

Despite its shortcomings the model is a valuable addition to the theory of the firm and its rich predictions have stimulated a considerable amount of empirical work. For example, the prediction that higher growth rates will lead to a lower valuation and an increased probability that a firm may be taken over was investigated by Singh (1971, 1975) and Kuehn (1975). Firms belonging to five UK industrial sectors (food, drink, electrical engineering, clothing and footwear) were studied by Singh with a view to finding out whether firms operating with managerial slack (Williamson's model) or those pursuing growth policies to the detriment of profit (Marris model) had a higher probability of being taken over. Singh examined four different indicators of profitability as well as the growth of assets and the valuation ratios and found, as expected, that on all these measures firms which had been taken over (victim firms) had performed on average worse than the rest of the industry. This difference in performance was not, however, statistically significant. The most important determinant of takeovers was size, with small and medium-sized firms having a much higher probability of being taken over than large firms. Low profitability was a significant contributing factor but only within the same size class. (Firms with low average profitability were twice more likely to be taken over.) This evidence suggests that the discipline imposed by the stock market is rather weak. Management of large firms seem to enjoy a large amount of managerial discretion so that large firms are quite likely to survive even if managed somewhat incompetently.

The prediction that managerially run firms will tend to adopt higher growth rates and lower profit rates was also tested by Radice (1971) with evidence from eighty-six UK firms. His research failed to confirm the theoretical prediction but he attributed the failure to econometric problems rather than to weaknesses of the theory tested. On the other hand, Holl (1975), who examined 183 UK firms, found that managerially run firms had, as expected, higher growth rates and lower profit rates although most of the difference tended to disappear when differences in market structure were taken into account. The evidence from the USA is also varied. For example, Monsen, *et al.* (1968) provide evidence of higher profit rates among owner-run firms (12.8 per cent compared with 7.3 per cent for managerial firms), while Larner (1970) and Kamerschen (1968) found no difference between the two types of firms.

Evidence has not resolved the controversy partly because of the statistical problems researchers are faced with and partly because managerial discretion is the result of an agency problem the nature of which and hence its solution varies from firm to firm, as the following section indicates.

THE AGENCY THEORY OF THE FIRM

The term managerial discretion is sometimes used to describe the behaviour of managers who enjoy excessive 'on-the-job consumption', such as expenditure on creating a pleasant environment, a good public image, avoiding very stressful tasks and opting for a quiet life or becoming powerful and influential. While owner–managers may take some of their profits in the form of on-the-job consumption, non-owners may be inclined to take more such consumption since they do not bear its full cost. Managerial discretion arises whenever non-owner managers behave differently than shareholders would wish them to behave. The difference is due to two reasons: (a) divergence of interests, the interests of managers do not necessarily coincide with those of the shareholders on whose behalf they run the business; and (b) monitoring or any other mechanisms designed to re-align the divergent interests is less than perfectly effective. A divergence of interests may exist quite independently of share ownership dispersion although monitoring difficulties may increase with ownership dispersion. Problems created by such divergences of interest and the related inducements and control mechanisms are addressed by agency theory.

The principal–agent relationship

An agency relationship exists when one individual (the agent) acts on behalf of another individual (the principal). Thus, a doctor is the patient's agent, a business consultant is the clients's agent and an executive manager is a shareholder's agent. Commonly, the principal compensates the agent and is entitled to the outcome of the agent's action. Therefore, the lower the agent compensation, given a particular outcome, or the higher the outcome for a given agent reward, the higher the residual claim of the principal is. Now if we assume that the outcome depends on the agent's work effort and that the agent enjoys higher compensations but dislikes extra work effort, it follows that when the outcome depends on the action (effort) of the agent a divergence of interests may arise. The principal's interest is better served by more effort but the agent's interest is not. If, additionally, information relating to agent action is not readily available to the principal, this divergence of interests may lead a self-interest seeking agent to act opportunistically. For example, managers on fixed annual pay may decide to take on-the-job consumption, which reduces profitability, in the knowledge that their behaviour cannot be detected by shareholders. In short, given information asymmetries we cannot expect agency relationships to function as well as they would when information is costlessly shared or when the interests of principals and agents coincide. Deviations from the ideal situation in which either interests coincide or there is perfect knowledge are referred to as *agency problems* or *agency costs*. To resolve the agency problem or minimise the relevant costs, agency contracts should be designed in a way that mitigates opportunistic behaviour and motivates agents to behave in accordance with a principal's interests. In particular, the remuneration of the agent might be specified in such a way as to achieve the required agent motivation. A contract which achieves this aim is called *optimal*. Its structure depends on the available information and its distribution between the two parties and on the risk attitudes of both agent and principal. To illustrate how risk attitudes and informational asymmetries determine the nature of the agency problem and the structure of optimal contracts (solutions), we examine three situations involving different informational assumptions.

Perfect knowledge

If perfect knowledge is assumed, so that both the behaviour (effort etc.) of the agent and any other factors influencing the outcome can be observed and measured without substantial costs, then all the details of the relationship can easily be specified in the contract and the agency problem does not arise.

Suppose, for example, that the outcome Q depends only on work effort E as follows:

$$Q = f(E). \tag{9.4}$$

For example, Q may be the number of boxes to be shifted manually. Since Q can be observed by both parties and it is known that it depends only on effort E, a contract can be designed specifying the required number of boxes to be shifted and the payment to be made to the agent when this is achieved. This is a paid worker contract. There is no need for the principal to monitor work effort.

Risk sharing under symmetric information

Consider, however, the possibility that Q depends on effort as well as on other factors whose influence may not be easily quantifiable. The relationship in (9.4) becomes

$$Q = f(E,S). \tag{9.5}$$

Q may in this case stand for agricultural output measured in bushels. E denotes the intensity of work effort (by a farmer or labourer) and S indicates the 'state of the world'. That is, S could refer to weather conditions such as degrees of temperature, inches of rainfall or hours of sunshine on particular days. Equation (9.5) can take different forms, depending on the particular way in which E and S influence Q. To simplify the problem suppose that the farmer's work effort can be either very intense (E_1) or less intense (E_2) and that the chances are equal that weather conditions will be very bad (S_a), very good (S_b), or average (S_c). Table 9.4 shows the level of production under these fictitious work and weather conditions.

An element of uncertainty is implied by Table 9.4. If weather conditions are very bad (S_a prevails) the harvest will be poor whatever the level of effort exerted by the agent (labourer). The opposite is true when S_b is the state of the world. In this case a good crop (3,000 bushels) will be achieved

Table 9.4 Output in different weather conditions and effort levels

Effort	State of the world		
	S_a	S_b	S_c
Very intense (E_1)	1,000	3,000	3,000
Less intense (E_2)	1,000	3,000	1,000

even if effort is not very intense. Work effort plays a crucial role when weather conditions are S_c in which case with intense effort the vagaries of the weather can be overcome and a good harvest can be secured.

In these circumstances, if S can be observed by both parties so that it is known which state of the world prevailed there is no need to observe effort and no incentives problem arises. A contract can specify work effort E_1 if S_c prevails and E_2 otherwise. But what compensation would induce such an agreement? The level of agent remuneration is difficult to determine because of the uncertainty regarding the level of outcome (risk is involved). A fixed agent remuneration would imply that the principal bears all the risks since his or her share will vary as the outcome varies. On the other hand an agreement to share the outcome, in some proportions, would imply sharing the risk of a poor outcome.

The question then arises as to whether risks should be shared between the two parties or whether they should be borne entirely by either party. The answer will depend on the risk attitudes of the two parties. For example, if the labourer (A) is a risk averse person while the landlord (P) is a risk neutral[11] person then it will be mutually beneficial if the landlord undertakes all the risks and offers insurance to the risk averse labourer. Figure 9.7 can help explain why such an agreement can be achieved, on the assumption that the principal is risk neutral and the agent is risk averse. This assumption would seem justified in the case of a landlord who owns several plots of land and can therefore diversify while the farmer on one plot may not be able to diversify. Similarly shareholders can diversify their portfolio of shares while managers (agents) may not be able to diversify to the same extent.

To facilitate the analysis, the example of Table 9.4 will be analysed in two stages. To begin with we assume that the probability of weather conditions being S_c is zero. It follows that whether work effort is E_1 or E_2 is immaterial. Output depends only on the 'state of the world'. If the weather is good output will be 3,000 bushels and if the weather is bad it will be 1,000 bushels whatever the efforts of the farmer. If it is known that the probability of S_b is P and that of S_a is $1-P$ then the probability of a good crop (X) will be P and that of a poor crop (Y) will be $1-P$.

Figure 9.7(a) shows the preference map of a risk averse labourer (A). The x axis measures A's share of the crop (X_A) when the harvest is good (X) and the y axis measures A's share of the crop (Y_A) when the harvest is poor (Y). Since both X and Y are uncertain events the indifference curves

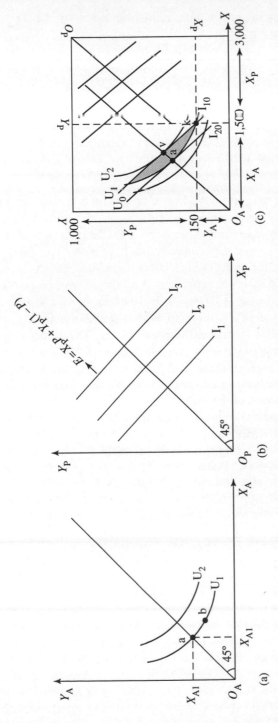

Figure 9.7 (a) The preference map of a risk averse agent (the slope of U at points on the 45° line is $-P_1/(1 - P_1)$, equal to the slope of the constant expected outcome line); (b) the preference map of a risk neutral principal; (c) optimal agent contracts: the case of a risk neutral principal undertaking all the risks. Note that, $X = X_A + X_P$ and $Y = Y_A + Y_P$

of A (a risk adverse person) will be convex to the origin (see Chapter 7). Points along the 45° line, such as a, indicate a certain reward (no risk portfolio) since A's share is the same whatever the harvest. The 45° line, therefore, is A's certainty line. It should be recalled (see pages 196–200) that

1 the slope of the indifference curves at points on the certainty line is equal to the negative ratio of the probabilities with which X and Y may occur, and
2 indifference curves further away from the origin indicate preferred positions.

Any point on the diagram indicates A's payment according to a different contract. Compare, for example, points b and a. Point a indicates an agreement with a fixed reward while b indicates that A's payment is higher when the harvest is good and lower when it is poor. The fact that both points lie on the same indifference curve indicates that A is indifferent between the reward schemes represented by these two points. Therefore, A would be willing to move from a to b. In other words, A is prepared to accept an increase in X_A combined with a reduction in Y_A, at a rate indicated by the slope of the indifference curve. The rate of increase of X_A required to compensate for a given reduction in Y_A (i.e. the curvature of U) varies from individual to individual reflecting the strength of risk aversion. This rate plays an important role in the selection of an optimal contract (as it will be seen below).

Figure 9.7(b) shows the indifference map of a risk neutral person. X_P measured along the x axis shows P's share of the harvest when the harvest is good. Y_P measured along the y axis refers to P's share of the harvest when the harvest is poor. P (the farmer) is assumed to be a risk neutral person. It should be recalled (from Chapter 7) that a risk neutral person maximises expected utility. Therefore, the indifference curves of a risk neutral person are the same as the lines of constant expected utility E. Since $E = X_P P + Y_P(1-P)$, P's indifference curves are straight lines with a slope equal to $-P/(1-P)$. Therefore, the rate at which P is prepared to trade off Y_P for X_P is equal to the ratio of the probabilities of good and bad weather occurring.

To find out what contractual agreements might be consistent with the preferences of both principal and agent and are therefore likely to be pursued, Figure 9.7(c) combines the information provided in Figures 9.7(a) and 9.7(b). To construct it, Figure 9.7(b) has been translated and then rotated by 180° so that a box is formed the north-east corner of which corresponds to the origin of Figure 9.7(b). The dimensions of the box are equal to the size of the two possible harvest levels, X and Y. The horizontal dimension (X) is 3,000 bushels of crop, in our example, and the vertical (Y) is 1,000 bushels, where

$$X = X_A + X_P$$
$$Y = Y_A + Y_P.$$

It follows that each point within the box indicates the distribution of a given outcome between the two parties. Each point, therefore, can be thought of as a specific contract. For example, point k corresponds to a contract specifying that if the harvest is good (3,000 bushels) it will be shared equally. When the harvest is only 1,000 bushels A receives 150 bushels and P receives the remaining 850 bushels.

Does point k represent an optimal contract? That is, does it indicate the best agreement that these two individuals can achieve? The answer is no. Inspection of Figure 9.7(c) can help explain why. At point k individual A is on indifference curve U_1 and individual P is on indifference curve I_{10}. A different distribution of the crop, e.g. one which gives A a higher share of a poor crop in exchange for a smaller share of a good crop, could move A to point a on the certainty line. A remains indifferent by this change while P benefits (moves to a higher indifference curve I_{20}). Similarly, another distribution corresponding to a move from point k to point v will benefit A (since A moves to a higher indifference curve U_2) without disadvantaging P. A move to any point along the certainty line between points a and v can benefit both parties. (Points along the line segment av are referred to as Pareto optimal.) Both parties, therefore, have an incentive to move to some point on A's certainty line. For any point within the shaded area there is a point between a and v which will be preferred by both parties. In fact for every point which is not on A's certainty line a point on this line can be found which will be preferred by both parties. It follows that the optimal contract will be on A's certainty line. That is, in these circumstances, A should be offered a certain reward whatever the harvest level. Moreover, inspection of Figure 9.7(c) shows that this reward will be located along line segment av. The exact point to be selected, i.e. the optimum contract, will depend on A's risk aversion which determines the curvature of U, on the probabilities of favourable and unfavourable 'states of the world' which determine the slope of I and possibly on the bargaining skills of the individuals concerned.

It can be concluded that when 'the state of the world' is observable by all, the effort incentives problem can be overcome. That is, given symmetrical information a Pareto optimal contract can be designed with the risk neutral principal undertaking the risk of a fluctuating outcome and offering the risk averse agent a certain reward (a wage contract). The converse is also true. That is, a risk neutral agent would offer a fixed amount of the outcome (rent) to a risk averse principal and keep the residual outcome. (Readers should be able to re-interpret Figure 9.7(c) to verify this well-known 'sharecropping' result.)

Effort incentives under asymmetric information

The analysis becomes somewhat more complicated when the outcome (the harvest in our example) depends on both effort and 'the state of the world' in a way that makes it difficult to observe the impact of each. Suppose that, in the example of Table 9.4, weather conditions are unknown when the action is performed but both parties agree that it is equally likely that any of the states (S_a, S_b, or S_c) may prevail. As mentioned earlier, it is to the principal's interest that effort should be E_1 (very intense) if the weather happens to be S_c and E_2 otherwise, so that the probability of a good harvest (3,000 bushels) is maximised (66.67 per cent in this case). If, however, effort, although known to the agent, cannot be observed or measured by the principal then remuneration according to effort E_1 or E_2 may not bring about the required result. Assuming that the agent prefers a higher to a lower monetary reward and less intense to more intense work effort,[12] a simple contract specifying work effort E_1 if S_c occurs and E_2 otherwise (or a contract offering a fixed reward independent of effort) cannot be optimal since it fails to discourage opportunistic behaviour. Since the agent's self-interest indicates that effort should always be E_2 if remuneration is fixed, E_2 will be chosen. Moreover, even if the contract specifies that E_1 should be the effort when the weather is S_c, it is possible that an agent may choose effort E_2 and make misrepresentations to the effect that despite effort E_1 a poor harvest resulted due to weather conditions S_a. It should be emphasised that opportunistic behaviour is possible because weather conditions are not clearly observable and the principal cannot observe the agent's work effort. That is, both risk and information asymmetry exist.

The question then arises as to whether the principal can design a contract incorporating sufficient incentives to induce A to select work effort E_1. Payment according to outcome may be considered so that the agent's remuneration will be higher when output is 3,000 bushels than when it is 1,000 bushels. However, such a scheme implies risks. The agent's reward will depend not only on effort but on chance factors as well. That is, despite hard work, the outcome (harvest) may be poor and A's income small. Would A be prepared to accept such a risk? It can be shown that even a risk averse agent may be induced to undertake risks by a compensation package which includes a sufficiently large share of a good outcome. The size of the required inducement will depend on the strength of A's risk aversion. The willingness or unwillingness of the agent to undertake risks, therefore, will influence the size and structure of the rewards in an optimal contract. Figure 9.8 may help illustrate these points.

An agent's preference for less rather than more effort will be reflected on the preference map. In Figure 9.8 the x axis measures, as before, A's share of a good harvest. But while in Figure 9.7 a good harvest required no extra effort, it now does depend on extra effort, which the agent finds unpleasant. To reflect this a new set of indifference curves, W_1 and W_2, have been drawn. These are steeper than indifference curves U_1 and U_2

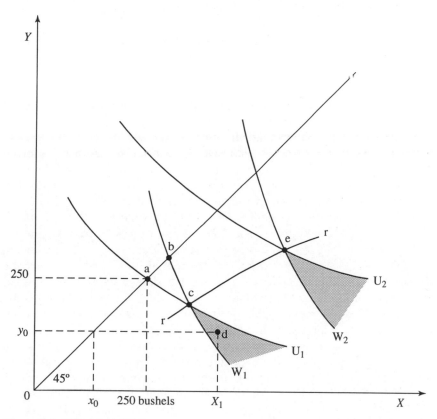

Figure 9.8 Effort incentives

since the latter were drawn on the assumption that no extra effort was
required for a good outcome.

To understand the change in the shape of the indifference curves,
consider A's remuneration and utility index at point a under the two
different assumptions about effort. Point a represents a contract specifying
that A's remuneration is 250 bushels when output is good (3,000 bushels)
whether this outcome requires extra effort or not. But remaining at a when
X requires extra effort means that A is not compensated for the extra work
so that she or he is worse off. Point a, therefore, must lie on a lower
indifference curve when X depends on effort than when it does not. To
remain on the same level of satisfaction A must be compensated for extra
effort. Increased compensation may be represented by a point such as b,
in which case the indifference curve through b corresponds to the same
level of satisfaction as that indicated by indifference curve U_1. The distance
ab represents the cost of extra effort.

Point c, where the two indifference curves cross, represents a remuneration which A finds indifferent to the remunerations implied by points a or b. This means that with a reward such as that indicated by point c, A's share of X_A is sufficiently large for A to overcome his or her aversion to extra effort. A further increase in A's share of a good harvest would ensure that A would prefer a contract implying extra effort. At points to the right of c and within the shaded area, A is better off when outcome depends on effort than when it does not. Point d is such a point. At d, A's share of the good harvest is sufficiently high to induce A to increase effort so as to improve the probability of a good harvest.

Similar reasoning shows that all points in the shaded area to the right of point e indicate contracts which involve extra effort and are preferred by A. Joining up all points located at the intersection of indifference curves, such as c and e, traces out the curve rr. Points to the right of rr correspond to contracts which include a sufficient remuneration, dependent on a good harvest, to induce the required extra effort. Such contracts require A to undertake some risks (they are not on A's certainty line).

Inspection of Figure 9.8 shows that the extent of agent risk and the related compensation depend on (a) A's risk attitudes (which affect the shape of the indifference curve), (b) A's aversion to extra effort and (c) the impact of effort on the probability with which a favourable outcome occurs. An improvement in this probability will also influence the preference map of the principal and the set of optimal contracts.[13] It should also be clear that a risk averse agent can be induced to undertake some risk but this requires a higher expected reward. Thus, the principal has to make a trade-off between offering more effort incentives and paying more to induce the agent to take higher risks. In general though, the solution to the effort incentives problem implies that risk sharing will not be optimal, since a risk averse agent undertakes some risks.

Provided that an optimal contract exists, it will be located to the right of curve rr. This indicates an agent remuneration consisting of a basic pay and some bonus related to the favourable outcome. If, for example, point d was optimal the basic pay would be $y_0 = x_0$ and the bonus $x_1 - x_0$. This bonus (incentive) in reality can take different forms. It could relate to physical or financial (profits) performance or it could take other than monetary forms such as policy commitments, improved promotional prospects, etc.

Further remarks

In the previous sections we assumed that the principal is a risk neutral person and the agent a risk averse person. This assumption can be justified in many business situations as, for example, in situations in which the principal can diversify his or her risk but the agent cannot. A landowner owning several plots of land can diversify more than a farmer and shareholders are more likely than managers or workers to keep a diversified portfolio of shares.

The analysis was carried out on the assumption of one principal and one agent during a single time period. It was shown that given symmetric information risk averse agents should be offered wage contracts (certain rewards) while under information asymmetry regarding work effort they should be offered effort incentives A trade-off between incentives and risk sharing arises in this case.

It is possible to extend the analysis to consider many agents and a multi-period time span. When a principal contracts with several agents comparisons among agents may be included in the contract. If at least one agent is risk neutral and has a rent contract then all the risk averse agents' outcomes can be compared with and expected to be at least as high as this rent. Alternatively if all agents are risk averse the performance of each can be compared with the average performance of all agents, provided that they all operate under the same external environment conditions. In multi-period situations rewards may depend on current and previous time period performance.

Managers as agents

Since a firm can be viewed as a nexus of implicit and explicit contracts between various groups (such as banks and other lenders, suppliers, employees, management and shareholders), managers may be viewed as principals in their relationships to lower level management and other personnel. As principals they need to provide a system of incentives and reward systems in order to cope with the agency problems that arise within the firm. Both the existence of these incentives and their structure and size depend on the risk attitudes of the members of the team that constitute a firm. Since agency problems arise when there is uncertainty and information asymmetry and when individuals act opportunistically, minimising agency costs requires both improvements in the flow of information and mitigation of opportunistic behaviour. These can be achieved, at least partly, by adopting an appropriate internal organisational structure. As Chapters 3 and 4 have shown, divisionalisation and decentralisation, the requirement that divisions remit profits to central office for reallocation on the basis of objective investment criteria and performance-related reward systems, are organisational features which can improve information flow and restrict management subgoal pursuit. Performance-related pay awards are also intended to cope with agency problems. They can be seen as incentives to enhance performance when monitoring work effort is either not practicable or too expensive. For example, the compensation of travelling salesmen is often heavily dependent on sales records. The difficulty of monitoring work effort implies that sales personnel have to tolerate substantial risks. When 'effort' is relatively easy to monitor but personal contribution to output is not measurable, because for example the work involves team effort, the incentive may take the form of promotion through a hierarchical ladder or bonuses related to the joint output of a group of employees or to the overall profitability of the firm. Both are quite common practices among UK firms.[14] In divisionalised firms the chief executive officer (CEO) is the principal in relation to divisional heads (agents) so that a multi-period and multiple agent relationship exists. Effort incentives in this case can be based on three things: (a) current divisional performance (total profit or return on investment), (b) performance in the previous time period(s) and (c) performance in comparison with other divisions (if they all operate in the same external environment, same industry, country, etc.) or with competing firms. An example is the Bacon and Bentham Inc's incentives discussed in the application at the end of Chapter 11.

Top managers, however, play a dual role. While they act as principals in their relationship to lower level management and other personnel they may act as agents in their relationship with shareholders. As Ricketts (1987) put it, 'Accepting . . . that managers are not, legally speaking agents of shareholders, it is still reasonable to argue that the manager does have a contract with the firm, that the provision of this contract and the incentive devices built into it will crucially influence the willingness of people to hold shares in a company' (p. 241). To the extent that there is a divergence of interest between managers and shareholders, and given that shareholders are not so well informed about the affairs of the firm, agency theory suggests that managers can pursue policies which are not necessarily the ones that owner–managers would pursue. Since agency problems may exist even if there is only one principal, the separation of ownership from control even in the absence of ownership dispersion creates agency problems. This means that shareholders need to devise a system of incentives and controls to ensure that managers act in accordance with their interests.

The most common direct incentives are rewards related to the financial performance of the firm such as bonuses linked to profitability or to the value of a firm's shares. For example, the compensation of Ian MacGregor as chairman of The British Steel Corporation was linked to the performance of the company over the contractual period (Ricketts 1987). Sir Ian MacLaurin, the chairman of the TESCO supermarket chain stores, received in 1989 a salary of £390,000 and an incentive payment of £1.09 million.

Incentive rewards can and do take a variety of forms and compensation packages may be complex in order to address various aspects of the constraints that shareholders wish to impose on managers. Thus, Sears, Roebuck and Company, base their bonuses on a combination of return to equity, sales growth, net sales, gross profits and growth in net premiums earned. The exact combination varies among divisions and executive level, and among companies (Lambert and Larcker 1985). Empirical evidence (Raviv 1985) has shown that, in general, managerial compensation depends on straight wages, bonuses, stock options, managerial tenure with the firm and the firm's relative performance compared with other firms in the industry. This is consistent with agency theory. As indicated above, if a substantial part of managerial compensation is related to the financial performance of the firm risk averse managers will be undertaking substantial risks. They may, therefore, avoid investing in risky projects despite expected positive returns to the detriment of shareholder wealth. Straight wages are intended to discourage this. Bonuses and other performance-related rewards are intended to induce managers to identify with shareholder interests so as to reduce managerial discretion.

The effectiveness of performance-related pay requires that it will not only improve when performance improves but that it will actually fall when performance indicators worsen. Thus, when the airline industry suffered massive losses in 1991, British Airways announced that all 50,000 staff will miss on profit-related bonuses and that a cut in performance-related bonuses is likely to apply to all 2,000 top managers. However, during the 1990–1 UK recession a large number of executives awarded themselves large pay increases in the face of worsening corporate performance causing a storm of shareholder protests. An example is the row over huge pay increases for senior management of UK's largest city investor, the Prudential. Its CEO Mick Newmarch was awarded a 43 per cent pay rise two months after the company announced a slump in pre-tax profits of almost 37 per cent and a 60 per cent decline in earnings.[15]

THE CONTROL OF MANAGERIAL DISCRETION

That compensation incentives may bring about improvements in performance is not seriously doubted. Their role, however, may be limited because in practice they may fail to be flexible enough, especially in the downward direction. Moreover, they are unlikely to be of an appropriate size given the difficulties involved in their calculation. Incentives cannot, therefore, be relied upon to totally eliminate managerial discretion. Several other control mechanisms, intended to reinforce them, operate in practice. These are now discussed.

Shareholder control

The right of shareholders to replace managers who are not acting according to shareholder interests is considered to be one of the most common managerial control mechanisms. The threat of replacement can be an important constraint on managerial behaviour whether ownership is concentrated in a few individuals or not, since share ownership dispersal can be overcome by the congealing of power at the annual general meeting

(AGM). Despite the fact that attendance at AGMs is in practice small, voting by proxy makes it possible for a dominant group to emerge. However, there are at least three reasons why this mechanism may fail to produce the required control.

1 Shareholders would wish to replace the existing management only if they believed that by doing so the value of their shares would improve by more than the costs involved in getting relevant information and acting upon it. To become well informed about managerial behaviour, however, may involve substantial costs since the observed performance of a firm may depend to a large extent on factors beyond managerial control. The more costly it is to acquire information and to act upon it, the more likely it will be that shareholders will see no benefit in attempting to replace the incumbent management.
2 Dissatisfied shareholders may find it difficult to acquire sufficient power to pose a credible threat to management when share ownership is dispersed. Voting by proxy, which is supposed to make this possible, may in reality tend to favour the incumbent management. Invitations to the AGM are usually accompanied by management letters giving relevant information and suggesting reasons why proxy votes should be given to the existing Board.
3 Finally, dispersed ownership may induce shareholders to shirk their monitoring responsibilities. Given informational and enforcement costs, an individual shareholder will have an incentive to let others bear the costs of removing the existing management. Since all shareholders have an incentive to free ride, the effectiveness of this control mechanism is compromised.

The market in corporate control

Shareholders dissatisfied with management performance may seek to take their capital to other companies whose management they believe more competent. If share sales occur at a sufficient rate the stock valuation of the firm will decline and the firm may be taken over by outsiders who feel that they can use the available resources more efficiently by replacing the existing management.

This method of managerial control, although potentially more effective than the displacement of management by existing shareholders, may also be hindered by information asymmetry, adverse selection and bounded rationality. In effect, potential acquiring firms may find it difficult to distinguish, without substantial costs, between a firm whose valuation is low because of poor management and a firm whose valuation is low despite a good managerial team. Poor performance in the latter firm may be due to circumstances beyond the control of a good management, but this is not known to outsiders and cannot be ascertained without costs. Asymmetric information may manifest itself in different forms and can cause the acquisitions market to utilise a variety of, possibly unreliable, informational signals. For example, the acceptance of a tender offer may be interpreted (rightly or wrongly) as a signal that the acquiring firm is simply paying too high a price to the acquired firm.

Moreover, the use of informational signals create free riding incentives, for both potential acquiring firms and existing shareholders, which can lead to a suboptimal allocation of resources to information acquisition. This is because firms considering external diversification need information relating to the merits of potential victims and information is not freely available. A potential acquirer can save on information costs by using takeover bids as signals about the existence of good target firms. But since all potential acquirers have a similar motive to reduce search costs by free riding on the search costs of others, the market operates with suboptimal information. Additionally, a takeover bid may, correctly, be interpreted by minority shareholders as a signal for the existence of an inefficient managerial team. They may refuse, therefore, the bid in the belief that after the firm has been taken over and the inefficient management replaced, returns on shares will improve substantially. Since this argument applies to all shareholders, no bid can succeed. This is a serious problem and attempts to overcome it have led to the adoption of several devices in practice. Two such devices are the oppression of minority interests and the compulsory acquisition of shares. In the UK, the takeover code attempts to limit the ability of management to act opportunistically in contesting or pre-empting bids which might be beneficial to shareholders. Management cannot attempt to stop a bid until an offer is imminent or has been made.

Finally an important weakness of this control mechanism may be related to the inability of potential acquiring firms to cope with the expansion associated with a successful takeover bid. A takeover implies that the resources directed and managed by the acquiring firm will expand so that top management may be faced with bounded rationality problems (i.e. difficulties arising from increased complexity, lack of expertise or sheer volume of work). Potential bidders, therefore, will be unwilling to expand unless they feel confident that they can themselves manage the acquired firm better than the existing management.

In this respect the diffusion of the M-form organisational structure can be seen as an institutional arrangement that facilitates the takeover mechanism, thus contributing to the control of managerial discretion. As Chapter 4 explained, this is due to the following: (a) the ability of M-form internal organisational structure to better control informational and bounded rationality problems; an acquired firm can be more easily appended and more effectively run as an autonomous division in an M-form firm than would be possible in a U-form firm; (b) the separation of strategic from operational decision making, in the M-form, implies that top management has more time and psychological commitment to long-term strategic decisions such as growth by acquisition; and (c) the M-form general office has monitoring advantages over the capital market both in access to information and in auditing and allocating resources. Williamson (1983b) goes as far as to claim that internal organisation has relieved shareholder versus management tensions and that 'the corporate control dilemma posed by Berle and Means has since been alleviated more by internal than by external (regulatory) organisational reforms' (p. 364).

Empirical evidence is not always consistent with the hypothesis that the takeover mechanism fully disciplines managers. Mueller, for example, claims that there is evidence from seven countries (Belgium, Germany, France, The Netherlands, Sweden, the UK, and the USA) which rejects the conclusion that mergers improve economic efficiency (as evidenced by profit and growth increases following a merger). The hypothesis that below average performing firms are acquired by firms performing better than themselves is supported by evidence from only two (Germany and the UK) of the seven countries studied. After reviewing this evidence and that of other studies Mueller concludes on the very sceptical note that to the extent that the market in corporate control works at all it 'does so with considerable slippage and uncertainty' (Mueller 1980: 312).

In brief, the takeover mechanism is fraught with informational complexities and bounded rationality problems which must be institutionally overcome if it is to operate as an effective control mechanism. Both external (regulatory) and internal (organisational) reforms have helped to mitigate managerial discretion. But mitigation is not the same as elimination.

The market for managers

The managerial labour market can play an important role in disciplining managers through the establishment or destruction of 'reputations'. Indeed some writers (Fama 1980) consider the managerial labour market as the prime mechanism of managerial control. They argue that firms compete for managerial services and in order to attract the best new managers and to keep the best of the existing ones they offer performance-related rewards. But a manager's performance and reputation is judged by the performance of the firm. A manager's association with failure or bankruptcy may be interpreted as managerial incompetence which will affect adversely future employment and earnings prospects. Since 'reputations' affect the valuation that firms place on managers, and hence a manager's earning potential, a desire to build and to maintain a good reputation may induce managers to behave according to shareholder interests. Managers may restrain from exercising managerial discretion or shirking their managerial responsibilities for fear that the disclosure of such behaviour will have detrimental effects on reputation.

Additionally, within a firm managers (even top managers) are disciplined by other managers. There is no doubt that senior managers monitor the behaviour of junior managers. What is claimed though is that managers at lower hierarchical levels can gain by stepping over shirking or incompetent managers. The motivation to do so is partly due to the knowledge that their marginal product and rewards depend on the marginal product of their superiors. Junior managers aspiring to climb up the hierarchical ladder will wish to see top management send the correct signals to the managerial labour market by not exercising managerial discretion. The mechanism through which they exercise their influence is the competition that exists among top managers for positions in the Board of Directors.

We cannot, however, assume that the managerial labour market is perfectly efficient. Even if it is accepted that the participants in the managerial market are experts who have the ability to receive and interpret signals better than other individuals, market efficiency will suffer (a) when information on managerial competence is incomplete and (b) if managers do not change jobs often. If managers move often it becomes harder to detect their efficiency since performance in the short run depends on decisions taken by their predecessors while the results of their own strategic decisions will be inherited by others. The idea that managers move often would also contradict the existence of internal labour markets which reward seniority and encourage long-term commitments (see Chapter 14). Besides, there is evidence that the Board of Directors is dominated by executives who have spent the bulk (over two-thirds in the UK) of their careers in the company they now direct (Cosh and Hughes 1987).

Finally, it has been suggested that the selection and appointment of (even the most senior) managers is undertaken by other managers, especially when ownership is dispersed, whose motives cannot always be trusted (because of opportunism) to select the best managers and to penalise the inefficient ones. The argument in this respect is that the appointment of a very competent manager may expose the weaknesses of the existing team. Alternatively, by appointing a less competent manager departmental managers may hope to show the superiority of the previous regime.

To conclude, both internal and external managerial markets can exert an influence on managerial discretion, but opinion is divided as to the significance of each kind of influence. Some writers (Alchian and Demsetz 1972; Ricketts 1987) believe that takeovers are the most important control of managerial discretion, although they acknowledge an influence by the market for managerial services, while others argue that the primary discipline of managers is exerted by the managerial labour markets (Fama 1980).

The product market

Competition in the product market may also act as a restraint on managerial discretion. Elementary economic theory suggests that under

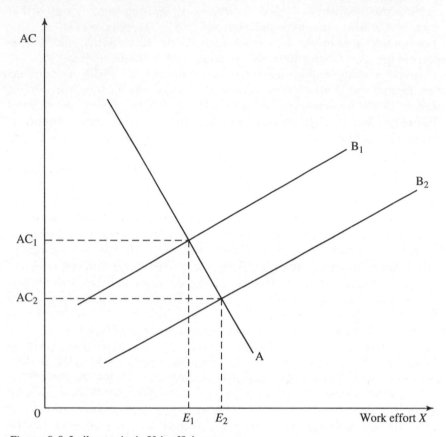

Figure 9.9 Leibensteins's X-inefficiency

conditions of perfect competition managers have no choice but to profit maximise since failure to do so forces a firm to exit the market. Managerial slack, therefore, can only exist in monopolistic situations. This conclusion, however, is derived from an analysis which ignores or assumes away the existence of informational and control problems.

By introducing monitoring costs into the analysis Leibenstein (1966) argued that managerial slack, in the form of production costs which are not minimised, may exist even in competitive markets. He called this form of slack *X*-inefficiency. Leibenstein recognised that employment contracts are incomplete and that monitoring work effort is expensive. He assumed that production can increase with work effort which in turn can increase with proper monitoring. But management may slack as monitors so that the output derived from given inputs may not be the maximum possible. Therefore, costs per unit of production may not be minimised even in competitive markets. Figure 9.9 illustrates this argument. The *x* axis refers to work effort per period of time while the y axis measures the average cost of production AC. Curve A shows that the average cost declines as effort increases. This is because as the effort of workers increases more is produced per worker so that the monetary cost per unit of output produced declines. Curve B illustrates another relationship that exists between effort and costs. The higher the per unit of production cost, the lower the profit for a given price. As costs increase and profitability is threatened the pressures on individuals to perform better increase. More effort is therefore forthcoming. The intersection of curves A and B_1 determines the equilibrium level of effort (E_1) and average cost (AC_1). Clearly this equilibrium will change if the position of either curve A or B_1 changes. The position of curve B_1 depends on market competition. The more competitive the market is or, as Leibenstein put it, the more 'environmental tightness' exists the more 'pressure' will be exerted by managers and supervisors and the more effort will be forthcoming. Given the average cost, increased environmental tightness will bring about increased work effort. Curve B shifts to the right. It is now shown as curve B_2. The new equilibrium is at E_2 showing more effort and lower average cost.

The significance of this analysis is that although it shows that competition will tend to reduce managerial slack, there is no presumption that it will eliminate it. This is because of monitoring costs (agency costs) which may vary among firms but which cannot be eliminated by competition.

More recently Hart (1983) has also shown that managerial slack will be lower (but not totally absent) when there is competition than when there is only one non-profit maximising firm. He also shows that the presence of profit maximising firms, what he calls 'entrepreneurial' firms, in an industry will tend to enhance the competitive pressure and reduce managerial discretion in the managerially run firms.[16] This is only true, however, when all the firms are subject to the same environmental conditions and pressures. For example, if the average and marginal costs of all the firms in the industry fall then the profit maximising firms will increase their output and the price of the product will tend to fall. This reduces profits and gives less opportunity for discretionary behaviour to the managers of a non-profit maximising firm. If environmental conditions do not affect all firms similarly, e.g. if the demand for the product of a managerially run firm increases but this increase is not industry wide, then an opportunity for managerial discretion arises.

In brief, product market competition may reduce but will not necessarily eliminate managerial discretion. Additionally entrepreneurial firms may be a source of discipline for managers.

Banks

The relationship between managers and their bankers or other lenders is similar to that of a principal–agent relationship. Banks as principals, therefore, will attempt to influence managers to behave in a way that will safeguard the interests of the Bank. Assuming that banks hold no equity capital then their main interest will be to minimise the risk of default. They might therefore attempt to encourage managers to avoid investment decisions which involve a high downside risk. The control mechanism used is the threat of liquidation or bankruptcy. Such a threat must have an important impact on management since its implementation would have devastating effects. As already mentioned under (c) a liquidation may be taken, in the managerial labour market, as a powerful signal of managerial incompetence. Prospective principals and shareholders may interpret failure of this nature as managerial inefficiency whether this were the case or not. The main investment of a manager, that of his or her human capital, might be irreparably damaged.

Given the significance of the above threat, one might conclude that managers will tend to minimise borrowing. Such a conclusion would be incorrect because a certain level of borrowing may be advantageous to managers since it may be interpreted as a signal of confidence and commitment to a good performance. This is referred to as 'bonding'. Bonding enhances reputations. Besides, the alternative sources of finance may be limited. Profit retention cannot be 100 per cent since dividends must be distributed. Additional equity finance may lead to dilutions of share ownership to a degree unwelcome by existing shareholders. Moreover, raising additional finance from shareholders might require disclosure of information useful to potential competitors. Therefore, managers may prefer to raise funds through banks which can guarantee confidentiality.

Banks can and probably do control managers more effectively than shareholders. However, they may not be interested in a profit maximising performance. Indeed it can be argued (Stiglitz 1985) that banks are only interested to see a satisfactory level of profitability despite the fact that banks together with other financial institutions (insurance companies, pension funds, etc.) have recently emerged as relatively significant shareholders in large corporations both in the USA and in the UK (see the first section of this chapter). Major financial institutions appear in many boards of large corporations and are well placed to exert substantial influence on managers. It is not certain, however, whether they are interested in utilising their potential influence for managerial discipline and control or whether they hold board positions for reasons of commercial intelligence and business generation.

In brief, several internal and external control mechanisms, operating independently or in conjunction with each other, seem to have a depressing effect on managerial discretion. However, the significance of their individual or cumulative impact has not been unequivocally demonstrated. Thus, it is safe to conclude that the existence of principal–agent relationships and the concomitant control mechanisms tend to mitigate but not necessarily eliminate managerial discretion.

SUMMARY

The diffusion of the joint stock company and the wide share ownership dispersion which are characteristic of modern capitalist societies have meant that many modern enterprises are run by professional managers who have a small or non-existent share interest in the companies they run. This divorce of ownership from control has led many economists and practitioners to question the profit maximisation assumption (see the section on 'The impact of the separation of ownership from control on business objectives') and to suggest that professional managers may be inclined to adopt policies which divert from those serving the best interests of their shareholders. They may pursue sales expansion and growth beyond the point justified by profitability or they may spend excessively on 'perquisites' and create discretionary investment in order to justify staff expansion. The implications for price, output, advertising and responses to changes in environmental conditions (costs, taxes, etc.) are analysed in the third section of the chapter.

Managerial theories provide an array of possible behavioural patterns and it is not always easy to empirically verify their predictions or select one model as better than another. This is not really surprising since at the heart of any managerial theory is an agency problem whose solution will vary with the circumstances surrounding it. An agency relationship exists when one party acts on behalf of another party for an agreed remuneration. In the presence of information asymmetry and information acquisition costs a divergence of interests may encourage opportunistic behaviour by an agent. An agency problem, therefore, may exist. To resolve this problem contracts should be designed incorporating incentives intended to discourage opportunistic behaviour. Such contracts are called 'optimal' and, as explained above, their characteristics will vary with the risk attitudes of people and the extent of uncertainty that prevails.

Several incentive and control mechanisms designed to reduce or eliminate agency costs or managerial discretion are examined. They operate either independently or in conjunction with each other. The significance of each mechanism or even their combined effect is difficult to assess. However, it is unlikely that managerial discretion has been eliminated. The combined effect of the incentive and control mechanisms in existence in modern economies seems to have mitigated managerial discretion. But mitigation is not the same as elimination.

APPLICATION: CONFLICT OF INTEREST AND ITS MITIGATION IN OIL AND GAS EXPLORATION PARTNERSHIPS

Market arrangements in some sectors of the oil and gas industry provide a good illustration of agency problems and some related control mechanisms.

The exploration and extraction of oil and gas is often undertaken by partnerships in which limited liability partners contribute capital and a drilling agent performs the exploration and further development of the business. A common contractual arrangement induced by US tax legislation is the so-called 'functional allocation'. In this arrangement limited partners contribute the capital for the exploration and when oil or gas is found the managing partner contributes the cost of completing the construction of the well. The oil or gas revenues are shared at agreed proportions. The managing partner's share was around 40 per cent of total revenue in the early 1980s. If gas or oil is not found in sufficient quantities the well is plugged and abandoned in which case the limited partner cannot recover the capital invested in the exploration while the managing partner bears no losses. The completion or non-completion decision is taken by the managing agent after drilling when it is found out whether gas or oil exists. This information is not, however, costlessly available to the limited partners. Therefore, decision making takes place in conditions of asymmetric information.

An agency relationship exists in the contractual arrangement described since the interests of the drilling agent do not always coincide with the interests of the limited partners. The problem arises when the expected oil or gas revenue R is higher than the cost C of completing the well but the managing partners' share (40 per cent of R) is less than C. In this case, the interest of the limited partners will be served if the well is completed (since some of the capital invested will be recouped) but the managing partner (drilling agent) will have an incentive not to complete in order to avoid private losses. A fictitious numerical example may clarify the problem. Suppose that drilling costs of £8 million have been incurred and oil worth £10 million was found. To extract it the managing agent has to incur £5 million. completion expenditure. The limited partners would benefit by this completion which would contribute £6 million towards their drilling cost, while non-completion means no revenue at all. The managing agent on the other hand is better off by not completing the well (incurring neither revenues nor costs) since completion means a loss of £1 million. As a result the managing partner will have an incentive to complete fewer than the optimal number of wells.

An alternative contractual arrangement such that the drilling agent's compensation consisted of a smaller percentage of total revenue (say 30 per cent) plus a larger percentage of completion cost recovery (70 per cent) would eliminate the divergence of interests and resolve the agency problem. Tax legislation, however, discourages such arrangements in practice. Agent monitoring is also not possible because of high costs.

A market control mechanism which tends to mitigate managerial discretion and reduce the conflict of interest has been developed in this industry. The way in which this market control operates is similar to that described in Section 5.3 and relates to the significance of sending proper signals to limited partners about the competence or reputation of the general partner. This is significant in gas and oil partnerships since the drilling partner usually forms new partnerships every year. Many non completions can be taken as a signal of opportunistic behaviour on the part of the agent with the serious risk that limited partners may in the future refuse finance for further explorations. To avoid this risk a self-interest motivated agent may be inclined to select for exploration a larger number of very risky projects. That is, the agent may concentrate on projects which will be either 'very successful' (bring in very high returns) or clearly unsuccessful (returns too low). In either case there will be no conflict of interest. The decision would be the same whether it was taken in the interest of the agent or in order to serve the interests of the partners. Wolfson (1984), who analysed a number of partnerships in the early 1980s, found that partnerships operating under the contractual arrangements described here tended to engage in more risky exploratory drilling compared with partnerships operating under other contractual arrangements. His statistical evidence also shows that 'reputation effects are at work in the market' which mitigate the conflict of interest although at the cost of undertaking risks. He actually concluded that without such mitigating forces this contractual form of partnership would not have survived as an organisational form.

FURTHER READING

Hay, D.A. and Morris, D.J. (1979) *Industrial Economics: Theory and Evidence*, 1st edn, Oxford: Oxford University Press.
Koutsoyiannis, A. (1979) *Modern Microeconomics*, 2nd edn, London: Macmillan.
Ricketts, M. (1987) *The Economics of Business Enterprise: New Approaches to the Firm*, Brighton: Wheatsheaf.
Strong, N. and Waterson, M. (1987) 'Principals, Agents and Information', in R. Clarke and T. McGuiness (eds) *The Economics of the Firm*, Oxford: Blackwell.

QUESTIONS

1 'Since ownership no longer implies control, business behaviour cannot be explained on the assumption of profit maximisation.' Discuss.

2 'The view that the firm is a coalition of individuals or groups of individuals with different and often irreconcilably contradictory objectives cannot be sustained, since the resulting conflict in decision making could not be resolved.' Discuss.

3 Explain (a) how managerial discretion may arise in Williamson's managerial utility maximisation model and what determines its size and (b) why the market in corporate control may fail to eliminate such discretion.

4 Since the Conservative Government took office in 1979, the rate of corporation tax has progressively declined in the UK. Examine the likely impact of this change on staff expenditure, the level of production and the rate of reported profits of a utility maximising firm.

5 A monopolist produces commodity X under the following cost and demand conditions:

$$TC = 43,000 + 4,000Q$$

$$P = 16,000 - 1,000 + \frac{24,000}{Q}$$

where Q denotes production and sales in tons and P is the price in pounds.

After careful consideration the management of this firm decided that they must pay a dividend of 50p per share. This implies that a total profit of at least £16,000 will be needed at the end of the financial year.

(a) Assuming that the objective of the firm is to maximise sales revenue calculate the price of X and the quantity that will be sold at this price.

(b) Would your answer to (a) be affected if the Government decided to reduce the rate of corporation tax?

6 'Since the threat of a takeover and the consequent risk to managerial job security increases with reductions in the value of a firm's shares, the suggestion that managerially controlled firms will adopt policies leading to higher growth rates and lower profit rates compared with owner-controlled firms cannot be valid.' Explain and evaluate this statement.

7 Examine the main constraints on corporate growth and explain whether you agree with the view that managers are disciplined by the market in 'corporate control' to act in the interest of shareholders.

8 Define agency costs and explain how they may arise.

9 Explain why managerial annual bonuses are usually related to some measure of the firm's performance while part of the total managerial compensation (e.g. salaries) is commonly fixed per time period and is independent of business performance.

APPENDIX 9.1: SALES REVENUE MAXIMISATION

Unconstrained sales maximisation

The problem is to determine the output Q which maximises TR = PQ where $P = f(Q)$ is the demand curve. Therefore, to maximise

$$TR = f(Q)Q$$

let

$$\frac{dTR}{dQ} = f'(Q)Q + f(Q) = 0$$

and

$$\frac{\mathrm{d}TR'}{\mathrm{d}Q} = f''(Q)Q + 2f'(Q) < 0.$$

Constrained sales maximisation

Assuming that sales can expand by advertising and other promotional activities, any excess profit will be spent. Production is such that total profit is just equal to the minimum required. Therefore, a simple profit equation has to be solved:

$$\Pi = TR - TC = \Pi_{min}$$

Where $TR = f(Q)Q$ and $TC = F(Q)$. Thus

$$\Pi = f(Q)Q - F(Q) = \Pi_{min}$$

or

$$f(Q)Q - F(Q) = \Pi_{min}.$$

A numerical example

A monopolist of product X is faced with the following demand and cost functions:

$$P = 120 - 4Q$$
$$TC = 6Q^2 + 40Q + 140$$

where Q denotes output and P the price of X. To calculate the sales maximising output, the total revenue must be differentiated with respect to Q and the derivative set equal to zero:

$$TR = PQ = (120 - 4Q)Q = 120Q - 4Q^2$$

$$\frac{\mathrm{d}TR}{\mathrm{d}Q} = 120 - 8Q = 0.$$

This gives $Q = 15$. The price at which this Q can be sold can be found by substituting this value into the demand curve:

$$P = 120 - 4(15) = 60.$$

Maximum revenue is $TR = PQ = 60 \times 15 = 900$ and total cost is $TC = 6(15)^2 + 40(15) + 140 = 2,090$. Therefore, profit $= TR - TC = 900 - 2,090 = -1,190$. This represents a substantial loss which implies that management will not be able or willing to pursue this unconstrained sales maximisation policy. Suppose that a minimum profit of £10 is required. The production policy in this case will be different. Price will have to be increased and less will be sold. Sales revenue will be smaller. To find the constrained sales maximising output set profits equal to £10.

$$
\begin{aligned}
\Pi &= TR - TC \\
&= (120 - 4Q)Q - (6Q^2 + 40Q + 140) = 10 \\
&= 120Q - 4Q^2 - 6Q^2 - 40Q - 140 = 10 \\
&= 80Q - 10Q^2 - 140 - 10 = 0 \\
&\quad Q^2 - 8Q + 15 = 0 \text{ or } (Q - 3)(Q - 5) = 0.
\end{aligned}
$$

Therefore $Q = 3$ or $Q = 5$. Since total revenue is higher at $Q = 5$ this is the output level that will be chosen. The corresponding price will be $P = 120 - 4(5) = 100$ $TR = 100 \times 5 = 500$.

APPENDIX 9.2: WILLIAMSON'S MANAGERIAL DISCRETION MODEL

Maximise $U = f(S, M, I)$ (A9.1)
subject to $\Pi_r \geq \Pi_{min} + T$

Where Π_r denotes reported profits and S staff expenditure. If Π stands for total profit possible, ρ is the proportion of reported to total profit and $T = t\Pi_r$ then by definition the following relationships hold:

$$\Pi = R - C - S$$

$$\Pi_r = \rho\Pi = \rho(R - C - S)$$

$$M = (1 - \rho)\Pi$$

and

$$I = \Pi_r - \Pi_{min} - T$$

where R is total revenue and C is total cost of production. It follows that

$$M = (1-\rho)(R - C - S)$$ (A9.2)

and

$$I = \rho(R - C - S) - \Pi_{min} - t\rho(R - C - S)$$

or

$$I = \rho(1 - t)(R - C - S) - \Pi_{min}.$$ (A9.3)

The definition of I implies that the constraint can be ignored. We can therefore substitute equations (A9.2) and (A9.3) into (A9.1) and maximise U with respect to output X, S and ρ:

Max $U = f[S, (1 - \rho)(R - C - S), \rho(1 - t)(R - C - S) - \Pi_{min}]$.
Define $\delta U/\delta S = U_a$, $\delta U/\delta M = U_b$ and $\delta U/\delta I = U_c$.

Provided that the sufficient conditions for a maximum are satisfied, the first-order conditions are

$$\frac{\delta U}{\delta X} = U_b(1 - \rho) \quad \left(\frac{dR}{dX} - \frac{dC}{dX}\right) + U_c\rho(1 - t) \quad \left(\frac{dR}{dX} - \frac{dC}{dX}\right) = 0 \quad \text{(A9.4)}$$

$$\frac{\delta U}{\delta S} = U_a + U_b(1 - \rho) \quad \left(\frac{dR}{dS} - 1\right) + U_c\rho(1 - t) \quad \left(\frac{dR}{dS} - 1\right) = 0 \quad \text{(A9.5)}$$

$$\frac{\delta U}{\delta \rho} = U_b(-1)(R - C - S) + U_c(1 - t)(R - C - S) = 0.$$ (A9.6)

The implications are as follows. For equation (A9.4) to hold, $dR/dX = dC/dX$. This means that production decisions are conventionally made. Output is such that $MR = MC$ (this does not mean that X will be the same as that under profit maximisation, because S influences demand). From equation (A9.5)

$$\frac{dR}{dS} = 1 - \frac{U_a}{U_b(1 - \rho) + U_c\rho(1 - t)}$$

Since U_a, U_b, U_c, $1 - \rho$ and $1 - t$ are all positive, it follows that $dR/dS < 1$, i.e. staff expenditure is carried beyond the profit maximising level. From equation (A9.6) we derive

$(R - C - S) [- U_b + U_c (1 - t)] = 0$

therefore, if $R > C + S$ (i.e. if there is any profit) then

$$\frac{U_b}{U_c} = 1 - t.$$

This means that the marginal rate of substitution between emoluments and discretionary investment depends on the tax rate. The higher the tax on profits the higher the proportion of profits that will be absorbed as emoluments and the smaller the amount of discretionary investment.

APPENDIX 9.3: GROWTH AND SHARE VALUATION

Determination of a firm's market value

In a growth context the owners' objective is assumed to be the maximisation of their wealth. Shareholder wealth depends not only on current dividends but on capital gains or losses which accrue when shares are sold. But since the price of shares at the time of sale will depend, at least partly, on expected future dividends, the market value of a firm is the same as the net present value of the stream of total dividends. Assuming away tax complications and the difficulties of defining an appropriate discount rate the following equation gives the present value of a stream of dividends:

$$V = PN = \frac{D}{1 + e} + \frac{D(1 + g)}{(1 + e)^2} + \cdots + \frac{D(1 + g)^n}{(1 + e)^{1+n}} \tag{A9.7}$$

where P is the share price, N is the number of shares, D is the dividend paid at the end of the year, e is the cost of capital (discount rate) and g is the rate at which both the firm and the dividends grow per year.

As n tends to infinity this sum can be written as

$$V = \frac{D}{1 + e} [1 + \frac{1 + g}{1 + e} + \frac{(1 + g)^2}{(1 + e)^2} + \cdots + \frac{(1 + g)^n}{(1 + e)^n}]$$

$$= \frac{D}{1 + e} [\frac{1}{1 - (1 + g)/(1 + e)}]$$

therefore,

$$V = \frac{D}{e - g} \tag{A9.8}$$

It is assumed that $e > g$ since share valuation would be infinite otherwise. Wealth maximisers would wish to adopt the growth rate that maximises V. Since D is total profit less retentions,

$$D = K\rho(1 - r)$$

Where K is the firm's capital, ρ is the rate of profit and r is the retention rate. Equation (A9.8) can be written as

$$V = K\rho \frac{1 - r}{e - g} \tag{A9.9}$$

But the growth rate is related to profitability, in two ways. Profit is required to finance both expansion, i.e. $g = r\rho$, and profitability, and the expansion of demand can be written as $\rho = f(g)$. Substituting these relationships into (A9.9) we derive

$$V = Kf(g) \frac{(1 - g/f(g)}{e - g}$$

so

$$V = K \frac{f(g) - g}{e - g.}$$

To maximise V

$$\frac{dV}{dg} = \frac{(e - g) K [f'(g) - 1] + K[f(g) - g]}{(e - g)^2} = 0,$$

so $dV/dg = 0$ when

$$(e - g)K[f'(g) - 1] + K[f(g) - g] = 0,$$

i.e. when

$$f'(g) - 1 = \frac{f(g) - g}{e - g}$$

but since $f(g) = \rho$ this implies

$$1 - f'(g) = \frac{\rho - g}{e - g}$$

or

$$f'(g) = \frac{e - \rho}{e - g}$$

but since the condition $\rho > e > g$ must hold if the firm is to be profitable at all, it follows that

$$f'(g) < 0.$$

That is, the rate of growth that maximises shareholder wealth occurs when the rate of change of the growth of demand curve is negative. This is denoted as g_v on Figure 9.6(b).

NOTES

1 This quote is in Book V, Chapter 1. See Putterman (1986: Chapter 1) for excerpts from Adam Smith *An Inquiry into the Nature and Causes of the Wealth of Nations*, originally published in 1776.
2 These findings, reported by Larner, are quoted by Ricketts (1987). Non-single important stock interest or 'management controlled' corporations were defined to be all the corporations in which the largest block of voting shares fell between 5 per cent and 20 per cent.
3 See Hay and Morris (1979: 246).
4 See Cyert and March (1963).
5 See *Business Observer*, 28 April 1991.
6 For a mathematical derivation of this rule, see Appendix 9.1.
7 For a discussion of this model see Koutsoyiannis (1979).
8 For a brief outline of this and other possible constraints see Hay and Morris (1979: 269–72).
9 This belief distinguishes Williamson from other managerialists who attribute managerial discretion to the separation of ownership from control.

10 The demand function is assumed to be $X = f(P, S, e)$ where X is output, S is expenditure on staff and e is a shift variable.
11 For definitions of risk aversion and neutrality see Chapter 7.
12 The agent's utility function is positively related to income and negatively related to the intensity of effort.
13 For a discussion of the derivation of the set of optimal contracts see Ricketts (1987).
14 Strong and Waterson (1987: 38) suggest that this form of pay may be a better incentive compared with flat- or piece-rate rewards since it encourages peer group monitoring.
15 See the *Guardian*, 30 May 1991. Shareholder concern over such practices has culminated in a decision to set up a Committee including the Bank of England and the Confederation of British Industry to examine, among other issues, directors' pay awards.
16 This does not imply that profit maximising firms may drive out of the market managerially run firms. (See Hart (1983) or Ricketts (1987) for the necessary proofs.)

10 Multi-market firms

INTRODUCTION AND EVIDENCE ON MULTI-MARKET FIRMS

Business growth by vertical, horizontal and transnational expansion is both widespread and growing over time. In the UK, for example, of all firms[1] employing over a hundred people, those considered as diversified to at least some extent controlled 55.75 per cent of net output in 1955 and 70.74 per cent in 1963. By 1970, 94 per cent of the one hundred largest UK manufacturing firms produced more than one product. Moreover, although expansion into unrelated products has shown a dramatic proportionate increase (see Table 10.1), firms have geared their diversification strategy towards related product areas.

Diversification by merger and takeover has been a popular method of expansion in recent years in all industrialised countries. Information on the growth strategies of the top 1,000 European industrial enterprises, for example, confirms this trend as Table 10.2 and Figure 10.1 show. The tendency of firms to expand their operations beyond national borders is indicated by Table 10.3.

Table 10.1 Diversification in the UK manufacturing industry, 100 largest firms (controlling approximately 60 per cent of sales and assets)

Category	1950	1960	1970
Single product[a]	34	20	6
Dominant product[b]	41	35	34
Related product[c]	23	41	54
Unrelated product[d]	2	4	6
	100%	100%	100%

Source: Adapted from Howe 1978: table on p. 121
Notes: [a] At least 95 per cent of sales were in a single product.
[b] Up to 30 per cent of sales were accounted for by secondary products.
[c] Firms produce related products no one of which accounts for more than 30 per cent of sales.
[d] Firms produce unrelated products no one of which accounts for more than 30 per cent of sales.

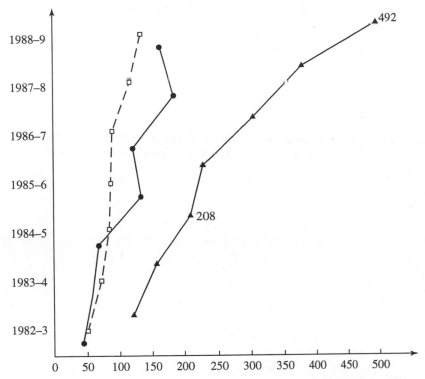

Figure 10.1 Number of takeovers (▲), acquisitions of minority holdings (●) and new jointly owned subsidiaries (□) (1,000 top EC industrial firms)
Source: Commission of the EC 1990.

Table 10.2 Number of mergers/takeovers and their distribution by nationality of firms involved

Year	National	EC	International	Total
1903 4	101	29	25	155
1984–5	146	44	18	208
1985–6	145	52	30	227
1986–7	211	75	17	303
1987–8	214	111	58	383
1988–9	233	197	62	492

Source: Commission of the EC 1990: p. 59

The dramatic increase in acquisitions in the European Community (EC) area during the 1980s is documented in Table 10.2. The number of acquisitions has doubled every four years, rising from 208 in 1984–5 to 492 in 1988–9. That mergers and takeovers have progressively become more preferred compared with other methods of expansion is shown by Figure

Table 10.3 The growth of multinational enterprises in Europe (as indicated by the stock of foreign investment)

Country	Direct investment stock* (billion current US dollars)		Percentage growth rate	Direct investment stock as percentage of GDP, 1988
	End 1982	End 1988		
Germany	39	89	128	7
France	24	66	175	7
Italy	17	33	94	4
Netherlands	53	82	55	36
UK	87	183	110	23
Total of five countries	220	453	106	–
USA	222	326	47	7
Japan	48	129	169	5

Source: Adapted from Commission of the EC 1990: Table 7.4
Note: Figures are not strictly comparable because of definitional differences.

10.1. Thus, although minority holdings accounted for 57 per cent of all acquisitions recorded in 1985–6, in 1988–9 they only represented 32 per cent.

Differences in vertical and lateral expansion are widespread even among firms in the same industry. Indeed, Wolf (1977) has shown that, depending on the attitudes of the research team of a firm, a trade-off may exist between the development of new products and the transfer of existing products to new national markets.

It is clear that multi-product and transnational firms have become a permanent feature of the industrial landscape, and economic theory that concentrates on single-product and single-plant firms has become progressively of less value to the business economist. Questions relating to motives and efficiency of multi-product firms have acquired significance both for businesses themselves and for policy makers. Thus, in this chapter we examine (a) the reasons why firms select to grow by diversification or vertical integration or to expand internationally and (b) the impact that such policies may have on pricing and competition. Efficiency as well as market power considerations are analysed under each heading in the following three sections and the main conclusions are drawn in the fifth section.

VERTICAL INTEGRATION

The production of any good or service usually involves several technically separable stages. Vertical integration (VI) is the term used to indicate the extent to which several stages of production are undertaken by a single business enterprise. The same term is also used, in a more dynamic sense, to refer to the process by which firms expand their operations vertically by investing new resources or by acquiring other firms in succeeding or preceding stages of production. When the process of expansion involves succeeding stages, such as final production or distribution, the term *forward (or downstream) vertical integration* is used, while *backward (or upstream) vertical integration* refers to expansion into preceding stages, such as the production of raw materials or semi-finished products. The extent of VI varies not only among industries but among firms of the same industry. Upstream VI, for example, is very common in the aluminium industry but not so common in the tin industry (Hennart 1988a). Within the British brewing industry large brewers who undertake their own malting and run their own public houses co-exist with small firms specialising in one stage of production. There are independent maltsters, breweries with very few if any tied public houses, as well as independent public houses or 'free houses' which buy beer from whichever brewer they choose. The question then arises as to what induces such diversity in business vertical strategy and what are its consequences.

VI brings into focus the question of why or to what extent firms, by internalising transactions, assume the co-ordinating function of the market. Whether they should do so is the concern of policy makers. Our earlier discussion on internalisation (Chapters 3 and 4) focused attention on efficiency to the exclusion of market power considerations. In this chapter we re-examine some of the efficiency considerations that apply specifically to vertical and to lateral expansion and we extend the analysis to include the pursuit of market power. Some policy implications of the co-existence of efficiency and market power pursuits will be drawn.

Efficiency motives

When corporate decisions on expansion are predominantly induced by attempts to economise on costs, VI enhances efficiency. There is some controversy, however, as to whether the efficiency motives of integration derive from production or transaction cost savings. The distinction may be of some significance in understanding the diversity of business behaviour.

Production efficiency

When two stages of production are technologically interdependent, integration may reduce production costs. The classic example of technological interdependencies arises in the production of steel and iron where substantial thermal efficiencies can be obtained from integrated production. Iron, produced from iron ore in blast furnaces, comes in molten form and at a high temperature. In the absence of integration, special handling and cooling of the molten iron is required to turn it into solid form[2] for transportation to the steel works. To be processed into steel the solid iron needs reheating. By integrating the iron and steel production the molten iron is carried straight into the steel making process with a substantial saving in handling and thermal costs. Similar thermal economies may be brought about by integration in other metal industries. Handling and other production cost efficiency motives for integration are observed in the petroleum industry, in other chemical industries, in the production of paper from pulp, etc. In addition to technological economies other cost savings can be achieved by integration. For example, advertising and other promotional expenditures and costs related to stock keeping may be reduced and managerial and research and development (R&D) economies[3] may be enhanced.

This does not mean that integration always enhances efficiency. If a firm specialises in one stage of production and sells an intermediate product to several other firms it may be possible to obtain economies of large-scale production which will not be present when production is restricted to the firm's own needs. For example, glass used in motorcars probably comes from a process involving economies of scale so that the requirements of any car assembler are not sufficient for economies of scale to materialise. It is for this reason, according to Waterson (1984: 95) that glass is not usually produced by car assemblers.

Economising on transaction costs

While technological interdependencies or other production cost savings may undoubtedly contribute to integration, Williamson (1975) and others have shown that production cost efficiency is rarely a sufficient explanation for integration. Moreover, scale economies may explain specialisation, as in the example of car glass production, but only when the inter-firm trade does not involve high transaction costs. In other words, transaction costs may be present to an extent that renders inter-firm trading inefficient and induces integration. Transaction costs is the decisive factor. It is the presence of transaction costs that leads to integration rather than any technological interdependencies. Technology may indicate that two stages of production must be in close proximity but this is an issue quite separate to the question of who owns each stage. When the ownership of the two stages does not coincide, however, a market exchange is required for the good to pass from one stage to the next. In circumstances in which such transactions become very costly, either because of contractual difficulties or because of post-contractual opportunistic behaviour, common ownership economises on transaction costs and integration becomes efficient.

It should be recalled that transaction costs are generated by the interplay of human attributes (bounded rationality and opportunism) and the characteristics of the transactions such as asset specificity, uncertainty and frequency. Since some degree of uncertainty is always present in a business environment and transactions are likely to be of a recurring nature, *asset specificity* is the most important single factor contributing to high transaction costs and hence to integration. Asset specificity is present when transactions require specialised investments, i.e. investments which have a small or no value to alternative users or uses. As asset specificity increases transaction costs increase and so do the potential benefits from VI.

When transactions are supported by highly specific investments, human or physical, the potential gains from integration, and hence transaction costs savings, are large. To illustrate how total cost economising may lead to VI consider an example from the petroleum industry initially provided by Klein *et al.* (1978). Suppose that several oil wells are located along a pipeline which transports crude oil to several oil refineries. The oil refineries have no alternative source of supply at comparable cost and the oil wells have no other means of transporting their oil. The oil wells and refineries are specialised investment to the pipeline. After construction, with the oil wells and refineries fully operational, the pipeline owner has substantial power. The price he or she offers for crude oil could be barely above the marginal cost of extraction (or its reservation value for future use) which may not be sufficient to cover all costs and give a return to recoup the initial exploration and drilling capital. Moreover, on delivery to the refineries, the pipeline owner could charge a price nearly as high as the cost of alternative sources of supply. Even if a price agreement existed, the owner of the pipeline could alter its terms (at the contract renewal or at any other time) in the safe knowledge that the well and refinery owners have no alternatives. Recourse to the courts may be both expensive and protracted. Besides, the pipeline owner can act opportunistically maintaining that business is bad and unless prices are as indicated business may have to cease. The anticipated vulnerability of the oil well and refinery owners is likely to lead to integration into oil transportation. However, if the well firms were to integrate forward and acquire ownership of the pipeline, the refineries would become vulnerable. Similarly, refinery integration into the pipeline could lead to the exploitation of the crude oil producers. Integration over all three stages of production would reduce the incentive for haggling and opportunistic behaviour. In practice, whenever several oil refineries (or oil wells) are served by the same pipeline we find that they jointly own the pipeline company with the shares of producers or refiners approximately equal to the shares of crude oil to be transported.[4]

The difference between the oil transportation example which requires integration and the glass production which does not lies in the different requirements for specific investments (asset specificity). In the case of glass, the product is standardised and has many different uses and users. This means that there is no asset specificity in its production or distribution and economies of scale favour specialisation in production and inter-firm trading. In the case of oil transportation asset specificity renders inter-firm trading prohibitively expensive and leads to integration. But these are two extreme cases. In reality the extent of asset specificity varies among products and more importantly perhaps both production and transaction costs depend on asset specificity (Williamson 1984a).

In general, production economies decline and transaction costs increase as the need for specific investments increases. In the extreme, when a transaction requires fully specialised investments, economies of scale will be the same whether the firm operates the asset under its own direction or acquires its services from another firm. Inter-firm trading, however, will be inhibited by high transaction costs and VI will enhance efficiency. At intermediate levels of asset specificity production costs may be lower without integration while transaction costs are lower with integration, or vice versa. A trade-off exists between transaction and production costs and the efficiency of VI will depend on the net effect.

The relationship between asset specificity and costs is shown in Figure 10.2. A certain output is assumed and the horizontal axis refers to the extent of asset specificity, A, while the vertical axis measures costs. ΔC denotes the difference in production cost between integrated and non-integrated production. It is positive everywhere indicating a production cost[5] disadvantage of integration. However, its shape shows that this disadvantage declines as A increases and in the limit it approaches zero. ΔT denotes the difference in transactions costs between market and internal transacting. When A is zero, or small, internalisation of transactions is more costly compared with market exchanges. However, as A increases internalisation saves on transaction costs. At A_0 transaction cost economising is sufficient to compensate for the production cost disadvantage of integration. When A is larger than A_0 integration is efficient since it economises on net production and transaction costs.

It is evident from Figure 10.2 that when the commodity produced and traded does not require specific investments (A is small) costs will be minimised by specialisation in production and inter-firm trading. Thus, if asset specificity is A_1 integration increases production costs by Oy and transaction costs by Oz. When asset specificity is high (A is large), efficiency favours VI. At A_2, for example, the net saving is equal to the distances A_2w. At intermediate degrees of asset specificity, however, there may not be much difference in efficiency between market transacting and integration. Thus, at A_0 producing one's own requirements would cost the same as acquiring them from another firm. In this case some firms in the industry will integrate while others will not and different forms of non-standard contracts may also co-exist.

The chemical industry provides a practical illustration of the issues discussed. Lieberman (1991) examined the incentives for backward VI of 203 US producers of thirty-four organic chemicals. He found that both the number of producers of each chemical and the extent of integration within each separate market varied. Some firms were not integrated and of those integrated some produced all of their requirements while others produced a surplus and yet others produced only part of their requirements. This diversity in industrial organisation was attributed to the differences in the extent of asset specificity among chemicals. Integration, for example, was

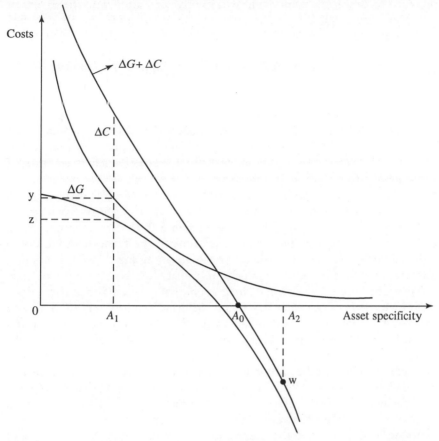

Figure 10.2 Cost differences between integrated and non-integrated production; ΔC denotes the production cost disadvantage of integration which declines as A increases; ΔG denotes the transaction cost disadvantage of non-integration which for high A becomes an advantage
Source: Reproduced from Williamson 1984a, p. 213, with permission of the editor of *Zeitschrift für die gestamte Staatwissenschaft*. Dotted lines and the symbols A_1, A_2, y, z and w do not appear on the original.

prevalent among producers of chemicals such as ethylene, ethylene oxide, propylene and chlorine, which are gases at room temperature and require large fixed investment in pipeline facilities to ship them between plants. These pipelines are highly asset specific. In general, Lieberman found that in this industry when asset specificity was high firms tended to integrate in order to avoid the bargaining problems they feared could arise after large funds were devoted to specific investments.

  Similar evidence has also been provided by Monteverde and Teece (1982) who examined 133 car components used by General Motors and Ford in 1976. They found that the extent of engineering investment required to develop a component was highly correlated with the extent of VI. They suggested that when components are technologically complex and expensive to develop there is a risk that the supplier can turn round and ask for a higher price at the last moment knowing that the car manufacturer has no alternative source of supply. By integrating the component production car manufacturers avoid such risks.

Evidence that integration depends on the characteristics of the transaction has also emerged from the US aerospace industry (see Application section of Chapter 3) investigated by Masten (1984). He concluded that design specificity and complexity were necessary if not sufficient conditions for the breakdown of co-operation in market exchanges and the subsequent production within the firm.

In addition to asset specificity the extent of *uncertainty* that surrounds a transaction and its possible *external effects* are considered to have an important bearing on integration. Lieberman (1991), for example, shows that in the US chemical industry, uncertainty in the form of variability in input demand tended to induce firms to integrate. More generally, uncertainty relating to quality or price of raw materials may induce vertical integration. Farmers concerned about seed quality often decide to produce their own seeds rather than buy them. Alternatives to integration may of course be available. For example, in order to reduce buyer uncertainty and to facilitate inter-firm transacting, sellers may allow buyer inspectors to monitor and even manage the production process. Such arrangements may be quite feasible and they are indeed widespread in cases where the sellers of branded goods subcontract their production. Retail chains such as Marks and Spencers and manufacturers assembling electronic products from components provide relevant examples. Contracts of this kind are also common in East–West trade according to Casson (1985). However, when the seller possesses know-how which cannot be protected from the buyers' agents present during production, such arrangements become infeasible.

Externalities (good or bad) are said to exist when transactions have an impact on individuals or firms other than those directly involved in the transaction. A detrimental externality may be avoided by integration. For example, if a distributor is likely to debase the quality of a product by poor instalment or service (even unintentionally), this may adversely affect the brand name of a firm and the sales from other distributors of the brand. Thus, unless it is easy to check and control for adverse externalities of this kind (by producer's warranties for example) forward VI or some other contractual agreement such as franchising will replace market exchanges.

VI may also be undertaken in order to resolve *informational problems* associated with innovation or quality of raw materials. Consider innovation. Suppose that an entrepreneur perceives of a new product (invention) which she or he believes to be profitable but which requires some specialised inputs or resources which the entrepreneur does not own. The supplier of such resources may have no way of knowing about the potential of the product without incurring substantial costs in order, for example, to investigate the marketing potential of the new product or its technical possibilities. She or he will be unwilling, therefore, to commit resources. This is a problem caused by informational impactedness. The nature of the difficulties that arise become more obvious when the commodity to be traded is the information itself. Suppose, for example, that the innovator has acquired and wishes to sell information useful to a prior or succeeding stage of production. The difficulty is that the product this innovator offers is not known to the potential buyer and must be kept secret. No samples or inspection can be offered since once information is given the supplier cannot charge for something the potential buyer has already acquired free of charge. To resolve this difficulty, called by Arrow (1971) the 'fundamental paradox' of information, the supplier of information has three choices:

1 pay extra premiums to potential suppliers of other resources used in conjunction with information;
2 write a detailed contract to foresee every eventuality, although, as we have seen in earlier chapters, this is not always possible and even if it is possible it is likely to be prohibitively expensive;
3 Purchase or rent the necessary resource to extend the operations of the firm so as to utilise the information internally – in other words, integrate – thus, depending on the extent of uncertainty and costs, VI or quasi-VI may result (Silver 1984).

Market power motives

While efficiency can undeniably be a major influence on integration the pursuit of market power, although potentially an equally strong motive, is not always acknowledged as such. It is, for example, claimed that a monopolist in one stage of production can appropriate any monopoly profits available at other stages in the production chain, whether integration has taken place or not. Monopoly power, if present, is therefore due to the horizontal expansion that created the monopoly in the first place and not to VI which is totally motivated by efficiency. This reasoning is not infallible however. The claim that full monopoly profits can be extracted without VI can only be sustained under very restrictive assumptions regarding input substitutability. In particular, it can be shown that a monopolist in one stage of production can extract full monopoly profits without integration only when the production technology involves fixed input proportions (FIP). That is, when there are no substitutes for the monopolised input or resource. In case of variable input proportions (VIP), integration can enhance monopoly power. To examine the validity of these claims we examine the impact of VI on price and output in each case.

Impact of vertical integration on price and output under fixed input proportions

In order to separate the market power from the efficiency effects of VI we assume that costs of production at each stage of production are not affected by integration. Additionally, since market power may depend on market structure, we examine the effect of VI under different market structures.

It should be intuitively obvious that there will be no enhancement of monopoly power and no effect on price when a firm operating in one stage under perfectly competitive conditions integrates with another firm in a succeeding (or preceding) stage operating also under perfect competition. The same is true when a monopolist in one stage takes over a single firm operating in a competitive industry. What is less obvious but equally true, under FIP, is that no power enhancement exists when a monopolist in one stage of production takes over the whole of a competitive industry of a succeeding (or preceding) stage.

Vertical integration between a monopoly and a perfectly competitive industry

To illustrate, consider Figure 10.3 showing a downstream perfectly competitive industry buying an essential resource A from an upstream monopolist and producing a final product X. Technology is such that the production of each unit of X requires one unit of A.[6]

D_X denotes the demand for product X and AC_X is the average cost of producing X excluding the cost of factor A. The demand for A, labelled D_A, is a derived demand. It shows the maximum amount the competitive industry can pay for any given quantity of A. Since, in the long run, the competitive price of X will be just equal to its average cost, D_A is simply the difference between D_X and AC_X. AC_A and MC_A indicate the average and marginal cost of producing A. Now assuming profit maximisation consider the price and output at each stage, before and after integration. Prior to integration, the monopolist profit maximises by charging price P_A and selling Q_A units of A (thus equating MC_A to MR_A). The per unit cost of the competitive industry (its supply curve) becomes then $AC_X + P_A$ and the industry is in equilibrium at output Q_X and price P_X.

Suppose now that the monopolist integrates forward by taking over all the firms of the competitive industry, the post-integration demand and cost conditions remaining the same. The demand for the final product, D_X, becomes now the demand facing the monopolist. The average cost of producing a unit of X is $AC_A + AC_X$. Therefore, both the monopolist's average cost and the monopolist's average revenue have increased by the same amount at each level of production. As a result, both the marginal cost and the marginal revenue curves have moved upwards by the same amount at each production level so that their intersection remains unaltered

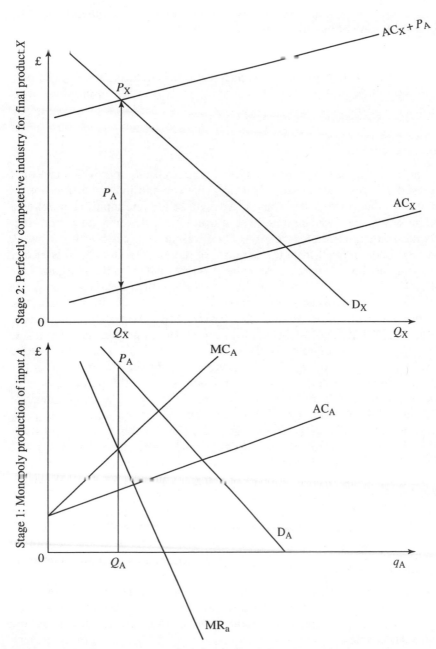

Figure 10.3 Vertical integration between a monopoly and a perfectly competitive industry

at output Q. Neither output nor price have been affected by integration. There are no market power enhancement gains.

The only possibility of gains, in the circumstances described, would be related to the revenue raising potential of forward integration. The monopolisation of the distributive outlets, for example, may facilitate price discrimination in which case some sectors of the market would be charged higher prices while others would experience price reductions. Thus, in addition to increased revenues which benefit the producer, some consumers gain but others lose so that the overall effect of price discrimination is difficult to evaluate *a priori*.

Bilateral monopoly

When a monopolist in stage 1 produces a specialised input which can only be used as a resource in stage 2, which is also monopolised, a situation of bilateral monopoly exists. That is, a single seller (monopolist) supplies a single buyer (monopsonist) and the market price depends on bargaining. To illustrate consider Figure 10.4. D represents the demand for input A and has been derived from the demand of the final product X. It is in fact the same as the net marginal revenue product of X. C is the marginal cost of producing A and MR is the marginal revenue corresponding to D. Since D is the demand (average revenue) curve for A, to profit maximise the monopolist will aim to produce Q_m (where MR intersects C) and charge price P_m. The buyer of A, being also powerful since no alternative markets for A exist, may refuse to trade at the monopoly price offering instead price P_b for quantity Q_b which maximises the buyer profits. To identify Q_b, the buyer's preferred solution, consider C from the point of view of the buyer. Since it is the marginal cost of A it indicates the minimum price that must be paid to induce the production of an extra unit of output A. It is, therefore, a supply (or average cost) curve as far as the buyer of A is concerned. The broken line (MC) represents the curve marginal to C. As already mentioned D is the net marginal revenue of A. To maximise profits, the buyer will attempt to buy such a quantity of A as to equate the net marginal revenue of A, i.e. D, to its marginal cost (MC). The simple outcome of this analysis is that there is disagreement. The buyer is offering a price lower than that demanded by the seller. The price is indeterminate. That is, given demand and cost conditions we cannot predict the price since its level will be determined by haggling, industrial muscle and bargaining strength. It will be somewhere between P_m and P_b and may fluctuate from period to period, even when market and cost conditions are stable.[7] There is, therefore, uncertainty regarding price and output and a contractual agreement may be fraught with difficulties and transaction costs.

Suppose, however, that the two independent producers integrate. Internal transfer pricing replaces market haggling. For a resource with no

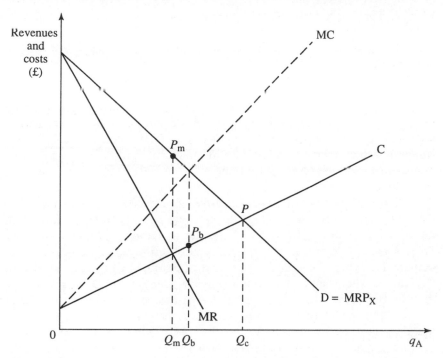

Figure 10.4 Vertical integration between a monopolist and a monopsonist

alternative markets the transfer price will be equal to marginal cost (see Chapter 11 for more details). In Figure 10.3 it will be P and the quantity Q_c produced increases to the competitive level. Thus, integration of bilateral monopolists improves resource allocation and reduces uncertainty and other transactional costs. This welfare enhancing result is not, however, necessarily valid when the bilateral monopolists are multi-product firms.[8]

A possible market outcome of bilateral monopoly is that the monopoly input price P_m prevails. This is likely when the buying firm is also a monopolist in its own product market. In this case the final product price which includes two monopoly mark-ups prior to integration will be reduced post integration since one of the two mark-ups will be eliminated. In general, the number of monopoly mark-ups is reduced when integration takes place in a chain of monopolised successive production stages.

It can be concluded that when fixed input proportions prevail VI is either innocuous (when a monopolist takes over the whole of a competitive stage) or has beneficial allocative and price effects (as in the bilateral monopoly market) and should not be discouraged by public policy. The stronger claim that VI is always desirable (associated with the Chicago school of thought) cannot, however, be sustained since integration when production involves variable input proportions may induce sufficient market power gains to negate any efficiency benefits.

Impact of vertical integration under variable input proportions

The term variable input proportions is used to describe a technology which allows input substitutability. That is, output can be produced by altering input proportions so that less of input A and more of other inputs can be used. In this case a monopolist supplier of A cannot necessarily extract full monopoly profits even when the buyer is a perfectly competitive industry. Integration may then be undertaken in pursuit of market power enhancement. A restriction of final output and a higher price may result from such integration.

To illustrate the market power incentive for integration, we assume that (a) VI has no impact on production costs and (b) a perfectly competitive final product industry is taken over by the monopolist producer of input A. In Figure 10.5, when substitutability between resources is possible the demand for factor A becomes more elastic (denoted by D_v) compared with its demand when substitution is not possible (denoted by D_f). D_v is flatter than D_f to indicate that as the price of A rises above its competitive level P_c, its users will tend to substitute other factors for A. Average and marginal cost of production is labelled AC. When D_f is the relevant demand curve the profit maximising price of A is P_f and a quantity Q is demanded by the second stage of production. When demand is D_v, the maximum price the monopolist can charge for the same output is P_v, which is lower than P_f.

The demand D_X for the final product, together with three possible long-run average cost (supply) curves, is illustrated in Figure 10.5(a). Each supply curve assumes a different price for A, given in parentheses. Under fixed input proportions the price of A is P_f and the competitive industry supply curve is AC_{P_m}. Final product output, therefore, is Q_m and price is P_m. However, when other factors can be substituted for A, the maximum price its producer can charge is P_v and the average cost of the final product is lower. The supply curve for X is denoted by AC_2. More of other resources are used to increase production to Q_v and the price P_v of the final product is lower. The final production is still not as high as the competitive output Q_c, which could only be achieved if factor A was priced at its marginal cost P. Marginal cost pricing of input A is associated with the supply curve $AC(P)$ at stage 2. In this case the final product output and price would be at the competitive level Q_c and P_c.

It follows that under variable input proportions the non-integrated monopolist cannot extract all the monopoly profit obtainable from the sale of final products. Following integration profits increase since (a) the monopolist uses more of A which is now priced at marginal cost rather than at P_m and (b) production of the final product is restricted to Q_m (as

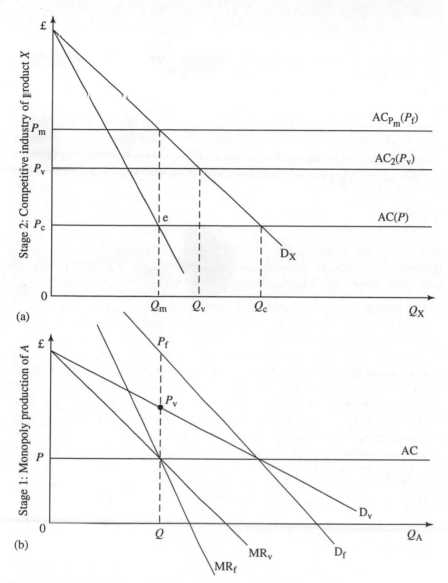

Figure 10.5 Vertical integration in case of variable input proportions

indicated by the profit maximising point e) and its price rises to P_m. The increase in price depends on the elasticity of demand and costs and on factor substitutability.

It should be noted that since factor A is not essential in the production of X, the enhanced monopoly profits, following integration, will be maintained only if there are other barriers to entry into stage 2. At the same time, monopolisation of stage 2 may give the producer of A some control over other resources used at this stage in which case integration can bring about improved utilisation not only of factor A but of other factors used with A.

Generally, an increase in the price of the final product indicates a trade-off between efficiency and enhanced market power. An example of increased product market power counterbalancing any efficiency improvements has been provided by Courtaulds, a monopolist producer of cellulosic fabrics, which integrated forwards into the textile industry by a series of acquisitions during the 1960s. A Monopolies Commission investigation into these vertical mergers concluded, in 1968, that continued acquisitions by Courtaulds in the textile industry could be against the public interest (Cowling *et al*. 1980).

Impact of vertical integration on potential competition

The monopoly power potential of VI may be further enhanced by its influence on potential competition. Integration may erect high barriers to new entry inhibiting potential competition for several reasons.

1 The backstream integration of a scarce raw material can make downstream entry impossible since the integrated firm may refuse to supply potential downstream competitors or may only supply at uncompetitive prices. Prior to integration there may have existed an upstream monopoly perhaps protected by high barriers to entry but downstream entry could none the less have been possible since there is no reason why the upstream monopolist would not be prepared to supply new buyers.
2 Forward integration may bring about the monopolisation of distributive outlets in which case a refusal to distribute the output of new entrants can be a serious barrier to entry at the preceding stage of production.

    If producers in stage 2 have control (even if not complete monopoly) of distributive outlets, they may refuse to buy from new entrants into stage 2 or be prepared to trade at very uncompetitive terms. Thus, potential entrants would have to either enter fully integrated or not at all. But entry into more than one stage of production increases the initial capital requirements which may constitute an obstacle to entry.
3 Finally, if VI is cost efficient, potential entrants will need to enter fully integrated so as to achieve the cost reductions that incumbent firms enjoy and be able to compete effectively. This, however, means higher initial capital requirements (as under (2)).

In brief, production efficiencies must be weighted against the allocative inefficiencies associated with increased market power if the overall social welfare effects of VI are to be assessed. Quantifying these effects is a difficult task of particular interest to those entrusted with government industrial policy, such as the Monopolies and Mergers Commission. Recognising the variety of inducements for, and effects of, integration, government regulatory provision and regulatory recommendations from bodies such as the Monopolies and Mergers Commission vary among industries. A Monopolies and Mergers Commission report (1990) has accepted, for example, that vertical links in the petrol industry are efficiency enhancing, but not in the supply of beer for which it has recommended (Monopolies and Mergers Commission 1989) that vertical agreements should be weakened. For similar reasons the EC regulatory provisions vary widely among industries such as beer, petrol and motor vehicles.

Measures of vertical integration

To be able to assess the extent and impact of VI we need to quantify it. Quantification, however, is fraught with problems raising from the difficulties of product definitions to measuring value added on each stage of production. As a result a variety of indices are used in empirical work the main ones of which are as follows.

1 *Value added/Total sales* This index is based on the idea that the higher the value added by a firm the more integrated the firm is. But there are serious limitations to this index since any price changes or changes in profitability or taxation, over time, will appear as changes in the extent of integration. Additionally, this index may not be very useful for comparative purposes because its size reflects the stage in which the firm operates and not just the extent of integration. Thus, two firms with the same value added but operating at different stages, one at the initial and the other at the final stages of production, will appear to have a different degree of integration.
2 *Value of inventories/Total sales* The rationale of this index is that the more stages of production undertaken by the firm the higher the inventories will be in relation to total sales. This may be misleading since integration reduces the uncertainty related to supplies and will tend to reduce the required volume of stocks at each stage. Thus, the overall value of inventories may or may not increase. Moreover, relative prices may change over time giving, as noted under (1), different indices even though integration has remained the same.
3 *Total inter-firm purchases or transfers/Total amounts of inputs used by the firm* This has been used as an index of backward integration and the equivalent for forward integration is

Total inter-firm transfers of output/Total output at a stage.

DIVERSIFICATION AND MERGERS

Diversification refers to the extent to which a range of products is produced by the same firm. It can be accomplished by internal (*de novo*) or external (merger or takeover) expansion into related or unrelated products. A threefold classification of diversification has emerged from the USA:[9] (a) product extension diversification, referring to diversification over a range of products related either on the demand side, in which case market concentricity is said to exist, or on the production side, when technological concentricity exists; (b) market extension diversification, referring to the sale of existing products in other geographic areas; and (c) conglomerate diversification, referring to diversification into unrelated product lines.

The more products a firm produces the more diversified, generally speaking, it is. The number of products produced may not, however, be a reliable index of the extent of diversification, especially when several secondary products contribute a small percentage to a firm's total revenue. As a result a number of other indices are commonly used,[10] such as the following.

1 The number of primary products as a percentage of the total number of products.
2 The specialisation ratio r. This is defined as the percentage of a firm's primary employment over its total employment. This ratio is frequently used because of its simplicity and the availability of data in census of production publications. A related index, known as the diversification ratio, $DR = 1 - r$, is also commonly used. Its value is 0 for a firm producing only one product.
3 An index analogous to the Herfindahl index of concentration, known as Berry's index, is defined as $D = 1 - \Sigma s_i^2$ where $i=1,2,3, \ldots, k$, s_i is the proportion of the ith product to total output and k is the total number of products produced by the firm. D is 0 for a specialist firm and approaches 1 as diversification increases.

Efficiency motives for diversification

Diversification is widespread but its extent varies significantly among industries. In 1972, for example, the diversification ratio of the chemical industry in the UK was 64.9, while that of the clothing and footwear industry was 28.0.[11] This section examines some of the motives contributing to such business diversity. It begins with a brief examination of 'economies of scope' and transaction cost economising. Risk spreading, financial cost considerations and power motives are analysed in subsequent paragraphs.

Economies of scope

Economies of scope arise when some resources are sharable or semi-public. A resource is defined as *sharable* when its use in the production of one good leaves excess capacity which could be utilised to produce another good. This is usually due to indivisibilities. A resource is *semi-public* when its utilisation in the production of a good does not diminish the quantity of it available for use in the production of another good. This property is usually associated with information or proprietary knowledge available for several products.

When resources are sharable or semi-public in the production of goods A and B, the minimum cost of producing a combined unit of A and B will be lower than the cost of producing each product separately. The cost reduction which joint production brings about is referred to as 'economies of scope'. In other words, economies of scope arise in the production of goods A and B when the cost of jointly producing the two goods is less than the sum of the cost of producing each one separately. Mathematically, if C denotes a cost function, economies of scope exist when

$$C(A,B) < C(A,0) + C(0,B).$$

Economies of scope can relate to a number of products and can result from technological interdependencies analogous to those sometimes found in vertically related products. An extreme form of interdependence exists in traditional joint products (see page 386) such as beef and hides or wool and mutton. If it is decided to raise sheep to produce mutton the same sheep is available to produce wool (sheep is the semi-public resource). The cost of producing wool and mutton jointly is much lower than raising sheep to produce only mutton and raising separate sheep to produce only wool. Similarly, a firm may have substantial expertise or know-how in, say, retail marketing which could be used, without congestion, to market a new product bringing about economies of scope. A machine used to produce one product may be idle for part of the day and, if not totally specialised, its utilisation for another product would bring an economy of scope. Managerial expertise or goodwill accumulated over the years are other common examples associated with economies of scope. Economies of scope are closely related to what businessmen refer to as 'operating synergies'.

It has been suggested that '[w]ith economies of scope, joint production of two goods *by one enterprise is less costly* than the combined costs of production of two specialty firms' (Willig 1979: 346, my emphasis). This suggestion presumes, however, that the sharable or semi-public resources or their service cannot be traded. This may be true in some cases but not in others. If selling or leasing the excess resource or its services is surrounded by complexity, or uncertainty and opportunism, so that the attendant transaction costs are very high, then intra-firm utilisation (i.e. diversification) will be more efficient. In other words, if selling the excess resource is not practicable, economies of scope will lead to multi-product operations but not otherwise. When economies of scope exist alongside an efficient inter-firm market, trading will take place alleviating the need for diversification. Conversely, economising on transaction costs may indicate diversification even if there are no economies of scope or in the presence of some degree of diseconomies of scope. What induces diversification is efficiency in the form of economising on transaction costs. In brief, economies of scope is neither a necessary nor a sufficient condition for diversification (Teece 1980, 1982).

Transaction cost economising

Enhanced human capital through learning-by-doing, the development of routines, the acquisition of information from R&D, indivisibilities and managerial specialisation are some of the reasons why excess capacity may exist within a firm at any point in time. Now assuming that because of demand limitations the firm cannot profitably expand its existing product lines at home or abroad, the choice is either to diversify or to sell this excess capacity or its services. When excess capacity, however, takes the form of a specialised asset so that the number of potential buyers is small, bilateral monopoly situations and opportunistic behaviour may imply high transaction costs. In this case firms may 'diversify in order to avoid the high transaction costs associated with using various markets to trade the services of various specialised assets' (Teece 1982). Excess resources of physical or human capital or know-how must, however, co-exist with market failures for diversification to be efficient.

That is, as already noted, the existence of economies of scope does not necessarily imply diversification. To illustrate consider the following example (initially suggested by Teece (1982)). Suppose that a machine used to stamp car bodies is subject to economies of scale which, given the market for cars, are not exhausted. In other words the machine remains idle for part of the day. The same machine, however, can be used to stamp light truck bodies so that its use means that there are economies of scope in jointly producing cars and light trucks. This does not, however, mean that the same firm must produce both trucks and cars. Assuming that the machine can be easily accessed three possibilities emerge for its effective use. The machine may be owned by the car manufacturer who contracts its use to the truck producer, or vice versa. Alternatively, a third firm could own the stamping machine and contract its services to both the car and the truck manufacturers.

Another example is the railroad trackage constructed to provide passenger services. Suppose that at current levels of passenger demand there is excess capacity which can be used to carry freight without congestion. Clearly the cost of providing both the passenger and freight services on the same track is lower than providing passenger and freight services independently on different tracks. The joint utilisation of the track provides economies of scope. This jointness in production does not, however, imply a multi-product firm. In principle, the owner of the track could contract out its spare services to an independent freight carrier. It is only when the costs of initiating and implementing such a contract are high that internalisation of the transaction will be more efficient and diversification will occur.

Transaction costs are likely to be very high when economies of scope arise from the sharing of intangible assets such as information resulting from R&D or human capital such as know-how. Proprietary knowledge related to know-how can be used in several non-competing applications without its value in any application being substantially reduced. Its marginal cost is likely to be less than the average cost of its production so that its application may produce substantial economies. But, since know-how involves tacit knowledge which makes inter-firm transfers very costly, to realise such economies firms must expand. The problems related to transferring tacit knowledge and information are threefold according to Teece (1980), i.e. recognition, disclosure and team organisation. To elaborate, suppose that a firm has accumulated technical or managerial know-how relevant to products other than its current range of output. To transfer this know-how the firm needs to find out who is it that it can transact with and in what terms. Once potential buyers of knowledge are located, the problem of negotiating the terms of the exchange must be tackled. Negotiations will prove rather difficult since information must be suppressed. The problem is how to sell information without divulging it (Arrow's paradox appears again). An additional difficulty arises when know-how includes a learning-by-doing element and working as a member of a team, so that it cannot be incorporated in a set of blueprints. Know-how may involve the way human beings, as team members, think and interact with each other. Thus, its transfer may require the transfer of a whole team. This may be possible for a once-for-all transaction but not in the case of recurring transactions. Thus, it is not uncommon for a contract to be signed and a 'consulting team' to be provided to help start-up a business or to give technical, marketing or managerial advice. However, when a succession of proprietary exchanges is required the reliance on long-term or repeated contracts is much more problematic. High transaction costs related to haggling and opportunism are likely to favour multi-product operations.

Internal capital markets and conglomerates

Economies of scope or the existence of surplus resources provide an efficiency rationale for product or market extension rather than for pure conglomerate diversification. The only excess resource that could profitably be utilised in pure conglomerate diversification is the entrepreneurial and managerial talents residing within a firm. Such talents may be released by the adoption of an M-form organisational mode. Indeed, Williamson (1975) considers conglomerates as the logical outgrowth of the M-form organisational structure. In assessing investment opportunities, conglomerate firms may have distinctive advantages over external capital markets.

Multidivisional firms can establish an internal capital market which is more efficient in allocating resources than the external capital market. The reasons for this were discussed in Chapter 4 (revise pages), but very briefly, shareholders and other members of the external capital market are not as well informed as managers about the opportunities available within firms. This information impactedness which renders capital markets less than perfect[12] is due to informational costs and difficulties (including 'Arrow's paradox'). Managers are not only better informed, they can better assess a diverse range of investment opportunities due to the monitoring and control systems employed by M-form firms. They can, for example, use fiat to transfer resources quickly and at minimum cost from less profitable to more profitable lines of production. The rationale for conglomerate firms, therefore, is the internal capital market. There are of course limitations to the superiority of the internal capital market. Bounds on rationality at the top may result in trade-offs between the breadth and the depth of investment opportunities. Managers may find it easier to acquire a better knowledge of a limited range of alternatives. More seriously perhaps, managers may not be motivated to pursue policies that maximise shareholder wealth. This possibility will be discussed in the section on 'Revenue raising and managerial motives' (pages 347–8); see also Chapter 9.

Risk spreading and other financial advantages

The benefits of spreading risks (or not putting all of one's eggs into the same basket) are commonly believed to contribute to an efficiency motive for diversification. The reasoning is that if diversification reduces risks then shareholders and lenders would be prepared to finance diversified firms at better terms compared with specialised firms. It is indeed statistically correct that the variability and, therefore, the risk of the combined anticipated earnings stream associated with a number of dissimilar productive activities is lower compared with the variability of the anticipated earnings associated with the individual activities. This may well induce managers to diversify but does not mean that diversified firms have an advantage over a group of specialised firms producing the same mix of products, as far as shareholders or lenders to the firm are concerned. Stockholders can achieve the same degree of risk reduction by diversifying their portfolios.

While it is not correct to claim that risk reduction in diversified firms will induce lenders to provide cheaper finance, the possibility of a reduction in the 'risk of default' may bring about this result. So, diversified firms may find it easier to raise debt capital. Lending to a group of specialised firms carries the risk that some of them may default. However, provided that the group of products as a whole is profitable, a diversified firm will not default. In other words, a profitable diversified firm cannot default on debts because losses occurred on a particular line. However, this advantage is counterbalanced once we consider raising equity capital. To the extent that diversified firms pay more interest compared with non diversified firms, profit will be lower and raising new equity capital will be more difficult. Thus, the cost of capital will, on balance, be the same, with more capital coming from debt finance and less via new issues.

Finally, a financial advantage may be derived from information impacted-ness. It is possible that loss of information regarding the performance of individual products might lead lenders and shareholders to over-estimate the expected returns from diversified firms and thus be prepared to provide capital at a lower cost.

Diversified firms may also enjoy tax advantages compared with specialist firms, so that their shares may become more attractive to shareholders. There are several reasons for this. (a) To the extent that diversification leads to more debt finance, the interest payments increase and the tax liability of the firm declines. (b) Given higher debt finance and less equity, as the tax liability declines, the increasing tax savings are distributed among a smaller number of shares. The after-tax profit per share increases. (c) Differential taxation on capital gains tax and dividends can benefit shareholders of diversified firms. If capital gains tax is lower than tax on dividends, shareholders can enjoy more after-tax income if their increase of wealth takes the form of capital gains associated with profit retentions which increase the value of their shares. It may be objected that specialist firms can retain profits. However, diversified firms may have more opportunities for re-investment. As noted above they can shift resources quickly and cheaply to the most profitable lines thus achieving higher returns. To move their capital to the most profitable lines shareholders of specialist firms would need to sell their shares and in the process they will have to pay capital gains tax and any other costs related to the buying and selling of shares. (d) Finally, diversified firms can offset losses of one activity against profits in others thus reducing their overall tax liability.

Revenue raising and managerial motives

Given a firm's size, diversification may be adopted because of its revenue raising potential. Two reasons can be identified for this potential: (a) diversification may be the only feasible way of differentiating products in a way that makes it possible to practice price discrimination and increase total revenue, and (b) demand interdependencies can be dealt with more effectively within a diversified firm. Given demand conditions, the total revenue from a group of products may be lower when they are produced by a number of specialist firms rather than by a diversified firm. The pricing strategy of a diversified firm can take into account any inter-dependencies that exist among the products. For a group of firms to achieve the same revenues requires that each firm anticipates correctly competitors's reactions, which is not normally feasible. Even if firms had an intention to collude, the maximisation of group revenues requires information and its communication among firms regarding the way in which the demand for individual products is affected by changes in the prices of each of the other products. Obtaining and communicating such information is easier within a diversified firm than among a group of firms. Additionally, the improved flexibility of the diversified firm in its resource allocation policy implies that diversification makes it easier for a firm to respond quickly and effectively when demand conditions change.

In addition to cost efficiency and its revenue raising potential, diversification may be induced by managerial objectives and behaviour. As we saw in Chapter 9, Marris's growth model postulates that diversification is the vehicle for a firm's growth and that managers will adopt a growth rate higher than that justified by the maximisation of the value of the firm. This means that diversification will be carried beyond the level indicated by efficiency considerations alone. An additional reason for this is that the opportunity cost of funds invested in the firm will be perceived to be lower by managers than by shareholders. The explanation for this is simple. For managers the opportunity cost of funds will equal the return on marginal projects in the firm rather than the return on the highest yielding investment projects in other firms, which is the opportunity cost as perceived by shareholders. Since managers have a lower discount rate they will tend to invest more in productive activities within the firm than the level required for shareholder welfare maximisation. This will raise the level of investment in horizontal, vertical and diversified expansion. The exact mix may well depend on external factors. If, for example, public policy constraints prevent horizontal and vertical expansion diversification will increase.

Finally, other influences may have a bearing on diversification. It can be argued that the degree of diversification depends on the attributes of the top decision makers and the authority structure of the firm. Thus, it would be more prevalent when those in authority are more likely to perceive new opportunities and have stronger incentives to pursue them.

Diversification and competition

Diversification may enhance the potential for price discrimination and may facilitate a better recognition of interdependencies among products, thus improving a firm's revenue raising potential. The impact on pricing, competition and overall welfare of the resultant policies, however, varies among products and industries and is not easy to assess *a priori*.

Practices commonly adopted by diversified firms which can have a significant impact on pricing and efficiency include the following.

1 *Tie-in sales* This is a contractual arrangement whereby the buyer of one commodity or service A (the tying good) is also required to buy

from the seller of A another good B (the tied good). This practice may aim to facilitate price discrimination on A, since the quantity demanded of B reveals the intensity of need for A. Alternatively the aim may be to make it possible for the seller to extract a higher price for the combined goods when the price of A is regulated. The success of this practice will depend on the price elasticities of the two goods and on whether they are complements or substitutes. Tie-in sales have pricing and allocative effects but their direction cannot be assessed on *a priori* reasoning.

Tie-in sales and other restrictive practices such as 'full-line' strategies (see (5) below) are often reported by the Monopolies and Mergers Commission. Almost half of the thirty-two Monopolies and Mergers Commission industries investigated in 1978 were found to have adopted such practices (Lyons 1988). Among the best known of these are the brewing and the petrol distribution industries.

2 *Cross-subsidisation* This practice refers to the pricing of one product below cost by utilising profits from other products. The aim is usually attributed to an attempt to drive competitors, especially specialised firms, out of the market. This practice will be feasible when re-entry is blocked or when the potential for predatory pricing constitutes a barrier to entry. It can, therefore, have a detrimental effect both on present and potential competition.

3 *Reciprocal dealings* These contractual arrangements require two or more firms to buy from each other alone. They could involve tie-in sales. The aim may be to avoid the market or to attenuate opportunistic behaviour in which case it saves on transaction costs. Thus, there may be potential efficiency gains in such practices although their market power motives should not be under-estimated.

4 *Other effects on competition* Diversification may impact on concentration and oligopolistic interdependence in various ways. For example, *de novo* expansion increases the number of competitors and reduces concentration. On the other hand, diversification by merger may have no impact on the number or the market share distribution of sellers operating in a market and hence on concentration. In both instances the presence of a large diversified firm in the market, however, may have an important influence on oligopolistic interdependence and competitive behaviour. Competition may be enhanced or reduced so that the effect of diversification on price and overall welfare is ambiguous and will vary from case to case.

5 *Effects on potential competition* Diversification may remove a recognised potential entrant into the firm's original market. If the producer of A takes over the producer of good B, who was the recognised potential entrant into market A, then competition in market A will be reduced, especially if B was the only potential entrant. Potential competition may be further reduced for two reasons: first, the loss of

information regarding the profitability of individual products coupled with the potential for cross-subsidisation may discourage entrants, and second, diversification can contribute to a strategy of 'product proliferation' by incumbent firms. This means that incumbents fill the product space in a way that leaves no profitable gaps for new entry (see Chapter 2).

In short, diversification can influence the way competitors interact (conjectural interdependence) to the detriment of existing competition and it can minimise the influence of potential competition. There is indeed some empirical evidence which supports the conclusion that diversification raises barriers to competition because of the potential for predatory pricing and the information loss on the profitability of individual markets (Rhodes 1973). Evidence also points to other reasons for diversification such as political or power motives. One of the reasons why Courtaulds entered the textile industry in the 1960s was a desire to be able to exert political influence to protect the declining UK textile industry.[13]

THE MULTINATIONAL ENTERPRISE

A multinational enterprise (MNE) is a firm which owns and operates production or distribution facilities in at least two countries. MNEs producing the same line of goods or services in different countries are referred to as horizontal MNEs and those producing resources or semi-finished products in one country to supply their facilities in another country are known as vertical MNEs. In either case an MNE is established when a firm (the parent company) creates or acquires a subsidiary in another country (the 'host' country). The parent company acquires control over the foreign facility and any movement of capital from the home to the host country is referred to as foreign direct investment (FDI)[14] to distinguish it from portfolio foreign investment (PFI) which involves either loans to overseas firms or the acquisition of minority (that is non-controlling) shareholdings.

The growth in numbers, size and power of MNEs, over the last three decades or so, has been very extensive. Today over half the world's traded output is conducted by the world's 500 largest MNEs, virtually all of which are based in the USA, Europe and Japan (Rugman and Verbete 1991). This unprecedented growth has stimulated voluminous work enquiring into the reasons for and the economic and political consequences of multinational expansion. The theoretical basis of this work lies in the interface of the theory of the firm, the theory of international trade and international finance. Here, we are mainly concerned with the question of why firms extending their operations beyond national borders do so by establishing subsidiaries rather than by co-operation with local firms or by exporting.

To establish an MNE the parent company usually supplies its subsidiary with assets comprising both tangible (finance, equipment, components, etc.) and intangible (managerial skills, trade secrets, technology, brand names, etc.) assets and retains control of important decision making such as the scale of production, pricing, exports, etc. In brief, the establishment of MNEs involves foreign control of domestic investment. This raises two questions: (a) what induces firms to expand their operations over national borders and (b) what makes foreign firms more successful than domestic firms in acquiring control of certain domestic investment opportunities? In answering the first question one can postulate that growing firms may attempt to expand their operations abroad when faced with limited home markets and impediments to exports. For example, the rising value of the yen in recent years coupled with curbs placed on European imports from Japan are believed to have forced Japanese firms to establish production outlets in Europe (Dunning and Cantwell 1991). The answer to the second question, however, is less straightforward. Since it is reasonable to assume that domestic firms are likely to be more familiar with the local economic, political, social and legal environment, foreign firms must have some other advantages that make them more successful than domestic firms. It is sometimes assumed, for example, that the cost of capital is lower for foreign firms, in which case, given the expected net revenues from an investment asset A, foreign firms will be able to offer higher prices for A compared with domestic firms and FDI will take place. To put it differently, the argument is that imperfections in the international capital market (ICM) induce firms to act as arbitrageurs of capital. Firms in countries with lower interest rates choose to invest where interest rates are high. According to this reasoning, the headquarters of MNEs should be found in countries where the marginal productivity of capital is relatively low.

The ICM imperfections thesis, however, has been challenged both on intuitive and on empirical grounds (Hymer 1976). Intuitively it is more reasonable to assume that ICM imperfections will be corrected by international lending and borrowing rather than by the investment decisions of firms which are more concerned with production and distribution. Besides, the suggestion that the emergence of MNEs may be attributed to differences in the cost of capital among countries contradicts several features of FDI and MNEs.

1 MNEs borrow substantial amounts of capital in the capital markets of their host countries.
2 FDI is concentrated in specific (oligopolistic) industries (cars, electronics, chemicals, petroleum, etc.) over many countries rather than in specific countries over many industries. It is indicative, for example, that, in 1987, almost one-third of all UK inward FDI was by oil companies. Moreover, while 20 per cent of total manufacturing is controlled by MNEs, over 40 per cent of motor vehicles are produced by foreign-owned subsidiaries (Ford, Vauxhall, Nissan).[15]

3 There are substantial cross flows of direct foreign investment. For
example, British MNEs invest in the USA and at the same time US
MNEs invest in Britain.
4 Some investors insist on ownership and control of assets acquired.

A theory of FDI based on differences in the expected net returns from
investment can more readily explain the above observations and the
occurrence of FDI even when there are no differences in the cost of capital.
If a foreign firm expects to earn sufficiently higher net returns compared
with domestic or other firms, it may undertake investment even at a
somewhat higher cost of capital. But why should foreign firms expect
higher returns compared with domestic firms? After all they have to
operate at a distance which implies that there are travel, communication
and other impediments to be overcome while domestic firms have informational advantages deriving from their familiarity with the economic, social,
cultural and legal conditions in the host country. Hymer (1976) suggested
that foreign firms may derive higher returns from investment because they
possess some specific monopolistically owned advantages. If a foreign firm
has such 'specific advantages' over rivals then it is possible that despite the
extra costs involved in operating at a distance, its expected returns may be
higher than those of local rivals. Monopolistically owned advantages may
derive from sources such as superior technology and skilled management,
differentiated products, diversification and international status which give
the MNE better access to markets, economies of scale at one stage of
production which makes it possible that subsidiaries at subsequent stages
can be supplied at better terms than local rivals, and so on. Moreover,
MNEs operate usually in oligopolistic markets which means that they may
have to establish subsidiaries for strategic reasons. That is, they may invest
abroad in order to prevent rivals from gaining an unanticipated advantage
or stealing a potential market. This is known as 'defensive' or 'rivalrous'
FDI.
   In brief, two main reasons for FDI have been identified by Hymer. The
first is a desire to remove competition among enterprises in different
countries (an example of this is discussed in the section on power motives).
The second is attempts by national firms to increase the returns from the
utilisation of their special advantages. This motive is analysed in the
following two sections.

The traditional approach to multinational expansion

Multinational expansion involves investment abroad so that the expected
net returns from the relevant projects are a decisive factor in the decision
to invest. In addition managerial attitudes may have an important bearing
on FDI decisions. Managers may be averse (resistant) to FDI in which case
the expected net returns from investment must be sufficiently high before

such aversion can be overcome. Richardson (1971)[16] has suggested that firms have a 'spatial preference' function which influences their foreign investment decisions through its influence on the expected profitability of investment. A simplified version of Richardson's model is employed here to indicate the traditional approach to MNEs.

For investment abroad to be undertaken its expected rate of return must be at least as high as the firms's 'target rate'. The latter is influenced by managerial spatial preferences and by the extent of the scarcity or abundance of internal resources. The expected profitability of a project will on the other hand depend on the demand for the products it helps to produce and on the costs of production. Since, however, MNEs often operate in oligopolistic markets they have some power in determining the price of their products. The price they expect to be able to charge abroad must be at least as high as the domestic price increased by the amount of transport costs and tariffs; otherwise exports would be more profitable. Given this minimum expected foreign price, the firm's investment criterion is to accept all investment projects whose expected rate of return is at least as high as the target rate of return. The set of all such projects is indicated in Figure 10.6 by the area below curve U which is the firm's investment opportunity curve. U is the locus of all points each of which is associated with a project whose sales volume Q and corresponding average cost AC just achieve the required (target) rate of return. Therefore, any point on the curve, such as a, shows an investment abroad which is just acceptable. U intersects the x axis at point x, which indicates the minimum level of sales below which FDI will not be contemplated whatever the corresponding cost of production. Points above the curve, such as z, indicate investments with expected rates of return lower than the firm's target rate. Such investments are not acceptable. Points below U, such as k, indicate desirable investment opportunities since their expected rate of return is higher than the target rate. Clearly the shape and the position of the curve will determine whether a firm will undertake initial FDI or not. Therefore, the factors which determine U are important determinants of FDI.

The numerical derivation of U and of the determinants of its slope and intercept is undertaken in Appendix 10.1 which shows that both economic and subjective factors are significant. Consider some such factors and their influence on the set of profitable foreign investment opportunities.

1 Managerial 'spatial preference' v. The more averse (resistant) management is to spatial expansion the higher is the required profitability of foreign investment, i.e. the further away x will be located from the origin point. The set of acceptable sales–costs combinations becomes smaller as v increases and the fewer investments will be undertaken. Any factors that reduce managerial resistance to FDI, such as improved communications, reduction in linguistic difficulties, freer flow of information, etc., shift U to the left and increase FDI. A period of exporting may bring about such improvements in knowledge of local conditions in the host

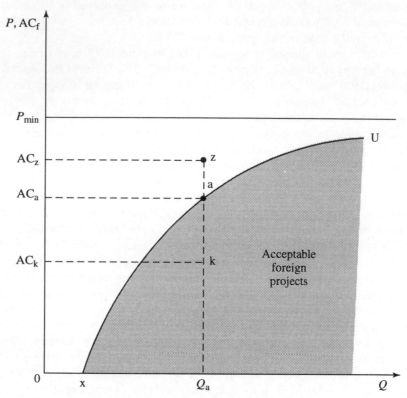

Figure 10.6 The foreign investment opportunity curve

country and reduce managerial resistance to FDI. This may be one of the reasons why in practice FDI is often undertaken after a period of exporting.

2 Given the target rate of return, a higher price abroad improves the expected profitability and acceptability of an investment. An increase in minimum prices which may be brought about by, for example, an increase in tariffs or export costs, shifts the U curve to the left and makes it steeper. Thus, a sufficient increase in tariffs may, for example, overcome managerial resistance to foreign investment.[17]

3 Costs of production. A reduction in costs, *ceteris paribus*, improves the expected profitability of an investment. Graphically a reduction in the foreign cost of production reduces the slope of U and increases the set of acceptable investment opportunities.

4 The size of the market.

5 The availability of spare resources.

Most of the factors traditionally thought to influence FDI are incorporated in this model directly or indirectly. Dynamic influences can also be seen to be consistent with this model, such as Vernon's (1965) life cycle hypothesis which suggests that FDI follows a period of exports from the home to the host country. Exporting improves a firm's familiarity with the host country, its institutions, its culture and its social and legal environment. This familiarity has a dual impact. First, it may help reduce managerial resistance to FDI, and second, it can reduce the cost of operating at a distance.

The transactions cost approach to multinational enterprises

The traditional approach to FDI outlined above has indicated that local cost advantages and impediments to international trade (tariffs, taxes, transport costs, etc.), coupled with the existence of abundant internal resources or 'specific advantages' such as skilled management and technological know-how, will induce firms to overcome any 'spacial preference' (resistance) and undertake foreign investment. This approach, however, fails to explain why firms will choose to establish wholly owned subsidiaries abroad rather than adopt other transactional arrangements such as subcontracting, licensing and joint ventures to transfer their technology or know-how.

In other words, neither favourable cost and demand conditions in the host country (the locational factor) nor the existence of abundant internal resources or 'specific advantages' (the strategic advantage factor) constitute a sufficient condition for FDI. In principle, firms could transfer internal resources or other advantages to the host country in collaboration with local firms. By such collaborations a firm could derive the benefits of expansion while avoiding the extra costs involved in operating at a distance and would, therefore, have 'the best of both worlds'. Indeed subcontracting and licensing arrangements can and do co-exist with FDI; but in most countries (in the early 1980s) licensing accounted for not more than 10 per cent of foreign activity while FDI was over 40 per cent and exporting made up the other 50 per cent (Rugman 1982).

Why does FDI take place in preference to other contractual arrangements? For Hymer the reason is that the transfer of 'specific advantages' involves the market for knowledge which is imperfect. Market imperfections create transaction costs which may favour internalisation of international transactions. In other words, firms expand by establishing foreign subsidiaries when the transaction costs incurred in inter-firm trading (local collaborations) can be reduced by more than the extra cost associated with increased intra-firm co-ordination and operating at a distance (the transaction cost factor). Conversely, co-operation with local firms such as subcontracting and licensing will be preferred to FDI when the costs of forming and managing a foreign subsidiary are higher than the costs of contracting with local firms.

In brief, MNEs will emerge when locational and strategic advantage factors induce firms to operate abroad but the transaction costs of subcontracting, licensing, etc. are relatively high. That is, 'the multinational enterprise and foreign direct investment represent a response to high transaction costs by firms with unique assets/capabilities which have value when utilized in production facilities located in foreign markets' (Teece 1986). But since transaction costs depend on the nature and frequency of the transactions involved, the reasons for the emergence of MNEs will vary according to whether FDI involves vertical or horizontal integration (Teece 1985). Let us consider each separately.

Vertical multinational enterprises

As noted in earlier chapters, asset specificity, uncertainty and externalities are among the attributes of transactions most likely to contribute to market failures and lead to integration. Vertical expansion, especially in the manufacturing sector, is due mainly to asset specificity. That is, vertical expansion commonly occurs when production technology and related cost savings require transaction specific investments. These are assets which are 'dedicated' to a transaction and have a significantly lower value in their next best use. Once such investments are made the market becomes a bilateral monopoly–monopsony in which buyers and sellers have market power. Long-term contracts become difficult to specify, monitor and enforce. Strategic manoeuvring and costly haggling may occur rendering inter-firm transacting inefficient. The aluminium industry is a good example. An alumina refinery once installed can only process a certain kind of bauxite. Bauxite is heavy and of low value which makes transportation costs very high, implying that the refinery must be located near the mine. The refinery investment is a dedicated investment and in the absence of integration can be held hostage to the mine. Post installation a bilateral monopoly situation arises. To protect themselves, traders could consider signing a long-term contract specifying the terms of the exchange, such as the price of the bauxite, for a period extending over the life of the investment. The investment required, however, is very substantial and has a long life. An efficiently sized mine costs one billion dollars and a refinery over half a billion dollars and their life span is 20–5 years. Environmental changes over that time span are both very likely and very difficult to foresee and specify *ex ante*. Contracts running over 20–5 years have to remain incomplete exposing the parties to opportunistic renegotiations (Stuckey 1983). Aluminium firms are therefore integrated. For similar reasons integration is extensive in the copper industry. By contrast, alluvial tin concentrates have a high degree of tin purity and since tin is a semi-precious product it has a high value and therefore a low transportation cost. Moreover, tin concentrates can be handled by any smelter. These two conditions mean that efficient spot markets exist where smelters can buy their inputs and mines sell their product without fear of opportunistic exploitation. Not surprisingly, therefore, integration is very low among the stages of production in this industry. In brief, differences in transaction costs can explain the different expansion patterns among otherwise similar industries. Thus, although economies of scale are significant in smelting aluminium, copper and tin, the supply of these ores is much more integrated in aluminium and copper than in tin production (Casson 1987).

The requirement for transaction specific investments and the associated transaction cost economising is believed to have contributed to the expansion of MNEs during the 1950s and 1960s since the vast bulk of this expansion took place in the manufacturing sector and among R&D intensive industries.

In addition to asset specificity, *externalities* and *uncertainty* regarding product or raw material quality may create transaction costs and induce vertical integration. When buyer uncertainty regarding the quality of a product cannot be reduced contractually, an incentive for backward integration arises (Teece 1983). Firms engaged in consumer marketing where quality control is essential may need to integrate backwards in order to ensure quality control of their goods and services. They then sell to the upper end of the market where the provision of good quality is demanded and higher premiums are paid for guaranteed good quality (Casson, 1982). The need to integrate is re-enforced when poor quality of a product or service in one location is likely to affect adversely a brand name and sales in other locations.

Both externalities and buyer quality uncertainty are believed to have induced integration over national borders in tropical agricultural products such as bananas. There is a limited number of locations where bananas can grow and their production is subject to economies of scale, due mainly to the indivisibilities of the infrastructure (road and rail link). Multinational food distributors have integrated backwards into the growing, shipping and ripening process in order to ensure a standard quality and distribution to their customers at the point of appropriate ripeness. This reduces buyer uncertainty 'to the extent that potential consumers identify the brand name of the MNE as synonymous with a risk-free choice' (Rugman 1982: 17). Uncertainty and externalities may also have contributed to the more recent MNE growth in other consumer product and service industries.

In summary, when international transactions are supported by dedicated assets, vertical FDI allows for the installation of cost saving investment in either upstream or downstream locations abroad with less risk that 'it will be idled by international disputes between enterprises of different nationality facing different incentives' (Teece 1985: 235). In addition externalities and uncertainty regarding product quality may induce VI internationally.

Horizontal multinational enterprises

Horizontal FDI will occur when two requirements are present: (a) 'firm-specific advantages' are due to technological or managerial know-how, which can be utilized in offshore facilities, and (b) inter-firm transacting (licensing, subcontracting, etc.) is inferior to FDI because of both the cost saving and the revenue raising properties of MNEs (Teece 1985).

The existence of a specific advantage is not sufficient for FDI to take place. When, for example, new technology is such that the formula for a chemical compound or the blueprint for a special device or the codes for a computer software is all that is needed for a transfer to take place, a contractual arrangement is quite feasible and more efficient than FDI. When, however, the transfer of technology or know-how involves information which cannot be patented or which is diffused among a number of individuals, each one of whom has only an intuitive understanding of their own contribution to the team effort, a contractual arrangement to transfer information may not be feasible (Williamson 1981). The frequency of the transaction may be a determining factor in this case. If a once and for all transfer is called for it may be quite feasible to send a small team of consultants abroad to carry out the transaction. When the transfer is of a recurring nature this may not be feasible.

As already noted, the difficulties of transferring information are three-fold: (a) a firm wishing to transfer information which can be useful to others cannot easily identify potential buyers, information cannot, for example, be sold by advertising it; (b) even if potential buyers were identified negotiations become very difficult because buyers cannot assess the sellers' claims regarding the quality of information; and (c) disclosure of information is not practical – if buyers were to be provided with all the information necessary to evaluate the know-how offered for sale then they would have acquired the knowledge free of charge.

Such transactional difficulties increase and the incentive to integrate (horizontally) is strengthened as the complexity of know-how to be transferred increases.

Informational rather than technological advantages contribute to horizontal international expansion. Where information asymmetry arises between buyers and sellers, MNEs may emerge to utilise their superior knowledge and internal control systems to ensure quality control and thus reduce buyer uncertainty (Casson 1987). In the consumer servicing sector, for example, the advantage owned by the MNE is an ability to generate sufficient know-how to guarantee a good quality product to consumers. Thus, in the international hotel industry, say, the firm's internal control systems and know-how ensure that the same high quality of service can be maintained internationally. This is important since customers such as business executives travel frequently from country to country so that lower standards in one country may debase the reputation of a firm and reduce bookings in other countries. Externalities, therefore, are important and ensuring a certain quality of service is instrumental in reducing customer uncertainty. To ensure the quality of service some backward integration may also be involved. The hotel industry, for example, is unskilled labour intensive so that maintenance of quality requires efficient management of unskilled labour which many MNEs achieve by training their own managers. In-house training can be the most efficient way of imparting firm-specific knowledge to senior personnel (Dunning and McQueen 1982). It is possible, however, to interpret the practice of vocational training as a method of quality control. Given the significance of external effects and the role of the manager in maintaining quality, the internalisation of training 'may be justified simply in terms of a lack of confidence in managers who have been college-trained or who have just quit jobs with competing firms' (Casson 1982: 39).

In brief, since asset specificity, uncertainty and externalities (particularly relevant in information transfers) imply high transaction costs, MNEs should be expected to be common in (a) industries in which technologically interdependent stages are supported by specific investments, (b) knowledge intensive industries, (c) communication intensive industries and (d) industries characterised by buyer uncertainty regarding product quality. A summary of indicative industries in which the theory predicts multinational expansion is given in Table 10.4.

Power motives for multinational enterprises

When firms possess a 'specific advantage' they have almost by definition some monopoly power and national and international expansion is a result

Table 10.4 Industries predicted by the theory to be dominated by international firms

Industry	Example
Primary	
Perishable agricultural products requiring careful monitoring of product quality	Bananas
	Tobacco
Raw materials whose deposits are geographically concentrated	Oil
	Copper
Manufacturing	
High technology, research intensive industries with intermediate flows of specialist knowledge and skills	Computers
	Pharmaceuticals
Capital intensive industries requiring the services of sophisticated plant and machinery	Earth moving equipment
	Heavy electrical machinery
Services	
Skill, knowledge and communication intensive services	Banking distribution
Location dependent services	Oil services industries

Source: Buckley and Casson 1985: 198

of their attempts to utilise this advantage while maintaining its ownership. Hymer (1976), however, maintains that MNEs may be formed in order to profit from reduced competition among enterprises operating in different countries. The following simple model is utilised by Casson (1987) to illustrate how this may occur.

Consider the case of two monopolists operating in two different countries (A and B) producing and selling a homogeneous product. If each monopolist were to try to profit maximise, independently of the other, each would set a price corresponding to the output where MR = MC. In Figure 10.7 the price in country A would be P_A and sales Q_A while those in country B would be P_B and Q_B respectively. This solution, however, will be stable only if transport costs are prohibitively high or other obstacles to exports and imports exist. Otherwise the solution described cannot be stable for two reasons. First, arbitrageurs may appear buying in country A and selling in country B, destabilising both markets. Second, since the marginal cost of each monopolist is lower than the price prevailing in the other country, each will have an incentive to sell in the other's market. In either case the monopoly prices cannot be sustained.

When entry barriers do not exist, the monopolists may be able to maintain their monopoly prices and profits by arriving at an agreement whereby they refuse to sell to arbitrageurs and they undertake not to export to each other's market. The sum of the profits from the two countries, however, can increase if the monopolists agreed to adopt the joint profit maximising strategy and share the extra profits.

The joint profit maximising output is indicated by Q in Figure 10.7(c). It is located at the intersection of the horizontal summation of the MC curves and the horizontal summation of the MR curves. The production of each firm must be such as to make $MC_A = MC_B$. This condition is necessary to ensure that Q is produced at minimum cost. This cost is denoted by c in Figure 10.7 and the corresponding production in each country is Q_A' and Q_B'. Cost minimisation, however, is a necessary but not a sufficient condition for profit maximisation. Profit maximisation requires that output Q is not only produced at minimum possible cost but it is additionally sold at prices that maximise total revenue. Maximum revenue will be achieved when the marginal revenue is the same in each country and equal to the common marginal cost c. Thus, the price in country A should be set at P_A' so that an output of S_A is sold. The corresponding figures in country B are P_B' and S_B.

In principle joint profit maximisation can be achieved either by an informal collusive agreement or by a formal cartel agreement. An informal agreement may be arrived at in which (a) sales are prohibited to arbitrageurs, (b) production is concentrated in the low-cost country and allows for a certain amount T of imports to the high-cost country, (c) firms undertake not to invade each other's market and (d) a profit sharing agreement is achieved. Such an informal collusive agreement, however, may be

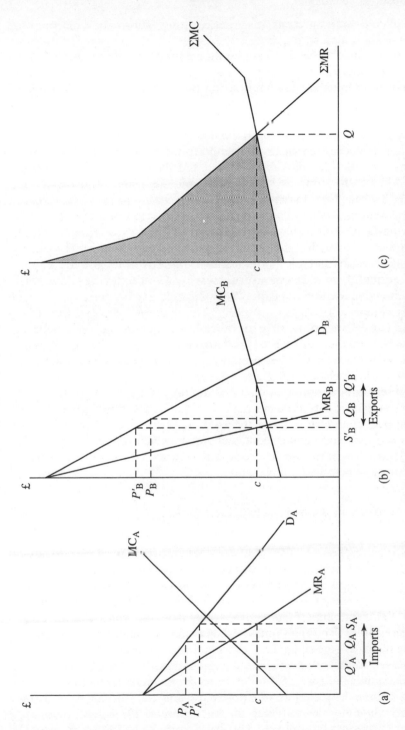

Figure 10.7 An international cartel: (a) monopoly in country A; (b) monopoly in country B; (c) cartel output and profit

Source: Adapted from Casson 1987, Figure 7.2

very difficult to implement in practice since substantial information communication may be required.

A formal cartel agreement may be more effective than an arm's length agreement because it allows for a sales agency (syndicate) to be formed. The firms then minimise the information they need to pass to each other. Having estimated demand and cost conditions the syndicate can offer to buy any quantity produced at a price c thus ensuring that both firms produce at the same marginal cost. To determine the price in each country the syndicate adds on c a mark-up related to the price elasticity of demand thus ensuring that the marginal revenues are the same in both countries. Prices will be the same as before (P_A' and P_B') and total profits are indicated by the shaded area in Figure 10.7.

The weaknesses of cartel agreements were noted in Chapter 8. The most serious one is that firms have an incentive to cheat by offering discounts to large buyers or by invading each other's market. An effective policing system is necessary but not always feasible. Moreover, non-price competition in terms of product innovation, servicing, etc. may develop which makes the administration of cartels very difficult. Finally cartels are illegal in many countries.

When cartels are not feasible an outright merger can achieve the same result and it might also save on monitoring and policing costs. When a merger takes place an MNE is formed. Competition has been avoided and profitability increased.

It is interesting to note that many of the horizontal MNEs of the 1950s and 1960s replaced cartelised markets. This can be attributed to (a) greater political stability which reduced the risks of expropriation, (b) improved communications and management techniques which reduced the costs of MNEs and (c) innovations in product design and diversity which made cartels more expensive to administer.

Joint ventures versus wholly owned subsidiaries

Equity joint ventures (JVs) arise when two or more firms own jointly a particular enterprise or when one firm takes over partial ownership of another firm. As with the establishment of wholly owned subsidiaries, JVs involve internalisation of transactions which can be attributed to transaction cost efficiency but constitute a governance structure distinct to that of an MNE. Firms entering foreign markets have the choice between a JV and a subsidiary. The question then arises as to what conditions induce firms to select to participate in a JV rather than establish a subsidiary.

In answer to this question several explanations have been offered such as (a) economies of scale, (b) a desire to overcome barriers to entry, (c) pooling complementary bits of knowledge and (d) allaying xenophobic reactions when entering a foreign market (Hennart 1988b). All these are, however, necessary but not sufficient conditions for MNEs to prefer a JV to whole ownership. The over-riding explanation is that a JV will be preferred when the transaction costs of this form of expansion are lower than the costs of establishing a wholly owned subsidiary. In other words, a sufficient condition for the development of JVs is that full ownership is associated with higher transaction costs.

Two groups of JVs, scale and link, are distinguished by Hennart. The distinction is based on the sufficient condition for their emergence. Scale JVs arise when firms seek to internalise a failing market but indivisibilities due to scale or scope economies make full ownership of the relevant assets inefficient. Examples are provided by the vertical JVs of the aluminium industry and the drilling consortia in the petroleum industry. In the case of aluminium production, MES are higher in refinery than smelting and fabrication. Forward integration of a mine into refinery and smelting would imply alumina surplus. Since the market for alumina is very thin and inefficient the firm has two choices: (a) invest in downstream facilities of sufficient size, which requires an enormous investment, or (b) establish an alumina JV with partners taking a specified share of output. The second option is common in the aluminium industry. For example, Comalco (a mining company) provides the bauxite to Queensland Alumina which it owns jointly (30.3 per cent of equity) with Kaiser (28.3 per cent), Alcan (21.4 per cent) and PUK (20 per cent).

Link JVs, on the other hand, arise from the simultaneous failure of at least two markets for the services of assets which are firm-specific public goods and where the acquisition of the firm owning them would involve significant management costs. An example is the JV between Dow Chemicals and BASF (German chemical company) by which BASF exploits its proprietary technology in the US market while Dow markets the JV output (i.e. it diversifies).

In brief, transaction cost considerations will determine whether MNEs would prefer to enter a market by establishing a subsidiary or by a JV or some other contractual arrangement. MNEs can be thought of as possessing a set of preferences over the available forms of transacting which can be ranked ordinally. The intensity of these preferences will be dependent on transaction costs and will influence the distance between the ranking of the different options (Gomes-Casseres 1990).

The choice of organisational form, however, will depend not simply on MNE preferences but on possible host government restrictions as well. As Gomes-Casseres put it we can conceptualise two processes. The first determining what the MNE wants and the second what it can get.

Multinational-enterprise–host-country relationships

Host country (HC) governments often treat MNEs differently to national firms by either providing inducements (taxation etc.) or by imposing various restrictions. Thus while firms may prefer to establish a wholly owned subsidiary, a host government may, under political and economic pressures, be more inclined to encourage collaborations with local firms. Thus, whether FDI or some other form of international expansion occurs will depend, at least partly, on the relationship between the MNE and the host government.

The most familiar framework for analysing this dynamic MNE–HC relationship relies on game theoretic bargaining models of a bilateral monopoly nature. On the one hand the MNE has skills, experience, employment, taxation opportunities and access to finance and markets which the host government needs and on the other hand the HC has mineral resources, cheap labour (usually unskilled) and control over taxes and other factors which when combined provide a good investment opportunity for the MNE. These factors set the scene for bargaining. Bargaining skills, political will and power (a gun boat in the harbour) will decide the outcome, i.e. the sharing of the rents associated with the development of natural resources etc.

Transaction cost theory improves on this setting by recognising that bargaining outcomes depend on the advantages of each party which determine the intensity with which it holds its preferences. If, for example, the transaction cost economising properties of whole ownership are very substantial, the intensity of preference for the establishment of a subsidiary may be so strong that the alternative may be no entry at all, rather than entry by JV or other local collaboration.

In reality, barring exceptional situations, both parties may make concessions. The HC may drop its insistence on JVs in collaboration with local firms in exchange for increases in the MNE's contribution to other goals (such as the use of certain local inputs, employment, etc.). The MNE might accept its second best choice (a JV) in exchange for access to a lucrative market.

Transaction cost theory also introduces a dynamic element into the analysis by pointing to what Williamson called 'the fundamental transformation'. With time the advantages of each party may change and recontracting may occur. In the case of expansion supported by specialised investment, the MNE possesses the required specific investment, know-how, etc. and has, prior to the installation, more bargaining power than the host government so that it can achieve favourable terms for the installation. Once the deal has been struck, however, and the investment is sunk the position of the MNE becomes much weaker. The MNE is vulnerable to opportunistic recontracting by the HC because the deployed assets cannot be withdrawn. According to Teece (1986) there is empirical evidence to show that HCs begin to cheat after installation. Few concession agreements in developing countries since the Second World War have remained unaltered and MNEs have been faced with renegotiations, adjustments, surtaxes, backtaxes, recomputations, etc.

The shift in bargaining power is repeated before and after each new major corporate investment. As the HC acquires skills (managerial and production) the skills of the MNE become less indispensable and additionally the HC becomes a more informed bargainer. In brief, the bargaining position of the HC improves over time (copper in Chile is an example) and the MNE threats of no further investment weaken.

Nationalisation is the ultimate risk. After nationalisation it is possible, however, that 'relational contracts' may develop. That is, the nationalised firm may persevere to provide the same services that the subsidiary had provided in the past so that a situation of trust and good business relations may develop which benefit both parties to the exchange. On the other hand hostility and mutual suspicion may develop (Teece suggests that this is the historical evidence). Several devices can be utilised to avoid hostilities.

1 Before investing the MNE may seek an agreement for a systematic divestment with a compensation agreed *ex ante*. To avoid the risk that the MNE may be induced to use a very heavy discounting rate, the HC may post a bond.
2 Hostility may be mitigated when not only the MNE but the HC as well dedicates investments such as roads or electric utilities to support the MNE project. In this case the HC may also require some guarantees against early withdrawal.

The argument of the obsolescence of benefits and the weakening of MNE power, however, varies among industries. Kobrin (1987), for example, who investigated 563 subsidiaries of US firms, concludes that 'although potential shifts in bargaining power cannot be ruled out, manufacturing is not characterized by the inherent, structurally based, and secular obsolescence that is found in natural resource-based industries'.

Empirical evidence

During the 1980s several pieces of research work in support of the bargaining model and the transaction cost theory have appeared. Lecraw (1984), for example, investigated factors that might influence bargaining power and has attempted to relate power to the degree of control that an MNE exercised over its subsidiary. He has suggested that MNEs are often able to reduce their equity shares in response to HC demands provided that they retain control of variables which are critical for investment success.

Kobrin (1987) confirms the existence of conflict between MNEs and the HC and shared gains, with bargaining over their distribution. Gomes-Casseres (1990) has attempted to empirically separate the factors that influence preferences regarding ownership from those that influencing bargaining. He suggests the following. MNEs prefer whole ownership when

1 they have a lot of experience in an industry or country
2 intra-system sales of the subsidiary are large
3 the subsidiary is in a marketing intensive industry.

MNEs prefer JVs when

1 they rely on local inputs or raw materials
2 local firms can contribute skills to a JV
3 they are relatively small (possibly because oligopolistic pressures to expand abroad stretches their organisational capabilities to the limit)
4 increased competition in markets leads to JVs (because of less scope for monopolistic pricing and lower transaction costs).

Finally he suggests that when governments impose ownership restrictions, large firms and those with high intra-system transfers are deterred from entry more than other firms.

SUMMARY

Multi-product and multinational expansion has become a permanent feature of the industrial landscape. Corporate decisions regarding vertical, horizontal and international expansion are examined in this chapter and a variety of influences are shown to have a bearing on the diversity of a firm's operations. A desire to economise on production and transaction costs is emphasised. In particular the following points were argued.

1 Economies of scope or the existence of surplus resources created by technological interdependence or from the development of proprietary knowledge is not a sufficient explanation of VI. Rather, it is transactional difficulties which impede the hiring or subcontracting of surplus resources that lead to vertical expansion.
2 Similarly, when a firm acquires shareable intangible assets such as proprietary knowledge and know-how which are relevant to several products but there are high transaction costs impeding their transfer, horizontal or conglomerate expansion occurs.
3 Firm-specific advantages, locational reasons and impediments to international trade induce firms to consider operating abroad. The choice of establishing a subsidiary in preference to adopting another transactional arrangement such as subcontracting, franchising or licensing, however, is due to transaction costs economising. Thus, the requirement for transaction specific investments, the existence of uncertainty and externalities, coupled with the efficiency of internal production and distribution systems, has contributed to the emergence of MNEs.

While efficiency considerations can undoubtedly influence a firm's vertical and horizontal expansion within and beyond national borders, market power motives cannot always be assumed away. Market power motives usually co-exist with efficiency considerations. Thus, the impact of business vertical or lateral expansion on prices and production will vary depending on the relative strength of the efficiency and market power gains. The net social welfare impact of this trade-off cannot be assessed on *a priori* grounds and must be assessed on a case by case basis. The same ambiguous conclusion applies to multinational expansion. As Buckley (1989) put it, 'The internalisation of markets may be welfare enhancing where efficiency is improved but may be welfare reducing where internal markets reinforce barriers to entry. Careful investigation rather than sweeping generalisation is called for in elucidating welfare effects'.

APPLICATION: VERTICAL INTEGRATION IN THE INTERNATIONAL ALUMINIUM INDUSTRY

Over 80 per cent of the world's bauxite is mined in six countries (Jamaica, Surinam, Guyana, Australia, Guinea and Brazil) and both

Table 10.5 Minimum efficient scale and integration in the aluminium industry

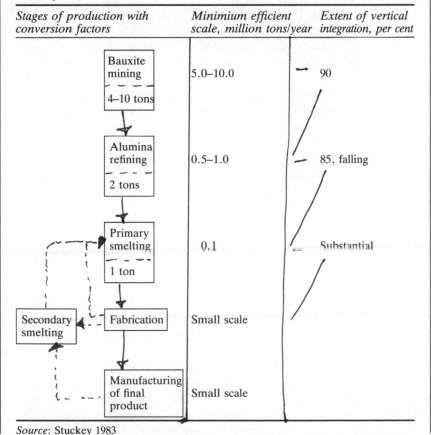

Stages of production with conversion factors	Minimium efficient scale, million tons/year	Extent of vertical integration, per cent
Bauxite mining — 4–10 tons	5.0–10.0	90
Alumina refining — 2 tons	0.5–1.0	85, falling
Primary smelting — 1 ton	0.1	Substantial
Secondary smelting / Fabrication	Small scale	
Manufacturing of final product	Small scale	

Source: Stuckey 1983

mining and processing are dominated by MNEs. The stages of production involved, from the mining of bauxite to the production of aluminium products, are shown in Table 10.5 together with the MES and the extent of VI. The industry is very concentrated. In 1979 the six largest MNEs (Alcoa, Alcan, Reynolds, Kaiser, PUK and Alusuisse) controlled 54.4 per cent of world bauxite, 73.8 per cent of alumina and 62.2 per cent of primary smelting production (Stuckey 1983). Stuckey's empirical evidence indicates that both efficiency and market power motives have played a role in shaping the organisation of the industry.

VI is extensive across the industry. Over 90 per cent of bauxite mined is passed on to the refining stage by internal transfers, 10 per cent of which is quasi-vertical integration (JV). Market trading (10 per cent) is mainly used to dispose of unexpected surpluses and deficits. The integration between alumina and primary production is also extensive at 85 per cent of the total production but there is a tendency of outright integration to be replaced by JV over time. VI is also substantial downstream (between primary smelting and fabric ation). Both the reasons for and the extent of vertical links vary, however, among stages of production. While mining–refining is mainly due to cost savings, an attempt to influence market structure and enhance market power seems to have been a motivating force for integration between alumina and primary producers and is the main reason for integration between primary and fabrication production.

The very high transaction costs which cause the arm's length trade in bauxite to collapse completely are created by asset specificity, informational problems and small-number exchanges due to the following reasons. First, bauxite is a heterogeneous product which requires a taylor-made refinery with specially designed technologies for chemical processing, material handling and waste disposal. Once a refinery is built it can process the bauxite of a particular mine. There is therefore a strong interdependence between refinery and mine which creates a bilateral monopoly situation with all the attendant costs of bargaining, opportunistic behaviour and uncertainty. Second, the wide geographic dispersion of the world's bauxite deposits combined with a small value of bauxite relative to freight creates substantial transportation costs which imply that once a refinery is built there is only one source of supply. This locks in mining and refining and a bilateral monopoly relationship arises. Site specificity is particularly significant in Australia, Guinea and Brazil (which produced 50 per cent of world bauxite in 1979) due to distances and the infrastructure costs involved. Third, even without the effects of VI there are high barriers to entry into bauxite mining and refining. A potential new entrant into refining would need to locate near a good potential supplier of bauxite. But information regarding the quality of mines (size of deposits etc.) is not freely available and can be distorted by opportunistic behaviour. To resolve this information impactedness problem potential entrants need to vertically integrate into exploration and mining. Internal control systems can then ensure that the exploration division is 'honest' in its dealings with other divisions of the firm.

VI between alumina production and primary smelting may also be attributed to 'small-numbers bargaining and financial risks resulting from commodity heterogeneity, transport costs and the technical and spatial specificity of plants that they cause' (Stuckey 1983). But these factors are not so strong as in stage 1 and they are weakening over time especially because of a lessening in product heterogeneity. Sandy alumina is becoming the predominant type of alumina and refineries can substitute aluminas without a great loss of efficiency. Transportation costs are also lower (alumina is more valuable than bauxite). The main cause of market failure at this stage seems to be high concentration on both sides of the market. Some new entry, however, has recently taken place mainly through JV and seems to have reduced the market power of the top six firms.

Market power motives dominate the third stage of production. Integration between smelting and fabrication has the main purpose of supporting a system of non-price rationing as market conditions change while keeping a stable price. Collusive price behaviour implies that non-integrated (independent) firms cannot compete effectively and creates substantial barriers to new entry.

The pattern of integration in the aluminium industry contrasts sharply to that of the tin industry. Integration in tin production is on the whole lower (approximately 60 per cent) with substantial variations among countries. The lower extent of integration has been attributed by Hennart (1988a) to the absence of any efficiency reasons for integration. This is particularly true in the case of the alluvial (low grade ore) sector. The sector is characterised by small-scale non-capital intensive production. Transportation costs are not high and extraction and smelting does not require specific investments. As a result spot market trading is used by miners and smelters.

FURTHER READING

Buckley, P.J. and Casson, M. (eds) (1985) *The Economic Theory of the Multi-national Enterprise: Selected Papers*, London: Macmillan. This is a selection of work previously published by the authors which gives valuable insights into the main aspects of MNEs.

Clarke, R. and McGuinness, T. (eds) (1987) *The Economics of the Firm*, Oxford: Blackwell. Chapters 5, 6 and 7 have adopted a similar approach to multi-product firms as that of this chapter.

Koutsoyiannis, A. (1982) *Non-Price Decisions: The Firm in a Modern Context*, London: Macmillan. This gives a detailed account of the traditional approach to vertical, horizontal and multinational expansion.

Williamson (1975, 1984a) and Teece (1980, 1982, 1983, 1985 and 1986) are some of the original sources of the transaction cost approach to multi-product firm operations.

QUESTIONS

1 'Cost conditions are not the only determinants of the product-structure of firms. Demand conditions can be just as important' (Bailey and Friedlaender 1982). Discuss.

2 'Economies of scope is neither a necessary nor a sufficient condition for vertical integration.' Discuss.

3 Briefly discuss the transactions cost economising motive for vertical integration and explain whether, in the absence of any efficiency gains, VI between a monopolist producer of input A and the whole of the perfectly competitive industry of final product X can have no effect on the price and output of X.

4 What are the likely effects of VI on a firm's price and output level?

5 Discuss motives for horizontal and conglomerate mergers and evaluate their possible impact on market structure and product pricing.

6 A manufacturing firm, the sole producer of product X in the UK, has just decided to expand vertically by taking over all the distributors of their product. The post-merger firm will be organised as an M-form enterprise with two independent divisions, a manufacturing division and a distribution division.

What advice would you give to the Managing Director of the company, who is faced with the following two tasks.

   (a) The establishment of a transfer pricing procedure which would contribute to the autonomy of the two divisions while leading to the adoption of transfer prices consistent with the company's objective to maximise global profits.

   (b) The publication of a report elaborating on and firmly backing the firm's contention that the proposed merger will not be against the interest of the consumers of product X.

7 Critically evaluate the view that VI is either socially desirable or innocuous and should not be discouraged by public policy.

8 'Neither favourable cost and demand conditions in the host country nor the existence of an abundance of firm-specific assets such as brand name, product differentiation, managerial skills or technological know-how constitute a sufficient explanation for the emergence of multinational enterprises.' Discuss.

9 A product X is produced in two countries A and B by a single firm in each country. Assuming that the two monopolists have formed an international cartel explain how the cartel syndicate may determine

   (a) the price of X and its total production
   (b) the volume and flow of exports and imports
   (c) the total joint profits.

Under what circumstances if any would you expect this cartel to be replaced by an MNE?

10 The Orbis Corporation produces its patented power-driven handsaws in Ugbar at a constant marginal cost of £200. A thoroughly researched estimate of the annual demand for these handsaws in Medonia yielded the following estimate:

$$P = £700 - 0.01Q.$$

Transport costs (inclusive of freightage, insurance and the Medonian import tariff) from Ugbar to Medonia is £70 per handsaw.

For a total annual fixed cost of £1.7 million the Orbis Corporation could install a plant in Medonia which would produce its handsaws at the same marginal cost as its plant in Ugbar.

(a) Should the Orbis Corporation export its handsaws from Ugbar to produce them in Medonia?

(b) How would your answer to (a) be affected if the demand for these handsaws in Medonia was increasing over time?

(c) Explain why the Orbis Corporation might successfully compete in the long run with indigenous Medonian producers of power-driven handsaws.

APPENDIX 10.1: A TRADITIONAL MODEL OF MULTINATIONALS

Assuming one time period, the expected total profit of an investment asset A producing output Q can be defined as

$$Z = (P_f - AC_f)Q_f \tag{A10.1}$$

Where P_f is the price in the foreign market, AC_f is the average cost of production and Q_f is the quantity sold. The following is assumed.

1 To invest abroad the level of profit Z should be high enough to give a rate of return r on the firm's internal resources IR which is at least equal to its 'target rate of return'. The latter depends on the firms's scarcity of internal resources and on its managerial 'spatial preference' function v.

2 MNEs operate in oligopolistic markets and provide differentiated products, hence the price P_f charged abroad must be at least as high as P_m where

$$P_m = P_d + EC + T$$

and $\tag{A10.2}$

$$P_d = AC_d + m_d$$

where P_d is the domestic price, AC_d is the domestic average cost, m_d is the profit mark-up, EC denotes export costs and T denotes tariffs.

3 The evaluation of projects depends on profitability adjusted for subjective spatial preferences. In particular,

$$U = Z^v. \tag{A10.3}$$

By substituting equation (A10.1) into (A10.3) we derive

$$U = Z^v = [(P_f - AC_f)Q_f]^v.$$

Rearranging we get

$$U^{*1/v} = (P_f - AC_f)Q_f. \tag{A10.4}$$

It follows from equation (A10.4) that

$$FDI = f(U, v, P_m, AC_f).$$

The firm's investment decision curve is the relationship between AC_f and Q_f that satisfies equation (A10.4), i.e.

$$AC_f = P_m - \frac{U^{1/v}}{Q_f} \tag{A10.5}$$

(see Figure 10.6) The x axis intercept is found by setting $AC_f = 0$ which gives

$$Q_f = \frac{U^{1/v}}{P_m}$$

(This is the quantity that would be produced abroad if there were no costs of production.) The slope of the investment decision function is found by differentiating equation (A10.5):

$$\text{Slope} = \frac{d(AC_f)}{dQ_f} = 0 - \frac{d\,(U^{1/v}/Q_f)}{dQ_f} = -\frac{d(U^{1/v}\,Q_f^{-1})}{dQ_f} = \frac{U^{1/v}}{Q_f^2}.$$

NOTES

1 For original sources see Howe (1978).
2 Non-integrated iron plants appear to have existed in the UK in the 1960s, see British Steel Corporation (1964).
3 For more details of this traditional approach to VI motivation see Koutsoyiannis (1982).
4 Other examples of joint ventures (JVs) include drilling consortia used by integrated oil companies, iron-ore JVs established by steel firms and car component JVs created by car manufacturers (Hennart 1988b).
5 At low levels of asset specificity internalisation would mean that economies of scale are forfeited.
6 The 1:1 proportion assumption is made in order to simplify the graphical exposition. It could easily have been 1:2 or any other relationship.
7 For a mathematical and diagrammatic analysis of this case see Waterson (1984: 83–6).
8 Salinger (1991) shows that when a two-product monopolist merges with one of its suppliers, three possible effects on downstream prices can result: (a) both prices may fall, (b) the integrated good price falls while the other product-price increases, and (c) both prices increase. He concludes that mergers among multi-product monopolies do not necessarily improve welfare.
9 See Roger Clarke (1985: 196).
10 See Roger Clarke (1985) for further details.
11 For more details see Roger Clarke (1985: 202).
12 This claim contradicts the finance literature's assertion that capital markets are efficient.
13 A. Knight, the then president of Courtaulds, is quoted to have explained the acquisition of one-third of the Lancashire textile works as 'necessary to have any prospect of influencing government attitudes about imports'. He also welcomed the entrance of ICI into fibres and textiles because the interests of ICI would coincide with those of Courtaulds in dealing with Whitehall, thus enhancing their potential influence on government policy (Cowling *et al.* 1980).
14 The OECD benchmark definition in 1983 of FDI was 'Direct investment is where the investor holds a lasting interest in an enterprise operating in an economy other than that of the investor, and where the investor has an effective voice in the management of the enterprise' (*Business Trends in British Business*, 29 September 1989: 14).
15 See Nigel M. Healey (1991).
16 See Koutsoyiannis for a similar but more detailed exposition of Richardson's (1971) model.
17 For a rigorous treatment of the impact of tariffs see Horst (1971).

11 Pricing policies of multi-market firms

INTRODUCTION

The managerial implications of a firm's vertical and lateral expansion will be examined in this chapter. The first section considers questions related to intra-firm transactions. As resources pass from one stage of production to the next within a vertically integrated firm, or products are traded between divisions within a multi-product firm, the question arises as to how such internal transfers should be priced. The determination of an 'appropriate' transfer price in different circumstances is examined. This section argues that traditional notions of transfer pricing must be extended to consider how transfer prices can be used as an instrument of resolving the agency problems that arise when internal trading decisions are delegated to divisions. The following section focuses on price and output decisions when a range of products is produced within a diversified firm. It is argued that the principles of single product pricing are inappropriate in the presence of demand or cost interdependencies which commonly arise within diversified firms. The argument is further developed in the following two sections which focus on technologically linked commodities. In particular, decisions related to production and pricing of 'joint products' are examined first and 'peak load' problems arising when products produced by the same resources are subject to demand curves which vary at different time periods peaking at some points (i.e. electricity available in the daytime and at night) are then discussed.

TRANSFER PRICING

A 'transfer price' can be defined as the price of a good or service traded between divisions of a business enterprise. Like any other price, a transfer price can affect the profitability and hence the willingness of divisions to trade with each other and has a bearing on the organisation of a firm's internal trade. When commodities produced by one division of a multi-product firm are used as inputs by another division two questions arise: (a) should trading among divisions be mandated or should general divisional heads (GDHs) independently select their suppliers and their buyers, and (b) provided that internal trade does take place, what is the 'appropriate' transfer price?

When divisions are independent units, as in the M-form organised firms, the price of the transferred commodity becomes very significant since it constitutes a cost to the buying division and a revenue to the selling division. As such, the transfer price has a direct bearing on the profitability of the divisions, the volume of internal trade, the firm's global profitability and the effectiveness of its strategic decisions. Top management, therefore, must ensure that the 'best' transfer price is adopted. What is 'best' or 'optimal', however, depends on the objectives a decision maker pursues so that the existence of divergent interests may create divergence of opinions as to the best transfer price.

If, for example, the aim of the chief executive officer (CEO) of a multidivisional firm is to maximise the overall profitability of the firm while the objective of GDHs is to maximise the profits of their divisions, a divergence of interest may arise and divisional heads may pursue divisional interests to the detriment of the global interests of the firm. Thus, if divisional independence and autonomy requires the CEO to delegate authority to GDHs regarding transfer pricing, it is necessary that any divergence of interests is minimised so that GDHs act in the interest of the firm as a whole.

The relationship between the CEO and GDHs is akin to that between a principal and his or her agents. As explained in Chapter 9, in any agency relationship the principal delegates decision-making authority to the agents and his or her problem is to devise a contract which ensures that self-interest-motivated agents will act in a way consistent with the principal's objectives. To achieve this aim the agency contract must include incentives as well as appropriate monitoring, evaluation and reward systems. In other words, divisional heads delegated with authority to determine the transfer price should be motivated, evaluated and rewarded in a way that ensures their decisions will maximise global profits. However, providing incentives, evaluating performance and rewarding agents involves the principal in monitoring and bonding costs. Such costs may increase when the relationship, as in transfer pricing, involves at least two agents since then the principal–agent relationship can be influenced by perceptions of fairness. 'If agents believe that they are been treated unfairly their incentive may be reduced and they may even work against the interest of the principal' (Eccles 1985: 154).

When transfer pricing is delegated to divisional heads the existence of agency relationships may necessitate modifications to the economically efficient price so as to give incentives, ensure fairness and minimise agency costs. Such modifications have not, so far, been incorporated formally into the economic theory of transfer pricing and it is for this reason that we observe a divergence between theory and practice (Eccles 1985). In this chapter we shall examine the theory of transfer pricing incorporating, wherever possible, examples of practices intended to arrive at transfer prices which serve both efficiency and fairness.

Agency problems apart, optimality in transfer pricing depends on the firm's objectives, the nature of the transferred good, the structure of the markets within which the firm operates, the relevant cost and demand conditions and any demand or cost interdependencies that might exist. The circumstances under which the firm operates, therefore, must be specified before the optimum transfer price can be determined. Following Hirsleifer (1956) the following assumptions can be made.

1 The firm's aim is to maximise profits. The internal organisation is that of an M-form structure with divisions being autonomous and independent profit centres. Each division attempts, therefore, to profit maximise independently of other divisions but it is assumed that it does not attempt to exploit other divisions monopolistically or monopsonistically.
2 Costs of production vary with output in the usual way, but there are no cost interdependencies. That is, the operating cost of each division is independent of the output level of the other divisions.
3 Any demand interdependencies are also assumed away for simplicity. In particular, it is assumed that the internal demand for a resource or a semi-finished product is neither dependent upon nor does it influence the demand from sources external to the firm.
4 All divisions are subject to the same taxation and other legal regulations which may impact on transfer price. The possible influence of import duties are also ignored.
5 The structure of both the intermediate and the final product markets can vary. An external market for the transferred commodity may or may not exist. When it does exist it may be perfectly or imperfectly competitive.

Transfer price when no external market for the transferred commodity exists

When firms undertake vertical integration in order to economise on transaction costs an external market for the transferred commodity may not exist. This is when, e.g. due to substantial asset specificity, certain components are produced for internal use only or when the manufacturing division produces a final product which it sells solely through the distribution division of the firm. If, in these circumstances, divisions are independent and autonomous profit centres the task of determining the transfer price may be delegated to divisional heads. The optimal price can be arrived at whether the price is set by the selling or by the buying division, with the only proviso being that divisions do not exploit each other monopolistically or monopsonistically. Efficiency will then be served when the transfer price is set equal to the marginal cost of the selling division.

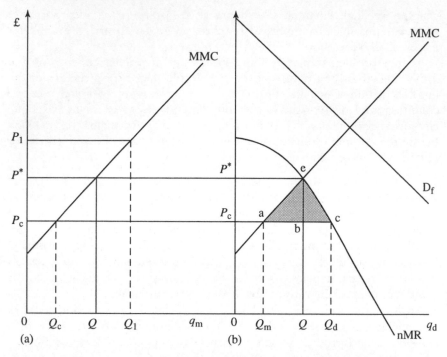

Figure 11.1 Transfer price, with or without an external competitive market for the transferred good: (a) manufacturing division; (b) distribution division

To illustrate, consider Figure 11.1 which shows a firm with two divisions. Division A manufactures product X and division B distributes it to the final consumers. There are no other manufacturers of X. The marginal cost of the manufacturing division is MMC. The consumer demand for X is shown by curve D_f. The marginal cost of the distribution division has been subtracted from the marginal revenue to derive the net marginal revenue (nMR) curve.

In hierarchically organised firms centralised decision making implies that the problem of transfer pricing does not arise. The firm profit maximises by selling output Q determined by the intersection of its marginal production and distribution cost with its marginal revenue. Under decentralised decision making the transfer price will be optimal if it induces the same output Q so that global profitability is maintained whichever division sets the price.

Let us consider whether this is indeed the case when division B sets the transfer price. To calculate the 'appropriate' buying price, B requires information regarding the supply possibilities or intentions of the manufacturing division. It could proceed by asking division A what quantities of X they would be prepared to supply at different prices. To profit maximise division A would wish to produce and supply, at each quoted price, a quantity determined by the intersection of the quoted price (which is the same as the marginal revenue) and the MMC schedule. For example, at P_1 the quantity supplied would be Q_1, at P_c it would be Q_c, etc. It follows that division A's quantity response to alternative quoted prices provides B with information regarding the marginal manufacturing cost. Having received this information, division B should not attempt to exploit division A by restricting purchasing in order to reduce the price. That is, division B should be instructed, or possibly induced, to treat MMC as a marginal cost rather than as an average cost,[1] in which case profit maximisation will be achieved at output Q (Figure 11.1(b)) where MMC = nMR. To secure Q, division B will set the transfer price at P^*. That is, the transfer price will be set equal to marginal manufacturing cost. This is optimal since both global profitability is maximised and divisional autonomy is maintained.

The same result can be obtained when division A determines the transfer price. In this case A requires information regarding the marketing potential of product X. It could proceed by asking division B what quantities of X they would be prepared to buy at different prices. Since the quoted price represents the marginal buying cost of the product, to profit maximise division B will demand such a quantity as to ensure that its net marginal revenue (nMR) is equal to the quoted price. As a result, the information it passes on to the manufacturing division traces the nMR curve. Division A should be instructed or motivated to treat the information received as a marginal revenue rather than as a demand curve. That is, A should not attempt to exploit division B by restricting output in order to raise the price. When the information received is treated as a net marginal revenue, profit maximisation (for division A) occurs where nMR = MMC, i.e. at price P^*.

In brief, when an external market for the transferred commodity does not exit, pricing at marginal production cost is optimal. Provided that internal monitoring of divisions or the provision of incentives discourages the development of bilateral monopoly, the transfer price will be set equal to the marginal cost of production whichever division is responsible for setting the price.

In reality monitoring may compromise the independence of the divisions and the provision of incentives creates further difficulties. Since incentives are usually rewards related to the financial performance of a division, the selling division will most probably insist on a transfer price which includes a profit margin. One way to overcome these problems, commonly adopted in practice, is either by designating the supplying division as a cost centre or by turning it into a quasi-profit centre. The performance of cost centres can then be evaluated by comparing actual costs with standard costs (i.e. engineering estimates of what the minimum unit costs should be for a given technology). On the other hand, when a supplying division is considered as a quasi-profit centre the transfer price usually includes a profit margin.

Transfer price when a perfectly competitive market for the transferred commodity exists

Primary products such as cotton, wool, wheat, etc. and some standardised (non-asset specific) manufacturing products such as nuts and bolts are often traded both internally and in external competitive markets. That is, the buying division of a firm can acquire part or all of their requirements of raw materials or semi-finished products at the competitive price. Similarly, the producing division can sell their output at the competitive price. External buying or selling is made possible without extra costs when divisions are technologically independent and the traded good is neither unique nor asset specific.

When a perfectly competitive external market exists, divisional independence and autonomy imply that (a) the volume of internal trade may diverge from the volume of production, the difference representing external trade, and (b) the profit maximising motive induces divisions to trade at the market price since the buying division will refuse to pay a price higher than the market price while the selling division will refuse to sell at a price lower than the market price. Moreover, global profits are maximised when the transfer price is equal to the market price and any surplus (deficit) production is sold (bought) externally. Thus, in Figure 11.1(b) if the perfectly competitive market price is P_c both divisions can trade any volume at this price. Since the manufacturing division can sell any quantity it wishes at price P_c it will refuse to sell at a lower transfer price. To profit maximise it would produce output Q_m (such that $P_c = $ MMC). Similarly, the distribution division can buy from external sources any quantity of X at price P_c. It would, therefore, refuse to accept a higher than P_c transfer price. To profit maximise it would acquire, for distribution, the quantity Q_d which is determined by the intersection of the combined marginal cost, MDC+P_c, and the marginal revenue. That is, the volume of internal trade would be determined by,

$$\text{MDC} + P_c = \text{MR} \tag{11.1}$$

or

$$P_c = \text{MR} - \text{MDC}.$$

But

$$\text{MR} - \text{MDC} = \text{nMR}$$

thus, in Figure 11.1(b), Q_d is determined at the point where

$$P_c = \text{nMR}. \tag{11.2}$$

Since Q_d is greater than Q_m, a number of $Q_d - Q_m$ units is bought in the external market. It is, of course, possible that, under different demand and cost conditions or at a competitive price higher than P^*, the manufacturing output would be greater than the volume of internal trade in which case the surplus would be sold externally.

In brief, when a competitive external market for the transferred commodity exists divisional and global profit maximisation and organisational efficiency indicate that the transfer price should be the same as the market price.

It should be emphasised that in these circumstances mandating internal trading to the exclusion of external trading would reduce global profitability. To see why consider Figure 11.1 again. In the absence of external trade the production of the manufacturing division must be exactly equal to the quantity taken by the distribution division. As equations (11.1) and (11.2) indicate, the transfer price which will achieve this objective is P^* and the common output is Q. Divisions may then be instructed to produce Q, or to trade at the transfer price P^* which, given the cost structure of Figure 11.1, is higher than the market price. Alternatively, to preserve some divisional autonomy top management may assign the task of the determination of the transfer price to either division while ensuring that the relevant information on costs is passed on. As explained in the previous section, if bilateral monopoly is avoided the pricing division combines the marginal costs and compares them with the marginal revenue of the final product. Consequently the transfer price will be set at P^* and the volume of internal trade will be Q.

However, restricting production to internal transfers, in the presence of a perfectly competitive market, has an adverse effect on the profitability of each division and of the firm as a whole. The manufacturing division produces at a marginal cost higher than the market price, indicating that it is not as efficient as other producers of X. The increased cost of production is passed on to the distribution division in the form of a higher transfer price which increases the price charged to final product consumers. Final product sales may thus suffer, reducing global profitability.

The shaded area in Figure 11.1(b) indicates the reduction in global profits when internal trade is mandated and the competitive price is P_c. Internal trade is Q. Each unit produced in excess of Q, where MMC$=P^*$, makes a negative contribution to profits since its production cost is higher than the cost of buying it at the competitive price. The total reduction in profit is indicated by the area of triangle eab. The area of triangle ebc, on the other hand, indicates the amount of extra profit that division B could have made by acquiring and selling Q_d-Q additional units of X at the market price. Any increase in distributive trade between Q and Q_d would add more to revenues than to costs, making a positive contribution to profits.

The analysis so far suggests that restricting divisional autonomy and disallowing the use of the competitive intermediate market should be avoided. It is possible, however, that such a restriction may be justifiable as part of an overall strategy expected to bring about future benefits sufficient to compensate for the suggested reduction in short-run profit-ability. For example, the decision not to use the external market may be related to an overall strategy aimed either at creating a brand name and enhancing brand loyalty or at preventing independent distributors from debasing the brand image by poor servicing. In either case future demand expansion may be enhanced sufficiently for long-term profitability to improve.

Transfer price when an imperfectly competitive intermediate market exists

The problem of transfer price and the determination of the right balance between internal and external trade become more complicated when an inter-firm market for the transferred commodity exists which is imperfectly competitive. Such a market may exist, for example, when a components division of a car manufacturing firm supplies components to the assembly division of other car manufacturers. In this case the assumption of demand independence may be violated since it is possible that efforts to sell more components to competing manufacturers contributes to their success and expansion of their share of the car market, to the detriment of sales of own cars and a reduced demand for components from the firm's own assembly division. Alternatively, restricting sales and charging a higher price to external firms may improve internal demand. Demand independence will not, however, be an unrealistic assumption if the competing manufacturers service a segregated market, or when a shoe manufacturer sells his or her shoes in the domestic market through independent distributors while the firm's own distribution division is the sole overseas exporter, or when an aluminium producing firm sells aluminium to the firm's own rod and wire making division and externally to the aluminium window making industry.

In these circumstances the firm operates in two independent markets, an internal market and an external market, with different demand elasticities. It is in a position akin to that of a discriminating monopolist. Global profit maximisation may indicate that the price charged to independent buyers is different to and higher than the transfer price. To elaborate, consider Figure 11.2 illustrating a firm whose manufacturing division A can sell its output either to division B for export or to independent local distributors. Both the domestic and the export markets are imperfectly competitive. Figure 11.2(a) illustrates the demand from independent distributors, d, and the corresponding marginal revenue, mr. It is assumed that selling directly to independent distributors involves no costs, so that mr is also the net mr. The demand for exports facing the distribution division is D and the corresponding marginal revenue is MR, shown in Figure 11.2(b). This figure also shows the marginal cost of this division, MDC, and the net marginal revenue nMR, where nMR = MR−MDC. Figure 11.2(c) shows the marginal cost of manufacturing, MMC, and the horizontal sum (mr+nMR) of the two marginal revenue curves.

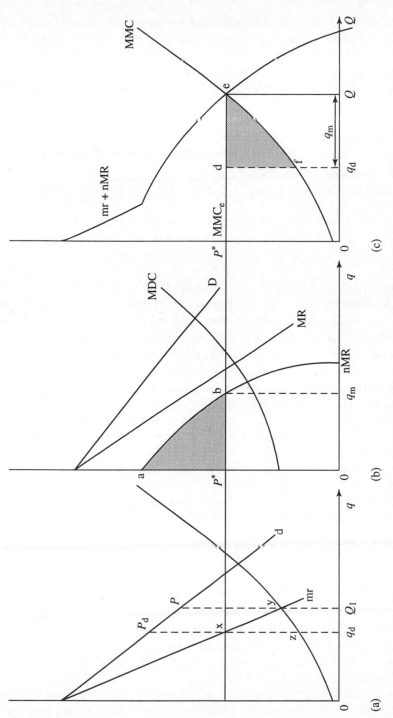

Figure 11.2 Transfer price when an imperfectly competitive intermediate market exists: (a) external market for the intermediate product; (b) distribution division, $nMR = MR - MDC$; (c) manufacturing division, $Q = q_d + q_m$

Global profit maximization requires (a) a total production level such that the sum of the net marginal revenues is equal to MMC, this is achieved at output Q in Figure 11.2(c), and (b) a distribution of Q such as to ensure that the marginal revenue is the same in both markets and equal to the common marginal cost of production; i.e. $\text{mr} = \text{nMR} = \text{MMC}_e$. To find diagrammatically the volumes that satisfy this equal marginal revenue rule the horizontal line through MMC_e is extended to Figures 11.2(b) and 11.2(a). Its intersection with each marginal revenue curve corresponds to the required output. Thus, sales to the external market should be q_d while the volume of internal transfers should be q_m, where $q_d + q_m = Q$. To achieve these volumes of trade the price charged to independent firms should be P_d and the transfer price P^* should be set equal to the marginal manufacturing cost. These are, by the way, the prices that the chief executive of a centrally run (U-form) firm would charge in order to profit maximise assuming that all the relevant information is made available to him or her.

Suppose, however, that the firm has adopted a decentralised internal structure (M-form) and the divisions are independent and autonomous profit centres. The question then arises as to whether the optimum transfer price would be adopted and what internal control mechanisms or assessment and reward systems would induce the divisions to arrive at the optimal solution. If, as is likely, the selling division sets the transfer price, the buying division should be instructed to provide as accurate information as possible regarding the quantities that they would wish to buy for export at alternative transfer prices. Since profit maximisation implies that at any given price the quantity demanded will be that at which the transfer price is equal to net marginal revenue, the buying division will be providing the selling division with an estimate of the net marginal revenue curve. The selling division, therefore, should be instructed that the information received should be treated as a marginal revenue and not as a demand curve. In other words, division A should not attempt to exploit monopolistically division B by restricting sales and charging a monopoly price. In essence, division A is asked to set the transfer price equal to MMC. It should, however, be allowed to determine freely the price charged to independent distributors and the total output Q, even though the volume of Q influences the cost of production and consequently the level of the transfer price. Thus, as each division attempts to profit maximise, the producer division will select the optimum output Q and charge the optimum transfer price P^*. The volume of output taken by the buyer division will be, equal to q_m as before, and the output sold to independent distributors, at price P_d, will be q_d.

It should be clear from Figure 11.2 that, when an intermediate market for the transferred commodity exists which is not perfectly competitive, (a) the price charged to independent distributors (P_d) is higher than the transfer price, its size depending on the price elasticity of d as well as on cost conditions, and (b) under the given demand and cost conditions any other configuration of output and prices would be suboptimal; in particular, should the manufacturing division be instructed not to trade in the external market or were the buying division to select an external source of supply, when spare capacity existed within the firm, total production and global profitability would suffer.

Transfer price and divisional viability

The analysis so far has indicated that divisional profits are subject to the constraint that inter-divisional transfers are based on the correct transfer price and that each division refrains from exploiting the other. It should, therefore, be clear that the contribution made by each division to the profitability of the firm is not limited to the net profitability of that division. Two serious implications follow. First, if divisional managers are to be motivated to act in the best interest of the firm, their performance evaluation and their rewards and incentives should not be based on divisional profitability alone. Second, strategic decisions regarding the closure of a loss making division or the expansion of the operations of a profitable division should not be based on the profits of that division alone. This is because even if a division is making a loss its contribution to the profits of another division may exceed that loss and thereby increase corporate profit.[2]

To illustrate the second implication consider Figure 11.2. The shaded area def in Figure 11.2(c) indicates the gross profit that division A earns from sales to division B. A large part of this profit might be eliminated if division B were to be shut down. Thus, assuming that the gross profit of division B (area abP* in Figure 11.2(b)) is less than its fixed costs, so that there is a net loss, it is still possible that the division is viable and should not be closed down. To assess divisional viability, top management should consider whether the net loss of division B is greater than any reduction in profit that division A might incur if the loss making division were closed down. Suppose, for example, that division B in Figure 11.2 were closed down. The manufacturing division could then sell only to the external market, producing output Q_1 at which mr = MMC (Figure 11.2(a)). Total production is lower and is sold to the external market at price P. The total profit from the external market increases by an amount equal to the area of triangle xyz but the profit which the manufacturing division earned from the internal sales (area def in Figure 11.2(c)) is eliminated. The gross profit of the manufacturing division is reduced by an amount indicated by the difference in areas def and xyz. The decision to close division B would be justified only if the net loss of the distribution division were more than this difference (see also the numerical example in Appendix 11.1).

Qualifying remarks and empirical evidence

The conclusion that transfer price should be set equal to the marginal cost of the producing division, unless a perfectly competitive intermediate market exists in which case the market price should be adopted, was derived assuming demand independence. The market for the intermediary commodity and for the final product may not, however, be entirely independent. An extreme form of demand dependence, termed by Hirshleifer (1956) 'perfect interdependence', exists when the distribution division of the firm sells its product in a perfectly competitive market while the manufacturing division is the sole producer of this product. Since in long-run equilibrium there is no excess profit in a competitive industry, there is no reason in this case for the firm to give preferential treatment to its own distribution subsidiary by charging a lower transfer price. On the contrary such preferential treatment may reduce overall profitability.

Perfect demand dependence, however, is an extreme case. It is more likely that any demand dependence will be less than perfect. Partial demand dependence arises (a) when the product of the distribution subsidiary of the firm is somewhat differentiated from its competitors, or (b) when the manufacturing division is not a sole monopolist but is sharing the market as an oligopolist. When the final and the intermediate markets are partially related an expansion of sales by the firm's subsidiary may cause the demand for the intermediate product from other distributors to decline. In this case, subsidisation of the distribution subsidiary, by lowering the transfer price, may still be beneficial to the firm. Suppose, for example, that the oligopolist suppliers of the intermediate product charge an agreed uniform price. Subsidisation of the distribution subsidiary may reduce the demand from other distributors but this reduction will be shared by the manufacturing division of the firm and its competitors. In general the optimal transfer price, in the case of demand dependencies, will be higher than the marginal cost of the producing division and lower than the price charged to independent distributors.

International transfer pricing should in principle be governed by the general pricing rules outlined above. However, multinationals dealing in various currencies and faced with differential tax and inflation rates may be tempted to use transfer prices strategically. Objectives such as a 'shift' of profits from one country to the other or the evasion of other restrictions and trade regulations may be pursued. Overseas subsidiaries, for example, may charge higher prices for imports from the parent company in order to circumvent any restrictions on the repatriation of profits. Alternatively, lower prices for imports from the parent company may be charged to avoid or reduce import duties in host countries.

The efficiency implications of such behaviour are a subject of debate among economists. Eden (1985), for example, concluded after reviewing the relevant literature that, when external markets either do not exist or function poorly, transfer prices improve global welfare by reducing the inefficiencies created by government interventions which segment the international markets. On the other hand, when international transfer prices are adjusted in response to tax differentials global welfare is reduced.

In short, strategic considerations and circumstances different to those assumed above will result in modifications to the pricing rules indicated. More importantly perhaps, empirical evidence suggests that in practice the economically efficient transfer prices are modified in order to give incentives and to ensure fairness so as to resolve the agency problem that arises in decentralised firms.

Empirical evidence indicates also that both market-based and cost-based transfer prices are used in practice. But cost-based prices are usually determined on a full cost rather than marginal cost basis (Eccles 1985; Al-Eryani *et al.* 1990). While this practice can be attributed to simplicity and objectivity, Eccles presents some evidence supporting the view that 'marginal cost pricing may interfere with the measurement of the selling division performance as a profit center' resulting in serious agency costs whose minimisation may require full cost pricing. Eccles, who investigated thirteen companies (chemicals, electronics, heavy machinery and machinery components), claims that 25–30 per cent of transfer prices are on the basis of full cost and the rest are (a) market prices defined in a variety of ways such as list prices, bid prices or competitors' prices, (market prices may be discounted to account for the fact that marketing, transport and other costs are lower in internal trade) (b) prices calculated on a full-cost plus a profit mark-up, and (c) prices negotiated between divisional heads.

The research by Al-Eryani and his colleagues, however, which is more recent and focused on multinational transfer prices, indicates 'that multinationals systematically used non-market-based transfer prices to reduce custom duties and taxes, and to circumvent government price and capital–profit remittance controls' (p. 411), and that the determination of transfer prices on a cost plus a mark-up basis is very popular among many US and Japanese multinationals. Al-Eryani's investigation of 164 US *Fortune 500* multinational enterprises tends to support the economic theory prediction that in imperfect markets management will use non-market-based transfer prices. However, where legal restrictions such as anti-trust and anti-dumping legislation, tax and custom regulations, etc. are important, US multinationals tend to use market-based transfer prices in an effort to prevent accusations of transfer pricing manipulation. Finally Al-Eryani's research concurs with earlier evidence supporting the claim that the larger a corporation is the more likely it is that it will use some market-based transfer price, possibly because the larger corporations are more visible to governments.

PRICING AND PRODUCTION DECISIONS OF DIVERSIFIED FIRMS

While vertical integration creates transfer pricing problems diversification into related products creates problems of demand and cost interdependences. The existence of market concentricity often implies that the price of one product can affect the sales and/or the price of another product produced by the same firm. Naturally such interactions cannot be ignored when pricing decisions are taken. The decision as to whether the price of one brand of a detergent should be altered will clearly depend partly on the impact that the proposed change may have on the sales of another brand produced by the same firm. Pricing decisions become further complicated when products compete for the use of a firm's limited resources such as managerial and other labour services, warehouse facilities, raw materials, machine time, etc. In the clothing industry, for example, the same resources can be used to produce ladies' wear, men's wear, children's wear or any combination of the three. Given limited resources an expansion in the production of one product line (say ladies' wear) implies restrictions in the output of another product line (men's wear). Charging a higher price for ladies' wear may constitute part of a policy aimed at releasing resources for men's wear. Pricing decisions, therefore, are interwound with decisions about the appropriate output mix.

The implication of such inter-relationships is that in the longer run both the scale of operations (i.e the size or the growth rate of the firm) and the optimum price and product mix need to be decided upon simultaneously.

To complicate matters, technology may be such that the production of one product may necessitate the production of another product. Commodities characterised by such technological links in production are known as 'joint products'. The proportion in which joint products are produced may be fixed or it may be variable, to a limited extent and normally at some expense which further affects the pricing and output decisions of firms. Before analysing such decisions we must examine demand and cost interdependences in more detail.

Demand interdependences

When firms undertake conglomerate diversification they extend their operations into unrelated products, i.e. products with independent demand and cost curves. In this case, the optimum price or output of one product neither will be affected by, nor will it affect, prices or quantities sold of other products. The principles of single-product pricing are applicable in this case. The profit maximising output of each product can be determined by the condition that MR = MC and the price charged will depend on each product's price elasticity of demand. The relationship between demand elasticity and price can be easily established by noting[3] that

$$MR = P(1 - \frac{1}{E_d})$$

and since MR is set equal to MC it follows that

$$MC = P(1 - \frac{1}{E_d})$$

which, by rearranging terms, gives

$$\frac{P - MC}{P} = \frac{1}{E_d}.$$

That is, a product's price will be higher than its marginal cost by an amount inversely dependent on its price elasticity of demand. Moreover, when the marginal cost is approximately equal to the average cost of production, a product's gross profit margin will be determined by its price elasticity.

The prediction that a product's own demand and cost conditions alone determine its price is a direct consequence of the assumption that the firm produces a range of unrelated products. Commonly, however, firms diversify into products (see Table 10.1) related on the demand side or on the production side of the market, or both. Such inter-relationships must be accounted for in pricing and output decisions. In order to focus, however, on demand dependences we begin by assuming no technological interdependences. That is, each product's marginal cost is assumed independent of the marginal cost of other products.

Products, however, may be related in consumption either as substitutes or as complements. The price or output of one product, therefore, will affect the quantity or price of other products sold by the same firm. On the common assumption of negatively inclined demand curves, when the price of a product, say A, increases, its sales fall by an amount dependent on its own price elasticity while the demand for substitute products increases and the demand for complementary products declines. The extent to which the sales of other products are affected by changes in the price of A depends on the cross-price elasticity of demand (see Chapter 7). Thus, a price change of one product will affect not only its own marginal revenue but the marginal revenues of other products as well, with an overall impact on total revenue dependent partly on the price elasticity of demand and partly on the sign and size of the cross-price elasticities. In other words, the overall direction of total revenue change will depend on how strong the product interactions are and on whether a firm's product range consists mainly of substitutes or complements. To arrive at an optimal price and production level all demand inter-relationships must be taken into account.

Assuming that demand elasticity and cross-price elasticities can be estimated a firm's range of optimum prices can then be determined simultaneously. While the formal analysis of this problem[4] goes beyond the scope of this book, it should be intuitively clear that in general when substitute relationships between products are dominant the optimal product price will be higher and the corresponding output lower than when there is no interdependence. When demand interactions are predominantly of a complementary nature a price reduction increases sales of both the product whose price has been reduced and its complementary commodities. The optimal price, therefore, will be lower than it would be in the absence of complementary demand inter-relationships.

Ignoring or neglecting the effects of demand interactions can lead to serious inefficiencies. In decentralised firms, for example, if divisional independence implies that divisions compete with each other so that demand inter-relationships are ignored, global profitability suffers.

Production interdependences

Optimal pricing, in the presence of demand dependences, presupposes that any alterations in production levels are feasible. This assumes that there are no limitations in resource availability and no technological interdependences among products which might inhibit the variation in output proportions. Resources, however, may be limited, especially in the short run. Moreover, several products may share the same limited resources so that increasing the output of one product may be possible only if the production of another product is reduced, in which case the problem of choosing an 'appropriate' output mix arises. This choice clearly depends on the range of products that the firm can produce given its limited resources, the available technology and its expertise and know-how. The production possibilities available can be described by what economists call a 'production possibility curve' or a 'production transformation curve' (PTC). From among the possible combinations of products described as feasible by the production possibility curve a single choice must be made each time period. This optimum choice will be affected by demand conditions and business objectives. Thus, assuming profit maximisation and given the production transformation curve the output mix which maximises expected revenues will be optimal.

The production transformation curve

The production possibilities of a fictitious firm are illustrated in Figure 11.3. Two products, X and Y, are assumed for simplicity. The set of all possible output combinations produced when all the resources are used fully and efficiently lies on curve FF, known as the production transformation curve (PTC) or the production possibility frontier. Curve FF is concave to the origin, to indicate that the resources available are not equally well suited to the production of the two products.[5] This means that to produce more of one product progressively more of the other product

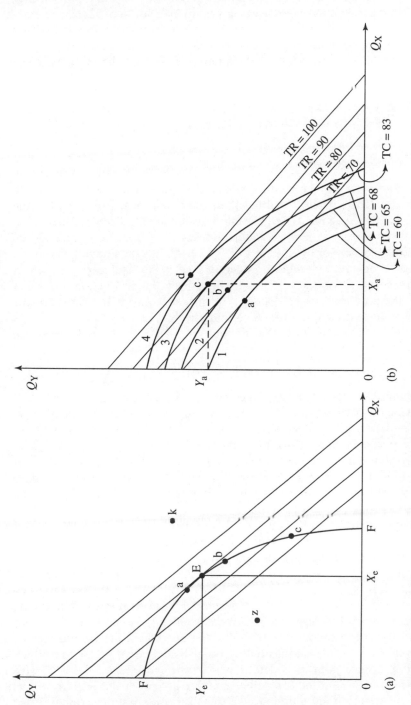

Figure 11.3 Scale of operation and output mix in perfectly competitive markets: in part (b) profit at a is 10, profit at b is 15, profit at c is 22 and profit at d is 17

must be given up. For example, a move from point a to b in Figure 11.3(a) indicates that one unit of Y must be given up in order to produce one extra unit of X, but a further unit expansion in X production requires a two unit reduction in Y production (move from b to c).[6] The rate at which products can be substituted (in production) is indicated by the shape of the PTC. At the margin the rate of product transformation is the same as the slope of the PTC at a point and is known as the marginal rate of transformation (MRT). The MRT_{XY} refers to products X and Y and is equal to the ratio of the marginal costs of the two products, i.e.

$$MRT_{XY} = \frac{MC_X}{MC_Y} .$$

All points on the production possibility curve (or frontier) indicate technically efficient and feasible output combinations. Points within the PTC boundary, such as z, are feasible but inefficient. They are inefficient since they represent output combinations which either do not use all the available resources or use them inefficiently.[7] Points outside the boundary, such as k, indicate infeasible production levels. The optimum output mix must therefore lie on the boundary. Thus, given the production possibility curve, the only managerial decision, in the short run, is the choice of the optimum output mix. In the long run, however, the scale of a firm's operations can be altered so that the optimum PTC must also be selected.

Choice of output mix in the short run

Given the PTC the selection of the profit maximising output mix requires that demand conditions must be considered. To simplify the analysis we assume that product demands are independent and to begin with we assume perfectly competitive markets.

Since all points on the boundary utilise the same resources they all refer to the same total cost of production, which implies that to profit maximise management must select the product combination which maximises total revenue. To identify this combination, revenues corresponding to alternative output mixes must be considered. In Figure 11.3(a) the combinations of X and Y which give the same total revenue at the prevailing market prices are represented by a straight line, called an 'iso-revenue' line.[8] A set of iso-revenue lines, each corresponding to a different level of total revenue, has been drawn. Since $TR = P_xX + P_yY$ the slope of the iso-revenue line is equal to $-P_x/P_y$. Iso-revenue lines further away from the origin correspond to higher levels of total revenue. Therefore, the profit maximising combination of X and Y is the one which lies on the highest iso-revenue line. This is indicated by point E and corresponds to outputs X_e and Y_e. Since point E is determined by the tangency of the PTC with an iso-revenue line it indicates that X and Y are produced in proportions which ensure that their marginal rate of substitution is equal to their price ratio. At point E, the MRT_{XY} is equal to the slope of the iso-revenue line. In other words, the profit maximising output configuration depends partly on the MRT and partly on relative product prices. It follows that any change which affects the shape or the position of the PTC and/or any price changes which alter the slope of the iso-revenue curves will affect the optimum output mix.

Scale of operation and output mix

In time resource availability may increase or decline, so that the assumption of a given PTC can only be valid in the short run. If technology and relative marginal costs also change over time then both the position and the shape of the PTC will change. Thus, in the long run the firm's scale of operations as well as the appropriate output mix must be selected. In Figure 11.3(b) each possible scale of operation is represented by a different PTC. Since each PTC refers to a different amount of resources, each represents a different total cost. Given the market prices the tangency between each PTC to the highest iso-revenue line determines the optimum output mix corresponding to each alternative amount of resources. The corresponding total cost, total revenue and total profit are also determined. The set of all feasible configurations of production levels, each corresponding to a different firm size, can therefore be determined. Figure 11.3(b) illustrates four such configurations. The long-run profit maximising output mix is shown to be X_a and Y_a, and the scale of operation is represented by PTC curve 3.

Pricing and choice of output mix in imperfect markets

When the assumption of perfect competition is relaxed, the firm is faced with negatively inclined demand curves which imply that the level of output affects price and the choice of the optimum output mix must be made simultaneously with the pricing decisions. Assuming two products X and Y with independent demand curves, the determination of the optimum output mix and price levels is illustrated in Figure 11.4. Quadrants 1 and 2 trace the demand and MR curves of X and Y (the demand and MR curve for Y are reflected in the *y* axis). Quadrant 3 contains a 45° line to transfer the quantity of Y to the fourth quadrant which contains two product transformation curves and the equal marginal revenue line MM.

As discussed earlier, profit maximisation occurs at that point on the PTC at which the price ratio is equal to the MRT_{XY}, i.e. where the following condition holds:

$$- \frac{P_X}{P_Y} = \frac{dQ_Y}{dQ_X} \text{ or } P_X dQ_X = P_Y dQ_Y.$$

But $P_X(dQ_X)$ is the marginal revenue of product X (MR_X) and $P_Y(dQ_Y)$ denotes the marginal revenue of product Y (MR_Y). Therefore, optimum

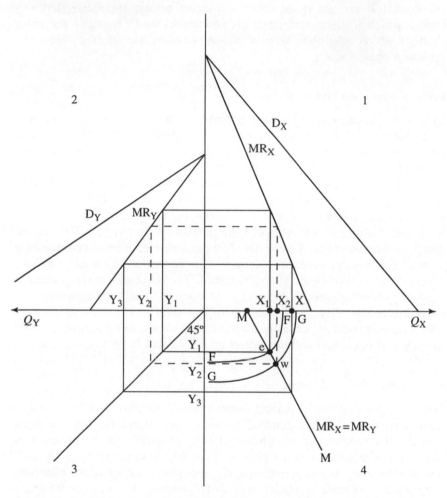

Figure 11.4 Pricing and output mix in imperfect markets

production is achieved at that point on the PTC at which the marginal revenues of the two products are equal.

The profit maximising requirement that marginal revenues must be equal for all products, known as the equal marginal revenue rule, should be intuitively clear. For suppose that the rule is violated, so that $MR_X > MR_Y$. Total profit can increase by a marginal reallocation of resources away from product Y and towards product X since total revenue would increase while total cost would remain the same. In quadrant 4 of Figure 11.4, all the output combinations which satisfy the equal marginal revenue rule are indicated by curve MM. Assuming that a full and efficient utilization of existing resources, with the given technology, implies the production possibilities represented by the curve labelled FF, point e, located at the intersection of line MM and curve FF, shows the optimum output mix (X_1 and Y_1). This mix is unique since any other points on MM are either inefficient (located inside the FF curve) or infeasible (located outside the boundary) in the short run.

In the long run the curve FF may shift outwards to, say, curve GG. In this case assuming that demand conditions remain the same the optimum output mix corresponding to the larger scale of operations is indicated by point w. A move from e to w represents an expansion in the scale of operation the desirability of which must be evaluated before the decision is implemented. A profit maximiser, for example, should compare the profitability at w with that at e before the expansion in resources involved is decided upon.

JOINT PRODUCTS

The PTC depicted in Figure 11.3(a) refers to products which are technically related in the sense that they can be produced from the same resources. Strictly speaking, however, there is no jointness in output since, as inspection of Figure 11.3 shows, all the available resources could be devoted to the production of either X or Y so that the production of one product does not necessitate the production of the other. The term 'joint products' refers to products which are technologically linked to each other in such a way that it is not possible to produce some quantity of one and none of the other(s). A classic example is that of cow hides and beef or wool and mutton. The production of beef necessarily means the production of cow hides and although the quantity of beef produced per cow may be increased by appropriate feeding and breeding methods it is not possible to produce beef without cow hides whether a market for hides exists or not. If a market for a joint product (hides) exists but its value is small compared with the value of the other product (beef), the less valuable product is called a by-product. When there are no appreciable differences in their values the joint products are referred to as co-products.

Provided that both (or all) joint products can be traded the problem of determining their optimal price and output (or sales) levels arises. Production interdependencies, similarly to demand interdependencies, imply that single-product pricing will not be efficient. Decisions on price or output of one product affect – via the jointness in production and costs – the output level and hence the price of its joint products. Any attempt to arrive at an optimal price without considering all the product linkages is likely to be suboptimal. This is because single-product pricing requires an allocation of the joint costs of production. As several authors have indicated,[9] however, the allocation of joint costs on some technical grounds is arbitrary and hence inefficient. *Optimal joint product pricing requires that the level of a number of decision variables is arrived at simultaneously.* That is, when considering a change in the output or price of one product it is necessary to consider not only the concomitant change in the marginal revenue and cost of this product but any changes in the marginal revenues and costs of its by-products and co-products. To profit maximise, a firm must choose that level of joint output which maximises the difference between total revenues and total costs. That is, the necessary condition for global profit maximisation is

$$\Sigma MR_i = \Sigma MC_i \qquad (11.3)$$

where $i = 1, 2, 3, \ldots, n$. Assuming only two joint products with joint marginal cost JMC and no other costs of further processing or distribution of either product, equation (11.3) becomes

$$MR_1 + MR_2 = JMC \qquad (11.4)$$

which gives

$$MR_1 = JMC - MR_2 = MOC_1 \qquad (11.5)$$

$$MR_2 = JMC - MR_1 = MOC_2. \qquad (11.6)$$

Where MOC denotes the marginal opportunity cost of each product. Not surprisingly, the profit maximising output of each joint product is that output at which marginal revenue is equal to marginal opportunity cost. This opportunity cost is not known, however, and cannot be calculated without reference to the demand curves for the two products. The reason, therefore, why an optimal allocation of the joint marginal cost is not possible on technical grounds alone is that the marginal opportunity cost of each joint product depends on the marginal revenues of the other product(s).[10]

In brief, the general principle for the identification of the optimum level of a firm's production (or pricing) is that the net effect of a marginal change in the level of output (or price) of any joint product on the level of the firm's profit (or other objective function) must be zero. To illustrate we shall examine pricing of joint products in the cases of fixed and variable output proportions.

Pricing of joint products produced in fixed proportions

When joint products A and B are produced in fixed proportions (A:B = k where k is constant) the analysis of a single product can be applied to determine the optimum output of a composite unit consisting of k units of A and 1 unit of B. Given the demand curves the prices of A and B are determined. Assuming independent demand curves the solution can be illustrated with the help of Figure 11.5. The demand curves of the two products are D_A and D_B and the corresponding marginal revenues are MR_A and MR_B. Product B is the by-product. The joint marginal cost of production is denoted by JMC. Curve MR denotes the vertical sum of the

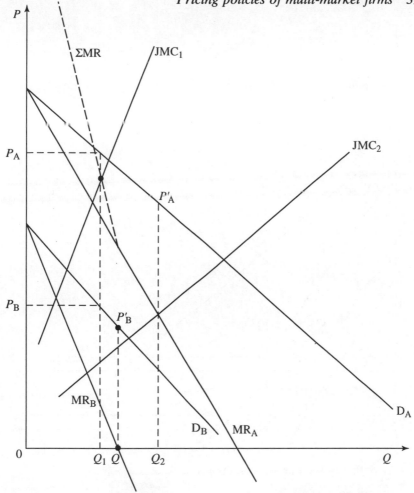

Figure 11.5 Joint products (fixed proportions) with independent demand curves

marginal revenues. The vertical axis denotes units of the composite output which are the same as units of each product when k is 1. For $k > 1$ the demand and marginal revenue of one product must be expressed in units of the other. Profit maximisation is achieved when output is Q_1 since then $\Sigma MR = JMC$. The corresponding prices are P_A and P_B.

The pricing policy should be modified when the composite output is higher than Q at which level the marginal revenue of product B becomes negative.[11] Thus, if JMC happened to be lower, say JMC_2, the optimum production would be Q_2. The price of product A should be P_A'. However, the optimum price of product B is the sales maximising price (P_B') which corresponds to output Q. To sell the entire output of B would reduce total revenue, while the cost remains the same, resulting in lower profits. Output $Q - Q_2$ should not, therefore, be traded. Disposing of unwanted

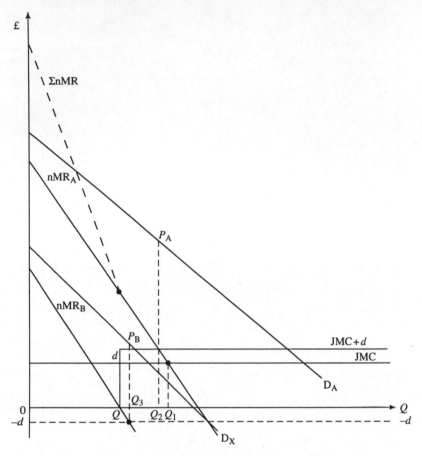

Figure 11.6 Pricing joint products in the presence of disposal costs

output is not only wasteful of production resources (in a world where poverty is widespread), it is also likely to incur disposal costs. The presence of disposal, or any other, costs requires modifications to the optimal production plan. To illustrate consider Figure 11.6.

Assume that excess production is disposed of at a cost of £d per unit. This means that the marginal cost of output higher than Q becomes JMC + d. It is also possible that each of the two products requires further processing and/or different marketing costs. In Figure 11.6 such 'private' marginal costs have been subtracted from the marginal revenue of each product and the net marginal revenues are illustrated. Equation (11.3) therefore is satisfied when

$$nMR_A + nMR_B = JMC.$$

But $nMR_B = -d$, therefore,

$$nMR_A + (-d) = JMC$$

or

$$nMR_A = JMC + d.$$

This is achieved at output Q_2 which denotes the optimum production level in these circumstances. The corresponding price for product A is P_A. The optimum price for product B is P_B, corresponding to output level Q_3 at which nMR_B is equal to $- d$. In short the presence of disposal costs not only induces a lowering in overall production (Q_1 to Q_2), it also induces the firm to sell more of this output (sales of B increase from Q to Q_3) so that the amount of dumping or disposal is minimized ($Q_3 - Q_2$).

Pricing of joint products produced in variable proportions

The case of joint products produced in fixed proportions (which has received more attention in the literature) is not the most useful from the point of view of its practical applications; this is for two reasons.

1 Management commonly attempt to alter the proportions in which joint products are produced in response to prevailing market conditions.
2 Even if proportions are fixed the optimum production and sales levels may diverge in which case the presence of disposal costs influences both the optimal production and price levels.

Joint products are usually produced in proportions which can be varied to a certain extent. Breeders, for example, can increase the quantity of beef produced per cattle raised or the proportion of wool and mutton produced by modifying the breeding and feeding methods they use. When proportions can be varied the firm will have to decide not only the optimum level of the composite output (size of the herd) but the optimum proportions of the joint products as well (more beef per hide). Moreover, costs may also vary not only according to the volume of the composite output (size of herd) but according to the relative outputs of the joint products. The production of more gasoline and less paraffin from a given volume of crude oil will require a better quality crude or a more expensive processing method.

To begin with let us assume that output proportions can vary and that the cost of production depends on the volume of the composite output but is invariant to the output proportions. An example often quoted is the production of different grades of lumber from a log or different sizes of bottles from the same raw material. Average and marginal cost may increase as the quantity of logs (or glass) to be processed increases, but the choice of different lumber grades (or bottle sizes) has no impact on costs. When, as in both these examples, output proportions can be altered without additional expense and to an extent associated with zero output for any joint product, jointness in production is more apparent than real. The assumption that output proportions can vary continuously and that the output of any product can be zero simply means that production interdependencies can be overcome. The possibility of zero output disposes of the technological interdependence which characterises joint products. The analysis of production and pricing decisions developed in the previous paragraph applies in this case and need not be repeated here.[12]

True jointness in production means that output proportions can vary but only within limits and at some expense. As already mentioned the quantity of beef per cattle can be varied but there is no possibility of producing beef without cow hides. Similar considerations apply to the distillation of crude oil which gives refinery gas, gasoline, kerosene, diesel oil and a residue. Different grades of crude oil contain these products in different proportions; the gasoline content of crude oil varies from 15 to 30 per cent. The quantity of gasoline produced, from a given quantity of crude, can increase compared with other products by either mixing crudes or by converting other components to gasoline by a method called cracking. Moreover, low grade gasoline can be converted to a high grade fuel by a method called 'reforming' (Hill and Holman 1987). Mixing crudes, cracking or reforming can increase the gasoline output, although at some expense, but cannot totally eliminate the production of residual products.

The optimal pricing of joint products produced in variable proportions is illustrated in Figure 11.7. We assume that two joint products, A and B, can be produced in two different output proportions so that the joint output can consist of either 1 unit of each product ($Q_A = Q_B$) or of 1 unit of A and 2 units of B ($Q_B = 2Q_A$). The horizontal axis denotes units of output when output proportions are equal. In this case the demand and marginal revenue curves for the two products are denoted as AA, MR_A and BB, BB' respectively. The joint marginal cost of production is JMC. The change in output proportions to $Q_B = 2Q_A$ indicates that relatively less of the main product and more of the by-product is produced. This may economise on production costs so that the joint marginal cost of production is lower at JMC'. When output proportions are not equal the demand and marginal revenue curve of one product must be expressed in terms of units of the other if the same diagram is to be used. Thus, B's demand curve and marginal revenue are now denoted as BB' and BC[13]. The vertical sum of the marginal revenues in each case is also given.

When output proportions are 1:2 the optimum combined level of output is Q^* as defined by the intersection of JMC' and curve MR_A+BC. Production of A is Q^* and that of B is twice as much ($2Q^*$). The quantity to be sold of B, indicated by point Q, is equal to $2Q$ since Q denotes units of A. The optimal prices consistent with this sales plan are P_A and P_B.

When output proportions are 1:1 the optimum production level is Q^{**}, indicated by the intersection of JMC and curve MR_A+BB'. Thus the output of A is Q^{**} and that of B is $2Q^{**}$. However, sales of B will be at R (where sales revenue is maximised) which is equal to $2Q$. The

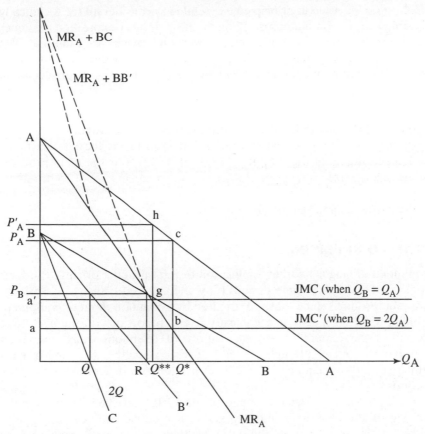

Figure 11.7 Pricing of two joint products when output proportions vary

corresponding prices are P_A' and P_B. The price of B remains the same but its overall production is lower so that the quantity of B to be disposed of has been reduced.

Having identified the optimum strategy under different output proportions, the overall optimum output/price combination can be deduced by comparing the gross profits in each case. Assuming that fixed costs are the same whatever the output proportions and since the revenue from product B is the same in both instances we need only consider the gross profit from product A. Now, when output proportions are equal the total gross profit (ignoring revenue from B sales) is indicated by area $a'ghP_A'$ while the profit when output proportions are 1:2 is $abcP_A > a'ghP_A'$. The optimum output proportion, therefore, is 1:2. Presumably, in this example changing the output proportions in favour of A (1:1) does not generate a sufficiently higher revenue to compensate for the required increase in JMC. The optimum choice, however, could be reversed by the presence of sufficiently high disposal costs.

The analysis could in principle be extended to consider all the technically feasible output combinations although the graphical exposition becomes more cumbersome the more alternatives one wishes to examine. The implications of this analysis, however, are generally valid. That is, given negatively sloping independent demand curves for the joint products the optimum output mix, sales volumes and corresponding prices will depend on the following factors:

1 the rate of increase in costs as output proportions change;
2 the price elasticity of demand for the main product; the less elastic its demand the more the output proportions will favour the main product;
3 the relative size of the price elasticities of demand in case of co-products; and
4 the existence and size of disposal costs.

PEAK LOAD PRICING

Peak load pricing is another application of joint product pricing. Products consumed at different time periods (day and night say), such as electricity, are joint products since they are supplied by a common input of equipment which provides capacity in technically fixed proportions during each time period. Other examples are the supply of telephone calls, television programmes, etc. Although capacity provision may be the same in each time period its demand and hence its utilisation may differ among the time periods.

Peak load pricing was developed in the 1950s and 1960s to analyse the pricing of the electricity industry and other public utilities which were either nationalised (as in the UK) or their prices were regulated by government (as in the USA). The assumption therefore employed was that the aim of the enterprise is to maximize social welfare rather than to profit maximise. Not surprisingly, the principles of joint product pricing of the previous section, although still applicable, indicate somewhat different pricing rules.

A well-known result of welfare economics is that, when perfectly competitive pricing prevails in the economy, to maximise social welfare an enterprise must set the product price equal to marginal cost. In the case of joint production, i.e. when the same capacity can sequentially supply a peak and an off-peak demand, social welfare maximisation requires that the total revenue from a group of joint products equals the group's marginal cost of production. That is, equation (11.3) must be replaced by

$$\Sigma P_i = \Sigma MC_i \tag{11.7}$$

where $i = 1,2,3, \ldots, n$, and n is the number of subperiods considered, and ΣMC is the joint cost of production JMC. The proper marginal cost concept to be utilised is the marginal opportunity cost (MOC) of production in each time period (each joint product). This is derived from equation (11.7) as follows:

$$P_j = \text{JMC} - P_{i-j}. \tag{11.8}$$

In the case of two time periods, a peak one and an off-peak one, this condition gives

$$P_p - \text{JMC} = P_o = \text{MOC}_p \tag{11.9}$$
$$P_o = \text{JMC} - P_p = \text{MOC}_o \tag{11.10}$$

where P_p and P_o are the peak and the off-peak period prices respectively.

Equations (11.9) and (11.10) are a modification of equations (11.5) and (11.6) which reflects the assumption that a different objective function prevails. They indicate that the marginal opportunity cost in each time period is equal to the joint cost of production reduced by the price of the output produced in the other time period. These equilibrium conditions were derived on the assumption that the only cost of production is the common cost. This is a simplifying assumption. Clearly it is likely that in each time period there exist other additional costs. If marginal operating costs exist in any time period they should be deducted from the corresponding demand curve to arrive at a net demand for the joint resources.

To illustrate graphically we assume in Figure 11.8 two time periods of equal length. The demands in the two time periods are different and completely independent. That is, a low price in the off-peak period will not affect the demand in the peak period and vice versa. D_p denotes the peak demand and D_o the off-peak demand.

It has been assumed that the capacity of the equipment (plant) can vary continuously prior to installation (different capacity generators exist) but is fixed after installation. The cost of installing a plant varies in proportion to its capacity, so that the marginal capacity cost per unit of output is constant at £b. Thus b is the JMC of production. The total operating cost is proportional to output in each time period, so that the marginal operating cost is £c.

The question is what prices to charge in each time period and what size plant to install so as to maximise welfare. Subtracting the operating cost from each period's demand curve gives the net demand for capacity d_1 and d_2 also called the effective demand for capacity. That is,

$$d_1 = P_p - c$$

and

$$d_2 = P_o - c.$$

The optimum plant size is that with capacity Q, at which the sum of the effective demand for capacity is equal to the joint marginal cost of capacity. That is, Q is determined by condition (11.7) such that

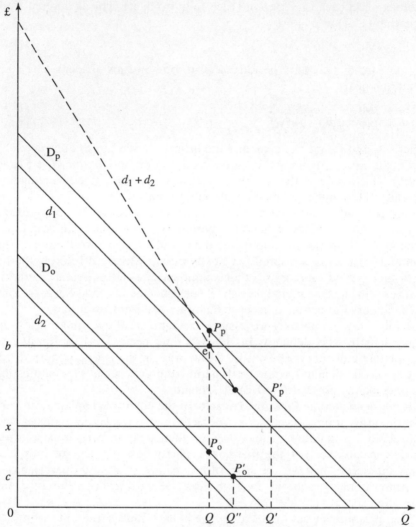

Figure 11.8 Peak load pricing (assuming different capacity cost and variable plant size): $P_p + P_o = 2c + b$ and $P_p' + P_o' = 2c + x$

$$d_1 + d_2 = b$$

or

$$P_p - c + P_o - c = b,$$

i.e.

$$P_p + P_o = 2c + b$$

which gives

$$P_p = b + 2c - P_o$$
$$P_o = b + 2c - P_p$$

where P_p and P_o are the optimum prices. Each is equal to the marginal opportunity cost of the time period it refers to as defined by conditions (11.9) and (11.10). Each is equal to the marginal opportunity cost which as already mentioned could not be defined without reference to the market value of the other joint products.

Finally when demand conditions are such that capacity is not fully utilised in the off-peak period, the proper marginal opportunity cost of the off-peak period is equal to the marginal operating cost. Since off-peak consumption, at the margin, makes no demand on capacity, the full marginal capacity cost is borne by the peak time consumers. To illustrate, assume that the marginal capacity cost is £x. The optimal plant size is now $Q'>Q$. Demand in the off-peak period is so low that attempting to produce at full capacity (sell Q') would result in a price insufficient to cover its marginal operating cost.[14] This is not optimal. Off-peak price must be set equal to its marginal operating cost which, in this example, is c ($MOC_o = x + 2c - P'_p = x + 2c - x - c = c$).

In reality further complications arise from the fact that more than one plant is used[15] and plants come in certain sizes rather than being perfectly divisible[16] as assumed here. Moreover, operating costs may differ among time periods. Recent, more efficient plants have lower costs and are operated continuously giving lower operating costs at off-peak time while more expensive capacity must be brought in to meet peak demand (Shepherd 1990). However, the general principles outlined are still applicable. Pricing according to the marginal opportunity costs will result in higher prices in peak periods and lower prices in off-peak periods. This is more efficient than charging a uniform price because it reduces the capacity needed to meet the peak demand even when demand curves are independent. Besides, charging different prices is not discriminatory when the differential reflects differences in marginal costs.[17] It is, however, possible that discriminating prices may be charged when the aim of the enterprise is to profit maximise.

SUMMARY

Some of the managerial implications of vertical and conglomerate business expansion are explored in this chapter. The choice of an appropriate transfer pricing policy is particularly significant when firms are organised into a number of autonomous and independent divisions. On the assumption that there is no divergence of interest between divisions and top management, and in the absence of demand or cost interdependencies between divisions, it is shown that when the transferred resource or commodity is sold in perfectly competitive markets, setting the transfer price equal to the market price will maximise corporate profits whether or not divisions trade with each other. Moreover, divisional independence and autonomy is consistent with global profitability which may suffer if internal trading is mandated. When an external market for the transferred commodity either does not exist or is imperfectly competitive the optimal transfer price is equal to the marginal cost of the selling division. This, however, requires that divisional heads act in the interest of the firm even in situations in which a divergence arises between divisional and global interests. In reality, when divisions are independent profit centres and decisions on internal trade and transfer pricing are delegated to divisional heads a divergence of interest may arise. Divisional heads may pursue divisional profitability to an extent detrimental to global profits. To induce behaviour consistent with corporate as opposed to divisional aims, appropriate incentives must be adopted and divisional evaluation must be based on the contribution that each division makes to corporate performance rather than on divisional financial performance alone. Such evaluations although feasible may compromise the independence of the divisions. To maintain divisional independence transfer prices can be used as behavioural instruments. That is, they may be allowed to deviate from the economically efficient level in order to enhance perceptions of fairness and to motivate self-interested divisional heads (the agents of top management) to achieve the objectives of top management (their principal). The section on transfer price concludes with some qualifying remarks and evidence on transfer prices in practice.

Some demand and cost interdependencies are explored in the third section of this chapter. It is pointed out that when product demands are related prices must be determined simultaneously and that the price of a single product will tend to be higher and its production level lower when the producer is a multi-product firm whose range of products are characterised by substitute relationships. The opposite is true when complementary product relationships predominate.

When a range of products can be produced from the same resources the question of selecting the optimum output mix arises. Resource availability and technology determine the production possibilities available to the firm. The range of feasible outputs is described by the PTC and the choice of the optimum product combination depends on the strength of the market demand for each product. The choice of output mix may change in the long run as resource availability, technology and demand conditions change.

Technological interdependencies may restrict substantially the potential for altering the output proportions. It is indeed possible that the restrictions are such that it is impossible to produce one product without at the same time producing at least some quantity of another product. Such jointness in production implies that the marginal opportunity cost of each product depends not only on the joint cost of production but on the marginal revenue of its co-products or by-products as well. The optimum production level of a composite unit of joint products is that at which the sum of the marginal revenues is equal to the joint marginal cost of production. The optimum sales level of a by-product, however, may diverge from the optimum production level in which case disposal costs may occur which modify the optimum output and pricing levels.

The final section of this chapter examines briefly the 'peak load' pricing problem. This refers to the pricing and production decisions of products produced by the same input but sold at different time periods sequentially under different demand conditions. Analytically the problem of peak load pricing is the same as that of joint products, in that it relates to the question of how to allocate common costs so as to arrive at prices and production levels that maximise the objective function of the decision maker. Commonly, however, peak load problems are analysed on the assumption of social welfare rather than profit maximisation. Optimal off-peak prices (i.e. prices set equal to their marginal opportunity cost) are lower than peak load prices. They are equal to or less than the off-peak period marginal operating cost depending on the size of the off-peak demand.

APPLICATION: TRANSFER PRICING PRACTICES; THE CASE OF ROUSSEAU CORPORATION AND BACON AND BENTHAM INC.

Bacon and Bentham Inc. and Rousseau Corporation were two of the thirteen enterprises whose transfer pricing policies were investigated by Robert Eccles (1985). In addition to providing an illustration of transfer price practices both case studies are indicative of the use made of transfer prices to facilitate the efficient organisation of the enterprise.

Case study No. 1

Bacon and Bentham Inc., a highly decentralised electronics firm, had twenty-four divisions at the time of the research. Internal trading of semiconductors produced by two divisions occurred but was small in volume since the buying divisions preferred external sources of supply. The transfer policy adopted was that described by Eccles as a 'market agency' method of transfer pricing. This exists when, as in Bacon and Bentham, the CEO delegates authority to GDHs who have complete freedom to decide on the price and the volume of internal trade. At Bacon and Bentham the transfer price was set by the selling division and was the same as the price charged to external buyers. The buying division was free to trade with internal or external suppliers.

Since the semiconductor market is not perfectly competitive, setting the transfer price equal to the market price suggests possible inefficiencies especially when managers are evaluated on the financial performance of their division in which case they may pursue divisional profitability to the detriment of corporate profitability or overall strategy. At Bacon and Bentham the performance of divisional heads was indeed evaluated primarily on the performance of their divisions in relation to the performance of firms competing with their division. Some 25–40 per cent of managerial salaries were derived from performance measures such as sales, profits and average return on investment. Failure to achieve the set objectives, for two years in a row, implied the removal of the general manager to another post. Moreover, buying divisions tended to select external sources of supply so that the volume of internal trade was rather small. Two reasons were given for this policy. (a) The buying divisions required small volumes of custom chips, while the manufacturing operations of the semiconductor divisions were not set up to produce efficiently for orders of this size and type. In essence the products demanded were not the same as those supplied. So resource allocation in the short run was not affected adversely by the reduction in the volume of internal trade. (b) The firm believed that setting price guidelines (in an attempt to arrive at the economically efficient price) or mandating internal trade would impinge on divisional independence and could create perceptions of unfairness and other agency costs. In these circumstances GDHs might raise complaints involving the CEO in settling disputes which could be very demanding in terms of CEO time. In general, monitoring and agency costs could increase to the detriment of corporate strategies. As a manager put it, '(the) transfer pricing method . . . depends on management philosophy. If we interfere with the management of profit incentives, we have to reimburse them. Once we interfere with their day to day operations they can complain to us' (Eccles 1985: 166).

It is clear that transfer price policy in this firm attempts to balance the costs and benefits of economic and organisational efficiency. Whether the right balance was achieved, however, is questionable since competition among divisions was so strong that managers recognised the need for better co-operation. In particular, one supplying division had taken steps to improve co-operation after discovering that an internal buyer was buying its products from outside distributors rather than directly from the division. Even if such obvious malpractices do not occur, lack of co-operation may have long-term implications as well. In this particular company, it may prevent the buying division from learning about the potential of some of the products of the semiconductor division which could have led to 'the development of proprietary semiconductor chips that would have provided a competitive advantage and increased profitability' (Eccles 1985: 163).

Case study No. 2

A management philosophy and transfer policy contrasting that of Bacon and Bentham's was adopted by Rousseau Corporation, a highly vertically integrated chemical company. As a manager put it, 'Our attitude is that we are not a conglomerate. We do better when we try to operate as a single unit, as a co-ordinated system. The corporate organisation co-ordinates the global strategy for all products. This is a very difficult way to operate but that's our mentality.' This attitude permeated throughout the firm. Another divisional manager suggested that he would be prepared to take decisions that would cost money to his division provided that they were profitable for the firm as a whole.

This management philosophy has been facilitated by a transfer price method called by Eccles a 'hierarchical agency' and by the adoption of appropriate incentives. In the hierarchical agency method of pricing the principal can order the agents to take certain actions such as to trade with each other. This limits the autonomy of the agents and creates team production in the sense suggested by Alchian and Demsetz (see Chapter 1). Rewards, therefore, must be based on joint outcomes to induce co-operation. A 'hierarchical agency' method was adopted at Rousseau with the transfer price set equal to standard full cost.

Managers were not concerned that this transfer pricing method created inefficiencies either in the short run or in the long run. Neither did they perceive the imposed limitations on their decision autonomy as unfair. This attitude can be attributed partly to the fact that divisions were highly inter-related because of the vertical strategy the firm pursued and partly by the incentives policies adopted. Divisional managers were not rewarded according to the performance of their own divisions but rather on their contribution to corporate profitability and strategy. Although this is difficult to measure there appeared to be no complaints about fairness. Their performance evaluation was subjective but included a poll of other divisional heads to make it fair and to induce managers not to act against the interests of other divisions.

Finally investment decisions in this company were in accord with the suggestions of our earlier analysis. Investment decisions were not based on the profitability of a division as determined by transfer prices. Decisions on the viability or expansion of a division, at Rousseau, depended on an evaluation of all the stages of the production process. Transfer prices had no influence on such evaluations.

FURTHER READING

Eccles, R.G. (1985) 'Transfer Pricing as a Problem of Agency', in J.W. Pratt and R.J. Zeckhauser (eds) *Principals and Agents: The Structure of Business*, Boston, MA: Harvard Business School.

Henderson, J.M. and Quant, R.E. (1980) gives a mathematical treatment of multiple product pricing.

Needham, D. (1978) *The Economics of Industrial Structure, Conduct and Performance*, London: Holt, Rinehart and Winston. This provides a brief but rigorous diagrammatic exposition of multiple product pricing in the presence of demand relationships (ch. 3), peak load pricing (ch. 11) and allocating costs between joint products (pp. 42–5).

Shepherd, W.G. (1990) *The Economics of Industrial Organisation*, 3rd edn, Englewood Cliffs, NJ: Prentice Hall International Editions.

QUESTIONS

1 Consider a multidivisional profit maximising firm. One of its divisions produces product X and another division produces product Y. Both products can be sold to external buyers but product X can also be used as an input in the production of product Y.

   (a) Assuming that the external demand for product X is negatively sloped, make any other assumptions necessary to determine the extent of internal trading and the optimum output and prices of goods X and Y.
   (b) Would your pricing and production strategy be affected if the two divisions were located in different countries?

2 Alpha Ltd, an M-form organised firm, is the sole producer of product X. Division 1 manufactures X and sells it either to division 2, a distribution division, or to independent distributors. Market research carried out by division 1 indicates that the demand for product X from independent distributors is given by

   $$P_1 = 170 - 2Q_1$$

   where P_1 is the demand price from independent distributors and Q_1 is the corresponding quantity demanded, and that due to market sharing agreements this demand is independent of the quantity of X which division 2 may decide to sell.

   The total manufacturing costs are estimated as

   $$TC = 500 + 40Q_1 + \frac{Q_1^2}{2}$$

   where Q_1 is the production of division 1.

   Division 2 have estimated that the demand function for their final product is given by

   $$P_2 = 250 - 3Q_2$$

   where P is the demand price and Q is the quantity demanded, and that distribution costs are £20.00 per unit of product handled.

   Assuming that the firm's object is to maximise total profits and that the two divisions are autonomous profit centres:

   (a) show that the economically efficient transfer price should be £85.3;
   (b) determine the total quantity of X that Alpha Ltd will manufacture and the proportion of it that is going to be sold to independent distributors; and
   (c) if the fixed cost of division 2 is equal to £1,600.00 should it be closed down and the firm sell its output through independent distributors?

3 BBI is a decentralised electronics firm. Its semiconductor manufacturing division produces a standardised type of chip which can be used as an input in its final product division. The cost of the semiconductor manufacturing division is given by

$$TC = 1,000 + 0.05Q_c^2$$

where Qc is a set of chips. The final product division requires one set of chips per unit of output produced and the cost of the division excluding the value of the chip is £50.00 per unit of output whatever the volume of production. The demand for the final product is

$$P = 150 - 0.1Q_f$$

where Q_f denotes units of final product. Chips of similar quality are produced by other firms and are traded at a constant price of £20.00 per set.

Although the two divisions are independent centres, the Managing Director has instructed the Divisional Managers that they should neither sell to nor buy chips from outside firms. They are, however, free to decide the price and volume of internal trade after consultation with each other and in a co-operative corporate spirit. In fact any attempts to exploit each other will not be tolerated.

You are required to

(a) determine the transfer price and the quantity of chips to be produced and transferred internally,
(b) determine the amount of profit that the firm forgoes by mandating internal trade, and
(c) suggest reasons why external trading is not permitted.

4 The Caxton company produces two goods, good X and good Z, and have estimated the own-price elasticity and the cross-price elasticity (with respect to good Z) of demand for good X to be -1.15 and -1.75 respectively. The income elasticity of demand for good X is estimated to be 0.7.

(a) What does the above information enable you to say about the nature of good X?
(b) The company is primarily concerned with its declining market share for good X, sales currently being 2,500 units. Since it takes time to mount and raise finance for an advertising campaign, the company is considering an immediate reduction in the price of X to stem the decline.

    (i) What effect will a 10 per cent reduction in the price of X have on the sale of X?
    (ii) Is this action the most effective that the company could take to stem the decline in its market share for good X?

5 The Woods company produces parquet flooring the demand of which, per day, is given by

$$P = 2,000 - 2Q$$

where P is the price in pence per square metre of flooring and Q is the quantity demanded in square metres.

The cutting and processing of timber involved in making parquet flooring produces a substantial quantity of sawdust, a waste product. However, it was recently found that with a negligible extra cost the sawdust can be compressed into briquettes which can be sold for burning in open fires (such as fire places, small furnaces, etc.). It is estimated that for every square metre of flooring one kilogram of briquettes is produced. The daily demand for briquettes is given by

$$P = 1,000 - 3Q$$

where P is the price in pence per kilogram and Q is the quantity in kilograms. The total production cost C of the parquet flooring and its by-product (briquettes) is proportional to the output of flooring such that

$$C = 600Q_1.$$

(a) Determine the quantity of parquet flooring and briquettes that Woods would produce per day and the price at which they will sell their products.
(b) Would your answer to part (a) be altered if you were told that in order to convert the sawdust to briquettes the company had installed a machine worth £100,000?

6 Goat plc, the producers of cheddar cheese, have estimated that the demand for their product is given by

$$P_1 = 600 - 0.3\,Q_1$$

where Q_1 is the quantity of cheddar in kilograms and P_1 is the price in pence (sterling) per kilogram of cheddar.
The total cost of production is given by

$$TC = 100,000 + 100Q_1.$$

The production process, however, is such that for every kilogram of cheddar produced a kilogram of whey, a by-product, is also produced. Fortunately there is a market for whey, although it is a small one. The relevant demand curve is given by

$$P_2 = 200 - 0.2Q_2$$

where P_2 and Q_2 denote the price in pence and the quantity in kilograms of whey.
Whey cannot be stored and any unsold quantity must be disposed of at a disposal cost given by

$$D = 1,000 + 20Q_d$$

where Q_d is the quantity in kilograms of either cheddar or whey to be disposed.

(a) How much cheddar cheese should Goat produce if they wish to profit maximise?
(b) How much cheddar and whey will be sold and what total profit will Goat make?

7 Assume that the demand for the product of a public enterprise fluctuates over the year so that for the six winter months demand is given by

$$P_1 = 1,200 - 0.8Q_1$$

whereas in the six summer months demand is given by

$$P_2 = 1,000 - 0.8Q_2.$$

Total capital cost K and total operating costs C both increase in proportion to output, more specifically

$K = £1,000Q$ per year
$C = £100Q$ per six months.

The enterprise is charged with maximising economic welfare rather than profits, subject to covering production costs.

(a) What size of plant (measured in terms of output capacity) should the enterprise install, bearing in mind that once installed its capacity cannot be changed quickly, certainly not within six months?
(b) What price should it charge in each time period? Explain the economic rationale underlying the fixing of prices at these levels.
(c) How would your answer to (a) and (b) be affected if capital costs were lower than stated, e.g. suppose capital costs were given by $K = 150Q$ per year?

(d) What criteria should the enterprise employ in deciding whether or not to install extra capacity (given that extra plants can be obtained in only one size with output equal to q) in response to an increase in demand?

APPENDIX 11.1: A NUMERICAL EXAMPLE ON TRANSFER PRICING

Consider the problem in question 2 above. The demand from independent distributors is

$$P_1 = 170 - 2Q_1$$

therefore,

$$MR_1 = 170 - 4Q_1 \text{ or } Q_1 = \frac{170}{4} - \frac{1}{4} MR_1 \tag{A11.1}$$

$$TC = 500 + 40Q + \frac{Q^2}{2}$$

thus

$$MMC = \frac{dTC}{dQ} = 40 + Q. \tag{A11.2}$$

The final product demand facing division 2 is

$$P_2 = 250 - 3Q_2$$

and the marginal distribution cost (MDC) is £20.00 Thus, its net marginal revenue (MR $-$MDC) is

$$nMR_2 = 250 - 6Q_2 - 20 \text{ or } Q_2 = \frac{230}{6} - \frac{nMR_2}{6} \tag{A11.3}$$

(a) In order to profit maximise, division 2 should set $\Sigma MR = MMC$. To find ΣMR vertically sum $MR_1 + nMR_2$ noting that $Q_1 + Q_2 = Q$, i.e.

$$Q = Q_1 + Q_2 = \frac{170}{4} - \frac{1}{4} MR_1 + \frac{230}{6} - \frac{1}{6} nMR_2$$

or

$$Q = \frac{970}{12} - \frac{1}{4} \Sigma MR - \frac{1}{6} \Sigma MR$$

$$Q = \frac{970}{12} - \frac{5}{12} \Sigma MR$$

or

$$\Sigma MR = \frac{970}{5} - \frac{12}{5} Q. \tag{A11.4}$$

Therefore, condition $\Sigma MR = MMC$ is satisfied when

$$\frac{970}{5} - \frac{12}{5} Q = 40 + Q$$

or when $Q = 45.3$ units and $MMC = 40 + 43.5 = 85.3$.

Total output must be distributed so as to ensure that the equal marginal revenue rule is satisfied, i.e. $MR_1 = nMR_2 = MMC$. Therefore, the quantity to be supplied to independent distributors must be such that

$85.3 = MR_1 = 170 - 4Q_1$

or $Q_1 = 21.2$, i.e. $Q_1 = 46.8$ per cent of total output and, similarly,

$85.3 = nMR_2 = 230 - 6Q_2$

or $Q_2 = 24.1$ units or 47.2 per cent of total output.

(b) The economically efficient transfer price is equal to MMC, i.e. TP = 85.3.
(c) To evaluate the viability of a division calculate and compare the profits of each division prior to and after a potential shut down.

Distribution division as a profit centre

To sell 24.1 units the maximum price that can be charged is

$P_2 = 250 - 3Q_2 = 250 - 24.1 = 177.7$.

Total gross profit is

$TR - TC = P_2\,Q_2 - TPQ_2 - dQ_2$,

i.e.
Total profit $= 177.7(24.1) - 85.3(24.1) - 20(24.1) = £1,744.84$.

Manufacturing division as a profit centre

Total profit $= TPQ_2 + P_1\,Q_1 - TVC - FC$
where $P_1 = 170 - 2Q_1 = 127.6$, thus
Total profit $= 85.3(24.1) + 127.6(21.2) - [500 + 40(45.3) + \frac{1}{2}(45.3)^2] - 1,600$

$= 1,422.8 - 1,600$
$= -£177,20$

Should this loss making division be closed down? The answer is not unequivocal. If the contribution that it makes to the profit of other divisions is no more than £177.2 it should be closed down, but not otherwise. To find out, calculate the firm's profits on the assumption that division 1 is shut down. Then, the profit of the manufacturing division becomes

Profit $= TR - TC = (170 - 2Q)Q - (500 + 40Q + \frac{1}{2}Q^2]$.

The necessary condition for profit maximisation is

$\dfrac{d(TR - TC)}{dQ} = 170 - 4Q - 40 - 2Q = 0$

or $Q = 26$ (total production is reduced and is sold entirely through independent distributors), therefore,

$P = 170 - 2Q = 170 - 2(26) = 118$
Profit $= 118(26) - [500 + 40(26) + \frac{1}{2}(26)^2] = £1,190$.

This is lower by $£1,422.9 - £1,190 = £232.8$. Therefore, the contribution that division 1 makes to the profits of division 2 is £232.8. Closing the division down would reduce the overall profitability by £232.8 - £177.2 = £55.6. In this example the division is therefore viable.

Note that the same solution can be arrived at by partial differentiation. Assuming that the manufacturing division has all the relevant information and sets the transfer price in a way that does not exploit the distribution division, the profit maximising quantities can be calculated as

$\text{Max}\Pi = P_1Q_1 + P_2Q_2 - 20Q_2 - (500 + 40Q + \frac{1}{2}Q^2)$

where $Q = Q_1 + Q_2$

$$\frac{d\Pi}{dQ_1} = 130 - 5Q_1 - Q_2 = 0$$

$$\frac{d\Pi}{dQ_2} = 190 - 7Q_2 - Q_1 = 0.$$

Which gives $Q_1 = 21.23$ and $Q_2 = 24.11$ and $Q = 45.34$. Therefore prices and profits are as above.

NOTES

1 If MMC is perceived as an average cost, division B would calculate the curve marginal to MMC and set the transfer price at the point where this new MC curve intersects with nMR. This would result in a lower than Q production level and a transfer price higher than the optimal one. Global profitability would decline, although the profits of division B would be higher.
2 Empirical evidence indicates the practical validity of both these suggestions. See, for example, the Rousseau case study given in the Application section of this chapter.
3 $$MR = \frac{d(\text{Total revenue})}{dQ} = \frac{d(PQ)}{dQ} = P + Q\frac{dP}{dQ}$$

$$= P\left(1 + \frac{Q}{P}\frac{dP}{dQ}\right) = P\left(1 - \frac{1}{E_d}\right).$$
4 For a mathematical formulation of the problem see Henderson and Quant (1980). A diagrammatic analysis is offered by Needham (1978: 71–4).
5 When the resources are equally well suited in the production of each product the PTC is a straight line.
6 This is because the marginal cost is either increasing for both products or increasing for one and constant for the other.
7 Non-utilisation of resources is inefficient from a profit maximising point of view. Recall, however, the role that organisational slack plays in the behaviouralist theory of the firm.
8 In numerical form an isorevenue line is $TR = Q_X P_X + Q_Y P_Y$ where TR, P_X and P_Y are constant, so that it shows all the linear combinations of Q_X and Q_Y which give the same TR.
9 See Needham (1978).
10 Similar reasoning can account for the failure of schemes to optimally allocate the costs of common inputs such as R&D or corporate image advertising among the divisions of a multidivisional firm. Cohen and Loeb (1982) have shown that for head office to efficiently allocate common costs, it needs information on marginal profitability of each division. In terms of joint products this is equivalent to requiring knowledge of the marginal revenues of by-products and co-products.
11 Note that the negative segment of MR_B is not included in the vertical sum MR.
12 For further expansion see Moschandreas (1985).
13 We simply substitute the relationship $Q_B = 2Q_A$ into the demand function $P_B = f(Q_B)$ so that it becomes $P_B = f(2Q_A)$.
14 This is similar to the production of a by-product whose demand is so low that part of its production is not offered for sale but is rather destroyed.
15 For an extension of the analysis to two plants see Crew and Kleindorfer (1971).
16 For the analysis of indivisible plants see Williamson (1966).
17 Profit maximisation would have also resulted in different peak and off-peak prices but these would have included an element of discrimination, since MR rather than P is set equal to JMC.

12 Ownership and the capital structure of firms

INTRODUCTION

This chapter investigates the relationships that arise between the firm and the providers of finance. Although finance is raised from a variety of sources one group of fund suppliers, the equity holders, are commonly considered to be the 'owners' of the firm. Strictly speaking this is incorrect. There is no ownership as such of labour or other resource providers by capital. To assume that there is, is not only factually incorrect but is to doubt the basis for the existence of firms (Alchian and Woodward 1988).

The term 'ownership', in the context of the firm, simply refers to a set of rights which can be assigned to any individual or group of individuals participating in the affairs of a firm. To examine how these rights are assigned to a particular group of firm participants this chapter begins by examining the definition of ownership. On the basis of the definition adopted it is shown that labour, capital or any other member(s) of the team which comprises the firm can become its owners.

Factors affecting ownership and control also have implications for the way in which a firm is financed. Issues relating to the optimal capital structure are examined in the second section which is followed by an analysis of the cost of capital. It is shown that informational asymmetries between outside investors who provide capital and the firm's managers who control its use imply that the capital structure of the firm can influence the cost of raising finance, the value of the firm and the way it responds to external environmental and policy changes (Greenward and Stiglitz 1990). The penultimate section evaluates the neoclassical approach to the cost of capital and the value of the firm in the light of recent developments in the theory of agency and transaction costs. The chapter concludes with a summary. The application following this chapter is a case study on the ownership structures and on the factors determining the size of debt finance in Japanese corporations.

OWNERSHIP

In a legal sense resource owners own their resources and although they may contractually acquire the right to direct resources owned by others they cannot, barring slavery, own other resource owners. Thus, if the firm is a coalition of individual resource owners governed by a set of contractual arrangements, there is, strictly speaking no ownership of the firm. Workers own their labour, lenders own their capital and customers own the products they buy. Neither group owns any of the other groups. They simply enter into contractual relationships and accept direction and some degree of authority. As indicated earlier (Chapter 4), resource owners form internal organisations, for reasons of efficiency. There are, however, costs relating to the organisation and operation of the internal structures (firm) that emerge. Efficiency will therefore be served when the internal costs of organisation and control are less than the costs of market contracting. To economise on internal costs a team requires a monitor who observes behaviour, meters productivity and apportions rewards. To induce the monitor to perform these duties effectively he or she must be assigned (a) the right to discipline resource owners by terminating their contracts and (b) the right to appropriate the firm's residual income.

These two formal rights, i.e. the right to monitor and direct the use of resources and the right to receive the residual earnings of the firm, define ownership. The individual or the group of individuals who acquires these two rights is the owner of the firm. When such rights do not exist ownership is absent. Non-profit making firms, for example, have no residual earnings and hence no ownership in the sense defined here.

An entrepreneur who internalises market transactions by forming a team may also undertake to monitor the behaviour of the team members, to assess their performance and determine their compensation. If, furthermore, this entrepreneur is rewarded for his or her endeavours by claiming the residual earnings of the team, this person is the 'owner' of the firm. The function of ownership, however, does not coincide with that of entrepreneurship which (as Chapter 5 explains) is a much broader function.

Often ownership is identified with the providers of equity capital so that shareholders are considered to be the owners of the modern corporation. Firms, however, can be owned by other member(s) of the team or any other individuals who transact with the firm such as customers, financial institutions, suppliers or workers; i.e. by any 'patrons' (to use the all embracing term coined by Hansmann 1988). Many firms are indeed owned by the suppliers of labour or raw materials or by their customers. The question then arises as to what factors determine which group of patrons will became the owners of the firm.

Who owns whom?

Theoretically, non-patrons could be the owners of a firm. This is rare, however, since non-patron ownership will normally be inefficient. The assertion, on the other hand, that firms are owned, controlled and administered by capital rather than labour is a myth. 'There are firms in which the human resources are firm-specific, and "labor" is the owner. To believe that "capital" is in some sense the "boss" and hires "labor" is to fail to understand the most basic forces that shape the firm' (Alchian and Woodward 1988).

Although in most large corporations the investors of capital are the firm's owners, other patterns of ownership are often present in many industries. Firms can be and often are owned by their customers, as in the case of consumer-owned co-operatives or, more commonly, businesses owned by their wholesale or supply co-operatives. Farm supply co-operatives are a good example of customer-owned firms. In 1984, there were 2,200 such firms in the USA accounting for 27 per cent of the overall market for farm supplies (Hansmann 1988).[1]

Co-operatives are prominent in the supply of petroleum products, fertilisers, farm chemicals and feed products. Retailer-owned wholesale co-operatives provide another example of customer-owned firms. These accounted, in 1985, for 14 per cent of all groceries distributed in the USA at the wholesale level and 31 per cent if internal distributions within chains are excluded. Other examples include the mutual insurance co-operatives, mutual banking institutions and co-operative housing (USA). Labour-owned firms are common in law practices, architecture, accountancy, engineering, economic consultancy, advertising, restaurants, computer software production and other services. But perhaps the most celebrated example of labour-owned manufacturing firms has been provided by the Plywood companies of the Pacific Northwest in the USA, the first of which, the Olympia Veneer Company, was established in 1921.

To understand this diversity in ownership patterns we must enquire into the factors which determine whether the formal ownership rights will be assigned to the lenders of capital, the suppliers of labour and other factors of production or to the customers of the firm.

By definition ownership includes the right to monitor, control and provide incentives to work. The assignment of ownership rights can therefore have an important impact on the efficiency and prosperity of the firm. In other words, if the exercise of ownership involves costs then it can be argued that efficiency will be best served if ownership is assigned in a way that minimises these costs. Two broad groups of relevant costs can be identified as follows:

1 *contractual costs* these are the costs involved in negotiating the membership of the team and in initiating, completing and implementing contracts relating to its organisation; and
2 *monitoring costs* these include the cost of controlling the management and of providing incentives intended to eliminate any divergencies of interests.

The factors which contribute to contractual difficulties and create transactional costs were analysed in Chapter 3. It was shown there that since individuals are limitedly rational and inclined to act opportunistically, three factors can contribute significantly to transaction costs: (a) small numbers of traders, which facilitate the acquisition of market power and may cause opportunism (see the exercise of dominance in Chapter 14), (b) asset specificity (human or physical) which can cause 'lock in' situations and may give rise to first mover advantages and/or opportunism, and (c) informational asymmetries which can lead to opportunistic behaviour and moral hazard.

It follows that high costs may exist in situations in which the firm has substantial market power over some of its participants which can inhibit the efficient functioning of the firm. In such situations it may be possible to reduce costs by assigning ownership rights to the patrons over whom the firm has market power. The firm might, for example, have substantial power over the owners of firm-specific assets or skills. The owners of such assets may be unwilling to commit resources to the firm because once resources are committed they are 'locked in'. They have no alternative users or uses and the firm can exploit them monopolistically. As we saw in Chapter 10, asset specificity is one of the main causes of vertical integration. When the transaction, and hence integration, is between two firms ownership is assigned to the firm which owns the 'asset specific' resources. When the transaction is between a firm and one or more individuals, however, integration is only possible if the individual(s) take(s) over the firm by becoming its owner(s), not the other way round. Similarly, in situations in which the firm has better information than a group of individuals it transacts with, so that transacting becomes hazardous and too expensive for the individuals concerned, ownership rights may be assigned to the group as a means of ensuring their continued participation in the firm.

Transaction costs economising is therefore an important, though not a unique, factor of ownership determination. Other factors include the size of expenses which the owners of a firm incur in monitoring the managerial function. Monitoring costs include the costs of becoming informed, communicating information among the owners, making decisions and ensuring that these decisions are carried out by the management of the firm (Jensen and Meckling 1976). Monitoring costs can vary substantially with the size and homogeneity of the owner group. The smaller the number of monitors the easier it becomes to communicate information and to arrive at decisions (see Chapter 3). Similarly communication costs fall the more homogeneous and closely related the group is. Thus, monitoring costs are relatively small when monitors 'reside in geographic propinquity to each other and the firm, and transact regularly and repeatedly with the firm over a prolonged period of time for amounts that are a significant fraction of their income' (Hansmann 1988).

A significant part of monitoring cost relates to the control of management. As explained in Chapter 9, failure to control managerial behaviour may cause managerial opportunism. This implies that despite legal, contractual and moral constraints, some managers may utilise slack in the form of an 'easy life' so that internal inefficiencies arise.

For some class of owners monitoring and control costs can be so high that it may be less costly to allow the existence of managerial discretion rather than to attempt to exercise fully effective control. When monitoring a particular group of patrons becomes so expensive that relatively effective control is infeasible, assigning ownership rights to this group is a way of overcoming the contractual difficulties involved. High monitoring costs become *ceteris paribus* the decisive factor in selecting the ownership group. However, as already noted, other costs and in particular transactions costs may not be equal among prospective owners. In this case it is the sum of transaction and monitoring costs that determine who the owner will be.

In sum, efficiency considerations indicate that ownership should be assigned to the group of firm participants associated with the smallest total transactions and monitoring costs of ownership. Since costs vary with the characteristics of transactions and with environmental features, diversity of ownership occurs. For certain groups of transactions worker ownership will be more efficient while in others capital ownership will be indicated for the reasons examined in the following sections.

Worker-owned firms

The majority of worker-owned firms are to be found in the service industry, especially among the professions, although there are notable exceptions. To the extent that efficiency has an impact on ownership the rationale of these firms and their weaknesses and strengths may be better understood in terms of the factors which contribute to the efficiency of ownership. As already indicated two groups of costs can be distinguished; transaction (contractual) costs and cost of controlling the managerial function or ownership costs.

Transaction costs

Human asset specificity can be a significant contributory factor to labour-related transaction costs. Investing in human skills and knowledge specific to the firm implies that workers may find it difficult to change occupation especially after long associations with a firm. Similarly, the firm will incur substantial costs in replacing personnel with highly specific knowledge and skills. The 'lock in' situations which develop could be overcome by assigning ownership rights to the workers concerned. This does not, however, seem to be a description of reality. Transaction costs stemming from human asset specificity although present do not appear to be a particularly significant factor in determining the ownership of many labour-owned firms. Human asset specificity, for example, is small among professionals such as engineers or architects who are relatively mobile and is insignificant in the case of refuse collectors and taxi drivers (who often own their firms).

An alternative source of transaction costs relates to monitoring of work effort. For many professions the nature of the work is such that substantial autonomy in labour behaviour is required. It is difficult to monitor, for example, artists, taxi drivers and other professionals without effectively repeating the work. So, it may be thought that substantial monitoring costs may lead to vertical integration between the firm and its employees, or, in other words, to employee ownership. Monitoring costs do not, however, constitute a sufficient condition for employee ownership. Difficulties in monitoring do not necessarily imply difficulties in assessing productivity. In law and other professional partnerships, for example, productivity can be easily quantified by, for example, the revenue that each partner brings to the firm. The need for monitoring work effort may not be that essential.

In brief, contractual difficulties although present do not appear to be insuperable so that the relevant transaction costs do not appear decisively high in many of the observed worker-owned firms.

Costs of ownership

These relate mainly to the difficulties associated with managerial control (agency costs). The costs of monitoring and control may be exceptionally high when the owners are other than the workers of the firm. This is because labour is on the whole in a better position than other firm participants to observe and assess the behaviour of management. And although workers may lack the knowledge and skills required to assess the marketing or financial performance of management, they have the incentive to acquire such knowledge or elect or appoint representatives who have the required ability and skills to perform this task. The benefits derived from effective management control may thus contribute to labour ownership and the existence of partnerships. This advantage of labour ownership, however, may be insufficient to compensate for the increase in risk which worker–owners undertake by providing part of the firm's finance themselves. Investing one's human capital plus savings in the same firm implies poor diversification and high risks which may explain the predominance of investor-owned firms even in labour intensive industries. It is, however, true that in many professional partnerships the organisation specific capital per partner is low so the increase in financial risk is not as important as in other industries. It can be concluded that in professional partnership the increase in risks may not be so high as to swap the benefits of a better management control. This is no proof, however, that effective management control is a sufficient reason why labour-owned firms emerge.

A feature that facilitates ownership and which is common to all well-established labour-owned firms is a strong homogeneity of interest among the individuals involved. There is an important homogeneity of jobs, skills and purpose. All worker–owners perform identical tasks within the firm which facilitates the adoption of equal pay or pay according to seniority (common in many law firms, for example). These features in turn facilitate decision making. Numbers of owners are invariably small which reduces communication costs. Worker–owners work independently and it is extremely difficult to find many examples of such firms organised hierarchically or with division of labour among the partners. Homogeneity of labour facilitates the selection process so that new recruitment to the team is of above average quality. This and a co-operative organisational structure may contribute to enhanced productivity. Economies in running costs and a reduction in the required size of capital funds are also achieved by sharing common resources such as library, secretarial and other staff and computer facilities.

It can be concluded that labour-owned firms emerge when a strong homogeneity of the labour input facilitates decision making and reduces the ownership costs of control.

Investor-owned firms

To examine the reasons why the providers of capital are often assigned ownership rights we must analyse possible transactional costs in the provision of finance as well as the relevant costs of ownership.

Transaction costs of equity

A firm could, theoretically, borrow 100 per cent of its capital requirements. The reason why this does not often happen in reality is because the cost of debt finance can become prohibitively high. Since lenders cannot be as well informed about the affairs of the firm as the owners, they could suffer from opportunism. The owners may promise to use the loan proceeds in the most efficient projects, but once a loan is granted incentives to act opportunistically arise. First, owner–managers may take for themselves dividends or perquisites which cannot be justified by the earnings of the firm, but perhaps more importantly they may be inclined to undertake risky projects, i.e. projects associated with a small probability of a lucrative gain and a high probability of a loss. This incentive for 'asset substitution' is provided by the fact that if the project is successful the owners will appropriate most of the gain but if unsuccessful the lenders will bear most of the loss.

In certain instances this problem which arises from information asymmetry could be overcome by offering a lien or outright ownership of the assets acquired by the proceeds of the loan. The difficulty, however, remains when the loan, or part of it, is used to acquire firm-specific assets (assets with no alternative uses or users). In this case the only alternative is to provide collateral on non-specific assets or have the owners offer security by personal assets or collateral on future earnings. This solution to the agency problem is indeed often adopted especially when the borrowers are small, owner-run firms. The costs of writing and enforcing such covenants, however, are prohibitive when the owner class is numerous.

As already emphasised (see Chapter 3) transactional difficulties associated with asymmetric information are magnified when long-term relationships are necessary. If loans could be withdrawn at will, the threat of withdrawal would be a sufficient check on borrowers. But business loans are often locked in since firms typically invest in long-term projects which require long-term financing. To finance long-term projects on short-term finance would require continuous refinancing which would be very expensive.

Ownership costs

When the contractual (agency) costs of raising debt finance are substantial, cost economising will be achieved by assigning ownership to the long-term investors, provided that the cost of ownership and in particular the cost of controlling the management of the firm is not higher than the agency costs saved by this arrangement.

When the group of owners is large costs of acquisition and communication of information combined with free rider problems (see Chapter 9) imply that owners have an incentive to shirk their monitoring responsibilities. As a result management has discretion in decision making which may be used against the interests of the owners. Although there is no general agreement as to the extent of managerial discretion some authors (of the Austrian school of thought) claim that the market in corporate control provides the necessary control of managers. The implication is that investor ownership not only economises on contractual costs but is also effective in controlling the firm.

The evidence of an efficient capital market, however, is neither a necessary nor a sufficient condition for investor ownership to occur. The effectiveness of the market in corporate control is an unnecessary consideration in explaining investor ownership since its existence post-dates that of the large dispersed share-ownership corporation by several decades. The efficiency of the investor-owned firm derives from transaction cost economising which exceeds the costs of monitoring management in large corporations requiring large long-term sums of finance. No other group of firm participants is in these circumstances more efficient as owners of the firm.

In brief, while labour-owned firms emerge when they enjoy low monitoring (ownership) costs, the existence of investor-owned firms is primarily due to transaction costs economising which compensates for high monitoring costs.

In general, the group of firm participants with the lowest sum of contractual and ownership costs become the owners of the firm. When transaction costs vary it is possible that large gains in transaction costs associated with ownership by a particular group may compensate for rather high monitoring costs. This is believed to be the reason why the owners of life insurance companies in the nineteenth century were their depositors and more importantly why most present-day corporations are investor owned.

THE CAPITAL STRUCTURE OF THE FIRM

Whether a firm is investor, labour or customer owned it requires finance for its normal daily functioning and in order to fund its long-term investment programme. Finance can be derived from a variety of sources (internal or external) and the ownership relationship can be used to facilitate the financing of the firm.

When referring to a firm's total financial requirements, the term *financial structure* is commonly adopted. It includes all current liabilities, long-term debt, common stock and preferred stock. *Capital structure* is a subset of financial structure. It includes long-term debt and equity (common or preferred) stock. If total debt is denoted by B and equity by E a firm's total capital K is $B+E$. The debt to equity ratio B/E is also known as the gearing ratio.

Since finance can be raised from a variety of sources each of which may be associated with a different per unit cost the determination of the most efficient method of finance is an important function of the finance department of a firm. This is because if capital structure affects the cost of capital, business financing decisions will affect the firm's investment and growth policies as well as the value of its stock.

To understand what determines a firm's optimal capital structure and the reasons why we observe firms with widely different gearing, we must inquire into the factors which may influence the cost of different methods of raising funds. Two strands of thought bearing on these issues, the so-called 'traditional' approach and the Modigliani–Miller approach, have dominated the financial management literature for some time now. We shall therefore outline these first before introducing the transactions cost approach to capital structure. Informational and other imperfections which influence the ownership structure of a firm can be seen to have an important influence in determining its optimal capital structure. Transaction costs between the providers and users of funds are reduced by merging the divergent interests into an ownership relationship. We begin, however, by defining the cost of capital.

The cost of capital

Since capital goods can be used over a number of years their acquisition requires an evaluation of current investments which bring returns in the future. That is, the price paid for capital goods must be compared with current and expected benefits. A discount rate, therefore, is needed in order to calculate the net present value (NPV) or to use as a yardstick with which the internal rate of return (IRR) can be compared. The discount rate which should be used is the cost of capital.

Furthermore, since value maximising firms adopt all investment projects with a positive NPV or invest till the IRR of the marginal project is just equal to the cost of capital (Hirshleifer 1958), the cost of capital is in equilibrium the same as the cost of the marginal project. But since the marginal project is that project whose benefits are just equal to the benefits forgone by not investing in the best alternative available, the cost of capital is an opportunity cost.

The cost of capital is theoretically easy to define, but its determination in reality becomes rather complicated by market imperfections and lack of information. If the capital market were perfect, so that firms could borrow or lend any desired funds at the given market rate, then clearly this market rate would represent the cost of capital. All projects with a positive NPV at the prevailing interest rate should be adopted and the IRR of the best alternative project forgone would be just equal to the current market rate. In reality, such a single market rate does not prevail. Lending and borrowing rates are not equal and would be expected to diverge, even if market imperfections were assumed away (or financial intermediaries could not exist). The difference between the two rates introduces complications, however, since the cost of capital in this case varies with the circumstances of the firm. For any firm either lending or borrowing may represent the cost of capital depending on the circumstances surrounding the investment decision. Thus, if the alternative to investing were to lend the money then the lending rate should be the appropriate rate to use in discounting and project evaluation. But, if the alternative to investing is to repay loans then the borrowing rate should be used as the cost of capital.

Further complications arise when lending and borrowing rates vary with the extent and/or the duration of the loans. That is, if the borrowing rate increases, as it commonly does, with the extent of indebtness, a simultaneity in the relationship between size of finance and its cost arises.[2] But perhaps the most important complication arises from the fact that neither the lending nor the borrowing rate is unique and independent of the source of finance. In fact the opposite is true. Several market rates exist depending on the source from which funds are raised. The cost of debentures, ordinary shares, retained profits and short-term loans vary and none need be equal to the cost of capital, in the sense of the opportunity cost of the best investment opportunity forgone. Which source of capital may be used will vary with the attitudes of firms regarding capital structure which in turn may depend on ownership structure and the characteristics of the projects which are financed. Tax considerations and the risk of bankruptcy may also influence the decision of the sourcing of finance.

For relatively small gearing ratios the cost of loan finance is likely to be smaller than the cost of equity simply because interest payments on loans are tax deductible while dividend payments are not. Thus, for a given gross earnings figure a higher gearing ratio implies higher interest costs which reduce the corporation tax liability of the firm and increase its net earnings.

Taxation, risks and other market imperfections imply that the cost of capital is not uniquely defined and finance managers are faced with the challenging task of estimating the most appropriate figure for their own firm.

The traditional approximation to the cost of capital

A practical approximation to the cost of capital is to calculate it as the weighted average of the cost of different sources of finance. Assuming that there are only two sources of finance, debt and equity, Figure 12.1 shows how the cost of each and the weighted average cost vary as the firm's gearing increases.

K_d and K_e represent the cost of debt and equity finance respectively. Curve K_d is drawn below curve K_e to indicate that the cost of loan finance is lower compared with the cost of equity finance. This is because loan finance is less risky than equity finance since interest payments are due whether the firm makes a surplus or not. The shape of Kd indicates how the cost of debt changes as the capital structure changes. As drawn, Figure 12.1 shows that at low levels of indebtness the cost of debt is fairly constant or increases slowly. As the debt to equity ratio reaches a certain level, however, the cost of debt begins to increase sharply because of increased risks associated with debt increases.

As the debt to equity ratio rises it becomes more likely that the net returns to share holders will deviate from their expected level. In other words the variability of earnings per share (EPS) increases as indebtness increases. In the absence of debt a given percentage increase in profit increases the EPS by the same proportion. With debt a fixed interest payment is due independently of gross earnings. Consequently, a given reduction in profits reduces the EPS by a higher proportion while a given profit increase results in a higher proportionate increase in EPS. The increase in variability in EPS is illustrated with a fictitious example in Table 12.1. It can be seen that for the same gross earnings stream the EPS of firm 2 varies more than that of firm 1.

The wider variation in EPS implies a higher financial risk. Consequently, as a firm's riskiness increases lenders require a higher compensation in order to invest in what they perceive to be a more risky firm. Thus, the

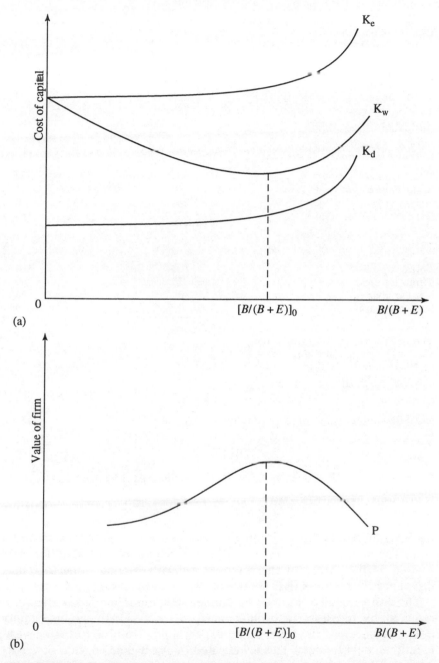

Figure 12.1 (a) The cost of capital as a function of the capital structure; (b) the value of the firm as a function of its capital structure

Table 12.1 Capital structure, financial risk and the cost of equity

	Firm 1 £	Firm 2 £
Equity (book value, £)	800	200
Debt (interest, 10%)	200	800
Total capital (book value)	1,000	1,000
Total earnings	200	200
Minus interest on debt	20	80
Total net returns on equity	180	120
Rate of return on equity	22.5%	60%
Earnings increase by 50 per cent		
Total returns	300	300
Minus interest on debt	20	80
Net earnings	280	220
Rate of return on equity	35%	110%
Earnings decline by 50 per cent		
Total earnings	100	100
Minus interest	20	80
Net earnings	80	20
Rate of return	10%	10%
The market value of a firm earning £200 in perpetuity at a discount rate of 15 per cent is 200/0.15	1,333.3	1,333.3
If the market value of debt is equal to its book value	200	800
Then the market value of the equity is	1,133.3	533.3
The cost of equity is	$\dfrac{180}{1,133.3} = 15.9$	$\dfrac{120}{533.3} = 22.5$

The higher cost of firm 2 is due to the increased financial risks associated with the higher debt

more highly geared firms become the higher the cost of debt they are faced with. The actual size of the debt ratio at which the cost of debt increases as well as the extent of the increase will vary among firms to reflect differences in business risks.

The cost of equity (K_e) can be defined as the minimum rate of return required by investors in ordinary shares. As residual earners, equity holders bear more risk and should expect higher returns to their investment than debt holders. This is indicated by the higher position of the K_e curve in Figure 12.1. Similarly to the cost of debt curve, the shape of the K_e curve reflects the increase in earnings variability associated with higher gearing ratios. Since the variability of the expected returns and hence the financial risks increase as the debt ratio increases so the equity holders would expect a higher return to their equity (as shown in Table 12.1). In addition, increased indebtness means an increased risk of bankruptcy. Thus, it can be said that the equity holders' required return and hence the cost of equity capital increases as the relative size of debt used to finance the firm increases.

The overall cost of capital (K_w) can be calculated, at different capital structures, as the weighted average of the cost of equity and the cost of debt with the weights being the debt B and the equity E ratios, $B/(B + E)$, and $E/(B + E)$, respectively. Thus, the weighted cost of capital shown in Figure 12.1 for different debt ratios is given by

$$K_w = \frac{E}{B+E} K_e + \frac{B}{B+E} K_d(1-t)$$

where t is the corporate tax rate.

At a zero debt (100 per cent equity) ratio, the weighted cost of capital is the same as the cost of equity. The K_w curve begins therefore at the same level as the K_e curve. As debt increases, however, K_w declines indicating that the overall cost of finance falls due to the lower cost of loan finance. As the proportion of debt finance increases the cost of capital declines until the debt ratio becomes so high that the cost of debt finance rises sharply causing K_w to start rising. The curve K_w, therefore, is U-shaped. The debt to equity ratio corresponding to the minimum point of this curve represents the optimal capital structure since at this capital structure the cost of capital is at a minimum. This happens at $[B/(B + E)]_0$ in Figure 12.1a.

Clearly the minimum point on the U-curve depends both on the position and the shape of both K_e and K_d and can vary among firms according to their characteristics. Thus, to understand the forces that shape the capital cost of each firm we need to investigate further the factors which determine at which gearing ratio costs begin to rise and at what speed. This requires an acknowledgement of the existence of informational and transactional costs which vary among enterprises as will be indicated below when we introduce transactions and agency costs into the analysis. Before doing so we must examine briefly the neoclassical (Modigliani–Miller) approach to these issues.

The Modigliani–Miller approach to the cost of capital

In their seminal contribution to the definition of the cost of capital and the value of the firm Modigliani and Miller (1958) argued that in the absence of taxes and given a well-informed and well functioning capital market, the cost of capital and the value of the firm are constant and independent of capital structure.

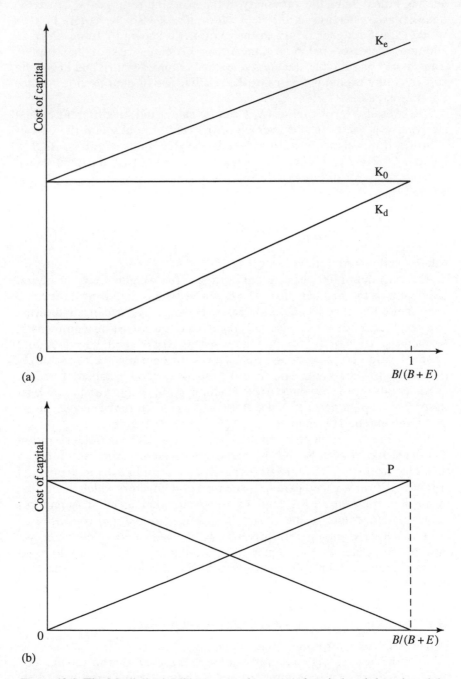

Figure 12.2 The Modigliani–Miller approach to cost of capital and the price of the firm: (a) the cost of capital is independent of capital structure; (b) market value is independent of capital structure

Very simply put, their argument is as follows. Since debt finance is more secure its cost is lower than the cost of equity so that as the gearing ratio increases the overall cost of capital to the firm should decline. However, an increasing debt ratio increases the financial risks to shareholders who in response expect a higher rate of return. This increase in the cost of equity is exactly equal to the reduction in cost brought about by the increase in debt so that the overall cost of capital remains the same whatever the debt to equity ratio. This is shown in Figure 12.2.

The cost K_0 *of capital is in fact the rate at which the firm's expected returns (ER) are capitalised,* so that the total price P (market value) of the firm, can be determined by

$$P = \frac{ER}{K_0} \tag{12.1}$$

or

$$K_0 = \frac{ER}{P}$$

When debt B is introduced, the value of the firm is $P = E + B$ and it follows from equation (12.1) that

$$ER = PK_0 = (E + B)K_0 \tag{12.2}$$

and the return on equity (E) is equal to the total expected returns (ER) minus the interest payment on debt (K_dB), i.e.

$$E = ER - K_dB$$

where K_d denotes the cost of debt and K_dB is the share of debt in total returns. Therefore, since the cost of equity (K_e) is defined as the rate of capitalisation of the expected returns on equity, it can be found by solving the following equation:

$$E = \frac{ER - K_dB}{K_e}$$

which by substituting ER from equation (12.2) and rearranging terms gives

$$K_e = \frac{K_0(E + B) - K_dB}{E}$$

or

$$K_e = K_0 + \frac{(K_0 - K_d)B}{E}$$

(12.3)

That is, the required return on equity is equal to the rate of return that would be expected if the firm had no debt at all (K_0) plus a financial risk premium which is proportional to the debt to equity ratio.

Modigliani and Miller (1963) recognised that the introduction of taxes alters the basic proposition that the cost of capital is constant. Since interest payments are tax deductible the cost of debt is effectively subsidised to an extent dependent on the corporate tax rate. Given its expected returns a firm's tax liabilities decline as the debt to equity ratio increases and the net returns per share increase. This implies that as debt increases the shareholders' increased financial risk is partly compensated by the reduction in tax (known as the tax shield). The required gross rate of return is correspondingly reduced. In other words, the compensation which equity holders expect for the increased risk associated with debt declines because of the tax shield. Since tax benefits increase with debt the cost of capital declines as the gearing ratio increases.

As indicated in Figure 12.3, the implication of the tax shield is that there is no equity in the optimum capital structure. In the absence of other costs a 100 per cent debt finance would be optimal. This is not, however, commonly observed in reality for the simple reason that other costs do exist, an important group of which relate to the increased risk of bankruptcy which is associated with increases in debt finance. The cost of both equity and debt will increase as the providers of finance seek compensation for increased risks. Thus, with bankruptcy costs, K^0 eventually increases (see the broken line in Figure 12.3).

The cost of capital and the value of the firm

The value of the firm, or the value of its equity or debt, is simply the capitalised value of the net expected returns on the corresponding investment. Since the capitalised value of an expected stream of net returns increases as the cost of capital declines, there is a correspondence between the cost of capital and the value of the firm. If the cost of capital varies with a firm's capital structure then the value of the firm will also depend on capital structure. Figures 12.1(b) and 12.2(b) indicate how the market price of debt and equity finance and the total value of the firm vary as a firm's debt ratio increases. At the optimal capital structure $[B/(B + E)]_0$ in Figure 12.1, the cost of capital is minimised and the value of the firm is maximised. In Figure 12.2, the cost of capital is constant and independent of the capital structure of the firm. The value of the firm, therefore, is also constant and independent of the firm's debt to equity ratio.

One of the assumptions of the above models is that a firm's expected

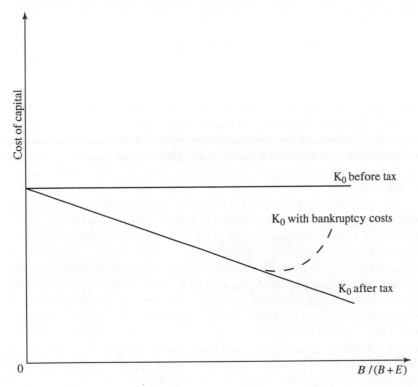

Figure 12.3 The impact of 'tax shield' and bankruptcy risks on the cost of capital

returns are constant over time. In reality, as we argued in Chapter 9, modern dynamic firms will seek to grow and the rate at which a firm grows is likely to have an important influence on the price of its shares (or its capital cost).

The value of a growing firm's equity as determined in Chapter 9 is repeated here for completeness. Recall that the cost of equity is the rate of return shareholders expect to earn, over the years, from holding the firm's shares (Reekie and Crook 1985). For a firm whose present dividend D_0 is expected to grow at a constant rate of g per cent per year, this is the rate r at which the sum of the discounted present value of future dividends is equal to the market price P_0. The cost of equity can be calculated by solving the equation (for further explanation see Appendix 9.3)

$$P_0 = \frac{D_0}{1+r} + \frac{D_0(1+g)}{(1+r)^2} + \frac{D_0(1+g)^2}{(1+r)^3} + \cdots + \frac{D_0(1+g)^n}{(1+r)^{1+n}}$$

which simplifies to

$$P_0 = \frac{D_0}{r - g} \qquad\qquad\qquad (12.4)$$

or

$$r = D_0/P_0 + g$$

where $r = K_e$. Thus, the cost of capital is equal to the rate of return on common stock increased by the firm's expected constant growth rate. This is correct on the assumption that the capital market is well informed and share prices reflect all the available information about the economy and the firm concerned. Assuming that share prices adjust quickly and cost-lessly to new information any changes in g (see Chapter 9) or r will be reflected on P.

It is clear, from equation (12.4), that given a firm's expected returns and growth rate, the value of its equity will vary inversely with the cost of capital. The higher the cost of capital the lower the capitalised value of an expected stream of returns.

The question remains as to whether the cost of capital depends on capital structure or whether the Modigliani–Miller (1958, 1961) hypotheses – that a firm's financial structure and its dividend policy are a matter of indifference in minimising a company's cost of finance and in determining its value – hold. Given the significance of these questions for financial management it is worth reiterating the fundamental assumptions behind the classical propositions so as to lay the foundation for a better understanding of the complexity of observed financial behaviour.

Classical economic theory views the firm as a set of production possibilities from which the most profitable one is always chosen. Consequently, financial securities are claims on a stream of expected net returns whose size or variability is exogenously determined. The fundamental premises of the Modigliani–Miller theorems are that the firm's gross earnings stream is exogenously determined and therefore unaffected by capital structure and that capital markets are well functioning so that investors can borrow on the same terms as firms. If these two premises are valid it follows that (a) capital structure and (b) dividend policy have no effect on the valuation of the firm.

To illustrate the irrelevance of capital structure suppose that two similar firms exist each expecting the same gross returns, ER. There are only two sources of finance; equity E and debt B. Firm 1 is totally equity financed while firm 2 has a 50 per cent debt to equity ratio. The market interest rate is r so that the net return on the equity of firm 2 after repayment of debt with interest is $ER - B(1 + r)$. An investor wishing to earn say 10 per cent of ER can do so by buying 10 per cent of the equity of firm 1. An alternative strategy would be to buy 10 per cent of the total finance of firm 2, i.e. 10 per cent of equity and 10 per cent of debt which would give the same cash flow:

0.10 [ER − B(1 + r)] + 0.10B(1 + r).

Since the second strategy gives the same cash flow, the total market price of firm 1 (equity) cannot be more than the market price of firm 2. If it were no one would invest in its shares. Therefore the price of equity of firm 1 is

$$P(\text{ER}) \leqslant B + P[\text{ER} - B(1 + r)].$$

Consider now another investor who wishes to earn say 20 per cent of the net returns of firm B (after principal and interest on debt has been repaid), i.e. 0.20[ER − B(1 + r)]. To achieve this she or he can buy 20 per cent of the equity of firm 2. An alternative strategy does exist however. The investor can buy 20 per cent of the shares of firm 1 and use them as collateral to borrow an amount equal to 20 per cent of the debt of firm 2. This leads to the same net returns since the investor receives dividends equal to 0.20ER and pays principal and interest on debt equal to 0.20B(1 + r). If investors can borrow at the same rate as firms (r) then for anybody to be prepared to buy shares of firm 2 the alternative portfolio which consists of shares of firm 1 and borrowing must not be cheaper. That is,

$$P[\text{ER} - B(1 + r)] \leqslant P(\text{ER}) - B.$$

The two inequalities imply that the value of the two firms is the same and does not depend on capital structure (Milgrom and Roberts 1992).

Intuitively the argument is that if two strategies offer the same pay-off they must have the same cost in equilibrium. That is, two firms with assets offering the same total returns will have the same market value despite any differences in the liabilities issued to finance their assets. This equalisation of values will be the result of arbitrage. In the absence of equal values, entrepreneurs will seize the opportunity to profit by selling shares of the higher valued firm and investing in shares in the lower-valued firm. The resulting arbitrage would tend to equalise the value of the two firms.

Such arbitrage arguments are at the heart of financial economics. They can be applied to show that when investment decisions, the firm's cash flow and investors' perceptions of it are independent of financial policies the market value P (= B + E) of the firm depends on the firm's total gross earnings and not on the way in which these earnings may be shared between shareholders and bondholders.

THE TRANSACTIONS AND AGENCY COSTS APPROACH TO THE FIRM'S OPTIMAL CAPITAL STRUCTURE

The classical hypothesis that a firm's capital structure is irrelevant to its value and its operating costs is refuted by observation and empirical evidence. The basic reason for this divergence is to be found in the primary premise of the neoclassical approach which is the existence of well functioning markets within which firms operate as mere production functions.

In reality a firm's relationship with the providers of capital, similarly to its relationship with other resource owners, is subject to informational asymmetries and contractual difficulties the extent of which varies with the characteristics of the transactions involved. Small-number exchanges under conditions of bounded rationality and information impactedness can create substantial contractual costs.[3] Similarly, informational asymmetries coupled with divergencies of interests create agency costs.[4]

A firm's capital structure can affect its market value not only through the effects of taxation and its influence on the probability with which bankruptcy costs may occur, but also by changing management incentives to work hard, by affecting the extent of the divergence of interests that can arise between shareholders and lenders and by providing incentives to stockholders to monitor management and to restrict the scope for discretionary behaviour.

Since transactions and agency costs vary with the sources of finance efficiency considerations indicate that the way in which a resource may be financed will depend on the attributes of that resource and in particular on its asset specificity (Williamson 1985). Furthermore, it follows that the transactions cost of debt and hence the debt to equity finance will vary inversely with the extent to which resources are firm specific and vulnerable to moral hazard (Alchian and Woodward 1988).

In short, the classical assumption of the irrelevancy of capital structure is misleadingly simple because it ignores the impact of transaction costs and agency relationships which can be influenced by financial decisions. Financial policies can affect a firm's expected returns by influencing the incentives and performance of various members of the firm and the behaviour of investors. Investors have typically less information compared with management regarding the true productive potential of the firm. A low current dividend, for example, may be interpreted as an indication that the firm's prospects are poor or a high gearing may be perceived as managerial confidence in the firm. In either case investor expectations about future returns are influenced and this is reflected in the market value of the firm. Finally investors may have ownership rights of decision and control which can influence the firm's returns and costs and hence its market value.

These ideas are developed in the following sections.

The agency cost of debt finance

Investors lending finance would want the firm to act in a way consistent with the debt holder's interests. However, if the assets financed are firm specific and costly to monitor then it becomes difficult for lenders (principals) to know what the firm will do in which case the agent (firm) can act in a way that serves its own interests rather than the interests of the principal. That is, debt finance is subject to moral hazard costs or, as the finance literature puts it, costs arising from *post-contractual opportunism*. In other words, once debt finance has been acquired the firm does not bear the full losses of its failure which implies that an owner–manager has an incentive to increase risks by investing in projects with a small probability of high earnings, which the firm enjoys, and a large downside risk which will be mainly borne by the lenders.

To illustrate the divergence of interests that exists between lenders and equity holders suppose that an individual seeks a £7,000 loan to invest in a project which has a fifty–fifty chance of yielding an end of period cash flow of either £9,000 or £11,000. This is a safe project since whatever the 'state of nature' the yield is sufficiently high to repay the loan. However, unknown to the lenders is the existence of another project (B) which yields £1,000 or £19,000 with an equal chance. After the loan has been granted the borrower will have an incentive to adopt the more risky project B since if successful the gain to the borrower will be much higher (£12,000 as opposed to £4,000 from project A) and if unsuccessful the loss will be mainly borne by the debtholder. Debtholders being aware of this incentive may (a) attempt to design appropriate contracts to safeguard their interests, in our fictitious example the lenders would want some guarantees or monitoring power to ensure that the loan is indeed used in project A rather than project B, and (b) be unwilling to lend when the debt ratio is extreme. It is highly unlikely that a firm with say £10,000 equity would be able to raise £10,000,000 in debt.

In principle, lenders may issue contracts with various covenant provisions which limit managerial behaviour in a way that safeguards the value of their loans. Indeed contracts imposing constraints on managerial decisions regarding the amount of dividend equity holders may award themselves or including clauses which restrict future debt issues or the sale of certain assets or referring to the maintenance of working capital are commonly observed in practice. To protect lenders completely, however, such contracts must be so detailed and covering so many aspects of the decision making that the relevant contractual costs would be prohibitively high. Besides, even if feasible such restrictive constraints could inhibit the efficient functioning of the firm by limiting the ability of management to respond quickly and effectively to profitable opportunities as they arise. In short, 'since management is a continuous decision making process it will be almost impossible to completely specify such conditions without having the bondholders actually perform the management function' (Jensen and Meckling 1976). Since lenders are unable to design perfect contracts they are likely to require higher interest payments to compensate them for the risks they are undertaking. Incidentally, since the difficulties in initiating and implementing contracts which protect lenders' interests increase as asset specificity and opportunism become more significant, it can be predicted that the more firm specific and more vulnerable to moral hazard a firm's assets are the lower its debt to equity ratio will be. This is in addition to and distinct from financial risks.

It must be emphasised that asset specificity and vulnerability to opportunism must be distinguished from other kinds of risks. In other words, agency costs are different from and additional to financial risk costs. The following examples suggested by Alchian and Woodward (1988) may illustrate this point. Compare the debt finance of a pharmaceutical firm with that of a public utility. The pharmaceutical company's activities are more diverse, include substantial research and development (R&D) and are difficult to monitor. Lenders may find it difficult to initiate and implement a contract that safeguards effectively their interests. This is not the case for public utilities whose activities are limited and easy to monitor. Prices are regulated and the possibilities of opportunistic behaviour are low. Debt finance will thus be cheaper for public utilities because of the nature of their resources and the monitoring possibilities and not because of the degree of riskiness involved. The distinction between the risk of the business and the debt-related risk is made clearer in the case of oil wells which although very risky are easy to monitor by lenders. Monitoring is easy since the optimal rate at which to pump oil depends on the pattern of prices over time. Prices may vary widely making the oil well a risky venture, but there is little in the way of possibilities of exploiting the lenders of an oil well either by increasing the riskiness of its value or by changing its product into personal consumption. As expected oil wells are highly debt financed while drilling and exploration of oil is not (for further details see the application at the end of Chapter 9).

Finally, as already noted, there are bankruptcy costs associated with debt which can help explain why debt finance does not predominate over a firm's capital structure. In the event of bankruptcy the pay-off to fixed interest debt holders is reduced. Since the probability of bankruptcy affects the net present value of the debt holders' returns, bankruptcy costs affect the cost of debt. Further, the cost of debt increases with the debt ratio since (a) managerial incentives to transfer wealth from bondholders increase with the size of debt, (b) the monitoring costs which these managerial incentive effects create also increase with debt, and (c) financial risks and managerial incentives to undertake risks increase with debt enhancing the probability of bankruptcy as debt finance increases.

Since the agency costs rise as debt increases, the question arises as to why firms use debt at all? There are several reasons for this. First, as noted earlier, there are often tax advantages related to debt. Second, shareholders may use debt as a means of preventing managers or trade unions from appropriating large parts of quasi-rents or windfall gains. This is most relevant when informational asymmetries are substantial since then managers of very profitable firms can utilize part of the profits in discretionary investment projects, perquisites or other status enhancing activities or unions may demand higher wages. High debt implies that a large part of the profit will be absorbed as interest payments reducing the incentives for opportunistic behaviour. Finally, even in the absence of any tax or other debt advantages, owner–managers with limited resources facing high equity costs will wish to raise debt finance when there are investment projects whose marginal revenue exceeds the marginal cost including the increased marginal cost of debt.

The agency cost of equity finance

Similarly to debt finance, equity may be subject to agency costs since the interests of an owner–manager may diverge from the interests of non-manager (outside) equity holders. To illustrate suppose that the firm of Figure 12.4 is owned exclusively by its manager. The market value of the firm is measured on the vertical axis while the market value F of any non-pecuniary benefits the manager may decide to take is measured along the x axis. Non- pecuniary benefits may include extra holidays, fewer working hours and expenditure on lavish offices or executive cars.[5] In the absence of such personal consumption the firm's value would be V. That is, V represents the maximum net present value of the firm's returns when the manager's consumption of non-pecuniary (fringe) benefits is zero. F_1, on the other hand, represents the maximum amount of fringe benefits a manager could possibly take. Line $V–F_1$ indicates a trade-off between V and F and is, therefore, a constraint under which the manager operates. Assuming that every £1 spent on non-pecuniary benefits reduces the value of the firm by £1 then the slope of this constraint is -1. If, additionally, managerial utility depends on the value of the firm and on non-pecuniary consumption then a utility maximising owner–manager whose utility is represented by indifference curves I_1, I_2 and I_3 will take F^* non-pecuniary benefits and the value of the firm will be V^*. This is because under the given constraint utility is maximised at point A (see Chapter 7). If it is possible, however, to sell part of the equity at the firm's current price V^* then the manager would have an incentive to do so if co-ownership implies that she or he will not bear the full cost of the fringe benefits.

To illustrate suppose that the owner–manager keeps a fraction a (80 per cent say) of the equity and sells the remaining fraction $1 - a$, to an outsider. If the buyer is unaware of the existence of F or believes that it will remain the same after the sale the price offered will be $0.2V^*$ for 20 per cent of the equity. After the sale, however, the owner–manager will have an incentive to take higher perquisites and to increase expenditure in luxurious office furnishings, executive cars and other status enhancing items since the cost of these benefits to the manager has been reduced to 80 per cent of their value. This is because fringe benefits reduce the firm's residual income part of which belongs to the new equity holder, the cost

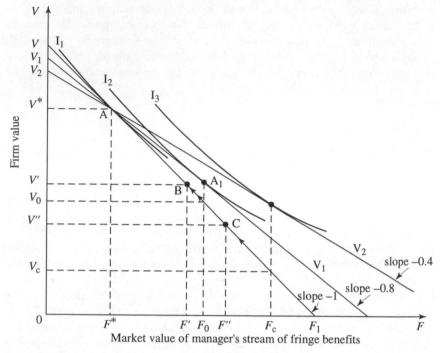

Figure 12.4 The value of thc firm and the level of managerial fringe benefits as a function of outside equity
Source: Adapted from Jensen and Meckling 1976, Figure 1

of these benefits is therefore shared between the two co-owners in proportion to their equity. Thus, the cost of F to the owner–manager becomes cheaper by a proportion dependent on the share of the outside equity. In fact the cost to the owner–manager has been reduced to £0.8 and the slope of the constraint is now -0.8 (instead of -1) as represented by line $V_1 V_1$. The owner–manager's utility will in this case be maximised at point A_1 which means that the value of F will increase to F_o and the value of the firm will fall to V_0. A further sale of equity say to 40 per cent of the total reduces the cost of F to the owner–manager and changes the slope of the constraint to -0.40 as shown by line $V_2 V_2$. The value of F increases (to Fc) and the value of the firm declines correspondingly (to Vc).

Generally, when management owns an insignificant part of the equity the divergence of interests between management and ownership creates several conflicts. First, management may be inclined to increase the value of financial and non-financial benefits for top management and to provide perquisitcs for other members of the team. Second, the firm's objectives may change. Management may be more interested in growth and long-term survival or in creating discretionary investment and stability rather than value maximisation (for details see Chapter 9).

Equity buyers aware of the existence of the divergence of interests, or the owner–manager's incentive to increase fringe benefits F, will be reluctant to pay $0.2V^*$ for 20 per cent or $0.4V^*$ for 40 per cent of the firm's shares. The price offered will clearly depend on the price that buyers expect the firm to have after the purchase. That is, for a claim on the firm of $1 - a$ the buyer 'will only pay $1 - a$ times the value he expects the firm to have given the induced change in the behaviour of the owner–manager' (Jensen and Meckling 1976: 318).

To the extent that expectations are rational, the price of equity would be just sufficient to compensate the owner–manager for the value of the equity sold after an adjustment has been made for the increase in non-pecuniary consumption. Thus, since the incentive to consume fringe benefits is enhanced as the share of the outside equity rises, the price at which shares are sold falls as equity increases. In other words, the cost of equity increases as outside ownership expands.

In a perfect world, the reduction in the value of the firm is entirely borne by the owner–manager[8] who would therefore only sell equity if the funds raised could be used in alternative ventures with a return to the owner–manager higher than the reduction in the value of the firm engendered by the increase in outside equity. If the funds are invested within the firm, the owner–manager will raise equity and expand the size of the firm up to the point at which the gross increment in value is just offset by the incremental loss associated with consumption of additional fringe benefits as the manager's share of equity declines.

In reality it is usually possible for shareholders to attempt to monitor the behaviour of managers in order to restrict their ability to enjoy fringe benefits. Several monitoring devices are used such as auditing, formal control systems, budget restrictions or the provision of compensation packages with incentives intended to align the interests of the two groups. As explained in Chapter 9 these are particularly useful in uncertain and complex situations.

Monitoring and the provision of incentives, however, are costly. Monitoring costs reduce the value of the firm to the shareholders by the net present value of the expected future monitoring expenditures. The maximum price shareholders will therefore be prepared to pay for any given fraction of the firm's equity will depend on the size of monitoring costs and on their effectiveness in reducing managerial discretion.

Managers may also expend resources in order to convince shareholders that discretionary behaviour will be restricted. Such expenditures are known as 'bonding costs' and can take the form of auditing by outside auditors or limitations in the manager's decision-making powers. The bonding cost of the latter can be very substantial since such limitations may restrict management's flexibility which can result in the loss of profitable opportunities for the firm.

Managers will in general undertake bonding costs to the extent to which the marginal benefits of such costs exceed the marginal bonding cost. And, since managerial incentives to act opportunistically (e.g. by taking high fringe benefits) increase with the percentage of outside equity, monitoring and bonding costs will also be positively related to outside equity.

In brief, the smaller the outside ownership the more convergent the management–shareholder interests are likely to be and the smaller the agency costs. The relationship is not, however, a precise one and it can vary with the personality of managers. Some managers may, by virtue of their personality or tenure or status as founder, identify with the interests of shareholders while holding a small percentage of equity. Others may be much less attached to the job despite holding more significant stakes (Morck *et al.* 1988).

Agency costs and the optimal capital structure

If the cost of equity increases with the extent of outside ownership why is it that we do not observe large corporations with a tiny or no equity capital owned by management and financed entirely by debt? As already suggested in the previous section, debt finance can also be very costly for three reasons: (a) the divergence of interests and the concomitant incentive effects associated with highly leveraged firms, (b) monitoring costs created by these incentives and (c) bankruptcy costs. Thus, any cost savings associated with reductions in outside equity may be more than offset by an increase in the debt ratio required to maintain a certain level of total outside finance.

In other words, both the cost of outside equity and the cost of debt vary with the firm's debt to equity ratio in a way dependent on agency costs. There is no reason to suppose, however, that the overall cost of capital may not also vary with the capital structure. On the contrary, differences in the agency costs of different sources of finance ensure that the optimal capital structure consists of various financial assets. To illustrate consider a firm of a given size with costs as shown in Figure 12.5. Curve AA' refers to the agency cost of equity. Since the x axis measures the debt ratio $B/(E + B)$, point A' represents a 100 per cent geared firm. There is no outside equity and consequently the equity cost is also zero. As the equity ratio increases (the debt ratio declines) the cost of co-ownership increases since the owner–manager's incentive to exploit the outside equity holders and/or the managerial monitoring and bonding costs increase. When debt finance is zero the agency cost of equity is A while that of debt is zero.

Curve 0T indicates how the cost of debt finance varies with the firm's capital structure. As the debt ratio increases so do the owner–manager's incentives to exploit bondholders by undertaking risky projects. The cost

of debt reaches its maximum at point T when all the external funding
derives from debt.

The sum of debt and equity cost at each debt ratio is indicated by curve
AT. As the debt to equity ratio expands beyond a certain level 'the
marginal agency cost of debt begins to dominate the marginal agency cost
of outside equity and thus the result of this is the generally observed
phenomenon of the simultaneous use of both debt and outside equity'
(Jensen and Meckling 1976). For the firm illustrated in Figure 12.5 the cost
of capital is minimised when the debt ratio is E^*. E^* denotes the optimal
debt to equity ratio when the outside funding requirements are assumed
to be at a given level. For a given size of firm, as the level of outside
funding increases the agency costs of finance increase. Agency costs,
therefore, are highest for firms run by professional managers especially
when they acquire firm-specific skills and knowledge. Graphically, an
increase in the level of outside finance is shown by an upwards shift of the
cost curves which may alter the optimal debt to equity ratio. Additionally,
since complexity increases with size, as the size of the firm increases it is
likely that the monitoring function becomes more complicated so that the
larger the firm the higher the agency costs.

The position and the shape of the cost curves and hence the optimum

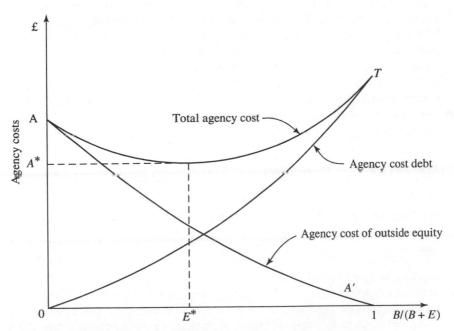

Figure 12.5 Agency costs as a function of debt to total outside financing
Source: Adapted from Jensen and Meckling 1976, Figure 5

debt ratio will also vary with the nature of the transactions in which the firm is involved. This is because the nature of transactions influences (a) the size of transaction costs and the ease or difficulty with which managers may pursue their own interests and (b) the costs of monitoring and bonding. Moreover, agency costs, and therefore the optimum capital structure, depend on the preferences of managers (the shape of the I curves in Figure 12.4), the ease or difficulty of evaluating and rewarding performance, the feasibility of incentive schemes and the costs of devising monitoring procedures.

In brief, agency costs relate to human and physical asset specificity and informational asymmetries which contribute to contractual difficulties.

CONCLUDING REMARKS

The 'irrelevance' of capital structure postulated by Modigliani and Miller in their seminal contribution of 1958 was based on the assumption of perfectly functioning capital markets and the absence of bankruptcy costs or tax advantages of debt finance. It is now accepted that the risk of bankruptcy and the tax benefits of debt imply that the probability distribution of the cash flows of the firm is dependent on capital structure and that an optimal capital structure exists. The suggestion, however, that the optimal capital structure can be determined solely on the basis of tax subsidies on debt and bankruptcy costs is seriously incomplete for two reasons: (a) it implies that 'no debt should be used in the absence of tax subsidies if bankruptcy costs are positive' (Jensen and Meckling, 1976: 333), which we know to be factually incorrect since debt finance was commonly used before the introduction of tax subsidies, and (b) the theory cannot explain the existence of preferred stock and warrants.[6]

The introduction of agency costs strengthens the theory of the determination of a firm's capital structure and resolves the 'irrelevancy' riddle posed by Modigliani and Miller.

SUMMARY

The question of the determination of the ownership of the firm and its capital costs is addressed in this chapter. Ownership was defined as two fundamental rights: the right to monitor and direct the use of resources and the right to receive the residual income of the 'firm'. Ownership can be exercised by any member of the team involved in the contractual relationships that define a firm.

Ownership by equity holders, although commonly observed, especially among large corporations, is by no means universal. Firms can be and often are owned by their workers, suppliers, customers or lenders. The exercise of ownership, however, is costly so that the assignment of ownership rights can be explained by efficiency considerations. Agency and other transaction costs related to the organisation and control of the firm can have an important influence in determining a firm's ownership structure as well as its optimal capital structure.

Given its practical importance, the question of the existence and determination of an optimal capital structure has been extensively debated over a number of years. The so-called 'traditional view' maintains that the cost of capital varies with the extent of debt finance so that the selection of the appropriate mix of debt and equity can minimise the cost and maximise the value of the firm. The U-shape of the cost of capital curve calculated as a weighted average is attributed, according to this view, to the beneficial influence of the initially cheaper cost of debt. Financial risks and the cost of bankruptcy mean that beyond a certain point increased gearing causes the cost of capital to rise.

The neoclassical view that in a tax free world a firm's capital structure is immaterial because any advantages of cheaper debt finance are exactly offset by the increased financial risks associated with debt has been challenged. The introduction of tax benefits and the costs of bankruptcy into the Modigliani–Miller model have modified this polar view so that it is now widely accepted that costs vary with the capital structure and there is an optimal gearing ratio.

The hypothesis that the cost of capital varies with its capital structure solely because of tax benefits and bankruptcy risks, is weak however, since it implies that in the absence of tax benefits the positive costs of bankruptcy would lead to no debt finance, a prediction which is contrary to experience. The contention that a firm's financing decisions affect its cost of capital and value, is strengthened when the agency costs of ownership are explicitly introduced into the analysis.

In brief, the irrelevancy of financial structures envisaged by Modigliani–Miller is invalid when the functioning of financial markets is impeded by informational asymmetries, in which case capital structures affect managerial incentives and the firm's expected returns. Moreover, informational asymmetries between principals (investors) and agents (decision makers) alter the firm's objectives so that decisions are no longer governed by simple valuation maximisation as assumed by the neoclassical theory (Greenward and Stiglitz 1990). In short, the capital structure or the equity to debt ratio is not immaterial when transaction and other agency costs are present. To reiterate, the agency costs of equity derive mainly from informational asymmetries and excessive perquisite consumption while the agency cost of debt derive from the same phenomena but are mainly related to risk incentives, investment incentives and bankruptcy costs.

APPLICATION: OWNERSHIP STRUCTURE AND DEBT FINANCE IN JAPANESE CORPORATIONS

There is evidence to suggest that the ownership structure of Japanese corporations differs, in certain important respects, to that of US corporations for reasons attributed to differences in the agency costs of finance. Such differences may arise because of the different institutional arrangements that prevail in Japan.

Institutional arrangements in Japanese markets differ from US and European markets in at least two important respects. First, financial institutions in Japan, unlike their US counterparts, are legally permitted to be and in practice are 'active investors'. They own shares, lend funds and actively participate in the running of the business they finance.[7] Japanese financial institutions exert, therefore, direct corporate control to an extent that is not observed in other countries. Second, Japanese industrial organisation is such that two broad groups of firms co-exist; the independent firms and those that belong to a *keiretsu*. A keiretsu is a group of firms from a variety of industries bound together by interlocking share ownership and by common dependence on one large commercial bank as a major lender. Large shareholders in keiretsu firms are often business partners as well as major creditors. Independent firms differ from keiretsu firms in that they have more distant relationships with other firms and financiers.

Such institutional differences may have an important influence on a firm's ownership structure, through their impact on the method and effectiveness of managerial monitoring and the provision of incentives. The existence of significant differences between Japanese and US corporate ownership concentration and composition can therefore be attributed at least partly to differences in the institutional environment of the firms. Before elaborating we must consider the evidence.

Table 12.2 summarises some recent research findings. The 1983 figures cover the Japanese manufacturing sector (Kester 1986), while the 1984 figures were derived from all listed Japanese corporations (67.3 per cent of total share ownership). The US sample represents 37.7 per cent of all corporate equity (Prowse 1992). Two observations

Table 12.2 The ownership structure of Japanese and US corporations

	Japanese manufacturing corporations (1983)	Various sectors (1984)	
		Japan	USA
Percentage of equity held by			
Financial institutions	37.69	43.30	26.60
Domestic corporations	25.73	24.00	11.10
Government	0.01	–	–
Individuals	29.53	26.70	58.10
Foreigners	7.04	5.00	4.20
Other	–	1.00	–
	100.00	100.00	100.00
Mean percentage held by			
Ten largest holders	44.44		
Five largest holders		33.10	25.40

Source: Kester 1986: Exhibit 1; and Prowse 1992: Tables I and II

follow from Table 12.2. First, there is a difference in ownership *concentration* between the two countries. Further data analysis confirms the conclusion that Japanese industry is more concentrated than the US industry and that financial institutions are the most important shareholders in Japanese corporation. There is no evidence, however, of any significant differences between keiretsu and independent Japanese firms (Prowse 1992).

Second, there is a significant difference in the *composition* of corporate ownership between Japan and the USA. A large part (43 per cent) of Japanese equity is owned by banks and other financial institutions. In addition almost a quarter of equity is held by other corporations. The corresponding figure for the USA is only 11 per cent. Individual share ownership is much more restricted. The percentage of ownership in the hands of individuals in the USA is double that observed in Japan. The small individual ownership implies a weak market in corporate control which has led to the erroneous view that shareholders have little control over management. In reality shareholder control in Japan is simply exercised differently than in the USA. Large shareholders have direct control on management and since they are also large lenders in the same keiretsu it is likely that they may preclude policies which attempt to transfer wealth from debt holders to shareholders (Prowse 1992). As explained in the text the prospect of such transfers (asset substitution) constitutes a significant part of the agency cost of debt. Its elimination implies therefore that Japanese firms are faced with lower agency costs of debt finance.

The agency costs of debt are further reduced because the ownership structure makes it possible for debt to be short term with secure characteristics. Most of the debt of Japanese companies is provided by banks in the form of promissory notes with 90 to 120 days of maturity which are renewed continually for a number of years. In contrast to the USA these loans are secured by collaterals on real estate, securities, obligation rights and inventory. Among the advantages of the use of this secured short-term method of finance are (a) a mitigation against incentives to under-invest, this is because shareholders can capture a higher percentage of net investment benefit than might be possible with unsecured loans and finance is available through the continuous renewal of debt, (b) a reduced need for monitoring the costs of debt and (c) a reduced scope for asset substitution. Informational asymmetries between management and lenders are also reduced by this structure.

Another financial benefit that arises from the Japanese ownership structure and which reduces the cost of debt is a lowering of the cost of financial distress. Temporary financial difficulties may cause costs by diverting corporate strategy and damaging the reputation of the firm even if bankruptcy is averted. In Japan the main bank of a company in

Table 12.3 Comparing Japanese with US corporation debt/equity ratios

	Japan (344)			USA (452)		
	Mean	Median	Standard deviation	Mean	Median	Standard deviation
Book value equity						
Gross debt	2.703	1.605	3.822	0.745	0.456	1.332
Net debt	1.910	1.000	3.098	0.577	0.340	1.342
Fully adjusted debt	1.494	0.636	2.860	NR	NR	NR
Market value equity						
Gross debt	1.416	0.949	1.444	0.882	0.490	1.184
Net debt	0.976	0.590	1.174	0.687	0.342	1.142
Fully adjusted debt	0.729	0.371	1.077	NR	NR	NR

Source: Adapted from Kester 1986: Exhibit 4

financial distress will co-ordinate the rescue effort and in the event of bankruptcy it will undertake to absorb the losses thus saving on the costs of protracted negotiations with other creditors. The Dai-Ichi Kangyo Bank, for example, as the main lender of the Kojin Corporation undertook, voluntarily, to repay all of Kojin Corporation's debts when Kojin went bankrupt (Kester 1986).

On the basis of economic reasoning we would predict that a lower cost of debt finance should lead to a higher debt to equity ratio, other things being equal. We would therefore expect Japanese firms to be more highly leveraged compared with US firms. The empirical evidence on this issue, although limited, provides some support for this view. As Table 12.3 indicates Japanese firms tend to operate with higher debt to equity ratios than US firms, although the difference is not always as large as sometimes suggested.

Kester (1986) shows that, at least for manufacturing firms, the leverage, on a market value basis, is not significantly different between Japan and USA if account is taken of firm differences in growth, profitability, risk, size and industry group. A significant difference does exist, however, when leverage is measured on a book value basis. This is particularly true for mature, capital intensive industries rather than for the whole Japanese manufacturing sector.

FURTHER READING

Barnea, A., Haugen, R.A., and Senbet, W.L. (1985) *Agency Problems and Financial Contracts*, Englewood Cliffs, NJ: Prentice Hall. This gives a rigorous and comprehensive, if somewhat technical, coverage of the nature of agency problems as they relate to corporate structure and financial management.

Copland, E.C. and Weston, J.F. (1988) *Financial Theory and Corporate Policy* 3rd edn, Reading, MA: Addison-Wesley. Chapter 13 gives a more advanced account of capital structure and cost.

Hansmann, Henry (1988) 'Ownership of the Firm', *Journal of Law, Economics and*

Organisation, IV (2). This gives a lucid and detailed account of the ownership issues raised in this chapter.

Milgrom, P. and Roberts, J. (1992) *Economics, Organisation and Management*, Englewood Cliffs, NJ: Prentice Hall. This adopts a similar approach to that adopted in this text, but gives a broader coverage to some of the issues raised here.

QUESTIONS

1 'The notion that firms are owned, controlled and administered by capital rather than labour is a myth.' Explain and critically evaluate this statement giving evidence wherever possible.

2 Explain why high levels of debt encourage risk taking when equity holders control the management of the firm.

3 'Information asymmetry coupled with managerial moral hazard implies that the cost of equity finance increases as the debt to equity ratio declines.' Explain whether you agree or disagree with this statement.

4 Since bankruptcy costs increase with the size of the debt, when interest payments are not tax deductible we would expect firms to have no incentive to raise debt finance. Firms would therefore be almost totally equity financed. Yet empirical evidence contradicts this expectation. Can you explain why?

5 Explain the concept of an optimal capital structure, examine its main determinants and comment on the implications of capital structure for the behaviour of the firm.

6 The debt to equity ratio of company A is 1:3. If the cost of debt is 9 per cent and the cost of equity is 18 per cent calculate the weighted average cost of capital assuming (a) a tax free world and (b) that the rate of corporation tax is 25 per cent.

Evaluate this method of calculating the cost of capital.

7 Do you agree with the view that transaction costs have resolved the riddle of the irrelevancy of capital structures? Explain.

NOTES

1 This section draws heavily on Hansmann (1988).

2 Investment may then depend crucially on the investor's time preference function. See Hirsleifer (1958).

3 For an elaboration on this point see pages 71–2.

4 For further details revise pages 295–305.

5 An example is F. Ross Johnson, the head of Standard Brands and then Nabisco Brands until 1988, who had built a reputation for spending corporate money lavishly. 'He doubled executives' salaries . . . and provided them (and himself) with company apartments, a private box at Madison Square Garden, and multiple country club memberships. He also put a variety of former athletes on the payroll' (Milgron and Roberts 1992: 493).

6 A warrant is a security issued by the firm in return for cash. It promises to issue shares of the firm to the holder of the warrant for a fixed price at any time up to the warrant's maturity date.

7 In 1984 commercial banks held over 20 per cent of the outstanding stock of all firms in Japan while in the USA they are prevented by law from holding any corporate stock on their own accounts. Even bank holding companies cannot hold more than 5 per cent of the voting stock of any non-bank corporation.

8 Following the partial sale of equity line V_1V_1 or V_2V_2, in Figure 12.4, moves inwards and equilibrium is established along the VF_1 line at point B or C.

13 The economics of human resource management

INTRODUCTION

Neoclassical economic theory asserts that in perfectly competitive markets wages adjust to the prevailing demand and supply conditions and settle at that level which clears the market. Consequently, all individuals who wish to work can find jobs. Pay depends on individual contributions to production and wage differences reflect differences in ability, educational attainment and other skills acquisition. Well functioning labour markets settle at the natural rate of unemployment which consists of those individuals changing jobs, temporarily out of work or voluntarily unemployed.

Such claims, however, are difficult to reconcile with the recent high and persistently rising unemployment levels prevailing in most Western countries or with the existence of widespread discrimination based on race, creed or sex. At the micro-level the industrial relations literature is replete with examples of a lack of correspondence between real wages and marginal productivity. Personnel departments adopt practices such as wages increasing with seniority rather than with productivity or promoting productive employees to senior posts where they are not so productive or maintaining high real wages even in periods of high unemployment. In brief, the traditional view of the firm as an employer who hires labour at fixed wages in well-defined labour markets does not correspond with reality in which many firms attempt to actively manage long-term employment relationships on wages higher than the market wage and motivate workers with carefully designed incentive schemes.

Issues of human resources management and the efficient organisation of the work place, neglected by traditional economics, have over the last decade or so been successfully addressed by reference to transaction cost economics and the agency theory of the firm. Concepts of production efficiency combined with considerations of transaction costs economising and the sharing of risks are utilised in this chapter to study how business firms organise and manage their personnel functions. The chapter begins with a brief outline of the basic concepts of marginal productivity theory. This is followed by a section on the traditional wage determination theory.

The fourth section examines the economic contributions to the organisation of work and analyses the efficiency features of current personnel practices, such as 'efficiency wages', 'dcfcrrcd compensations' and 'hierarchies', which comprise what is come to be known as the new economics of personnel. The role and economic impact of trade unions is examined next and the chapter concludes with a summary of the main points. The cnd of chapter application is drawn from the UK construction industry.

MARGINAL PRODUCTIVITY THEORY OF FACTOR DEMAND

In traditional economics the theory of income distribution in private markets is simply the theory of price applied to factors of production. That is, the price and employment of any factor is determined by the prevailing demand and supply conditions in the relevant market. Factors are demanded by firms to be utilised in the production process. Factor demand, therefore, is a derived demand and as such it depends on the value of the output produced. Factor supply on the other hand originates from the owners of various resources who may be firms (in the case of machinery, raw materials, etc.) or individuals (as in the case of labour).

To profit maximise firms would wish to employ labour (or any other factor) up to the point at which the value of the last employee's contribution to output is just equal to his or her marginal cost (wages plus any other expenses). Labour demand, therefore, is determined by its marginal productivity. Labour supply, on the other hand, is determined by employee wage–leisure preferences. Given perfectly competitive markets the interaction of employer demand and labour supply determines the level of employment and the market clearing wage rate. It is almost self-evident that the equilibrium wage is equal to the value of the marginal product.

The equilibrium price of any other factor of production is determined similarly. To illustrate, suppose that only one variable factor of production, called k, is used in conjunction with a fixed factor to produce product Q, so that $Q = f(k)$. If Q is sold in a competitive market at price P, the price of k is P_k, the fixed cost is denoted by F and total profit by Π, it follows that

$$\Pi = PQ - P_k k - F.$$

To maximise Π the firm would demand such a quantity of k as to ensure that

$$\frac{d\Pi}{dk} = Pf'(k) - P_k = 0$$

or

$$Pf'(k) = P_k \qquad\qquad (13.1)$$

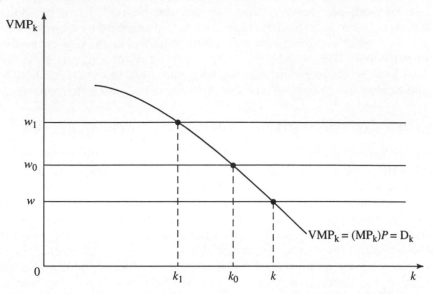

Figure 13.1 The demand for a single factor of production in perfect competition

where $f'(k)$, the marginal product MP_k of factor k, indicates by how much total output changes when the employment of k changes marginally. Condition (13.1) is fulfilled when the quantity of k employed by this producer is such as to make the value of the marginal product equal to the factor price. In other words, given P and P_k a firm's demand for a factor of production is determined by the value of this factor's marginal product.

In Figure 13.1 a firm's demand for k is derived graphically.

It is assumed that output increases with k but at a diminishing rate. That is, the law of diminishing marginal productivity holds and the MP_k curve slopes downwards. In perfect competition the value of the marginal product (VMP_k) is simply the marginal product multiplied by the constant product price. That is, $VMP_k = P(MP_k)$ and since P is constant VMP_k has the same shape as MP_k. If the price of k is w_o ($P_k = w_o$) condition (13.1) is fulfilled when the quantity of k demanded is k_o. At the lower price w, the quantity demanded increases to k while at the higher price of w_1 less is demanded (k_1). In fact the demand for k is the same as VMP_k. Given the price of k, an increase in productivity shifts VMP_k to the right and increases the demand for k.

It should be noted that if the producer is a monopolist the price of the final product would vary inversely to the quantity sold according to the demand curve $P = F(Q)$, so that to expand sales the price of the product must be reduced. This implies that the additions to total revenue (i.e. marginal revenue) decline as the employment of k and, hence, output expands. The contribution made to total revenue by each additional unit of k is equal to $(MP_k)MR$ and is called the marginal revenue product. Since $(MP_k)MR$ is less than VMP a monopolist's demand for k is smaller compared with its demand under perfect competition, everything else being the same. Even so, increases in productivity induce a monopolist to demand more of k.

The market demand for k is simply the sum of the individual demand curves of all producers using k. The supply of k depends on the preferences (utility)[1] of the individual owners of k (if k refers to labour services) or on costs of production, business objectives and market structures if k denotes any other factor of production. Market supply is then the sum of the individual supply curves. Assuming that the supply of k increases as P_k increases we derive a conventional upwards sloping market supply curve. Employment and price will be determined by the intersection of total demand and supply.

The analysis becomes more complicated when we consider that several variable factors co-operate in the production of most products. In this case, the productivity of k depends only partly on the inherent qualities of k and partly on the quantity and productivity of the other factors it co-operates with in production. The firm has therefore to decide simultaneously on the quantities of several factors of production it wishes to employ.

Suppose, for example, that three factors A, B and C are used in production and that technology is such that some degree of substitutability among factors is possible. How are they to be combined? The answer depends on relative prices and productivity. For profit maximisation, given factor prices P_A, P_B and P_C, the firm would employ quantities Q_A, Q_B and Q_C such that

$$VMP_A = P_A$$
$$VMP_B = P_B$$
$$VMP_C = P_C.$$

Therefore, the optimum input proportions are those for which the ratio of the value of the marginal product (i.e. the marginal rate of substitution) of any two inputs is equal to the ratio of their prices (for a further explanation of this result refer to Chapter 6).

WAGE DETERMINATION IN THEORY AND PRACTICE

Casual labour market observation, however, would suggest that wages actually paid by firms are subject to a host of influences not accounted for by the simple traditional labour market model just outlined. To begin with markets are not perfectly competitive. Information flows are imperfect, costly and asymmetrically distributed among the members of a team. There are obstacles to entry into certain markets, investment in human capital varies among individuals and learning-by-doing may result in human asset specificity which creates monopoly power. More importantly perhaps, work takes place in teams and under circumstances which make measuring marginal productivity infeasible or very costly.

It is thus not surprising that empirical evidence often indicates that individuals do not get paid according to the value of their marginal products. Frank (1984), for example, who examined evidence relating to productivity and pay awards of automobile and real estate sales workers and full university professors in the USA, reports that individuals with lower productivity receive wages in excess of their marginal products while the wages of higher productivity employees are lower than their marginal products. This he attributes to the notion that individuals care about their position in the income hierarchy because of the status level associated with different positions. Since top positions carry more status individuals at posts higher up the income ladder are prepared to accept remunerations lower than their marginal product while those at lower income levels are compensated for loss in status. Thus, the income distribution of the groups examined showed less variation than the marginal productivity of labour.

Moreover, marginal productivity theory cannot explain the observed segmentation of labour markets and the operation of a 'primary' alongside a 'secondary' market, each with distinct characteristics and pay norms. Employment and wage discrimination along the lines of sex, race or ethnicity would seem to contradict a firm's incentive to employ according to marginal productivity alone. Industrial relations practices such as wages attached to jobs rather than to individual workers, payments according to seniority or the maintenance of high real wages in the presence of widespread unemployment cannot be explained by marginal productivity theory.

That the simple neoclassical model of wage determination is very remote from the reality of labour markets and industrial relations practices is not surprising when considering that traditional neoclassical economics is interested in trends rather than in explaining the functioning and wage setting of individual firms. The consequence has been that until recently economics has neglected the significant contribution that the organisation and management of human resources can make to the overall success of the firm and to the national economy. Recent developments in transaction cost economics and agency theory seek to remedy this imbalance.

THE NEW ECONOMICS OF PERSONNEL

The transactions cost approach to work organisation

As already emphasised in previous chapters the basic proposition of transaction cost economics is that efficiency is enhanced when the features of an organisational structure match the attributes of the transactions it governs. Labour transactions, similarly to any other transactions, are characterised by different degrees of frequency, complexity/uncertainty and asset specificity. These characteristics are therefore critical in devising efficient organisational structures for personnel. In the words of Williamson, 'governance structures for labour need to be matched with the attributes of labour transactions in a discriminating way if transaction cost economising is to be achieved' (1984b: 89).

When considering the organisation of human resources we are interested in long-term employment relations within firms. Frequency is therefore always present so that complexity and specificity are the critical dimensions which should influence the organisation of work. In other words, the organisation of labour should reflect (a) the extent to which human asset specificity is involved in labour relations and (b) the ease or difficulty of evaluating the productivity of individual employees.

Human asset specificity

When employees acquire skills specific to a particular employer, i.e. skills which cannot be transferred to other employers, human asset specificity exists. The labour relationship involved in such cases has been termed by Williamson *et al.* (1975) 'an idiosyncratic exchange'. On-the-job training may, but need not, be the cause of idiosyncratic exchanges. Word processing, for example, and other information technology skills may be acquired or enhanced with experience but they are not specific to a firm as normally they can be transferred to other firms. Knowledge of a firm's filing system or of the unwritten and informal ways in which a particular team interacts is specific to a firm and cannot be utilised by other firms.

Since skills, whether general or specific, enhance productivity their acquisition should be compensated. Payment according to marginal productivity is not, however, a sufficient safeguard or the only feature of an efficient labour organisation in circumstances in which the work performed involves substantial learning by doing which is specific to the firm and hence non-transferable. The presence of firm-specific skills or human asset specificity implies transactional difficulties since (a) workers acquire monopolistic power but lose their skills if dismissed and (b) firms need to incur extra expenses to train new employees when the existing ones quit or are dismissed. Efficiency, in the presence of human asset specificity, requires a protective labour organisation. That is, a governance structure which ensures stability and continuity of the employment relation and safeguards the interests of both employer and employees. For if the employment contract breaks down the employee cannot transfer the acquired knowledge to other users and the employer incurs costs and delays in training another employee. Since these costs increase with the extent of human asset specificity the more idiosyncratic the exchanges involved the more carefully crafted the work organisation must be.

The difficulty of evaluating productivity

Payment according to marginal productivity pre-supposes that the productivity of each individual can be measured and evaluated costlessly. When team production is involved, however, attributing output to the individual members of a team may not be possible. The classic example is that of two men shifting a cargo into trucks. The output of the joint effort is clearly observable but the effort of each person cannot be quantified easily. Although occasionally it may be possible to assess employee productivity by observing the intensity with which individuals work and co-operate as members of a team, this is not always possible. Depending on the nature of the work and the technology involved, measuring inputs in order to evaluate productivity can be achieved with different degrees of difficulty.

In short both the extent of human asset specificity and the ease or difficulty of productivity measurement can vary from labour market to labour market. Assuming for simplicity that each can take only two values, a low and a high one, we can distinguish four different labour organisation structures (Williamson 1984b). If A_1 and A_2 represent low and high levels of human asset specificity and M_1 and M_2 represent easy and difficult to measure individual productivity, then the four combinations of A and M describe four types of labour exchanges requiring different organisational structures in order to operate efficiently. These are as follows.

Internal spot markets (A_1, M_1)

An internal spot market exists when work involves no human asset specificity and individual productivity can be measured easily. Any on-the-job training that might exist can be easily transferred among firms. Workers, therefore, can change jobs without loss in productivity and employers can replace workers without incurring start-up or training costs. Since measuring inputs and evaluating productivity is also easy, payment according to marginal productivity presents no serious problems. Workers are paid according to their contribution to output and the employment relationship can be terminated when there is dissatisfaction on either side. Examples of internal spot markets are provided by the market for migrant farm workers. Some professional employees such as craftsmen and engineers may fall into this group of employees.

Primitive team $(A_1$ and $M_2)$

These are labour markets bearing the characteristics of an Alchian and Demsetz (1972) team discussed in Chapter 3. Workers have no firm-specific skills but production functions are non-separable so that there are problems in measuring individual contributions to output. Total output is easily observable and payment is according to the average output of the team. This implies that any output loss brought about by an individual's reduction in work effort (shirking) will be shared among the members of the team rather than be borne by the individual concerned. The cost of shirking (or increased leisure) is thus reduced for the shirker. Assuming that all individuals enjoy leisure it follows that all have an incentive to shirk. In other words, difficulties in measuring individual productivity coupled with opportunistic behaviour may lead to shirking which reduces output. A monitor may be able to reduce shirking and enhance production in these circumstances by observing behaviour. To be effective the monitor should have the right to discipline workers and if necessary to terminate individual contracts. This is possible since the absence of human asset specificity implies that the membership of the team can change without loss of productivity. To reduce a monitor's incentive to shirk monitors should become residual income claimants. A simple hierarchical structure of work organisation, which Alchian and Demsetz termed the 'classical capitalist firm' thus evolves for reasons of efficiency (see Chapter 3).

The simple hierarchical structure of primitive teams becomes ineffective, however, in situations in which not only inputs but total output is difficult to measure. When both inputs and outputs are difficult to measure it is possible that employers may attempt to exploit employees by paying them less than their average productivity. It has been suggested, however, that such exploitation will not be possible since employees without firm-specific skills may, when dissatisfied, sever the employment relationship so that the threat of quits will protect workers from this moral hazard. It is unlikely, however, that this threat will be a sufficient protection for employees especially when labour markets are not perfectly competitive or when there is widespread unemployment. The required protection though may be forthcoming through another mechanism: the impact of reputational effects. That is, employers may refrain from acting opportunistically in the knowledge that they may acquire a bad reputation which will make it difficult for them to recruit productive employees in the future. For reputational effects to operate, however, it is important to devise a work organisation which secures continuity of employment so as to have repeated output observations and adjustments in employee payments so that firms can establish their reputation.

To conclude, when it is difficult to measure both individual and total labour productivity a primitive team is superseded by a 'reputational team'.

Obligational markets (A_2, M_1)

Tasks are easy to measure in obligational markets but there is a great deal of firm-specific knowledge. On-the-job learning enhances skills and productivity but such skills cannot be transferred to other users. Specific human knowledge may refer to the particular technology of a firm or the internal communication systems such as accounting and data processing conventions or other internal rules and procedures. Whatever their source, specific skills create bilateral monopoly situations with the associated potential for wasteful bargaining and the enhanced risk of employment severance and skill losses. Efficiency in this case requires continuity of employment. Work organisation should therefore include procedural safeguards intended to discourage arbitrary dismissals. Moreover, employees should be given incentives which discourage unwanted quits. Occupational pension schemes and other benefits fulfil this role. The presence of unions and collective bargaining can ensure continuity of employment and enhanced efficiency. The organisation of labour in these markets will be very elaborate and 'jobs of this kind are candidates for early unionisation, since mutual gains can thereby be realised' (Williamson 1984b: 272).

Relational teams (A_2, M_2)

These exist when human assets are specific to the firm and productivity is very difficult to measure. Efficiency in this case requires that employees are dedicated to the purpose of the firm. Social conditioning and the provision of absolute job security may be used by firms in order to induce employee dedication to the firm. Although the creation of relational relationships, i.e. a workforce totally dedicated to the firm, is difficult in practice, it is sometimes claimed that large Japanese firms are organised along these lines.

It should be noted that the four-way market classification described is only indicative and that in reality both A and M can take a range of values rather than only two as assumed above. It clearly demonstrates, though, that to be efficient the organisation of work must match the characteristics of the work involved and since the latter vary there is no single efficient way of organising work. Rather, there is a variety of efficient structures. An organisational structure is efficient not only when it promotes production efficiency but also when it attenuates opportunism and reduces bounded rationality thus saving on transaction costs. A simple structure cannot effectively cope when work is complex while a complex structure would be unnecessarily costly when the work it governs is simple.

Generally speaking the existence of vertical or horizontal hierarchy can contribute to transaction costs economising through monitoring and performance evaluation. But since monitoring and auditing can offend they may induce perfunctory behaviour. To counter this an optimal structure must provide incentives, both to employers and employees, to behave co-operatively rather than opportunistically. The need for such incentives increases with the complexity of the work involved. When work effort and/ or output is difficult to measure and there is substantial human asset specificity structural features characterising what are known as 'internal labour markets' may enhance efficiency. That is, the presence of skills implies high productivity which implies high pay. Moreover, transaction costs are reduced by protective employment structures which reduce labour turnover. Stability of employment, high pay, well-defined promotion ladders and the restriction of 'ports of entry' to lower levels in the hierarchy are among the main features of a 'primary labour market', while lack of skills, low pay, instability of employment and high labour turnover characterise the 'secondary labour market'. The high degree of work stability in primary markets is well documented. A study of occupational mobility in the UK, for example, showed that 90 per cent of the primary market workers surveyed had remained in the same occupation throughout the decade of the survey period. Workers in the secondary market, however, were more mobile. Indeed one in four of them had moved from the secondary to the primary market (Metcalf and Nickell 1982).

In brief the existence of dual labour markets operating along the lines suggested by Deoringer and Piore (1971) is well documented and can be attributed to transaction costs economising and the need to provide work incentives.

Agency theory and the organisation of work

Work incentives are at the centre of agency theory. Their significance derives from the fact that labour differs from other factors of production in some important ways. To begin with, in the absence of slavery, labour contracts cannot be life-long. Labour services are therefore provided on the basis of renewable implicit or explicit contracts. In addition labour owners, unlike the owners of other hired factors, are always present in the production process and can influence performance by adjusting the intensity of the work effort. The quality of other factors of production, even if difficult to detect initially, can be revealed with utilisation. Labour quality is more difficult to assess since labour performance depends both on ability and effort. Employees, unlike other factors of production, may have an interest in working less hard or slow enough, for example, to ensure overtime rates of pay. If employees prefer to exert less rather than more effort while employers prefer the opposite, a divergence of interests arises which creates agency costs (see Chapter 9). Effort incentives may therefore play a significant role in the organisation of work. The introduction of incentive schemes, however, may involve employees in taking some risks since performance may depend on factors beyond their control. When, for example, remuneration depends, at least partly, on profitability, employees undertake the risk that profit may be low despite an intensified work effort. The success and efficiency of incentive schemes depends therefore on whether employees are prepared to undertake risks.[2]

Depending on employee risk attitudes and the risks and benefits of shirking, it is possible that an efficient organisation may allow a certain degree of employee discretion regarding work effort. When the value of reduced effort to the worker is so high that the incentives required to induce high effort are too costly for the firm it is efficient to allow a certain level of shirking. In other instances, however, it is possible that not only the firm but also its employees may benefit from reduced shirking. In this case workers prefer high-wages–high-effort packages to low-wages–low-effort packages. Efficiency requires then an organisational structure which brings this about.

Both work incentives and the desire to economise on transaction costs (by reducing bounded rationality and attenuating opportunism) can have an important role to play in devising efficient work structures. This is not to deny the significance of power relations, however. Labour transaction features, such as the existence of firm-specific skills, which contribute to transaction costs and to the efficiency of incentive schemes may also contribute to monopolistic and monopsonistic power situations. Power motives can have a significant bearing on personnel organisation and practices. Some power motives are explored briefly below, but for present purposes we concentrate on efficiency.

Current industrial practices on pay

As already noted many employment compensation arrangements in large corporations are, for the most part, inconsistent with the simple notion that workers are paid according to the value of their marginal product in each time period. We observe, for example, equally productive workers receiving different wages and wage variations across workers which do not correspond to variations in their productivity. In addition the following features of employment organisation are currently prevalent especially among large organisations.

1 Wages are hierarchically structured in the sense that the number of employees receiving higher wages tends to be smaller than the number receiving lower wages (this is known as horizontal hierarchy).
2 Promotions to higher level posts are often internal and new recruitment is at the lower levels of the job ladder.
3 Wages rise with seniority. Both internal promotions and seniority payments often exist even in the absence of any on-the-job training and improvements in productivity.
4 The variance of earnings increases with experience.
5 Wages are attached to jobs rather than to individual employees. This, Williamson (1975) suggests, reduces the scope for individual bargaining over pay. Besides, the wages differentials among jobs are often set by administrative procedures (and union agreements) rather than by any reference to market wages.

These features are 'for the most part, inconsistent with the simple notion of employees being paid a wage in every period equal to their marginal product in that period' (Malcomson 1984a: 489). Efficiency considerations in the form of transaction cost economising and the need to provide incentives so as to reduce agency costs can lead to labour organisations and payment structures consistent with the above observations. The following personnel practices are believed to contribute to such efficient work organisation.

Efficiency wages

It is non-controversial to assert that wages induce workers to offer labour power to firms but the view that wages determine the productivity of each hour spent working is less easily acceptable.

The claim that labour productivity depends on wages, known as 'the efficiency wage hypothesis', was initially advanced in relation to labour pay in Third World countries where increased wages were thought to improve productivity through improvements in nutrition and health. More recently several authors[3] have suggested that efficiency wages operate in advanced Western countries as well and they constitute an industrial relations practice which contributes to better personnel management and improved efficiency. The reason why firms may offer wages which are higher than the prevailing market rates and why they are reluctant to reduce them even in periods of widespread unemployment is 'that the productivity of a firm's employees increases as their wage is increased, at least over an economically relevant part of its range' (Malcomson 1981: 848), this is for several reasons which will now be discussed.

Reduced shirking

In many jobs measuring individual effort is difficult, so that workers have some discretion in choosing the intensity or speed of their work effort. This coupled with difficulties in measuring individual output may provide an incentive to shirk. To reduce or eliminate shirking, firms introduce monitoring systems with attached penalties for shirking including the possibility of dismissal.

The penalty of dismissal increases when efficiency wages are paid since alternative employment, even if available, will be at a lower wage. The so-called 'cheat-threat' theory suggests that the higher the premium included in the efficiency wage the higher the cost of dismissal and therefore the lower the tendency to shirk.

Firms do not only benefit by the increase in output that reduced shirking brings about, they also gain by the reduced need for monitoring which saves on monitoring and supervision costs.

Reduced labour turnover

Firms may pay higher than the current (or the market clearing) wage in an attempt to reduce labour turnover and economise on recruitment and retraining costs. Labour turnover costs increase with the extent to which work involves on-the-job training especially when learning-by-doing is of a firm-specific nature as, for example, in relational and obligational labour markets. When recruiting and re-training staff is particularly expensive firms can offer very generous remunerations in order to ensure loyalty and firm attachment. The high remunerations offered by firms like IBM are sometimes thought (Main 1990) to be due to this motive and are referred to as 'golden handcuffs'.

Self-selection

Assuming that workers differ in their ability to perform certain tasks and that such differences are not easily detectable by recruiting firms, the problem of adverse selection discussed in Chapter 3 arises. Low productivity individuals may make misrepresentations regarding their abilities so that firms may incur high selection costs or recruit individuals of a lower performance potential.

In these circumstances efficiency wages may help alleviate selection problems by attracting high productivity employees. The hypothesis is that a self-selection mechanism is initiated among applicants with the more productive ones applying to the firms offering wages higher than marginal products. For this to occur individuals of higher productivity must have higher reservation wages. Reservation wages increasing with productivity potential would be observed, for example, when higher productivity individuals believe that they have a higher earnings potential in self-employment (Malcomson 1981).

In brief, efficiency wages can (a) improve productivity by attracting a more productive workforce and (b) reduce a firm's screening and selection costs especially in circumstances in which personal traits are difficult to screen for and individuals cannot be relied upon to reveal their true characteristics.

Improved morale and co-operation

Firms may pay labour higher wages in an attempt to improve the work atmosphere by inducing a feeling of belonging and a sense of fair treatment. As a result motivation is enhanced which increases productivity. The most celebrated example of efficiency wages is that provided by the Ford motor company when in 1914 Henry Ford introduced the $5.00-a-day minimum wage for the workers of the Detroit plant, more than doubling the then current wage of $2.34. As a result job applications rocketed, labour turnover plummeted and productivity showed a dramatic increase pushing up profitability.

To summarise, offering wages above the going rates fulfils several personnel management objectives. It provides a better quality and more motivated workforce which is strongly attached to the firm. Improved co-operation reduces monitoring costs, and a lower labour turnover reduces hiring and firing costs. A high calibre and well-motivated workforce improves productivity and overall efficiency.

It should be noted, however, that the advantages of efficiency wages vary according to the nature of work and the related labour requirements. Since the costs associated with labour turnover increase with the extent of human asset specificity, firms find it beneficial to increase the premium included in the efficiency wages as the significance of the firm-specific skills of a job increases. Thus, both the extent to which efficiency wages are used as a personnel policy and their size will vary with the circumstances of the firm. Different firms will offer different efficiency wages which explains, at least partly, why equally well qualified individuals with the same experience working in similar jobs in the same location but within different firms may receive different wages.

Since efficiency wages are an incentive to reduce shirking and labour turnover they should be more prevalent where the nature of work is such that shirking can be a serious problem and where labour stability is valued. Jobs which require training and those which involve substantial learning-by-doing are more likely to be associated with efficiency wages. Unskilled work which is easy to monitor and to replace, on the other hand, requires no strong incentives and its organisation is unlikely to depend on efficiency wages. Given the motives behind their practice, efficiency wages contribute to the existence of dual labour markets consisting of a primary sector which pays higher wages and offers job stability and a secondary sector employing less-skilled workers with a high turnover and lower pay.

Deferred compensations

Deferred compensation incentive schemes can take different forms but, broadly speaking, they pay lower wages during the first years of employment and higher wages in subsequent years. Worker compensation increases with seniority and experience for reasons of efficiency rather than because of learning-by-doing and any related improvements in productivity. Lazear (1981) has shown that 'it is optimal to construct age–earnings profiles which pay workers less than the value of marginal products (VMP) when they are young and more than the value of marginal products when they are old' even if the marginal product has remained constant throughout an individual's working life. If productivity increases with age, because of learning effects for example, earnings may increase at a faster rate as indicated by the age–earnings profile of Figure 13.2.

The efficiency enhancing properties of deferred compensations derive from reduced shirking and labour turnover. Workers who accept contracts with deferred payments are committed to the firm. By accepting lower initial payments they are effectively posting a bond which will be repaid

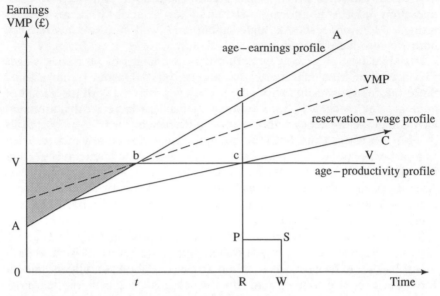

Figure 13.2 Deferred compensation theory
Source: Adapted from Lazear 1981, Figure 1

with interest in the future. The value of this bond is indicated in Figure 13.2 by area AbV. It is repaid in later years by payments in excess of marginal product. Total repayment is indicated by area bcd, for an individual retiring at year R, plus the net present value of the employer's contribution to pension funds (area RPSW).

It should be noted that the age–earnings profile indicated by curve AA in Figure 13.2 can vary among individuals and firms. The steeper the curve the higher the value of the bond an employee is expected to post and the lower the incentive to shirk. A horizontal VV line indicates that the value of the marginal product is constant, while the positively sloping line VMP indicates that productivity increases with seniority. The important point is that wages increase with age even in the absence of any productivity improvements.

The optimality of deferred compensation schemes derives from (a) a reduction in shirking and the concomitant increase in work effort – if shirking workers are penalised by losing their jobs, the cost of shirking becomes very high since workers forfeit the value of their bond, in addition to any loss in firm-specific skills and any difficulties in finding alternative employment – and (b) reduced monitoring. Since workers have reduced incentives to shirk the need for monitoring declines which lowers monitoring costs and promotes a more co-operative work environment with further improvements in productivity.

Deferred compensation schemes are not, however, devoid of problems.

Difficulties may arise in the implementation of seniority payments because of moral hazard. A firm may, for example, be induced to dismiss workers for shirking even when they do not shirk in order to appropriate the cumulative difference between marginal products and wages paid. The optimum point of default occurs at point t (Figure 13.2) when the difference between the cumulative marginal product and the cumulative real wage is at a maximum

Defaulting at point t is optimum on the assumption of no default costs. If, however, firing and hiring costs vary with age the optimum default point will vary and excessive default costs can render defaulting altogether unprofitable. Even in the absence of hiring and firing costs, reputational effects may deter firms from behaving in this opportunistic fashion. A firm that defaults groups of workers will acquire a bad reputation which means that it will not be able to use the deferred compensation incentive in the future and will incur higher labour costs per unit of output (Malcomson 1984b). Defaulting endangers a firm's future survival.

The second area of problems relates to the impact of wages on the desired hours of work and the retirement age. The supply of labour responds to actual wages so that if young workers are paid less than VMP they would offer fewer hours of work while older workers would be eager to work overtime. Hours restrictions may therefore need to be incorporated into the work contracts. Moreover, workers with a reservation wage–age profile AC would never wish to retire. Assuming that their age–productivity profile is VV, their optimum retirement age is R after which point the reservation wage becomes higher than the value of the marginal product. Even after point c, however, real wages are higher than the reservation wage which exceeds the marginal product and voluntary retirement will not be sought. The problem does not arise, however, when mandatory age for retirement is included in the employment contract, which may explain why companies commonly adopt a mandatory retirement age. Mandatory retirement, however, is illegal in some countries[4] in which case termination of employment must be encouraged by other means. Pension schemes are often designed with the terms favouring early retirement. This is why the actuarial value of a firm's contribution to pension often falls with age.

To test whether earnings patterns reflect productivity patterns one needs to empirically measure individual productivity, which is not an easy task. Researchers have, as a result, utilised a variety of productivity indicators. Medoff and Abraham (1980), for example, used in their research performance ratings determined annually for each employee within a given grade by the grade supervisor. They have attempted to analyse the factors contributing to the positive association between earnings and experience by drawing on a sample of managerial and professional employees of two large US corporations. The data analysed were derived from personnel department records of all male employees in full-time employment at managerial and professional grades, during 1977. Information on personnel records included age, education, service date, current work location and, most importantly, individual performance ratings. The latter were used as ordinal indicators of individual productivity; a higher rating was assumed to represent a more productive individual.

The evidence presented shows that greater experience moves employees towards the upper end of the earnings distribution within a given job grade but it does not move them towards the upper tail of the performance (productivity) distribution. In other words, this evidence rejects the human capital theory contention that earnings increase with experience because productivity improves with experience. The authors conclude that 'the facts presented indicate that while, within grade levels, there is a strong positive association between experience and relative earnings, there is no association or a negative association between experience and relative performance' (p. 735).

The evidence is consistent with earlier findings based on 2,500 mana-

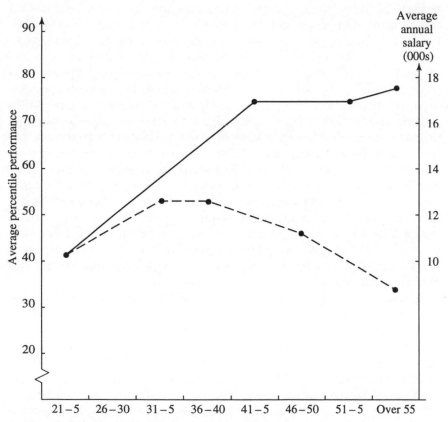

Figure 13.3 Age, performance and salary of engineers
Source: Medoff and Abraham 1980, Figure 1, p. 731.

gerial and professional employees of six technology based US companies. A typical finding of this work is shown in Figure 13.3.

More recently Kotlikoff and Gokhale (1992) estimated the age–productivity and the age–earnings profiles of 300,000 employees of a *Fortune 100* firm covering the period 1969–83. For each of the five occupation/sex groups considered productivity was found to fall with age, with productivity exceeding earnings for young workers and earnings exceeding productivity for older workers.

The rank order tournament theory of incentives

Both efficiency wages and seniority payments assume a wage–productivity relationship. This is a serious weakness since it is precisely in situations where productivity cannot be measured objectively that work incentives are required.

Employment contracts rarely specify productivity levels precisely. Although some aspects of work are specified the presence of bounded rationality and difficulties in measuring inputs or outputs imply that contracts are incomplete. For example, payment by time rate specifies the hours of work but cannot precisely specify the number and the details of the tasks to be performed during the contracted time. When some aspects of performance can only be assessed subjectively it may not be possible to specify individual performance 'in a way that is sufficiently objective for it to form an enforceable clause of a contract' (Malcomson 1981: 851). Production must be stated in terms of a measure that can be verified by both parties to the contract and which a third party can arbitrate. If this is not possible employees would be unwilling to accept contracts relating wages to performance, or 'payment by standard' as it is often called, because they may be faced with a moral hazard problem. Firms could potentially deny that performance was up to the specified level even if it was.

It is possible, however, to devise work incentive schemes in these situations based on relative rather than absolute performance. Malcomson (1984b) and Lazear and Rosen (1981), for example, have shown that provided that one principal (employer) employs a number of agents (employees) a modified version of the simple deferred compensation scheme discussed above can overcome both problems related to performance information asymmetries and a firm's incentive to default workers on seniority payments. This modified scheme of deferred payments is an efficient and enforceable system of incentives based on the rank order tournament.

The essence of the rank order tournament scheme is simple. The firm offers its employees a contract (possibly implicit) specifying that a certain proportion of the workforce will be paid more than the rest and that the higher pay will be offered to the most productive employees. Whether the firm abides by the contractual obligation to pay more to a certain proportion of employees is easily verifiable and once committed to higher payments the employer has every incentive to pay the higher wages to the most productive members of the team. Production levels are not, however, specified and the best workers receive the higher pay whatever the actual overall performance of the team. All that is required, therefore, is a ranking of employees' performance according to a relative measure of performance. In other words an ordinal rather than a cardinal ranking system is required. Since measuring individual performance in absolute terms is not necessary information asymmetries do not create serious problems.

The rank order tournament has strong efficiency implications since the entire workforce is motivated to work harder in the hope of receiving the higher payments.

In considering the salary structure for top executives Lazear and Rosen (1981) note that presidents of large corporations are commonly selected from among the existing vice-presidents. On the day of the promotion a vice-president's salary may increase by a factor of three which makes it difficult to suggest that the level of his or her productivity tripled over night. It is more reasonable to suggest that the salary scale is such in order to provide incentives. Presidents do not necessarily earn high salaries because they are that much more productive as presidents but because this particular type of payment structure makes them and all the other employees more productive over their entire working lives.

The organisation of work along the lines of the rank order tournament is also compatible with the five features of labour organisation commonly observed in practice. That is: hierarchical pay structures; promotions to higher level posts being mainly by internal promotion while ports of entry occurring at the lower levels of the hierarchy; wage rates rising more with seniority rather than productivity; and wage rates being attached to jobs rather than to individuals.

THE ROLE OF TRADE UNIONS

Trade unions are the principal institutions of labour. They are complex organisations whose purpose and impact has been debated for over 200 years but is still causing widespread disagreement. Economists like A. Marshall and J. S. Mill considered unions to have a positive overall influence while others like Fritz Macklup believe them to have a negative influence. The positive view of unions was predominant during the 1930s and 1940s while the negative view has prevailed over the last two decades or so.

The publicity commonly afforded to management versus trade union disputes over wages and to the strikes and work to rule that may result from such confrontations is, at least partly, responsible for the widely held belief that the main aim of a trade union is to raise wages. This view can be very misleading as it tends to ignore the very significant but not newsworthy non-wage functions of unions. It is commonly accepted that the aims of trade unions are to improve pay as well as conditions of work. In their attempt to improve working conditions and to protect employment, trade unions fulfil several efficiency enhancing functions. For example, they act as agents of labour. In this capacity they provide management with useful information regarding the preferences of the workforce about conditions of work, compensation packages, etc. A better flow of information improves managerial decision making. Unions facilitate collective bargaining which attenuates opportunism and reduces bounded rationality thus improving the organisation of work to the benefit of both employers and employees. Additionally, unions provide labour with a voice with which to communicate with management. Such communication may further improve industrial relations and raise productivity. In short, in addition to their attempts to improve wages unions perform a multiplicity of functions as labour agents, communicators of information and as a labour voice.

Asserting the existence of a multiplicity of union functions is not to deny the significance or predominance of any of these functions. It is, however, the case that different aspects of a union's functions may be predominant under different sets of circumstances and that the influence of unionisation on the efficiency of labour markets may be positive or negative depending on the relative influence of different union motives and management's response to trade unions. Following Freeman and Medoff (1979) we can distinguish three broad aspects (or faces) of unionism; monopoly, efficiency and voice. We now consider each in turn.

The monopoly face of unionism

The monopoly view of unionism is that unions form the institution through which workers monopolise the labour market creating contrived scarcity and economic inefficiencies. They impose work rules which decrease productivity and they reduce national output through frequent strikes. They cause unemployment whose detrimental effects extend to the non-unionised markets since unemployed workers from the unionised sector move to the non-unionised sector increasing the labour supply and reducing wages.

Unions, according to this view, aim to control the labour supply and create scarcity so as to raise wages above competitive levels. As a result unionised firms use too little labour in relation to capital. There are factor distortions and unemployment. Figure 13.4 illustrates this view by examining the impact of the introduction of a trade union in a previously competitive labour market. The union as a monopolist can reduce labour supply by restricting entry into the market (craft or profession) to L_1, so as to raise the wage to w_1. Alternatively, it can bargain for or impose a

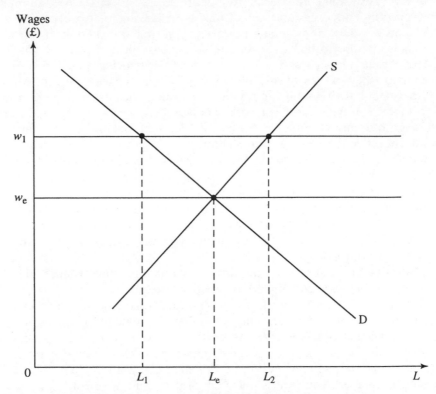

Figure 13.4 The unionisation of a perfectly competitive labour market

minimum wage of w_1. In either case the competitive equilibrium employment level L_e declines to L_1 while the labour supply expands as more
workers wish to work at the higher wage. As a result unemployment (L_2
$- L_1$) is created which may have repercussions onto other markets as
unemployed workers seek alternative employment.

The above effect of unionism, however, is totally dependent on the
assumption that unions are introduced in otherwise perfectly competitive
markets. The effects could be totally different if unions are introduced in
non-competitive labour markets. Consider, for example, the monopsonised market in Figure 13.5. A single firm employs labour whose value of
marginal product is shown by curve VMP and the competitive labour
supply curve is S. In the absence of a union and in order to profit maximise
the firm employs L_1 workers (as indicated by the intersection of VMP and
the marginal cost of an extra worker MFC) and offers a wage of w_1 which
is lower than the VMP. In these circumstances a trade union might demand
a higher wage for its membership of L_1 or, acting as a monopolist, it might
aim to maximise the wage bill or the difference between real wages and
the reservation wages of its members. The implementation of these aims

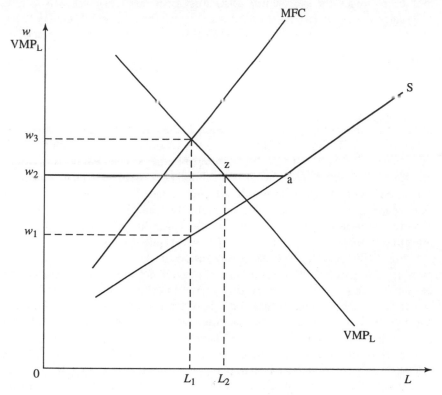

Figure 13.5 Unionisation of a monopsony labour market

is far from secured since the union is confronted by a single buyer of labour. In technical jargon the unionisation of labour has created a bilateral monopoly market in which employment and wages will be determined by the relative bargaining power of the two participants. The outcome is unknown and it is possible that both the employment level and the real wage rate may increase. For suppose that the trade union aims at and is successful in increasing the current wage to any level up to w_3, say w_2. Since no worker is prepared to work for less than w_2 the supply curve in Figure 13.5 becomes w_2aS. Profit maximisation now occurs at z and employment increases to L_2. Since this is closer to the competitive equilibrium the efficiency of the market may have improved.

The efficiency face of unionism

The view that the unions may have an overall positive influence on firms and the economy does not derive, however, from their role as a counter-vailing power in monopsony markets. Unions may enhance economic efficiency through their role as agents of labour, as a governance structure that economises on transaction costs and provides work incentives and efficiency in risk sharing, or as a labour voice. These three efficiency faces of unionism may co-exist but can be distinguished at least conceptually.

Agency

As agents of labour trade unions provide management with information regarding labour preferences over benefits and industrial relations practices. They also help employees to assess and evaluate complex compensation packages. Unions have the necessary resources to hire experts such as actuaries or lawyers to evaluate benefits and policies which individual employees would be unable to do. In this respect union officials concerned with their election prospects would attempt to gather and provide information regarding the average rather than the marginal member. In the absence of unions the firms' information would be derived from the marginal workers who would be prepared to quit their jobs.

While Williamson (1984b) sees this function of unions as purely instrumental and suggests that even non-unionised labour can recognise the benefits of an agent and can develop a mechanism to realise them, Malcomson (1983) suggests that the role of trade unions as agents of labour has a positive influence on economic efficiency. At an intuitive level, if information flows between employer and employees improve, decision making improves with concomitant improvements in productivity. Malcomson's rigorous analysis shows that trade unions facilitate the introduction of incentive schemes designed to overcome the problems of measuring productivity. They may therefore improve efficiency by enabling an improved allocation of risks between a firm and its employees. Malcomson contends that the observation that employees are prepared to undertake substantial risks such as the risk of lay-off, redundancy and changes in the real value of their wages is indicative of the fact that firms are risk averse. They are rarely prepared to guarantee wages or employment for life. Given that both employers and employees are risk averse and that (a) individual performance is not possible to be assessed and specified in a legally enforceable way and (b) employees interests do not coincide with employer interests, the problem arises of designing optimum contracts which motivate workers to increase work effort. Certain contracts may not be possible to introduce in the absence of collective action since the risk that firms may default would make them unacceptable to employees, e.g. contracts specifying that at least part of the compensation be dependent on an employer's subjective evaluation of performance or payment according to a certain occurrence (a state contingent contract) such as the market position of a firm which workers may not be able to observe or enforce legally.

Since the employment relation involves non-specific contracts with compensation dependent partly on the 'state of the world' that prevails, individual workers may lack the information to ascertain *ex post* whether the contractual conditions have been met and the power to enforce an agreement in the case of a firm defaulting on its obligations. A union can fulfil both these roles since it has sufficient power to enforce agreements (when a firm defaults) and sufficient power and resources to undertake the necessary investigation or to hire professionals (lawyers, accountants, etc.) to ascertain what state of the world prevailed. Although this role of unions may not be perfect, it can reduce the scope of firms to benefit by defaulting their employees.

By reducing the risk of default unions make it possible for firms to introduce contracts with incentives for productivity which both enhance production and are preferred by those employees who choose to work harder or more carefully in order to achieve higher remunerations. Moreover, the bargaining power of unions makes it possible for certain aspects of a contract to be negotiated *ex post*, which may be after workers have performed the required work. In this case an individual has no bargaining power since the only power of withholding labour is no longer available. A trade union still has, by collective action, the power to deprive a firm of all labour services.

In brief, trade unions can improve efficiency by making state contingent contracts possible, thereby providing incentives and improving productivity. These efficiency gains are greater the more risk averse a firm is and the more non-unionised firms emulate union-induced policies.

Governance

The existence of trade unions may contribute to improved efficiency in the form of economising on transaction costs. For Williamson (1984b) transactions costs economising, although not the only factor, 'has a pervasive and significant influence' (p. 89) on work organisation. To improve efficiency work organisation must match the characteristics of the jobs involved and since the nature of work and the associated transactions costs vary it is simply wrong to assert that there is a unique way of organising work. When the work involved is of a simple non-specialist nature a complex organisation will be unnecessarily expensive while a simple structure would be inefficient when work is of a complex nature. It is therefore possible that both employers and employees can gain benefits by moving from an individualistic to a collective bargaining structure through unionisation.

Trade unions can be part of a governance structure which matches the characteristics of labour transactions thus economising on transaction costs. The basic argument as explained in Chapter 4 (see page 82) is simple. When jobs involve substantial human asset specificity of a firm-specific nature, i.e. when workers acquire firm-specific skills, they may act opportunistically. They may attempt to exploit their monopolistic power or make misrepresentations. This is not to the interest of either workers or management since individual bargaining involves time, expense and risks for both parties. An important risk is the discontinuation of employment which for the employee implies a loss of firm-specific training in addition to possible difficulties in securing alternative employment and for employers implies extra expense in appointing and training replacements. In addition, efficient adaptations to environmental change may be delayed or curtailed by individual bargaining. In these circumstances unionisation facilitates the introduction of the efficiency features associated with the organisational structure known as an 'internal labour market' (ILM).

Collective organisation is an essential feature of an ILM. It reduces bargaining costs by eliminating the need for individual bargaining and by rationalising the internal wage structure. Wages are collectively negotiated – and are attached to jobs rather than to persons – and grievance procedures are introduced. Collective action attenuates opportunism and reduces bounded rationality. Bounded rationality is reduced since, unlike individuals, unions have the time and the required resources to gather and evaluate information. Collective agreements and bargaining reduce the incentives for individuals to act opportunistically. Moreover, when contracts specify remuneration depending on the 'state of the world' the incentive for firms to default declines since unions can (a) seek specialist advice (lawyers, accountants, etc.) in order to evaluate *ex post* what state of the world has occurred and (b) impose a general labour withdrawal, even though an individual's sanction of labour withdrawal has been lost. To the extent that opportunism is reduced and the negotiation and implementation of work contracts is facilitated, the continuity of work is enhanced which promotes investment in human capital of an idiosyncratic nature and facilitates adaptation to change. Co-operative behaviour is promoted which further enhances efficiency.

Since the benefits associated with a reduction in quit rates and other transaction cost savings increase with the extent to which human asset specificity is present, the prediction is that the incentive to collective organisation increases and the organisational structure becomes more elaborate the higher the degree of human specificity involved. It is for this reason that (a) unions appeared earlier in industries such as the railways where skills are highly specific and (b) work organisation is much more elaborate with well-defined job ladders, grievance procedures, pay schemes, etc. in industries with greater human asset specificity.

Unions as collective voice

The view that unions provide workers with a voice, i.e. with a means of communicating with management, has been developed by Freeman and Medoff (1979). The need for a collective voice arises because (a) many aspects of the work environment are 'public goods' and (b) workers acting individually are subject to dismissal and, therefore, feel vulnerable which may inhibit their behaviour.

The public good nature of aspects of work organisation derives from the fact that it affects all, or large groups of workers, creating incentives for free riding. Conditions referring to safety, lighting, noise, lay-off policy, the speed of the production line, pension plans, etc. affect all employees and would involve any one individual in extensive investment in time and effort to negotiate changes. Each individual would, therefore, have an incentive to let others undertake any necessary changes. But since all individuals have a similar incentive to free ride, insufficient time and resources will be devoted to negotiating improvements. Furthermore any one individual initiating demands for changes runs the risk of dismissal which is not present for collective action.

In addition to eliminating the free riding problems in negotiations, unionism as a voice institution can provide management with information regarding worker preferences which if properly utilised can have a significant positive influence on managerial efficiency.

In the absence of unions workers faced with unfavourable work conditions have the choice of seeking alternative employment and employers can dismiss opportunistic or shirking employees. This might suggest that the efficiency of the labour market, like that of any other market, can be achieved through free entry and exit. Labour mobility, however, may be very costly or infeasible. Apart from personal (family) circumstances, or other barriers that might inhibit labour mobility, changing jobs can be very costly and inefficient especially when on-the-job training is firm specific and hence non-transferable. In this case a change of job may mean that the employee loses the firm-specific human capital acquired and the employer needs to incur expenses in selecting and retraining a replacement. In addition, labour mobility may be infeasible in periods of widespread unemployment or when labour markets are monopsonised. For example, to work as a coal miner in the UK means to work for the National Coal Board. A coal miner involved in a dispute with his employer would find it impossible to change employer unless he changed his profession.

Through their collective voice employees, however, can influence their environment favourably by talking to their employer rather than by seeking alternative employment. This reduces quit rates and improves efficiency through economising on transaction costs. Changes that may be brought about through negotiation include methods of production and administrative procedures as well as employee compensation packages and personnel policies. Additionally, information flows between management and labour can improve which enhances the efficiency of management decision making.

Some empirical evidence

The question then remains as to whether the monopoly or the efficiency role of trade unions predominates. The answer must be sought in empirical evidence and it may well vary with the circumstances and managerial attitudes and responses to unions.

Freeman and Medoff (1979) provide evidence which supports the main predictions of the collective voice/institutional response theory of unionism. Their research, based on the analysis of extensive US data in the 1970s, confirms the prediction that 'unionised workers have significantly lower quit rates than nonunion workers who are comparable in other respects'. Unionised quit rates were reduced by as much as 86 per cent for all workers in 1973–5 (USA May Current Population Survey) and tenure among unionised workers, in the male sample of the National Longitudinal Survey, showed an increase of 38 per cent (p. 79). There are variations, however, with older workers showing larger reductions in quit rates and higher increases in tenure.

In addition to reducing labour turnover unions had further improved productivity by an estimated average of 20–5 per cent in the manufacturing industry (wooden household sector, 15 per cent; cement, 6–8 per cent; underground bituminous coal in 1965, 25–30 per cent.) However, during the 1970s, due to management inability to cope with union issues during growth of the United Mine Workers, unionism was associated with a negative impact on productivity of 20–5 per cent.

Freeman and Medoff quote evidence indicating that the average estimated union effect on wages is an increase of the order of 10–15 per cent. Additionally, as predicted by the monopoly model of unions, the capital–output ratio is higher than optimal but only slightly so. The loss of output due to this effect was insignificant at 0.3 per cent of gross national product (GNP) in 1975. The output loss due to strikes during the two decades 1960 and 1970 was also very small, at 0.2 per cent on average and never more than 0.5 per cent of GNP. On the other hand there is evidence of improvements in personnel practices and of a reduction in income inequalities in the unionised sector.

Freeman and Medoff conclude that unions 'can and do affect positively the functioning of the economic and social systems' and that 'enough work has been done to yield the broad outlines of a new view of unionism' (p. 70).

Clark (1980) reports, on the basis of econometric evidence, a positive union effect on the US cement industry of the order of 6–8 per cent. British evidence on union/non-union wage differentials based on studies utilising the New Earnings Survey data of 1973 show a wide disparity in their findings, from an estimated 4–8 per cent differential to an 8–40 per cent differential. Finally, there is some evidence that organised workers prefer fringe benefits of a deferred compensation nature.

SUMMARY

The observation that wages differ from marginal products does not necessarily indicate that human resources are managed inefficiently.

Labour is heterogeneous and labour transactions vary with regard to the extent to which labour skills are transferrable or specific to a particular transaction and with regard to the ease or difficulty involved in measuring inputs and outputs. Efficient labour organisation requires structures which minimise the related transaction costs by mitigating opportunism and reducing bounded rationality. Moreover, when work effort is difficult to observe or measure and employee and employer interests regarding levels of work effort divert, work incentives can contribute to improved productivity and to an optimum sharing of risks provided that both firms and workers are risk averse.

In brief, the structure of internal labour markets can be attributed both to attempts to reduce transaction costs when work involves skills of a specific nature (Williamson 1984b) and to the provision of incentives intended to overcome problems associated with difficulties in measuring productivity and in achieving an optimum allocation of risks (Malcomson 1981, 1984b).

Personnel practices such as paying wages higher than the market rate (efficiency wages), paying young workers less than their marginal product and older workers more than their marginal product (deferred compensation theory) and adopting hierarchical pay structures can be seen to have efficiency enhancing implications. Efficiency wages can help attract a better qualified, well-motivated and strongly attached to the firm workforce which improves productivity and reduces labour turnover and the associated firing and hiring costs.

Efficiency wages can explain the existence of dual labour markets and the observation of equally well qualified personnel earning different wages. They can also contribute towards an explanation of the persistence of high wages in the face of unemployment.

Deferred compensations, i.e. the practice of paying workers less when they are young and more when they are older, combined with generous occupational pension schemes and a mandatory retirement age aim to reduce shirking and labour turnover. Both improve efficiency.

Hierarchical pay structures, i.e. the existence of relatively few senior posts and the promotion of a small proportion of employees on the basis of a relative rather than absolute measurement of performance, can also have a strong efficiency enhancing potential since they motivate the entire workforce rather than only those promoted to work hard.

Section 5 analyses the monopoly motive of unionism and indicates that in addition to their interest in raising wages trade unions perform a selection of other functions which can significantly improve economic efficiency. Evidence especially from the USA indicates that the efficiency enhancing impact of trade unions may well compensate for increased wages and the minuscule effects of strikes and work to rule supporting the view that unions can have an overall positive effect on the economy. To achieve the positive effects management must be able to respond in an effective and productive way to the presence of unions.

APPLICATION: PERSONNEL MANAGEMENT IN THE UK CONSTRUCTION INDUSTRY

To evaluate the personnel management of an industry we must examine the nature of the product produced and the conditions under which it is traded.

The output of the construction industry is highly customised and diversified by type, size, function, form and method of production. To meet the individual requirements of a large number of customers productive activity cannot precede orders. Work is carried out under contract.

The demand facing the industry is geographically dispersed and localised. While some work may be produced in factory conditions (pre-fabricated), production, in the main, takes place on site and cannot be transported so that any efficiency benefits of centralised production are absent.

The lack of economies of large-scale production results in a small minimum efficient scale of operations. This coupled with the low capital intensity[5] of the industry implies the absence of natural barriers to entry. Customised design and production means that innovation is also small and there are no great advantages to advertising. Inter-industry labour mobility, the lack of vertical integration and the availability of a large number of raw materials imply easy entry into the industry. The work requires the services of a large number of specialist traders which are usually provided by small specialist firms operating under subcontract. More than half the number of all construction firms were, in 1985, specialists, as Table 13.1 indicates. Both specialist and general contractors are small firms and there is substantial self-employment. Ninety per cent of all firms operating in the UK in 1985 employed fewer than eight persons. There were a few very large firms although each of those controlled a small percentage of industrial output. John Laing, the largest UK firm, had approximately 2–3 per cent of total domestic construction work and Barratt Developments had about 7 per cent of the private house building market (Johnson 1988).

The market demand for capital products, being a derived demand, tends to be extremely sensitive in periods of economic recession. Indeed the demand for construction projects shows strong cyclical and seasonal variations creating substantial uncertainty. In 1980, for example, at the beginning of the previous UK recession, the top ten contractors shed 15 per cent of their workforce and the second ten largest 14 per cent. The current recession has contributed to a further reduction in the size of production and employment in construction. Over 250,000 jobs were lost during the past two years, including a 30 per cent reduction in the number of working architects, and over

Table 13.1 Number of firms, employment and output by size of firm in Great Britain, 1985 (percentages)

Size of firm (number of employees)	Percentage of firms in main trade	Percentage of firms in specialist trade	Percentage of all firms	Employment, %	Value of work (third quarter), %
1	38.2	47.6	43.4	7.2	6.4
2–7	51.2	43.4	46.8	24.3	19.2
8–24	7.3	6.8	7.0	6.4	15.5
25–79	2.3	1.8	2.0	14.8	15.6
80–299	0.8	0.4	0.5	13.6	15.5
300–1,199			0.1	12.2	14.7
1,200	0.2	0.1	–	11.5	13.0
All firms	100	100	100	100	100
Total	73,760	94,065	167,825	941,000	£5,974.3 million

Source: Flemming in P. Johnson (ed.) 1988: Table 10.2

100,000 more jobs are expected to be lost by the end of 1992 (J. Willcott, *Guardian*, 27 July 1992). In general, the unemployment rate of the construction industry is approximately double that of the other industries.

Construction is very labour intensive and many different trades are involved (architects, engineers, plumbers, electricians, surveyors, carpenters, plasterers, etc.). A high proportion of the personnel is skilled but labour skills are transferrable within the industry rather than firm specific. This lack of human asset specificity accounts for inter-industry mobility of labour which has important personnel management implications.

Union organisation is, on average, very low at about 30 per cent of the workforce but it is concentrated in the crafts with 75 per cent of crafts persons belonging to one of a variety of unions in 1982–3.

In summary, the construction industry is characterised by a cyclically and seasonally fluctuating demand, the production of mainly customised products based on small value orders, a labour intensive production process utilising a variety of inter-industry transferrable skills and unionisation restricted mainly to crafts trades.

These characteristics denote the absence of significant benefits to labour internalisation and to the development of an internal labour market in the organisation of work. The intermittent number of small value orders and the instability of demand signify the absence of managerial advantages from a stable employment and a long employee attachment to the firm. On the contrary, the protective features of internal labour markets would imply that employers would bear the total risk of a reduction in demand, for no obvious reason. Given that there are no substantial benefits to a reduced labour turnover it is efficient for management to attempt to reduce the risks of a fluctuating demand by shifting them to labour in the form of either redundancies (when demand is low) or self-employment and subcontracting.

Apart from its risk reduction benefits, subcontracting is an efficient system of assigning individuals to tasks since the subcontractor is likely to be more knowledgeable than the main contractor (principal). Adverse selection problems are thus alleviated and work intensity is enhanced especially when quality is easily monitored. The innovation incentives of subcontracting are also good since the individual who innovates enjoys the concomitant benefits.

Transaction difficulties under subcontracting, however, do exist and they are mainly related to product flow, tools and machinery utilisation and lack of incentives to co-operative behaviour. Of these product flow and tool utilisation problems are not important in this industry. What may present more serious problems is a subcontractor's lack of reliability with regard to start and completion dates and the quality of work. The problem of reliability, however, is mitigated by the easy availability of relevant information in the industry. Similarly the quality of work can be controlled at least partly by controlling the quality of materials and plant used. To ensure quality the main contractors usually provide the materials and bear the cost of wastage which is not very difficult to monitor.

The main disadvantages of subcontracting are as follows. (a) A lack of incentives to use equipment carefully. Related costs are, however, minimised by hiring plant or hiring both plant and operator. Additionally a significant part of equipment is in the form of hand tools which are normally owned and used by the individuals employed under subcontract. (b) Co-operative behaviour and adaptability to changing circumstances is not encouraged by subcontracting especially when such behaviour may increase the work load of subcontractors remunerated on a lump-sum basis. On balance the advantages of subcontracting seem to outweigh the possible disadvantages.

Subcontracting has indeed been widespread and growing. The number of workers operating under-labour only subcontracting has grown between 1965 and 1982 from 160,000–200,000 to 600,000. In 1981, a third of gross construction by value was subcontracted (Buckley and Enderwick 1989).

FURTHER READING

Freeman, R.B. and Medoff, J.L. (1979) 'The Two Faces of Unionism', *Public Interest*, Fall: 69–93.
Mallier, A. and Shafto, A. (1989) *Economics of Labour Markets and Management*, London: Hutchison.
Williamson, O.E. (1985) *The Economic Institutions of Capitalism, Firms, Markets, Relational Contracting*, London: Collier Macmillan.

QUESTIONS

1 'Transaction costs must not be identified with marketing costs' (Stephen 1984). Discuss.
2 With reference to Figure 13.2 explain the personnel management consequences of the introduction of a law which abolishes the mandatory age for worker retirement.
3 The observation that brilliant teachers are often promoted to become mediocre headmasters, or that excellent salespersons become mediocre managers, or the promotion of a company's vice-president to president with an overnight trebling of salary, indicates the existence of widespread labour market inefficiencies. Discuss.
4 'A survey of Britain's oldest directors shows that more than 700 directors of public companies are on or above the official retirement age of 65.' The average age of those over retirement age is 71. 'Pride of place goes to Lord Shawcross who at the age of 91 said that he has no plans to step down from his post as deputy chairman of Caffyns, a Sussex based motor distributor' (*Sunday Times*, 9 May 1993).

Give an economic explanation for this phenomenon and comment on its possibly beneficial effects on the companies concerned.

5 'Trade unions can improve efficiency by making state contingent contracts possible thereby providing incentives and improving productivity.' Discuss.

NOTES

1 Individual utility functions are supposed to be independent.
2 Transaction cost economics assumes that labour is risk neutral. Agency theory allows for risk aversion. The extent of risk aversion is an important dimension of labour markets.
3 For references see Yellen (1984).
4 'In the USA the 1978 and 1986 amendments to the Age Discrimination and Employment Act exempted most workers from mandatory retirement' (Main 1990).
5 'The total stock of fixed capital in the industry is equivalent to little more than one year's wage and salary bill' (Johnson 1988).

14 Competition policy, privatisation and de-regulation

INTRODUCTION

Government economic policy is commonly designed to serve a variety of economic and political objectives. Macroeconomic policies aim to influence aggregate variables such as economic growth, inflation, unemployment, the balance of payments or the public sector borrowing requirements, while microeconomic or industrial policies focus directly on industries and firms. Although both macroeconomic and microeconomic policies have a direct or indirect impact on industry this chapter focuses on the latter.

At the risk of over-simplification we can distinguish two broad approaches to industrial policy; a *laissez-faire* approach which views the role of government as unnecessary and advocates that its activities should be strictly limited to supporting and re-enforcing the operation of market forces, and the extreme opposite, an *active* approach which argues for government intervention to improve the functioning of the market. In reality industry policy lies typically between the two extremes. It consists of competition policy which attempts to influence the conduct of certain markets and firms, regional policy which focuses on the location of industry, innovation policy which aims to promote technological advancement and trade policy designed to protect specific firms and industries. Both the mixture and the extent of these policies vary among countries reflecting the prevailing political and economic philosophies.

During the 1980s the UK competition policy underwent a substantial transformation. A radical programme of widespread privatisation and deregulation was introduced, prior to and possibly in view of the European integration of 1992. Over £38 billion worth of assets were transferred from the public to the private sector between 1979 and 1992. The tradable public sector was reduced to a third of its size. This chapter focuses on the impact of these transfers or 'privatisation' and the related issues of competition policy and de-regulation. The first section builds on economic arguments developed in earlier chapters to examine the theoretical basis of competition policy and privatisation. The second focuses on competition policy in practice and compares the UK, European Community (EC) and US policies. The debate on the UK privatisation programme is briefly summarised in the third section. The fourth section examines de-regulation and franchising and the chapter concludes with a brief summary. The privatisation of the Electricity Supply Industry is the subject of the end of chapter application.

THE ECONOMIC FOUNDATIONS OF COMPETITION POLICY

The rationale of government industrial policy is usually declared to be a desire to improve market failures and the allocative inefficiencies associated with monopoly. Other objectives may intrude, however. To achieve these aims governments utilise a variety of instruments the nature and extent of which vary among countries and over time reflecting the prevailing economic theories and political philosophies. For example, the emphasis of the 'new industrial economics' on the endogeneity of market structure and the interdependence between environmental characteristics and the behaviour of decision makers has been reflected in the significance which current UK competition policy places on incentives and entrepreneurship. Thus, the 1989 UK White Paper on Restrictive Trade Practices states that the Department of Trade and Industry will strive, through its competition policy, to promote open markets because 'open markets are the best guarantee of incentive and efficiency' while 'closed, insular markets kill enterprise and effort'.

The emphasis on incentives and enterprise reflect theoretical developments on transaction cost economics, agency theory and contestability theory, all of which shed doubt on the belief that there is a one-way causal link between a firm's conduct and performance (in terms of allocative efficiency) and the structure of the industry. As Chapter 2 shows, this causal link derives from the structure–conduct–performance (SCP) paradigm which postulates that perfectly competitive markets lead to an optimal allocation of resources while monopolies induce allocative inefficiencies. The implication is that the efficiency of markets depends directly on their structure and in particular on the extent of seller concentration. The more firms there are the more competitive a market is and the better the performance of the firms while the more concentrated the market the more closely its behaviour resembles that of a monopoly and the more inefficient the resource allocation is. This paradigm remained influential for over thirty years in directing industry policy to the adoption of measures intended to change the structure of the industry in order to improve performance. Competition policy was accordingly aimed at creating less-concentrated market structures as a means to achieving the objective of a better performance.

The concept of competition underlying the SCP paradigm, however, is a static one derived from the neoclassical economic theory which treats the firm as a 'black box'. As indicated throughout this book, however, firms are not mere production devices. Rather, they consist of a set of transactional relationships which take place in a world characterised by uncertainties and informational asymmetries and in which competition is a dynamic process manifesting itself in a variety of ways through entrepreneurial actions. Entrepreneurs in their search for personal gain tend to correct market inefficiencies and excessive profits. Their actions, however, are influenced both by the internal organisational systems within which they function and by the external incentives provided and controls imposed by the product and capital markets.

Although competitive pressures are important in inducing managers to operate more efficiently, it cannot be presumed that unfettered markets will lead to an ideal allocation of resources. Markets may fail to operate efficiently and it is precisely because of such failures that firms emerge (see Chapter 3) and supersede the market by expanding vertically, horizontally and spatially (see Chapter 10). Efficiency in the form of economising on transaction and production costs may thus lead to expansion and the acquisition of a dominant market position. Despite its possible efficiency origin, the acquisition of market power can lead to business practices that run against the public interest.

Monopolies may increase costs, for example, by expending resources in activities aimed at reducing competition in order to maintain dominance. The removal of competitive pressures may further reduce managerial incentives to improve performance. The combined effect is that the cost of producing any given level of output may not necessarily be the lowest possible. Production inefficiency, in other words, exists in addition to the allocative inefficiency associated with the pursue of profit maximisation (see Chapter 8). Production and other inefficiencies can also arise from the fact that dominant firms often compete in terms of non-price decision variables such as expenditure on research and development (R&D) and innovation, product proliferation and advertising.

Non-price competition, often the only form of competition, can be more significant than price competition since it has a direct effect on costs and an indirect effect on price through its influence on competitiveness and on the choice offered to consumers. Expenditure on R&D, for example, has significant welfare implications since it leads to product and process innovation which is essential for economic growth and prosperity. The lack of threat to monopoly profits coupled with a desire to avoid the risks inherent in R&D may induce dominant firms to under-invest in research. Expenditure on R&D and the concomitant innovation may, therefore, be less than optimal in markets dominated by a few firms. Expenditure on other non-price variables can, on the other hand, be excessive. Advertising, investment in excess capacity and product proliferation can be manipulated strategically in an attempt to influence competitive behaviour favourably or in order to prevent new entry. Firms may devote resources to signalling intentions in order to built a desired form of reputation and impede incumbent or potential competition (see Chapter 8).

To summarise, both price and non-price decisions by dominant firms can contribute to social welfare losses. Compared with perfectly competitive markets, advertising can be excessive, innovation too slow and internal inefficiencies may develop. Perfectly competitive markets, however, are unrealistic and it can be argued that it is more useful to make comparisons between feasible alternative market structures rather than between existing markets and an infeasible theoretical ideal.

What matters for efficiency is not the static concept of perfect competition postulated in the neoclassical economic model but whether in reality competition from other firms or potential entrants is sufficiently strong to mitigate against strategic behaviour and to induce incumbent firms to operate efficiently. Considerations of effective as opposed to 'perfect' competition, therefore, have an important bearing on competition policy. With this proviso in mind this chapter begins with an examination of the theoretical reasons why market dominance occurs and how firms may attempt to maintain and exercise it, before describing and evaluating current competition policies.

The acquisition and maintenance of market dominance

Two main routes to the acquisition and maintenance of dominance can be distinguished; efficiency or the pursuit of market power.

Dominance through efficiency gains

The reasons why large multi-product and multinational firms emerge were analysed in Chapter 10 which shows that a firm's expansion may be due, at least partly, to efficiency. Firms may acquire spare resources either because of economies of scale or scope or because of organisational improvements, enhanced know-how and expertise. If hiring or subcontracting the use of these surplus resources is very costly (due to transactional difficulties), efficiency is enhanced by internal expansion which, depending on the nature of the resources, will be vertical or horizontal, national or international. Expansion, however, may lead to dominance. The dominant position of Alcoa, for example, was attributed by the US anti-trust authorities to 'skill, foresight and industry' (Hay and Vickers 1987). Similarly Nestle's dominance was acquired 'by operating efficiently and by developing products and brands that offer consumers good value for money' (Monopolies and Mergers Commission 1991b).

If the exercise of dominance causes inefficiencies the fact that its acquisition may be due to efficiency creates a serious dilemma for competition policy. Policy makers have to strike the right balance between the gains of effective competition which lead to dominance and the detrimental effects arising from the market power associated with dominance.

A similar dilemma arises in the case of natural monopolies. A natural monopoly arises when technology is such that economies of scale exist which are exhausted at a scale of operation which is so large in relation to the market that only one firm can operate efficiently. That is, in the relevant range of production the average cost declines as output expands which means that if more than one firm operated independently the average cost of production of each could increase to an extent outweighing any benefit derived from enhanced competition. In other words, a trade-off may exist between production efficiency and the benefits derived from enhanced competitiveness.

The difficulties in designing an appropriate policy are exacerbated by the fact that it is not always easy to empirically establish whether a firm has become dominant because of efficiency, as in the case of ALCOA and Nestle, or whether its profitability is due to the exercise of market power.

Other means to dominance

Firms may acquire market power by various means some of which are described below.

Legal protection

Public authorities often grant monopoly rights to public utilities (electricity, water, gas, telecommunications, etc.) for reasons of productive efficiency since these industries are believed to be natural monopolies. To mitigate against the allocative inefficiency which in such industries can be very substantial, firms are controlled either by subjecting them to a framework of regulation (as in the USA) or by bringing them under public ownership (as in the UK).

Patents are another way of granting market power. They give protection from competition to innovators of new products, processes or techniques by prohibiting imitation or reproduction of the patented product for a number of years. The aim of the provision of this form of protection is clearly to encourage invention and innovation. Without this protection, firms would be unwilling to spend sufficiently on R&D since potential competition by imitators would reduce the net expected returns. The length of time during which a patent is valid must therefore be determined in a way that encourages innovation by providing a monopoly right to the innovator against the disadvantage of the stifling of competition that the patent necessitates.

Collusion

Collusive agreements were examined in Chapter 8. It should be recalled that they can be explicit or implicit and their aim is invariably to reduce competition and facilitate monopolistic pricing. Given their adverse effects on competition, horizontal collusive agreements are usually banned in most jurisdictions. Exemptions are few, but R&D joint ventures are sometimes permitted on the premise that duplication of effort is avoided although strategic reasons may also be present.

Mergers

One of the most common routes to market dominance is via mergers. Their impact on competition and pricing is not dissimilar to that of cartels. Despite this, mergers in the UK are not prohibited for two reasons; first, they may occur for reasons of efficiency and, second, they are necessary for the takeover mechanism to exist which is at the heart of the market in corporate control. The threat of takeover is considered to be one of the most important controls on managerial discretionary behaviour.

Predatory behaviour

Predatory or strategic behaviour may be used to either eliminate existing competition so as to acquire dominance or in order to discourage potential competition so as to maintain dominance, or both. Predatory pricing, for example, aims to eliminate incumbent competition but as a credible threat it can also avert potential competition. When BOC was investigated by the Monopolies and Mergers Commission in 1956 it was reported that it used 'fighting' subsidiaries to undercut small competitors, in several parts of the UK, which were then taken over. This tactic not only eliminated existing competitors, it was a credible threat which deterred potential entrants.

Price is not the only variable that can be strategically used. Predatory policies can be based on innovation, advertising, investment and even on the manipulation of patent laws (DuPont was accused of this practice as reported on page 43).

In summary, both the acquisition and the maintenance of dominance may affect competitiveness and costs of production. It is thus concern with the impact of dominance on social welfare that necessitates the existence of competition policy.

The impact of Market Dominance

Allocative inefficiencies

Concern over the existence of dominant firms derives from the possibility that market power may be exercised in a way which leads to a misallocation of resources. The traditional economic analysis of dominance focuses on this possibility by indicating how dominant firms may restrict production

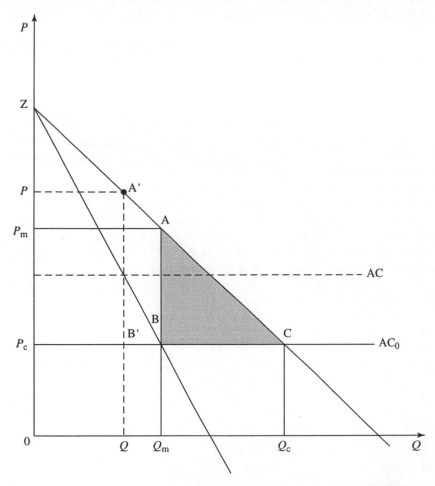

Figure 14.1 The welfare loss of monopoly (monopoly deadweight loss ABC increases to A'B'C in the presence of production inefficiency)

in order to charge prices higher than unit production costs. Assuming profit maximisation the price P_m and output Q_m of the single-product monopolist whose cost and demand curves are AC_0 and D respectively are illustrated in Figure 14.1 (ignore the broken lines for the time being). Compared with the perfectly competitive or perfectly contestable market price P_c and output Q_c, the monopoly output is too small and the price too high. That is, price is higher than marginal cost implying that resource allocation under monopoly is less efficient compared with the competitive ideal. To identify the extent of the distortion (net welfare loss) we must compare the monopoly price and output with that which maximises social welfare. This requires knowledge of the social welfare function. A simple specification, commonly adopted, is that social welfare is the sum of consumers' and producers' surplus; i.e. $W = S + \Pi$, where W denotes social welfare, S is consumers' surplus and Π is the producers' surplus.

It should be recalled that perfectly competitive pricing throughout the economy results in an optimum resource allocation provided that prices reflect the true valuation that consumers attach to products and that marginal costs indicate the true opportunity costs of production. If furthermore it is assumed that the identity of the beneficiaries of market power, or its removal, is immaterial then it can be shown that the welfare loss associated with monopoly is indicated by the area ABC in Figure 14.1. This loss, also known as the *deadweight loss*, is derived as follows. In perfect competition the price is P_c and there is no producer surplus (no long-run profit). Consumers' expenditure on Q_c units is equal to area OP_cCQ_c but their true valuation of Q_c is the total area under the demand curve so that consumers' surplus is equal to area P_cZC. The exercise of dominance implies that price increases to P_m which creates producers' surplus (profit) equal to area P_cP_mAB but reduces consumers' surplus which is now equal to area P_mZA. The reduction in consumers' surplus, P_cP_mAC, is larger than the increase in profit by an amount equal to the area of triangle ABC (shaded area).

It follows that, given the cost curves, the welfare loss of monopoly depends on the size of the industry and the price elasticity of demand. The larger the extent of industrial monopolisation and the more essential the monopolised products the larger the deadweight loss will be and the more significant the role of competition policy. The quantification of the welfare loss of monopoly is a matter for empirical verification and many researchers have indeed attempted to estimate its size in different countries. Table 14.1 gives some examples. These show that the size of the welfare loss associated with monopoly as a percentage of gross domestic product (GDP) varies greatly, from 0.1 to 13 per cent. Such disparities reflect partly difficulties in estimation and partly differences in the underlying economic circumstances.

The deadweight loss provides the basis for the condemnation of monopolies. It shows the extent to which consumers would benefit by a transfer

Table 14.1 Empirical evidence on the welfare loss of monopoly

Country	Year	Author	Welfare Loss
USA	1963–6	Cowling and Mueller (1978)	4.0–13.1
USA	1950–66	Masson and Shaanan (1984)	2.9
USA	1962–75	Wahlroos (1984)	0.04–0.9
USA	1977	Gisser (1986)	0.1–1.8
Canada	1965–7	Jones and Laudio (1978)	3.7
UK	1968–9	Cowling and Mueller (1978)	3.9–7.2
Finland	1970–9	Wahlroos (1984)	0.2–0.6
France	1967–70	Jenny and Webber (1983)	0.13–8.85
Korea	1983	Oh (1986)	0.02–3.0

of resources from other industries (where $P = $ MC) to the monopolised sector where they are more highly valued ($P > $ MC). In the absence of this transfer resources are misallocated; too few being employed in the monopolised industry and too many in the competitive industries.

Production efficiency

The above analysis implies that monopolisation leads to allocative inefficiency, a conclusion which is correct on the assumption that industrial structure has no impact on demand and cost conditions. As already indicated, however, the acquisition of market dominance may affect both market shares and production costs. Dominant firms often adopt price and non-price practices in an attempt to influence market shares and they expend resources in order to acquire or maintain market power. On the other hand, firms expand by internalisation when the costs of internal organisation are smaller than the costs associated with market transacting. As Chapter 3 explained, firms will tend to integrate vertically, e.g. when producing their own requirements rather than buying them from other firms economises on transaction costs by more than the extra costs of organising the additional transactions internally. Economies of scale or scope or rather the transactional difficulties that may arise in their presence can be among the most significant factors contributing to vertical, horizontal and spatial expansion of firms. Market dominance may therefore be associated with production efficiency in which case a trade-off arises which is central to government policy regarding mergers and monopolies. To illustrate consider Figure 14.2.

It is assumed that Figure 14.2 shows a competitive structure associated with transaction costs so that the average cost is AC_0. In order to focus on efficiency we assume that the market demand remains the same whatever the market structure. The competitive price and output are denoted by P_c and Q_c respectively. Now suppose that if all the firms merged, transaction costs economising would reduce the cost of production to AC_1. To profit maximise the post-merger monopoly produces the smaller output Q_m and charges price P_m. Consumers are worse off since they acquire fewer units of the product and they pay more per unit. Consumers' surplus has been reduced to an extent indicated by the sum of the areas of triangle 1 and rectangle 2. Producers, however, are better off since they now enjoy a surplus indicated by the area of rectangles 2 and 3. This is derived partly from a transfer from consumers to producers (area 2) and partly from the cost saving associated with dominance (area 3). The deadweight loss, i.e. the reduction in consumer surplus that does not represent benefit to producers, is indicated by area 1.

Is monopolisation overall beneficial in this case? Assuming that social welfare improves by a net improvement in $W = S + \Pi$ then the net welfare effect of the merger illustrated in Figure 14.2 depends on the relative sizes

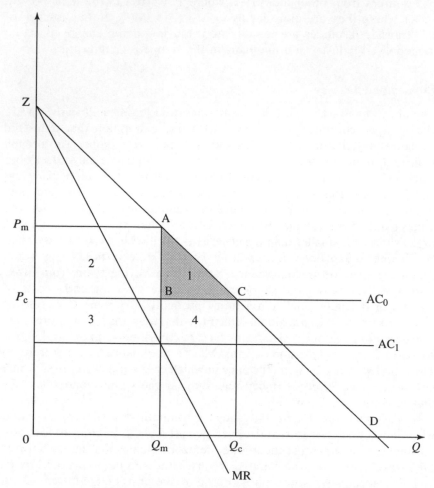

Figure 14.2 The trade-off between productive and allocative efficiency

of areas 1 and 3. Social welfare remains the same, improves or deteriorates as the deadweight loss (area 1) is equal to, smaller or larger than the production cost saving (area 3).

Whatever the effect of monopoly on W, allocative inefficiency is present so long as profit maximisation is pursued. This means that even if monopoly improved W the improvement could have been higher since output $Q_c - Q_m$, which is valued more than the resources required for its production, is not produced. Therefore the relevant resources, if employed at all, are producing a less valuable product.

In reality the assumption that the identity of the beneficiaries or losers of a policy is immaterial may not be valid. Both political considerations and notions of fairness may induce a government to consider the distributional implications of monopoly policy. Such considerations seem to have led the US anti-trust authorities to turn down a merger application by Santa Fe and Southern Pacific railroads, in 1986, despite an estimated net gross welfare benefit. The annual operating cost saving of the proposal (area 3 in Figure 14.2) was estimated by the Interstate Commerce Commission at $188.2 million (4.3 per cent of total cost) Assuming a price elasticity of -0.75 and a post-merger price increase of 22.5 per cent, Pittman (1990) estimated the deadweight loss of monopoly at $98.2 and the transfer from shippers to the railways (area 2 in Figure 14.2) at $336.9 million, which implies a net increase in W of $246.9. Thus a merger promising production efficiency twice as large as the deadweight loss was banned presumably because the adverse effect on consumers (more than twice as much as the promised cost efficiency) was given a higher weight than that associated with the beneficial effect on the owners of the railroads.

Production inefficiency and other effects of market dominance

The exercise of dominance does not simply imply a higher price. Dominance can manifest itself in the form of price discriminatory practices, vertical restraints and other restrictive conditions of sale or as an influence on the speed of innovation, the extent of advertising, investment and the variety and quality of output.

Price discrimination and vertical restraints raise the question of whether they are detrimental to social welfare and competition and whether their presence is indicative of a lack of effective competition. The welfare implications of both these practices vary with the specific circumstances under which they are exercised. As explained in Chapter 8 and as Schmalensee (1981) has shown, simple price discrimination is undesirable since it allocates resources among existing customers inefficiently. This adverse effect, however, may be outweighed by an increase in output which may occur by opening up new markets.

Similarly, ambiguities arise regarding the welfare effects of vertical restraints such as exclusive dealings, reciprocal sales or territorial quotas often imposed by manufacturers to the retailers of their products. It can be argued, for example, that intra-brand restraints may enhance efficiency by mitigating free-rider problems. An example is the pre-sale services for which a price cannot be charged. Although such services are desirable each retailer will have an incentive to reduce their size expecting to benefit by the services provided by other retailers.

Retail price maintenance (RPM) agreements are widely believed to be anti-competitive and are therefore illegal in many jurisdictions, but other non-price restraints associated with dominance have more ambiguous effects. Bundling, the practice of selling several goods as a package, is justified by those practising it (IBM for example) on the grounds that it can reduce production and transaction costs. The practice, however, is condemned when it is used as a means of segregating groups of consumers with different elasticities in order to practice price discrimination.

Advertising is a means of information dissemination which is often used as a competitive weapon or as a means of influencing tastes and preferences. Since informational asymmetries can create substantial transactional costs, to the extent that advertising facilitates the acquisition of information it can contribute towards improvements in efficiency both within firms and in market transacting. But although in its informative role advertising can enhance efficiency, its strategic use implies that it can be carried to an excess and contribute to productive inefficiencies. There is indeed evidence that 'the market equilibrium level of advertising is socially excessive even when judged by post-advertising tastes. The result holds for a variety of market structures' (Hay and Vickers 1987).

Innovation and its relationship to market dominance is a more significant and more complex issue. It is possible, however, to show that a firm can over-invest in R&D or capital expenditure in order to gain a strategic advantage over existing or potential competitors. Strategic entry deterrence is socially inefficient because it raises production costs and thwarts competition.

The production inefficiency associated with dominance can be further enhanced through its adverse effect on managerial incentives and controls.

Lack of competitive pressures may allow managers to create slack, employ excessive staff, spend on discretionary investment projects or simply opt for a 'quiet life'. As Leibenstein argued in 1966, in competitive product markets the fear of bankruptcy and unemployment compels management and workers to behave in a profit-maximising/cost-minimising way, but when competitive forces weaken, as in a monopoly, then the scope for management and workers to pursue personal objectives (leisure, security, easy life) increases so that they may work neither as hard nor as efficiently as they could. As a result actual costs increase by an amount referred to as X-inefficiency (see page 311–13). For Leibenstein the welfare loss to society due to X-inefficiency within firms outweighs the loss due to inefficiency in the operation of markets. In other words, in addition to its allocative inefficiency dominance implies an increase in production costs (indicated by the broken line in Figure 14.1). There is no trade-off of the kind described in Figure 14.2. X-inefficiency exacerbates the deadweight loss increasing the welfare loss to an extent indicated by area A′ABB′ in Figure 14.1.

Ownership and incentives

When the welfare losses associated with dominance are expected to be large, as for example in the case of essential commodities such as electricity, water or gas, governments intervene to control the behaviour of their producers. Various methods of control from taxation to price or profits regulation or outright nationalisation have been used over the years. The nationalisation of many UK industries which occurred after the Second World War meant that a large public sector co-existed with the private sector for many years. Dissatisfaction with the performance of public enterprises, however, has contributed to recent government decisions to transfer many productive units (public enterprises) from the public to the private sector.

Although privatisation has commonly been accompanied by other measures intended to improve competitiveness, such as removals of legal barriers to entry and the creation of a more liberal market structure, it is often claimed that the change of ownership itself will contribute to a better performance because of its influence on the constraints and opportunities under which management operates (Kay and Thompson 1986).

Managers in the public sector, like their private sector counterparts, act as the agents of the owners of the firm. If ownership alters a firm's behaviour it must be either because it changes business objectives or because management motivation and behaviour is different under different ownership. Let us examine each possibility in turn.

Ownership objectives and performance

The legislation which brought many UK enterprises into public ownership prescribed their objectives in most general terms and saw their managers as the trustees of the public interest. Consequently, economists assumed the objective of public enterprises to be the maximisation of social welfare and prescribed the pricing and investment rules that their management should follow to achieve its objective.

Public sector managers, however, are likely to pursue their own objectives rather than those of their principals unless effective monitoring and control systems operate which eliminate discretionary behaviour. If managers have no discretion their decisions will reflect the objective of the owners which in the case of public enterprises is generally assumed to be 'the public interest'. As already suggested the economic literature has associated the public interest with the maximisation of a social welfare function which in its simplest form is the sum of consumers' and producers' surplus. But since consumers' surplus is defined as the difference between the value that consumers place on a given quantity q minus the price they have to pay to acquire that quantity while producers' surplus is simply the profit, we can write

$$W = S(q,x) + \Pi (q,x)$$

Where $\Pi = [p - c(x)]q$, $S = V(q) - c(q)$, x denotes expenditure on cost reducing activities and p is the price in the case of perfectly competitive markets or the demand curve in the case of a monopoly.

Now if the objective of privately owned firms is to profit maximise, this is achieved by maximising $\Pi = [p - c(x)]q - x$ which implies marginal cost pricing and allocative efficiency in the case of perfectly competitive markets. When the market, however, is dominated by one firm profit maximisation is achieved when output is such that marginal revenue equals marginal cost and the price is higher than marginal cost implying allocative inefficiencies.

Public sector managers, on the other hand, select the output that maximises W. They therefore produce more output (where $P = MC$) and set a lower price compared with private sector managers of dominant firms. The public firm production is indicated by point C in Figure 14.1 and price is equal to AC_0. There is no deadweight loss.

Thus, for given demand and cost conditions, public enterprises would be more efficient than their private sector counterparts. The achievement of allocative efficiency, however, was derived on the assumption that managers actively pursue the public interest. Doubts, however, have been expressed as to whether this is a realistic assumption to make. For managers would, in this case, have followed the pricing and investment rules which the economic literature carried on prescribing for over twenty years. It appears, however, that at no time did this literature, or the legislation prescribing specific objectives (e.g. White Papers of 1961, 1967 and 1978), have much of an impact on what managers actually did do. For, had managers pursued the public interest with vigour, the performance of their industries would have been better compared with the performance of private firms (Kay and Thompson 1986). The reason why managers did not pursue the objectives prescribed must be sought in managerial incentives and discretion. If public sector managers are motivated by personal objectives such as a desire to expand the size of the enterprise or seek a quiet life, thus neglecting to pursue innovation and change, productive efficiency will suffer. The question is to what extent.

Ownership and managerial incentives

While ownership objectives imply that a dominant firm's behaviour improves under public ownership, the behaviour of public sector managers can cause serious deviations from optimality. Public sector managers, as agents, are likely to pursue their own objectives under the constraints facing them rather than strive to achieve the public interest. And, since public sector firms face neither a bankruptcy nor a takeover threat the constraints under which they operate may not be as effective as the control mechanisms facing private sector managers. Furthermore, government interference and lack of appropriate incentives may mitigate against work effort and productive efficiency.

To illustrate, suppose that control mechanisms and incentives, although present in both the private and the public sector, are not equally effective in controlling managerial discretion. Thus, the existence of a difference in incentives can take the form of a difference in work effort or in expenditure on cost-reducing activities between the two sectors. In terms of the simple model used above this means that private sector managers will attempt to maximise profits adjusted for work effort. That is,

$$\max A(q,x) = \Pi(q,x) - (a - 1)x = [p - c(q)]q - (a - 1)x$$

where a indicates the cost of effort to the manager relative to the benefit he or she derives from the increase in profit. If $a = 1$ there is no managerial discretion and the manager's profit maximises. In general we would expect managers to be able to exercise some discretion in which case $a > 1$.

Similarly under public ownership managers maximise a social welfare function adjusted for work effort. That is,

$$\max B(q,x) = S(q,x) + \Pi(q,x) + (b - 1)x.$$

Similarly to a, the parameter b measures the cost of effort to the manager in relation to the benefits he or she derives from enhanced social welfare. Again if $b = 1$ there is no managerial discretion. Normally we would expect $b > 1$. That is, public sector managers would be expected to deviate from pursuing rigorously the interests of their principals. The question, however, is whether private sector incentives are keener, as often advocated, than public sector incentives in which case $b > a$ or vice versa.

Assuming that $b > a$ private sector managers would spend more on cost reducing activities than public sector managers, thus achieving an improvement in production efficiency. In this case a transfer of ownership from the public to the private sector would be associated with a trade-off since allocative efficiency deteriorates but production efficiency improves. The result of the trade-off depends on the relevant magnitudes of the changes involved. As Vickers and Yarrow (1988) show, an overall improvement under private ownership is only possible if managerial incentives are distinctly more effective in the private sector, otherwise the opposite is true. That is, if $a \geqslant b$ then public ownership is superior to private ownership in terms of both allocative and productive efficiency. Public firms not only produce more and charge a lower price than private dominant firms, their unit costs are lower since more is spent on cost reducing activities and the resulting savings are spread over a larger volume of output. Social welfare is enhanced.[1]

But is $b > a$? As Chapter 9 shows, the most important management control mechanisms in the private sector are the market in corporate control, product market competition and the risk of bankruptcy. The fear of a takeover, financial constraints and risks or competitive pressures contribute to a mitigation, if not elimination, of managerial discretion. Most of the public enterprises are not, however, subject to these or similar controls. Since there are no tradable shares or shareholders, there is no market in corporate control. There is no possibility of a takeover bid and no risk to job security relating to the valuation of the firm. Furthermore, there is no risk of bankruptcy since deficits are covered by the government. Finally, the discipline imposed by competition in the product markets is often non-existent especially when the firm is a natural monopoly.

Further disincentives may arise in the case of a natural monopoly since allocative efficiency (marginal cost pricing) implies losses the financing of which creates two major problems. First, government financing of the deficit requires taxation which means that tax payers subsidise the consumers of the subsidised output. This income redistribution may in turn be politically undesirable. More importantly, perhaps, the existence of a loss and the requirement for subsidies may have adverse effects on staff morale. Working for a loss making enterprise may be demoralising to an extent that it could reduce labour productivity. To avoid such problems average cost pricing was more frequently adopted which is only a second best as far as social welfare optimisation is concerned.

The above arguments seem to suggest that public sector controls and incentives are weaker than those in the private sector, an argument often used in support of privatisation. Care, however, must be taken to ensure that in arriving at this conclusion like is compared with like. This is not always the case, since the assumed superiority of private markets is strictly dependent on the existence of well functioning capital and product markets. Given that the absence of product market competition is likely to lead to allocative inefficiency in the private sector, the question is not whether perfectly competitive private firms operate better than public enterprises but whether private firms which do not face competition are likely to perform better than public enterprises.

As already indicated the incentive to productive efficiency comes from the need of private firm managers to achieve a certain level of profitability so as to be able to maintain their share valuation high in order to avert the risk of a takeover or bankruptcy. If there is little or no competition, however, the risk of bankruptcy is virtually non-existent and the risk of a takeover is minimal especially for large monopolies. The pressures on private sector managers may not be any more substantial than those facing the public sector managers.

There is some empirical evidence in support of the above claim. Singh (1971, 1975) has conducted the most extensive empirical work so far on UK acquisitions. His work shows that there was no significant difference between the performance indicators of firms that had fallen victim to takeover and the rest of the industry, casting doubt on the notion that poor performance increases the risk of a takeover. What Singh's findings show is that the risk of a takeover diminishes significantly for firms over a certain size. And although it has been suggested that large firms may have become more vulnerable to hostile bids since the period studied by Singh, 'it remains true that the size of newly privatized firms . . . provide incumbent management with substantial protection against takeover threats' (Vickers and Yarrow 1988: 22).

In other words, the issue of market competition must be treated separately since market liberalisation can be introduced in the public sector either via domestic competition (electricity showrooms) or from imports (steel) or both, and can often be absent in the private sector (British Aerospace).

In brief, privately owned competitive firms are likely to achieve both productive and allocative efficiency since the controls and incentives that operate under private ownership tend to promote productive efficiency while competition promotes allocative efficiency. When competitive pressures are absent or ineffective, however, it is likely that privately owned firms may not perform better than publicly owned firms. It is the effectiveness of competition that induces managers to operate efficiently rather than ownership *per se*. That is not to deny that public ownership may impede market competitiveness. The opposite may indeed be true since public enterprises often operate under legal protection which makes the market non-contestable. But in this case it is the absence of contestability or competition that has the adverse effect on performance rather than public ownership. The empirical evidence reviewed after the section on competition policy in practice provides some support for this claim.

COMPETITION POLICY

The analysis so far suggests that incumbent or potential competition is necessary for allocative efficiency and for providing the necessary managerial incentives. To promote economic efficiency competition policy must enhance competitiveness while ensuring that dominance when present has no adverse effects on resource allocation. A variety of policy instruments can be used, however, for this purpose. The particular ones a government adopts will depend on distributional effects and on political philosophies. It is for this reason that competition policy can vary over time and among countries. In this section we examine the development of UK competition policy since the Second World War and compare it with that of the USA and the EC.

UK competition policy

The total resource mobilisation which occurred during the Second World War acted as a catalyst which promoted the assumption that the government had an overall responsibility for economic management. This altered the relationship between industry and government and resulted in a wave of nationalisation which led to one-fifth of the UK commercial and industrial enterprises coming under public ownership. The rationale for nationalisation was to be found in the interplay of political and economic reasons.

Despite a gradual deceleration in state intervention, the influence of government on industrial activity was, by the early 1950s, very significant. A major step towards establishing a competition policy in the UK was taken by the introduction of the Monopolies (Inquiry and Control) Act of 1948. The Act established a Monopolies Commission which was to investigate and report on cartels and monopolies. Subsequently, the Restrictive Trade Practices Act of 1956 transferred the control of cartels to a court while the Monopolies and Mergers Act of 1965 added mergers to the responsibilities of the Commission which became the Monopolies and Mergers Commission (MMC).

The 1965 Act has not had any dampening effect on the favourable attitudes towards mergers and government intervention in industry which prevailed throughout the 1960s and 1970s. A number of agencies were consequently formed to implement relevant policy. The National Economic Development Council (NEDC) was formed in 1961–2 with a tripartite membership drawn from government, employers and trade unions. The National Board for Prices and Incomes (NBPI) was established in 1965. The Industrial Reorganisation Council (IRC) established in 1966 actively promoted mergers as a means of improving the UK's international competitiveness. The predominant view in the UK during this time was that British firms were too small to successfully compete internationally. Consequently, mergers were favourably viewed in the belief that they would facilitate the tapping of economies of scale and scope, thus enhancing performance and international competitiveness.

During the 1970s doubts were raised, however, as to whether the internal efficiency of monopolies would necessarily outweigh the allocative inefficiency that results from monopoly pricing and strategic behaviour. Consequently, the focus of the tripartite framework was to strengthen the control of the monopolies and mergers. The Fair Trading Act of 1973 was passed which defined a monopoly as any firm or group of inter-connected companies with a market share of at least 25 per cent of the relevant market. Any monopolies, or even oligopolies, acting in a way that restricted competition could be referred to the MMC by the Director General of Fair Trading (DGFT). Further industrial legislation was introduced in 1975 and 1976. The 1975 Industry Act provided a successor to the IRC by establishing the National Enterprise Boards (NEBs) which were considered as instruments for the regeneration of industry by expanding, modernising and restructuring certain sectors. The NEBs acted as holding companies and provided loans at commercial rates for long-term investment. They also acquired equity in private firms. The overall aim was to assist the operation of competitive markets and to amend the myopic attitudes of the private sector in regard to long-run investment and risk.

The establishment of the NEBs, IRC and NEDC reflected the belief that markets can fail and should be assisted to achieve the commercially and socially efficient allocation of resources. At the same time industrial policies were pursued aiming to moderate the effects of profit seeking conduct which resulted in some firms acquiring market power through monopolisation, mergers and restrictive practices. It is in pursuit of this objective that the MMC Act of 1948 was strengthened in 1965 and 1973.

The view that under certain circumstances society may be better off with a monopoly than without it has meant that monopolies were not ruled out *per se*. As permissive attitudes towards monopolies weakened, however, competition policy was strengthened. Thus, the 1980 Competition Act allows for the referral to the MMC for investigation of any firm (not just monopolies) if there are grounds to believe that it engages in anti-competitive practices. A changing attitude regarding the efficiency of public sector firms has also been reflected in the 1980 Competition Act which provides that public bodies may be referred to the Commission for investigation.

During the 1980s the influence of economic theories (such as contestability) which question the need for anti-monopoly legislation and strengthen the belief in the efficacy of effective competition has resulted in a radical alteration in competition policy. By far the most important change has been a reversal in the tendency for state intervention in the production of goods and services. The emphasis on reduced state involvement culminated in the transfer of the majority of public firms from the public to the private sector and on the de-regulation of several markets.

The extensive programme of privatisation and de-regulation has been accompanied by a change in policy regarding restrictive practices. Policy in this respect has so far been governed by the 1976 Restrictive Trade Practices Act which requires that restrictive practices be notified to the Office of Fair Trading which enters them into a register and refers them to the Restrictive Practices Court for a ruling on whether they operate against the public interest in which case the practice is discontinued. The 1989 White Paper on 'Open Markets; New Policy on Restrictive Practices' set out the government intention to adopt a much stricter policy on restrictive practices. The legislation is expected to lead to

a more effective means of rooting out anti-competitive agreements which raise costs and prices;
a reduction in the unproductive administrative burden on firms;
a welcome consistency with the approach pursued in EC competition legislation.

This represents a significant change in policy since it proposes to abolish the requirement that agreements should be registered, in favour of *a prohibition of any agreement which has anti-competitive effects*. Thus, certain practices like retail price maintenance, collusive tendering, market sharing and collective boycotts will be prohibited although the prohibition will not apply to small firms. In addition, since it is recognised that some restrictive practices may have economic or technical benefits outweighing their disadvantages, firms have been granted the right to apply to the DGFT for an exception from the prohibition. The proposed penalties for violation of the law are severe; a fine of up to 10 per cent of the UK turnover or £250,000 whichever is the highest to a maximum of £1 million.

The policy is not only consistent with EC policy it is also more in line with US policy especially as far as the exception of small firms from prohibitions relating to vertical restraint practices is concerned.

US and EC competition policy

The Commission of the European Communities views competition policy as a means to promoting market competitiveness and structural readjustment, the main aim of which is to prevent practices which eliminate competition between member states and affect adversely the economic integration of Europe. The fundamental provisions of EC policy are included in Articles 85 and 86 of the Treaty of Rome. Article 85(1) prohibits

> all agreements between undertakings, decisions by associations of undertakings, and concerted practices which . . . have as their object or effect the prevention, restriction or distortion of competition within the Common Market.

Article 86(1) is concerned with market dominance. It condemns

> any abuse by one or more undertakings of a dominant position within the Common Market or a substantial part of it . . . in so far as it may affect trade between Member States.

Article 86 specifies that abuse may consist in unfair purchasing or selling, restricting production or technical development, discrimination, etc., while a dominant position has been defined by the Court of Appeals as

> a position of economic strength enjoyed by an undertaking which enables it to prevent effective competition being maintained on the relevant market by affording it the power to behave to an appreciable extent independently of its competitors, its customers and ultimately of the consumer.[2]

Suspected violations of Articles 85 and 86 are investigated by the European Commission which may ask for the termination of the practice and can impose fines of up to 10 per cent of the annual world-wide turnover of the guilty firm. Appeals can be heard by the European Court of Justice. A case at hand is Rover's former practice of limiting dealers' discounts to the public. The practice clearly violated Article 85 of the Treaty and as such it was discontinued in 1990. The Commission, according to current press reports,[3] is likely to fine Rover – Britain's leading car manufacturer – for the breach of EC competition policy by as much as £2.5 million and to bring a court action for compensation for an estimated amount of £65 million.

In brief, rather than prohibit certain business practices the EC policy condemns dominance and abusive behaviour that derives from it. A particular difficulty in relation to the implementation of this policy has arisen in determining the extent of dominance. This is because dominance can only be defined with reference to a particular market and markets cannot be defined unambiguously for the reasons discussed in Chapter 2. Extending the boundaries of a market reduces dominance and vice versa. Thus, some decisions of the European Court of Justice have been criticised as condemning a particular practice and then defining the market in a way that shows the abuse to be an abuse of a dominant position. An example is the condemnation of Michelin's practice of giving annual bonuses to dealers who have achieved a certain sales target. The practice was condemned as deriving from the dominant position of Michelin, whose market share was found to be 65 per cent of total sales. The market, however, was defined to be the heavy tyres market in the Netherlands, a definition criticised as too narrow since it excludes competition from other tyres and from other EC countries (Hay and Vickers 1987).

The US competition policy is based on four main pieces of legislation; the Sherman Act 1890, the Clayton Act 1914, the Federal Trade Act 1914 and the Merger Regulation 1990.

The Sherman Act prohibits trade restrictions and outlaws monopolisation or attempts and conspiracies to monopolise. This was supplemented in 1914 by the Clayton Act (which was amended by the Robinson–Patman Act 1936). The Clayton Act outlaws price discrimination and prohibits certain vertical restraints such as tie-in sales as detrimental to competition. The Federal Trade Act 1914 set up an agency (the FTC) to investigate competition matters. The FTC together with the Department of Justice are responsible for enforcing competition policy. Violations of competition law are severely punished with fines and imprisonment.

The emphasis of US anti-trust law, as it has been enforced by the Court of Justice, has been on the promotion of competition by the prevention of dominance. The influence of the SCP paradigm is strong. An early example is provided by the dismantling of Standard Oil into thirty-three regional companies. The Vertical Restraints Guidelines provide further examples. Non-price restraints are legal in industries where concentration is low or where a small part of the industry practices the restraint. Tie-ins are not disallowed provided that the firm involved has less than 30 per cent of the market.

Contrary to UK law, US anti-trust law has long been hostile to mergers (and collusive practices). The 1968 Merger Guidelines lay down criteria for challenging mergers which were based on market shares. Attitudes have been changing, however.

Since the early 1980s there has been a tendency to limit the scope of the anti-trust laws. 'A number of bills sent to Congress early in 1986 propose relaxation of antitrust policy with a view to promoting competitiveness of American companies' (Hay and Vickers 1987, p. 46). The President has been empowered to give exceptions for up to five years to companies faced with international competition. Similarly a merger may be allowed if it is deemed to enhance international competitiveness. Such developments coupled with increased de-regulation reflect the anti-interventionist government philosophies developed during the 1980s in the USA as well as in the UK and other European countries.

To conclude, while competition policy in the USA is essentially consistent with the SCP paradigm (until the late 1970s), in the UK it has adopted a more pragmatic approach. The EC policy favours more a 'free-market' Austrian approach. During the 1980s the influence of the Austrian school of thought has brought about significant changes in the UK and even in the US policy. As a result there has been a convergence in policy and enhanced consistency despite the differences that may still exist.

PRIVATISATION

The 1980s has been described as the decade of the UK privatisation. Between 1979 and 1991 over 50 per cent of the public sector had been transferred to the private sector; 650,000 workers were involved; 1,250,000 council houses were sold mainly to sitting tenants and contracting out has been well established in the NHS and the local authorities (Marsh 1991). The number of shareholders increased from 3 million in 1979 to 11 million by 1993. Even the privatisation of parts of the police service is currently under consideration according to press reports. The major transfers of assets are given in Table 14.2 in chronological order.

The term 'privatisation' has been used with reference to a number of distinct and often alternative government policies. Prominent among these are the sale of publicly owned assets to the private sector (denationalisation) and the deregulation of statutory monopolies and franchises (or contracting out) of the production of state-financed goods and services. The transfer of ownership from the public to the private sector will be examined in this section and de-regulation and other policies will be covered briefly in the next section.

Several aims have been attached to privatisation prominent among which are the following:

1 to improve the economic performance of the enterprise or service transferred to the private sector;
2 to improve competition by market liberalisation;
3 to widen share ownership as a means to popular capitalism;
4 to reduce the public sector borrowing requirement (PSBR);[4]

Table 14.2 Major asset transfers from the public to the private sector 1971–91

Sale of	Year
British Petroleum	1979–87
National Enterprise Board Investment	1980–6
British Aerospace	1981 and 1984
Cable and Wireless	1981–5
Amersham International	1982
National Freight Corporation	1982
Britoil	1982 and 1985
British Leyland (Rover)	1984–8
British Telecom	1984 and 1991
British Gas	1986
British Airport Authority	1987 (first issue)
British Airways	1987
British Steel	1988 and 1989
10 Water Cos	1989 and 1990
Electricity Distribution	1990
Electricity Generation	1991

British Shipbuilders and National Bus Company were deregulated and sold off piecemeal at various dates since 1985

5 to resolve conflicts that had arisen between public sector management and the government by reducing the government involvement in industry;
6 to discipline public sector trade unions; and
7 to gain a political advantage (this is often thought to be an implicit objective).

Although it is quite possible for a policy to fulfil a number of aims the multiplicity of objectives attached to privatisation has often been seen as a justification for, rather than the real purpose of, the policy. The UK privatisation policy has in fact been criticised as lacking clarity of purpose and effect and as 'a policy in search of a rationale' (Kay and Thompson 1986). It is indeed the case that at the early stages of its development the government failed to articulate any objectives while later on several objectives evolved with the focus on each shifting from project to project. Thus, despite an emphasis on liberalisation of markets, research shows that privatisation was pursued even when it did not promote competition (gas, BA) and was promoted even when it contributed to increased public expenditure. (The cash flow impact of removing BT from the public sector was according to Kay and Thompson very much smaller than the stream of earnings forgone.)

The existence of several and often contradictory objectives makes the task of evaluation rather complex since the achievement of one objective may have a negative effect on another or it may depend on the fulfilment of a third. Thus, widening of share ownership could best be achieved by distributing the shares of the newly privatised firms free to every citizen in the country. But this would contradict the revenue raising objective. More importantly, the existence of a variety of objectives renders difficult the task of determining the cause of a particular outcome. It is not, for example, always easy to find out whether an improved performance is due to a change in ownership or market structure and competition. Such difficulties are common and should be borne in mind as we proceed to examine whether privatisation has achieved its main aims.

Improvements in economic efficiency

Economic theory suggests that a change in ownership can affect performance through its influence on objectives and incentives. The expectation is that privately owned firms, operating in competitive markets, perform better than publicly owned firms. In imperfectly competitive markets, however, publicly owned firms are more likely to perform better in terms of allocative, if not in terms of productive, efficiency. The discipline imposed on private firm management by the capital market is the reason why privately owned firms may out-perform publicly owned firms. In terms of production efficiency the argument is that inefficient nationalised firms are immune to takeovers while the fear of hostile takeover bids and bankruptcy ensures cost efficiency in the private sector.

Doubts have been raised, however, as to whether managerial control and incentive mechanisms are necessarily successful in mitigating managerial discretion in the private sector. First, there are several reasons (see Chapter 9) why the capital market may not operate effectively and, second, the fear of takeovers may cause 'short-termism' leading to lower investment which is detrimental to long-term economic growth. That the capital market discipline may not be always effective is indicated by some empirical evidence (Singh 1971, 1975).

To evaluate the performance of the newly privatised firms many researchers have attempted to analyse the empirical evidence. This is not an easy task given that the relative performance of firms depends on a variety of influences, such as the extent of competition, the regulatory framework and the market structure. To evaluate the economic performance of firms these other factors must therefore be taken into account. Unfortunately, empirical studies often fail to do so, either due to data limitations or to inappropriately specified models (Vickers and Yarrow 1988). Due to lack of data empirical investigation has not often attempted to estimate consumers' and producers' surplus but rather relied on more easily observable indicators such as labour productivity and profitability. Furthermore, it has not always been possible to quantify differences in quality and variety of products and services provided following a change in ownership. The consequence of both these limitations is that the results may be biased especially in favour of privatisation. Despite this the evidence fails to unequivocally confirm that privatisation has brought about the expected improvements in efficiency.

Thus, Marsh (1991) after reviewing the recent empirical evidence concluded that economic efficiency was compromised. The evidence he reviewed includes several references to the performance of British Telecommunications following privatisation. The reported results are mixed. Profitability has increased and a 'more aggressive management style' has been adopted. There is no evidence, however, of efficiency improvement since in comparison with total factor productivity in the European Telecommunication industry British Telecom (BT) does not appear to perform better than its European state-owned counterparts.

BT, British Aerospace, the National Freight Corporation (NFC) and the Royal Ordnance Factories (ROF) were among a sample of companies investigated by Dunsire *et al.* (1991). This research examined whether a change of ownership can improve performance as measured by productivity, employment or several conventional financial ratios. The hypothesis tested was that a change in ownership status from pure government department through trading fund to public company to owner manager firm improves efficiency. This was generally confirmed in only three cases; the National Freight, British Airways and the privatised British Aerospace. However, when productivity was compared with national trends only one of the privatised companies (NFC) showed an improvement. In terms of profitability there was also an improvement but only in one case (ROF). The performance of Rolls Royce improved under nationalisation and deteriorated after privatisation contradicting the hypothesis tested.

Profitability has actually improved in many privatised industries. In 1990 eight former nationalised industries were included among the fifty most profitable UK companies in terms of profitability per employee (Parker 1991). The British Airport Authorities occupies eighth position followed by five water companies, British Steel and BT. Profitability in terms of return on capital improved marginally in the case of British Gas, BT and Rolls Royce but has declined in other industries such as the Associated British Ports, Jaguar and Enterprise Oil. It is possible, however, that these changes could have occurred even in the absence of privatisation, since (a) the competitive structure has not changed following privatisation and (b) there does not seem to have been a change in the managerial culture. Contrary to the expected stricter discipline and control, managerial discretion at least as manifested in managerial remunerations has been enhanced since managerial pay packages increased to an extent that is not always justified by increased profitability, as the sample in Table 14.3 indicates.

The argument that the observed improved performance of newly privatised firms would have occurred without privatisation is credible for two reasons: (a) the nationalised industries improved their productivity, during the 1980s, faster than the private sector, 'Treasury figures show that, in every year between 1984 and 1991, the productivity of nationalised industries outpaced that of manufacturing industry by anything up to three

Table 14.3 Changes in return on capital and managerial remuneration since privatisation

	British Gas		British Telecom		Rolls Royce		Associated British Ports		Jaguar		Enterp Oil	
	1987	1990	1986	1990	1987	1989	1986	1990	1986	1988	1985	1989
Return on capital, %	22.7	23.4	18.3	21.3	15.2	16.3	14.9	8.8	47.7	13.2	27.8	10.7
HDS[a] £000s	109	183	172	308	130	171	79	155	86	180	98	167

Source: Parker 1991: Table 3
Note: [a] Highest Director's salary £000s in real terms.

Table 14.4 Labour productivity in nationalised industries (annual percentage change)

Year	Nationalised industries	Whole economy	Manufacturing
1979–80	0.1	0.7	0.9
1981–2	6.5	3.5	6.9
1982–3	2.4	4.0	6.4
1983–4	7.2	4.0	8.3
1984–5	6.0	2.9	4.8
1985–6	9.6	1.1	2.4
1986–7	6.2	3.6	4.8

Source: Parker 1991: Table 4

times' (V. Keegan, *Guardian*, 3 March 1993); and (b) nationalised industries increased their profitability as a percentage of GDP as Table 14.4 documents.

There is, consequently, no reason to believe that privatisation has necessarily caused the observed increased profitability and productivity. As Bishop and Kay (1988) argue, rather the opposite may be true. That is causation may run from economic efficiency to privatisation rather than the other way round.

Furthermore, it is difficult to argue that improved profitability following privatisation is an indication of enhanced efficiency when the transfer of monopoly assets to the private sector had not been accompanied by market liberalisation or by any widespread change in managerial culture.

The evidence from other countries and especially from the USA, where often public and private firms operate in the same market, also fails to confirm the view that public firms are less efficient. The investigation of the relative achievements of public and private firms has been very active.[5] The industries most thoroughly covered are electricity, gas, water and refuse collection. These studies do not support the view that private firms are always more efficient than the publicly owned firms especially in terms of costs.

Most studies show that public utilities in the electricity industry have either lower unit costs than privately owned firms or there is no significant difference between them. Some of the studies showing that public firms have lower unit costs have been criticised for failing to take into account the fact that public firms often have a lower cost of capital. When this is done the difference in unit cost disappears, but is not reversed. With regard to allocative efficiency the presumption that publicly owned firms perform better has not always been confirmed. The reason for this is that private firms were often adopting the – time of day – pricing rule which leads to allocative efficiency. As Vickers and Yarrow (1988) point out, however, the nationalised electricity industries in Britain and France were among the pioneers in developing the peak load pricing policies. The evidence from the US water industry gives similar results. Public firms are no less efficient than their private sector counterparts. In Canada the performance of the two railroad companies, one privately owned and the other publicly owned, which operate in the same competitive environment indicates ownership has no effect on costs.

Empirical work in the UK has been hampered by the fact that nationalisation of industries such as electricity, gas and water meant the absence of private firms for direct comparisons. Empirical work by Pryke (1982) and others on airlines, ferries and hovercraft and the sale of gas and electricity appliances has concluded, however, that the private firms investigated were more profitable and more efficient. Pryke inferred that the inefficiency of the public enterprises he studied was due to public ownership.

Pryke's conclusion, however, has been criticised on several grounds. The main criticism is that he failed to always compare like with like. Thus public firms were often compared with the most efficient of the private firms. Also, in the case of domestic appliances, public enterprise showrooms which performed extra services like dealing with payments of bills and safety regulations were compared with private firms which did not perform such services, thus biasing the results. More importantly the conclusion that relative inefficiency is due to ownership type has been called into question. For example, the inefficiency of British Airways compared with other national flag and UK operators, which was reported by researchers in 1984, can be attributed, according to Kay and Thompson (1986), to the regulatory environment within which British Airways operated rather than to its ownership structure. This view is supported by the fact that within the sample studied in 1984 the most efficient carrier was the publicly owned Air Canada which operated in the competitive North America Market.

The sharp contrast between the performance of the companies privatised as monopolies and those operating in competitive conditions is highlighted by some recent statistics reported in the *Guardian* (3 March 1993). British Steel has recently announced heavy losses and the closure of its Ravenscraig steelworks. Rover is still making losses and its parent British

Aerospace has announced a loss of £1.2 billion (the biggest ever private sector loss). Rolls Royce has also been experiencing problems.

Where privatised firms were not subjected to very fierce competition or when they maintained their monopolies their profitability did not suffer. Thus, British Airways and Cable and Wireless, as well as gas, electricity and water companies, have been achieving enhanced profits.

In conclusion, the claim that privatisation enhances efficiency is not generally supported by the evidence.

Enhanced competition

Competition in the product market is a more reliable way of creating an environment within which management has the necessary incentives to pursue economic efficiency than switching a monopoly from the private to the public sector. Liberalisation of natural monopolies, however, is fraught with difficulties. Complex structures would need to be devised which, especially if opposed by management, would have meant substantial delays in the implementation of the transfer. In the case of the UK privatisation speed was essential for political expediency. Besides delays, the success of the privatisation programme would have been threatened if the monopoly position of the companies concerned were seriously undermined so that managerial support for privatisation was not forthcoming.

Many privatised companies were indeed successful in fighting off the threat of competition (Beauchamps 1990). For example, BT management have been credited with success in inducing the Government to abandon many of its initial ideas about liberalisation in the telecommunications industry. The proposal that local operating companies should be created (as in the USA) was rejected as well as the idea of separating the international division. Similarly, British Airways convinced the government to reject a Civil Aviation authority recommendation which established a route network that ensured British Caledonian was an effective competitor. Since then British Airways has enhanced its monopoly position by taking over Dan Air and British Caledonian. Another example is the privatisation of the British Airport Authorities as a single entity, after its management convinced the Government to reject a re-organisation of the airport services provision along a competitive market plan. The list of examples can be extended. The gas industry was privatised as a 'monolith' and has been described as three monopolies in one. British Gas is a monopoly in the purchasing of gas and the largest single owner of UK offshore gas fields. It owns and controls the gas pipeline and storage system and it has the right to supply more than 98 per cent of all gas customers.

Market liberalisation has often been sacrificed. This is because there is a tension between increased competition which is necessary for enhanced efficiency and the broader government political aims of success which require management co-operation. In circumstances like these where trade-offs exist 'the political aims appear to have been paramount' (Marsh 1991: 467). As a result, in the privatisation programme the choice has not always been between dynamic, competitive firms and lethargic state monopolies. State monopolies have been replaced by private monopolies. Private monopolies can exploit consumers. Companies such as gas, electricity and water have been profitable but have been in trouble with the regulators and the public for overcharging.

More recently, however, the government and the regulators of the privatised monopolies seem to be responding to criticisms and attempts at market liberalisation have been strengthened.

The regulator of the privatised gas industry (OFGAS) has proposed to the MMC that British Gas should be broken up into fourteen separate companies. The new structure should consists of twelve regional gas companies similar to the regional electricity companies (RECs), but unlike the RECs the gas companies should not have control of the distribution networks and should compete with each other and other traders for business. (This system contrasts with the complicated price pooling system operating in electricity). Gas buying should be a free standing operation and the group's gas and oil exploration and production should be another business. But as Kay and Thompson (1986) noted well before the gas privatisation, 'fragmentation into smaller operating units is harder to impose on a private firm than a public one' (p. 29). British Gas fiercely opposes the proposed restructuring, claiming that a re-organisation along the suggested lines would cost £3 billion leading to large price increases costing each household £166 or each shareholder £1,500. The MMC report is expected to be published shortly.

Since 1991 any firms may apply for a telecommunication licence to operate in the UK. The aim is clearly to encourage more firms to compete with BT and Mercury. AT&T, the US telecommunication conglomerate, has already applied for a UK public operator's licence. Government decision is pending and there is opposition to granting this licence till the US market is opened to BT. Meanwhile MCI and Sprint (long distance US operators) are also expected to apply for UK licences.

Widening share ownership

Privatisation has been credited with success in achieving wider share ownership. It is indeed the case that individual shareholders have increased from 3 million in 1979 to 11 million in 1993. This, however, has failed to reverse a long-term trend for shareholding concentration since the percentage of total shares held by individuals (as opposed to institutions) has fallen from 28 per cent in 1979 to 20 per cent today. Thus, ownership has become wider but not deeper, as a result of privatisation.

To induce individuals who were never interested in shares to invest in the newly privatised firms the government had to provide substantial incentives. Thus, extensive advertising was combined with the sale of shares to individuals at reduced prices and with a variety of bonuses.

The perceived benefits of wider share ownership are both political and economic. First, wider share ownership has been associated with the belief that the more individuals that become shareholders the wider the interest in profits and private ownership so that political views would change in favour of capitalist values. Doubts, however, have been expressed as to the impact of privatisation on the pattern of share ownership and the promotion of 'popular capitalism' since the widening of share ownership has not been followed by a deepening of ownership. Only a small proportion of total shares are in the hands of individuals. '54% of investors hold shares in only one company and only 17% have shares in more than four enterprises' (Parker 1991: 157). Second, wider share ownership implies more employees become shareholders with the implication that this provides them with incentives to increase work effort and efficiency. A contradiction, however, arises since wider share ownership implies increased share dispersion which weakens the effectiveness of the market in corporate control and hence the argument that the capital market will contribute to the efficiency of the privatised industries.

Raising revenues

Political expediency may have contributed to selling assets at heavily discounted prices compromising the revenue raising potential of privatisation. The process of privatisation has thus been expensive for tax payers. By 1987 the cost to the government has been estimated to be between £600 million and £1,300 million. By the time of the electricity privatisation the cost has reached £2,375 million over 50 per cent of which will have been spent on water and electricity. Despite this, privatisation has made some contribution towards reducing the PSBR although it was not till 1987–8 that the deficit was turned into a surplus as indicated in Table 14.5

It can be concluded that financial objectives do not appear to have been a primary aim, or achievement, of privatisation.

Table 14.5 Privatisation receipts as a percentage of the public sector borrowing requirement

Year	Proceeds	Year	Proceeds
1979–80	2.9	1985–6	31.8
1980–1	3.1	1986–7	56.7
1981–2	5.4	1987–8	282.3
1982–3	5.2	1988–9	–[a]
1983–4	10.5	1989–90	–[a]
1984–5	17.3		

Source: Marsh 1991: Table 2, p. 471
Note: [a] In 1989 and 1990 the PSBR was in surplus.

Reduced government intervention in the running of business

The potential of privatisation to resolve public administration problems has been deceptive since in many instances it has fostered the need for regulating the newly created private monopolies. Thus, despite its declared objective to reduce its market intervention, the government has formed a series of regulatory agencies, such as OFGAS (gas), OFTEL (telecommunications), OFWAT (water) and OFFER (electricity). In addition seve ral other bodies such as the MMC, the water authorities and environmental organisations have been involved with issues of regulating privatised industries.

The role of senior management in privatisation has already been noted. They have seen privatisation as a means of avoiding the burden of Treasury control while ensuring that this is achieved without a change in organisational structure or a move to a more competitive environment.

The control of trade unions

There is no doubt that government saw privatisation as a means to curbing union power. There are doubts, however, as to whether privatisation has indeed fulfilled this aim.

Both the TUC and independent observers point to massive reductions in employment, deteriorating pay and worsening industrial relations practices. This pattern is clearly evident in the case of contracting out and competitive tendering but there are variations when considering the sale of nationalised industries. Thus while BT announced 15,000 job losses in the run up to privatisation others like the National Freight Corporation and BT increased employment in 1987 and 1990. Moreover during the 1980s many UK companies experienced job losses both in the private and the public sector. Most of the dramatic loss in employment in the steel industry (71 per cent between 1979 and 1988) occurred in the 1980–1 recession long before any plans about the privatisation of steel were made. Over the same period non-privatised companies shed more jobs than the 18 per cent reduction in gas and electricity and the 17 per cent in British Airways. Losses, however, were particularly heavy in the non-privatised coal (55 per cent) and rail (36 per cent) industries.

The impact of privatisation on industrial relations practices has generally been to emphasise flexibility, quality and changing working patterns. But there are substantial variations in management style and approach to their relationship with trade unions. The gas and electricity industries, for example, have adopted a non-confrontational policy. They have perceived advantages to their shareholders from a record of labour relations stability and have sought to maintain a harmonious relationship with unions. British Gas has been reported to have promised no job losses, no compromise on safety standards and no change in pension rights as a result of privatisation (Ferner and Colling 1991: 403).

BT, on the other hand, has adopted a more aggressive management style. Prior to privatisation in addition to redundancies the company announced its intention to withdraw from certain long standing agreements with the unions. A confrontational strategy and the deteriorated industrial relations led to the two-week strike by telecommunication engineers in 1987 and the first strike by managerial and professional staff in 1990.

The observed differences in industrial relations cannot, however, be accounted for by privatisation. It is more likely that business pressures not experienced by other privatised firms contributed to BT's aggression. Differences in competition (BT faced some competition from Mercury while British Gas did not) or technological changes (new electronic exchange systems) can partly explain the difference in behaviour.

Falling unionisation has been used as another indicator of reduced union power. It is true that overall union membership fell by 21 per cent between 1979 and 1985. It is difficult, however, to attribute this reduction to privatisation since the most dramatic reductions took place in industries least affected by privatization (coal, railways and the civil service) and in the private sector (Transport and General Workers Union, 31 per cent; engineering, 20 per cent; Construction Workers Union, 28 per cent). At the same time the membership of public sector unions such as NALGO and NUPE remained stable (Marsh 1991).

It is more likely that any reduction in union power that may have occurred may be due to government legislation rather than privatisation as such. It can indeed be argued that private firms are both less able and less motivated to resist unions than the government. They are less able financially to withstand long drawn confrontations with the unions and less motivated since each firm would tend to ignore the external effects that their resistance to unions may have on other firms. The events of the year-long miners strike of 1984–5 have demonstrated both these points (for further expansion see Vickers and Yarrow (1988)). Finally firms may be more appreciative of the beneficial effects that a co-operation with unions may have on morale and efficiency within the firm (see Chapter 13 for an expansion on this point).

General impact

It must be concluded that the scale of privatisation has been immense and is likely to have lasting effects. An undisputed result it has had is to wipe off the political agenda the issue of nationalisation and to change the balance between the public and private sectors to an extent that it can be claimed that 'Britain is no longer a mixed economy; it has moved decisively in the direction of the market'.

With regard to its impact privatisation has failed to enhance efficiency because increased efficiency required improved competition which was often sacrificed for speed of implementation and in order to ensure management co-operation without which privatisation would not have been possible.

Finally the evidence suggests that privatisation has not always been successful from the point of view of consumers, since the quality of services has not necessarily improved and in some instances it has deteriorated despite increased prices. Some commentators even predict that prices are likely to increase by as much as 40–90 per cent in the next twenty years (Marsh 1991). In brief, privatisation represents at best a missed opportunity.

DEREGULATION AND FRANCHISING

Deregulation is the policy of removing regulatory constraints on a market. It occupies a central position in recent UK competition policy on the premise that it facilitates the introduction of competition and thus induces a better economic performance. Deregulation is sometimes identified with privatisation. This is incorrect, however, since deregulation is a policy quite distinct to and independent of ownership. It can apply to any market whatever the ownership of the firms that operate within it and leads to liberalisation. State and private firms can co-exist in a liberalised market.

Formally deregulation is a simple policy. All that is required for its implementation is for the government to repeal its regulatory statutes. Market liberalisation has indeed occurred in several UK industries since 1979. One of the early industries to be deregulated was Express Coaching (in 1980). Several others followed such as telecommunication apparatus, airlines and parts of the energy industries. Solicitors have lost their exclusive conveyancing rights, opticians have lost their monopoly in dispensing spectacles, local bus services have been given freedom to determine routes and fares, etc.

The suggested simplicity, however, is deceptive. The deregulation of a natural monopoly can lead to inefficiencies and deadweight losses and even if the industry is not a natural monopoly the incumbent dominant firms may be able to impede new entry following liberalisation with similar results. These are real problems if it is assumed that regulation was introduced initially precisely because of market failures inhibiting efficiency.

Given market imperfection the introduction of regulation aims to influence behaviour in a way that promotes efficiency. The theory of regulation, however, suggests that the relatively imperfect knowledge of the regulator can induce business behaviour associated with trade-offs between productive and allocative efficiency. It is well known for example that the US-type rate-of-return on capital regulation leads to over-capitalization and higher production costs. The removal of regulation, therefore, can lead to benefits especially where market failures were not the main reason for the initial regulation.

But as already noted deregulation does not imply the automatic enhancement in competition. As indicated above the expected benefits from the transfer of state assets to the private sector did not always materialise partly because market liberalisation was either absent or insufficient to enhance competitiveness. In investigating the impact of liberalisation in telecommunication apparatus, coaching, airlines and part of the energy industries, Thompson (1987) came to a similar conclusion with regard to deregulation. That is, deregulation was not always accompanied by increased competition and efficiency.

In brief to achieve the full benefits of liberalisation it is not sufficient to remove the statutes; the policy must ensure the minimisation of other entry barriers. This may not always be feasible. The liberalisation of some industries can actually create more problems than it can solve. Parts of the public utilities, for example, such as gas, electricity and water, are 'sustainable' natural monopolies. This means that the emergence of competition is not only improbable but is actually inefficient. Having more than one producer at the transmission stage of these products would imply huge cost increases.

This does not necessarily imply that sustainable natural monopolies cannot be liberalised. Contestability theory has revived interest in an old solution to market liberalisation in these cases; franchising. The essence of franchising is the 'argument . . . that excess profits can lead to competition *for* the market rather than competition *in* the market' (Bailey and Friedlander 1982).

Since introducing competition in production is inefficient, what is suggested is that the government retains state ownership or regulation of production but introduces competition, by, for example, auctioning the right to the monopoly. The winner of the auction gains the contractual right (franchise) to be the monopolist for a certain period of time, at the end of which the contract is renewed by competitive bidding. Franchising enhances productive efficiency since the holder of the franchise will attempt to minimise production costs in order to increase profits. If the franchise is awarded to the lower bidder it can be shown that allocative efficiency will also improve.

Franchising has been adopted in television wavebands, in North Sea oil exploration licenses, in cable and even BT privatisation is on a 25 year franchise (although it is unlikely that it will not be renewed).

Franchises refer simply to the contractual arrangements that support certain market transactions. As such, they are subject to transaction costs whose size varies with the characteristics of the transaction and the extent of complexity and uncertainty surrounding such transactions. Franchise specifications and monitoring become more complicated the more variables are involved. Price is rarely the only variable of a transaction. In cable television, for example, the franchise refers to a service that can differ in terms of channels offered, variety and quality of programmes, reliability and disruption in installation, etc. Organising the bidding system and more importantly monitoring and policing the contract can involve very high transaction costs.

It should be recalled that transaction costs increase with asset specificity, uncertainty and complexity. When the transactions involve learning-by-doing and require specific investments and know-how it is possible that the benefits of competition may be outweighed by increased transaction costs resulting in a reduction in economic efficiency. Thus if franchises are introduced in the case of natural monopolies usually requiring long-term investments, particular difficulties may arise in relation to the transfer of assets at the end of the contractual period. The contract must ensure that the franchisee invests, but does not over-invest, in sunk costs.

Deregulation or liberalisation via franchising may not be sufficient to ensure efficiency as the deregulation of industries such as the telecommunication, coaching and electricity examples indicate. The introduction of competition in these and other industries has been worthwhile but de-regulation has been only partially successful in promoting competition even in sectors where entry costs are low. This is because incumbents which have achieved dominance during the statutory period have considerable technical, financial and political advantages over potential entrants.

When, for example, the Express Coach market was deregulated some new entry did occur but most new entrants subsequently exited. National Express, the dominant firm, controls now most of the routes to which it formerly had exclusive rights. Nevertheless there has been a price reduction, on average, and some innovatory changes in the service provided. The reasons why National Express has remained a dominant firm are several; the reputation acquired during the regulatory period, its control of the main coaching terminals and its refusal to give access to competitors which makes it very difficult for new entrants to operate efficiently, aggressive pricing and the establishment of co-operative ventures with new entrants.

Similar reasons assisted BT to retain its dominant position in the PBX (Private Branch Exchange) market following liberalisation. BT benefits from its established product reputation and, more importantly, from a customer perception of BT as a more committed supplier than new entrants into the market. Additionally BT established exclusive supply agreements with manufacturers and has taken over Mitel which manufactures over 50 per cent of the PBXs supplied by the new entrants (Thompson 1987).

In brief, obstacles to entry in deregulated markets may arise from (a) established product reputation and a perception that incumbents are more committed to the market and (b) incumbents being financially strong (possibly from operating in other protected markets) with a low bankruptcy risk are often able to adopt policies that discourage entry.

SUMMARY

This chapter examines government competition policy and its impact on the environment within which firms operate. It begins with the theoretical underpinnings of competition policy. It explains that the possibility that dominance may lead to allocative and productive inefficiency induces governments to interfere in the market. The allocative inefficiency of monopoly is known as the 'deadweight' loss.

Firms causing deadweight losses may have acquired their dominant position for reasons of (productive or transaction cost) efficiency. In this case a trade-off between the allocative and productive efficiency arises. On the other hand the managerial control mechanisms are weaker in dominant markets so that the management of dominant firms enjoys enhanced discretion. Moreover dominant firms may adopt strategic behaviour designed to maintain if not to enhance dominance. Both managerial discretion and strategic behaviour may lead to production inefficiency which exacerbates the allocative inefficiency of dominance.

State-owned firms tend to price according to costs so that a change in ownership from private to public should enhance allocative efficiency. State ownership, however, may have an adverse effect on managerial incentives and control mechanisms in which case a trade-off between productive and allocative efficiency may develop.

The existence of managerial discretion and the weakening of incentives in monopolistic conditions imply that there is no presumption that privately owned firms will necessarily perform better than publicly owned firms. This is an important conclusion given the current emphasis of competition policy on privatisation, the scale of which has been immense, particularly in the UK, over the last ten years or so.

Privatisation has had some undisputed political success in that nationalisation is no longer an issue. Its economic success is less clear however. Privatised firms have improved efficiency but not by as much as the nationalised industries. Where costs have been reduced, as in the case of electricity generation, they have failed to take into account extra costs that this has created in other parts of the economy in terms of unemployment or imports. Market liberalisation by deregulation has not proved sufficient for enhanced competitiveness. Incumbents long protected by statutes have acquired technical, reputational and financial advantages which have often been used to prevent new entry. When price is not the only dimension of a transaction franchising is accompanied by the transactional costs which had led to regulation in the first place.

As a result privatisation has not been an unequivocal success. It has in fact failed to enhance economic efficiency mainly because it was not always accompanied by enhanced competitiveness. Many factors contributed to this failure not least among which was the need to ensure the co-operation of incumbent managements which had an interest in transferring ownership without strict market liberalisation. As a result there are customer complaints of high prices in the public utilities and calls for the introduction of competition by breaking up the newly created private monopolies (gas).

APPLICATION: PRIVATISATION OF THE UK ELECTRICITY SUPPLY INDUSTRY

The 1988 White Paper on electricity privatisation signalled the end of the thirty-year-old Central Electricity Generating Board's (CEGB's) monopoly. Until then the CEGB operated all thirty-six cold stations, nine oil fired stations, nine gas turbines, twelve nuclear plants, six hydroelectric plants, two storeys and one windmill. It also had control of the high tension transmission lines and had a 130,000 strong workforce. The CEGB supplied electricity to twelve Area Boards which distributed it to their local customers. The rationale for the tightly vertically integrated structure is to be found in the natural monopoly of the National Grid. Integration, however, gives extreme power to the owner of the Grid which could lead to anti-competitive behaviour (see Chapter 10).

By March 1990 the new privatised structure was in place. The vertically integrated structure has been replaced by a de-integrated structure in an attempt to remove the industry's monopoly power. The three distinct stages of production have been segregated in the new Electricity Supply Industry (ESI). Generation is independent of transmission and an attempt to introduce horizontal competition at the generation stage has meant that the capacity of the CEGB has been passed on to two new companies; National Power which controls approximately 52 per cent of generating capacity and Power Gen which has 33 per cent while Nuclear Electric generates about 15 per cent. In addition the National Grid transmits electricity generated in Scotland and France and from some small independent generators. The National Grid, a natural monopoly, has remained intact but its ownership is shared by the twelve RECs which administer the Grid at arm's length. The third stage, the distribution and supply to customers, was privatised in December 1990 as it stood creating some widely profitable local monopolies. The twelve RECs who replaced the twelve Area Authorities also have the right to generate their own electricity.

Although it is too early for the full effects of privatisation to be assessed, it has been suggested (Goldring 1993) that following privatisation the workforce was reduced by 50 per cent, the consumption of coal has fallen by 800 tons per day and prices to the final consumer have increased substantially. Profits are high. Political meddling with the industry is still present. The decision to close thirty-one coal pits created an uproar and fierce public opposition forcing the government to reconsider this decision and interfere with input decisions of the industry.

Electricity is an essential commodity for industry and domestic customers which cannot be stored. While it must be used as it is generated its demand varies every half hour of the day. Variations can be large and unpredicted (they may, for example, vary with the popularity of television programmes). This implies that a very delicate balance must be struck almost instantaneously between demand and supply by the operator of the National Grid. Prior to privatisation this was based on planning, post-privatisation the delicate planning continues but it also takes account of the list of half hourly prices submitted, every twenty-four hours, by the generating companies (the pooling system).

To avoid shortages and blackouts the Grid operator builds in excess capacity (around 10 per cent of predicted demand) which means that generators are kept on wait and are paid even if they produce nothing, thus increasing the cost to the customer. It also follows that a generator provides electricity to the pool for transmission by the Grid operator and cannot direct its output to a designated point of demand.

A good knowledge of the interdependencies and intricacies of the system places the Grid operator in a unique position to make decisions on what stations should be built, where, and when, so as to avoid bottlenecks in the system. The operator is uniquely informed to decide on whether more transmission lines or more stations should be built. But in the privatisation restructuring market forces rather than the operator are to provide all the solutions.

Given the natural monopoly elements in the (transmission and distribution) system, the government has retained some regulatory powers over transmission and distribution charges and the prices charged to small users. Regulating prices, however, can act as disincentives to sunk investment.

The fear that the government or the regulator may tighten prices in the future can lead the generators to under-invest. It is therefore essential for the government to find ways to commit itself and its successors not to behave opportunistically in the future.

The main objective of the ESI de-integration was, as noted above, the introduction of competition. However, competition in generation seems to have been limited since the RECs are local monopolies. Large consumers, however, have been given the right to shop around and some progress has been noted. Next year customers consuming between 600 kW and 1 MW, will also be able to shop around thanks to a new invention; the 'smart meter' which can record hourly electricity consumption. The expected fall in the price of the smart meter from the current £250 to around £50 by 1998 will make it possible for domestic customers to switch from REC to REC in search of cheaper electricity. RECs will then have an incentive to shop around for the cheapest generator and to reduce their costs and possibly profit margins in order to be able to gain and sustain customers. What the OFFER regulator has not yet achieved the smart meter may soon achieve; competitive electricity prices.

FURTHER READING

Ferguson, P.R (1988) *Industrial Economics: Issues and Perspectives*, Basingstoke: Macmillan Education.
Roper, B. and Snowdon, B. (eds) (1987) *Markets, Intervention and Planning*, Harlow: Longman.
Vickers, J. and Yarrow, G. (1988) *Privatisation; An Economic Analysis*, Cambridge, MA: MIT Press

QUESTIONS

1 In comparing the efficiency of the transfer of assets from the public to the private sector Vickers and Yarrow (1988) contend that 'Given some degree of market power, it might be expected that private firms will tend to be the more profitable, but this in itself has no direct bearing on the question of economic efficiency. Similarly, a finding that private firms have lower unit costs than their public counterparts does not necessarily imply that their contributions to social welfare are greater; questions relating to allocative efficiency and to the quality of goods and services provided also need to be taken into account.'

   (a) Define 'allocative efficiency' and 'social welfare'.
   (b) Explain and evaluate the statement.

2 'Inherent in the government's policy of floating the nationalised industries on the stock exchange is a conflict of objectives. The government can aim either at maximising the contribution to cuts in taxation and the PSBR or it can aim at optimising the post-privatisation performance of these industries. It cannot do both.' Explain why you agree or disagree with this claim.

3 Why is it that a government which declares its belief in free markets fails to liberalise when it de-nationalizes?

4 (a) Explain how the inefficiencies associated with the existence of 'sustainable natural monopolies' might be eliminated by market liberalisation through franchising.
   (b) Would your answer to (a) be altered with the realisation that incumbent producers develop know-how advantages and that the existence of economies of scale is due to sunk costs?

5 'In view of the economic welfare loss attributable both to the X-inefficiency of monopolists and to their exercise of market power, the benign attitude of the UK Monopolies & Mergers Commission towards mergers cannot be justified. That mergers are merely a device for avoiding competition was demonstrated by the merger boom which followed the implementation of Restrictive Practices legislation.' Explain why you agree or disagree with this analysis.

NOTES

1 For further details please see Chapter 2 of Vickers and Yarrow (1988).
2 This was in the case of Hoffman-La Roche as quoted by Hay and Vickers (1987: 37).
3 See the *Guardian*, 12 January 1993.
4 In fact privatisation has been seen as a U-turn in government policy since the sales of assets have made it possible to circumvent the fiscal constraints associated with a strict monetary policy (Marsh 1991).
5 For references see Ferguson (1988) and Vickers and Yarrow (1988).

REFERENCES

Akerlof, M.A. (1970) 'The Market for Lemons: Qualitative Uncertainty and the Market Mechanism', *Quarterly Journal of Economics*, 84: 488–500.

Alchian, A.A. and Demsetz, R. (1972) 'Production, Information Costs and Economic Organisation', *American Economic Review*, LXII(5): 777–95.

Alchian, A.A. and Woodward, S. (1988) 'The Firm is Dead; Long Live the Firm. A Review of O. Williamson's *The Economic Institutions of Capitalism*', *Journal of Economic Literature*, XXVI, March: 65–79.

Al-Eryani, M.F., Alam, P. and Akhter, S.H. (1990) 'Transfer Pricing Determinants of US Multinationals', *Journal of International Business Studies*, 21(3): 409–25.

Armour, H.O. and Teece, D.J. (1978) 'Organisational Structure and Economic Performance: a Test of the Multidivisional Hypothesis', *Bell Journal of Economics*, 9: 106–22.

Arrow, K.J. (1971) *Essays in the Theory of Risk-bearing*, Chicago, IL: Marcham Publishing.

Bailey, E.E. and Friedlaender, A.F. (1982) 'Market Structure and Multiproduct Industries', *Journal of Economic Literature*, XX: 1024–48.

Bain, J.S. (1956) *Barriers to New Competition*, Cambridge, MA: Harvard University Press.

Bain, J.S (1959) *Industrial Organisation*, New York: Wiley.

Bakkal, I. (1991) 'Characteristics of West German Demand for International Tourism in the Northern Mediterranean Region', *Applied Economics*, 23: 295–304.

Barnea, A., Haugen, R.A. and Senbet, L.W. (1985) *Agency Problems and Financial Contracting*, Englewood Cliffs, NJ: Prentice Hall.

Baumol, W.J. (1959) *Business Behavior, Value and Growth*, London: MacMillan.

Baumol, W.J. (1961) *Economic Theory and Operations Analysis*, Englewood Cliffs, NJ: Prentice Hall.

Baumol, W.J. (1972) *Economic Theory and Operations Analysis*, 3rd edn, Englewood Cliffs, NJ: Prentice Hall.

Baumol, W.J. (1982) 'Contestable Markets', *American Economic Review*, 72: 1–15.

Baumol, W.J., Panzar, J.C. and Willig, D.R. (1982) *Contestable Markets and the Theory of Industrial Structure*, Jovanovich, NY: Harcourt Brace.

BBC (1992) 'Follow the Money: The Fix', Programme broadcast on 8 March.

Beauchamps, C. (1990) 'National Audit Office; its Role in Privatisation', *Public Money and Management*, 10, (2): 55–8.

Berle, A.A. Jr. and Means, G.C. (1932) *The Modern Corporation and Private Property*, London: Macmillan.

Bishop, M. and Kay, J. (1988) *Does Privatisation Work?* London: London Business School.

British Steel Corporation (1964) *A Simple Guide to Basic Processes in the Iron and Steel Industry*, Revised edn.

Brozen, Y. (1971) 'Bain's Concentration and Rates of Return Revisited', *Journal of Law and Economics*, 14: 351–69.

Buckley, P.J. (1989) *The Multinational Enterprise: Theory and Application*, London: Macmillan.

Buckley, P.J. and Casson, M. (1985) *The Economic Theory of the Multinational Enterprise. Selected Papers*, London: Macmillan.

Buckley, P.J. and Enderwick, P. (1989) 'Manpower Management in the Domestic and International Construction Industry', in P.J. Buckley (ed.) *The Multinational Enterprise: Theory and Application*, London: Macmillan, ch. 9.

Casson, M. (1982) *The Entrepreneur: An Economic Theory*, Oxford: Martin Robertson.

Casson, M.C. (ed.) (1983) *The Growth of International Business*, London: Allen and Unwin.

Casson, M.C (1985) 'Multinational Monopolies and International Cartels', in P.J. Buckley and M. Casson (eds) *The Economic Theory of the Multinational Enterprise*, London: Macmillan.

Casson, M.C. (1987) 'Multinational Firms', in R. Clarke and T. McGuiness (eds) *The Economics of the Firm*, Oxford: Basil Blackwell.

Chandler, A.D. (1962) *Strategy and Structure: Chapters in the History of the Industrial Enterprise*, Cambridge, MA: MIT Press.

Chandler, A.D. (1977) *The Visible Hand: The Managerial Revolution*, American Business, Cambridge, MA: Belknap Press.

Chang, H.S. and Hsing, Yu (1991) 'The Demand for Residential Electricity: New Evidence on Time-Varying Elasticities', *Applied Economics*, 23: 1251–6.

Channon, D.F. (1978) *The Service Industries: Strategy, Structure and Financial Performance*, London: MacMillan.

Chen, J-S.A. and Walters, J.S. (1992) 'Estimating Telephone Usage Elasticities: A Shares Equation System Approach', *Applied Economics*, 24: 1219–24.

Clark, Kim, B. (1980) 'Unionisation and Productivity: Micro-econometric evidence', *Quarterly Journal of Economics*, 95, December: 613–39.

Clarke, Roger (1985) *Industrial Economics*, Oxford: Basil Blackwell.

Clarke, Rosemary (1984) 'Profit Margins and Market Concentration in UK Manufacturing Industry: 1970–1976', *Applied Economics*, 16: 57–71.

Clarke, Rosemary (1985) *Applied Microeconomic Problems*, Oxford: Philip Allan.

Clarke, R. and Davies, S.W. (1982) 'Market Structure and Price–Cost Margins', *Economica*, 49: 277–87.

Clarke, R. and McGuiness, T. (eds) (1987) *The Economics of the Firm*, Oxford: Basil Blackwell.

Coase, R.H. (1964) 'The Nature of the Firm', *Economica*, 1937, New Series, IV: 386–405, reprinted in *Readings in Price Theory, The American Economic Association*, New York: Allen and Unwin, pp. 331–51.

Cohen, S.I. and Loeb, M. (1982) 'Public Goods, Common Inputs, and the Efficiency of Full Cost Allocations', *The Accounting Review*, LVII (2), April: 336–47.

Commission of the EC (1990) *European Economy*, Special edn.

Copland, E.C. and Weston, J.F. (1988) *Financial Theory and Corporate Policy*, 3rd edn, Wokingham: Addison Wesley.

Cosh, A.D. and Hughes, A. (1987) 'The Anatomy of Corporate Control: Directors, Shareholders and Executive Remuneration in Giant US and UK Corporations', *Cambridge Journal of Economics*, 11: 285–313.

Cowling, K. and Mueller, D. (1978) 'The Social Costs of Monopoly', *Economic Journal*, 88: 727–42.

Cowling, K., Stoneman, P., Cubbin, J., Cable, J., Hall, G., Domberger, S. and Dutton, P. (1980) *Mergers and Economic Performance*, Cambridge MA: Cambridge University Press.

Crew, M. and Kleindorfer, P. (1971) 'Marshall and Turvey on Peak Load or Joint Product Pricing', *Journal of Political Economy*, 79, December: 1369–77.

Curry, B. and George, K.D. (1983) 'Industrial Organisation: A survey', *Journal of Industrial Economics*, 31: 203–56.

Cyert, R.M. and March, J.G. (1963) *A Behavioural Theory of the Firm*, Englewood Cliffs, NJ: Prentice Hall.

Davies, S. (1988) 'Concentration', 3 in S. Davies and B. Lyons with H. Dixon and P. Geroski (eds) *Economics of Industrial Organisation*, Surveys in Economics, Harlow: Longman.

Davies, S. and Lyons, B. with Dixon, H. and Geroski, P. (1988) *Economics of Industrial Organisation*, Surveys in Economics, Harlow: Longman.

Dean, J. (1969) 'Pricing Pioneering Products', *Journal of Industrial Economics*, XVII (3): July, 165–79.

Demsetz, H. (1982) 'Barriers to Entry', *American Economic Review*, 72: 47–57.

Demsetz, H. (1983) 'The Structure of Ownership and the Theory of the Firm', *Journal of Law and Economics*, XXVI(2): 375–90.

Deoringer, P.B. and Piore, M.J. (1971) *Internal Labor Markets and Manpower Analysis*, Lexicon, MA: Heath Lexicon Books.

Dixit, A. (1979) 'A Model of Duopoly Suggesting a Theory of Entry Barriers', *Bell Journal of Economics*, 10(1), Spring: 20–32.

Dixit, A. (1980) 'The Role of Investment in Entry Deterrence', *Economic Journal*, 9: 95–106.

Dixit, A. (1982) 'Recent Developments in Oligopoly Theory', *American Economic Association, Papers and Proceedings*, 72(2), May: 12–17.

Downie, J. (1958) *The Competitive Process*, London: Duckworth.

Drake, L. (1992) 'Economies of Scale and Scope in the UK Building Societies; An Application of the Translog Multi-product Cost Function', *Applied Financial Economics*, 2: 211–19.

Drucker, P.F. (1985) *Innovation and Entrepreneurship: Practice and Principles*, London: Heinemann.

Dunning, J.H. and Cantwell, J.A. (1991) 'Japanese Direct Investment in Europe', in B. Burgenmeier and J.L. Mucchielli (eds) *Multinationals and Europe 1992, Strategies for the Future*, London: Routledge.

Dunning, J.H. and McQueen, M. (1982) 'The Eclectic Theory of the Multinational Enterprise and the International Hotel Industry', in A.M. Rugman (ed.) *New Theories of the Multinational Enterprise*, London: Croom Helm.

Dunsire, A., Hartley, K. and Parker, D. (1991) 'Organisational Status and Performance: Summary of the Findings', *Public Administration*, 69: 21–40.

Eccles, R.G. (1985) 'Transfer Pricing as a Problem of Agency', in J.W. Pratt and R.J. Zeckhauser (eds) *Principals and Agents: The Structure of Business*, Boston, MA: Harvard Business School, ch. 7.

Eden, L. (1985) 'The Microeconomics of Transfer Pricing', in A.M. Rugman and L. Eden (eds) *Multinational Transfer Pricing*, London: Croom Helm.

Fama, E.F. (1980) 'Agency Problems and the Theory of the Firm', *Journal of Political Economy*, 88: 288–307.

Ferguson, P.R. (1988) *Industrial Economics: Issues and Perspectives*, Basingstoke: Macmillan Education.

Ferner, A. and Colling, T. (1991) 'Privatisation, Regulation and Industrial Relations', *British Journal of Industrial Relations*, 29(3): 393–409.

Fitzroy, F. and Mueller, D.C. (1984) 'Cooperation and Conflict in Contractual Organisations', *Quarterly Review of Economics and Business*, 24: 24–50.

Fleming, M. (1988) 'Construction', in P. Johnson (ed.) *The Structure of British Industry*, 2nd edn, London: Unwin Hyman, ch. 10.

Frank, R.H. (1984) 'Are Workers Paid their Marginal Products?' *American Economic Review*, 74(4): 549–71.

Freeman, R.B. and Medoff, J.L. (1979) 'The Two Faces of Unionism', *Public Interest*, Fall: 69–93.

Friedlaender, A.F., Winston, C. and Wang, D.K. (1982) 'Costs Technology and Productivity in the U.S. Automobile Industry', Working Paper No 294, Department of Economics, Massachusetts Institute of Technology.

Fudenberg, D. and Tirole, J. (1984) 'The Fat-Cat Effect, The Puppy-Dog Ploy, and the Lean and Hungry Look', *American Economic Association*, *Papers and Proceedings*, 74(2): May, 361–6.

Geroski, P. (1981) 'Specification and Testing the Profits–Concentration Relationship: Some Experiments for the UK', *Economica*, 48: 279–88.

Gisser, M. (1986) 'Price Leadership and Welfare Losses in US Manufacturing', *American Economic Review*, 76: 756–67.

Goldring, M. (1993) 'The Goldring Audit', BBC Broadcast on the Privatisation of the Electricity Industry.

Gomes-Casseres, B. (1990) 'Firm Ownership Preferences and Host Government Restrictions: An integrated approach', *Journal of International Business Studies*, 21(1): 1–22.

Greenward and Stiglitz (1990) 'Asymmetric Information: The New Theory of the Firm, Financial Constraints and Risk Behaviour', *American Economic Review*, 80(2) May.

Grinyer, P.H., Yassai-Ardekani, M. and Al-Bazza, S. (1980) 'Strategy, Structure, the Environment and Financial Performance in 48 United Kingdom Companies', *Academy of Management Journal*, 23: 193–220.

Hannah, L. and Kay, J.A. (1977) *Concentration in Modern Industry*, London: Macmillan.

Hansmann, H.B. (1988) 'Ownership of the Firm', *Journal of Law, Economics and Organisation*, IV(2): 267–304.

Harrison, B. (1989) 'Elasticities of Demand', *British Economy Review* 18(2), Spring: 61–2.

Hart, O.D. (1983) 'The Market Mechanism as an Incentive Scheme', *Bell Journal of Economics*, 14: 366.

Hay, D.A. and Morris, D.J. (1979) *Industrial Economics: Theory and Evidence*, 1st edn, Oxford: Oxford University Press.

Hay, D.A. and Morris, D.J. (1991) *Industrial Economics and Organisation: Theory and Practice*, 2nd edn, Oxford: Oxford University Press, No 2, April.

Hay, D.A. and Vickers, J.S. (eds) (1987) *The Economics of Market Dominance*, Oxford: Blackwell.

Healey, N.M. (1991) 'The Role of Multinational Corporations in the British Industry', *British Economy Survey*, 20(2): 51–5.

Henderson, J.M. and Quant, R.E. (1980) *Microeconomic Theory; A Mathematical Approach*, 3rd edn, New York: McGraw Hill.

Hennart, J.-F. (1988a) 'Upstream Vertical Integration in the Aluminum and Tin Industries', *Journal of Economic Behaviour and Organisation*, 9: 281–99.

Hennart, J.-F. (1988b) 'Transaction Costs Theory of Equity Joint Ventures', *Strategic Management Journal*, 9: 361–74.

Hill, C.W.L. (1984) 'Organisational Structure, the Development of the Firm and Business Behaviour', in (eds) J.F. Pickering and T.A.J. Cockerill *The Economic Management of the Firm*, Oxford: Philip Allan.

Hill, G.C. and Holman, J.S. (1987) 'Chemistry in Context'. Nelson.

Hirshleifer, J. (1956) 'On the Economics of Transfer Pricing', *Journal of Business*, 29: 172–84.

Hirshleifer, J. (1958) 'On the Theory of Optimal Investment Decision', *Journal of Political Economy*, August: 329–52.

Holl, P. (1975) 'Effect of Control type on the Performance of the Firm in the UK', *Journal of Industrial Economics*, 23: 257–72.

Holtermann, S.E. (1973) 'Market Structure and Economics Performance in UK Manufacturing Industry', *Journal of Industrial Economics*, 27: 359–69.

Horst, T. (1971) 'The Theory of the Multinational Firm; Optimal Behaviour under Different Tariff and Tax Rates', *Journal of Political Economy*, 79: 1059–72.

Howe, W.S. (1978) *Industrial Economics: An Applied Approach*, London: Macmillan.

Hughs, Steward (1988) *The Structure of Industry*, Economies Briefs, London: Economist Books.

Hymer, S. (1976) 'The Efficiency (Contradictions) of Multinational Corporations', *American Economic Review, Papers and Proceedings*, 60(2): 441–8.

Jenny, F. and Webber, A.P. (1983) 'Aggregate Welfare Loss Due to Monopoly Power in the French Economy: Some tentative Estimates', *Journal of Industrial Economics*, 32: 113–30.

Jensen, M.C. and Meckling, W.H. (1976) 'Theory of the Firm: Managerial Behaviour, Agency Costs and Ownership Structure', *Journal of Financial Economics*, 3: 305–60.

Johnson, Peter (ed.) (1988) *The Structure of British Industry*, 2nd edn, London: Unwin Hyman.

Jones, J.C.H. and Laudio, L. (1978) 'The Empirical Basis of Canadian Antitrust Policy; Resource Allocation and Welfare Losses in Canadian Industry', *Industrial Organisation Review* 6: 49–59.

Jones, P. (1989) 'Price Elasticity of Demand', *Business Studies*, November: 36–9.

Kamerschen, D. (1968) 'Influence of Ownership and Control on Profit Rates', *American Economic Review*, 58: 432–47.

Karatzas, George (1992) 'On the Effect of Income and Relative Price on the Demand for Health Care – the EEC Evidence: A Comment', *Applied Economics*, 24: 1251–3.

Kay, J.A. and Thompson, D.J. (1986) 'Privatisation: A Policy in Search of a Rationale', *Economic Journal*, 96, March: 18–32.

Kay, N.M. (1982) *The Evolving Firm, Strategy and Structure in Industrial Organisation*, London: MacMillan.

Kay, N.M. (1984) *The Emergent Firm: Knowledge, Ignorance and Surprise in Economic Organisation*, London: MacMillan.

Kester, W.C. (1986) 'Capital and Ownership Structure: A Comparison of United States and Japanese Manufacturing Corporations', *Financial Management in Japan*, Spring.

Khalilzadeh-Shirazi, J. (1974) 'Market Structure and Price–Cost Margins in UK Manufacturing Industries', *Review of Economics and Statistics*, 54: 64–76.

Kirzner, I.M. (1979) *Perception, Opportunity, and Profit: Studies in the Theory of Entrepreneurship*, Chicago, IL: University of Chicago Press.

Kirzner, I.M. (1982) 'Uncertainty, Discovery, and Human Action: A Study of the Entrepreneurial Profile in the Misesian System', in Israel M. Kirzner (ed.) *Method, Process, and Austrian Economics*, Lexington, MA: Lexington Books.

Klein, B., Crowford, A. and Alchian, A. (1978) 'Vertical Integration, Appropriable Rents and the Competitive Contracting Process', *Journal of Law and Economics*, 21: 297–326.

Knight, F. (1921) *Risk, Uncertainty and Profit*, Chicago, IL: Chicago University Press.

Kobrin, S.J. (1987) 'Testing the Bargaining Hypothesis in the Manufacturing Sector in Developing Countries', *International Organisation*, 41(4), Autumn: 609–38.

Kotlikoff, L.J. and Gokhale, J. (1992) 'Estimating a Firm's Age–Productivity Profile using the Present Value of Workers' Earnings', *Quarterly Journal of Economics*, CVII: 1215–42.

Koutsoyiannis, A. (1979) *Modern Microeconomics*, 2nd edn, London: MacMillan.

Koutsoyiannis, A. (1982) *Non Price Decisions: The Firm in a Modern Context*, London: MacMillan.

Kuehn, D. (1975) *Takeovers and the Theory of the Firm*, London: Macmillan.

Lambert, R.A. and Larcker, D.F. (1985) 'Executive Compensation, corporate Decision – Making and Shareholder Wealth; a review of the Evidence', *Midland Corporate Finance Journal*, 2(4): 6–22.

Larner, R. (1970) *Management Control and the Large Corporation*, New York: Dunelless.

Lazear, E.P. (1981) 'Agency, Earnings Profiles, Productivity, and Hours Restrictions', *American Economic Review*, 71(4): 606–20.

Lazear, E.P. and Rosen, S. (1981) 'Rank-Order Tournaments as Optimum Labor Contracts', *Journal of Political Economics*, 89(5): 841–64.

Lecraw, D.J. (1984) 'Bargaining Power, Ownership, and Profitability of Transnational Corporations in Developing Countries', *Journal of International Business Studies*, Spring/Summer: 27–43.

Leibenstein, H. (1950) 'Bandwagon, Snob, and Veblen Effects in the Theory of Consumers' Demand', *Quarterly Journal of Economics* May: 183–207.

Leibenstein, H. (1966) 'Allocative Efficiency vs X-Efficiency', *American Economic Review*, 56: 392–415.

Lieberman, M.B. (1991) 'Determinants of Vertical Integration: An Empirical Test', *Journal of Industrial Economics*, XXXIX: 451–65.

Lyons, B. (1987) 'Strategic Behaviour by Firms', in R. Clarke and T. McGuiness (eds) *The Economics of the Firm*, Oxford: Basil Blackwell.

Lyons, B. (1988) 'Barriers to Entry', in S. Davies and B. Lyons with H. Dixon and P. Geroski (eds) *Economics in Industrial Organisation*, Surveys in Economics, Harlow: Longman, ch. 2.

Machlup, F. (1967) 'Theories of the Firm: Marginalist, Managerialist, Behavioural', *American Economic Review*, LVII(1): 1–33.

Main, G.M. (1990) 'The New Economics of Personnel', *Journal of General Management*, 16(2): 91–103.

Malcomson, J.M. (1981) 'Unemployment and the Efficiency Wage Hypothesis', *Economic Journal*, 91, December: 848–66.

Malcomson, J.M. (1983) 'Trade Unions and Economic Efficiency', *Economic Journal*, 93, Supplement March: 51–65.

Malcomson, J.M. (1984a) 'Efficient Labour Organisation; Incentives Power and the Transactions Costs Approach', in F.H. Stephen (ed.) *Firms Organisation and Labour: Approaches to the Economics of Work Organisation*, London: Macmillan.

Malcomson, J.M. (1984b) 'Work Incentives, Hierarchy, and Internal Labour Markets', *Journal of Political Economy* 92(3): 486–507.

Mallier, A. and Shafto, A. (1989) *Economics of Labour Markets and Management*, London: Hutchinson.

Mansfield (1983) 'Technological Change and Market Structure: An Empirical Study', *American Economic Review, Papers and Proceedings*, 73(2): 205–9.

Marris, R. (1963) 'A Model for the Managerial Enterprise', *Quarterly Journal of Economics*, 7: 185.

Marris, R. (1964) *The Economic Behaviour of Managerial Capitalism*, London: Macmillan.

Marsh, D. (1991) 'Privatisation under Mrs Thatcher: Review of the Literature', *Public Administration*, 69: 459–80.

Masson, R.T. and Shaanan, J. (1984) 'Social Costs of Oligopoly and the Value of Competition', *Economic Journal*, 94: 520–35.

Masten, S.E. (1984) 'The Organisation of Production: Evidence from the Aerospace Industry', *Journal of Law and Economics*, XXVII, October: 403–17.

Medoff, J.L. and Abraham, K.J. (1980) 'Experience, Performance, and Earnings', *Quarterly Journal of Economics*, 95, December: 703–36.

Metcalf, D. and Nickell, S. (1982) 'Occupational Mobility in Great Britain', in R.G. Ehrenberg (ed.) *Research in Labor Economics: A Research Annual*, vol. 5, Greenwich: JAI Press.

Milgrom, P. and Roberts, John (1992) *Economics, Organisation and Management*, Englewood Cliffs, NJ: Prentice Hall.

Milne, R. and Molana, H. (1991) 'On the Effect of Income and Relative Price on Demand for Health Care: EC Evidence', *Applied Economics*, 23: 1221–6.

Mises von, L. (1966) *Human Action*, Chicago, IL: Henry Regnery.

Modigliani, F. and Miller, M.H. (1958) 'The Cost of Capital, Corporation Finance and the Theory of Investment', *American Economic Review*, 48: 261–97.

Modigliani, F. and Miller, M.H. (1963) 'Corporate Income Tax and the Cost of Capital: A Correction', *American Economic Review*, LIII(3): 433–43.

Monopolies and Mergers Commission (1989) *Report on the Supply of Beer*, Cmnd 651, London: HMSO.

Monopolies and Mergers Commission (1990) *Report on the Supply of Petrol*, Cmnd 972, London: HMSO.

Monopolies and Mergers Commission (1991a) *Carbonated Drinks*, Cmnd 1625, London: HMSO.

Monopolies and Mergers Commission (1991b) *Soluble Coffee*, Cmnd 1459, London: HMSO.

Monopolies and Mergers Commisssion (1991c) *Razors and Razor Blades*, Cmnd 1472, London: HMSO.

Monopolies and Restrictive Practices Commission (1956) *The Supply of Certain Industrial and Medical Gases*, London: HMSO.

Monsen, R., Chin, J. and Cooley, D. (1968) 'The effect of the Separation of Ownership and Control on the Performance of the Large Firm', *Quarterly Journal of Economics*, 82: 435–51.

Monteverde, K. and Teece, D.J. (1982) 'Supplier Switching Costs and Vertical Integration in the Automobile Industry', *Bell Journal of Economics*, 13: 206–13.

Morck, R. (1988) 'Management Ownership and Market Valuation. An Empirical Analysis', *Journal of Financial Economics*, 20: 293–315.

Moschandreas, M. 'Pricing of Joint Products', Discussion Paper in Economics No 5, Middlesex Polytechnic, September.

Mueller, D.C. (1980) *The Determinants and Effects of Mergers: An International Comparison*', Cambridge, MA: Oelgeschlager, Gunn and Hain Publishers.

Needham, D. (1978) *The Economics of Industrial Structure, Conduct and Performance*, London: Holt, Reinehart and Wiston.

Oh, S.J. (1986) 'The Magnitude of Welfare Losses from Monopoly in the Korean Economy', *Economic Research*, 7: 219–34.

Oni, W.Y. (1971) 'A Disneyland Dilemma: Two-part Tariffs for a Mickey Mouse Monopoly', *Quarterly Journal of Economics*, 85: 77–90.

Orr, D. (1974) 'An Index of Entry Barriers and its Application to the Market Structure–Performance Relationship', *Journal of Industrial Economics*, 23: 39–50.

Palay, M.T. (1984) 'Comparative Institutional Economics: The Governance of Rail Freight Contracting', *Journal of Legal Studies*, VIII, June: 265–87.

Panzar, J.C. and Willig, D.R. (1977) 'Economies of Scale in Multi-product Production', *Quarterly Journal of Economics*, 91: 481–94.

Parker, D. (1991) 'Privatisation Ten Years on: A Critical Analysis of its Rationale and Results', *Economics*, Winter: 154–63.

Parkin, D., McGuire, A. and Yule, B. (1987) 'Aggregate Health Care Expenditure and National Income; Is Health Care a Luxury Good?', *Journal of Health Care Economics*, 6: 109–27.

Penrose, E. (1959) *The Theory of the Growth of the Firm*, Oxford: Blackwell.

Pittman, R.W. (1990) 'Railroads and Competition: The Santa Fe/Southern Pacific Merger Proposal', *The Journal of Industrial Economics*, XXXIX(1): 25–45.

Prais, (1976) *The Evolution of Giant Firms in Britain*, Cambridge: Cambridge University Press.

Pratt, J.W. and Zeckhauser, R.J. (eds) (1985) *Principals and Agents: The Structure of Business*, Boston, MA: Harvard Business School.

Prowse, S.D. (1992) 'The Structure of Capital Ownership in Japan', *Journal of Finance*. Vol XLVII(3), July: 1121–40.

Pryke, R. (1982) 'The Comparative Performance of Public and Private Enterprise', *Fiscal Studies*, 3: 68–81.

Putterman, L. (ed.) (1986) *The Economic Nature of the Firm*, A reader, Cambridge: Cambridge University Press.

Radice, H. (1971) "Control Type, Profitability and Growth in Large Firms: An Empirical Study', *Economic Journal*, 81: 547–62.

Raviv, A. (1985) 'Management Compensation and the Managerial Labor Market: An Overview', *Journal of Accounting and Economics*, 7: 239–45.

Reekie, W.D. (1984) *Markets, Entrepreneurs and Liberty: An Austrian View of Capitalism*, Brighton: Harvester Wheatsheaf.

Reekie, W.D. (1989) *Industrial Economics: A critical Introduction to corporate enterprise in Europe and America*, Aldershot: Edward Elgar.

Reekie, W.D. and Crook, J.N. (1985) *Managerial Economics*, 2nd edn, Oxford: Philip Allan.

Rhodes, S.A. (1973) 'The Effects of Diversification on Industry Profit Performance in 241 Manufacturing Industries: 1963', *Review of Economics and Statistics*, 55: 146–55.

Richardson, G. (1964) 'Limits to a Firm's Rate of Growth'. *Oxford Economic Papers*, 16, March: 9–23.

Richardson, J.D. (1971) 'Theoretical considerations in the Analysis of Direct Foreign Investment', *Western Economic Journal*, 9: 87–98.

Ricketts, M. (1987) *The Economics of Business Enterprise; New Approaches to the Firm*, Brighton: Harvester Wheatsheaf ch. 7.2.

Ronen, J. (ed.) (1983) *Entrepreneurship*, Price Institute for Entrepreneurial Studies, Toronto: Lexington Books.

Ronen, J. (1989) 'The Rise and Decay of Entrepreneurship: A Different perspective', *Journal of Behavioral Economics*, 18(3): 167–84.

Roper, B. and Snowdon, B. (eds) (1987) *Markets, Intervention and Planning*, Harlow: Longman.

Rugman, A.M. (ed.) (1982) *New Theories of the Multinational Enterprise*, London: Croom Helm.

Rugman, A.M. and Eden, L. (eds) (1985) *Multinational Transfer Pricing*, London: Croom Helm.

Rugman, A.M. and Verbete, A. (1991) 'Competitive Strategies for Non-European firms', in B. Burgenmeier and J.L. Mucchielli (eds) *Multinationals and Europe 1992*, London: Routledge.

Rumelt, R.P. (1974) *Strategy, Structure and Economic Performance*, Division of Research, Graduate School of Business Administration, Harvard University.

Salinger, M.A. (1991) 'Vertical Mergers in Multi-product Industries and Edgeworth's paradox of Taxation', *Journal of Industrial Economics*, XXXIX(5): 545.

Schelling, T. (1980) *The Strategy of Conflict*, Cambridge, MA: Harvard University Press.

Scherer, F.M. (1980) *Industrial Market Structure and Economic Performance*, 2nd edn, Chicago, IL: Rand McNally.

Schmalensee, R. (1981) 'Economies of Scale and Barriers to Entry', *Journal of Political Economy*, 189: 1228–38.

Schmalensee, R. (1982) 'Product Differentiation Advantages of Pioneering Brands', *American Economic Review*, 82: 349–65.

Schumpeter, J.A. (1943) *Capitalism, Socialism and Democracy*, London: Unwin University Books.

Shackle, G.L.S. (1984) 'To cope with time' in F.H.S. Stephen (ed.) *Firms, Organisation and Labour: Approaches to the Economics of Work Organisation*, London: Macmillan.

Shaked, A. and Sutton, J. (1987) 'Product Differentiation and Industrial Structure', *Journal of Industrial Economics*, XXXVI (2): 131–46.

Shepherd, W.G. (1990) *The Economics of Industrial Organisation*, 3rd edn, Englewood Cliffs, NJ: Prentice Hall.

Shughart, W.F.S. (1990) *The Organisation of Industry*, Homeward, IL: Richard D. Irwin.

Silver, M. (1984) *Enterprise and the Scope of the Firm*, Oxford: Martin Robertson.

Simon, H.A. (1957) *Administrative Behaviour*, London: Macmillan.

Singh, A. (1971) *Takeovers: Their Relevance to the Stock Market and the Theory of the Firm*, Cambridge: Cambridge University Press.

Singh, A. (1975) 'Takeovers, Economic Natural Selection and the Theory of the Firm', *Economic Journal* 85: 497–515.

Spence, A.M. (1977) 'Entry, Capacity, Investment and Oligopolistic Pricing', *Bell Journal of Economics*, 8, Autumn: 534–44.

Steer, P. and Cable, J. (1978) 'Internal Organisation and Profit: An Empirical Analysis of Large U.K. Companies', *Journal of Industrial Economics*, 27: 13–3.

Stephen, F.H.S. (ed.) (1984) *Firms, Organisation and Labour: Approaches to the Economics of Work Organisation*, London: Macmillan.

Stigler, G.J. (1947) 'The Kinky Oligopoly Curve and Rigid Prices', *Journal of Political Economy*, 55: 432–49.

Stigler, G.J. (1966) *The Theory of Price*, 3rd edn, London: Macmillan.

Stigler, G.J. (1968) *The Organisation of Industry*, Homewood, IL: Irwin.

Stiglitz, J. (1985) 'Credit Markets and the Control of Capital', *Journal of Money, Credit and Banking*, 17: 133–52.

Strong, N. and Waterson, M. (1987) 'Principals, Agents and Information', in R. Clarke and T. McGuiness (eds) *The Economics of the Firm*, Oxford: Basil Blackwell.

Stuckey, J.A. (1983) *Vertical Integration and Joint Ventures in the Aluminum Industry*, Cambridge, MA: Harvard University Press.

Sweezy, P. (1939) 'Demand under Conditions of Oligopoly', *Journal of Political Economy*, 47: 568–73.

Teece, D.J. (1980) 'Economies of Scope and the Scope of the Enterprise', *Journal of Economic Behaviour and Organisation*, 1: 223–47.

Teece, D.J. (1982) 'Towards an Economic Theory of the Multiproduct Firm', *Journal of Economic Behaviour and Organisation*, 3: 39–63.

Teece, D.J. (1983) 'Technological and Organisational Factors in the Theory of Multinational Enterprise', in M. Casson (ed.) *The Growth of International Business*, London: Allen and Unwin.

Teece, D.J. (1985) 'Multinational Enterprise, Internal Governance, and Industrial

Organisation', *American Economic Association*, Papers and Proceedings, 75(2): 233–8.

Teece, D.J. (1986) 'Transaction Cost Economics and the Multinational Enterprise', *Journal of Economic Behaviour and Organisation*, 7. 21–45.

Thompson, D.J. (1987) 'Privatisation in the UK; DE-regulation and the Advantage of Incumbency', *European Economic Review*, 31: 368–74.

Utton, M.A. (1970) *Industrial Concentration*, Harmondsworth: Penguin Books.

Varian, Hal R. (1990) *Intermediate Microeconomics; A Modern Approach*, 2nd edn, London: Norton.

Vernon, R. (1965) 'International Investment and International Trade in the Product Cycle', *Quarterly Journal of Economics*, 80: 190–207.

Vickers, J.S. and Hay, D.A. (1987) 'The Economics of Market Dominance', in D.A. Hay and J.S. Vickers (eds) *The Economics of Market Dominance*, Oxford: Blackwell, ch. 1.

Vickers, J. and Yarrow, G. (1988) *Privatisation; An Economic Analysis*, Cambridge, MA: MIT Press.

Wahlroos, B. (1984) 'Monopoly Welfare Losses under Uncertainty', *Southern Economic Journal*, 51: 429–42.

Waterson, M. (1984) *Economic Theory of the Industry*, Cambridge: Cambridge University Press.

Weizsacker, C.C. von (1980) 'A Welfare Analysis of Barriers to Entry', *Bell Journal of Economics* 11: 399–420.

Williamson, O.E. (1964) *The Economics of Discretionary Behavior. Managerial Objectives in a Theory of the Firm*, Englewood Cliffs, NJ: Prentice Hall.

Williamson, O.E. (1966) 'Peak Load Pricing and Optimal Capacity under Indivisibility Constraints', *American Economic Review*, 56, September.

Williamson, O.E. (1971) 'Managerial Discretion, Organisation Form and the Multi-division Hypothesis', in R. Marris and A. Wood (eds) *The Corporate Economy; Growth, Competition and Innovative Potential*, London: Macmillan.

Williamson, O.E. (1975) *Markets and Hierarchies: Analysis and Antitrust Implications: A Study in the Economics of Internal Organisation*, New York: Free Press.

Williamson, O.E. (1981) 'The Modern Corporation: Origins, Evolution, Attributes', *Journal of Economic Literature*, 19: 1537–68.

Williamson, O.E. (1983a) 'Organisational Innovation: The Transaction Cost Approach', in J. Ronen (ed.) *Entrepreneurship* Price Institute for Entrepreneurial Studies, Toronto: Lexington Books.

Williamson, O.E. (1983b) 'Organisation Form, Residual Claimants, and Corporate Control', *Journal of Law and Economics*, XXVI (2): 351–66.

Williamson, O.E. (1984a) 'The Economics of Governance: Frame Work and Implications', *Zeitschrift fur die gesamte Staatswissenschaft*, 140: 195–223.

Williamson, O.E. (1984b) 'Efficient Labour Organisation', in F.H. Stephen (ed.) *Firms, Organisation and Labour: Approaches to the Economics of Work Organisation*, London: Macmillan.

Williamson, O.E. (1985) *The Economic Institutions of Capitalism. Firms, Markets, Relational Contracting*', London: Collier Macmillan.

Williamson, O.E., Wachter, M.L. and Harris, J.E. (1975) 'Understanding the Employment Relation: the Analysis of Idiosyncratic Exchange', *Bell Journal of Economics*, Spring: 250–78.

Willig, D.R. (1979) 'Multiproduct Technology and Market Structure', *American Economic Review*, 69: 346–51.

Wiseman, J. (1991) 'The Black Box', *The Economic Journal*, 101 (404): 149–55.

Wolf, B.M. (1977) 'Industrial Diversification and Internationalisation: Some Empirical Evidence', *Journal of Industrial Economics*, 26: 177–91.

Wolfson, M.A. (1984) 'Empirical Evidence of incentive Problems and Their

Mitigation in Oil and Gas Tax Shelter Programs', in J.W. Pratt and R.J. Zeckhauser (eds) *Principals and Agents: The Structure of Business*, Boston: Harvard Business School.

Yarrow, G.K. (1976) 'On the Predictions of the Managerial Theory of the Firm', *Journal of Political Economy*, 24(4): 267–79.

Yellen, J.L. (1984) 'Efficiency Wage Models of Unemployment', *American Economic Review*, 74(1): 200–5.

Index